Praise for *Russia Against Napoleon*

Winner of the Wolfson History Prize, 2009

"The central point made by Mr. Lieven's witty and impeccably scholarly book is that Russia owed its victory not to the courage of its national spirit or to the coldness of the 1812 winter, as some French sources have argued, but to its military excellence, superior cavalry, the high standards of Russia's diplomatic and intelligence services, and the quality of its European elite."   —*The Economist*

"Lieven not only makes his case in rich, probing detail; he also encases it in a fluent reading of Russia's larger political and social dynamics during this period."   —*Foreign Affairs*

"*Russia Against Napoleon* achieves that rare thing of taking a story we thought we knew and recounting it in a new and more convincing light."   —*The Seattle Times*

"*Russia Against Napoleon* is illuminating, highly readable, a book that probably could not have been written anytime before now. For those who love corrective histories (of which probably everyone's first favorite is Barbara Tuchman's *The Guns of August*), Lieven's story stands with the best."   —*The Dallas Morning News*

"His [Lieven's] book is a masterpiece of military writing. He presents extraordinary detail in crisp, rich prose."   —*The Washington Times*

"With *Russia Against Napoleon* Lieven has written a Tolstoyan masterpiece of nonfiction, an answer to the classic that is indeed as filled with as much great sweep and drama as *War and Peace*. This one is truly a monument and labor of love."

—Blogcritics.com (review also ran on Seattle Post-Intelligencer.com)

"What Lieven does in this monumental, two-pound tome, subtitled *The True Story of the Campaigns of War and Peace*, is take on much of *Western* Conventional Wisdom (as well, it might be said, as Tolstoyan and Soviet C.W.) about this war."   —*Russian Life*

PENGUIN BOOKS

RUSSIA AGAINST NAPOLEON

Dominic Lieven is a professor of Russian history at the London School of Economics. His previous books include *Empire: The Russian Empire and Its Rivals* and *Nicholas II: Twilight of the Empire*. Three of his direct ancestors were generals in the Battle of Leipzig. He lives in London.

DOMINIC LIEVEN

Russia Against Napoleon

The True Story of the Campaigns of
War and Peace

PENGUIN BOOKS

PENGUIN BOOKS

Published by the Penguin Group
Penguin Group (USA) Inc., 375 Hudson Street, New York, New York 10014, U.S.A.
Penguin Group (Canada), 90 Eglinton Avenue East, Suite 700, Toronto,
Ontario, Canada M4P 2Y3 (a division of Pearson Penguin Canada Inc.)
Penguin Books Ltd, 80 Strand, London WC2R 0RL, England
Penguin Ireland, 25 St Stephen's Green, Dublin 2, Ireland (a division of Penguin Books Ltd)
Penguin Group (Australia), 250 Camberwell Road, Camberwell,
Victoria 3124, Australia (a division of Pearson Australia Group Pty Ltd)
Penguin Books India Pvt Ltd, 11 Community Centre,
Panchsheel Park, New Delhi – 110 017, India
Penguin Group (NZ), 67 Apollo Drive, Rosedale, North Shore 0632,
New Zealand (a division of Pearson New Zealand Ltd)
Penguin Books (South Africa) (Pty) Ltd, 24 Sturdee Avenue,
Rosebank, Johannesburg 2196, South Africa

Penguin Books Ltd, Registered Offices:
80 Strand, London WC2R 0RL, England

First published in Great Britain by Allen Lane, an imprint of Penguin Books Ltd. 2009
First published in the United States of America by Viking Penguin,
a member of Penguin Group (USA) Inc. 2010
Published in Penguin Books (UK) 2010
Published in Penguin Books (USA) 2011

1 3 5 7 9 10 8 6 4 2

THE LIBRARY OF CONGRESS HAS CATALOGED THE HARDCOVER EDITION AS FOLLOWS:
Lieven, D. C. B.
Russia against Napoleon : the true story of the campaigns of War and Peace / Dominic Lieven.
p. cm.
Includes bibliographical references and index.
ISBN 978-0-670-02157-4 (hc.)
ISBN 978-0-14-311886-2 (pbk.)
1. Napoleonic Wars, 1800–1815—Campaigns—Russia. 2. Russia—History—
Alexander I, 1801–1825. 3. Tolstoy, Leo, graf, 1828–1910. Voina i mir. I. Title.
DC235.L49 2009
940.2'70947—dc22
2009042564

Printed in the United States of America

For my courageous wife, Mikiko, and in memory of the
regiments of the Imperial Russian Army who fought, suffered
and triumphed in the great war of 1812–14

Contents

CONTENTS

Illustrations

Page 14
Borodino: the Raevsky Redoubt after the battle

Page 15
Spring 1813: the Cossacks in Hamburg

Page 16
Fère-Champenoise: the Cossack Life Guard Regiment attacks the French infantry

Picture credits:
Page 1: George Dawe painting, Bridgeman Art Library/Getty Images
Page 3 Christoph von Lieven: British Library
Page 4 Aleksei Arakcheev: British Library
Page 7 Alexandre de Langeron and Fabian von der Osten-Sacken: British Library
Page 8 Andrei Kologrivov: British Library
Page 14: Albrecht Adam sketch: AKG Images
Page 15: V. Bezotosny
Page 16: Don Cossack Life Guard Club/Courbevoie

Maps

Acknowledgements

So many people and institutions helped me to research and write this book that in normal circumstances it would be difficult to know where to start with my thanks. But the help of one institution, the Leverhulme Trust, was so fundamental that beyond question it must come first. In 2006 I was awarded a Leverhulme Major Research Fellowship, which left me free to work on my book for the next two years and also funded most of my research in the Russian archives. I owe a huge amount to the generous support of the Trust. Professors Paul Bushkovitch, William Fuller and Geoffrey Hosking supported my application for the fellowship, and to them too I owe many thanks.

In the summer of 2006 I had a two-month fellowship from the British Academy which enabled me to work in the Slavic Library in Helsinki. During these two months I was able to read all the regimental histories of Russian units which participated in the Napoleonic Wars. I also read or at least copied all the journal articles published in Russia before 1917 which were relevant to my topic. For any historian of imperial Russia the Helsinki Library is a unique asset, made all the better by the friendly and efficient help of its staff, led by Irina Lukka. My deep thanks are owed not just to Irina but also to Ulla Tillander, who helped so much to organize my expedition and make it pleasant. Richard Stites and the community of historians working in the Library were also very kind to me.

One part of the Russian State Military Historical Archive's (RGVIA) holdings on the Napoleonic Wars was microfilmed shortly before I began my research. This is Fond 846, the so-called Voenno-uchenyi Arkhiv (VUA). As anyone looking at my references will see, it contains priceless information for my book. The Librarian of the LSE Library (BLPES), Jean Sykes, and the Library's main Russian specialist, Graham Camfield, acquired this immensely valuable collection, and left me for ever in their debt.

Even so, the main archival sources for my book had to come from holdings in the Russian State Military Historical Archive (RGVIA) in Moscow other than the VUA. Above all these were the papers of the wartime recruit levies (Fond 1), most of the materials relating to the feeding, equipment and arming of the field armies (Fond 103), the documents of the Reserve Army (Fond 125), and the immensely useful personnel records of Russian regiments (Fond 489). Thanks to Tatiana Iurevna Burmistrova and the staff of RGVIA, I was able to get through all the materials I needed during my six research trips to Moscow.

I would never have been able to do so, however, without the help of Vasili Kashirin. My research was complicated by family needs and by the fact that for part of this time the archive closed for repairs, sometimes with minimal notice. Without Vasili's help in finding materials and ensuring that I received them this book would be much weaker than it is. More than any other individual, he made an enormous contribution to my research. A number of archivists also deserve my special thanks, and not least Aleksandr Kapitonov. Professor Apollon Davidson and his wife Liudmilla kindly put me up in Moscow on a number of occasions and coped with my grumpiness when something went wrong with the archive.

I owe a big debt to the friends who took me to battlefields. Viktor Bezotosnyi showed me the field at Maloiaroslavets, and was also a constant source of advice, information and friendship. Paul Simmons and Vasili Kashirin spent a memorable day at Borodino with me. Dominic Herbestreit and Christin Pilz took me around the battlefields of Leipzig and also drove me to Kulm, now in the Czech Republic. Even more heroic was my sister, Professor Elena Lieven, who drove me deep into rural Poland to the battlefield of the Katzbach. Our expedition was helped hugely by Alexandra Porada, who helped us negotiate the area.

My agent, Natasha Fairweather, has been a key ally and so have my publishers, Simon Winder and Wendy Wolf, as well as Alice Dawson and Richard Duguid of Penguin. Elizabeth Stratford was an exceptionally efficient copy-editor. I have wanted to write this book since childhood but they encouraged me to do so. I think that the initial spur to write the book in time for the bicentenary in 2012 came, however, from my colleague, Professor James Hughes.

Among others at LSE who helped me enormously, Sue Starkey stands out. She coped with my frequent hysteria when confronted by computers, photocopiers and other technological challenges. Her colleagues in the Government Department's General Office (Jill Stuart, Cerys Jones, Madeleine Bothe, Hiszah Tariq) also helped me and calmed me down. My colleague, Professor Janet Hartley, very kindly read the text for me and suggested changes. So too did our students, Conor Riffle and Megan Tulac. In my first twenty-four years at LSE I kept as far from the School's management as possible. While working on this book, however, I was initially head of department and subsequently a member of LSE's governing council. That gave me some insight into the intelligent, efficient and good-humoured manner in which the School was run by (Sir) Howard Davies, its director. Tony (Lord) Grabiner, chairman of the Board of Governors, showed not just wisdom but great unselfishness, devoting an immense amount of his time to unpaid service to the School to a degree that few members of the academic community realize.

I must also thank Professor Patrick O'Brien for his advice on war, finance and economic issues, and Alexis de Tiesenhausen for his help and advice as regards illustrations.

For the first eighteen months of my research I lived mostly off the excellent holdings of the British Library and owed much to the help of its staff. After joining the London Library halfway through my research, I discovered just how splendid a resource it is for scholars in general and historians of imperial Russia in particular.

I published an article outlining the theme and purpose of this book in *Kritika* in spring 2006 and would like to thank the editors of the journal and readers of the piece for their useful criticism and advice.

My family – Mikiko, Aleka, Max and Tolly – suffered during my research and writing of the book but helped to keep me going.

A Note on the Text

In the era covered by this book Russia ran on the Julian calendar, which in the nineteenth century was twelve days behind the Gregorian calendar used in most of the rest of Europe. The events covered by this book occurred partly in Russia and partly abroad. To avoid confusion, I have used the Gregorian – i.e. European – calendar throughout the text. Documents are cited in the notes in their original form and when they have dates from the Julian calendar the letters OS (i.e. Old Style) appear after them in brackets.

I have used a modified version of the Library of Congress system for transliterating words from Russian. To avoid bewildering anglophone readers I have not included Russian hard and soft signs, accents or stress signs in names of people and places in the text. A point to note is that the Russian *e* is usually pronounced *ye*. Sometimes, however, the *e* is accented and stressed, appearing in Russian as *ë*. In this case it is generally pronounced as *yo*, though after some consonants as just *o*. Among words frequently found in this book, for example, are Petr (i.e. Peter) which is pronounced Pyotr, Potemkin which is pronounced Patyomkin and the Semenovsky Guards Regiment, which is pronounced Semyonovsky. The surname of Aleksandr Chernyshev, who figures prominently in this story, sounds like Chernyshoff in English. Very many Russian surnames end like an adjective in the letters -*ii* but in deference to English custom I use the letter -*y*. Thus the reader will come across, for example, Petr Volkonsky, who served as Alexander's chief of staff, not the grammatically more correct Volkonskii.

When faced with surnames of non-Russian origin I have tried – not always successfully – to render them in their original Latin version. My own name thereby emerges unscathed as Lieven rather than depressed and reduced as Liven. As regards Christian names I also transliterate for

Russians but in general use Western versions for Germans, Frenchmen and other Europeans. So Alexander's chief of staff is called Petr Volkonsky but General von der Pahlen is rendered as Peter, in deference to his Baltic German origins. No system is perfect in this respect, not least because members of the Russian elite of this era sometimes spelt their own names quite differently according to mood and to the language in which they were writing.

Where an Anglicized version of a town's name is in common use, I have used it. So Moscow rather than Moskva burns down in this book. But other towns in the Russian Empire are usually rendered in the Russian version, unless the German or Polish version is more familiar to English readers. Towns in the Habsburg Empire and Germany are usually given their German version of a name. This is to simplify the lives of baffled readers trying to follow the movements of armies in texts and maps, though when any doubts might exist alternative versions of place names are given in brackets.

The names of Russian regiments can also be a problem. Above all this boils down to whether or not to use the adjectival version (i.e. ending in -skii) as in the Russian. I prefer Moscow Regiment – to take one example – rather than Moskovskii Regiment but I make some exceptions for the Guards. The senior Guards infantry regiments, for example, were named after obscure villages outside Moscow. It makes far more sense to render them in their habitual adjectival form: in other words Preobrazhensky Guards rather than Preobrazhenskoe. Where confusion might occur the alternative variants of the regiment's name are placed in brackets: so, Lithuania (Litovsky) Guards. I have also accepted tradition in using the habitual French version – Chevaliers Gardes – rather than the Russian Kavalergardsky for this regiment and by referring to the Cossack Life Guards.

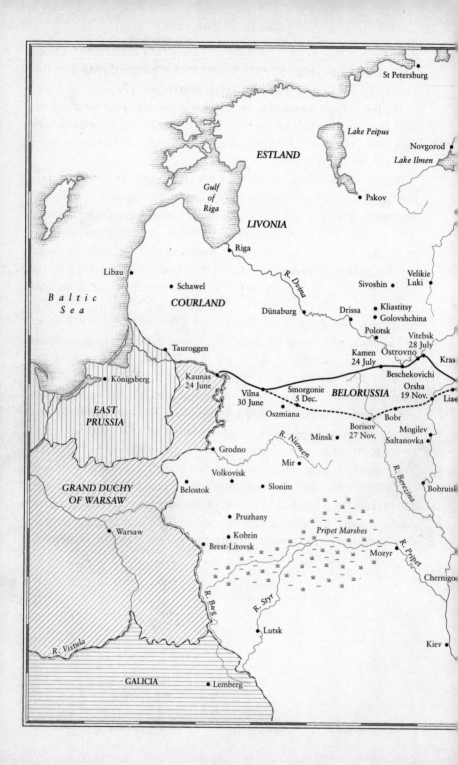

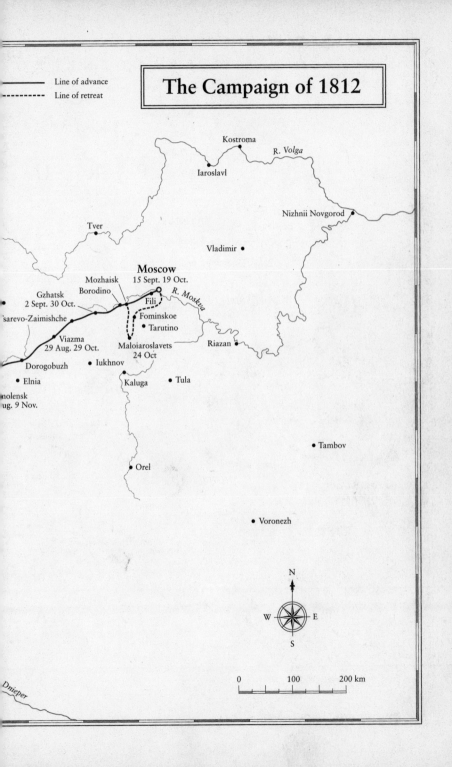

The Campaign of 1812

Line of advance

Line of retreat

Kostroma

Iaroslavl

R. *Volga*

Nizhnii Novgorod

Tver

Vladimir

Moscow
15 Sept. 19 Oct.

Mozhaisk

Borodino

Gzhatsk
2 Sept. 30 Oct.

Fili

R. *Moskva*

sarevo-Zaimishche

Fominskoe

Tarutino

Viazma
29 Aug. 29 Oct.

Maloiaroslavets
24 Oct

Riazan

Dorogobuzh

Iukhnov

Elnia

Kaluga

Tula

nolensk
ug. 9 Nov.

Tambov

Orel

Voronezh

N

W ✦ E

S

0   100   200 km

Dnieper

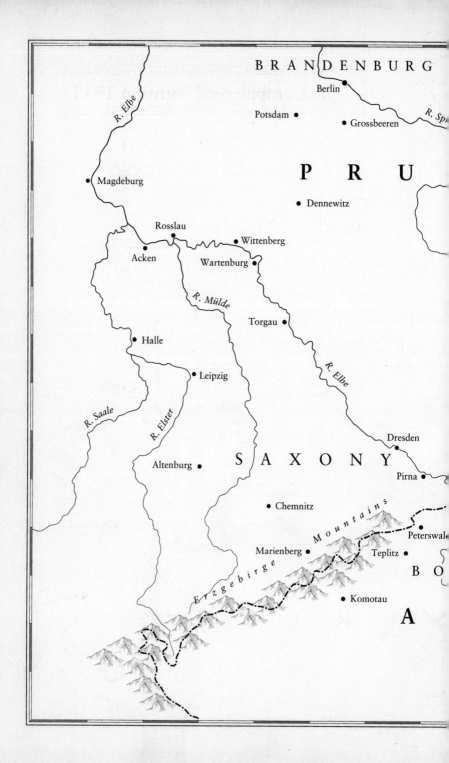

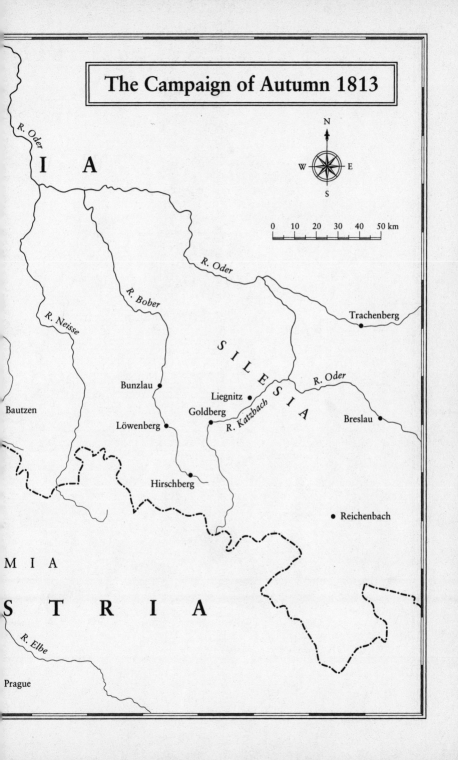

The Campaign of Autumn 1813

R. Oder

N

W · E

S

0 10 20 30 40 50 km

I A

R. Oder

R. Bober

R. Neisse

R. Oder

Trachenberg

S I L E S I A

Bunzlau

Liegnitz

Goldberg

R. Oder

Bautzen

Löwenberg

R. Katzbach

Breslau

Hirschberg

Reichenbach

M I A

S T R I A

R. Elbe

Prague

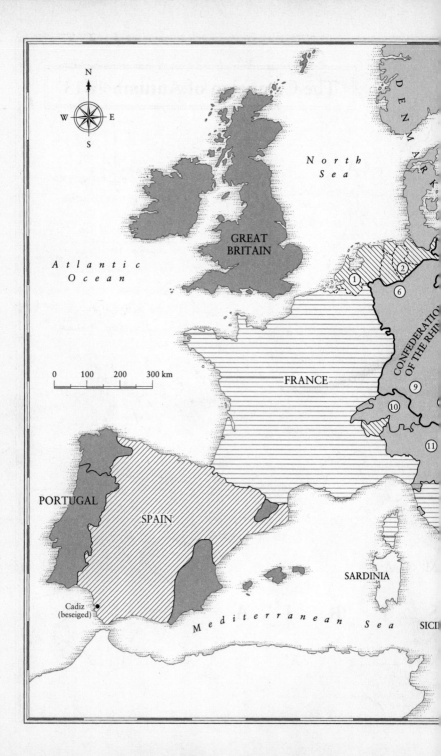

Europe in May 1812

1. Holland
2. Oldenburg
3. Swedish Pomerania
4. Danzig
5. Lithuania
6. Westphalia
7. Saxony
8. Bavaria
9. Württemberg
10. Helvetic Confederation
11. Kingdom of Italy
12. Illyrian Provinces
13. Silesia
14. Serbia
15. Montenegro
16. Moldavia
17. Bessarabia (to Russia, 1912)
18. Wallachia
19. Ionian Islands (disputed)
20. Malta

French frontiers, December 1809

French annexations 1810–12

French occupation/administration

French satellites/allies

Great Britain and dependencies

Frontier of Confederation of the Rhine

PRUSSIA

GRAND DUCHY
OF WARSAW

RUSSIA

AUSTRIA

Black Sea

OTTOMAN
EMPIRE

NAPLES

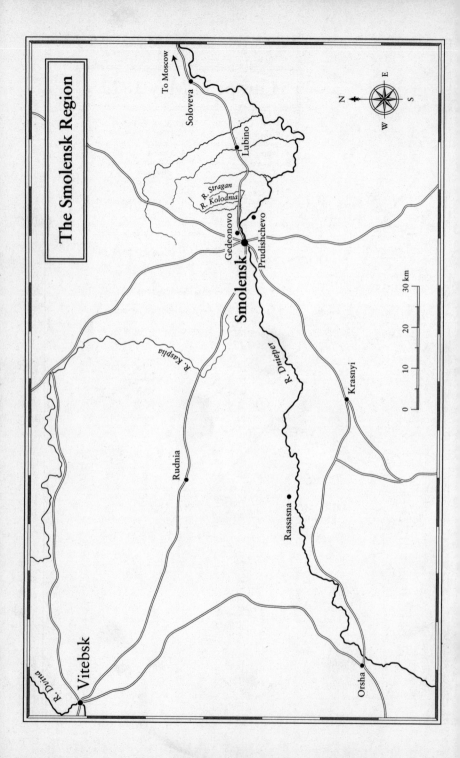

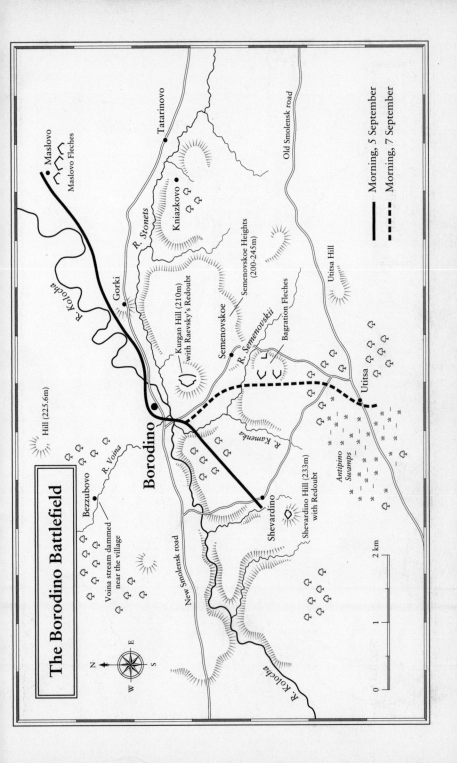

The Borodino Battlefield

Maslovo
Maslovo Fleches

Tatarinovo

Kniazkovo

R. Stonets

R. Kolocha

Semenovskoe Heights
(200-245m)

Gorki

Kurgan Hill (210m)
with Raevsky's Redoubt

Semenovskoe

Utitsa Hill

R. Semenovskii

Bagration Fleches

Hill (225.6m)

R. Voina

Borodino

R. Kamenka

Utitsa

Antipino
Swamps

Bezzubovo

Voina stream dammed
near the village

Shevardino

Shevardino Hill (233m)
with Redoubt

New Smolensk road

Old Smolensk road

R. Kolocha

N
E · · W
S

——— Morning, 5 September
- - - - Morning, 7 September

2 km

0   1   2

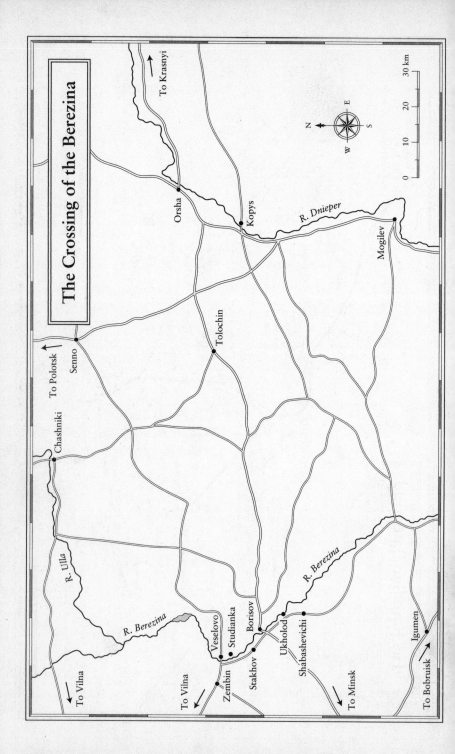

The Crossing of the Berezina

To Krasnyi

Orsha

Kopys

R. Dnieper

Mogilev

Senno

To Polotsk

To Polotsk

Tolochin

Chashniki

R. Ulla

R. Berezina

R. Berezina

Veselovo

Studianka

Borisov

Ukholod

Shabashevichi

Zembin

Stakhov

Igumen

To Vilna

To Vilna

To Vilna

To Minsk

To Bobruisk

30 km

0   10   20

N   E
W   S

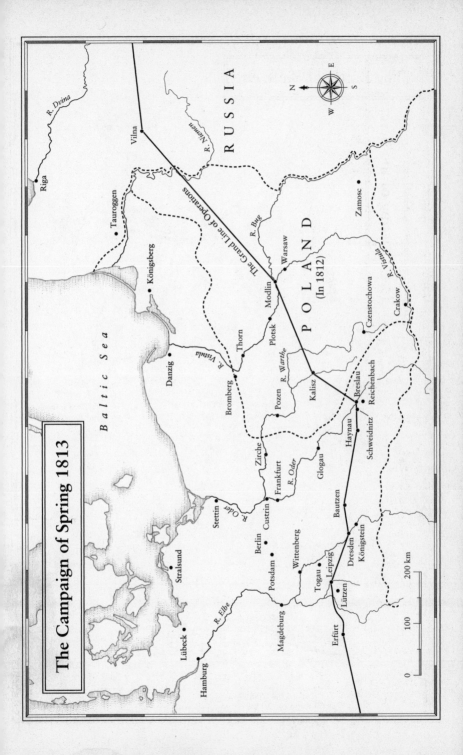

The Campaign of Spring 1813

R. Dvina

Riga

Tauroggen

Königsberg

Baltic Sea

Danzig

R. Vistula

Bromberg

Thorn

Plotsk

Modlin

Warsaw

Vilna

R. Niemen

RUSSIA

R. Bug

The Grand Line of Operations

POLAND (In 1812)

Zamosc

Czenstochowa

R. Vistula

Crakow

Kalisz

Breslau

Reichenbach

Haynau

Schweidnitz

Pozen

R. Warthe

Zirche

Frankfurt

R. Oder

Glogau

Bautzen

Stettin

Custrin

Berlin

Wittenberg

Potsdam

Togau

Leipzig

Lützen

Dresden

Königstein

Magdeburg

R. Elbe

Erfürt

Stralsund

Lübeck

Hamburg

N
E
W
S

200 km

100

0

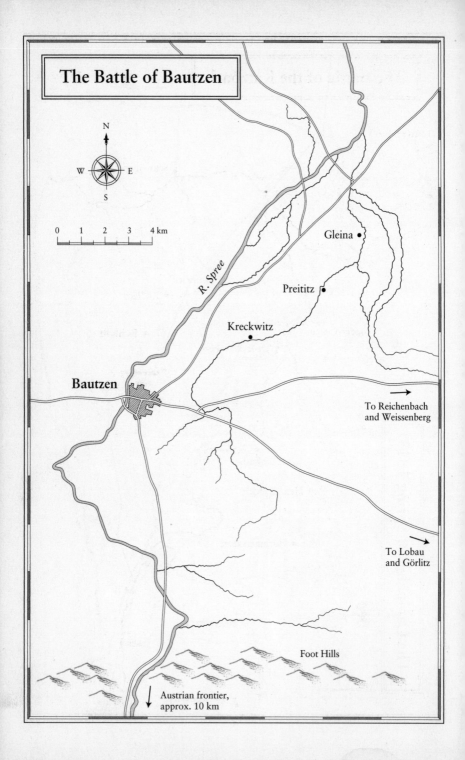

The Battle of Bautzen

N
W E
S

0 1 2 3 4 km

R. Spree

Gleina •

Preititz •

Kreckwitz •

Bautzen

To Reichenbach
and Weissenberg

To Lobau
and Görlitz

Foot Hills

Austrian frontier,
approx. 10 km

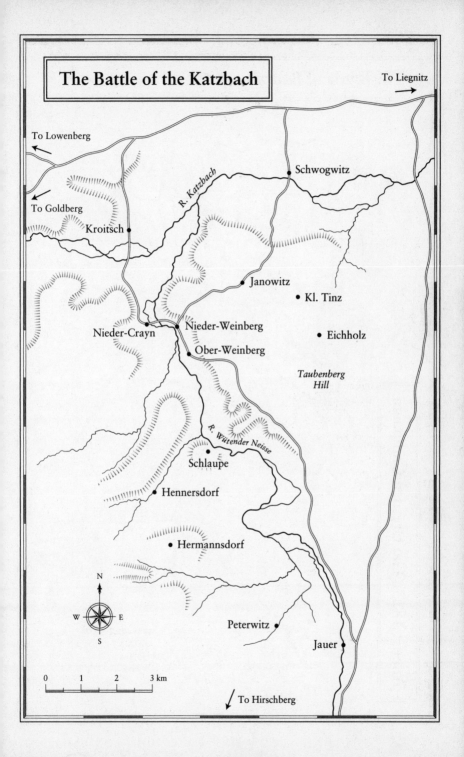

The Battle of the Katzbach

To Liegnitz

To Lowenberg

To Goldberg

R. Katzbach

Schwogwitz

Kroitsch

Janowitz

Kl. Tinz

Nieder-Weinberg

Eichholz

Nieder-Crayn

Ober-Weinberg

Taubenberg Hill

R. Wütender Neisse

Schlaupe

Hennersdorf

Hermannsdorf

N

W   E

S

Peterwitz

Jauer

0   1   2   3 km

To Hirschberg

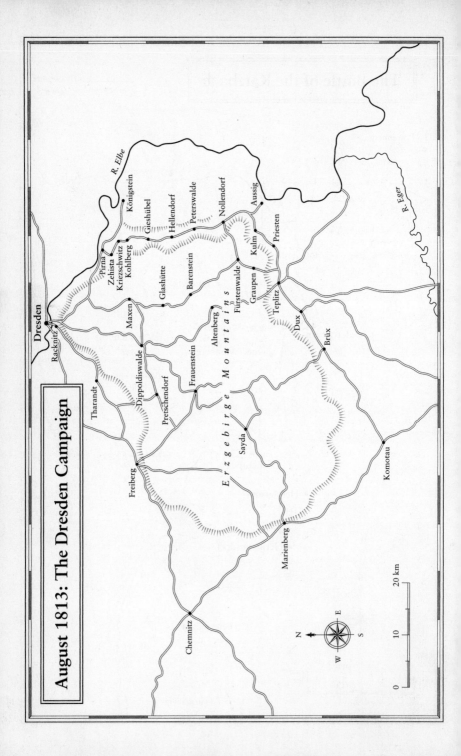

August 1813: The Dresden Campaign

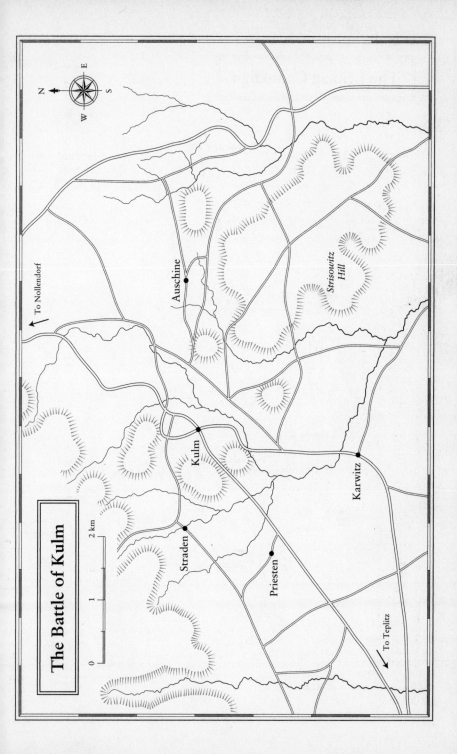

The Battle of Kulm

N E W S

To Nollendorf

Auschine

Strisowitz Hill

Kulm

Karwitz

Straden

Priesten

To Teplitz

0   1   2 km

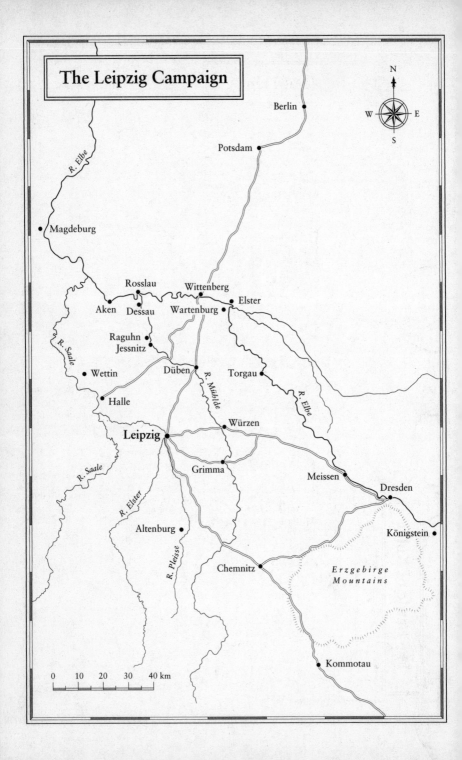

The Leipzig Campaign

Berlin

Potsdam

R. Elbe

Magdeburg

Rosslau
Wittenberg
Elster
Aken
Dessau
Wartenburg

Raguhn
Jessnitz

R. Saale

Wettin
Düben
Torgau

Halle

R. Mulde

R. Elbe

Leipzig
Würzen

Grimma
Meissen
Dresden

R. Saale

R. Elster
Altenburg
Königstein

R. Pleisse
Chemnitz
*Erzgebirge
Mountains*

Kommotau

0   10   20   30   40 km

N
W   E
S

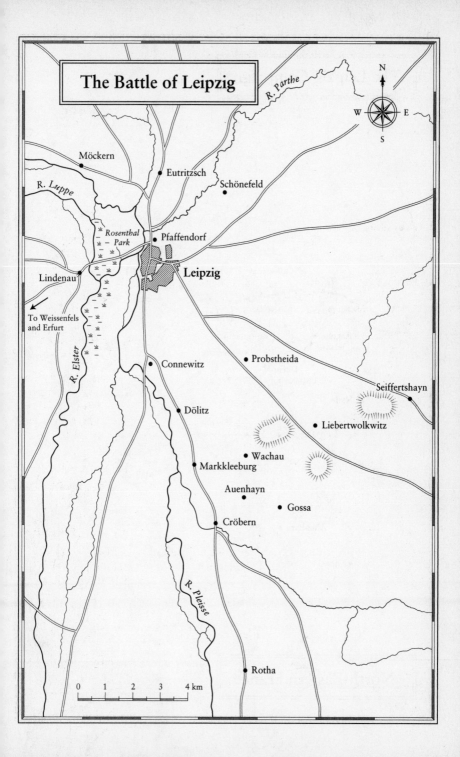

The Battle of Leipzig

R. Parthe

N
W   E
S

Möckern

Eutritzsch

Schönefeld

R. Luppe

Rosenthal
Park

Pfaffendorf

Leipzig

Lindenau

To Weissenfels
and Erfurt

R. Elster

Connewitz

Probstheida

Seiffertshayn

Dölitz

Liebertwolkwitz

Wachau

Markkleeburg

Auenhayn

Gossa

Cröbern

R. Pleisse

Rotha

0   1   2   3   4 km

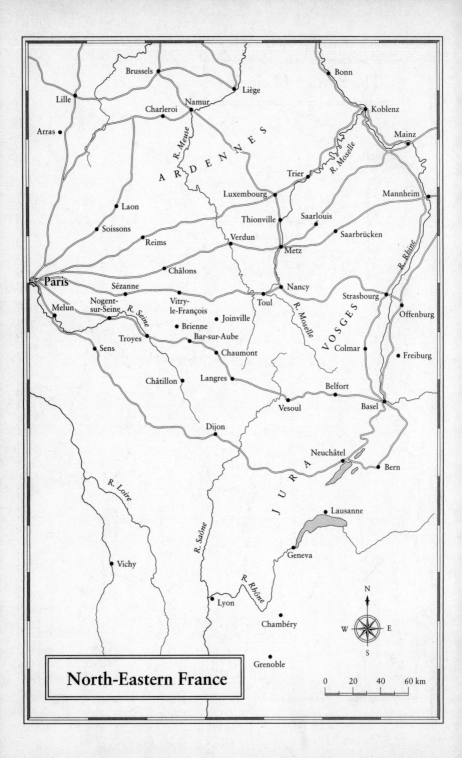

North-Eastern France

0   20   40   60 km

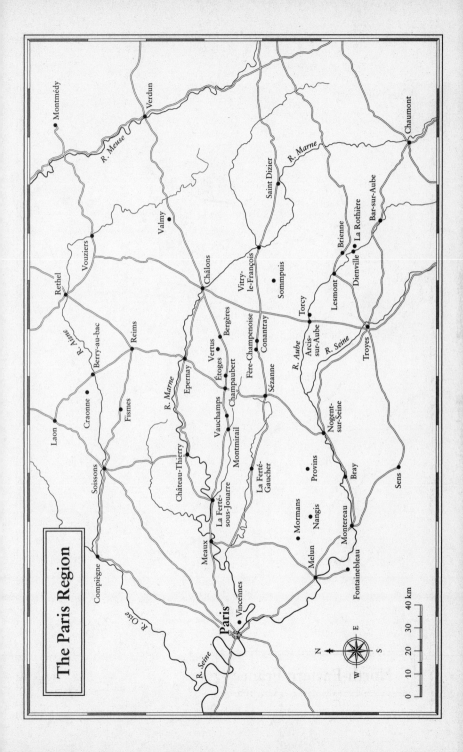

The Paris Region

Montmédy • Verdun •

R. Meuse

Chaumont •

R. Marne

Saint Dizier •

Bar-sur-Aube •

Valmy •

Vouziers •

Brienne •
La Rothière •

Châlons •

Vitry-le-François •

Sommpuis •

Lesmont •
Dienville •

Rethel •

R. Aisne

Torcy •
Arcis-sur-Aube •

Reims •

Berry-au-bac •

Bergères •

Fère-Champenoise •

Conantray •

R. Aube

R. Seine

Troyes •

Vertus •
Etoges •

Sézanne •

Craonne •

Fismes •

Epernay •

Champaubert •

Nogent-sur-Seine •

Laon •

R. Marne

Vauchamps •

Montmirail •

Soissons •

Château-Thierry •

La Ferté-Gaucher •

Provins •

Bray •

Sens •

La Ferté-sous-Jouarre •

Mormans •
Nangis •

Montereau •

Meaux •

Compiègne •

R. Oise

Melun •

Fontainebleau •

Paris
Vincennes •

R. Seine

N E
W S

0   10   20   30   40 km

Russia Against Napoleon

I

Introduction

Russia's defeat of Napoleon is one of the most dramatic stories in European history. It has many twists and turns. Not just in 1812 but also for much of 1813 the outcome remained very uncertain with most of the odds seemingly in Napoleon's favour. His personal history in these years is a tale of hubris and nemesis. There is a rich supporting cast of fascinating personalities who enliven the story and with whom it is often easy to empathize. The story contains two of the greatest battles in European history, Leipzig and Borodino, and many other episodes of great fascination for the military historian. It also tells one much about European society, culture and politics in that era. From the Russian perspective the story has that crucial element, a happy ending. Napoleon's first *Grande Armée* was destroyed in Russia in 1812. His second was defeated on the battlefields of Germany in 1813. In the longest campaign in European history, the Russian army pursued the French all the way from Moscow to Paris and led the victorious coalition into the enemy capital on 31 March 1814.

For very many years I have wanted to tell this story. At one level that is the simple purpose of this book. But I am an old-fashioned historian who likes his stories to be true, or at least as close to the truth as an honest, knowledgeable and meticulous study of the available evidence allows. Many years ago I came to the conclusion that the story as told in Western Europe and North America was very far from the truth. Hearing an untrue tale told over and over again annoyed me. Another purpose of this book is therefore to tell the story of how and why Russia defeated Napoleon in what seems to me to be a more truthful way.[1]

It is not surprising that what happened in 1812–14 is usually distorted in British, French and American books. Popular works on the Napoleonic era necessarily follow a rather set pattern. In Britain, for example, the bookshelves groan under the weight of works on Nelson and Trafalgar, or Wellington and Waterloo. These are the heroic narratives and the icons of British national identity. Napoleon and his army have also retained their fascination for the English- as well as French-speaking public. In any case, most authors cannot be expected to read many languages or consult archives in a range of countries. They expect to draw their information from the research of specialists. As regards Russia's role in the defeat of Napoleon, this research and these specialists do not exist. No Western professor has ever written a book on the Russian war effort against Napoleon. The surest way to make yourself unappointable in any British, let alone American, university is to say that you wish to study the history of battles, diplomacy and kings.[2]

In many areas of military history the gap left by the universities is filled by army staff colleges. There are some excellent books by military specialists – often but not always serving officers – on the Napoleonic era but almost none of this work covers Russia.[3] One reason why military specialists have avoided Russia is that the military archives have only become accessible to foreign researchers since 1991. More important, however, has been the belief that the French and Prussian armies of the Napoleonic era are much more worth studying, because they appear more modern. In the case of Napoleon, one had the timeless lessons to be learned from military genius, but the French army was also seen as pioneering aspects of modern warfare such as the all-arms division and corps. In the Prussian case one had Clausewitz, generally seen as the greatest of all thinkers on modern war. In addition, Prussia was believed to have created two other key elements of military modernity in this era: the first modern general staff and a highly effective and motivated mass conscript army. By contrast, there seemed little point in struggling to learn Russian and scrounge for information outside the archives in order to study an army that was still unequivocally Old Regime. The result is that the Russian side of the story is ignored or misinterpreted, with historians largely seeing Russia through the prism of French- or German-language sources.

As regards the French sources,[4] there are obvious dangers of interpreting any army or campaign largely through enemy eyes. Of course French officers usually wrote reports or memoirs to win promotion, boost their egos, achieve glory or justify their actions. No one who looks at the uniforms of the era can expect to find much modesty or self-effacement from the men who wore them. On the contrary, aggressive and boastful self-promotion often flourished in the armies of both Napoleon and his enemies. If the French were more boastful than most of the others, they had some reason to be, since their army was in most respects the best in Europe until 1812. When facing the Russians, their normal sense of superiority was sometimes heightened by an almost colonial scorn for the irrational barbarians of Europe's borderlands. Napoleon himself set the tone by finding few words of praise for any Russian troops other than Cossacks. This to some extent perhaps reflected a French variation on the theme of exoticism and Orientalism. Blaming defeat on the Cossacks or the weather was also useful. Since the French army had no Cossacks and the weather was an 'unfair' act of God, no French officer need fear that by invoking these sources of disaster he was questioning his own superior virility or professional skill. The way in which the English-language literature often uncritically repeats French accounts is likely to drive to distraction anyone who has studied the Russian sources or even just walked over the battlefields in question.

The German-language sources are much more mixed. In 1812–14 Germans fought both with and against Russia. Germans who fought with Russia in 1812 were either ethnic German subjects of the tsar or officers who had left their own armies in order to fight against Napoleon. There are actually a number of German-language memoirs which tell one a great deal about the Russian army and the Russian war effort in 1812. For example, of all the Russian generals' memoirs, probably the best are those of Prince Eugen of Württemberg, which are written in German.[5] Even so, they are very little used by English-language authors. The same is true of a number of other valuable memoirs written in German, for the most part by men who were Alexander's subjects.[6] By far the most frequently cited source is Clausewitz, both because of his fame and because his history of the 1812 campaign is translated into English.[7]

Clausewitz's history is extremely interesting and useful but one does nevertheless need to remember the context in which it was written. Under Frederick the Great the Prussian army had been considered the best in Europe. Foreign officers studied it as a model. But in 1806 it was not just defeated but humiliated, with rearguards and garrisons sometimes disintegrating and surrendering in the face of much smaller enemy forces. When Frederick William III sided with Napoleon in 1812 the humiliation increased, especially among those hyper-patriotic officers who like Clausewitz resigned their commissions and entered the Russian service. The xenophobic and faction-ridden Russian army of 1812 was a deeply frustrating place to be for a foreign officer such as Clausewitz who spoke no Russian and had inevitable difficulties in understanding the army and society he had joined. When reading Clausewitz I sometimes think of parallels with an intelligent staff officer in the Free French forces in London in 1940–44. Such an officer might have written a fascinating corrective to standard accounts of the British war effort but it would be surprising if we were to understand the conflict through his eyes alone.[8]

Studies of the 1812 campaign in English mostly concentrate on Napoleon's mistakes, on the problems created for the French by Russia's geography and climate, and on the horror but also the heroism in evidence in Napoleon's army during the retreat from Moscow. The year 1813 traditionally belongs to German authors celebrating the resurgence of Prussia and the triumph of German patriotism. Some of the Prussian general staff historians, and above all Rudolph von Friederich, are excellent.[9] But of course most of the memoirs and many of the histories put forward a Prussian view of events, which subsequently influenced British and American authors. So too do the views of the Austrian official history, not written until just before 1914, some volumes of which have a distinctly anti-Russian tinge.[10] If anything, the Russian angle on events gets even less attention or sympathy when it comes to the 1814 campaign. Military historians enthuse about Napoleon's reinvigorated genius after his disappointing performance in 1813. Historians of diplomacy and international relations on the other hand focus on Metternich and Castlereagh as the creators of a stable and orderly European system. Sometimes this literature has a Cold War feel to it, celebrating the alliance of British and German statesmanship to secure Europe against a threat of Russian hegemony.[11]

Of course national bias in the writing of history exists in all countries and especially when it comes to writing about war. War is generally the best source of heroic nationalist myths.[12] The Napoleonic Wars occurred at the dawn of modern European nationalism. It was exactly at this time that many of the ideas behind modern nationalism were first expressed. Shortly afterwards the Industrial Revolution would create cities, mass literacy and all the other aspects of modern society which helped nationalism to flourish. Traditionally, for example, the British grabbed Waterloo for themselves and it is only very recently that the decisive Prussian contribution to victory has been recognized in the English-language literature.[13] In this context it is not at all surprising that the Prussians elbowed Russia aside when it came to interpretations of 1813 or that French historians of the period have gloried in the exploits of Napoleon and his army, without paying too much attention to what enemy accounts and foreign historians had to say.

One crucial area of Napoleonic warfare has attracted too little attention from historians of every nationality. This is logistics, in other words the equipment and feeding of the armies. Commissariat officers had little status in any of the rival armies and societies. Their efforts have won little attention from historians. This is unfortunate because their role was often crucial. Napoleon destroyed his army in 1812 in large part because of logistical failures. By contrast, one of the key triumphs of the Russian war effort was its success in feeding and supplying more than half a million troops outside Russia's borders in 1813–14. How this was done in a European continent which in those days only had two cities with populations of more than 500,000 is a key part of the present book. The contrast with the Seven Years War (1756–63), when logistics helped to cripple the Russian military effort, is very much to the point.[14]

In many ways the greatest hero of the Russian war effort in 1812–14 was not a human being but the horse. To some extent this was true of all European land warfare at that time. The horse fulfilled the present-day functions of the tank, the lorry, the aeroplane and motorized artillery. It was in other words the weapon of shock, pursuit, reconnaissance, transport and mobile firepower. The horse was a crucial – perhaps even the single most decisive – factor in Russia's defeat of Napoleon. The enormous superiority of the Russian light cavalry played a key role in denying food or rest to Napoleon's army in the retreat from Moscow and thereby destroying it. In 1812 Napoleon lost not just almost all the men but virtually all the horses with which he had invaded Russia. In 1813 he could and did replace the men but finding new horses proved a far more difficult and in the end disastrous problem. Above all it was lack of cavalry which stopped Napoleon winning decisively in the spring 1813 campaign and persuaded him to agree to the fatal two-month summer armistice, which contributed so much to his ultimate defeat.

The final allied offensive in 1814 which led to the fall of Paris and Napoleon's overthrow was sparked off by the Russian light cavalry's interception of secret French dispatches revealing all of the emperor's plans and his capital's vulnerability. This was a fitting end to two years of warfare in which the Russian light cavalry had been superior from the start and totally dominant after September 1812. But this dominance was not an act of God or nature. The historian needs to study the Russian horse industry and how it was mobilized by the government in 1812–14. Also crucial is a grasp of how the Russians managed, preserved and reinforced their cavalry regiments during these campaigns. Again, this is a key part of the present book.[15]

Naturally, humans in general and nationalist historians in particular were interested in soldiers' heroics on the battlefield, not in how their stomachs were filled or their horses kept healthy. This was just as true in Russia as elsewhere. Like the other great powers, Russia mined the Napoleonic era for national myths. The official tsarist myth of 1812 was that the Russian people had united around the throne and under the leadership of the nobility to destroy the invader of the country's sacred soil. There was if anything rather more truth to this Russian myth than to its Prusso-German equivalent, which stated that the Prussian nation had sprung to arms in 1813 to liberate Germany after Frederick William III's appeal 'To My People'.

One entirely true reason why Russia defeated Napoleon was that many able young officers were promoted on merit to key positions during the war. Among the Russian leaders, Aleksandr Chernyshev and Johann von Diebitsch became lieutenant-generals aged 28, and Mikhail Vorontsov aged 30. They were just the tip of the iceberg. Count Karl von Nesselrode was only 28 when he took control of Russian espionage in Paris in 1808. He served subsequently as Alexander's chief diplomatic adviser in 1813–14. Even the older generation of military leaders was often not that old: Petr Mikhailovich Volkonsky, who served as Alexander's chief of staff, was only 38 when the war ended. These men were to dominate Russia's army and government for many subsequent decades. The official histories of the war by Dmitrii Buturlin and Aleksandr Mikhailovsky-Danilevsky were very careful not to offend these grandees. There are British parallels. The Duke of Wellington lived for almost four decades after Waterloo and was in a position to make his own view on the battle almost canonical in Britain.[16]

There were, however, important differences between Wellington and the Russian leaders. Although the duke had many political enemies in the 1820s and 1830s, by the time he died he was a national icon. The same was far from true of the Russian generals who lived as long as him. Just after Alexander I's death in 1825 a group of officers, the so-called Decembrists, attempted to overthrow the absolute monarchy and install a constitutional regime or even a republic. Among them were officers such as Mikhail Orlov and Prince Serge Volkonsky who had distinguished themselves in the wars. The coup was crushed. Key heroes of the wars such as Aleksandr Chernyshev, Alexander Benckendorff and Petr Volkonsky played a part in its suppression and went on to serve as ministers under Nicholas I well into the mid-nineteenth century.

The Decembrist revolt and its suppression was the beginning of the exceptionally bitter split between right and left in Russia which ended in the revolution of 1917. The violent hatred between the two camps helped to poison and distort memories of 1812–14. In the Winter Palace in Petersburg there is a fine gallery with portraits of almost all the generals from 1812–14. As a graduate student in the Soviet Union in the 1970s I once got into a fierce argument with a young woman who was furious at the fact that among the portraits is that of Alexander Benckendorff, who subsequently served as Nicholas I's chief of the security police. My attempts to argue that Benckendorff was a war hero got nowhere. When I called him a partisan leader, which is exactly what he was for much of 1812–14, she stormed off in disgust. The young student was not at all pro-Communist but she was a product of the Moscow radical-liberal intelligentsia. For her, heroes of 1812 in general and partisans in particular were 'friends of the people' and therefore by definition honorary members of her radical political camp and tradition.

When it took over the 1812 myth and made it an integral part of Soviet patriotism, the Communist regime to a great extent set such ideas in stone. The historical reality of Russia's war effort had to be startlingly distorted to suit official ideology in the Stalinist era. Alexander I had to be marginalized and vilified, and the war's international context distorted; Kutuzov was elevated to the level of Napoleon or higher, while his aristocratic origins and court connections (together with those of Prince Petr Bagration) had to be overlooked; the significance of mass resistance to Napoleon had to be exaggerated and occasional resistance to landlords and government officials somehow interpreted as constructive elements in the people's war against both domestic tyranny and the French. Official norms of this sort crippled Russian scholarship on the Napoleonic era for a time and have left a mark on how many ordinary Russians of the older generation think about 1812–14. Contemporary Russian historians have mercifully long since escaped the Stalinist myths about the Napoleonic era, however.[17]

Nevertheless, for all its crude distortions, the Soviet-era official interpretation of the Napoleonic Wars still in many ways remained true to the spirit of Leo Tolstoy, who was by far the most important nineteenth-century mythmaker as regards his impact on Russian (and foreign) understanding of Russia's role in the Napoleonic era. Tolstoy depicts elemental Russian patriotism as uniting in defence of national soil. He paints Kutuzov as the embodiment of Russian patriotism and wisdom, contrasting him with the idiocy of so-called professional military experts, whom he sees as Germans and pedants. His conception of history in any case leaves little room for skilful leadership or even for the attempt to direct events in rational fashion. Instead, he celebrates the moral strength, courage and patriotism of ordinary Russians. Perhaps most important in the context of the present book, Tolstoy ends his novel *War and Peace* in December 1812 with the war only half over and the greatest challenges still to come. The long, bitter but ultimately triumphant road that led from Vilna in December 1812 to Paris in March 1814 plays no part in his work, just as it was entirely marginalized in the Soviet patriotic canon and in contemporary Russian folk memory. For every one publication in Russian on 1813–14 there are probably more than one hundred on 1812. The most recent attempt to write a grand history of 1812–14 which is both popular and scholarly devotes 490 pages to 1812 and 50 to the longer and more complicated campaigns of the two following years.[18]

The popular or 'Tolstoyan' Russian interpretation of the war fits rather well with foreign accounts that play down the role of Russia's army and government in the victory over Napoleon. Napoleon himself was much inclined to blame geography, the climate and chance; this absolved him from responsibility for the catastrophe. Historians usually add Napoleon's miscalculations and blunders to the equation but many of them are happy to go along with Tolstoy's implied conclusion that the Russian leadership had little control over events and that Russian 'strategy' was a combination of improvisation and accident. Inevitably too, Russian lack of interest in 1813–14 left the field free for historians of other nations who were happy to tell the story of these years with Russia's role marginalized.

Of course it is not difficult to understand why Russians found it easiest to identify with a war fought on national soil in defence of Moscow and under a commanding general called Kutuzov. It was harder to be as enthusiastic about campaigns waged in Germany and France under commanders called Wittgenstein and Barclay de Tolly in defence of a true but somewhat metaphysical concept of Russian security rooted in ideas about the European balance of power. As the war's centenary approached in 1912 there was great interest, and many new publications resulted. By this time, however, Russia was on the eve of war with those very same Hohenzollerns and Habsburgs with whom she had allied herself in 1813. Obviously, this was not the best of moments to celebrate Russo-German solidarity. In 1813–14 the two most brilliant Russian staff officers were Karl von Toll, a Baltic German, and Johann von Diebitsch, the son of a Prussian staff officer who had transferred to the Russian service. Almost two-thirds of the troops in the most successful allied force – Field-Marshal Blücher's so-called Army of Silesia – were in fact Russian but Blücher's two Russian army corps' commanders were Alexandre de Langeron and Fabian von der Osten-Sacken. By now too Nikolai Rumiantsev and Aleksandr Kurakin had been marginalized and there were no ethnic Russians at all among Alexander's chief advisers on foreign policy. Meanwhile the emperor himself gave many Russians even at the time the feeling that he saw Russia as backward and unworthy of his ideals, and was willing to sacrifice Russian interests in the name of European security or even so as to win applause for himself in fashionable Europe.

At the root of all these issues is the contrast, very familiar to historians, between Russia as empire and Russia as nation and people.[19] In 1814 the British, French and Germans were, or were in the process of becoming, nations. The nationalist myths generated from the Napoleonic Wars suited this reality and endeavour. Russia in 1814 was a dynastic, aristo-cratic and multi-ethnic empire. Its core was the Russian land, people and nobility but these did not yet constitute a nation and could never entirely do so as long as the dynastic empire existed. The Russian Empire won the war of 1812–14 but the myths which have subsequently lived in Russian memory have above all been ethno-national ones. That is the most important reason why – uniquely, and in total contrast to the Germans, French and British – Russian national myths derived from the Napoleonic Wars greatly underestimate the Russian achievement in 1812–14.[20]

A key aim of this book is to get back beyond the Russian myths to the realities of the Russian war effort in 1812–14. I am above all interested in establishing how and why Russia overcame the enormous challenge presented by Napoleon in these years. There are also other reasons for questioning aspects of Russian mythology about the Napoleonic era.

One reason is a reflection on empires and nations. Both generally and in the Russian case it seems to me a mistake to see everything in the imperial tradition as harmful and the nation as the inevitable embodiment of virtue. This is in no sense a justification for neo-empire in today's world. But empire in its day – unlike very many nations – was often relatively tolerant, pluralist and even occasionally benevolent in its attitude towards the many communities who sheltered under its protection. This was true too as regards the Russian Empire's treatment of most non-Russians, most of the time. It was certainly one of the empire's strengths in the era of Alexander I that it was willing and able to employ and trust the loyalty of so many non-Russian elites. More specifically, it seems a mistake to see Alexander's foreign policy as 'imperial' and as not serving the interests of Russia, however 'Russia' is understood. Before 1812 Napoleon had shown rather clearly why his domination of Europe was a great threat to Russian security and economic interests. In 1813 Alexander was entirely right to seize the opportunity of driving the French out of Germany and restoring the foundations of a European balance of power. The subsequent decision to take the Russian army over the Rhine and remove Napoleon is more debatable. In my view, however, Alexander was once again right to believe that Russia above all needed peace and stability in Europe, and that Napoleon's survival would make both peace and stability impossible. The Napoleonic era is a classic example of how interdependent are Russian and European security. It was also a time when Russia made a great contribution to restoring peace and stability in Europe.

Russians therefore have every reason for pride in what their state and army achieved in 1812–14. Ironically, the traditional obsession of Russian historians with military operations in 1812 at the expense of the two following years does no service to the Russian army's reputation. Even more than in most activities, there is a huge difference between training for war and its reality. By 1813–14 the army had learned from experience. By then many of the generals were first-rate and staffs were performing much better than at the beginning of the 1812 campaign. On the battlefield in 1813–14 reserves were often utilized and cavalry, infantry and artillery coordinated much more effectively than had previously been the case. Given the enormous distance of military operations from the army's bases, the reinforcement and supply of the field armies was managed with remarkable skill. Discipline, regimental pride, loyalty to comrades, and pre-modern religious and monarchist loyalties motivated the ordinary soldiers of the emperor's army whether they fought on Russian soil or abroad. To anyone who has read accounts of the battles of (to take three examples) Kulm, Leipzig and Craonne, the idea that the army's motivation or fighting spirit declined after 1812 seems very strange.

The final crucial reason for not forgetting 1813–14 is that the history of 1812 makes no sense without it. Alexander and his war minister, Mikhail Barclay de Tolly, planned before 1812 for a war which would last two years at a minimum and probably longer. They made their plans partly on the basis of excellent intelligence about Napoleon's intentions and about the strengths and weaknesses not just of his army but also of his regime. From the start, their plan was to wear down Napoleon by a defensive campaign in Russia, and then to pursue the defeated enemy back over the frontier and raise a European insurrection against him. There is ample evidence of this thinking in Russian military, intelligence and diplomatic documents. The whole manner in which Russian resources and manpower were mobilized makes sense only in the context of a long war. One key reason why Russia defeated Napoleon was that her top leaders out-thought him. In 1812 they planned and then successfully imposed on him a drawn-out campaign, knowing full well that it was precisely the kind of war he was least equipped to wage. In 1813–14 Alexander's combined diplomatic and military strategy contributed to isolating Napoleon first in Europe and then even from French elites. Of course Napoleon played a huge part in his own downfall. But his enemy's capacity for self-destruction was always part of

Alexander's calculation. Russian policy in these years was intelligently conceived and was executed with consistent purpose. It was very far removed indeed from Tolstoyan mythology.

The core of this book is a study of grand strategy, military operations and diplomacy, in other words of power politics. Military and diplomatic policy were closely intertwined in these years and must be studied together. This is particularly true as regards the Russo-Austrian relationship, which was the most sensitive but also probably the most important aspect of Russian foreign policy in 1813–14.

From the summer of 1810 until Napoleon's invasion, though in principle diplomacy was central, Russian policy was strongly affected by military considerations. The exceptionally valuable information provided by Russian intelligence in Paris persuaded Alexander I that Napoleon was intent on attacking Russia and greatly influenced Russian diplomacy and strategic planning. The Russian emperor's preference for adopting a defensive military strategy more or less ruled out any possibility that his attempts to secure an alliance with Prussia would succeed. In the campaigns of 1812 and autumn 1813 diplomacy was of little importance and military operations were decisive. This was not true in the spring 1813 and 1814 campaigns, in which diplomatic and political considerations influenced and at times even determined military strategy. In the spring 1813 campaign this almost resulted in disaster. Alexander I decided Russian grand strategy and diplomacy, and often had a big influence on military operations. His views, personality and modus operandi were of crucial importance. Without him the Russian army would probably not have pursued Napoleon into Germany in 1813 and would certainly never have reached Paris. So this book truly is a study of kings and battles.

Power politics requires the existence of power and is influenced by how much power a state has and what forms this power takes. The book looks at the sources of Russian power in Alexander's reign. That of course means the imperial army, and in particular its structure of command, tactics, 'doctrine' and personnel. But it also means Russian military industry, public finance, horse industry and manpower. Russian strengths and weaknesses in these areas help to explain how the empire fought the war and why it triumphed. As is always the case, the political regime and the social context heavily influenced both the mobilization and the use of the empire's resources. The basis of the Russian political and social order was serfdom. The imperial army was a professional force whose soldiers were a separate estate of the realm and who served for twenty-five years of their lives. How could and did such a society and army meet and overcome Napoleon's challenge? The Russian officer corps, and in particular its senior ranks, were very much a part of the overall imperial elite, itself still largely aristocratic. Army, aristocracy and government were a maze of family and patronage networks. It is often impossible to understand how the army functioned unless we take this into account.

The same is true as regards the values and culture of the imperial army's generals and officers. Honour, publicly displayed courage, and loyalty to regiment and fellow-officers all mattered greatly. So too did living up to one's status and rank. The battlefield, like the duel, allowed honour to be publicly displayed and defended. In some respects the 'field of honour' – in other words the battlefield – was also the ancestor of today's sporting match. 'Winning' meant holding one's ground and capturing trophies such as cannon and standards. These male warrior values appear not just archaic but also sometimes childish: nevertheless they mattered greatly because they affected morale and kept officers steadfast in the face of death and mutilation. A key problem in the 1812 campaign was that these values cut right across Russia's strategic imperative to retreat.[21]

Though the historian can write with some confidence of officers' values and motivation, understanding the mentalities of the rank and file is far more difficult. In 1812–14 more than 1.5 million men served as privates or NCOs in the army and militia. Only two left memoirs.[22] These can be eked out by a few oral reminiscences recorded decades later and by the personnel records of many regiments preserved in the archives. Often, however, one is forced to interpret soldiers' values through their actions and through what their officers said about them. This has obvious dangers. But a book which simply took as a given the courage, endurance and loyalty of Russian soldiers in the face of awful privations and – sometimes – brutal treatment by their superiors would be ignoring one of the most vital but also at times puzzling elements in the wars.

Russia is the biggest gap in contemporary Western understanding of the Napoleonic era. The aim of this book is to fill that gap. But a more knowledgeable and realistic understanding of Russian power and policy can also change overall perspectives on the Napoleonic era. In this period Russia was less powerful than Britain. Its global reach was much weaker. Unlike Austria or Prussia, however, Russian interests and perspectives were not just narrowly continental. For a significant section of the ruling elite the Napoleonic Wars were in one sense a distraction and a sideshow. They saw Russia's main interests as lying in expansion southwards against the Ottomans and Persians. These men seldom saw France itself as Russia's main or inevitable enemy. Most of them believed that the Napoleonic empire was a transient phenomenon, born of exceptional circumstances and Napoleon's genius. The most impressive member of this group was Count Nikolai Rumiantsev, who was in practice Russia's minister of foreign affairs from late in 1807 until Napoleon invaded Russia. In his view the greatest long-term challenge to Russia lay in Britain's growing domination of global finance, trade and industry, and in her monopoly of naval power. This view of Russian interests was ultimately overruled by Alexander I. Above all, it was undermined by Napoleon, who forced the Russian government to make fighting France its top priority. But Rumiantsev's perspective had some impact on Russian policy in 1812 because it was shared in part by Mikhail Kutuzov. It also provides an interesting insight into some of the underlying realities of the Napoleonic era.

The Napoleonic Wars of 1800–1815 were a global, not just a European struggle.[23] This may seem a strange view since the overwhelming majority of the battles in these years occurred in Europe. In that sense the Napoleonic Wars were more European and less global even than the Revolutionary Wars of the 1790s. They were far less global than the Seven Years War or the American War of Independence, in both of which much of the most significant fighting occurred in the Western hemisphere and in Asia. In reality, however, the Napoleonic Wars were largely confined to Europe because the British were getting closer to winning their hundred-years-war with France for global supremacy. The most basic fact about the Napoleonic Wars was that British seapower locked French imperialism into Europe. For many reasons it was far harder to create any species of empire in Europe than overseas. As a number of Russian observers understood, it was in the Revolutionary and Napoleonic eras that Britain consolidated its hugely powerful global empire, both territorial and commercial. Looked at from one angle, Napoleon's attempt to create a European empire was simply a last, heroic effort to balance British imperialism and avoid defeat in France's century-long conflict with Britain. The odds were very much against Napoleon, though by 1812 he had come seemingly very close to success.

It is in fact possible to study the Napoleonic Wars on many different levels. At one extreme one has the God's-eye view. This looks at events in the round and in the long term. It is interested in the impact of geopolitics, at shifts in European ideology and cultural values after 1789, and at global patterns of trade and finance. At the other extreme one has what might be described as the view of the worm. This includes the day-to-day perceptions of ordinary people in this era. It includes, too, important details such as the firing locks and cartridge paper which contributed to the unreliability of Russian musketry. Here, too, for example, one finds discussion of the events of the afternoon of 21 May 1813, when Marshal Michel Ney's mistakes robbed Napoleon of decisive victory in the battle of Bautzen and probably thereby denied him the chance to decide the 1813 campaign and keep Austria out of the war. Between the levels of God and the worm one finds the other matters commonly discussed by historians. As regards this book, for example, they include Russian infantry tactics, the Russian armaments industry, or Russian perceptions of Austria and the Balkans. In the present book all these levels are covered, since all of them are relevant to understanding how and why Russia defeated Napoleon.

The basic approach of the book is chronological. I begin with the negotiations at Tilsit in 1807 and end with the Russian army's entry into Paris in 1814. One reason for doing this is that any other approach would ruin the story. Not even a professor has the right to do this to one of the best stories in European history. But another reason for using narrative and chronology is that this is usually much the most truthful way to explain what happened in these years. On the battlefield an opportunity for victory that existed at two o'clock in the afternoon had often gone by four. Chance, misperception and confusion accounted for much of what happened. Decisions had consequences which rippled through the following days and weeks. At a number of points in the book I pause from the narrative to explain the background, however. In Chapter 7, for example, I turn aside from the narrative of the 1812 campaign to explain what was happening on the crucial Russian home front.

The book progresses as follows. Chapter 2 introduces the reader to two of the book's 'heroes', namely the imperial army and Emperor Alexander I. It provides essential information on the Russian political system, the sinews of Russian power, and the nature of international relations in the Napoleonic era. It concludes with the negotiations at Tilsit in 1807 and seeks to explain Russian thinking at the conference and the bases of the Franco-Russian 'deal' to run Europe and put their relations on a long-term peaceful footing. Chapter 3 is a narrative of Franco-Russian relations from Tilsit until Napoleon's invasion of Russia in June 1812. It is mostly but by no means exclusively about diplomacy. A crucial element of this chapter is a discussion of Russian intelligence operations, above all in Paris, and of their impact. The chapter ends with an attempt to put Franco-Russian relations into the broader global context. It is this chapter which most obviously combines all levels of explanation, from God to the worm. Chapter 4 looks at how the Russian army prepared and planned for war between 1807 and 1812.

There follow four chapters on 1812 and four on 1813. Six of these eight chapters are essentially narratives of the campaigns. In all six chapters, however, I devote much attention to how the armies were fed and supplied. This is always important. At some points in 1812 and 1813 it was decisive. The chapters on 1812 and autumn 1813 are largely military in content. Once these campaigns had begun, diplomacy took a back seat. On the contrary, in the first eight months of 1813 Russian strategy was largely determined by the need to bring Prussia and Austria into the war if Alexander's goals were to be achieved. Diplomacy therefore plays a big role in Chapter 9 on the campaign of spring 1813. Two of these eight chapters are devoted to the Russian home front and to how Russian resources were mobilized in 1812 and 1813. It is impossible to understand the war effort or Russian victory without them. Chapters 13 and 14 cover the 1814 campaign. They too are a narrative, though a complicated one because of the need to weave together military operations, diplomacy, logistics and even French domestic politics, since all four elements were closely intertwined and essential to understanding Russian policy and the eventual allied victory.

2

Russia as a Great Power

For the Russian state the eighteenth century had been an era of victories. Before the reign of Peter the Great (1689–1725) European elites had seen the Russians as barbarous, alien and unimportant. Like the Ottomans, they were regarded as outsiders to Europe: unlike them, they did not earn even the grudging respect born of fear. By the time of Peter's death, however, attitudes had begun to change. Russia had smashed Sweden in the Great Northern War (1700–21) and had replaced it as the most powerful state in north-eastern Europe. In the Seven Years War (1756–63) Russia made an even bigger impact on European minds. Her armies occupied East Prussia, defeated Frederick II's forces on many occasions, and even briefly captured Berlin. Only the death of the Empress Elizabeth in 1762 and the dramatic reversal of Russian policy by her successor, Peter III, saved Prussia from destruction.[1]

There followed the reign of Catherine II (1762–96) during which Russia's territory, power and international status grew enormously. Most of the Polish commonwealth as well as huge territories in what we now call southern and eastern Ukraine but which was then known as 'New Russia' were annexed. Having become the leading Baltic power under Peter, Russia now came to dominate the Black Sea as well and to send her fleets into the Mediterranean. The fertile Ukrainian grasslands conquered by Catherine began to fill up with colonists. As the economy of New Russia boomed, there seemed almost no limits to possible future Russian power. Catherine and her most famous lover, Grigorii Potemkin, contemplated restoring the Byzantine Empire and putting her grandson, the Grand Duke Constantine, on its throne. The scheme was ambitious and fantastic but so too was not just Catherine's own life but also Russia's dramatic rise in the eighteenth century.[2]

One effect of these triumphs was to accustom Russian elites to victory and to feed their pride, confidence and arrogance. For better and worse, this had an impact on how Russia fought in 1812–14. Inevitably too, victory increased the legitimacy of the Romanov dynasty and of the autocratic system of government. Russia was a strong supporter of constitutional principles in Sweden and Poland because it knew that the weakness of the Swedish and Polish monarchies undermined these neighbours and rivals. Russia's spectacular victories over the Ottomans between 1768 and 1792 also owed much to the inability of weak sultans to control court factions and provincial satraps. Both the Russian tsars and the Ottoman sultans faced the challenge of out-of-date military forces which blocked the creation of a modern, European-style army. These regiments – the *strel'tsy* (musketeers) in Russia and the janissaries in the Ottoman Empire – were all the more dangerous because they were deployed in the capitals and linked to conservative political and religious groups which opposed a swath of necessary reforms. Peter the Great destroyed the *strel'tsy* in the 1690s. Not until the 1820s was an Ottoman sultan powerful and resolute enough to destroy the janissaries. By then the tsarist state had long since overtaken the Ottomans in terms of power.[3]

The foundations of this power were the political alliance between the Romanov monarchy and the landowning aristocracy and gentry. In this respect Russia was similar to the other four European great powers (Britain, France, Austria and Prussia), all of which rested on a similar alliance between the crown and the landowning elites. In each case this alliance had its specific traits. In Britain, for instance, monarchical power was not absolute and the aristocracy was the senior partner in a coalition which included financial and commercial elites.[4]

Though all four continental great powers were in theory absolute monarchies, no one doubted that the power of the Russian emperor was more complete than that of his French, Austrian or even Prussian peers. He could make laws and tax his peoples without their consent, and no laws protected even his most aristocratic subjects against his arbitrary whims. By contrast, especially in France and Austria, aristocratic assemblies and judicial institutions inherited from medieval feudalism inhibited a monarch's power, as indeed did the ethos of the social elites, including sometimes of the monarchs themselves and their relatives. Other factors also enhanced the power of the Russian autocrat. For example, in Protestant Europe the previously enormous landholdings of the Catholic Church had been confiscated during the Reformation and had mostly fallen into the hands of the aristocracy. In eighteenth-century Catholic Europe most of these lands were still held by the Church. In Russia, however, the monarchy had confiscated the vast wealth of the Orthodox Church by the 1760s and largely held on to it for itself. That was one key reason why by the 1790s more than 40 per cent of the entire serf population 'belonged' not to private landlords but to the crown.[5]

The immense and arbitrary power of the autocrat was an everyday reality in Russian politics and government. The autocrat's policies and the skill with which he or she managed both the machinery of government and the aristocratic elite were of crucial importance. But a Russian monarch was simultaneously all-powerful and yet in some respects strongly constrained. Even European Russia was vastly larger than any other great power. Its population did not exceed that of France until the 1750s and remained widely scattered by European standards in Alexander I's reign. Land-based communications were primitive and disintegrated into impassable mud in the spring and autumn. The state bureaucracy was small, corrupt and incompetent. In 1763 Russia had only slightly more state officials than Prussia, though the latter was a hundredth the size of Russia-in-Europe. A Prussian monarch could recruit bureaucrats trained in law and administration from the many German universities which in some cases had existed since medieval times. When Alexander I came to the Russian throne in 1801 Russia had just one university, founded in Moscow in 1755. After the reform of provincial government in 1775 the state administration in the countryside began to thicken but in the great majority of cases these new officials were drawn from, and often elected by, the local landowning gentry. Very often these men had served as army officers for a few years before returning to the provinces to marry and inherit small estates. The extension of local administration therefore deepened the mutual dependence of the monarchy and the landowning class.

On the one hand the Romanovs could not do without the landowners, whom one monarch called the state's involuntary tax-collectors and recruitment agents in the villages. Nor could the state survive without the service of noblemen in its bureaucracy and, above all, as officers in its army. But the gentry also badly needed the state. Employment as officers or officials was a crucial additional source of income. The state also provided security for the landowners against peasant recalcitrance or insurrection. In 1773 a revolt of Cossacks and peasants spread across a huge area in the Urals and along the lower Volga, headed by Emelian Pugachev. It took many months of campaigning by thousands of regular troops to suppress the rebellion, which cost hundreds of nobles their lives and left a deep scar on the consciousness of the elites. For a small but nevertheless significant number of minor nobles the army and even bureaucracy provided a channel by which they could rise into the aristocratic elite and thereby acquire wealth. The constant wars of the eighteenth century provided many opportunities for young nobles to prove themselves.

Apart from the Romanovs, the greatest beneficiaries of eighteenth-century Russia's growing wealth were the small group of families who dominated court, government and army in this era and formed the empire's aristocratic elite. Some of these families were older than the Romanovs, others were of much more recent origin, but by Alexander I's reign they formed a single aristocratic elite, united by wealth and a web of marriages. Their riches, social status and positions in government gave them great power. Their patron–client networks stretched throughout Russia's government and armed forces. The Romanovs themselves came from this aristocratic milieu. Their imperial status had subsequently raised them far above mere aristocrats, and the monarchs were determined to preserve their autonomy and never allow themselves to be captured by any aristocratic clique. Nevertheless, like other European monarchs they regarded these aristocratic magnates as their natural allies and companions, as bulwarks of the natural order and hierarchy of a well-run society.

The aristocracy used a number of crafty ways to preserve their power. In the eighteenth century they enlisted their sons in Guards regiments in childhood. By the time they reached their twenties, these sprigs of the aristocracy used their years of 'seniority' and the privileged status of the Guards to jump into colonelcies in line regiments. Catherine the Great's son, Paul I, who reigned from 1796 to 1801, stopped this trick but very many of the aristocrats in senior posts in 1812–14 had benefited from it. Even more significant was the use made by the aristocracy of positions at court. Though mostly honorific, these positions allowed young gentlemen of the bedchamber (*Kammerjunker*) and lords in waiting (*Kammerherr*) to transfer into senior positions in government of supposedly equivalent rank.

In the context of eighteenth-century Europe there was nothing particularly surprising about this. Young British aristocrats bought their way rapidly up the military hierarchy, sat in Parliament for their fathers' pocket boroughs and sometimes inherited peerages at a tender age. Unlike the English, Russian aristocrats did not control government through their domination of Parliament. A monarch who bungled policy or annoyed the Petersburg elite too deeply could be overthrown and murdered, however. Paul I once remarked that there were no *Grands Seigneurs* in Russia save men who were talking to the emperor and even their status lasted only as long as the emperor deigned to continue the conversation. He was half correct: Russian magnates were more subservient and less autonomous than their equivalents in London or Vienna. But he was also half wrong and paid for his miscalculation with his life in 1801, when he was murdered by members of the aristocracy, outraged by his arbitrary behaviour, led by the governor-general of Petersburg, Count Peter von der Pahlen.

The Russian aristocracy and gentry made up the core of the empire's ruling elite and officer corps. But the Romanovs ruled over a multi-ethnic empire. They allied themselves to their empire's non-Russian aristocracies and drew them into their court and service. The most successful non-Russian aristocrats were the German landowning class in the Baltic provinces. By one conservative estimate 7 per cent of all Russian generals in 1812 were Baltic German nobles. The Balts partly owed their success to the fact that, thanks to the Lutheran Church and the eighteenth-century Enlightenment in northern Europe, they were much better educated than the average Russian provincial noble.[6]

There was nothing unusual at the time in an empire being ruled by diverse and alien elites. In its heyday, the Ottoman ruling elite was made up of converted Christian slaves. The Ching and Mughal empires were run by elites who came from beyond the borders of China or the subcontinent. By these standards, the empire of the Romanovs was very Russian. Even by European standards the Russian state was not unique. Very many of the Austrian Empire's leading soldiers and statesmen came from outside the Habsburgs' own territories. None of Prussia's three greatest heroes in 1812–14 – Blücher, Scharnhorst or Gneisenau – was born a Prussian subject or began his career in the Prussian army.

It is true that there were probably more outsiders in the Russian army than in Austria or Prussia. European immigrants also stood out more sharply in Petersburg than in Berlin or Vienna. In the eighteenth century many European soldiers and officials had entered Russian service in search of better pay and career prospects. In Alexander's reign they were joined by refugees fleeing the French Revolution or Napoleon. Above all, European immigrants filled the gap created by the slow development of professional education or a professional middle class in Russia. Doctors were one such group. Even in 1812 there were barely 800 doctors in the Russian army, many of them of German origin. Military engineers were also in short supply. In the eighteenth century Russian engineers had been the younger brothers of the artillery and came under its jurisdiction. Though they gained their independence under Alexander, there were still too few trained engineer officers trying to fulfil too diverse a range of duties and Russia remained in search of foreign experts whom it might lure into its service. On the eve of 1812 the two most senior Russian military engineers were the Dutchman Peter van Suchtelen and the German Karl Oppermann.[7]

An even more important nest of foreigners was the quartermaster-general's department, which provided the army's general staff officers. Almost one in five of the 'Russian' staff officers at the battle of Borodino were not even subjects of the tsar. Fewer than half had Slav surnames. The general staff was partly descended from the bureau of cartography, a very specialized department which required a high level of mathematical skill. This ensured that it would be packed with foreigners and non-Russians. As armies grew in size and complexity in the Napoleonic era, the role of staffs became crucial. This made it all the more galling for many Russians that so large a proportion of their staff officers had non-Russian names. In addition, Napoleon's invasion in 1812 set off a wave of xenophobia in Russia, which sometimes targeted 'foreigners' in the Russian army, without making much distinction between genuine foreigners and subjects of the tsar who were not ethnic Russians. Without its non-Russian staff officers the empire could never have triumphed in 1812–14, however. Moreover, most of these men were totally loyal to the Russian state, and their families usually in time assimilated into Russian society. These foreign engineers and staff officers also helped to train new generations of young Russian officers to take their places.[8]

For the tsarist state, as for all the other great powers, the great challenge of the Napoleonic era was to mobilize resources for war. There were four key elements to what one might describe as the sinews of Russian power.[9] They were people, horses, military industry and finance. Unless the basic strengths and limitations of each of these four elements is grasped it is not possible to understand how Russia fought these wars or why she won them.

Manpower was any state's most obvious resource. At the death of Catherine II in 1797 the population of the Russian empire was roughly 40 million. This compared with 29 million French subjects on the eve of the Revolution and perhaps 22 million inhabitants of the Habsburgs' lands at that time. The Prussian population was only 10.7 million even in 1806. The United Kingdom stood somewhere between Prussia and the larger continental powers. Its population, including the Irish, was roughly 15 million in 1815, though Indian manpower was just becoming a factor in British global might. By European standards, therefore, the Russian population was large but it was not yet vastly greater than that of its Old Regime rivals and it was much smaller than the human resources controlled by Napoleon. In 1812 the French Empire, in other words all territories directly ruled from Paris, had a population of 43.7 million. But Napoleon was also King of Italy, which had a population of 6.5 million, and Protector of the 14 million inhabitants of the Confederation of the Rhine. Some other territories were also his to command: most notably from the Russian perspective the Duchy of Warsaw, whose population of 3.8 million made a disproportionate contribution to his war effort in 1812–14. A mere listing of these numbers says something about the challenge faced by Russia in these years.[10]

From the state's perspective the great point about mobilizing the Russian population was that it was not merely numerous but also cheap. A private in Wellington's army scarcely lived the life of a prince but his annual pay was eleven times that of his Russian equivalent even if the latter was paid in silver kopeks. In reality the Russian private in 1812 was far more likely to be paid in depreciating paper currency worth one-quarter of its face value. Comparisons of prices and incomes are always problematic because it is often unclear whether the Russian rubles cited are silver or paper, and in any case the cost of living differed greatly between Russia and foreign countries, above all Britain. A more realistic comparison is the fact that even in peacetime a British soldier received not just bread but also rice, meat, peas and cheese. A Russian private was given nothing but flour and groats, though in wartime these were supplemented by meat and vodka. The soldiers boiled their groats into a porridge which was their staple diet.[11]

A Russian regiment was also sometimes provided not with uniforms and boots but with cloth and leather from which it made its own clothing and footwear. Powder, lead and paper were also delivered to the regiments for them to turn into cartridges. Nor was it just soldiers whose labour was used for free by the state. A small minority of conscripts were sent not to the army but to the mines. More importantly, when Peter the Great first established the ironworks which were the basis of Russian military industry he assigned whole villages to work in them in perpetuity. He did the same with some of the cloth factories set up to clothe his army. This assigned labour was all the cheaper because the workers' families retained their farms, from which they were expected to feed themselves.[12]

So long as all European armies were made up of long-serving professionals the Russian military system competed excellently. The system of annual recruit levies allowed the Russian army to be the largest and cheapest in Europe without putting unbearable pressure on the population. Between 1793 and 1815, however, changes began to occur, first in France and later in Prussia, which put a question mark against its long-term viability. Revolutionary France began to conscript whole 'classes' of young men in the expectation that once the war was over they would return to civilian life as citizens of the new republic. In 1798 this system was made permanent by the so-called *Loi Jourdain*, which established a norm of six years' service. A state which conscripted an entire age group for a limited period could put more men in the ranks than Russia. In time it would also have a trained reserve of still relatively young men who had completed their military service. If Russia tried to copy this system its army would cease to be a separate estate of the realm and the whole nature of the tsarist state and society would have to change. A citizen army was barely compatible with a society based on serfdom. The army would become less reliable as a force to suppress internal rebellion. Noble landowners would face the prospect of a horde of young men returning to the countryside who (if existing laws remained) were no longer serfs and who had been trained in arms.[13]

In fact the Napoleonic challenge came and went too quickly for the full implications of this threat to materialize. Temporary expedients sufficed to overcome the emergency. In 1807 and again in 1812–14 the regime raised a large hostilities-only militia despite the fears of some of its own leaders that this would be useless in military terms and might turn into a dangerous threat to the social order. When the idea of a militia was first mooted in the winter of 1806–7, Prince I. V. Lopukhin, one of Alexander's most senior advisers, warned him that 'at present in Russia the weakening of ties of subordination to the landowners is more dangerous than foreign invasion'. The emperor was willing to take this risk and his judgement proved correct. The mobilization of Russian manpower through a big increase in the regular army and the summoning of the militia just sufficed to defeat Napoleon without requiring fundamental changes in the Russian political order.[14]

Next only to men as a military resource came horses, with which Russia was better endowed than any other country on earth. Immense herds dwelt in the steppe lands of southern Russia and Siberia. These horses were strong, swift and exceptionally resilient. They were also very cheap. One historian of the Russian horse industry calls these steppe horses 'a huge and inexhaustible reserve'. The closest the Russian cavalry came to pure steppe horses was in its Cossack, Bashkir and Kalmyk irregular regiments. The Don Cossack horse was ugly, small, fast and very easy to manoeuvre. It could travel great distances in atrocious weather and across difficult terrain for days on end and with minimal forage in a way that was impossible for regular cavalry. At home the Cossack horse was always out to grass. In winter it would dig out a little trench with its front hoofs to expose roots and grasses hidden under the ice and snow. Cossacks provided their own horses when they joined the army, though in 1812–14 the government did subsidize them for animals lost on campaign. Superb as scouts and capable of finding their way across any terrain even in the dark, the Cossacks also spared the Russian regular light cavalry many of the duties which exhausted their equivalents in other armies: but the Russian hussar, lancer and mounted jaeger regiments also themselves had strong, resilient, cheap and speedy horses with a healthy admixture of steppe blood.[15]

Traditionally the medium (dragoon) and heavy (cuirassier) horses had been a much bigger problem. In fact on the eve of the Seven Years War Russia had possessed no viable cuirassier regiments and even her dragoons had been in very poor shape. By 1812, however, much had changed, above all because of the huge expansion of the Russian horse-studs industry in the last decades of the eighteenth century. Two hundred and fifty private studs existed by 1800, almost all of which had been created in the last forty years. They provided some of the dragoon and most of the cuirassier horses. British officers who served alongside the Russians in 1812–14 agreed that the heavy cavalry was, in the words of Sir Charles Stewart, 'undoubtedly very fine'. Sir Robert Wilson wrote that the Russian heavy cavalry 'horses are matchless for an union of size, strength, activity and hardiness; whilst formed with the bulk of the British cart-horse, they have so much blood as never to be coarse, and withal are so supple as naturally to adapt themselves to the manege, and receive the highest degree of dressing'.[16]

If there was a problem with the Russian cuirassier horse it was perhaps that it was too precious, at least in the eyes of Alexander I. Even officially these heavy cavalry horses cost two and a half times as much as a hussar's mount, and the horses of the Guards cuirassiers – in other words the Chevaliers Gardes and Horse Guard regiments – cost a great deal more. Their feeding and upkeep were more expensive than that of the light cavalry horses and, as usual with larger mounts, they had less endurance and toughness. Since they came from studs they were also much harder to replace. Perhaps for these reasons, in 1813–14 the Russian cuirassiers were often kept in reserve and saw limited action. Alexander was furious when on one occasion an Austrian general used them for outpost duty and allowed them to sustain unnecessary casualties.[17]

Russian military industry could usually rely on domestic sources for its raw materials with some key exceptions. Much saltpetre needed to be imported from overseas and so too did lead, which became an expensive and dangerous weakness in 1807–12 when the Continental System hamstrung Russian overseas trade. Wool for the army's uniforms was also a problem, because Russia only produced four-fifths of the required amount. There were also not enough wool factories to meet military demand as the army expanded after 1807. The truly crucial raw materials were iron, copper and wood, however, and these Russia had in abundance. At the beginning of Alexander's reign Russia was still the world's leading iron producer and stood second only to Britain in copper. Peter the Great had established the first major Russian iron-works to exploit the enormous resources of iron ore and timber in the Urals region, on the borders of Europe and Siberia. Though Russian metallurgical technology was beginning to fall well behind Britain, it was still more than adequate to cover military needs in 1807–14. The Ural region was far from the main arms-manufacturing centres in Petersburg and in the city of Tula, 194 kilometres south of Moscow, but efficient waterways linked the three areas. Nevertheless, any arms or ammunition produced in the Urals works would not reach armies deployed in Russia's western borderlands for over a year.[18]

Arms production fell into two main categories: artillery and handheld weapons. The great majority of Russian iron cannon were manufactured in the Alexander Artillery Works in Petrozavodsk, a small town in Olonets province north-east of Petersburg. They were above all designed for fortresses and for the siege train. Most of the field artillery came from the St Petersburg arsenal: it produced 1,255 new guns between 1803 and 1818. The technology of production was up to date in both works. In the Petersburg Arsenal a steam-powered generator was introduced in 1811 which drove all its lathes and its drilling machinery. A smaller number of guns were produced and repaired in the big depots and workshops in Briansk, a city near the border of Russia and Belorussia. Russian guns and carriages were up to the best international standards once Aleksei Arakcheev's reforms of the artillery were completed by 1805. The number of types of gun was reduced, equipment was standardized and lightened, and careful thought went into matching weapons and equipment to the tactical tasks they were intended to fulfil. The only possible weakness was the Russian howitzers, which could not be elevated to the same degree as the French model and therefore could not always reach their targets when engaged in duels with their French counterparts. On the other hand, thanks to the lightness of their carriages and the quality of their horses the Russian horse artillery was the most mobile and flexible on the battlefield by 1812–14.[19]

The situation as regards handheld firearms was much less satisfactory. Muskets were produced in three places: the Izhevsk works in Viatka province near the Urals turned out roughly 10 per cent of all firearms manufactured in 1812–14: many fewer were produced at the Sestroretsk works 35 kilometres from Petersburg, though Sestroretsk did play a bigger role in repairing existing weapons; the city of Tula was therefore by far the most important source of muskets in 1812–14.[20]

The Tula state arms factory had been founded by Peter the Great in 1712 but production was shared between it and private workshops. In 1812, though the state factory produced most of the new muskets, six private entrepreneurs also supplied a great many. These entrepreneurs did not themselves own factories, however. They met state orders partly from their own rather small workshops but mostly by subcontracting the orders to a large number of master craftsmen and artisans who worked from their own homes. The war ministry complained that this wasted time, transport and fuel. The state factory was itself mostly just a collection of smallish workshops with production often by hand. The labour force was divided into five crafts: each craft was responsible for one aspect of production (gun barrels, wooden stocks, firing mechanisms, cold steel weapons, all other musket parts). Producing the barrels was the most complicated part of the operation and caused most of the delays, partly because skilled labour was in short supply.

The biggest problem both in the factory and the private workshops was out-of-date technology and inadequate machine tools. Steam-powered machinery was only introduced at the very end of the Napoleonic Wars and in any case proved a failure, in part because it required wood for fuel, which was extremely expensive in the Tula region. Water provided the traditional source of power and much more efficient machinery was introduced in 1813 which greatly reduced the consumption of water and allowed power-based production to continue right through the week. Even after the arrival of this machinery, however, shortage of water meant that all power ceased for a few weeks in the spring. In 1813, too, power-driven drills for boring the musket barrels were introduced: previously this whole job had been done by hand by 500 men, which was a serious brake on production. A Russian observer who had visited equivalent workshops in England noted that every stage in production there had its own appropriate machine tools. In Tula, on the contrary, many specialist tools, especially hammers and drills, were not available: in particular, it was almost impossible to acquire good steel machine tools. Russian craftsmen were sometimes left with little more than planes and chisels.[21]

Given the problems it faced, the Russian arms industry performed miracles in the Napoleonic era. Despite the enormous expansion of the armed forces in these years and heavy loss of weapons in 1812–14, the great majority of Russian soldiers did receive firearms and most of them were made in Tula. These muskets cost one-quarter of their English equivalents. On the other hand, without the 101,000 muskets imported from Britain in 1812–13 it would have been impossible to arm the reserve units which reinforced the field army in 1813. Moreover, the problems of Russian machine tools and the tremendous pressures for speed and quantity made it inevitable that some of these muskets would be sub-standard. One British source was very critical of the quality of Tula muskets in 1808, for example. On the other hand, a French test of muskets' firing mechanisms concluded that the Russian models were somewhat more reliable than their own, though much less so than the British and Austrian ones. The basic point was that all European muskets of this era were thoroughly unreliable and imperfect weapons. The Russian ones were undoubtedly worse than the British, and probably often worse than those of the other major armies too. Moreover, despite heroic levels of production in 1812–14 the Russian arms industry could never supply enough new-model muskets to ensure that all soldiers in a battalion had one type and calibre of firearm, though once again Russia's was an extreme example of a problem common to all the continental armies.[22]

Perhaps the quality of their firearms did exert some influence on Russian tactics. It would have been an optimistic Russian general who believed that men armed with these weapons could emulate Wellington's infantry by deploying in two ranks and repelling advancing columns by their musketry.[23] The shortcomings of the Russian musket were possibly an additional reason for the infantry to fight in dense formations supported by the largest ratio of artillery to foot-soldiers of any European army. However, although the deficiencies of the Russian musket may perhaps have influenced the way the army fought, they certainly did not undermine its viability on the battlefield. The Napoleonic era was still a far cry from the Crimean War, by which time the Industrial Revolution was beginning to transform armaments and the superiority of British and French rifled muskets over Russian smoothbores made life impossible for the Russian infantry.

The fourth and final element in Russian power was fiscal, in other words revenue. Being a great power in eighteenth-century Europe was very expensive and the costs escalated with every war. Military expenditure could cause not just fiscal but also political crisis within a state. The most famous example of this was the collapse of the Bourbon regime in France in 1789, brought on by bankruptcy as a result of the costs of intervention in the American War of Independence. Financial crisis also undermined other great powers. In the midst of the Seven Years War, for example, it forced the Habsburgs substantially to reduce the size of their army.

The impact of finance on diplomatic and military policy continued in the Napoleonic era. In 1805–6 Prussian policy was undermined by lack of funds to keep the army mobilized and therefore a constant threat to Napoleon. Similarly, in 1809 Austria was faced with the choice of either fighting Napoleon immediately or reducing the size of its army, since the state could not afford the current level of military expenditure. The Austrians chose to fight, were defeated, and were then lumbered with a war indemnity which crippled their military potential for years to come. An even more crushing indemnity was imposed on Prussia in 1807. In 1789 Russia had a higher level of debt than Austria or Prussia. Inevitably the wars of 1798–1814 greatly increased that debt. Unlike the Austrians or Prussians, in 1807 Russia did not have to pay an indemnity after being defeated by Napoleon. Had it lost in 1812, however, the story would have been very different.

Even without the burdens of a war indemnity Russia suffered financial crisis in 1807–14. Ever since Catherine II's first war with the Ottomans (1768–74) expenditure had regularly exceeded revenue. The state initially covered the deficit in part by borrowing from Dutch bankers. By the end of the eighteenth century this was no longer possible: interest payments had become a serious burden on the treasury. In any case the Netherlands had been overrun by France and its financial markets were closed to foreign powers. Even before 1800 most of the deficit had been covered by printing paper rubles. By 1796 the paper ruble was worth only two-thirds of its silver equivalent. Constant war after 1805 caused expenditure to rocket. The only way to cover the cost was by printing more and more paper rubles. By 1812 the paper currency was worth roughly one-quarter of its 'real' (i.e. silver) value. Inflation caused a sharp rise in state expenditure, not least as regards military arms, equipment and victuals. To increase revenue rapidly enough to match costs was impossible. Meanwhile the finance ministry lived in constant dread of runaway inflation and the complete collapse in trust in the paper currency. Even without this, dependence on depreciating paper currency had serious risks for the Russian army's ability to operate abroad. Some food and equipment had to be purchased in the theatre of operations, above all when operating on the territory of one's allies, but no foreigner would willingly accept paper rubles in return for goods and services.[24]

At the death of Catherine II in 1796 Russian annual revenue amounted to 73 million rubles or £11.7 million; if collection costs are included this sinks to £8.93 million, or indeed lower if the depreciating value of the paper ruble is taken into account. Austrian and Prussian revenues were of similar order: in 1800, for example, Prussian gross revenue was £8.65 million: in 1788 Austrian gross revenue had been £8.75 million. Even in 1789, with her finances in deep crisis, French royal revenue at 475 million francs or £19 million was much higher. Britain was in another league again: the new taxes introduced in 1797–9 raised her annual revenue from £23 million to £35 million.[25]

If Russia nevertheless remained a formidable great power, that was because crude comparisons of revenue across Europe have many flaws. In addition, as we have seen in this chapter, the price of all key military resources was far cheaper in Russia than, for example, in Britain. Even in peacetime, the state barely paid at all for some services and goods. It even succeeded in palming off on the peasantry part of the cost of feeding most of the army, which was quartered in the villages for most of the year. In 1812 this principle was taken to an extreme, with massive requisitioning and even greater voluntary contributions. One vital reason why Russia had been victorious at limited cost in the eighteenth century was that it had fought almost all its wars on enemy territory and, to a considerable extent, at foreign expense. This happened too in 1813–14.[26]

In 1812–14 the Russian Empire defeated Napoleon by a narrow margin and by straining to breaking point almost every sinew of its power. Even so, on its own Russia could never have destroyed Napoleon's empire. For this a European grand alliance was needed. Creating, sustaining and to some extent leading this grand alliance was Alexander I's greatest achievement. Many obstacles lay in Alexander's path. To understand why this was the case and how these difficulties were overcome requires some knowledge of how international relations worked in this era.[27]

In the second half of the eighteenth century Europe contained five great powers. Of this fivesome, Britain and France were inveterate enemies and so were Austria and Prussia. Russia was the only one of the five without a bitter rival and this worked greatly to its advantage. On the whole Russia sided with Britain in its conflict with France. Above all, this was because France was the traditional patron of the Swedes,

Poles and Ottomans who were Russia's immediate neighbours and rivals. Britain was also much the biggest market for Russian exports. Nevertheless relations between the two powers were sometimes strained. Like other Europeans, the Russians resented Britain's high-handed treatment of neutral trade in wartime and led a coalition of Baltic powers to defend neutral rights during the American War of Independence, at a time when British naval power was at its weakest. In 1787–91 France's domestic crisis seemed to have undermined her power and thereby allowed British diplomacy more room for manoeuvre. At precisely this moment Russian armies were smashing the Ottomans and advancing deep into the Balkans. The first shadow of the Victorian-era 'Great Game' between Britain and Russia for the domination of Asia came over the horizon. William Pitt, the prime minister, took up the role of Turkey's saviour against Russia and attempted without success to force Catherine II to give up some of her conquests. Soon afterwards French expansion pushed such concerns aside and they remained on the margins of European diplomacy for a generation. But Pitt's efforts were not forgotten in Petersburg.[28]

Even more useful to Russia was Austro-Prussian rivalry. The lesson learned by both the Habsburgs and the Hohenzollerns from the Seven Years War was that their security, let alone future expansion, depended on Russian goodwill. Catherine II conducted a shrewd auction for Russian support. By the 1770s she had come to the correct conclusion that Russia had most to gain by expanding southwards against the Ottomans. For such a policy Austria was more useful than Prussia. The empress therefore graciously allowed Vienna to win the auction for her favour. For this the Austrians paid a high price. In 1788 they found themselves involved in an expensive war against the Ottomans which served Russian not Austrian interests.

Already by the Napoleonic era many of the issues which were to take Austria to war against Russia in 1914 were causing friction between the two empires. Above all there was Austrian fear of ever-growing Russian power. By the 1790s, for example, not merely did the Russian navy dominate the Black Sea, it also had a powerful squadron operating in the Adriatic, in other words in the Habsburgs' back yard. During Russia's three wars against the Ottomans between 1768 and 1812 her armies occupied present-day Romania. Russian annexation of this territory was a very real possibility and a major threat to Austrian interests.

Russian power and Russia's victories over their Ottoman overlords won Russia many adherents among the Christian population of the Balkans. In addition, these Christians were Orthodox, as were the Russians. In 1804–12 the Serbs were in rebellion against their Ottoman rulers and looked to Russia for support. In a manner very familiar to historians of Russian foreign policy before 1914 Russian diplomats wavered between wanting the Serbs as loyal clients and fearing that Serbian ambitions would drag Russia into disastrous conflicts with the Habsburgs. Still worse from an Austrian perspective, Russia had a growing number of sympathizers among the Habsburgs' own Orthodox subjects, thousands of whom emigrated to the steppe lands of southern Russia and Ukraine in the second half of the eighteenth century.[29]

Initially the French Revolution and French subsequent expansion was of less concern to Russia than to any other European power. Catherine disliked the Revolution and locked up a handful of Russian dissidents. She crushed 'Jacobinism' in Poland, using this as a good excuse to destroy the last remnants of Polish statehood. No sensible person could fear a French-style revolution in Russia, however. There was no Russian 'Third Estate'. To the extent that it existed at all, the professional middle class was mostly of foreign origin and in the state's employ. Russian merchants and artisans were still with few exceptions deeply traditional, Orthodox and monarchist in their mentalities and loyalties. Enlightened public opinion, still almost the monopoly of nobles, saw the monarchy as the most enlightened force in Russia and looked to it to modernize and Europeanize the empire. In the land of Pugachev any idea of mass revolution was anathema to every educated or property-owning Russian.[30]

As regards French territorial expansion, Russia could initially also take a relaxed view. France was at the other end of Europe. It would have to expand some distance before Russia's interests were challenged. By contrast, any advance would quickly carry French troops into the Rhineland and into Belgium, thereby touching on essential Habsburg and British interests. With Britain, France, Austria and perhaps even Prussia embroiled at the other end of Europe, Russia need have no fears for its security and could pursue her interests with confidence, not least in Poland.[31]

By the late 1790s Russia could no longer afford to be quite so relaxed. De facto French annexation of the Rhineland, Switzerland, the

Netherlands and parts of Italy added up to a worrying increase in French power. With French eyes turning to the eastern Mediterranean and even Ottoman Egypt, Paul I had some reason to join the Second Coalition. The manner in which he did so showed, however, that he regarded Russia as an auxiliary in a war whose front-line belligerents were Austria and Britain. Moreover, within a year of Russian troops going into action Paul had fallen out with his allies. By the last year of his reign he had reversed his position entirely. Russia withdrew from the coalition, banned all trade with Britain, headed a new league to secure neutral countries' maritime rights, and even sent off a Cossack force on a fanciful expedition towards India. By the time Paul was assassinated in March 1801 Russia to most intents and purposes had allied itself to France in its war against Britain.

The new emperor, Alexander I, immediately restored good relations with Britain but his main initial priority was to steer clear of international entanglements and devote himself to internal reforms. Only in 1804 did Russo-French relations once again begin to slide towards war. The main reason for this was that the geopolitical concerns that had taken Russia into the Second Coalition had reappeared but in sharper form. France was now considerably more powerful than it had been in 1798. Under French pressure the Holy Roman Empire was being dismantled and Germany was being rearranged without reference to Russian interests. By proclaiming himself King of Italy in 1804 Napoleon was not just asserting his domination of the peninsula: he was also establishing powerful bases for French expansion into the eastern Mediterranean, the Balkans and Constantinople. To these fundamental concerns Napoleon's abduction and subsequent murder of the Duc d'Enghien, a junior member of the exiled French royal family whom he had lifted from the territory of Alexander's father-in-law, added an element of moral outrage. Many French royalist émigrés lived in Petersburg and the Russian aristocracy saw in Enghien's murder a confirmation that Napoleon was the true heir of Jacobin terror. Alexander himself was much less of a legitimist than these Petersburg grandees but Napoleon's treatment of Enghien was by no means the only example of the French leader's contempt for international treaties and norms.[32]

All these factors took Russia to war in 1805. On this occasion the Russian commitment was more whole-hearted than it had been in 1798. Nevertheless Alexander still saw Austria, Britain and Prussia as the front-line antagonists, to whom Russia was offering unselfish assistance though its own vital interests were not directly engaged. Annoyance that Prussia was unwilling to do its duty led him to plan to coerce Berlin into joining the coalition. Though he kept a clear eye on Russian interests, Alexander also floated grandiose principles to underpin lasting European peace and security. A child of the Enlightenment, he liked to speak and see himself in such terms. But his at times almost Wilsonian tendency to proclaim great principles of international order was also rooted in a rather American sense that a country of Russia's power and geopolitical security could afford to stand on a hill above the common ruck of states and lay down rules for the common good.[33]

The war of 1805–7 was a disaster for Russia. Instead of awaiting the arrival of Mikhail Kutuzov's Russians, part of the Austrian army advanced into Bavaria at the beginning of the 1805 campaign and was cut off and forced to surrender. Kutuzov extricated his army from a potential trap and retreated with great skill eastwards into Moravia. The Russian troops behaved with their habitual calm discipline and held the French at bay in a number of hard-fought rearguard actions. Most notable was the battle at Schongraben on 16 November 1805, immortalized by Leo Tolstoy in *War and Peace*. In this action the Russians were commanded by the fiery and charismatic Prince Petr Bagration. By the beginning of December the campaign appeared to be swinging in the allies' favour. Napoleon's lines of communication were very stretched and Prussia seemed to be on the verge of joining the Austrians and Russians. But Alexander I overrode Kutuzov's advice and launched the allied army into an attack that led to the catastrophic battle of Austerlitz on 2 December. As a result Austria made peace and the Russians retreated back across their borders.[34]

For almost a year there followed a strange interlude in which the Russians and French neither made peace nor actually fought each other. This period ended when war broke out between Napoleon and Prussia in October 1806. In the previous decade the Prussians had tried to protect their security and expand their territory by remaining neutral and balancing between France and its enemies. By the autumn of 1805, however, the implications of French hegemony in Germany were drawing Prussia towards the allies. But Berlin prevaricated for too long and Napoleon's victory at Austerlitz left them at his mercy. In the following months they learned the humiliating price of being his client. In the autumn of 1806 Prussia went to war to regain its position as a proud and independent great power. Instead of trying to hold the line of the river Elbe and await Russian help, however, the Prussian army advanced and was destroyed at the battle of Jena-Auerstadt on 14 October 1806.[35]

For the remaining eight months of the war the Russians found themselves fighting Napoleon in Poland and East Prussia almost on their own, since only a small remnant of the Prussian army had survived. In these months the Russian army fought well and inflicted heavy losses on the French, especially in the drawn battle of Eylau in February 1807. Their commander was General Levin von Bennigsen, an intelligent strategist and a skilful tactician, who had left his native Hanover as a young officer and transferred to the Russian service. The odds were always heavily against the Russians, however. Napoleon now controlled most of western Europe, Germany and Poland. A coalition able to draw its resources only from Russia and the small province of East Prussia was bound to be outmatched. In any case the Russians had not expected or prepared to wage a life-and-death struggle on their own against Napoleon. The empire's resources were far from fully mobilized.

Thousands of Russian troops fell ill or deserted for lack of food in the winter of 1806–7. The Russian commissariat was notoriously slow and corrupt. Bennigsen was better at tactics than logistics. He put far too much faith in local Prussian contractors and failed to organize transport, communications and supply bases in his rear. To do him justice, however, the Russians had been plunged into a winter campaign with no warning. Lithuania and Belorussia – in other words the areas immediately behind his army – were much poorer and more sparsely populated than the Great Russian core of the empire or the rich agricultural provinces of south Russia and Ukraine, let alone Germany, Bohemia or France. Bad harvests were frequent and made it doubly hard to procure food for men and horses. Transporting food and fodder into the region from Russia was difficult and expensive because of primitive communications. In addition, there was the currency issue. In Russia itself the paper ruble was almost universally accepted. In the empire's western borderlands it was either shunned entirely or accepted only at heavy discounts against the silver ruble. This made the cost of sustaining an army in the region ruinously expensive.[36]

Politics and geography were the most important reasons for Napoleon's triumph in 1805–7. The three eastern great powers had not united against him: Prussia was neutral in 1805, Austria in 1806. In fact at no time were the main armies of even two of the eastern powers united on the battlefield against Napoleon. By the time Russian troops arrived in the theatre of operations their allies' armies had already been defeated. To some extent this was due to foolish Austrian and Prussian strategy, but geography dealt the allies a losing hand. In 1805 it was possible both financially and logistically to concentrate the French armies in the area of Boulogne and to use this as a base from which the entire army could be deployed against the Austrians. For the same reasons it was inconceivable to concentrate the Russian army anywhere near the Austrian or Prussian borders for weeks, let alone months, on end. Even had it been possible, it would probably have made little difference. The distance from the Channel to the Bavarian–Austrian frontier was much less than from the Russian borderlands. Moreover, the French could march through fertile country down many excellent roads, requisitioning as they went to cover their needs. An army which attempted to move at this speed and in this way in the Russo-Austrian borderlands would have starved and disintegrated. The Austrians and Russians managed the movement of Kutuzov's troops with fair efficiency in 1805; even so, partly thanks to Mack, they arrived too late.[37]

In 1806 the geographical dilemma of the allies was far worse because Napoleon now had a string of bases and allies in western and southern Germany. His troops were much closer than the Russians to Berlin and the Prussian heartland. Perhaps the Prussians could have held Napoleon on the Elbe long enough for the Russians to arrive but this is anything but certain. If not, the heirs of Frederick II were hardly likely to avoid decisive battle, abandon almost all Prussia and retire to the Oder to await deliverance from Russia. The basic lesson of 1805–7 was that not only must the three eastern monarchies unite but the Russian army must already be positioned in central Europe when military operations began. This finally happened in 1813 but under unique circumstances which no one could have predicted.

Politics and geography were a more important source of disaster in 1805–7 than any failings of the Russian army. Even in 1805 the army was in many respects formidable. Above all this was because of the near legendary courage, resilience and loyalty of the rank and file. Ethnic solidarity contributed to the army's strength. Most soldiers were Russians, though a significant minority were Belorussians and Ukrainians.

Ukrainians were particularly common in the cavalry, which made good sense since the average Ukrainian was far more likely to be familiar with horses than a peasant from northern or central Russia. In this era, however, it was class and religion that mattered above all. What counted therefore was that these men were peasants and Orthodox. In any case in ethno-linguistic terms Russians, Ukrainians and Belorussians were if anything closer than the soldiers of a French regiment drawn from Brittany, Lorraine and Aquitaine.[38]

Most important in creating solidarity were the conditions of military service. Military historians stress that what usually matters most in war is not grand allegiances to country or ideology but the loyalty that binds soldiers to their comrades and their units. In Alexander I's army this loyalty existed to the highest degree. In the decade before 1812 the average age of conscripts was just under 22[39] and soldiers served for twenty-five years. Given high mortality rates even in peacetime, for many soldiers this was a life sentence. Few conscripts were literate, so they could not maintain contact with their homes by letter. The regimental personnel records show that most NCOs never took home leave. Most soldiers did not return to their villages even after retirement from the army. Parents were long since dead and siblings might well not welcome an extra mouth to feed. Particularly on private estates, conscription was sometimes used as a means to rid the community of restless young men and was often conducted unjustly. Neither the landowner nor the village community necessarily welcomed the return of an ageing man, possibly unfit for agricultural work and maybe nursing a grievance against those who had sent him off as a recruit. The noble landowner could forbid a retired soldier to return to his village.[40]

Meanwhile, once the conscript had adapted to military life, the regiment could become a new home. The new soldier's messmates became a sort of substitute family. If a man died, his possessions went to his comrades. Each company had its own mess cooperative (artel'), into which part of a soldier's pay, half his outside earnings, and most of any money given as a reward for good service was invested. Particularly in the Guards, the funds of the regimental artels could add up to many thousands of rubles. This money was used to buy the soldiers 'luxuries' to supplement their diet of bread and porridge, and to save money by purchasing food, kettles, transport and other items in bulk. Ideally a soldier would serve in the same regiment all his life and many did so.

Even when men were moved into new regiments, however, they usually transferred with their whole company, so many collective loyalties and solidarities remained.[41]

Prince Eugen of Württemberg, Emperor Alexander's first cousin, commanded initially a Russian brigade, next a division and finally a corps between 1807 and 1814. He admired his soldiers and had a reputation not just for courageous leadership but also for 'mucking in' with them and forgetting his royal dignity. His memoirs are probably the most useful written by any Russian general in the Napoleonic era. He recalled that

the young recruit is normally patient and very eager to learn, and he accepts his unavoidable fate more readily than is the case with the peoples of other countries who are compulsorily conscripted ... In time the regiment becomes his new home and to understand the attachment which can inspire a Russian soldier for this home you must witness it with your own eyes. No wonder then that, armed with such sentiments, the Russian soldier fights so well.[42]

Alexander I understood the power of regimental solidarity and tried to preserve it by ensuring that as far as possible officers remained within a single regiment until they reached senior rank. Sometimes this was a losing battle since officers could have strong personal motivation for transfer. Relatives liked to serve together. A more senior brother or an uncle in the regiment could provide important patronage. Especially in wartime, the good of the service sometimes required transferring officers to fill vacancies in other regiments. So too did the great expansion of the army in Alexander's reign. Seventeen new regiments were founded between 1801 and 1807 alone: experienced officers needed to be found for them. In these circumstances it is surprising that more than half of all officers between the rank of ensign and captain had served in only one regiment, as had a great many majors. Particularly in older regiments such as the Grenadiers, the Briansk or Kursk infantry regiments, or the Pskov Dragoons the number of officers up to the rank of major who had spent their whole lives in the regiments was extremely high. As one might expect, the Preobrazhensky Guards, the senior regiment in the Russian army, was the extreme case, with almost all the officers spending their whole careers in the regiment. Add to this the fact that the overwhelming majority of Russian officers were bachelors and the strength of their commitment to their regiments becomes evident.[43]

Nevertheless, the greatest bearers of regimental loyalty and tradition were the non-commissioned officers. In the regiments newly formed in Alexander's reign, the senior NCOs arrived when the regiment was created and served in it for the rest of their careers. Old regiments would have a strong cadre of NCOs who had served in the unit for twenty years or more. In a handful of extreme cases such as the Briansk Infantry and Narva Dragoons every single sergeant-major, sergeant and corporal had spent his entire military life in the regiment. In the Russian army there was usually a clear distinction between the sergeant-majors (*fel'dfebeli* in the infantry and *vakhmistry* in the cavalry) on the one hand, and the ten times more numerous sergeants and corporals (*unterofitsery*) on the other. The sergeants and corporals were mostly peasants. They gained their NCO status as veterans who had shown themselves to be reliable, sober and skilled in peacetime, and courageous on the battlefield. Like the conscript body as a whole, the great majority of them were illiterate.

The sergeant-majors on the other hand were in the great majority of cases literate, though particularly in wartime some illiterate sergeants who had shown courage and leadership might be promoted to sergeant-major. Many were the sons of priests, but above all of the deacons and other junior clergy who were required to assist at Orthodox services. Most sons of the clergy were literate and the church could never find employment for all of them. They filled a key gap in the army as NCOs. But the biggest source of sergeant-majors were soldiers' sons, who were counted as hereditary members of the military estate. The state set up compulsory special schools for these boys: almost 17,000 boys were attending these schools in 1800. In 1805 alone 1,893 soldiers' sons entered the army. The education provided by the schools was rudimentary and the discipline was brutal but they did train many drummers and other musicians for the army, as well as some regimental clerks. Above all, however, they produced literate NCOs, imbued with military discipline and values from an early age. As befitted the senior NCO of the Russian army's senior regiment, the regimental sergeant-major of the Preobrazhenskys in 1807, Fedor Karneev, was the model professional soldier: a soldier's son with twenty-four years' service in the regiment, an unblemished record, and a military cross for courage in action.[44]

Although the fundamental elements of the Russian army were

immensely strong, there were important weaknesses in its tactics and training in 1805. With the exception of its light cavalry, this made it on the whole inferior to the French. The main reason for this was that the French army had been in almost constant combat with the forces of other great powers between 1792 and 1805. With the exception of the Italian and Swiss campaigns of 1799–1800, in which only a relatively small minority of regiments participated, the Russian army lacked any comparable wartime experience. In its absence, parade-ground values dominated training, reaching absurd levels of pedantry and obsession at times. Partly as a result, Russian musketry was inferior to French, as was the troops' skill at skirmishing. The Russians' use of massed bayonet attacks to drive off skirmishers was costly and ineffective. In 1805–6 Russian artillery batteries were often poorly shielded against the fire of enemy skirmishers.[45]

The army's worst problems revolved around coordination above the level of the regiment. In 1805 there were no permanent units of more than regimental size. At Austerlitz, Russian and Austrian columns put together at the last moment manoeuvred far less effectively than the permanent French divisions. In 1806 the Russians created their own divisions but coordination on the battlefield remained a weakness. The Russian cavalry would have been hard pressed to emulate Murat's massed charge at Eylau. The Russian artillery certainly could not have matched the impressive concentration and mobility of Senarmont's batteries at Friedland.

Most important, however, were weaknesses in the army's high command, meaning the senior generals and, above all, the supreme commanders. At this level the Russians were bound to be inferior to the French. No one could match a monarch who was also a military genius. Although the Russian military performance was hampered by rivalry among its generals, French marshals cooperated no better in Napoleon's absence. When Alexander seized effective command from Kutuzov before Austerlitz the result was a disaster. Thoroughly chastened, Alexander kept away from the battlefield in 1806–7. This solved one problem but created another. In the absence of the monarch the top leader needed to be a figure who could command obedience both by his reputation and by being unequivocally senior to all the other generals. By late 1806, however, all the great leaders of Catherine's wars were dead. Mikhail Kutuzov was the best of the remaining bunch but he had been out of favour since Austerlitz. Alexander therefore appointed Field-Marshal Mikhail Kamensky to command the army on the grounds of his seniority, experience and relatively good military record. When he reached the army Kamensky's confused and even senile behaviour quickly horrified his subordinates. As one young general, Count Johann von Lieven, asked on the eve of the first serious battles with the French: 'Is this lunatic to command us against Napoleon?'[46]

Kamensky quickly abandoned the army and took himself off to the rear. He was ordered by Alexander to retire to his estates, where soon afterwards he was murdered by his peasants. In Kamensky's absence the more junior of his two corps commanders, Levin von Bennigsen, more or less seized control of the army, consolidating his position by exaggerating the Russians' success in the rearguard actions at Golymin and Pultusk in his reports to the monarch. Bennigsen's allies in Petersburg whispered in Alexander's ear about his skill and achievement. The emperor responded by overlooking Bennigsen's role in his father's murder, appointing him to be supreme commander and loading him down with decorations and financial rewards. To do Bennigsen justice, he certainly was the most competent replacement available for Kamensky, and somebody needed to take control of the situation quickly. He also performed creditably in extricating the army from the dangerous position in which it found itself at the beginning of the campaign. This did not stop his army from becoming a nest of intrigue among the senior generals. The other corps commander, Friedrich von Buxhoeweden, loathed Bennigsen, refused to collaborate with him, and challenged him to a duel. Alexander himself sent General Otto von Knorring to keep an eye on his supreme commander.

A particularly bitter dispute broke out at the beginning of the spring 1807 campaign between Bennigsen and his senior divisional commander, Lieutenant-General Baron Fabian von der Osten-Sacken, yet another Baltic German. The battle between the two men is worth a moment's attention, not just because it was symptomatic of a major and lasting problem in the army's upper ranks, but also because the individuals concerned were to play vital roles in the years 1812–14.

Like many of the senior Russian commanders, Osten-Sacken was tough, jealous, stubborn, ambitious and proud. Charming and witty in society, he could be a very different man in his treatment of the officers and men under his command. His personality was probably affected by a sense of unfairness and bitterness which did not finally leave him until he achieved glory and universal respect in 1813–14. In 1740 his father Wilhelm had been the aide-de-camp to Field-Marshal Münnich, the key figure in the army and government of the Empress Anna. Had the regime of Anna and her nephew Ivan VI survived, Wilhelm could have expected a glorious career. His son Fabian would have been enlisted in the Guards almost from birth and by his mid-twenties he would have been a colonel and an imperial aide-de-camp. Instead, Ivan VI was toppled, Münnich exiled, and Wilhelm von der Osten-Sacken banished to a garrison regiment, where he spent the rest of his long career without any further promotion. His son Fabian lived a childhood of poverty and made his way up the military ladder the hard way, through the ranks of the line infantry with every step won by courage and hard work. The progress began when he won promotion to the rank of ensign, the first officer rank, for bravery in action against the Turks in 1769.[47]

Osten-Sacken loathed Bennigsen. His diaries in 1806–7 are a list of complaints against a commander whom he considered to have mismanaged the army's medical and commissariat services, failed to seize the opportunities for victory at Eylau, and – perhaps most significantly – neglected ever to consult his second-in-command, namely Osten-Sacken himself, about how to conduct the campaign. At the beginning of the 1807 campaign Bennigsen planned to surprise and trap the isolated corps of Marshal Ney by coordinated movements from different directions by the Russian divisions. Osten-Sacken moved slowly and Ney escaped. Bennigsen accused Osten-Sacken of deliberately sabotaging his plans in order to discredit him and take over the army. Osten-Sacken claimed that the orders were contradictory. The initial inquiry got nowhere: in predictable fashion Bennigsen and Osten-Sacken were supported by their networks of 'friends'. The process then dragged on for months and only in 1808 did a court martial find against Osten-Sacken.[48]

By then the war had long since been concluded. On 14 June 1807 Napoleon defeated the Russian army at the battle of Friedland and drove it back to the empire's border. Friedland was a serious defeat: initial Russian estimates suggested that they had suffered up to 20,000 casualties. Nevertheless it was not a rout like Austerlitz, let alone on the scale of Jena-Auerstadt. The great majority of the Russian army got back safely and in relatively good order across the river Neman. With the river between themselves and Napoleon, the Russian regiments quickly regained their habitual discipline, order and fearlessness. Two fresh divisions under princes Dmitrii Lobanov-Rostovsky and Andrei Gorchakov had just arrived from Russia to reinforce them. Two hundred thousand militiamen had been mustered in Russia and would in time be used to fill the ranks of the army. New regular regiments were being raised, and new recruit levies witnessed to the fact that Russia's manpower resources were far from exhausted. At present Napoleon had not even crossed the Russian border. He still had a very long way to go before he could threaten the centres of Russian military, political and economic power in the Moscow and Petersburg regions. If Russia needed to continue the war after Friedland, there was no doubt that she could do so.

Nevertheless there were excellent reasons for the Russians to seek peace. The treasury was bankrupt, the army's arsenals and stores were empty and it would take a long time to train, arm, officer and equip the new recruits. Tens of thousands of soldiers and many generals had been lost to wounds and sickness in the previous six months. Alexander no longer had any faith in Bennigsen but saw no other general as adequate to replace him. If the war continued then in practice Russia would be fighting alone. Prussian military power had been destroyed and the British not merely had no troops on the continent but were unwilling to allow Russia subsidies or even loans. Meanwhile London still seemed able to send military expeditions to conquer the Cape and parts of Spanish America. By now Napoleon controlled most of western and central Europe and could mobilize enormous resources for a war against Russia. No doubt it would take him some months to mount an invasion of the Russian heartland but this was not a major concern of Alexander's advisers. What worried them enormously was that Napoleon was now positioned on the borders of the provinces – most of them in present-day Ukraine and Belarus – which Russia had acquired after Poland was partitioned in the previous generation. Polish landowners and officials still dominated this region. There was every reason to fear that, if Napoleon invaded the empire's western borderlands, the Poles would rise up in his support.[49] After hearing the news of Friedland Alexander agreed to Bennigsen's appeal for an armistice and sent Lieutenant-General Prince Dmitrii Lobanov-Rostovsky to conduct the armistice negotiations with the French. The emperor's instructions to Lobanov told him 'not himself to propose peace negotiations but if the French were the first to express a desire to put an end to the war then he should respond that the Emperor Alexander also desires peace'.[50]

In some ways Lobanov was a strange choice for what was a semi-diplomatic mission. He had no diplomatic experience and neither looked nor behaved like a diplomat. On the contrary, he was a rather brusque, impatient and slightly awkward man, not at all the person to smooth over misunderstandings by flattery and politeness. Of medium height, with a somewhat oriental slant to his eyes, Lobanov's posture may not have been improved by the fact that he had twice been severely wounded in the Russo-Ottoman war of 1788–92, once in the head. The fact that he was a courageous soldier, however, might perhaps win him respect among the French generals with whom he was to negotiate. Lobanov did also have other advantages. Having just arrived from Russia with his division, he was wholly independent of Bennigsen and of the other generals in his faction-ridden army. Lobanov was also loyal and dependable. Unlike some senior officers and officials, he could be relied on to carry out Alexander's orders to the letter.[51]

Lobanov quickly discovered that Napoleon wanted not just peace but also an alliance with Russia. On the Russian side the detailed negotiations for both peace and an alliance treaty were conducted by Lobanov and Prince Aleksandr Kurakin. In June 1807 Kurakin was the most senior statesman and diplomat at Alexander's headquarters. For a time in Paul I's reign he had run Russian foreign policy. Currently he was preparing to depart for his new post as ambassador in Vienna. Kurakin was obsessed with the minutiae of rank, status and appearance. He could be pedantic. But he was more intelligent, shrewder and more worldly-wise than his critics allowed. He belonged to that section of the ruling elite which had always seen Anglo-French competition for global dominion as the key cause of the wars that had wracked Europe since 1793. Kurakin believed that if possible Russia must remain neutral in this conflict, using Anglo-French rivalry to enhance Russian interests. Though after Austerlitz he had come to see Napoleonic France as a threat to Russian security, he believed that the best way now to protect Russia was to come to an agreement with Napoleon to divide Europe into French and Russian spheres of interest.[52]

Lobanov and Kurakin were first cousins. Both came from ancient aristocratic families. Whereas the Kurakins were rich, by 1800 Dmitrii's branch of the Lobanov-Rostovskys was relatively poor. Above all that was because Kurakins had occupied top positions in government throughout the eighteenth century in an era when political power usually brought rich financial rewards. Their marriage alliances placed them at the very heart of the Russian aristocracy. The Kurakins also produced only one or at most two sons in each generation, so the family's wealth was not dissipated. By contrast, it was a long time since a Prince Lobanov had played a key military or political role and Dmitrii Lobanov's wealthy great-grandfather seems to have sired twenty-nine children from three marriages. When Tolstoy in *War and Peace* needed a fictional family to embody the world of the court and Petersburg high society he called them the Kuragins, though the real-life Kurakins were much more inter-esting and many-sided than Tolstoy's parody of the cynical aristocratic courtier, Prince Vasilii Kuragin, and his unpleasant brood of spoiled children. Like Tolstoy's fictional character Prince Boris Drubetskoy, Dmitrii Lobanov was brought up and educated in the family of his rich cousins, in this case the Kurakins.[53]

Although Kurakin and Lobanov discussed details with Talleyrand and Marshal Berthier, Russia's true chief negotiator was Alexander I, who spent hours in one-to-one conversations with Napoleon. The first meeting between the two monarchs was the famous encounter on a ceremonial raft which took place in the middle of the river Neman on 25 June 1807. The river was the dividing line between the two armies, with the Russians on the east bank and the French on the west.

Of the six men – all of them generals – who accompanied Alexander to his meeting with Napoleon, the senior was his younger brother and heir, the Grand Duke Constantine. The emperor was fortunate in resem-bling his tall and handsome mother rather than his short, ugly and snub-nosed father. Constantine was not so lucky, and he resembled his father not just in looks but also in personality. Both men were obsessed with the minutiae of correct military drill and uniforms. More important, they were both very excitable and inconsistent, swinging between moods and ideas in a bewildering fashion. Above all, both were subject to terrifying fits of temper, in which threats and insults would rain down on anyone unfortunate enough to be the target of their wrath. Both men were actually also capable of great generosity and kindness but for proud aristocrats, acutely sensitive to public dishonour, Paul's insults had been as intolerable as his wayward policies or his blows to their careers.

In 1807–14 Constantine was not just the heir to the throne but, apart from Alexander, the only adult male in the Romanov family. In the Russia of that time, it was unthinkable to overthrow the monarchy or displace the Romanov family by other candidates for the throne. Memories of the anarchy two hundred years before – the so-called Time of Troubles – when the extinction of the ruling dynasty had led to civil war, foreign invasion and the state's disintegration, put a taboo on any such ideas. But however frustrated Russian aristocrats might be with Alexander, few would dream of putting Constantine on the throne in his place. In any case, to do the Grand Duke justice, he revered his brother and was very unlikely to offer support to any conspiracy. If this strengthened the emperor's position at home, the fact that Constantine was one heartbeat from the throne had to worry foreign statesmen. Both Constantine's father and his grandfather, Peter III, had been notorious for sudden and dramatic shifts in foreign policy. The inherently unpredictable nature of foreign policy under an autocracy was already sufficient reason to worry about relying on Russia, even without a personality such as Constantine's lurking in the wings.[54]

The youngest general in Alexander's entourage was Major-General Count Christoph von Lieven. Calm, tactful, self-effacing and hardworking, Lieven occupied the modest-sounding job of head of the emperor's personal military secretariat. In reality this was a position of great power. Paul I had introduced into Russia the Prussian system of military administration, whereby the monarch operated as his own commander-in-chief and ran the army through his adjutant-general, who in principle was no more than a glorified secretary. The actual minister of war sat in Berlin, rarely met the king, and ensured that the army had proper boots. Even in Prussia, the king's adjutant-general inevitably accrued great power. In Russia neither Paul nor Alexander could equal Frederick's detailed knowledge of military affairs. That necessarily increased the role of their adjutant-general, Lieven, whom one historian rightly called the 'first deputy of the emperor for military affairs'.[55]

Though his family's medieval origins were Livonian rather than German, Lieven is best defined as a member of the Baltic German aristocracy. As was true of many Baltic German generals and senior officials, however, Lieven's identity was mixed but his loyalties were unequivocal. Being German above all meant that he was a convinced

Lutheran, with all that religion's stress on duty, hard work and obedience. Born in Kiev, of which his father was the military governor, he was educated in Petersburg and spent his entire adult life at the imperial court and as an ambassador. Not surprisingly, his two preferred languages were French – the lingua franca of international high society – and Russian, the language of the army. His political loyalties were entirely Russian but to an even greater extent than most Balts this meant a strong personal loyalty to Alexander I and to the Romanov family.[56]

This personal link owed something to the fact that Christoph Lieven was an officer of the Semenovsky Guards Regiment, of which Alexander had been colonel-in-chief from adolescence. Founded by Peter the Great in 1683, along with their sister regiment, the Preobrazhenskys, the Semenovskys provided many of Alexander's closest aides, including Lieven's former deputy, Prince Petr Mikhailovich Volkonsky. In a system of government made up of many networks and 'families', the Semenovskys were one of the emperor's private followings. It was this regiment which had been on guard around the palace on the night of Paul I's overthrow.

Above all, however, Lieven's life and loyalties were determined by the fact that his mother was the closest friend of the Dowager Empress Marie, Alexander's mother; she was her chief lady-in-waiting and the governess of the imperial children, who remained devoted to Charlotta Lieven throughout their adult lives. One of her former charges, the Grand Duchess Anna – later the Queen of the Netherlands – wrote: 'Was it not her exclusive privilege to scold the family, for this is granted neither by decree nor by hereditary title?' Links to the imperial family of this strength were literally golden. Titles, estates and patronage rained on the heads of Charlotta and her children. Christoph's elder brother was a general who served subsequently as Minister of Education. His younger sibling, Johann, had distinguished himself in 1807 and been wounded at the battle of Eylau. Leo Tolstoy's novel opens at the soirée of Anna Scherer, devoted confidante of the Empress Marie. In real life the closest equivalent to Anna Scherer was Charlotta Lieven.[57]

Alexander and Napoleon talked on their own for almost two hours during their first meeting on 25 June. Both men were experts in flattery and seduction, and each was intent on winning the other's sympathy and goodwill. No doubt many ideas were floated which neither monarch would readily have committed to paper, let alone enshrined in a treaty. In the older literature, Russian as well as French, it is sometimes said that Alexander was bowled over by Napoleon and that this partly explains the terms of the Franco-Russian treaties. One has to be very careful in taking Alexander's admiration of Napoleon at face value, however, particularly when he was speaking to French diplomats. The secret instructions he gave to Kurakin and Lobanov after he had held a number of discussions with the French emperor were rooted in a coolly realistic grasp of the interests, weaknesses and strengths of both Russia and Napoleon.[58]

In the end Alexander got most of what he wanted in the treaties agreed at Tilsit. Above all, he gained a peace which would be more than a temporary truce, without paying the vanquished side's usual price of territorial concessions and a war indemnity.[59] Apart from this, his overriding concern was to save Prussia, both out of a sense of loyalty to the Prussian king and queen, and because Russia wanted Prussia as an ally against further French expansion eastwards. To achieve this goal Alexander would have to pay a high price. The French now occupied the whole of Prussia and there was no chance that the Russian army could regain it. Napoleon would have preferred to partition Prussia, leaving its eastern – largely Polish – territories to Alexander and distributing the rest of the kingdom among his German clients.

Prussia's survival was therefore a victory for Russian diplomacy, though an equivocal one. Prussia lost half her territory and population. Her Polish provinces became a new small state, the so-called Duchy of Warsaw. Its ruler was to be the King of Saxony, whose ancestors had been kings of Poland for much of the eighteenth century. The new duchy would be totally obedient to Napoleon and was potentially very dangerous for Russia, both as a base for a future invasion across the empire's western border and as a source of hope for all Poles who dreamed of the restoration of the Polish kingdom in all its former territories. Forced to reduce its army and pay a vast war indemnity, the newly truncated Prussia was too vulnerable to Napoleon's power to act as a defensive barrier for Russia, as became clear in 1811–12. Nevertheless, Alexander's insistence on preserving Prussia was to prove hugely important in 1813, when the Prussians played a vital role in Napoleon's overthrow.

The main price paid by Russia for Prussia's survival was agreeing to join Napoleon's war with Britain. Above all, this meant adherence to Napoleon's Continental System and therefore the exclusion of British ships and goods from Russian ports. By the terms of the Treaty of Tilsit the Russians were also bound to impose the Continental System on the Swedes, if necessary by war. In June 1807 Alexander was angry at Britain's failure to support the Russian war effort but he certainly did not want conflict with London and understood the damage it would do to the economy and the state's finances. He believed, however, that at this moment Russia had no room for manoeuvre between Britain and France, and that subordinating Russia's economic interests to Napoleon's overriding concern – in other words blockading British trade – was the only way to ensure an acceptable peace. The emperor comforted himself with the hope that if British trade was excluded from the continent and Napoleon's terms were moderate, then London would probably make peace. A compromise peace which checked both British expansion outside Europe and French advances on the continent would of course serve Russia's interests perfectly. Alexander could take more realistic comfort from the fact that the Tilsit treaties did not bind Russia to military action against Britain and that a successful war with Sweden might allow the annexation of Finland, and thereby make Petersburg much more secure against any future Swedish attack.[60]

The one area where Alexander may have made an unnecessary concession to Napoleon was Russia's relations with the Ottoman Empire. Egged on by France, the Ottomans had been at war with Russia since 1806, hoping to use Russia's defeat at Austerlitz to regain some of the provinces lost in the previous three decades. In the Tilsit treaties France pledged itself to mediate between Russia and the Ottomans, and to support her new ally should the Turks prove intransigent. Alexander hoped that Napoleon would accept Russian predominance in the Ottoman Empire to balance France's domination of western and central Europe. In reality, for all Napoleon's grandiose talk about Russo-French collaboration in the Orient and about the impending demise of the Ottoman Empire, his basic policy was to block Russian expansion. No doubt he would have pursued this policy quietly whatever the Treaty of Tilsit said. Giving him a role as mediator merely allowed him more opportunities to realize his goal.[61]

To make negotiating easier, Alexander and his advisers moved to Tilsit, on the west bank of the river Neman, where Napoleon had his headquarters. The two monarchs spent many hours together, indulging in conversations which ranged far beyond the treaty negotiations and inspecting Napoleon's troops. Half of Tilsit was handed over to the Russians and the First Battalion of the Preobrazhensky Guards moved in to protect their emperor. All eyes were on the French army, however. A chance to inspect the men who had conquered Europe and to listen as one of history's greatest generals explained the secrets of his success was not to be missed, especially by a monarch as interested in military matters as Alexander. In any case it suited the emperor's purposes to play the role of deferential disciple and thereby flatter Napoleon. But the French monarch would have done well to have a careful look at the Preobrazhenskys, because his eventual downfall was to owe much to the Russian army's veteran regiments.

In most respects the Preobrazhensky Guards were typical of the Russian army, or perhaps more truly, were the perfect embodiment of what a Russian regiment should be. Of course, its officers and veteran NCOs were very committed to their famous regiment. Like all Russian regiments the Preobrazhensky Guards were in many respects a self-contained little world. Soldiers doubled as tailors, cobblers and builders. In addition, a Russian regiment had full-time armourers, blacksmiths, joiners, carpenters, wagon-repairers, farriers and other artisans in its ranks. Doctors were a rather new addition: very unusually the Preobrazhenskys had four. Far more traditional and to be found in every Russian regiment were priests and other junior clergy. Full Orthodox masses were held on Sundays and major holidays. The priests addressed the troops, preaching the duty of loyal service to the tsar as protector of the Orthodox faith and community. Proper treatment of enemy prisoners and civilians was another common theme. In battle some priests were found right up in the firing lines. Their usual place was with the doctors, comforting the wounded and – very importantly – performing the proper burial services for the dead.[62]

Least typical of the army as a whole were the officers of the Preobrazhensky Guards. Although the great majority of Russian officers were nobles, 6 per cent were the sons of labourers, peasants or, most often, soldiers. In any case most Russian nobles scraped along on small incomes and the same was true of most officers. Roughly one-quarter of them in 1812 owned estates or were their heirs, and most of these estates were small. It was a very rare officer in a line regiment whose family owned more than 100 'souls' (i.e. male serfs). In Alexander's Russia there was almost no free education of any quality. Artillery officers were usually educated at cadet corps (i.e. military schools designed to train boys to be officers) and most had essential mathematical knowledge as well as foreign languages. But the great majority of infantry and even cavalry officers of the line read and wrote Russian, might have a smattering of arithmetic but had no other educational attainments.[63]

The officers of the Preobrazhensky Guards were very different. Though the personnel records underestimate officers' wealth, even they show that two-thirds of the regiment's officers came from families with 100 'souls' or more. More than one-quarter owned more than 1,000 'souls' and the commander of the First Battalion, Count Mikhail Vorontsov, was the heir to 24,000. With wealth went education and culture. The overwhelming majority of the officers spoke two or more languages and almost half spoke three or more. The Guards officers' memoirs and diaries speak of literature, history and philosophy. Their education for the most part made them rounded gentlemen and interesting conversationalists rather than professional officers in any narrow sense. They were members of a Russian and European aristocratic elite that was nourished on French literature and Roman history.[64]

The relationship between Alexander and his Guards officers was strangely ambivalent. On the one hand the emperor took enormous pride in his Guards and felt at home amidst cultured, aristocratic officers. But in a curious way the officers of the aristocratic Guards regiments formed a species of republic in the heart of the Russian absolute monarchy. One officer recalled that 'in service matters strict subordination existed but outside this all officers were equal'. If this is an exaggeration, it remains true that relations between officers of very different age and rank were surprisingly informal. This was helped by the fact that very many of these men's families were related or had known each other for generations. For the monarch, this republic of Guards officers could be a source of concern. When 'outsiders' were put in charge of Guards units to tighten up discipline and treated the officers rudely, they were apt to face what amounted to strikes. At the back of an emperor's mind there must also have lurked the memory of the many coups mounted by the Guards in the eighteenth century, the last of which had happened only six years before Tilsit. Indeed, the last great attempted coup by Guards officers was to occur in 1825, immediately after Alexander's death. Its aim was to replace absolutism with a constitutional monarchy or even a republic.[65]

On 9 July, after the ratification of the Tilsit treaties, the two emperors took the salute at a parade of the French and Russian guards. After the parade, in a dramatic gesture which aptly concluded two weeks of play-acting between the monarchs, Napoleon asked Alexander's permission to award the Légion d'honneur to the bravest soldier in the Preobrazhensky Guards. Mikhail Kozlovsky, the regiment's commander, was thoroughly taken aback by this piece of Napoleonic populism and simply summoned forward the battalion's right-hand marker, Grenadier Aleksei Lazarev. The bewildered Lazarev, a soldier's son, suddenly found himself embraced by Napoleon, an officer of the Légion d'honneur, and the recipient of a pension of 1,200 francs a year.

But Alexander's Russia in general and the Preobrazhensky Guards in particular were not best suited to such dramatic examples of French-style 'social mobility'. Two years later Lazarev was ejected from the regiment for cheek to a sergeant-major. In 1819, back in the invalid (i.e. veterans) battalion of the Preobrazhenskys as an ensign, he was arrested for assaulting two civilians. Maybe Lazarev was just a difficult character. But soldiers' sons who rose into the officer corps sometimes faced prejudice and had a hard time adapting to their new status. Even in line regiments a number of them were dismissed or censured after the war, their personnel records citing drunkenness, incompetence and other failings. If officers risen from the ranks faced difficulties in line regiments, Lazarev may well have found life even as a semi-retired ensign of the Preobrazhenskys quite a struggle. He committed suicide before his case could be resolved.[66]

After the treaties were ratified and the parades finished, Alexander left Tilsit and headed back to Petersburg. He divulged his innermost thoughts about recent events to no one. Just how much hope or confidence he had in his new relationship with France it is impossible to say. No doubt he believed that, whatever might follow as regards Russo-French relations, at least he had gained time for his empire and rescued it from a situation of great danger. Perhaps the truest guide to his thoughts is the comment he is said to have made to the Prussian king and queen about Napoleon: 'He will break his own neck. Despite all my performance and external behaviour I am your friend and hope to prove that to you by my actions.'[67]

Neither contemporaries nor historians found Alexander an easy man to understand. An excellent actor, who operated behind a screen of charm and flattery, he remained secretive, opaque, distrustful and elusive. To many observers both in his lifetime and subsequently he appeared to be a mass of contradictions. On the one hand he was a champion of enlightened and liberal principles, but on the other he did very little to ameliorate the authoritarian system of government he inherited, or the world of serf and master on which it rested. He sounded like his grandmother, Catherine II, when he spoke of liberal reforms, but acted like his father, Paul I, in his obsessive concern for the correct drill and appearance of his soldiers on the parade ground. In foreign affairs he put forward high-minded schemes for international peace and order, while simultaneously pursuing a policy of realpolitik. All this has persuaded some critics that he was simply confused and hypocritical.[68]

It is true that the emperor combined very different interests and enthusiasms, inherited from his grandmother and father. He also played to the European gallery, as Catherine had done, seeking to depict himself as a truly enlightened European man and monarch. Brought up on enlightened European ideas by his Swiss tutor and then forced to operate within a Russian context, at one level Alexander believed that Russia was unworthy of him. One side effect of this was a tendency to trust foreign military advisers more than his own generals. There was something in Alexander's nature which made him want to seduce and win the sympathy of every person he met. If this applied most strongly as regards women, he used seduction, sensibility and charm on men too. Alexander was sensitive and highly strung. He evaded confrontations, disliked hurting people's feelings and acted by indirect means to get his way. These elements of Alexander's personality had a big influence on the way he ran his government and his army. In foreign policy he sometimes received information and operated through private channels unknown to his foreign minister and ambassadors. In the army he used private links to subordinates as a means to watch over his commanding generals. Excessive sensitivity, even an element of moral cowardice, stopped him from pruning the military structure of command of a number of superfluous generals. He was also very inclined to avoid overt responsibility for difficult decisions, operating from behind the backs of his generals to get his way, and distancing himself from them if failures occurred.

Alexander's personality was of crucial importance in determining how Russia faced up to the challenge of Napoleon in 1807–14. Nevertheless his actions and even his ideas are incomprehensible unless one understands the context and the constraints within which a Russian monarch operated. Not just Alexander's father but also his grandfather, Peter III, had been overthrown and murdered. So had the previous male monarch, Ivan VI. From his earliest days Alexander had been surrounded by court and political faction and intrigue. As emperor, he was the supreme source of honour, wealth and status. Most people to whom he spoke wanted to use him to advance their own interests or policies. They operated in patron–client networks which hid the truth from him and tried to reduce his independence. These networks spread across court, government and army, which were still essentially one community. The arrogant, ambitious and jealous men who peopled the networks were often very exhausting to manage. But the emperor had to manage them if he was to survive and if the army and bureaucracy were to function effectively. Faced with this Petersburg milieu, an emperor could be forgiven a large degree of suspicion, evasiveness and duplicity. Over the years a world-weary despair about human nature was almost bound to grow. As one of his confidants once remarked, 'in your position an angel would have developed a suspicious personality'.[69]

During these years the shrewdest foreign observer in Petersburg was Joseph de Maistre, the envoy of the King of Sardinia, whose mainland territories had been annexed by Napoleon. He commented that it was 'in the nature of Alexander's personality and his system of rule that top officials operate only in their own limited sphere. He cheerfully and without repugnance employs simultaneously two mortal enemies, not allowing either of them to swallow the other.' By this method the chances of conspiracy were reduced. Usually more to the point, the emperor had a better chance of knowing what was really going on behind his ministers' always deferential and obedient façade. The iron fist was always present and sometimes used but in general Alexander preferred subtler methods. To an extent, secrecy became second nature, almost an end in itself. To do Alexander justice, however, it was usually not just safer but also more efficient for the monarch to operate by manipulation, seduction and bribery. It was also only natural that a monarch sometimes sought advisers who were not part of the Petersburg networks but were entirely dependent on himself. Foreigners were one obvious source of such advice.[70]

When Alexander looked over the heads of the Petersburg networks he saw a vast Russia administered by a woefully inadequate government bureaucracy. In the countryside, where over 90 per cent of his subjects lived, public order, taxation and conscription depended entirely on the cooperation of the landowners. Alexander disliked serfdom but he could not destroy the foundations on which his entire system of government rested and least of all when faced with the need to mobilize all his empire's resources against Napoleon. In any case, was not the weakening of the landowners' power more likely to lead to anarchy than progress, given the current level of development of Russian government and society? He did begin to chip away at serfdom by making voluntary emancipation easier and above all by breaking with his ancestors' policy of 'donating' thousands of state peasants to private owners.[71]

There are many reasons to believe that, in principle, Alexander favoured representative institutions but Russian realities were a powerful disincentive to constitutional reform. Given the weakness of the state administration and the power of the Petersburg patron–client networks, did the emperor really want to strengthen these networks by giving them a parliament through which to exert extra influence on laws, taxation and government? Any representative institutions in Russia would be dominated by the serf-owners: no other group could remotely match their wealth, education or status. Would not such institutions make it harder to modernize Russia and abolish serfdom? Did it not make more sense to improve the bureaucracy so that it could bring enlightened reform to a conservative society? Still less could the emperor be blamed for his approach to foreign affairs. In desiring a more peaceful and cooperative international order while pursuing his own country's interests he was no more hypocritical than the allied leaders after both twentieth-century world wars.[72]

Though in retrospect one can advance these arguments in Alexander's favour, at the time he was widely perceived as well-meaning but feminine and weak. In 1812 this perception mattered greatly. The Austrian foreign minister, Count Metternich, spoke for most foreign diplomats and many members of the Russian elite when he wrote that 'I count on no shred of firmness from the Emperor Alexander', as the French penetrated ever deeper into Russia and finally took Moscow. Napoleon's own strategy makes little sense unless one takes such calculations into account. But in fact Alexander's courage did not desert him in 1812. It also sufficed to overcome the enormous risks and difficulties of invading central Europe in 1813, building an international coalition, and leading it all the way to Paris.[73]

Back in September 1810, as Franco-Russian relations began their descent into war, the French ambassador in Petersburg tried to warn his government that Alexander was much tougher than he seemed.

People believe him to be weak but they are wrong. Undoubtedly he can put up with many upsets and hide his discontent but that is because he has before him an ultimate goal, which is peace in Europe, and one which he hopes to achieve without a violent crisis. But his amenable personality has its limits, and he will not go beyond them: these limits are as strong as iron and will not be abandoned. His personality is by nature well-meaning, sincere and loyal, and his sentiments and principles are elevated but beneath all this there exists an acquired royal dissimulation and a dogged persistence which nothing can overcome.[74]

3

The Russo-French Alliance

After ratifying the treaties of peace and alliance with France Alexander left Tilsit and travelled back to Petersburg, where he arrived on 16 July 1807. The previous day the capital had witnessed a twenty-one-gun salute and a service in the Kazan cathedral to celebrate peace. Similar celebrations occurred in Moscow, where Bishop Augustin put a good face on events by telling his congregation that Napoleon had been so impressed by the Russian troops' courage that he had decided he needed Russia for a friend. The Orthodox Church did have some explaining to do since, on the orders of the government, it had been declaiming from the pulpit for many months against Napoleon the Antichrist. Apparently, the story now went round many Russian villages that the tsar had met Napoleon in the middle of a river in order to wash away his sins.[1]

Alexander could afford for the moment to ignore the bafflement of his peasant subjects over his sudden friendship for the former Antichrist. He could not be so nonchalant about the opinion of the Moscow and Petersburg aristocracy, and of the generals and Guards officers who formed a key element in this elite. In the autumn of 1807 Count Nikolai Rumiantsev took over as foreign minister. Subsequently he told the French ambassador, the Marquis de Caulaincourt, that

the Emperor Napoleon and in general everyone in France makes a mistake about this country. They don't know it well and believe that the emperor governs as a despot, whose simple decree is enough to change public opinion or at least to determine all decisions . . . [This] is wrong. For all his goodness and the gentleness of character for which he is famous, the Emperor Alexander perhaps imposes his views on public opinion more than any previous monarch. The Empress Catherine, who was beyond question the most imperious of women and the most absolute sovereign who ever reigned, did this much less than him. Of that you can be sure. Nor did she ever find herself in such difficult circumstances as he now faces. She understood this country so well that she won over all elements of public opinion. As she herself once told me, she handled carefully even the spirit of opposition of a few old ladies.[2]

In fact Rumiantsev was preaching to the converted and the French embassy in Petersburg kept a very wary eye on public opinion. It was widely believed that the coups which overthrew Alexander's father and grandfather had been motivated in part by opposition to their foreign policies, though Caulaincourt himself stressed the manner in which these monarchs had infringed the personal interests of key members of the Petersburg aristocracy. In his dispatches he told Napoleon that memories of Emperor Paul and dislike of the Grand Duke Constantine were some guarantee against an attempt to overthrow Alexander I. When the Russian monarch travelled to Erfurt to meet Napoleon in September 1808, Caulaincourt noted that with the totally dependable Dmitrii Lobanov-Rostovsky as military governor of Petersburg and the very loyal Fedor Uvarov in command of the Guards nothing untoward was likely to happen in the emperor's absence. Subsequently, however, the ambassador noted that the cultivation of Russian nationalist circles by the emperor's sister, Grand Duchess Catherine, represented a potential threat to the throne. With the exception of some rather brief moments, above all in 1809, Caulaincourt stressed that, though few Russians wanted war, the support of Alexander and Rumiantsev for the French alliance made them isolated and unpopular figures in Petersburg.[3]

To some extent hostility to France was due to a sense of injured pride. Eighteenth-century Russia had won its wars, so Austerlitz and Friedland were a humiliating shock. Needless to say, such public humiliation was all the harder to bear for proud aristocrats brought up to feel an acute concern for their honour and reputation. Prince Serge Volkonsky recalls that he and his young fellow-officers of the Chevaliers Gardes regiment burned with desire to revenge Austerlitz and took out their frustrations by breaking the windows of the French embassy and then racing off before anyone could catch them.[4]

Nor were matters necessarily much different among the army's senior officers. Alexander's first ambassador in Paris after Tilsit was Lieutenant-General Count Petr Tolstoy. Tolstoy was an ambassador of heroic bluntness: he was in fact not a diplomat but a fighting general and longed to escape from the Paris embassy, where in his opinion he was wasting his time on a fool's errand. He told his superiors in Petersburg repeatedly that Napoleon (whom in general he pointedly continued to call Bonaparte) was bent on the domination of all Europe, and 'wants to make us an Asiatic power, to push us back behind our old frontiers'. Repelled and humiliated by French arrogance and vainglory, Tolstoy came close to fighting a duel with Michel Ney after the ambassador had sung the praises of the Russian army a bit too loudly for the Frenchman's taste and had argued that French victory in 1807 was due to luck and to overwhelming numbers.[5]

Such feelings were shared by members of Alexander's family. Even while the emperor was negotiating at Tilsit, his sister the Grand Duchess Catherine wrote to him that Napoleon was 'a blend of cunning, personal ambition and falseness' who should feel honoured just to be allowed to consort with the Russian monarch. She added: 'I wish to see her [i.e. Russia] respected, not in word but in reality, seeing that she certainly has the means and the right to be so.' Catherine's mother, the Dowager Empress Marie, became the centre of Petersburg aristocratic opposition to the French alliance. Most of Petersburg high society closed its doors to Caulaincourt when he first arrived and some of these doors remained closed throughout his stay, despite Alexander's annoyance. Many French royalist émigrés lived in Petersburg or served in the Russian army. Their manners, education and style won them much sympathy in Petersburg high society and contributed to its hostility to Napoleon. Among the most prominent émigrés was the Duc de Richelieu, who became governor-general of New Russia (i.e. southern Ukraine) but returned to France after the Restoration to serve Louis XVIII as prime minister. Also to the fore were the Marquis de Traversay, who served as Minister of the Navy from 1811, and the two sons of the Count de Saint-Priest, France's ambassador to the Ottoman Empire before 1789. Best known of all was Joseph de Maistre, along with Edmund Burke the most famous political thinker of the European counter-revolution, who served as the exiled King of Sardinia's envoy to Petersburg in these years.[6]

The 'legitimist' sympathies of the Petersburg drawing rooms were not just a product of snobbery and nostalgia for Old Regime France, how-ever. They were also rooted in the sense that Napoleon's actions were a challenge to the religious and historical principles on which their own state and society rested, as well as to any stable system of international relations in Europe. Baron Grigorii Stroganov, for example, had been Russia's envoy to the Spanish court for many years. When Alexander requested him to continue to serve in the same capacity at the court of Joseph Bonaparte, Stroganov refused. Stroganov wrote to the emperor that Napoleon's deposition of the Bourbons violated 'the most sacred rights', indeed precisely those rights on whose basis Alexander himself ruled. In kidnapping and deposing his own Spanish allies, Napoleon had also violated in the crudest manner 'the holiness and the good faith of treaties'. If Stroganov continued to represent Russia in Madrid he would feel personally dishonoured before the Spanish people and 'of all the sacrifices which I am ready to bear for the glory and the service of Your Imperial Majesty that of my honour is the only one which I am not in a position to offer'.[7]

In addition to these sentiments, there was a strong strain of Anglophilia in Petersburg society. Britain was seen as not just very powerful but also as the freest of the European states. Unlike other countries, Britain's freedoms actually seemed to enhance its power, allowing the state to sustain a huge level of debt at very manageable cost. The wealth, entrenched rights and values of its aristocracy were seen as a key to both British freedom and British power, and were compared favourably with Napoleon's bureaucratic despotism. If the Vorontsov and Stroganov families were Petersburg's most prominent aristocratic Anglophiles, some of Alexander's closest friends from his own generation also belonged in this camp.

In addition, Adam Smith was widely read and the British economy much admired by many of the key individuals who shaped Russian economic and financial policy. Nikolai Mordvinov, the elder statesman of Russian economic policy, was a great disciple of Smith and Ricardo for example. Dmitrii Gurev, the minister of finance, called the British system of public finance 'one of the most extraordinary inventions of the human understanding'. All this admiration was by no means merely abstract. These men believed that Russia's interests were closely aligned with Britain's. Britain was the main market and the main carrier of Russian exports. In 1808–12 Mordvinov in particular was terrified that if Russia continued to adhere to Napoleon's economic blockade of Britain these export markets would be lost for good. In his opinion mutually profitable trade relations with Britain were by no means incompatible with selective protection of fledgling Russian industries. Meanwhile not just these Anglophiles but almost all Russia's senior diplomats in 1808–12 came to agree that Napoleon's drive to dominate the continent was the main threat to Russian interests and that Britain was a natural ally in the face of this threat. If, unlike Petr Tolstoy, they did not bombard Petersburg with these opinions that was because they wished to keep their jobs and often sympathized with Alexander's own view that it was in Russia's interests to postpone the inevitable conflict with France for as long as possible.[8]

The papers of General Levin von Bennigsen, the commander-in-chief in 1807, go to the core of Russian geopolitical thinking at this time. Like most members of the ruling elite, Bennigsen supported peace in 1807 but disliked the French alliance. Equally common was his view that, although British naval power was sometimes used in ways that damaged Russian pride, French domination of continental Europe was much more of a threat to key Russian interests. In particular, it was in Napoleon's power to re-establish a Polish state of 15 million people on Russia's borders and this would be a huge threat to Russian security. Bennigsen also believed that if Napoleon was allowed to strangle Russia's foreign trade then the economy would no longer be able to sustain Russia's armed forces or the European culture of its elites. The country would revert to its pre-Petrine, semi-Asiatic condition.

In Bennigsen's view, Britain's global position was so strong that it would be immensely hard for Napoleon to break, even if all of continental Europe united behind this goal. A crucial factor in British global power was its hold on India, which Bennigsen considered unassailable. He argued that the British had created a European-style military system in India funded by local taxpayers. This army, 'formed on the same principles as our European regiments, commanded by English officers, and excellently armed, manoeuvres with the precision of our grenadiers'. In the past Asiatic cavalry armies had invaded India over its north-west frontier and conquered the subcontinent but these had no chance against the Anglo-Indian infantry and artillery. Meanwhile no rival European army could reach the subcontinent because the British dominated the sea-routes and the logistical problems of getting a European-style army across Persia or Afghanistan were insurmountable. Having himself campaigned in northern Persia, Bennigsen spoke with authority on this point. The conclusion which Bennigsen drew from this analysis was that for Russia to ally with France against Britain was suicidal. In the first place French victory over Britain was flatly contrary to Russian interests. Secondly, Russian finances and the economy would disintegrate long before any economic war with Britain could be successful.[9]

The alliance with Napoleon always had many more potential enemies than friends in Petersburg. Nevertheless there were possible sources of support. Any sensible official concerned with the empire's internal affairs knew that Russia faced many domestic problems with very inadequate resources to meet them. Hugely expensive foreign policies and wars were a disaster from this perspective. In 1808–12 the key figure in Russian internal affairs was Mikhail Speransky, whom Tolstoy – still very much the provincial aristocrat when he wrote the novel – caricatures unfairly in *War and Peace*. Speransky was an unlikely person to find in the top ranks of Russian government. The son of a penniless provincial priest, sheer ability had resulted in him being sent to Russia's leading ecclesiastical academy in Petersburg. From there, his obvious career would have been as a bishop and a senior administrator in the Orthodox Church. He was plucked from this life by Aleksandr Kurakin's brother, who made Speransky his private secretary and then transferred him to the state bureaucracy to help him in his official duties.

Speransky's great intelligence, his skill as a draftsman of laws and memoranda, and his astonishing work ethic won him the admiration first of a range of top officials, and then of Alexander himself. Though there is no reason to doubt Alexander's enthusiasm for Speransky, the emperor will also have realized that a chief adviser without connections in the Petersburg aristocracy posed no threat and could easily be thrown to the wolves in case of necessity. In 1808–12 Speransky was in reality the emperor's main adviser on financial matters, the restructuring of central government, and the affairs of newly acquired Finland. In 1809–12, as Alexander began to run aspects of Russian diplomacy and espionage behind Rumiantsev's back, he used Speransky as the conduit for secret reports designed for the monarch's eyes alone. Alexander also discussed secretly with Speransky plans for the fundamental reform of Russian society and government, entailing both the emancipation of the serfs and the introduction of elected assemblies at central and regional level.

Any individual with this degree of imperial favour would have attracted enormous jealousy and criticism in Petersburg society. The fact that Speransky was a parvenu and lacked the time or the skill to forge useful connections made him all the more vulnerable. Rumours floated about concerning Speransky's plans to emancipate the peasants. Some of his reforms, designed to improve administrative efficiency, damaged the interests of members of the aristocracy. Much of noble opinion saw Speransky as a 'Jacobin' and a worshipper of that heir of the Revolution, Napoleon Bonaparte. There was little truth in this. Speransky admired some of Napoleon's administrative and legal reforms but his plans for representative institutions were closer to English models than to Napoleon's bureaucratic despotism. Moreover, though Speransky would have loved to be allowed to get on with domestic reform untroubled by external complications, he was under no illusions that Napoleon would leave Russia in peace to do this.[10]

A somewhat more real 'Bonapartist' was the minister of the navy, Admiral Pavel Chichagov. The admiral was a far more familiar type than Speransky in the Russian government of Alexander's day. Though from a run-of-the-mill gentry family, Chichagov was well educated and himself the son of a prominent admiral. The French ambassador believed that Chichagov was one of the strongest supporters of the Franco-Russian alliance, and so too did many Russians. In September 1807, for instance, the admiral wrote to Alexander denouncing British maritime tyranny and hailing Napoleon's genius. Aged only 40, still relatively young for a minister, the admiral was an intelligent and energetic man, with a lively mind. There were those who said that his conversation was more impressive than his deeds, but both Caulaincourt and Joseph de Maistre considered Chichagov to be one of the most intelligent and interesting figures in Petersburg. Among the admiral's failings was a tendency to get somewhat carried away by his own wit and to go too far in conversation. Like most Russian noblemen, he was also very quick to take offence if he considered his pride to have been affronted. That could make him a poor subordinate and an overbearing commander. Much worse, Chichagov was generally disdainful of Russian backwardness and inclined to compare his own country unfavourably with others, above all with Napoleonic France. When he did this to a flagrant degree during a long stay in Paris, Russian diplomats there were very unamused. They kept a close eye on him in case he blurted out Russian secrets. Alexander actually shared many of Chichagov's views, admired him and forgave him his outbursts. But by 1812 there were many knives in Petersburg long since sharpened and waiting to plunge into Chichagov's back.[11]

If the Russo-French alliance was to survive, however, the key group which Napoleon needed to cultivate in Petersburg was what Caulaincourt called the 'Old Russians' and whom one might realistically call the Russian isolationists. In almost all cases ethnic Russians and often from the older generation, these men saw no reason why Russia should involve itself in European affairs because of (as they would have whispered) Alexander's infatuation with Queen Louise of Prussia or his fantasies of universal peace and brotherhood. In some cases a desire to avoid diplomatic and military entanglement in Europe went along with a dislike of Frenchified manners and values invading Russian society and 'subverting' its traditions. Many of the aristocratic isolationists, however, were highly cultivated men, as much at ease conversing in French as in Russian. Often isolationism also had its own aggressive strategic agenda. It saw expansion to the south against the Ottomans as Russia's truly national interest and objective, looking back to the victorious wars of Catherine II as a model for future Russian grand strategy. Isolationists also recalled that the great leaders of Russian southward expansion under Catherine – field-marshals Petr Rumiantsev, Grigorii Potemkin and Alexander Suvorov – were all ethnic Russians, unlike so many of the men who commanded Alexander's armies in the Napoleonic era.

There were parallels between these Russian isolationists and eighteenth-century British debates about grand strategy. Many English politicians demanded a truly 'national' policy of colonial and maritime expansion, and denounced involvement on the continent of Europe as mere pandering to the Hanoverian dynasty. Opinions which could be shouted from the rooftops in Britain could only be whispered in Russia. Nor were the Romanovs as obviously foreign as the Hanoverians. But when the male line of the dynasty died out in 1730, the succession had passed down through a daughter of Peter the Great who had married into the princely house of Holstein. The deference of Peter III and his son Paul I to the 'Great Frederick' and his Prussian army suggested to some Old Russians that a distinctly German and poisonous element had entered the Romanovs' bloodstream. In August 1809, thoroughly disillusioned by Alexander's foreign policy, Field-Marshal Prince

Prozorovsky wrote to Prince Serge Golitsyn, fellow 'Old Russian' aristo-crat and veteran of Catherine's wars, that if Napoleon continued to trick and weaken Russia then no doubt the Prozorovskys and Golitsyns would hang on to their estates one way or another but the 'House of Holstein' would cease to sit on the Russian throne.[12]

The parallels between Russian and British debates on strategy reflected a basic common geopolitical reality. Britain and Russia were great powers on the European periphery. For both countries it was more profitable to use their power outside Europe, where pickings were easier and other European rivals found it almost impossible to intervene. Acquisitions in the European heartland were far more expensive to acquire and defend. By 1800, however, if both Britain and Russia could benefit from their peripheral position the key advantages rested with Britain. In terms of the security of the two empires' core territory, the seas were a better barrier than the plains of Poland and Belorussia. To an extent, what Poland was to Russia, Ireland was to the English, in other words a vulnerable frontier territory inhabited by religious and historical enemies. Having expropriated almost the entire native elite, however, the English were confident that the Irish back door into Britain was secure unless the country was invaded by a large French army. The power of the Royal Navy made it almost certain that it would not be. No Russian statesman could feel a similar security about Poland.[13]

The British were also much better placed as regards new acquisitions on the periphery. As Russian southward expansion brought them within range of Constantinople and even sent their fleet into the eastern Medi-terranean they were entering a region which other great powers con-sidered as crucial and where they could intervene effectively to block the Russians. Moreover, though southward expansion brought Russia gains in 'Ukraine' and on the Black Sea shore which were of great significance, they could not compare with the enormous advance of British power between 1793 and 1815. With the French, Spanish and Dutch navies all more or less eliminated, the British were able to take over much of South America's trade, eliminate their key rivals in India, begin to use Indian exports to break into the Chinese market and consolidate their hold on naval bases which stretched across the globe and greatly enhanced their control of international trade. The basic geopolitical realities underlying the Napoleonic era pointed towards future British global predominance, especially since geopolitics was reinforced by the first signs of Britain's Industrial Revolution. This had to cause unease in some Russian minds. On the other hand, the overriding current geopolitical priority was that both Russian and British security would be in great danger if any other power dominated continental Europe.[14]

The most prominent representative of the 'Old Russians' between 1807 and 1812 was Count Nikolai Rumiantsev, the foreign minister in this period. Before Peter the Great's time the Rumiantsev family had been middling gentry, far beneath the status of the princes Volkonsky, Lobanov or Golitsyn, but Nikolai's grandfather, Aleksandr Rumiantsev, had been a close associate of Peter from childhood and throughout his reign. He died a full general, a count and a wealthy man. Peter ensured that Aleksandr Rumiantsev married into the core of the old Muscovite aristocracy. As a result, his grandson Nikolai's connections were formidable: he was for example the first cousin of Aleksandr Kurakin.

The relationship which really mattered, however, was with Nikolai's father, the great hero of Catherine's reign, Field-Marshal Count Petr Rumiantsev. As the Foreign Minister once said to Caulaincort, 'only the hope of achieving a great benefit for his country could inspire the son of Field-Marshal Rumiantsev' to remain in public service. Acutely conscious of his heritage, Nikolai Rumiantsev was a ferociously proud Russian patriot, determined that his country should be second to none. One aspect of his patriotism was his enormous interest in old Russian manuscripts and other artefacts. Not only did he fund the collection, publication and display of these treasures, he also participated enthusiastically in expeditions across Russia to find them. Many of the greatest old Russian and Slavic collections in contemporary Russian libraries and museums owe their origins to this remarkable man, who ultimately bequeathed his treasures to the public.[15]

In Rumiantsev's youth not only had Russia been on the march southwards under his father's command, it had also been Europe's leading producer of iron. As Rumiantsev was well aware, however, by 1807 its relative economic position was slipping. During Rumiantsev's service as Foreign Minister, Russia established diplomatic relations with the United States. The first American envoy to Russia was John Quincy Adams, the son of an American President and himself to hold this office in the 1820s. Rumiantsev once confided to Adams that 'it was no subject for exaltation to a great empire that the choicest of its productions for exportation were hemp and tallow, and bees-wax and iron'. His interest in economic affairs was partly that of an immensely wealthy landowner, very aware of the impact of new farming methods in western Europe. In addition, however, he had run the empire's canals and other water-ways for many years, and had served as minister of trade since 1802. This was a unique background for a Russian foreign minister.[16]

For Rumiantsev, Napoleon was in one sense a sideshow, in another an opportunity. What really concerned him was growing British domi-nation of the global economy. The foreign minister welcomed Napo-leon's economic blockade of Britain: 'It would be better that the whole commerce of the world should cease to exist for ten years, than to abandon it for ever to the control of England.' As he told Adams, Russia would not go the way of India. As minister of trade, he had introduced new laws to ensure that foreigners did not take over Russian domestic trade or production. Meanwhile British control of Russian overseas trade threatened 'a dominion, something like they had in India' and this 'could not be endured'. Rumiantsev cultivated the United States both as an alternative carrier of Russian trade and as a potential check on British domination of the global economy. He was constantly on the search for new markets for Russian goods in the Americas and China.[17]

Rumiantsev faced an uphill task, however. Granted that Napoleon's throttling of European trade offered involuntary protection to a number of nascent Russian industries such as sugar production, was Russian society or the Russian economy yet in a position to take advantage of this? Of course Caulaincourt welcomed Rumiantsev's ideas, but even he believed that the absence of a middle class and of large numbers of skilled artisans would heavily constrain Russian economic potential. To a great extent, too, the Industrial Revolution depended on the marriage of coal and iron, but in Russia only the coming of the railways could span the distance between the country's huge deposits. In more immediate and policy-related terms, Rumiantsev came to despair of Napoleon's Continental System, the Pan-European blockade of British trade by which the emperor hoped to bring his arch-enemy to its knees. In Rumiantsev's opinion it was actually harming Britain's competitors and handing global trade to the British on a plate.[18]

In political terms too the success of Rumiantsev's strategy lay in Napoleon's hands. Isolationism was only a viable strategy if Napoleon refrained from threatening Russian security. Above all, in Rumiantsev's view, that meant no encouragement to the Poles. Any restored Polish state would be bound to want back its pre-partition frontiers, thereby depriving Russia of much of Ukraine and Belorussia. As he told Caulaincourt, though all his own political capital had been invested in the French alliance, 'I will myself be the first person to tell the Emperor to sacrifice everything rather than consent to Poland's re-establishment or to agree to any arrangements which even indirectly lead to its restoration or convey any idea about it'.[19]

If Alexander himself did leave Tilsit with any illusions about the French alliance they were soon dissipated. The first dispute revolved around Moldavia and Wallachia, Ottoman provinces occupied by the Russian army during the ongoing war. The Russians wished to annex them to compensate for the costs of the war started by the Ottomans in 1806. Very possibly the arrival of Nikolai Rumiantsev as Foreign Minister increased their appetite for expansion at Turkey's expense. Since this acquisition was not written into the Treaty of Tilsit the French claimed compensation for themselves to balance Russia's gain. Alexander believed that Napoleon had encouraged him to annex these provinces in conversations at Tilsit, so he was taken aback by this demand. What truly appalled him, however, was the French claim for Silesia as compensation. Not only was Silesia far more valuable than the two Turkish provinces, it was also the richest remaining province of Prussia. To remove it would both dishonour Alexander before Frederick William and reduce Prussia to the status of a petty principality, totally incapable of shielding Russia's western borders. In addition, Silesia was situated between Saxony and the Grand Duchy of Warsaw, whose sovereign was the Saxon king. The Saxon-Polish monarchy was Napoleon's leading outpost and client-state in eastern Europe. If (as was likely) Napoleon added Silesia with its large Polish population to the Saxon-Polish monarchy then Russian fears of a reborn Polish threat would increase enormously.

This dispute over the Ottoman 'principalities' was sidelined by beginning Franco-Russian negotiations on the future of the whole Ottoman Empire. These revealed both Rumiantsev's great appetite for Ottoman territory and total French unwillingness to give Russia Constantinople and access to the Mediterranean. These discussions were then overtaken by the crises caused by French and Russian efforts to implement the terms of the Treaty of Tilsit which called for the imposition of the Continental System on the rest of Europe. The Russian share of this enterprise was to impose the Continental System on the Swedes, which they achieved (at least on paper) as a result of defeating Sweden in the war of 1808–9. From the Russian perspective, the key justification for this expensive war was that it would lead to the annexation of Finland, thereby making Petersburg far more secure against Swedish attack in the event of any future conflicts. The peace treaty was signed at Friedrichsham in September 1809: Alexander signalled his satisfaction by promoting Rumiantsev to chancellor (the top position in the Russian civil administration) and granting the Finns a generous degree of autonomy.

Meanwhile the French attempt to impose the Continental System on Iberia had gone disastrously wrong. The Portuguese government and royal family fled to Brazil, escorted by the British navy. Now completely dependent on British goodwill, they immediately opened the whole Portuguese Empire to British trade. Far worse were the results of Napoleon's deposition of the Spanish Bourbons and attempted takeover of Spain. This exposed Alexander and Rumiantsev to even more criticism in Petersburg society for supporting Napoleon. It opened up not just Spain but also the Spanish Empire to British trade, thereby driving a further enormous hole into the Continental System. The Spanish insurrection also persuaded the Austrians that this might be their last opportunity to strike while Napoleon was absorbed elsewhere and their finances could still sustain the army of a great power.

Alexander had explained his support for the Continental System to Frederick William by arguing that 'I have reason to hope that this will be a means to hasten the general peace of which Europe has so urgent a need. So long as the war between France and England continues, there will be no tranquillity for the continent's other states.' Some of his advisers had warned him all along that it was fanciful to imagine that even combined Franco-Russian pressure could make Britain negotiate. Now Alexander himself was forced to acknowledge that Napoleon's policy had made the peace which Russia needed more remote than ever. France's blundering aggression in Spain had given Britain 'immense advantages' and spurred Austria into a military build-up which could unleash further war on the continent.[20]

It was in the middle of this threatening international situation that

Alexander travelled to Erfurt in central Germany in September 1808 for the long-awaited follow-up meeting to Tilsit. Amidst great festivities and a cascade of mutual admiration in public, the relationship between the two monarchs had noticeably chilled since the previous year. To an extent this simply reflected the fact that Russia's relative position had improved, so there was more room for bargaining and less need for unlimited deference to Napoleon. Russia had long since recovered from the defeat of Friedland. French armies were no longer deployed threateningly on her borders. Instead they were struggling in Spain or awaiting the possibility of a new war with Austria. France needed Russia and therefore abandoned her opposition to Russian annexation of Moldavia and Wallachia. In return, Alexander promised to support Napoleon in the event of an Austrian attack but since this was already implicit in the Treaty of Tilsit the Russians were not making any real concession.

Much more interesting than the rather meaningless negotiations and agreements at Erfurt were the letters between Alexander and his family concerning the meeting with Napoleon, for they reveal much about his innermost thoughts. One week before the emperor's departure his mother had written him a long letter imploring him not to go. In the light of Napoleon's kidnapping of the Spanish royal family, the Empress Marie was nervous about her son's safety in a foreign town garrisoned by French troops and controlled by a man devoid of any scruples or limits. Though she admitted that peace had been a necessity at Tilsit, she spelled out the dangerous subsequent results of the alliance with France. Napoleon had manipulated Russia into waging an expensive and immoral war against Sweden, while blocking peace with the Ottomans and even trying to insinuate himself into Russo-Persian relations. Still worse were the domestic consequences of the disastrous break with Britain and adherence to the Continental System. Commerce had collapsed and prices of basic necessities had shot up, halving the real value of salaries and forcing officials to steal in order to feed their families. Declining state revenues and the demoralization and corruption of government officials threatened a crisis. However, Napoleon's difficulties in Spain and Austrian rearmament offered Russia a chance to unite with France's enemies and end her dominion of Europe. At such a moment, argued the empress, it would be disastrous for Alexander's prestige and Russia's interests if he made a pilgrimage to visit Napoleon and consolidate the Franco-Russian alliance.[21]

Marie's arguments were not new. Many of Alexander's diplomats could have made exactly the same points, and Count Tolstoy had indeed frequently done so in his dispatches from Paris. Alexander could ignore his officials much more easily than his mother, however. Though often exasperated by Marie, he was at heart not just a loyal and polite son but also a devoted one. So before departing for Erfurt he set out and justified his policies in a long handwritten letter to her.

Alexander opened by stating that in a matter of such huge importance, the only consideration had to be Russia's interests and well-being, to which all his cares were devoted. It would be 'criminal' if he allowed himself to be swayed by ignorant, shallow and shifting public opinion. Instead he must consult his own conscience and reason, looking realities squarely in the eye and not giving way to false hopes or emotions. The basic reality at present was that France was immensely powerful, more powerful and better placed than even Russia and Austria combined. If even republican France in the 1790s, weakened by misgovernment and civil war, could defeat all Europe, what must one say now about the French Empire, led by an autocratic sovereign who was also a military genius and sustained by an army of veterans hardened by fifteen years of war? It was an illusion to think that a few setbacks in Spain could seriously shake this power.

At present Russia's salvation lay in avoiding conflict with Napoleon, which could only be done by making him believe that Russia shared his interests. 'All our efforts must be devoted to this so that we can breathe freely for some time. During this precious time we can build up our resources and our forces. But we must do this in complete silence and not in making our armaments and preparations public or in declaiming in public against this man whom we distrust.' Not to go to a meeting with Napoleon which had been planned for so long would arouse his suspicions and could prove fatal at such a moment of international tension. If Austria started a war now, it would be blind to its own interests and weaknesses. Everything must be done to save Austria from this folly and to preserve her resources until the moment arrived when they could be used for the general good. But this moment had not yet come and, if his expedition to Erfurt resulted in 'stopping so deplorable a catastrophe' as Austria's defeat and destruction, it would repay with interest all the unpleasant aspects of meeting with Napoleon.[22]

There is good reason to believe that in this letter to his mother

Alexander was speaking from the heart. Knowing her loathing for Napoleon, however, it is possible that he was exaggerating his dislike and distrust of the French monarch. Alexander had no such reason for pretence when writing to his sister Catherine, who was probably the person whom he trusted more than anyone else in the world. After departing from Erfurt and bidding an unctuous farewell to Napoleon he wrote to her that 'Bonaparte thinks that I am nothing but an idiot. "They laugh longest who laugh last!" I put all my trust in God.'[23]

During the six months which followed the meeting at Erfurt the main aim of Russian foreign policy was to avoid a Franco-Austrian war. Alexander and Rumiantsev were convinced that if war came, Austrian hopes of effective help from risings in Germany or British landings would prove false. The Habsburg army would certainly be defeated and Austria would either be destroyed or weakened to such a degree that she would be forced to become a French satellite. Russia would then be the only independent great power left to oppose Napoleon's domination of the whole European continent. The emperor remained committed to the French alliance as the only way to buy time for Russia. If Petersburg openly sided with Austria not merely would Napoleon destroy the Habsburg army before Russian help could arrive, he would then turn all his forces against a Russia which was still far from ready for a life-and-death struggle.

Alexander refused Napoleon's demand for concerted Franco-Russian warnings in Vienna, partly because he did not want to insult the Austrians and partly because he feared that too strong Russian support might even inspire Napoleon himself to start a war aimed at eliminating the Habsburg monarchy or simply at raiding the Austrian treasury to pay for the upkeep of his bloated army. Nevertheless he did warn the Austrians that if they attacked Napoleon Russia's obligations under the Treaty of Tilsit would force her to fight on France's side. On the other hand, since he believed that Austrian armaments could only be explained by fear of French aggression, he promised that, if the Austrians partially disarmed, Russia would publicly guarantee to come to their assistance in the event of a French attack. Right down to the outbreak of war on 10 April 1809 Alexander found it almost impossible to believe that Austria would take the suicidal risk of attacking Napoleon. When this actually happened, the emperor blamed the Habsburg government for allowing itself to be carried away by public opinion and its own emotions.[24]

The Austrian attack on Napoleon left Alexander no alternative but to declare war. Had he failed to meet his clear treaty obligations the Russo-French alliance would have collapsed and Russia and France would probably have been at war within a matter of weeks. While in theory Austria's enemy, Russia's overriding war aim was that the Austrian Empire should be weakened as little as possible. The last thing Russia wanted to do was damage the Austrian army, since its survival was the main guarantee against Napoleon imposing crushing peace terms on the Habsburgs. In addition, the Russians were strongly opposed to any addition of territory to the Duchy of Warsaw. The Russian army which invaded Austrian Galicia therefore devoted much of its efforts to avoiding the Habsburg forces and impeding the advance of the Duchy's Polish army, which was supposedly its ally. Of course it was impossible to hide such tactics, especially when Russian correspondence intercepted by the Poles made their intentions clear. Napoleon was furious and never really believed again in the usefulness of the Russian alliance. Predictably, the war ended in Austria's defeat. In the peace treaty of Schönbrunn, signed in October 1809, Napoleon revenged himself on Alexander by handing a large slice of Galicia to the Poles.

The war between Austria and France was the beginning of the end of the Russo-French alliance but two developments over the winter of 1809–10 disguised this for a time. Napoleon agreed that his ambassador in Russia, Armand de Caulaincourt, should draft a Franco-Russian convention which would lay to rest Russian fears about Poland's possible restoration. More or less simultaneously he divorced his wife, the Empress Josephine, and sought the hand of Alexander's sister. Rumours that Napoleon was in pursuit of a Russian grand duchess had been floating around for some time. In March 1808 a very worried Empress Marie had asked the ambassador in Paris to find out whether this was a real danger. At that time the obvious target would have been the Grand Duchess Catherine. The marriage of this extremely feisty and strong-willed young woman with Napoleon would have been interesting and combustible. For all her ambition, however, Catherine could not stomach the idea of marrying the Corsican bandit. Perhaps to avoid any possibility of this, in 1809 she married her distant cousin, Prince George of Oldenburg, instead. This left the only possible Russian bride as the Grand Duchess Anna, just turned 16 when Napoleon's proposal arrived.[25]

Napoleon's request for Anna's hand was very unwelcome to Alexander. He neither wanted to marry his sister to a Bonaparte nor to insult the French emperor by refusing to do so. Paul I had decreed in his will that his daughters' marriages should be in their mother's hands and in a sense this was a glorious excuse for Alexander to dodge the issue, though by pleading inability to impose his will on a mere woman he confirmed all Napoleon's suspicions about his weakness. Alexander rather dreaded a tantrum from the empress on this issue but in fact mother and son saw eye to eye on the matter and this was just one sign of their growing agreement on political questions. Of course Marie was horrified by the idea of the marriage but she fully understood the dangers of annoying Napoleon. She wrote to her daughter Catherine that Alexander had told her that Russia's western frontier was very vulnerable, with no fortresses to cover the likely invasion routes: 'The Emperor told me that if God granted him five years' peace, he would have ten fortresses, and his finances in order.' The Empress accepted the fact that it was the duty of the imperial family to sacrifice themselves for the good of the state but she could not bear the thought of losing her daughter, who was still a child, to Napoleon. The fact that two of her older daughters had been married young and that both had died in childbirth strengthened this revulsion. In the end the Grand Duchess Catherine came up with a compromise: Napoleon would not be refused outright but merely told that, having lost two daughters, the Empress was determined that her last one should not marry before the age of 18.[26]

By the time the Russian semi-rejection reached Napoleon in February 1810 he had long since opted for his second-best option, namely marriage with the daughter of the Austrian emperor, the Archduchess Marie-Louise. Alexander stifled both his resentment that Napoleon had been simultaneously negotiating with both courts and his deep fear that an Austrian marriage would contribute to the breakdown of the Franco-Russian alliance and Russia's isolation. Almost simultaneously he was shocked to learn that Napoleon had refused to ratify the convention barring the restoration of Poland. Napoleon assured the Russians that he had no intention of restoring a Polish kingdom but could not sign a convention which bound France to stop anyone else, including the Poles themselves, from doing so. In a sense the dispute over the convention's wording was nonsensical: no one could hold Napoleon to any agreement he signed and his record of fidelity to treaties was not impressive. In a way, however, that made his refusal even to pretend to meet Russian wishes as regards Poland even more suspicious in Russian eyes. From this moment on Franco-Russian relations went into a steep decline, which continued until the outbreak of war in June 1812. It was no coincidence that in early March 1810 the new minister of war, Mikhail Barclay de Tolly, drafted his first memorandum on measures for the defence of Russia's western border from French attack.[27]

Meanwhile the Continental System was beginning to cause Russia major difficulties. Alexander recognized always that Russian adherence to Napoleon's economic blockade of Britain was 'the basis of our alliance' with France. To restore relations with Britain would be to breach the core of the Treaty of Tilsit and make war with Napoleon inevitable. For that reason he refrained from doing this until French troops actually crossed his border in June 1812. By 1810, however, it was clear that something had to be done to reduce the damage being caused to Russia by the Continental System.[28]

The biggest single problem was the collapsing value of the paper ruble, which by 1811 was almost the only currency in use in the empire's Russian heartlands. In June 1804 the paper ruble had been worth more than three-quarters of its silver equivalent: by June 1811 it was valued at less than one-quarter. This had two key causes. In the first place, the only way the state could pay for its enormous military expenditures in 1805–10 was by printing more and more paper money. Secondly, the Continental System, added to general economic and political uncertainties, had resulted in a collapse in business confidence. Even the silver ruble lost one-fifth of its value against the pound sterling in 1807–12. The value of the paper ruble on the foreign exchanges plummeted. This had a dramatic effect on the cost of sustaining Russian armies fighting in Finland, Moldavia, the Caucasus and Poland: Caulaincourt reckoned that the campaign against the Swedes was costing Alexander the equivalent of fifteen French silver francs per man per day, commenting that 'the Swedish war is ruining Russia'. By 1809 state income was less than half of expenditure and crisis was looming. The real value of the government's tax income that year was 73 per cent of what it had been five years before. At a time when Russia needed to prepare for war against Napoleon's empire this was nothing short of a potential catastrophe.[29]

The government's response to this crisis took a number of forms. A resounding statement was issued pledging that the paper rubles were seen as a state debt and would be redeemed. No more printing of paper money was to be permitted. All unnecessary expenditures were to be cut and taxes raised. Above all, the import of all luxury or inessential items was to be banned outright or charged prohibitive duties. Meanwhile encouragement and protection would be given to neutral ships docking at Russian ports and carrying Russian exports. The emergency taxes brought in little cash and when war broke out again in 1812 the pledge on new printing of paper money had to be forgotten. But the ban on imports and the encouragement of neutral shipping did make an immediate impact on Russian trade and finance.

Unfortunately, they also made a big impact on Napoleon. He claimed – in fact falsely – that French imports to Russia were being targeted. With more truth he argued that neutral ships were being used as a cover for trade with Britain. Since he himself at this very time was annexing much of north Germany in order to tighten controls on trade, Russian and French policy was diametrically opposed. Alexander refused to back down in the face of French protests, however. He argued that necessity forced these changes and that it was his right as a sovereign ruler to determine tariffs and trade rules so long as these did not contravene his treaty obligations.

Dire financial crisis as well as Russian pride was involved in his stubbornness. Both the emperor and Rumiantsev might have been more inclined to compromise had they not come to the correct conclusion that the Continental System had largely been transformed from a measure of economic war against Britain into a policy whereby France bled the rest of Europe white in order to boost its own trade and revenues. At a time when Napoleon was demanding the virtual elimination of Russian foreign trade, he was issuing more and more licences for French merchants to trade with Britain. To rub salt into Russian wounds, the occasional French vessel armed with such licences even tried to sell British goods in Russia. As Caulaincourt told Napoleon, the Russians could hardly be expected to accept the costs of France's economic war with Britain when France itself was increasingly evading them. The Continental System's effects had long since been denounced by many

Russian statesmen. By early 1812, however, even Rumiantsev admitted that Napoleon's policy lacked any honesty or coherence, telling John Quincy Adams that 'the system of licences is founded upon falsehood and immorality'.[30]

By now, however, the key issue had long since become not specific sources of disagreement between France and Russia but the clear evidence that Napoleon was planning a massive invasion of the tsar's empire. At the beginning of January 1812 the French minister of war boasted that Napoleon's army had never before been so well equipped, trained and supplied for a forthcoming war: 'We have been making preparations for more than fifteen months.' In keeping with the general level of French security before 1812 the boast was made within earshot of a Russian informant. The Russians were in fact exceptionally well informed about French intentions and preparations. Already in the summer of 1810 a number of young and usually very competent officers had been sent as attachés in the Russian missions scattered throughout Germany's princely courts. Their job was to gather intelligence. Within Germany the greatest source of intelligence was the Russian mission in Berlin, since January 1810 headed by Christoph Lieven. The majority of Napoleon's units preparing to invade Russia either travelled across Prussia or deployed within it. Since the Prussians loathed the French it was not difficult to gain abundant information about all these units and their movements.[31]

By far the most important source of intelligence, however, were Russia's diplomatic and military representatives in Paris. Petr Tolstoy was recalled in October 1808 and replaced as ambassador to Napoleon by Aleksandr Kurakin. By 1810, however, Kurakin had been partly sidelined not just by Napoleon but also by Alexander and Rumiantsev. In part this was because the ambassador, already a martyr to gout, was badly burned in a fire at the Austrian embassy early in 1810 during a great ball to celebrate Napoleon's marriage to the Archduchess Marie-Louise. It was also, however, because Kurakin was overshadowed by two exceptionally able younger Russian diplomats in Paris.

One of these men was Count Karl von Nesselrode, who served as deputy head of mission under first Tolstoy and then Kurakin. Nesselrode in fact was secretly in direct communication with Alexander via Mikhail Speransky. The other Russian was Aleksandr Chernyshev, not a diplomat but an officer of the Chevaliers Gardes, an aide-de-camp of

Alexander I and the emperor's former page. When first appointed deputy head of mission in Paris Nesselrode was 27 years old. When Chernyshev was first sent by Alexander with personal messages for Napoleon he was only 22. Partly as a result of their brilliant performance during these crucial years in Paris both men made outstanding careers. Ultimately Nesselrode was to serve as foreign minister and Chernyshev as war minister for decades.

In certain respects the two young men were very different. Karl Nesselrode came from an aristocratic family from the Rhineland. His father's career in the service of the Elector Palatine ended in dramatic style when the elector took objection to his wife's infatuation with young Count Wilhelm. After serving the kings of France and Prussia, Wilhelm von Nesselrode worked as Russian minister in Portugal, where his son Karl was born and christened as an Anglican at the church of the British legation in Lisbon. Not until late adolescence did Karl Nesselrode have any experience of life in Russia but his subsequent marriage to the daughter of the finance minister, Dmitrii Gurev, strengthened his position in Petersburg society. Nesselrode was a calm, tactful and even at times self-effacing man. That led some observers to miss his great intelligence, subtlety and determination.

No one ever called Aleksandr Chernyshev self-effacing. On the contrary, he was a genius at self-promotion. Chernyshev came from the Russian aristocracy. An uncle, Aleksandr Lanskoy, had been one of Catherine II's lovers. Aleksandr Chernyshev first gained the Emperor Alexander's attention at a ball given by Prince Kurakin to celebrate the tsar's coronation in 1801. The poise, wit and confidence of the 15-year-old immediately struck the emperor and resulted in Chernyshev's selection as an imperial page. This was to be a fitting start to the career of an elegant and handsome man who glittered in society and always loved the limelight. Chernyshev once wrote of a fellow-officer that he was 'full of that noble ambition which obliges any individual who feels it to make himself known'. This certainly was a self-portrait too. But Chernyshev was much more than mere ambition and glitter: he was a man of outstanding intelligence, courage and resolution. Though an excellent soldier, in common with other intelligent aristocratic officers of his day his vision was far broader than the narrow military world. Just as Nesselrode's reports sometimes discussed grand strategy, so too Chernyshev was deeply aware of the political context of Napoleonic warfare.[32]

Together the two young men ran the Russian espionage operation in Paris. It helped that they saw eye to eye as regards French intentions and became firm friends. On the whole, as one would expect, Nesselrode's sources were mostly diplomatic and Chernyshev's most often military but there were many overlaps. Nesselrode, for example, procured one report on the military resources of the Duchy of Warsaw. He spent a good deal of money buying secret documents, paying 3,000–4,000 francs for some memoranda. The serving French minister of police, Joseph Fouché, and the former foreign minister, Charles-Maurice de Talleyrand, both appear to have been providers of these materials but whether there were other intermediaries and precisely how payments were arranged and documents acquired are matters which Nesselrode – very sensibly – did not go into in his reports.

The information he bought or otherwise acquired covered a range of topics. One report, for instance, concerned Napoleon's eccentricities, eating habits and growing forgetfulness during a period at the palace of Rambouillet. Given the extent to which the survival of Napoleon's empire and the fate of Europe hung on this one man's life and health such reports were significant. Nesselrode begged Speransky to ensure that only he and the emperor saw or mentioned this material. These details of Napoleon's behaviour were so private that any leak would result in his source being revealed. Nesselrode made a similar plea for total secrecy about another purchased memorandum detailing intelligence operations in Russia's western borderlands and naming many names. He added that his source for this document was extremely valuable and could produce further such documents if protected. The crucial point was that Russian counter-intelligence must watch the individuals mentioned but stage its arrests in a manner to protect his source at all costs.[33]

Probably the single most important document bought by Nesselrode was a top secret memorandum on future French policy submitted by the French foreign minister, Champagny, to Napoleon at the emperor's request on 16 March 1810, in other words at precisely the crucial turning point when the plan to marry a Russian princess had failed, Napoleon had refused to ratify the convention on Poland, and Barclay de Tolly was drawing up his first report on the defence of Russia's western frontier. Champagny wrote that geopolitics and trade meant that Britain was Russia's natural ally and a rapprochement between the two powers was to be expected. France must return to its traditional policy of building up Turkey, Poland and Sweden. It must, for instance, ensure that the Turks were kept ready as allies for a future war with Russia. Indeed, French agents were already working quietly on the Ottomans to this end.

As regards Poland, even Champagny's more modest scenario was to increase the power of the King of Saxony, who was also Grand Duke of Warsaw, by giving him Silesia. A second scenario, which Champagny called 'more grandiose and decisive and perhaps more worthy of Your Majesty's genius', envisaged a full-scale restoration of Poland after a victorious war with Russia. This would entail pushing the Russian border back beyond the river Dnieper, turning Austria eastwards against Russia and compensating it in Illyria for Polish lands it would have to give to the new Polish kingdom. In all circumstances Prussia must be destroyed since it was an outpost of Russian influence in Europe. Within a matter of weeks the memorandum was on Alexander's desk. In the circumstances its contents were little short of dynamite.[34]

Aleksandr Chernyshev also had a number of permanent, paid agents. One of them worked in the council of state near the heart of Napoleon's government, another was in military administration, and a third served in a key bureau of the war ministry. There may well have been more, at least on an occasional basis. The published documents provide rather more details about the content of their reports than is the case with most of the memoranda purchased by Nesselrode. We have everything from general memoranda on the domestic political situation and the position in Spain to detailed information about the redeployment of artillery to infantry battalions, the organization of transport and rear services for future campaigns, and reports on new arms and equipment.

Some of these documents bore explicitly on the coming war with Russia. Chernyshev reported that Napoleon was rapidly increasing his cavalry arm, his measures proving 'how much he fears the superiority of our cavalry'. Special wagons – larger and stronger than the previous models – were being built to survive Russian conditions. Chernyshev disguised himself to get into one of the workshops where they were being constructed and drew sketches. He reported that one of his sources stated that Napoleon intended to deliver the decisive blow by his central column, which would advance on Vilna under the emperor's own command. He expected to be able to recruit large numbers of Polish soldiers in Russia's western borderlands. Probably Chernyshev's most valuable agent was the officer in the heart of the war ministry who had worked previously for the Russians but whom Chernyshev now exploited to maximum effect. Every month the ministry printed a secret book listing the numbers, movements and deployment of every regiment in the army. On each occasion a copy was delivered to Chernyshev, which he re-copied overnight. The Russians could follow the redeployment of Napoleon's army eastwards in precise detail. Given the sheer scale and cost of this redeployment one could hardly imagine that it would end without a war, as Chernyshev himself remarked.[35]

Both Chernyshev and Nesselrode were far more than mere purchasers of secret memoranda. They moved in Paris society, gleaning an immense amount of information along the way. Some but by no means all of this information was provided by Frenchmen who disliked Napoleon's regime. Chernyshev in particular was accepted into the heart of Napoleon's own family and intimate circle. King Frederick William wrote to Alexander that Prussian diplomats reported that Chernyshev's 'relations with many individuals provide him with means and opportunities that no one else possesses'. Because of their intelligence and political sophisti-cation Nesselrode and Chernyshev could evaluate the huge amounts of information they received and encapsulate it in the very shrewd appreciations they sent to Petersburg. Both men, for instance, were at pains to disabuse Alexander of any illusions that Napoleon would not or could not attack Russia so long as the war in Spain continued. They stressed the enormous resources he controlled but also the implications of his domestic problems for his campaign in Russia. Both men reported that the longer the war dragged on and the further Napoleon was pulled into the Russian interior the more desperate his situation would become.[36]

The last report that Chernyshev submitted to Barclay de Tolly from Paris gives one a flavour of his overall views and methods, as well as of the aristocratic confidence with which this young colonel wrote to a minister far his senior in age and rank. He noted that 'I speak often to officers who are of great merit and knowledge and who have no affection for the head of the French government. I have asked them about what strategy would be best in the coming war, taking into account the theatre of operations, the strength and the character of our adversary.' With one accord these Frenchmen had told him that Napoleon would long for big battles and rapid victories, so the Russians should avoid giving him what he wanted and should instead harass him with their light forces. The French officers told him that 'the system we should follow in this war is the one of which Fabius and indeed Lord Wellington offer the best examples. It is true that our task will be more difficult in that the theatre of operations is for the most part open countryside.' Partly for that reason, it was crucial to have large reserve forces held well in the rear so that the war could not be lost by a single battle. But if the Russians could 'sustain this war for three campaigns then the victory will certainly be ours, even if we don't win great victories, and Europe will be delivered from its oppressor'. Chernyshev added that this was very much his own view too. Russia must mobilize all its resources, religion and patriotism included, to sustain a long war. 'Napoleon's goal and his hopes are all directed towards concentrating sufficient strength to deliver crushing blows and decide the matter in a single campaign. He feels strongly that he cannot remain away from Paris for more than one year and that he would be lost if this war lasted for two or three years.'[37]

From the summer of 1810 onwards it was clear to Alexander and most of his key advisers that war was inevitable, and sooner rather than later. At best its outbreak might be postponed for a year or so. In these circumstances the key point was to prepare as effectively as possible to fight the coming war. Preparation for war occurred in three distinct spheres: there were the purely military plans and preparations (to be discussed in the next chapter); the diplomatic efforts to ensure that Russia fought Napoleon with as many friends and as few enemies as possible; and, last but not least, the government needed to create the greatest possible degree of internal unity and consensus if Russia was to survive the enormous shock of Napoleon's invasion. Though in principle distinct, the military, diplomatic and domestic political spheres in fact overlapped. For example, whether or not Prussia fought in the Russian or enemy camp depended greatly on whether Alexander adopted an offensive or defensive military strategy.

Inevitably too, as war loomed, the influence of the army and, above all, of Mikhail Barclay de Tolly grew. The war minister invaded the diplomatic sphere by, for example, insisting on the need to end the war with the Ottomans immediately. He also stressed the key importance of raising the morale and national pride of the population. In an important letter to Alexander in early February 1812 Barclay noted that, apart from narrowly military preparations,

we must try to raise the morale and spirit of Russia's own population and arouse its commitment to a war on whose outcome Russia's very salvation and existence will depend. I make bold to add here that for the last twenty years we have been doing all we can to suppress everything that is truly national but a great nation which changes its customs and values overnight will quickly go into decline unless the government stops this process and takes measures for the nation's resurrection. And can anything aid this process better than love for one's sovereign and one's country, a feeling of pride at the thought that one is Russian in heart and soul? These feelings can only be brought forth if the government takes the lead in this matter.[38]

Mikhail Barclay de Tolly was of course not an ethnic Russian. Originally of Scottish origin, his family had settled in the Baltic provinces in the mid-seventeenth century. To most Russians he was just another Baltic German. During the 1812 campaign this made him the target of savage attacks and libels by many Russians. But Barclay's advice to Alexander in February 1812 echoed exactly what the nationalists in the 'Old Russian' and 'isolationist' camp had been saying for many years. The best-known public figures in the 'Old Russian' camp were Admiral Aleksandr Shishkov in Petersburg and Count Fedor Rostopchin in Moscow. Russia's leading historian, Nikolai Karamzin, and Serge Glinka, the editor of a patriotic journal, were close to Rostopchin. Karamzin was a scholar and a 'public intellectual', with no personal political ambitions. Though an admiral, Aleksandr Shishkov had not served afloat since 1797 and behaved much more like a professor than a military officer. A kind and generous person in his personal relations, he became a tiger when defending the cause to which he devoted much of his life, which was the preservation of the national purity of the Russian language and its ancient Slavonic roots from corruption by imported Western words and concepts.

Count Fedor Rostopchin shared the commitment of Karamzin and Shishkov to preserving Russian culture and values from foreign influences. The fictional stories he published between 1807 and 1812 all aimed at this goal and made a big impact. His fictional hero, Sila Bogatyrev, was a no-nonsense squire who stood up for traditional Russian values and thoroughly distrusted all foreigners. In his view,

French tutors were corrupting Russian youth. Meanwhile the Russian state was being manipulated by the English and tricked by the French into sacrificing its blood and treasure for their interests. Unlike Karamzin and Shishkov, Rostopchin was extremely ambitious and a politician to his fingertips. A favourite of Paul I, he had been out of office ever since Paul's death. Alexander distrusted the Russian nationalists and disliked their ideas. He particularly disliked Rostopchin. The count was indeed in many ways a ruthless and unpleasant man. Though a great nationalist, he had none of Karamzin's or Glinka's generous or warm feelings towards the ordinary Russian. On the contrary, in Rostopchin's view 'the rabble' could never be trusted and must be ruled through repression and manipulation.

Rostopchin was a sharp and amusing conversationalist. He could be unguarded. It is said that he once commented that Austerlitz was God's revenge on Alexander for the part he had played in his father's overthrow. The emperor took his own high-mindedness very seriously and did not take kindly to sly comments at his expense. His father's murder and his own role in the disaster at Austerlitz were the bitterest memories of his life. But Alexander too was an exquisite politician. He knew that he had to use even men he disliked, particularly at a moment of supreme crisis such as the impending war with Napoleon. However much he disliked Rostopchin and distrusted his ideas, Alexander knew that the count was an efficient and resolute administrator, and a skilful politician. Above all he was a fine propagandist, absolutely loyal to the regime but with a handle on the emotions of the masses, whose behaviour would matter greatly in the event of a war on Russian soil. In 1810 Rostopchin was given a senior position at court, though encouraged not to put in too many appearances. He was kept available in case of need.[39]

The person who brought Alexander and Rostopchin back into contact was the Grand Duchess Catherine. After her marriage, Catherine's husband was appointed governor-general of three central Russian provinces in 1809. He and his wife took up residence in Tver, within easy distance of Moscow. Catherine's salon in Tver attracted many intelligent and ambitious visitors, including Rostopchin and Karamzin. Her reputation as the most 'Russian' member of the imperial family was well known. It was she who commissioned Nikolai Karamzin to write his *Memoir on Ancient and Modern Russia*, which was to be the most influential and famous expression of the 'Old Russian' viewpoint. The influence of the

Memoir had nothing to do with any impact on public opinion. The work was designed for Alexander's eyes alone. Given its sharp criticism of government policies the *Memoir* could never have been published at that time and remained unknown to any but a tiny circle for many decades. Karamzin delivered the *Memoir* to Catherine in February 1811. The next month, when Alexander stayed in Tver with his sister, Catherine summoned Karamzin to meet the emperor, to read passages from the *Memoir* to him, and to discuss its ideas with the monarch.

Karamzin sharply criticized Russian foreign policy in Alexander's reign. In his view, the empire had been dragged into quarrels which were not its concern and had often lost sight of its own interests. The crafty British were always alive to the possibility of getting other countries to bear the main burden of Britain's ancestral struggle with France. As for the French and Austrians, whichever empire dominated European affairs would deride Russia and call it 'an Asiatic country'. Apart from reflecting these deep-rooted Russian insecurities and resentments, Karamzin also made many specific criticisms. In the winter of 1806–7 either Bennigsen's army should have been massively reinforced or Russia should have made peace with Napoleon. The actual peace treaty signed at Tilsit was a disaster. Russia's overriding interest was that Poland must never be resurrected. Allowing the creation of the Duchy of Warsaw was a major error. To avoid this, no doubt Silesia would have had to be left to Napoleon and Prussia abandoned. This was unfortunate but in foreign affairs one had to consult one's own self-interest alone. The alliance with France was fundamentally flawed.

Shall we deceive Napoleon? Facts are facts. He knows that inwardly we detest him, because we fear him; he had occasion to observe our more than questionable enthusiasm in the last Austrian war. This ambivalence of ours was not a new mistake, but an inescapable consequence of the position in which we had been put by the Tilsit peace. Is it easy to keep a promise to assist one's natural enemy and to increase his power?[40]

If anything, the analysis of Alexander's domestic policy was even more critical. Alexander had kept Catherine informed of his discussions with Speransky and some of this she had passed on to Karamzin. The core of his *Memoir* was a defence of autocracy as the only form of government which could stop the Russian Empire from disintegrating and guarantee ordered progress. For Karamzin, however, autocracy did not mean despotism. The autocrat must rule in harmony with the aristocracy and gentry, as Catherine II had done. State and society must not become divorced, with the former simply dictating to the latter. Karamzin conceded that Paul had indeed acted despotically but after his removal Alexander should have returned to the principles on which Catherine's rule was founded. Instead he had allowed the introduction of foreign bureaucratic models which, if developed, would turn Russia into a version of Napoleonic bureaucratic despotism. Aristocrats rooted in the Russian social hierarchy were being displaced in government by mediocre bureaucrats with no stake in society. Moreover, if the peasants were emancipated anarchy would ensue, because the bureaucracy was far too weak to administer the countryside.[41]

Karamzin's arguments made a lot of sense. Catherine II had ruled in harmony with the 'political nation', in other words the elites. In subsequent decades a bureaucratic monarchy was created without strong roots in society, even among the traditional elites. That was a major factor over the much longer term in the isolation and ultimate fall of the imperial regime. On the other hand, to the extent that Karamzin's criticisms were directed against Speransky, they were mostly unfair. Russia was woefully under-governed. A much larger and more professional bureaucracy had to be developed if Russia was to flourish. Society could not control the growing bureaucratic machine by old-fashioned methods such as aristocrats hopping from positions at court into top posts in government. Only the rule of law and representative institutions could hope to achieve this goal, and Speransky – perhaps unknown to Karamzin – was planning to introduce them.

Even if he had known all Speransky's plans, however, Karamzin would probably still have opposed them. Given the cultural level of the provincial gentry he might well have considered the introduction of representative assemblies premature. Certainly he would have argued that the eve of a great war with Napoleon was a mad moment at which to throw Russia into chaos by fundamental constitutional reform. Unlike most of Speransky's opponents, Karamzin was in no way motivated by personal enmity or ambition. Nevertheless he would probably have pointed out to Alexander that most Russian nobles considered Speransky to be a Jacobin, a worshipper of Napoleon and a traitor, and that this was a very dangerous state of affairs on the eve of a war in which national unity was crucial and the war effort would depend enormously on the voluntary commitment of the Russian aristocracy and gentry.

In fact the emperor was far too good a politician not to understand this himself. In March 1812 Speransky was dismissed and sent into exile. In these weeks that preceded the outbreak of war Alexander was overworked and under great pressure. He also hated confrontations like the long private meeting with Speransky which preceded the latter's removal. The emperor was also outraged by reports of snide comments by Speransky about his indecisiveness, faithfully passed on by the Petersburg grapevine. The result was a hysterical imperial outburst, culminating in a threat to have Speransky shot. Since Alexander sometimes enjoyed histrionics and on this occasion his audience was a rather dimwitted and deeply impressed German professor, we can take all this hysteria as the performance of a brilliant actor letting off steam. Alexander's actions after Speransky's fall betray a politician's cool rationality. Speransky was to some extent replaced by Aleksandr Shishkov, appointed imperial secretary in the following month and largely employed to draft resounding patriotic appeals to the Russian people during the subsequent years of war. In May Fedor Rostopchin was named military governor of Moscow, with the job of administering and maintaining morale in the city which would be not just the army's major base in the rear but also crucial to sustaining public enthusiasm for the war throughout the empire's interior.

As regards diplomatic preparation for war, Alexander put little effort into mending fences with Britain. This partly reflected his wish to postpone the outbreak of war for as long as possible and deny Napoleon any legitimate justification for invading Russia. He also knew that the moment war began Britain would automatically become his enthusiastic ally so preparation was not necessary. In any case there was not much direct help that Britain could offer for a war fought on Russian soil, though the 101,000 muskets it provided in the winter of 1812–13 were to be very useful. In terms of indirect help, however, the British in Spain were doing far more than they had ever managed before 1808. The performance of Wellington and his troops had not just transformed perceptions of the British army and its commanders. In 1810 it had also shown how strategic retreat, scorched earth and field fortifications could exhaust and ultimately destroy a numerically superior French army. In 1812 Wellington's great victory at Salamanca not only boosted the morale of all Napoleon's enemies but also ensured that scores of thousands of French troops would remain tied down in the Iberian peninsula.

The key issue before 1812, however, was which way Austria and Prussia would go, but here Russian diplomacy faced a very uphill struggle. It is true that Rumiantsev, and probably Alexander, did not help matters by their stubborn determination to hang on to Moldavia and Wallachia. There were influential figures in Vienna who saw Russia as a greater threat than France because Napoleon's empire might well prove ephemeral whereas Russia was there to stay. Probably, however, Austria would have swung into Napoleon's camp whatever Russia did.

Francis II was embarrassed to have to own up to the existence of the Franco-Austrian military convention aimed against Russia, and all the more so because the terms of this convention had been discovered by Russian espionage in Paris. But he told the Russian minister, Count Stackelberg, that he had been forced into this convention by the 'strict necessity' to preserve the Austrian Empire; the same necessity, added Francis, which had led him to sacrifice his daughter to Napoleon. The basic point was that Austria had made a similar decision in 1810 to the one that Russia had made at Tilsit. Confronting Napoleon was too dangerous. Another defeat would spell the end of the Habsburgs and their empire. By sidling up to Napoleon Austria preserved its existence for better times. If the French Empire survived, so would Austria as its leading satellite. If on the contrary Napoleon's empire disintegrated then Austria, having regained its strength, would be well placed to pick up many of the pieces. The main difference between Russia in 1809 and Austria in 1812 was that the Habsburgs were in a much weaker and more vulnerable position. For that reason the Habsburg war effort in support of Napoleon in 1812 was far more serious than the Russian campaign against Austria had been in 1809. Nevertheless the two empires did quietly maintain diplomatic relations throughout 1812 and the Austrians stuck to their promise made on the eve of the war never to increase their auxiliary corps above 30,000 men and to move their troops into Russia through the Duchy of Warsaw, keeping the Russo-Austrian border in Galicia neutralized.[42]

The Prussian situation was even clearer. King Frederick William loathed and feared Napoleon. All other things being equal, he would have far preferred to ally himself with Russia. But things were not equal. Prussia was surrounded by French troops who could overrun the country long before Russian help could arrive from the other side of the river Neman. In the king's view, the only way in which Prussia could ally itself with Russia was if the Russian army surprised and pre-empted Napoleon by invading the Duchy of Warsaw. To be effective this would require Austrian assistance and Polish consent. To that end Frederick William urged Alexander to support the re-establishment of an independent Polish kingdom under a Polish monarch.[43]

The Russians might well have conceded this had they been defeated by Napoleon, but they were unlikely to do so before the war had even begun. The emperor was in fact discussing the restoration of Poland with his old friend and chief adviser on Polish affairs, Prince Adam Czartoryski. Conceivably, had his feelers to the Poles met an enthusiastic response, he might have considered a pre-emptive strike to occupy the Duchy of Warsaw and win Prussian support, but there is no evidence in the Russian diplomatic or military archives of preparations for an offensive in 1810 or 1811. Alexander was in any case convinced that Russian security and Russian public opinion made it essential that any reconstituted Poland had the Russian emperor as its king. In 1811–12 this idea could not compete in Polish hearts with the hope of a restored Poland, within its full old borders, and guaranteed by the all-conquering Napoleon. The union of the Russian and Polish crowns was also unacceptable to the Austrians.[44]

By the summer of 1811 Alexander had decided on a defensive strategy. He made this clear to both the Austrians and the Prussians, thereby ruling out the last faint hopes that either country would join him against Napoleon. In August 1811 the emperor told the Austrian minister, the Count de Saint-Julien, that although he understood the theoretical military arguments for an offensive strategy, in the present circumstances only a defensive strategy made sense. If attacked, he would retreat into his empire, turning the area he abandoned into a desert. Tragic though this would be for the civilian population, he had no other alternative. He was arranging echelons of supply bases and new reserve forces to which his field army could retreat. The French would find themselves fighting far from their bases and even further from their homes: 'It is only by being prepared, if necessary, to sustain war for ten years that one can exhaust his troops and wear out his resources.' Saint-Julien reported all this to Vienna but added, significantly, that he doubted whether Alexander could hold his nerve and pursue such a strategy when the invasion actually occurred.[45]

To Frederick William, Alexander was even more explicit. In May 1811 he wrote to the king:

We have to adopt the strategy which is most likely to succeed. It seems to me that this strategy has to be one of carefully avoiding big battles and organizing very long operational lines which will sustain a retreat which will end in fortified camps, where nature and engineering works will strengthen the forces which we use to match up to the enemy's skill. The system is the one which has brought victory to Wellington in wearing down the French armies, and it is the one which I have resolved to follow.

Alexander suggested to Frederick William that he set up his own fortified camps, some of which should be on the coast where they could be supplied by the British navy. Not at all surprisingly, this prospect did not appeal to Frederick William, whose country would first be abandoned by the Russians and then fought over and ravaged as enemy territory by the French. In his last letter to Alexander before war began, Frederick William explained that he had seen no alternative but to succumb to Napoleon's pressure and join the French alliance. 'Faithful to your strategy of not taking the offensive, Your Majesty deprived me of any hope of prompt or real assistance and placed me in a situation where the destruction of Prussia would have been the preliminary to a war against Russia.'[46]

Though it failed as regards Austria and Prussia, Russian diplomacy did achieve its other key goals by ending the war against Turkey and neutralizing any threat from Sweden.

The Ottomans had declared war against Russia in 1806 in the wake of Austerlitz. This seemed a good opportunity to win back some of the territories and other concessions which the empire had been forced to make to Russia in the last forty years. The Russians instead soon overran the principalities of Moldavia and Wallachia, and made their acquisition the key Russian war aim. No doubt over-impressed by his father's achievements, Rumiantsev in particular was hell-bent on acquiring the provinces and too optimistic about how easy it would be to get the Turks to concede them. As war with Napoleon loomed and most Russian diplomats and generals yearned to end the sideshow in the Balkans,

Rumiantsev's stubbornness made him many enemies but in fact there is not much evidence that Alexander was any more willing to give way than his foreign minister.

One reason the Turks proved so recalcitrant was that they were urged to resist Russian demands first by the British and then by the French. Since by 1810 they were well aware that a war between Napoleon and Russia was in the offing, they had every incentive to hold out and wait until the Russians became desperate to cut their losses and redeploy their troops northwards against the French.

There were also military reasons why the war dragged on. In the field the Ottoman army was hopeless. To win battles in this era required infantry trained to deliver rapid volleys and to move in formation across the battlefield. The troops must be able to shift between column, line and square according to circumstances and to do so rapidly and in good order. The infantry needed to be supported by mobile artillery and by cavalry trained to charge home in massed formation to exploit any wavering by the enemy. Though all this sounds simple, amidst the terrors of the battlefield it was anything but. To achieve this an army required good training, a strong core of veterans, and experienced officers and NCOs. Behind the army there had to stand a state and a society capable of providing reliable officers and of paying the large sums needed for men, arms, food and equipment. The main European armies achieved this and so did the British in India. The Ottomans did not, for many reasons, of which inadequate financial resources was probably the most important. By the 1770s their untrained and ill-disciplined levies could seldom stand up to the Russians in open battle.

In siege warfare the Ottomans remained formidable, however. Napoleon discovered this in his Egyptian campaign. Having scattered Muslim armies on the battlefield without difficulty, he came to a halt before the fortress of Acre. The Balkans were the Ottomans' main strategic theatre. Fortresses here were far stronger than Acre. They were generally defended, often from house to house, not just with skill but also very great tenacity. Perhaps the only comparison in the Napoleonic Wars was the siege of Saragossa, which the French finally took after immense bloodshed and resistance. The terrain of the Balkans helps to explain why siege warfare often prevailed in this theatre. Unlike in western Europe, there were few good roads and population densities were low. A good fortress could block the only viable invasion route into a district. The Ottomans were also experts at ravaging the country-side, and at raids and ambushes. An army which sat down to besiege a fortress would find its supply columns raided and its foraging parties forced to scatter over great distances. In 1806–12 the Russians faced all these problems. Pressed by Alexander to end the war, on occasion the Russian commanders attempted premature storming of fortresses and suffered heavy casualties. At Rushchuk in 1810, for example, 8,000 men of a force of barely 20,000 became casualties in an unsuccessful attempt to storm the town.[47]

Finally, in the winter of 1811–12 the crafty new Russian commander-in-chief, Mikhail Kutuzov, cut off the main Ottoman army as it attempted to manoeuvre against him, and forced it to surrender. In so doing he made one of his greatest contributions to the 1812 campaign before it had begun. With his main armies lost, his treasury empty and intrigue rife in Constantinople, the sultan agreed to peace, which was signed in June 1812. The peace came too late to allow the Army of the Danube to be deployed northwards to face Napoleon's invasion, but soon enough for the troops to reach Belorussia by the autumn and pose a huge threat to Napoleon's communications and his retreating army.

At the other, northern end of the Russian line the obvious danger was that, with French power resurgent, Sweden would revert to its traditional role as a French client. When Marshal Jean-Baptiste Bernadotte was elected as heir to the Swedish throne in August 1810 this danger appeared to be confirmed. Since he was Joseph Bonaparte's brother-in-law as well as Napoleon's marshal, on the surface Bernadotte appeared likely to prove a reliable French client. In fact, he had stored up a good deal of resentment against Napoleon and moved quickly to reassure Alexander I about his peaceful intentions regarding Russia. It helped greatly that Aleksandr Chernyshev had established a close relationship with Bernadotte before any question of the Swedish throne came up and was able to act as a trusted intermediary between him and Alexander both in Paris immediately after his election and in an important special mission which he undertook to Stockholm in the winter of 1810. Even before Bernadotte's final selection as Swedish crown prince, Chernyshev was able to reassure Petersburg that he had got to know the marshal well, that Bernadotte was well disposed towards Russia and that he was certainly no admirer of Napoleon.[48]

Although personal factors mattered, cool calculation guided Berna-dotte's actions as the de facto ruler of Sweden. He realized that if he joined Napoleon and helped to defeat Russia this would bring about Europe and Sweden's 'blind submission to the orders of the Tuileries'. Swedish independence would be better assured by Russian victory and he did not despair of Alexander's chances, given 'the immense resources of this sovereign and the means he has to offer a well-calculated resist-ance'. Moreover, even if Sweden did succeed in recapturing Finland from Russia this would not be the end of the story. Russia would not go away, she would always be stronger than Sweden, and she would also always seek to regain Finland in order to increase the security of Petersburg. Much better therefore to seek compensation for Finland's loss by taking Norway from Denmark.

The British stance must also have been a key factor in Bernadotte's thinking. If Napoleon attacked Russia, Britain and Russia would become allies. Since Sweden's crucial foreign trade was totally at Britain's mercy, to join Napoleon in attacking Russia could spell ruin. By contrast, neither London nor Petersburg would mind too much if Sweden despoiled Napoleon's faithful ally, the Danish crown, of its Norwegian territories. On these considerations the Russo-Swedish alliance was signed in April 1812. It stored up some problems for the future by promising Bernadotte a Russian auxiliary corps to help him defeat the Danes, and by giving this task priority over a joint landing in Napoleon's rear in Germany. In the spring of 1812, however, what concerned the Russians was that they did not need to guard Finland or Petersburg from a Swedish invasion.[49]

Any overview of the years between Tilsit and Napoleon's invasion of Russia is likely to come to the conclusion that the collapse of the Russo-French alliance and the descent into war were not surprising. Napoleon was aiming at empire in Europe or at the least for a degree of dominance which did not allow for the existence of independent great powers not subject to French orders. In these years the Russian Empire was much too powerful and its elites far too proud to accept French dominion without putting up a stiff fight. Eighteen-twelve was the result.

To an extent, the main difficulty in making sense of these years is that Napoleon 'blundered towards empire'. In other words he did not always sort out priorities or match ends to means, and often used tactics of bullying and intimidation which harmed his own cause. In the famous expression of the American historian Paul Schroeder, Napoleon could never see a jugular without going for it. In addition, his views on economics were often crude and his grasp of naval matters limited. Though true, this is not however the whole truth.[50]

The Napoleonic empire was above all the result of the sudden increase in French power brought about by the Revolution of 1789. This increased power took everyone by surprise. French expansion was partly driven by the army's desire for plunder and the French government's wish that other countries should pay this army's costs. Napoleon's personality was also a major factor. But French grand strategy has to be judged within the context of the policies of the other great powers and, above all, of the century-old struggle with Britain. After 1793 British naval superiority more or less confined French imperialism to the European continent. The enormous gains made by the British outside Europe since 1793, not to mention their ever-growing economic power, meant that, unless Napoleon created some form of French empire within Europe, the struggle with Britain was lost. It is true that Napoleon undermined his own cause by never working out a coherent and viable plan for the creation and maintenance of this empire. On the other hand, the whole Napoleonic episode was so brief that this is not altogether surprising.[51]

Napoleon's greatest rivals, the British and Russian empires, were not peace-loving democracies anxious to stay at home and cultivate their gardens. They were themselves expansionist and predatory empires. Many of the criticisms aimed at Napoleon's empire could, for example, be applied to British expansion in India in this period. They would, for example, include the repatriation of Indian wealth back to Britain by the subcontinent's British rulers and the impact on Indian manufacturing of incorporation into the British Empire on terms set by London. In 1793–1815, too, the main engine for British territorial expansion in India was a formidable but very expensive European-style army, which needed to conquer new lands to justify its existence and pay its costs, and which was itself fuelled by plunder. Particularly under Richard Wellesley, British territorial expansion was pursued with a single-mindedness worthy of Napoleon, and justified in part by reference to the need to preserve Britain's position in India against the French threat.[52]

The basic point was that it was far harder to create an empire in Europe than overseas. Ideology was a factor here. Within Europe, the

French Revolution had glorified concepts of nationhood and popular sovereignty which in principle were the antithesis of empire. The experience of Napoleon's wars – economic as much as military – did nothing to legitimize the idea of empire in Europe to Europeans. Meanwhile, however, on the whole European opinion was becoming more inclined than before to accept the idea of Europe's civilizing mission and inherent cultural superiority over the rest of the world. The French, with some justice, saw themselves as the leaders of European civilization and they regarded the continent's eastern periphery in particular as semi-civilized. Even they, however, would hardly have applied to Europeans a British senior official's view of 'the perverseness and depravity of the natives of India in general'. Nor would many Europeans have believed them had they done so.[53]

More immediately important was the fact that the British in India were the heirs of the Mughals. Empire was hardly a novelty in India and the regimes which the British overthrew were not in most cases very ancient or deeply rooted in their regions. Despite some subsequent claims by nationalist myth-makers, in Europe too Napoleon was not usually faced by nations in the full modern meaning of the word. But many of the regimes he faced were deeply rooted in the communities they ruled. History and ancient myths, common religions and vernacular high cultures linked rulers to ruled.[54]

Above all, the geopolitics of Europe was different. General Levin von Bennigsen's comments go to the heart of British geopolitical invulnerability in India. A would-be European emperor was faced with a much harder task. Any attempt to dominate the continent would bring down on one's head a coalition of great powers with a common interest in preserving their independence and with military machines honed by generations of warfare at the cutting edge of technology and organization. Even if, as with Napoleon, the would-be emperor could conquer the continent's heartland, he was still faced by two formidable peripheral concentrations of power in Britain and Russia. To make things worse, the conquest of these peripheries demanded that the conqueror mobilize simultaneously two different types of power. In the British case this meant seapower, in the Russian a military-logistical power sufficient to penetrate and sustain itself all the way to the Urals. This challenge – subsequently faced by the Germans in the twentieth century – was very difficult.

There are usually three stages in the creation of empires, though these stages often overlap. First comes the conquest of empire and the elimination of foreign threats. This is generally a question of military power, diplomatic craftiness, and geopolitical context. To survive, however, an empire needs institutions, otherwise it will disintegrate with the death of the conqueror and his charisma. Establishing these institutions is the second stage in creating an empire and is often harder than the first stage, particularly when huge conquests have occurred in a short period. The third stage requires the consolidation of imperial loyalties and identities in the subject populations, and above all, in the pre-modern world, in their elites.[55]

Napoleon made great progress in the first stage of empire-building, took some steps towards creating imperial institutions but still had a very long way to go in legitimizing his power. To do him justice, he faced a daunting task. A thousand years after the death of Charlemagne, it was rather late in the day to dream of restoring a European empire. Three hundred years after the printing of the vernacular Bible, the imposition of French as a pan-European imperial language was unimaginable. An imperial project backed by a universalist, totalitarian ideology might have gone some way towards establishing empire in Europe for a time. But Napoleon was in no sense a totalitarian ruler, nor was his empire much driven by ideology. On the contrary, he had put the lid on the French Revolution and done his best to banish ideology from French political life. Even the uprooting of local elites in conquered Europe went well beyond Napoleon's desires or his power. In 1812 his empire was still very dependent on his personal charisma.[56]

Many European statesmen understood this and acted accordingly. On the eve of his departure for the Americas in 1809, Count Theodor von der Pahlen, the first Russian minister to the United States, wrote that

despite the triumphs of France and its current dominance, within less than fifty years nothing will remain to it but the empty glory of having overthrown and oppressed Europe. It will have acquired no real benefits from this for the French nation, which will find itself exhausted of men and treasure once it can no longer raise them from its neighbours. France's immense current influence depends wholly on the existence of a single individual. His great talents, his astonishing energy and impetuous character will never allow him to put limits on his ambition, so that whether he dies today or in thirty years' time he will leave matters no more consolidated than they are at present.

Meanwhile, added Pahlen, as a new European Thirty Years War continued, the Americas would grow enormously in strength. Of the European powers only the English would be in a position to derive any advantages from this.[57]

The implication of this comment is that in the eyes of history the triumphs and disasters of the Napoleonic era would seem the proverbial tale full of sound and fury, not (let us hope) told by an idiot but also not adding up to much. There is some truth in this. Aspects of the Napoleonic saga were more spectacular than significant. Nevertheless it would be wrong to be too dismissive of the fears and efforts of Europe's statesmen in these years.

Like all political leaders, Russia's rulers had to confront pressing contemporary realities. They could not live on hopes for a distant future. They might well share Theodor Pahlen's longer-term perspectives and believe that, if they could buy time and postpone the conflict with Napoleon, it might actually pass them by. The emperor himself could die or lose his fire. That after all was the rationale behind Nesselrode's spies assiduously reporting whether Napoleon was still eating a good breakfast. Unless fortune intervened, however, Russia's leaders from mid-1810 had to confront the reality that Napoleon was preparing to invade their empire. No doubt if they caved in to his demands war might be averted for a time. But to subscribe to his current version of the Continental System was to undermine the financial and economic bases of Russia's position as an independent power. By definition, this would leave it open to Napoleon to establish a powerful Polish client state which would shut Russia out of Europe.

The chances of Napoleon establishing a lasting empire across Europe may have been poor, though this was far from self-evident in 1812. His regime certainly could put down deep roots west of the Rhine and in northern Italy. It was also well within his power to implement the strategy set out in Champagny's memorandum of 1810, which Russian espionage had acquired for Alexander. There was every reason to fear in 1812 that Napoleon would defeat the Russian army and force peace on Alexander I. This would have resulted in the creation of a powerful Polish satellite kingdom, with its own ambitions in Ukraine and

Belorussia. Austria could easily have become the loyal client of Napoleon after 1812, as it became Prussia's first lieutenant after 1866. With its ambitions turned to the Balkans and against Russia, it would have been a useful auxiliary of the French Empire against any threat from the east. Within Germany, a stroke of Napoleon's pen could have abolished Prussia and compensated the King of Saxony for losing his largely theoretical sovereignty over Poland. Meanwhile for at least a generation the combination of French power and regional loyalties would have kept the Confederation of the Rhine (Rheinbund) under Paris's thumb. Russia would be permanently under threat and at the mercy of a Europe organized along these lines. On top of this the consequences of defeat might well include a crushing indemnity and the sacrifices a victorious Napoleon might require Russia to bear in his ongoing war against the British. In 1812 the Russian state had much to fight for.[58]

4

Preparing for War

On 25 January 1808 General Aleksei Arakcheev was appointed minister of war. Joseph de Maistre commented that 'opposed to Arakcheev's nomination there were *only* both empresses, Count Lieven, General Uvarov, all the imperial aides-de-camp, the Tolstoys – in a word, everyone who has weight here'. Moreover, in appointing Arakcheev the emperor broke his own first rule of government, which was never to allow undivided authority over a key area to any one adviser. Previously the war minister had been balanced by the very powerful head of the emperor's military chancellery. Arakcheev's price for becoming minister was undisputed authority over the army and therefore the chancellery's emasculation. Christoph von Lieven was diverted into a diplomatic career. His deputy, Prince Petr Mikhailovich Volkonsky, had already been sent to Paris to study the French general staff system. In the opinion of Joseph de Maistre, the Sardinian envoy in Petersburg, Alexander had acted in this way because of 'the terrible disorder' in the commissariat and victualling departments revealed in 1806–7. In addition, opposition sentiment within the Petersburg elite required an absolutely loyal 'iron hand' at the head of the army.[1]

At the time of his appointment Arakcheev was 38. He was of above average height, round-shouldered and with a long neck; one of his many enemies in the Petersburg aristocracy recalled that Arakcheev resembled an outsize monkey in uniform. His earthen complexion, big fleshy ears and hollow cheeks completed the impression. Perhaps matters might have improved had he ever smiled or joked but he very seldom did. Instead, a cold, gloomy and sardonic look greeted most of those who met him. Amidst the extravagant, fun-loving society of Petersburg and the glittering festivities of the imperial court he cut a strange figure. Up every morning at four, he dispatched his private and estate business first and then got down to affairs of state by six. He sometimes played cards for pennies with his few friends, but never went to the theatre or to balls, and ate and drank very sparingly.

To an extent, Arakcheev's austere behaviour reflected his origins. Like most sons of run-of-the-mill gentry families at this time, the young Arakcheev was educated initially by the village sexton on his father's small estate. His father owned just twenty male serfs and had to tighten his belt to pay for his son's entry into a cadet corps, even though Aleksei's place was subsidized. A strict, austere and very resolute mother formed the character and aroused the ambition of her eldest son. Starting well behind many of his peers, Arakcheev quickly made his mark at the Second Cadet Corps because of his excellent brain, his astonishing work-rate, his ambition, and his rigid discipline and obedience to orders. These qualities won him a succession of patrons, ending with the Grand Duke and later Emperor Paul.[2]

Arakcheev was very much Paul's ideal subordinate. He was blindly obedient to his superiors, very efficient, meticulous to the point of pedantry, and relentlessly strict in his treatment of wayward juniors, whatever their social origins or aristocratic connections. Arakcheev himself never belonged to any Petersburg faction, remaining wholly dependent on the monarch's favour and support. Of course, this too was a comforting thought for a Russian autocrat. Though his cadet corps training had taught him French and German, Arakcheev possessed none of the cultural or intellectual interests or the witty conversational skills of the Petersburg elite. Fascinated by mathematics and technology, his mind was entirely practical. In modern jargon, he was a problem-solver and an enforcer. For an emperor trying to govern Russia through a grossly overstretched, poorly paid and corrupt bureaucracy, men like Arakcheev could seem a precious asset. Joseph de Maistre wrote that 'I consider him to be evil and even very evil . . . but it is probably true that at present only such a man can restore order'.[3]

Arakcheev was an artillery officer by training and had been inspector-general of the Russian artillery since 1803. At least in retrospect, even his enemies usually acknowledged his success in this position. In 1800 the Russian artillery had poor guns and equipment, a corrupt administration, confused doctrines, and disorganized (usually civilian) drivers and trains. Thanks above all to Arakcheev, by 1813 it had solved almost all these problems and was superior to its Austrian and Prussian counterparts. By the time he became minister, Arakcheev had already transformed the weapons and equipment, greatly improved the quality and upkeep of the horses, and militarized the drivers and ammunition trains. He studied campaign reports from 1805–7 carefully, in order to understand what made artillery effective on the Napoleonic battlefield. Though the key reforms of the Russian artillery had already occurred before 1807, a number of important improvements to weapons and ammunition were brought in while Arakcheev was minister.[4]

As minister, Arakcheev also encouraged the creation of the *Artillery Journal* (*Artilleriiskii zhurnal*) so that an intelligent public debate could contribute to modernizing the Russian artillery and educating its officers. He introduced stiff exams for officers wishing to enter the Guards artillery and then used the Guards as a training ground and model for all artillery officers. He assigned and often subsidized sixty cadets a year to train with the Guards batteries and rotated officers and gunners from the line artillery through short spells with the Guards in order to learn best practice. On the eve of 1812 General Neithardt von Gneisenau, the Prussian military reformer, submitted a memorandum to Alexander I which in many respects was critical of the Russian army. Even Gneisenau conceded, however, that 'the Russian artillery is in wonderful condition . . . nowhere else in Europe can one find such teams of horses'.[5]

On his appointment as minister of war, Arakcheev sent word to the ministry that he would turn up for work at 4 a.m. on the following day and that he expected all officials to be there to meet him in their correct uniforms. This set the tone for his two subsequent years in the job. Strict obedience to the regulations was the watchword. All communications with the emperor must go through the minister. Commanding officers must record all failings of their juniors in the latter's service records. Tight rules were drawn up as regards supplying the army with uniforms and equipment on time and in the correct manner: laggards were threatened with fines and dismissal. Arakcheev took pride in the fact that whereas the arsenals were empty when he became minister, within two years all new recruits were armed and there were 162,000 spare muskets in store. Some bottlenecks restricting production at the Tula arms factory were also being overcome. The minister insisted that officials must make payments according to the agreed budgets, and no longer simply dole out the cash provided by the finance ministry whenever it became available to whatever need appeared most pressing.[6]

The new model musket introduced by Arakcheev was lighter and less clumsy than its predecessors. Given time, he believed that it could become the standard firearm for all infantry regiments. One clear lesson of 1805–7 was that Russian musketry was far inferior to French. The new firearm was intended to help here but in addition Arakcheev issued repeated orders that troops must be trained to aim and shoot accurately. He also produced a very useful booklet on the components, maintenance and cleaning of firearms. Meanwhile energetic measures had been taken to boost production of gunpowder and of cloth for uniforms. By the time he left office in 1810 Arakcheev was able to claim that future demand for military uniforms could now be met from Russian production without the need for the emergency ban on sales to the civilian market which he had been forced to introduce on becoming minister.[7]

Arakcheev's management certainly did improve matters. His successor as minister, General Mikhail Barclay de Tolly, was also extremely strict when it came to failings in the military administration. Shortly after his appointment, however, he noted that the commissariat was being run with outstanding efficiency and was in 'the very best order'. Supplies and uniforms were beginning to flow into the stores. On the eve of Arakcheev's retirement as minister, the French ambassador noted that 'there has never previously been this level of order in the military administration, above all in the artillery and the victualling departments. In general, military administration is in excellent condition.'[8]

Nevertheless, through no fault of Arakcheev, there remained many problems. In reality the Russian textile industry was still very hard pressed to meet military needs. New factories and sheep farms could not be created overnight and a bankrupt government was poorly placed to provide subsidies to encourage their development. Arakcheev had partly 'solved' shortfalls by extending the lifetime of existing uniforms. In addition, for example, demand had been reduced by requiring the provincial administration to clothe all new recruits in so-called 'recruit uniforms' which would have to last them for their first year in the army. Usually grey, and always made of inferior 'peasant cloth', these uniforms were much shoddier and less durable than the dark-green woollen tunics of the regular infantry. The ministry of war struggled to provide uniforms for a growing army in 1809–12. It had no chance of stockpiling large reserves for wartime needs, though Alexander tried to encourage this. When war came in 1812 the commissariat had spare uniforms and equipment for only one-quarter of the existing field army. The so-called 'recruit uniforms' quickly disintegrated when worn by soldiers on campaign.[9]

Similar problems affected Russian firearms. The new musket was an improvement but accurate shooting was still affected by the varying thickness of the paper in Russian cartridges. To accommodate these cartridges, calibres had to be greater than initially planned. Though the new model musket was well designed, Russian labour and machine tools were not capable of mass production of top-quality interchangeable parts.[10] Some cartridges still rattled around in the barrel. In addition, lead was in short supply and was very expensive during these years in Russia. In part it was imported secretly and at great cost from Britain. As a result Russian infantry on average had six rounds of live ammunition a year for shooting practice and had to make do with clay bullets. Ordinary British foot soldiers received thirty rounds, light infantrymen fifty. Perhaps most important, efforts substantially to increase the production of muskets failed, above all because of shortages of skilled labour. More than anything else, it was this that sabotaged efforts to boost production at the new arms works near Izhevsk in the Urals, which Arakcheev set up in 1807. Luring skilled foreign labour to the borders of Siberia was a difficult and expensive business. Meanwhile inadequate labour and machine tools, added to a shortage of water to power the machinery, greatly undermined efforts to boost production at Tula in the pre-war years. Although the ministry tried hard to introduce suitable steam-powered machinery at Tula, when the war began Russia had a danger-ously small reserve of muskets to arm new units and replace losses in existing ones.[11]

Probably the most radical change introduced during Arakcheev's two years as minister concerned the treatment of recruits. Under the system he inherited new recruits were delivered straight to their regiments, where they received all their military training. This was particularly difficult in wartime but even in normal circumstances the shock of sudden immersion in their regiments could be too much for the peasant recruits. Very heavy sickness and mortality rates resulted. To avoid this, a new system of Reserve Recruit Depots was established in October 1808. Men would be given their initial military training for nine months in these depots. The tempo of training was rather slow, discipline rela-tively mild and the training cadres were in any case entirely devoted to this task, rather than being subject to the other pressures of regimental service. Arakcheev expressed the hope that this would do something to ease the inevitable psychological stress when – as he put it – a peasant was torn from his accustomed village life and subjected to the totally different society and disciplines of the army.[12]

In January 1810 an important new institution was created at the heart of Russian government. The new State Council was Speransky's brainchild. It was designed to debate and to advise the emperor on all legislation and budgets, and to oversee the ministries. Mikhail Speransky saw the State Council as the first step in the complete transformation of central government. This never happened, but major changes in the ministries' structure and responsibilities were also under way in these years. In these circumstances it was difficult to predict in which institutions most power would lie. Alexander offered Arakcheev the choice of either remaining minister of war or becoming chairman of the military committee of the new state council. Arakcheev chose the latter, commenting that he preferred to supervise rather than be supervised. Since the new war minister, Barclay de Tolly, was junior to Arakcheev and to some extent owed his promotion to him it may be that Arakcheev believed that he would retain a degree of indirect control over the ministry. In fact, however, Barclay soon showed that he was very much his own man and quickly became Alexander's chief military adviser, thereby earning the enmity of Arakcheev, who was intensely jealous of anyone who rivalled him for the emperor's favour.[13]

Though his family originated from Scotland, Barclay was in reality a member of the German professional middle class. His ancestors had settled in the Baltic provinces, but Barclay himself was brought up by relatives in the German community of Petersburg. The dominant Lutheran values of his childhood home were obedience, duty, conscience and hard work. He reinforced these values and his own place within the German community in Russia by marrying his cousin, as commonly happened in this era. At the age of 15 he entered Russian military service as an NCO, being promoted to officer rank two years later. Better educated than the normal officer drawn from the Russian gentry, he rose on merit and at modest speed. It took him twenty-one years to rise from cornet to major-general. His skill and courage in the East Prussian campaign of 1806 won him promotion to lieutenant-general, brought him to Alexander's attention, and secured him a key role in the subsequent war with Sweden. Urged on by Arakcheev, Barclay invaded southern Sweden from Finland across the ice of the Gulf of Bothnia in March 1809, thereby helping greatly to bring Swedish resistance to an end. A grateful monarch promoted Barclay to full general and made him commander-in-chief and governor-general of Finland.[14]

Tall, well built and with an upright, commanding presence, the new head of the army looked the part. His slight limp and stiff right arm, both the product of wounds, added to his distinction. But in the jealous world of Petersburg Barclay's rapid promotion to full general and minister won him many enemies. By temperament, background and experience he was not well suited to Petersburg high society and the imperial court, milieux which a minister ignored at his peril. At court he was respectful but awkward, wooden and insecure. The earnest, proud and sensitive Barclay knew that he lacked the culture, wit or broad education to win respect in this world. The Petersburg aristocracy, many of whose members held top military posts, looked down on him as a solemn, boring German and a parvenu. Barclay did not make friends easily, though men who served near him in time came to admire him greatly. Like all senior Russian generals and ministers, he had acquired his own clients in the course of his career, many of whom were Germans. This did not help his popularity. Whatever Barclay did, however, criticism was inevitable in this world of jealousy and carping: when subsequently he appointed Ivan Sabaneev to be his chief of staff he was criticized for favouring an old regimental colleague over other, abler (and in this case Baltic German) staff officers.[15]

Barclay de Tolly had Arakcheev's virtues without his vices. He was an efficient, incorruptible, hard-working and meticulous administrator but he was never a pedant. He could also be very tough, even ruthless, when necessary: given the habits of the Russian commissariat this was essential. Unlike Arakcheev, however, Barclay never indulged in superfluous cruelty, rudeness or vendettas. He was both a more efficient administrator and a tougher disciplinarian than Bennigsen, in whose army hunger, indiscipline and banditry had become endemic in 1806–7. As minister and commander-in-chief Barclay did everything possible to stop mistreatment of troops by their officers. His circulars condemned officers who used fear as a means to train and instil discipline into their troops: 'The Russian soldier has all the highest military virtues: he is brave, zealous, obedient, devoted, and not wayward; consequently there are certainly ways, without employing cruelty, to train him and to maintain discipline.'[16]

Given the emperor's skill at manipulation, it is quite possible that Alexander nudged Arakcheev into abandoning his ministerial post and joining the State Council in January 1810. In 1808 a war minister had been needed who would restore order to military administration, where necessary by terror. No better candidate for such a task existed than Arakcheev. By 1810, however, the job requirements had changed. An efficient and hard-working administrator was necessary but not sufficient. With conflict against Napoleon beginning to loom over the horizon the army needed a chief who could prepare and plan for war. Arakcheev had never served in the field and was barely competent to discuss strategy or war plans. Barclay de Tolly on the other hand was a front-line soldier with an outstanding wartime record. If Barclay lacked the daring or imagination of a great commander-in-chief, he nevertheless had a solid grasp of tactics and a quick eye to spot the possibilities and dangers of a battlefield. More important, he had not just a realistic grasp of strategy but also the patriotism, resolution and moral courage to sustain this strategy in the face of many obstacles and ferocious criticism. To an extent which was rare, Barclay would put the 'good of the service' above personal interests and vendettas. In 1812 Russia was to owe him much for these qualities.

In the two and a half years between his appointment as minister and Napoleon's invasion Barclay was immensely active. In the sphere of legislation, the new law on the field armies was of greatest significance. It was extremely detailed, taking up an astonishing and unprecedented 121 double-columned pages in the collection of laws. Known as the 'yellow book' because of the colour of its cover, the law encompassed all the departments, functions and key officers of the field army, and set out their powers and responsibilities. It also, however, went far beyond this, acting as a handbook for officers on how they should fulfil their tasks.[17]

Of course there were some errors in such a vast and complicated piece of legislation. The dual subordination of chiefs of staff, both to their own general and to the chief of staff at the next level of command, caused problems. Prussian commentators claimed that their own model, in which all departments had access to commanding generals only through their chiefs of staff, reduced inter-departmental wrangling and freed the supreme commanders from worrying about trivia. The division of responsibility for hospitals between the commissariat (supply and administration) and the medical department (doctors and paramedics) caused much inefficiency in 1812–14. Inevitably, too, the regulations sometimes had to be adapted to wartime realities. For example, the law envisaged a situation in which a Russian commander-in-chief commanded a Russian army operating in the absence of the emperor and on foreign soil. Actually in 1812–14 this never happened: the army was either fighting on Russian soil or operating abroad in Alexander's presence, though often under the command of foreign generals.

None of this mattered too much, however. For the first time, clear rules were set out for how an army should be run in wartime. Most of the principles established by Barclay worked well in 1812–14. Where necessary these rules could easily be amended to suit conditions on the ground. Six weeks after the army law was issued in early 1812, for example, it became clear that the future war would initially be fought on Russian territory. As regards the feeding and supply of the army, an amendment was immediately published which stated that the law was to be applied to any Russian provinces which the emperor declared to be in a state of war. In these provinces all officials were thereby subordinated to the army's intendant-general, who had the right to requisition food, fodder and transport at will in return for receipts. The law therefore goes far towards explaining how the Russian treasury sustained the 1812 campaign at such small cost to itself, at least in the short run of the wartime emergency. The clear lines of command and responsibility it established also laid the groundwork for the generally good collaboration of the army and the provincial governors in 1812.[18]

The other crucial pre-war legislation transformed the organization of internal security within Russia. To some extent the new law on internal security, issued in July 1811, was a spin-off of efforts to shake out manpower from the army's rear echelons in order to get the maximum number of soldiers into the ranks of the field armies. Above all this meant combing out men capable of service in the field from the many so-called garrison regiments distributed very unevenly across the empire's cities and fortresses. Thirteen newly formed regiments, roughly 40,000 trained men, were added to the field army in this way without recourse to an additional levy. Most of the soldiers released from the garrison units were potentially of good quality. Very many of the officers were not, however, since assignment to a garrison regiment (except in the key front-line fortresses on the Baltic coastline) implied that an officer was either physically incapable of front-line service or had a poor record.[19]

Roughly 17,000 men of the garrison regiments were deemed unfit for service in the field. They were to form the nucleus of the new internal security forces, with a half-battalion (in other words two companies) deployed in each of the empire's provincial capitals. They joined the small internal security units which already existed in the provinces and the more numerous but less mobile companies of veterans (*invalidy*) who were often deployed in the smaller provincial towns. All these units were now integrated into a single command which covered the whole of European Russia. It might have seemed logical to subordinate the internal security troops to Aleksandr Balashev, who, as minister of police, had overall responsibility for preserving order within Russia. But Alexander distrusted his police chief's growing power and was unwilling to add the internal security forces to his empire. He therefore made the internal security troops a separate organization, commanded by his own aide-de-camp general, Count Evgraf Komarovsky, who reported directly to the monarch.[20]

The internal security forces guarded public buildings, and helped to enforce judicial verdicts and to uphold public order, though in the event of widespread unrest they would need reinforcements from the regular army. What really mattered in 1812–14, however, was that they were responsible for guarding prisoners of war and, above all, for mustering recruits and escorting them to the camps where the army's reserves were being formed. As one would expect, many of the officers of the internal security forces who commanded these escort parties were of low quality. Prince Dmitrii Lobanov-Rostovsky, who commanded the Reserve Army in 1813–14, complained about them constantly and no doubt many recruits suffered at their hands. From the point of view of the Russian war effort, however, the new internal security forces were a godsend. Before 1811 regiments had been obliged to send officers and men back to the provinces to collect and escort the new recruits. Even in peacetime this had been a major distraction. In 1812–14, with a vastly expanded army operating far from the empire's interior, the diversion of effort would have been crippling.[21]

It is relatively easy to assess the impact of the new legislation on the field army and the internal security forces. Coming to firm conclusions about the results of Barclay's efforts to improve military training is more difficult. Hundreds, even sometimes thousands, of kilometres from Petersburg the effect of even the most intelligent and best-intentioned circulars might be muted. It is true that in 1808–12 bright young officers of the line were seconded to the Guards training camps outside Petersburg and were then expected to take the lessons they learned in tactics back to their regiments and teach them to their soldiers. Most generals commanding divisions in these years also did their utmost to ensure effective training of their soldiers. For much of the year even an infantry division, let alone a cavalry one, was quartered over a wide area, however. A great deal therefore depended on the regiments' commanding officers.[22] Some commanders were brutes and pedants. Only rarely were they punished for their brutality if it was seen to threaten the army's effectiveness. The commander of the Kexholm Infantry Regiment, for example, was actually court-martialled and dismissed the service in 1810 for mistreatment of soldiers on a scale to cause near mutiny.[23]

Most commanders were not brutes, however, and some were excellent. Count Mikhail Vorontsov, for example, was the chief of the Narva Infantry Regiment in this period. He echoed Barclay in condemning the use of beatings to train and discipline Russian soldiers. Vorontsov once commented that discipline was far better in the Narva regiment, where such beatings were forbidden, than in the neighbouring 6th Jaegers, whose commander, Colonel Glebov, thought that Russian troops could only be controlled by the rod. Like some other regimental commanders, Vorontsov issued instructions to his officers outlining how they were to fight on the battlefield. Petr Bagration thought these instructions to be a model and reissued them to his whole army.

Vorontsov put a heavy stress on the example that officers needed to set. In some regiments, he stated, one found officers who were strict and demanding in peacetime but weak and irresolute in war: 'There is nothing worse than such officers.' Putting on a good show at parades was useless. It was battles that mattered. Officers who won the men's trust in peacetime by decent behaviour would be able to turn that respect to good effect on the battlefield. Leadership was everything. No officer who caused even a whiff of doubt about his courage had ever been tolerated in the Narva regiment. When the regiment was advancing the company commanders must march in front of their men to show an example. But an officer must combine courage with calm and good judgement. When the enemy fled in the face of the regiment's attack – which was to be expected because 'Russians always were and always will be much more courageous' – the officers must keep their heads and rally their men. Only a detachment from the third rank should be sent off in pursuit. When commanding skirmishers the officer must try to conceal his men if the terrain permitted but he himself must move ceaselessly up and down the skirmish line to encourage his soldiers and keep an eye out for unexpected danger.

Under artillery fire the regiment must stand upright. Any ducking was quickly noticed by the enemy and boosted their confidence. If there was better cover in the immediate neighbourhood then it was permitted to move there but the regiment must not retreat under any circumstances. Before a battle began every soldier should have two reserve flints and sixty cartridges, all in proper repair. No unwounded soldier should accompany wounded comrades to the casualty station in the rear. If the regiment was attacking an enemy under cover in a village or broken ground the key to success was to charge in with the bayonet, since the defenders would have all the advantages in a fire-fight. When firing at the enemy the men must take careful aim and remember what they had been taught about judging ranges and not shooting over the heads of their target. In 1806–7 regiments had sometimes been thrown into disorder by panicky cries that the enemy was attacking their flank or rear. Any repetition of such behaviour must be punished severely. Officers seeing enemy attempts to outflank the regiment must report this calmly to the colonel and must remember that a well-trained unit like the Narva regiment would have no difficulty redeploying to its flank or rear. Finally, the officers must encourage their men by noting their exploits, bringing them to the colonel's attention and recommending them for promotion, where appropriate even promotion to officer rank. 'The officer corps always gains by taking in a truly brave man, from whatever background he comes.'[24]

Another outstanding commander was Dmitrii Neverovsky, who was appointed to the crack Pavlovsky Grenadier Regiment in November 1807. Neverovsky was the kind of general that the Russian army loved. His background was typical of the officer corps. His father owned thirty male serfs and was a middle-ranking provincial official elected by his fellow nobles. With no less than fourteen children to care for, life at home was spartan. Though Neverovsky came from Poltava in present-day Ukraine, in the world of 1812 he was regarded (realistically in his case) as a Russian. Like many inhabitants of Ukraine, he was a fine horseman. He was actually rather better educated than the average product of the provincial nobility, having Latin and mathematics as well as being able to read and write in Russian. Possibly this was because he was befriended by a local grandee, Count Petr Zavadovsky, who liked Neverovsky's father, took the son into his own home, and helped him in the first stages of his career. Nevertheless the young Neverovsky enjoyed the tough, free, adventurous youth of a provincial nobleman. His loud voice, upright bearing and confidence inspired respect in his leadership. So did his size. At almost two metres tall he topped most of his grenadiers.

Above all Neverovsky was honest, direct, generous and hospitable. He was also very courageous. These were the legendary qualities of a Russian regiment's commander. Neverovsky kept a close eye on his soldiers' food and health. When he took over the regiment he found a high level of desertion in two of the companies. Like many other senior officers he believed that if Russian soldiers deserted it almost certainly meant that their officers were incompetent, cruel or corrupt. Both company commanders were quickly forced out of the regiment. Meanwhile he set up a regimental school to train NCOs and teach them to read and write. Above all, he put a heavy stress on training the men in marksmanship, personally overseeing the upkeep of muskets and participating in shooting practice alongside his men.[25]

If good shooting was important for infantry of the line such as the Pavlovskys, it was even more so for the light infantry (in Russia called jaegers), whose job it was to skirmish and to pick off enemy officers and artillerymen with accurate fire. Here, however, one needs to be a little cautious. The history of light infantry in the Napoleonic era has acquired a certain degree of mythology and ideological colouring. Given the nature of the weapons available at the time, it was still in most cases only close-order massed formations of infantry that could deliver the firepower and shock which brought victory on the Napoleonic battlefield. Nor was every *chasseur* a freedom-loving citizen-in-arms. Light infantry had existed before the French and American revolutionary armies. In 1812–14 perhaps the best light infantry in Europe were the hard-bitten, professional soldiers of Wellington's Light Division, who were about as far removed from being citizens-in-arms as it is possible to imagine.[26]

General George Cathcart had served with the Russian army and was well placed to make international comparisons. His comments on the Russian army's jaegers are balanced and realistic. Cathcart believed that where light infantry were concerned,

individual intelligence is the main requisite; and the French are, without question, by nature the most intelligent light infantry in the world ... The Russians, like the British, are better troops of position than any of the other nations; but it is difficult to excel in all things, and their steadiness in the ranks, which after all is the great object to be desired, as well as their previous domestic habits, render them naturally less apt for light infantry purposes than more volatile nations: yet in both services particular corps, duly practiced in this particular branch, have proved themselves capable of being made by training equal to any men that could be opposed to them.[27]

Russian jaeger regiments had existed since the Seven Years War. By 1786 there were almost 30,000 jaegers in the Russian army. Mikhail Kutuzov commanded jaeger regiments and actually wrote the general rules for jaeger service. The 1789 regulations for training jaegers stressed the need for marksmanship, mobility, craftiness and skilful use of terrain for concealment. The jaeger must, for example, learn how to reload lying on his back and to fire from behind obstacles and folds in the ground. He must trick his enemy by pretending to be dead or by putting out his shako as a target. The jaegers became associated with Grigorii Potemkin and Russia's wars against the Ottomans. Potemkin introduced comfortable, practical uniforms to suit the climate and the nature of operations on the southern steppe and in the Balkans. The jaeger regulations told the men not to waste time polishing their muskets.

None of this endeared the jaegers to Paul I, who reduced the number of light infantry by two-thirds. Though one needs to be wary about Russian nationalist historiography's attacks on German pedantry, in this case the Russian historians were right to believe that Paul's obsession with complicated drill on the parade ground damaged the Russian army in general and its jaegers in particular. George Cathcart was undoubtedly also correct in believing that serfdom was not the perfect background for a light infantryman. Nor was the discipline to which the new recruit was subjected in order to turn the peasant into a soldier. After 1807 the need to expand and re-train the jaegers was widely recognized at the top of the army. Both Mikhail Barclay de Tolly and Petr Bagration, for example, had been commanders of jaeger regiments. Some senior officers found it hard to believe that Russian peasants could make good light infantry, however. This could easily serve as an excuse for their own failure to train the men intelligently. As Gneisenau noted in the spring of 1812, the training of Russia's jaegers was often much too rigid, complicated and formalistic.[28]

Nevertheless one should not exaggerate the failings of Russia's jaeger regiments. On the whole the jaegers performed well in the rearguard actions during the retreat to Moscow and at Borodino. The key point was that by 1812 the Russian army had over fifty jaeger regiments, which in principle meant well over 100,000 men. Differences in quality between regiments were inevitable. Fourteen line infantry regiments were redesignated as light infantry in October 1810 and one would expect them initially to be poor skirmishers since all sources agree that in the Russian army true jaeger units were much better at operating independently than the infantry of the line. On the other hand, those jaeger regiments which had fought in Finland, in the Caucasus or against the Ottomans in 1807–12 were likely to be best.[29]

On active service there were plenty of targets and no constraints on the use of live ammunition. The historian of the 2nd Jaegers writes that the campaign in Finland's forests was excellent training for light infantry in marksmanship, use of terrain and small-scale warfare. General Langeron recalls that the 12th and 22nd Jaegers were among the best marksmen in his corps, since they had years of experience fighting Circassian sharpshooters in the Caucasus. According to the historian of the 10th Jaegers the same was true of the Ottoman campaigns, during which the regiment was sometimes required to cover more than 130 kilometres in five days as it fought a 'small war' of skirmishes and ambushes in the foothills of the Balkans. Ottoman raiding parties often had better guns and were better marksmen than the Russian jaegers, at least until the latter learned from experience.[30]

The difference in quality between Russian jaeger regiments in 1812 was often evident to their enemies. The first Russian skirmishers encountered by the Saxon army after invading Russia were the inexperienced troops of General Oertel's corps. A Saxon officer recorded that 'the Russian army was not yet that which it became in 1813 . . . they did not understand how to skirmish in open order'. Some weeks later the Saxons got a great shock when they first encountered the veteran jaegers of the Army of the Danube, fresh from many campaigns in the Balkans. These men were 'the excellent Russian jaegers of Sacken's corps. They were as skilled in their movements as they were accurate in their shooting, and they did us great harm with their much superior firearms which were effective at twice our range.'[31]

How to train and use light infantry was one of the themes debated in the *Military Journal* (*Voennyi zhurnal*), published for the first time in 1810–12 under the editorship of the highly intelligent Colonel P. A. Rakhmanov. The *Journal* was designed to encourage officers to think about their profession. Some of its articles were translations from foreign 'classics'. They introduced Russian officers to the ideas of key foreign thinkers such as Antoine de Jomini, Friedrich Wilhelm von Bülow and Henry Lloyd. Other pieces concerned military history or were anecdotes about recent Russian wars. Very many of the articles concerned the key issues of the day, however, and were written by serving officers, often anonymously. Of course the *Journal* could not openly debate aspects of a future war with France but it was easy to read between the lines of some of its articles on questions such as the role of fortifications and the relative advantages of offensive and defensive war. The *Journal* also debated issues such as the proper deployment of artillery on the battlefield, the role of general staffs, and what values and skills military education should seek to instil into the officer corps. The subscription list for the *Journal* was impressive. Some regimental commanders bought many copies of it for their officers. But there were also very many individual subscriptions, above all of course from what one might describe as the emerging military intelligentsia.[32]

The core of this intelligentsia was the general staff, which grew in size and in quality during these years. In fact one could truthfully say that it was in 1807–12 that a real Russian general staff emerged for the first time. The need for such a staff was very evident from the debacle in 1805–7. The Russian army set off for war in 1805 guided by too few staff officers, who were poorly educated for the job. Kutuzov's chief Russian staff officer was a fine hydrographer of German origin, who had virtually no experience of wartime operations. In all respects Major-General Gerhardt was in fact typical of Russian staff officers of the time, the best of whom were cartographers, engineers, even astronomers but very seldom soldiers in the full meaning of the word. Even the minority of staff officers who had military experience had usually only served against the Ottomans. Fighting against the Turks was no preparation for a number of key tasks of staff officers facing Napoleon in 1805–14, including picking advantageous battlefields on which Russian troops could counter the tactical mobility, concentrated artillery and skilled skirmishing of Europe's best army.[33]

The two most informed Russian staff officers in Kutuzov's entourage were Prince Petr Mikhailovich Volkonsky and Karl von Toll. These two men learned the lessons of 1805 and were the key figures in the creation of an effective general staff in the subsequent years. Volkonsky was a small, stocky man who, as an officer of the Semenovsky Guards, had known Alexander from his adolescence. Nevertheless he stood in some awe of the monarch, to whom he was absolutely loyal and whose will he never questioned. Kindly, tactful and modest, Volkonsky was quite well educated and exceptionally hard-working. He was an efficient administrator who cut quickly to the heart of problems. His calm, patient good manners made him a useful diplomat at allied headquarters in 1813–14 when wrangling between rival egos and national perspectives threatened to get out of hand. Nobody ever claimed that Volkonsky had an outstanding brain, let alone that he was a great strategist. But he selected first-class subordinates – above all Karl von Toll and Johann von Diebitsch – and had the good sense to trust and support their judgement. Without Volkonsky's hard work, political skills and connections the Russian general staff would have been much more weakly positioned and less effective in 1812–14. Even after all his efforts, when the war began in 1812 there were still too few staff officers and too many of those that existed were young and inexperienced.[34]

On returning from Paris, where he had studied the French staff, Volkonsky struck up a good working relationship with Barclay de Tolly which endured throughout the period. In the two years that preceded Napoleon's invasion he got the Russian general staff on its feet. Acting as Volkonsky's assistant, Toll produced a manual to guide staff officers. It set out their key responsibilities as being all issues linked to the army's deployment, movements and choice of battlefields. Meanwhile A. I. Khatov was running the education of an increasing number of bright young cadets who would become junior staff officers and Volkonsky himself was luring some very able officers to transfer into the general staff, of whom Diebitsch, another officer of the Semenovskys, was subsequently the most famous. Bringing into the staff a number of officers who had front-line military experience and some young Russian aristocrats helped to reduce the gap and the suspicion between the fledgling general staff and the generals commanding corps and divisions. So too did the wartime experience gained by staff officers in 1805–12.

Nevertheless distrust remained. A key moment came in 1810 when Alexander decreed that henceforth all staff positions at headquarters should be reserved for trained general staff officers. Traditionally, commanding generals had run their headquarters through a duty general and a bevy of aides-de-camp, many of whom were relatives, friends and clients. In a manner typical of the Russian army and bureaucracy, headquarters resembled an extended family household. Now professionalism was attempting to upset and nose its way into this comfortable and traditional arrangement. Commanding generals might find the principle hard to swallow. They might also wonder whether the unknown, young and often non-Russian staff officers foisted on them were truly competent at real war, as distinct from organizing marches and drawing maps.

In addition, one great point about the friends and clients who had traditionally manned headquarters was that they were loyal to their patron. Could one be so sure of this with unknown staff officers appointed on supposedly impersonal professional grounds? In his manual for staff officers Toll had stressed loyalty to their commanding general as being of paramount importance. That did not stop Alexander from telling the chiefs of staff of both Barclay's and Bagration's armies to write directly to him about all matters of interest in their commands. Not at all surprisingly, it took Russian command structures some time to settle in 1812–13. The historian of the general staff suggests that if Tormasov's Third Army did so more quickly than Barclay's First or Bagration's Second that was because Tormasov himself and all his key staff officers came from the old network of Field-Marshal Prince Repnin.[35]

As this suggests, if in some ways the Russian army had been renewed in 1807–12, in other ways old habits and problems remained. On the whole the Russian army in June 1812 was not just bigger but also better than the one that had faced Napoleon in 1805. Over and above the specific reforms which had taken place in 1807–12, the army benefited from having far more experience of European warfare than had been the case seven years before. Nowhere was this more true than in the Guards. Paul I had begun their transformation from ornaments at the imperial court to a fighting elite but when the Guards regiments went on campaign in 1805 they had minimal experience of war. In the Preobrazhenskys, for example, no officer under the rank of colonel, no sergeant-major and very few sergeants had ever seen action.[36] Blooded in 1805–7 and reinforced in subsequent years by veterans drawn from the line regiments, the Guards were now much closer to being an elite reserve fighting force whose commitment could decide the fate of a battle. Nevertheless the army's most fundamental strengths and weaknesses remained unchanged from 1805. On the credit side stood the numbers and quality of the light cavalry, and the immense courage, discipline and endurance of the infantry. On the other side of the balance were problems in the high command. Above all this meant rivalries between the generals and the difficulty of finding a competent and authoritative supreme commander.

Once one goes into detail, the deployment of Russian forces to meet the threat of invasion inevitably becomes complicated. For that reason it is useful to think of the Russian forces as divided in principle into three lines of defence.

The front line was filled by the Guards, the Grenadiers and most of the line army. Initially it was divided between Barclay de Tolly's First and Bagration's Second armies. When Petersburg learned of the Franco-Austrian alliance a Third Army was formed in May 1812 under General Aleksandr Tormasov to defend the invasion routes into northern Ukraine. These three armies combined and including their Cossack regiments added up to only 242,000 men, which was barely half the first wave of Napoleon's invading forces. If they were destroyed, the war would be over. Without their cadres it would be impossible to rebuild an army capable of challenging Napoleon during the course of a war.

Since in principle the Russian army was said to have almost 600,000 men on its rolls in June 1812, the fact that it could put less than half of this number in the front line against Napoleon appears surprising. To some extent this merely reflected the usual gap in the Russian army of that time between men on the rolls and soldiers actually present in the ranks. There were always many men who were either ill or detached on a range of duties, or even dead and not yet removed from the rolls. In addition, however, many troops were deployed on other fronts. These included 42,000 men in the Caucasus, many of whom were engaged in the ongoing war with the Persians. Most important were the 31,000 men in Finland, the 17,500 in Crimea and southern Ukraine, and the nearly 60,000 soldiers of the Army of the Danube who had just become available as a result of the peace treaty with the Ottomans. These troops were not just numerous but also battle-hardened veterans. They were too far away to join the fray in the summer of 1812 but if the war could be prolonged their impact might be decisive.[37]

The second line of defence was manned by reserve units. Part of this force was made up of the line regiments' reserve infantry battalions and cavalry squadrons. In this period Russian infantry regiments were composed of three battalions, each in principle approximately 750 men strong. In the event of war, the first and third battalions set off together on campaign, while the second battalion was designated as 'reserve' and remained in the rear. Cuirassier and dragoon regiments were formed of five squadrons, one of which was left behind as a reserve. Two of the ten squadrons of light cavalry regiments were called 'reserve' and left in the rear. The function of these reserve units was to fill up the front-line regiments, guard regimental stores, train recruits and (in the cavalry's case) muster and break in remounts.[38]

Unfortunately, matters were a little more complicated than this simple picture suggests. As was so often the case, the Guards were an exception to the rule. Their infantry regiments set off to war in full three-battalion strength.[39] In addition, all Russian infantry battalions – Guards, line or light – were composed of four companies. Of these the elite company was called 'Grenadier', the other three usually 'Musketeer'. Though the second battalions of the line infantry remained in reserve, they detached their Grenadier companies for front-line service. These companies were united into so-called 'Combined' Grenadier battalions, brigades and divisions. Between them the First and Second armies had two such divisions and both fought at Borodino.

In 1812 there was a lively exchange between successive governors of Riga (Dmitrii Lobanov-Rostovsky and Magnus von Essen) and army headquarters about the quality of the reserve battalions which formed the Riga garrison. Not only the governors but also the senior Russian military engineer, General Karl Oppermann, complained that reserve battalions were by their nature very under strength and often poorly trained. Alexander denied this, arguing that good regiments had good reserve battalions and vice versa. Common sense suggests that Lobanov, Essen and Oppermann were at least partly right. Any sensible colonel taking his regiment off to war was likely to try to slip weaker elements into a reserve battalion designated for service in the rear. By definition, a battalion which shed its elite Grenadier company declined in quality as well as size. Nevertheless, Alexander was right in insisting that many of the reserve battalions which served under Bagration or joined Count Peter Wittgenstein's First Corps fought very well in 1812.[40]

The other half of the Russian 'second line' was made up of battalions formed from the Reserve Recruit Depots initially created by Arakcheev back in 1808 to ease peasants' transition to military service. In 1811, with war looming, it was decided to form the recruits who had almost completed their training in the so-called 'first-line' depots into reserve battalions. These were officially called the fourth battalions of their respective regiments. Their cadres were provided by the officers, NCOs and veterans who had been detached from the parent regiments to train the recruits in the depots. The fourth battalions were then united into reserve brigades and divisions. In March 1812 proposals were hatched to unite all the reserve units of the 'second line' into three reserve armies. In time these reserve armies would be able to reinforce Barclay, Bagration and Tormasov. In the event that the front-line armies were defeated or forced to retreat, they would be able to fall back under the cover of these rear formations.[41]

This plan never came to fruition and in reality reserve armies never existed in 1812. One reason for this was that Napoleon advanced more quickly than anticipated and the Russian reserve units were forced to decamp before they could form such armies. More importantly, many reserve battalions had to be redeployed in 1812 to stiffen the front line of defence. In May 1812 when Tormasov's Third Army was created in response to the new threat from Austria, it included many reserve (i.e. second) battalions. Reserve battalions also comprised most of the 18,500-strong garrison of Riga, as well as the smaller forces assigned to hold the fortresses of Bobruisk, Kiev and Dünaburg. When Dünaburg was abandoned its garrison joined Wittgenstein's corps in defending the approaches to Petersburg.

Meanwhile, of the eighty-seven fourth battalions from the Recruit Depots twelve joined the Riga garrison and six fought under Wittgenstein but the rest were incorporated into the retreating First and Second armies on the march. General Mikhail Miloradovich joined Kutuzov's forces on the eve of the battle of Borodino with most of the last remaining group of battalions, some 13,500 men. The fourth battalions were all broken up and their men distributed to refill the ranks of Kutuzov's regiments. This made good sense. The recruits in the fourth battalions had never seen their parent regiments and had little sense of regimental identity. In addition, battalions packed with men who had never seen action could not be relied on in battle. But these men all had basic military training and would be a safe and valuable addition when distributed among Kutuzov's veteran units. In addition, this policy allowed the fourth battalions' officers and NCOs to be detached to instruct the horde of new conscripts mobilized by the wartime levies.[42]

In principle Russia's third line of defence was the entire able-bodied manpower of the empire. During the war more than a million men were to be mobilized into the armed forces, over and above the hundreds of thousands of soldiers already in the ranks when the war began. Very few of this million saw active service in 1812, however, and it might seem strange that with such resources at his disposal Alexander allowed himself to delay mobilizing his potential manpower and thereby to be seriously outnumbered by Napoleon at the war's outbreak.

A number of plausible explanations exist. The full dimensions of Napoleon's invasion force only became apparent early in 1812. Alexander was also intent on not provoking Napoleon by ostentatiously increasing the size of the Russian army. Probably even more to the point were issues of cadres and finance. There was no sense in mobilizing hordes of recruits to fill their stomachs at the government's expense unless there were officers and NCOs to train and lead them. The government did all it could to create effective military cadres in 1807–12. Regiments were instructed to train junior NCOs. Three so-called Grenadier Training battalions were established to train likely looking young soldiers to become sergeant-majors and quartermaster-sergeants. A range of inducements were offered to potential officers. For instance, the widows of officers killed in action would receive their full salaries as pensions. Above all the ministry of war created the so-called Noble Regiment, which offered free, compressed officer-training courses and was attached to the Second Cadet Corps. Between 1807 and the end of 1812 more than 3,000 young men had passed through this regiment and received commissions, the great majority of them entering the line infantry. Nevertheless both before and during the war finding reliable officer and NCO cadres was always a bigger problem than netting recruits.[43]

Alexander's actions and words around the time of Napoleon's invasion provide some clues to his thinking. He told a Finnish official in August 1812 that the only way to unite Russian society behind the immense sacrifices needed to defeat Napoleon was for the latter to be seen as the aggressor and to invade Russian territory. Fighting on Russian soil, the emperor clearly felt he could appeal for 'voluntary' contributions towards the military build-up in a way that would not have been possible had he begun the war himself or fought it abroad, like all the other wars of the previous century. He had already begun to appeal for these contributions on the eve of Napoleon's invasion. There was therefore a political and financial logic for a bankrupt government to delay full-scale mobilization until war was in sight and it could tap society for contributions. It continued to follow this policy throughout 1812.[44]

Planning for war began early in 1810. In March of that year Barclay de Tolly submitted a memorandum to Alexander entitled 'The Defence of Russia's Western Frontiers'. The document is crucial both for what it did and did not say. Most of its ideas underlay all subsequent planning by Barclay and Alexander, who in the end were the only two people who truly mattered when it came to deciding how to fight the war.

Barclay stressed that of all Russia's borders the western one was the most vulnerable. It was enormously long and poorly defended by nature or man. Unlike most of Russia's other borders, there had been no threat on the western frontier since Charles XII's defeat at Poltava a century before. That explained its lack of fortifications. The minister argued that, if the territories annexed from Poland since 1772 were invaded by an enemy whose forces greatly outnumbered the Russian army, it would be impossible to defend them. The network of fortresses which alone would make it possible to hold this region would cost a fortune and take at least twenty-five years to build. In these circumstances the Russian army must stage a fighting withdrawal across the whole of Belorussia and Lithuania. It must eat up, remove or destroy all the food and fodder available in the region, leaving the enemy to sustain itself in a desert.

The key priority was to establish a strong defensive line along the rivers Dvina and Dnieper, where the Russians must make their stand. A number of fortresses and fortified camps must be constructed to strengthen this line. Barclay believed that it was 'most probable' that the enemy's main thrust would be south-eastwards towards Kiev, though an advance north-eastwards into Courland and Livonia was also possible. In either case, the Russian army facing this advance would seek to slow it down by a fighting withdrawal, without, however, risking a major battle. As the threatened army retreated into its fortified camp, the Russian army at the other end of the line would seek to advance into the enemy's rear. Barclay added that 'one cannot expect that the enemy would dare to advance in the centre' – in other words towards Minsk and Smolensk – but if it did so then the small 'Reserve Army' deployed there would draw the enemy onwards and the two main Russian armies would strike into its flanks and rear.

Of Russia's twenty-three existing divisions, Barclay argued that eight would need to remain in Finland, the Caucasus and the Ottoman border to defend these regions. This assumed some construction of fortresses in Finland, peace with the Ottomans and no Austrian invasion of Wallachia and Moldavia. Even given this optimistic scenario only fifteen divisions – barely 200,000 men – would be available for the western front. Seven of these divisions were to be deployed in the south, in other words on the left of the Russian line. They would block an enemy advance towards Kiev. Four divisions were to be concentrated on the right in Courland. In the enormous gap between these two armies the Reserve Army of just four divisions would deploy between Vilna and Minsk.

For whatever reason, Barclay said nothing about what would happen if the defence line along the Dvina and Dnieper was breached. Nor did he venture an opinion as to whether 200,000 men would be sufficient. Only weeks into his new job, perhaps he felt that he had risked enough by advocating the abandonment of the whole of Belorussia and Lithuania in his first discussion of strategy with the monarch.[45]

For two years after Barclay wrote this memorandum Russian generals debated whether to adopt a defensive or offensive strategy in the face of the threat from Napoleon. Given the fact that the defensive strategy initially suggested by Barclay in March 1810 was the one which was finally adopted and which ultimately proved successful it might seem self-evident that this was the correct option. In fact this was far from clear at the time. A number of intelligent proposals for an offensive strategy were put forward by key generals. A point to note is that for much of the period between March 1810 and April 1812 both Barclay de Tolly and Aleksandr Chernyshev advocated at least a limited initial offensive into Prussia and the Duchy of Warsaw. The leading advocate of a purely defensive strategy was Lieutenant-General Karl von Pfühl, a former senior Prussian staff officer accepted into Russian service in December 1806. Pfühl's chief assistant was Lieutenant-Colonel Ludwig von Wolzogen, who was responsible for choosing the position of the famous fortified camp at Drissa on which Pfühl's defensive strategy rested. But in October 1811 even Wolzogen argued that an offensive strategy made more sense.[46]

The reasons for this were partly political. It was clear to everyone that unless the Russian army advanced at the beginning of the war there was no chance of keeping Prussia as an ally. Right down to the winter of 1811–12 this issue hung in the balance, with a Russo-Prussian convention pledging Russia to an offensive signed but ultimately never ratified by the Prussian side. Another vital political issue was the competition to secure Polish loyalty. As Bennigsen argued in February 1811, a Russian offensive into the Duchy of Warsaw would stymie Napoleon's wish to mobilize Polish support in Russia's western borderlands. If the moral effect of a Russian offensive was combined with attractive political concessions to the Poles, large sections of the Polish army might fight on the Russian side.[47]

There were also powerful military reasons for an offensive. Invading the Duchy of Warsaw meant that Polish rather than Russian soil would bear the costs of war. More important, if Napoleon was to invade Russia, the Duchy of Warsaw and East Prussia would be his key bases. Huge stores would need to be amassed well in advance to sustain the invading army. As this army made its way across Europe to take up position on the Russian border their stores and their sources of food and fodder in the Duchy would be vulnerable to a Russian pre-emptive strike. For a sensible invader, the campaigning season in Russia was short. It was lunacy to invade before early June, when there would be sufficient grass in the field to feed the horses. That allowed less than five months before the snows began to fall in November. At the very least, a Russian pre-emptive strike might delay Napoleon's plans for an offensive and gain an additional year for Russian defensive preparations.

Above all, Russian generals advocated an offensive because they understood how very risky and difficult a purely defensive strategy would be. The western border was immensely long. If Russia was still at war with the Turks, French or Austrian troops could invade Bessarabia and threaten the entire Russian position on the north shore of the Black Sea, at the same time as Napoleon's main army was tying most of the Russian forces down in Belorussia and Lithuania. In the spring of 1812 peace with the Ottomans and the Austrian promise not to invade Russia from Galicia at least ended these worries.

Nevertheless the border with East Prussia and the Duchy of Warsaw alone remained very long. The Russians had to defend the approaches to Petersburg and Moscow. The latter could be threatened directly via Smolensk in the west or from Kaluga and the south-west. The defence of Kiev and Ukraine was also a top priority. Russian armies would therefore be stretched very thin. Communications through the huge area of the Pripet marshes were extremely poor. The Russian southern army defending Ukraine would be on its own. It would be within Napoleon's power to block the two main roads across the marshes and turn most of his army against one or other half of the Russian defensive screen.

It was in the nature of a defensive strategy that it gave the enemy the initiative. Added to the geography of the western borderlands, it would give Napoleon every opportunity to drive through the Russian forces, keep them separated and defeat them in detail. Moving through the centre of the Russian armies, he would then have the advantage of being between them and using interior lines. Bagration, Petr Mikhailovich Volkonsky and the emperor's uncle, Duke Alexander of Württemberg, all stressed this danger in the early months of 1812.[48]

To make the situation worse, in the impoverished western borderlands it was very difficult to keep large armies concentrated and static for weeks on end, except possibly in the weeks immediately after the harvest. Sickness rates also shot up once the army was concentrated. In addition, much the most effective way to eat up the region's food supplies and deny them to the French was to quarter the Russian army across a large swath of the area and use it to requisition supplies in lieu of tax. A state of war was declared in the border provinces in late April, which helped with requisitioning, but army headquarters was loath to concentrate its forces too early and too narrowly. In any case, once Napoleon left Paris the sources of Russian intelligence partly dried up. Napoleon himself was hoping for a Russian offensive and did not make final plans for an invasion until very late. He then of course did his utmost to hide where he intended to make his main thrust. Not until late May 1812 did the Russians begin to get a clear sense of where the main enemy attack was likely to come.[49]

In his March 1810 memorandum Barclay had stated that Russia's western borderlands were very weakly defended by man or nature. Many other officers expanded on this theme in reports written between then and June 1812. Russian military engineers were badly overstretched in these years. In 1807–11 the small corps of engineers was deployed in the Baltic seaport fortresses against possible British attack, in the Caucasus and in attempts to refortify strong-points taken from the Ottomans in the Balkans. From March 1810 it was also lumbered with the immense task of fortifying the western borderlands at breakneck speed. As was pointed out in a number of memorandums, fortresses bypassed by Napoleon would be a big threat to his fragile communications. This would slow down his advance. More importantly, a retreating army with no fortresses in its rear had nowhere secure for its supplies and baggage, and was therefore always obsessed with the need to protect them. In this situation an army tended to retreat quickly since only distance provided security.[50]

But fortresses, however necessary, could not easily be built from scratch in two years. On their southern flank, the Russians succeeded in preparing Kiev's defences for a siege and constructed a strong fortress at Bobruisk. On their northern flank, Riga was strengthened though the commander of the corps of engineers, General Oppermann, doubted whether it could hold out for long against a serious siege unless its garrison was very large. Once the new fortress of Dünaburg on the Dvina was completed, Oppermann wanted to move all supplies and stores there from Riga, since he feared that the latter's fall to the French would otherwise threaten the logistics of the main Russian armies.

Unfortunately, however, Dünaburg could not be completed by the summer of 1812. This meant that the entire central sector of the Russian defence line was open. As Bennigsen pointed out, this central sector gave access to the core territories of the Russian Empire, including the army's likely supply bases in Moscow and Smolensk. To make matters worse, this huge central sector had no natural defences of real value. Wolzogen

had obeyed his orders to choose a defensive position on the river Dvina
and had selected the spot for a fortified camp at Drissa. Nevertheless he
warned that the upper two-thirds of the Dvina was shallow and easily
forded in summer. Moreover at most points the west bank was higher
than the east, which put defenders at a serious disadvantage. Barclay
received the same advice from an even more authoritative voice, namely
General Oppermann, who told him in August 1811 that the river Dvina
could not be defended against a serious enemy advance, 'however good
any specific position may be'. The reason for this was that 'in summer
the river is easily crossed, the areas close to its banks are almost everywhere open and easily traversed, and any position on or near the river's
banks can be outflanked'.[51]

Between Riga on the Baltic coastline and Bobruisk far to the south
the only significant defence-works in June 1812 were the fortified camp
at Drissa, way upriver on the Dvina towards Vitebsk, whose construction
began in the spring of 1812. Alexander's unofficial adviser, General
Pfühl, made the camp at Drissa the key to his plan for the defence of the
empire's heartland. By the time Napoleon's forces approached Drissa,
Pfühl expected them to be exhausted and reduced in number after
crossing a devastated Belorussia and Lithuania. If they attempted to
storm the fortified camp in which the bulk of First Army had taken
refuge they would be at a great tactical disadvantage. If they tried to
move beyond Drissa then First Army could attack their flank. Meanwhile
Bagration and Platov's forces would be striking deep into Napoleon's
rear.

In principle Pfühl's plan had much in common with Barclay's proposals in March 1810. There was the same reliance on strategic retreat
and devastating the abandoned territory; on fortified camps as a means
to strengthen the defending army when it finally turned at bay; on the
role of other Russian forces in striking into Napoleon's flanks and rear.
Pfühl had merely transported Barclay's concept from the two flanks,
where Barclay had seen the greatest threat, to the centre of the Russian
line, which now seemed the likeliest target for Napoleon's main blow.
But Barclay's fortified camps were to rely on the support of fortresses,
Riga in the north and Bobruisk in the south. With Dünaburg gone,
Drissa must stand alone. In addition, in 1810 Barclay had not anticipated
that Russia would be invaded by an army of anything like half a million
men.

Even in 1812 Pfühl was probably not fully aware of the size of Napoleon's invasion force. Access to Russian intelligence material was confined to a very tight circle. By March 1812 Alexander, Barclay and their de facto chief intelligence officer, Petr Chuikevich, knew that even the first wave of Napoleon's army would be 450,000 strong. A force of this size could both mask and outflank Drissa without danger. It could also block any attack by Bagration and Matvei Platov without difficulty. If First Army took refuge in Drissa, it might be surrounded and captured as easily as Mack's troops in Ulm had been at the beginning of the 1805 campaign.

Nevertheless Alexander's plan of campaign in 1812 at least on the surface revolved around the fortified camp at Drissa. The Russian army was to make a strategic withdrawal to Drissa at the war's outbreak and would then attempt to hold the French on the line of the river Dvina. Perhaps Alexander genuinely believed in Pfühl's plan. He always tended to value foreign soldiers' opinions above those of his own generals, in whose abilities he usually had little confidence. In addition, Pfühl's 'scientific' predictions as to the precise moment when Napoleon's supplies would run out may have appealed to Alexander's liking for tidy, abstract ideas. Undoubtedly the emperor believed that Pfühl's plan was based on the same concept as Barclay's earlier proposals. He will also have remembered that in 1806–7 Bennigsen had kept at bay for six months an enemy double his numbers. Nevertheless there is room for some cynicism. Alexander did not want Napoleon to penetrate into the Russian heartland, though he feared that he might do so. Any open admission that Napoleon might reach Great Russia in his initial campaign, let alone the circulation of plans based on such an idea, would have destroyed the emperor's credit. If Napoleon was to be stopped short of the Great Russian border, Pfühl's plan seemed the only one currently available. Should it fail, Alexander knew that Pfühl would be the perfect scapegoat. A foreigner without protection, he was also despised by the Russian generals as the epitome of a German pedantic staff officer who knew nothing about war.[52]

Though Alexander may have retained faith in Pfühl's plan even in June 1812, it is very hard to believe that the experienced Barclay allowed it greatly to affect his thinking on how the war should be conducted, given the advice he had received from the army's chief engineer. From Barclay's perspective, however, the camp at Drissa did no harm. It absorbed almost none of his resources, since it was built with local labour. It was also a useful stopping point in the army's retreat and almost unique as a place where stores could be established for the retreating army under some kind of protection. In any case, final decisions on Russian strategy rested with the emperor, not with Barclay. But the best guide to Barclay's thinking immediately before the war is provided by a memorandum written by Chuikevich in April 1812. It says nothing about fortified camps in general or the camp at Drissa in particular.

Chuikevich's analysis was close to the ideas expressed earlier by Aleksandr Chernyshev. He argued that Napoleon's whole system of war depended on big battles and rapid victories. For the Russians, the key to victory was 'to plan and pursue a war exactly contrary to what the enemy wants'. They must retreat, raid enemy communications with their much superior light cavalry, and wear down Napoleon's forces. 'We must avoid big battles until we have fallen right back on our supply bases.' In previous wars, when frustrated, Napoleon had made serious mistakes but his enemies had not exploited them. Russia must not miss this opportunity. Its cavalry could prove lethal in pursuit of a beaten foe. Determination not to negotiate and to continue the war until victory was vital but so too was caution; Fabius, the Roman general whose refusal of battle had so frustrated Hannibal, must be their guide. So too must Wellington's policy of strategic withdrawal in the Peninsula. 'However contrary this strategy based on caution is to the spirit of the Russian people, we must remember that we have no formed reserve units behind our front-line forces and the complete destruction of the First and Second armies could have fateful consequences for the Fatherland. The loss of a few provinces must not frighten us because the state's survival depends on the survival of its army.' Chuikevich also advocated a number of ways in which Europe might be incited to rise up in Napoleon's rear. Though unrealistic, they do serve as a useful reminder that for him, Barclay and Alexander the 1812 campaign in Russia was merely the first act in a longer war designed to destroy Napoleon's domination of Europe.[53]

Chuikevich's memorandum did not go into details. It said nothing specific about where Napoleon's advance might be stopped. Unlike Pfühl, Chuikevich was a practical soldier who understood the uncertainties of warfare. But no one who read the memorandum could be confident that Napoleon's advance would be halted within the western borderlands. The danger that the war would spread into the Russian heartland was obvious. In reality Barclay and Alexander had always understood this possibility. Any Russian leader knew how Charles XII had marched deep into the empire's interior and had been destroyed by Peter the Great. The parallels were clear enough. On the very eve of Napoleon's invasion, Count Rostopchin wrote to Alexander that 'if unfortunate circumstances forced us to decide on retreat in the face of a victorious enemy, even in that case the Russian emperor will be menacing in Moscow, terrifying in Kazan and invincible in Tobolsk'. While recovering from his wounds in 1807 Barclay himself apparently spoke at length of the need to defeat Napoleon by drawing him into the depths of Russia and inflicting on him a new Poltava. Before 1812 Alexander and his sister Catherine spoke privately about the possibility of Napoleon taking both Moscow and Petersburg in the event of a war. Early in 1812 the emperor made quiet arrangements to evacuate his mistress and child to the Volga if the need arose.[54]

All this was a long way from concrete plans to lure Napoleon into the Russian interior or prepare for his destruction there. In reality no such plans or preparations existed. This was sensible. Barclay's brother was a colonel on the general staff: he wrote in 1811 that it was pointless to make plans for military operations beyond the first stages of any war, so great were the uncertainties involved in any campaign. This was doubly the case in 1812 since Russia's defensive strategy had left the initiative in Napoleon's hands. If Napoleon crossed the Dvina he might head for Moscow. On the other hand, he could make for Petersburg or even shift the main thrust of the war southwards towards Ukraine, as his Polish advisers were urging. More likely, he could end his campaign with the conquest of Belorussia and devote his energies to restoring the Polish kingdom and organizing a supply base for a campaign into the Russian heartland in 1813. Before the war began Napoleon told Metternich, the Austrian foreign minister, that this was what he intended to do and at least one senior Russian general staff officer believed that if Napoleon had stuck to this idea the consequences for Russia would have been disastrous.[55]

For the Russian leadership, how their own subjects would respond to the French invasion was a matter of immense importance and uncertainty. Above all, this meant the Poles, not least because they dominated the region which Russian strategy intended to surrender to the invaders. There was considerable debate among Russian generals and statesmen before the war began about how the Poles would respond to a French invasion. It was felt that many of the great landowners preferred Russian rule because they disliked the abolition of serfdom in the Duchy of Warsaw and feared further radical measures. As to the region's peasants, they might indulge in anarchic assaults on property and order but the Russian leadership was confident that they neither understood nor cared about nationalist or Jacobin ideas. The big danger was the mass of the Polish gentry. Most Russian generals agreed that, if Napoleon invaded Russia and proclaimed Poland's restoration, the great majority of educated Poles in Lithuania and Belorussia would support him, partly out of nationalist enthusiasm and partly because they believed that he would win. Of course this reinforced the generals' unwillingness to withdraw from the borderlands, not least for fear that Napoleon would turn them into a fruitful base for subsequent operations against the Russian heartland. Alexander and Barclay could not deny this possibility. But they believed that Napoleon's overwhelming numbers left them no alternative to their strategy. They knew that restoring the Polish kingdom could not be done overnight. They banked on Napoleon's temperament, as well as on the nature of his regime and military system, making a strategy of sustained patience unlikely.[56]

As regards the emperor's Russian subjects, much the most important 'constituency' was the army itself. For any army, maintaining discipline and morale during a long retreat is extremely difficult. The Prussian army disintegrated after Jena-Auerstadt and the French were little better during the retreat from Moscow in 1812 and from Leipzig in the autumn of 1813. British discipline collapsed during Sir John Moore's retreat to Corunna in 1808 and again during the retreat from Burgos back into Portugal in 1812. As one historian of the Peninsular War comments, 'retreats were not the British army's forte'. Though the Russian army was famous for its discipline, a retreat not just across the whole of Belorussia and Lithuania but also deep into Russia itself was bound to test morale and order within the regiments to the limit. In stressing the impact of retreat on his troops' morale just before the war Prince Bagration had his own axe to grind because the very idea of retreating in the face of an enemy was anathema to him. Nevertheless, his fears were by no means groundless.[57]

It is a truism among military historians that armies can only fight wars in line with their 'military doctrine', which is elaborated in the pre-war years. In the early nineteenth century formalized military doctrine in the modern sense existed nowhere. This would have to wait for staff colleges and the whole paraphernalia of modern military education and training. In an informal sense, however, the Russian army did have a 'doctrine' in 1812 and it was wholly committed to offensive strategy and tactics. From his first moments in his regiment the young officer was encouraged to be daring, fearless, confident and aggressive. Every lieutenant was expected to believe that one Russian was worth five Frenchmen. Male pride was at stake in the 'game' to capture trophies such as flags and drive the enemy off the battlefield. Many Russian generals in 1812 had this mentality too. To retreat before the enemy was almost as shocking as failing to defend one's honour in a duel when challenged. In addition, in the previous century the army had experienced only victory. Its great triumphs over Frederick II and the Ottomans had been won on the offensive and on enemy soil. The greatest eighteenth-century Russian generals, Aleksandr Suvorov and Petr Rumiantsev, stressed speed, aggression, surprise and shock. An army bred on such ideas and traditions was bound to mutter if forced to retreat hundreds of kilometres deep into Russian territory on the basis of calculations about logistics and numbers made by 'German' staff officers.[58]

It was also hard to predict how the Russian civilian population would respond if Napoleon entered the Great Russian provinces. After all, the army of a great power was supposed to protect the property of its compatriots, not retreat for hundreds of kilometres without a battle and open the country's core to devastation. Above all, the elites had to worry about how their serfs would react to Napoleon, particularly if he issued promises of emancipation. In pre-war military documents there is very little on this subject. One interesting (though unique) war ministry document did raise the spectre of Russian peasant disturbances, arguing that the experience of the Pugachev rebellion showed that house serfs and peasants working in factories were the least reliable elements.[59]

Inevitably such fears grew as Napoleon approached the Russian borders in July 1812. The private secretary to Alexander's wife Empress Elizabeth, Nikolai Longinov, wrote in July that 'although I am convinced that our people would not accept the gift of freedom from such a monster, it is impossible not to worry'. In December 1812, with the danger passed, John Quincy Adams wrote that among the Petersburg elite there was great relief that 'the peasants had not shown the least disposition to avail themselves of the occasion to obtain their freedom. . . . I see this is what most touches the feelings of all the Russians with whom I have conversed on the subject. This was the point on which their fears were the greatest, and upon which they are most delighted to see the danger past.' The influence of such fears on pre-war planning or wartime operations must not be exaggerated, however. Petersburg's salons might shiver at the word 'Pugachev' but fears of peasant insurrection barely figure in the correspondence of Alexander, Barclay or Kutuzov.[60]

At the beginning of April 1812, as they struggled to prepare their armies to oppose the invasion, Russia's generals had more pressing concerns than serf rebellion. At this time Barclay was still hoping to mount a pre-emptive attack into the Duchy of Warsaw and East Prussia, though he realized that by now this could only be a quick and limited spoiling action. He awaited with impatience the emperor's arrival at headquarters and permission to start the attack. In fact, however, Alexander was delayed and permission never came. The emperor had always preferred to await the attack and to adopt a defensive strategy. His determination to follow that line was confirmed by news of the Franco-Austrian alliance. If a Russian army advanced into the Duchy of Warsaw, Austria might well be impelled by this treaty to mobilize all its military forces and could push forward from Galicia into the rear of the advancing Russian armies.[61]

With all chances of a pre-emptive strike gone and the Austrian army also now to be reckoned with, the Russians were forced to redeploy their troops quickly. As Petr Mikhailovich Volkonsky wrote on 11 May, currently more than 800 kilometres separated the headquarters of Barclay's right-hand corps at Schawel and Bagration's headquarters at Lutsk. The armies were deployed for an advance into the Duchy of Warsaw. Above all, they were well placed to feed themselves off the countryside. But they were very poorly deployed to resist invasion. Volkonsky admitted that a pre-emptive strike had been the best option but it was no longer possible even in military terms because Napoleon had now gathered his stores into fortresses and 220,000 enemy troops were already deploying along the border. A new, 'Third', army was set up under Aleksandr Tormasov to guard the approaches to Ukraine. Bagration would detach part of Second Army to reinforce Tormasov and would bring the rest of his command northwards to link up with Barclay. Volkonsky reckoned that it would take fifteen days' uninterrupted marching for Bagration's men to reach their new positions. Even then First and Second armies would still hold a front of not much less than 200 kilometres.[62]

By 6 June Bagration's army, now really no more than the size of a big corps, was deployed around Pruzhany. The Russians were evacuating cash, food, transport and archives from the border region. They were also trying to 'evacuate' local Polish officials who would be of service to the enemy. Having reached Pruzhany, Bagration was soon ordered to move still further northwards, since Russian intelligence now correctly believed that Napoleon's main thrust would be further north than previously thought, from East Prussia and through the centre of First Army's deployment in the direction of Vilna. This order was dispatched on 18 June, only six days before Napoleon crossed the border.[63]

Bagration was becoming distinctly unhappy. His army was drawing further and further away from Tormasov's men. He wrote to Barclay that Volhynia (i.e. western Ukraine) was a juicy target for the French since it contained great reserves of food and horses, and its Polish nobles were certain to collaborate with Napoleon if given the chance. With Second and Third armies now beyond the range of mutual support, the road into Ukraine's richest provinces was opening up. Meanwhile, in an effort to draw closer to First Army, his much reduced force was strung out over a front of more than 100 kilometres. Nor was it possible to execute his orders to destroy or drag away all local food supplies. Most local carts had been requisitioned by the army and if he drove all the local horses and cattle to the rear they would eat out the meadows on which his own army's horses depended.[64]

In all these complaints there was, without doubt, an element of foot-dragging. Bagration loathed the idea of retreating without a fight and appealed to Alexander on 18 June to be allowed to mount a pre-emptive strike. In a fiery letter he set out all the disadvantages of a retreat. To do Bagration justice, his understanding of realities was not helped by the fact that Alexander had not passed on Russian intelligence's estimates about the size of Napoleon's forces. Nor had Bagration any clear overall picture of Napoleon's deployment on the other side of the border. Before he could receive a response from the emperor Napoleon had crossed the border on 24 June and the war had begun.[65]

5

The Retreat

In March 1812 Mikhail Barclay de Tolly was appointed to command First Army, whose headquarters were in Vilna, much the biggest city in Lithuania. Though he retained the title of minister of war, Barclay handed over the day-to-day running of the ministry to Prince Aleksei Gorchakov, who remained in Petersburg when Barclay and many of the other most able officers departed the capital for army headquarters.

First Army was roughly 136,000 strong. This made it bigger than Prince Bagration's Second Army (around 57,000 men) and General Tormasov's Third Army (around 48,000) combined.[1] Together these three armies guarded Russia's western borders against invasion by Napoleon. Barclay was in no sense the supreme commander of all three forces. In fact he was junior to both Bagration and Tormasov, which mattered greatly in the acutely rank-conscious elite of imperial Russia. The only supreme commander was Alexander himself, who arrived in Vilna in April.

The bulk of First Army was made up of the five infantry corps which by June 1812 were arrayed along the frontier of East Prussia and the northern border of the Duchy of Warsaw. Each of these corps contained two infantry divisions, which in turn were made up of three brigades. Two of these brigades were formed from regiments of the line, one from jaegers. As we have seen, a Russian infantry regiment went on campaign with its first and third battalions, which fought side-by-side. An infantry brigade usually therefore contained two regiments of four battalions. At full strength at the beginning of a war it should in principle be almost 3,000 strong. A Russian infantry division should therefore have 6,000 infantry of the line and 3,000 light infantry, though in reality sickness and the many men absent in detachments meant that no formation ever actually reached these numbers. A Russian division also usually contained three twelve-gun artillery batteries. Two of these batteries were designated as 'light' and most of their guns were six-pounders. The other was a heavy battery, with twelve-pounder cannon. Both heavy and light batteries included a section of howitzers, designed to shoot at high angles.

A small number of Cossack and regular light cavalry regiments were attached to infantry corps. Most of the light cavalry, however, was formed into separate mounted formations. Confusingly, these were called 'Reserve Cavalry Corps' though in fact they were neither reserves nor corps. The three so-called 'Reserve Cavalry Corps' of First Army were each roughly 3,000 strong, and contained anything from four to six regiments of dragoons, hussars and lancers, and one battery of horse artillery. Fedor Uvarov commanded the first of these cavalry corps. The Second Cavalry Corps was commanded by Baron Friedrich von Korff and the Third by Major-General Count Peter von der Pahlen, the son and namesake of the man who had led the conspiracy which overthrew and murdered Alexander I's father in 1801. His ancestry does not seem to have damaged greatly the career of the younger Pahlen, who was to prove himself an exceptionally able cavalry commander in 1812–14.

First Army's actual reserves stood behind the front line in the vicinity of Vilna. They were the Grand Duke Constantine's Fifth Corps, made up of nineteen battalions of Guards infantry and seven battalions of Grenadiers. To them were attached the four heavy cavalry regiments of First Cuirassier Division, which included the Chevaliers Gardes and the Horse Guards. The Grand Duke Constantine also commanded five artillery batteries, though in addition three heavy batteries formed the overall army reserve.[2]

With very few exceptions the men and horses of First Army were in excellent shape when the war began in June 1812. They had been well fed and well quartered for many weeks, unlike the often already hungry and exhausted men of Napoleon's army who had been marching across Europe and finding it increasingly hard to feed themselves as they packed into their cramped quarters in the Prussian and Polish border areas. As one might have predicted, the main problems in the Russian army concerned not the soldiers and their regiments but the staffs and the high command.

Barclay's first chief of staff was Lieutenant-General Aleksandr Lavrov. His first quartermaster-general was Major-General Semen Mukhin.

Their inadequacy for senior staff positions was quickly revealed once the war began. Mukhin lasted seventeen days into the campaign, Lavrov just nine. He was succeeded by Lieutenant-General Marquis Philippe Paulucci, who was hanging around in Alexander's suite and whom the emperor offered to Barclay on a take-him-or-leave-him basis. Paulucci had previously served in the Piedmontese, Austrian and French armies. He was one of a number of individuals scooped into Russian service as a result of Russia's campaigns in the Adriatic and Mediterranean in 1798–1807. Paulucci described himself in a letter to Alexander as possessing a 'lively and impetuous' character which must not be restrained since it boiled over with zeal for the emperor's cause. Certainly Paulucci possessed a very lively egoism and a bad habit of insinuating that anyone who disagreed with him was an idiot or a traitor. For all Paulucci's brains and energy, Russia had quite enough generals of this temper already without needing the services of a Piedmontese *enfant terrible*. Barclay trusted neither Paulucci's competence nor his loyalty and immediately sidelined him. Paulucci promptly resigned. In early July Colonel Karl von Toll became First Army's acting quartermaster-general. Paulucci was replaced as chief of staff by Major-General Aleksei Ermolov. Now the right men were in their correct posts. Both Toll and Ermolov were formidable soldiers who would play crucial roles in the campaigns of 1812–14.[3]

Though Karl von Toll's family was ultimately of Dutch origin, it had long since settled in Estland and become part of the Baltic German minor gentry. Both Toll's parents were Germans, and he himself remained a Lutheran all his life. In 1814 he married a Baltic German noblewoman. Although this appears to make him a thoroughgoing Balt, in reality matters were more complicated. For many years of his adolescence he attended a cadet corps in St Petersburg. The school's director at that time was the later Field-Marshal Mikhail Kutuzov, who always regarded Toll not just as a brilliant officer but also almost as an adopted son. On leaving the cadet corps Toll served all his career in the quartermaster-general's section of the emperor's suite, in other words the general staff. Here his great patron came to be Prince Petr Mikhailovich Volkonsky. An officer whose two key patrons were leading members of the Russian aristocracy was by definition likely to be seen as an honorary Russian. According to one contemporary, Toll was very careful to portray himself in these terms, always speaking Russian whenever possible, though this did not stop him using his position to find jobs for his German relatives. In doing this he followed the universal custom of the time, which saw such behaviour not as nepotism but as praiseworthy loyalty to family and friends – unless of course the patron happened to be a German and the job was one on which one had set one's own hopes.

A cynic might remark that with patrons as powerful as Kutuzov and Volkonsky Karl von Toll could hardly fail, but this would be unfair. He earned their patronage by his intelligence, efficiency and hard work, as well as by his loyalty. His main problem was his proud, impatient and passionate temperament. His temper was notorious and he found it very difficult to tolerate opposition or criticism, including from superior officers. On a number of occasions in 1812 this almost ruined his career. After a ferocious argument in August with the equally explosive Bagration, Toll was demoted, only to be rescued by the arrival of his old patron Kutuzov as commander-in-chief. Although Toll could be an infuriating colleague, let alone subordinate, he was neither petty nor vindictive. He was deeply committed to the army and to Russia's victory over Napoleon. His outbursts of fury and impatience were usually directed not by personal ambitions and slights but against anything which he saw as impeding the efficient prosecution of the war.[4]

As quartermaster-general of First Army Toll's immediate boss was Aleksei Ermolov. An extremely courageous and inspiring front-line commander, Ermolov did not have the trained staff officer's meticulous attention to detail and careful recording of all orders on paper. At times in 1812 this caused problems. Trained as an artillery officer, Ermolov had done brilliantly in the East Prussian campaign of 1807. Together with a number of other young artillerists – of whom Count Aleksandr Kutaisov, Prince Lev Iashvili and Ivan Sukhozhanet were the most famous – he had done much to restore the reputation of the Russian artillery after the humiliation it had suffered at Austerlitz. Subsequently, however, Ermolov contributed to deepening the factional cleavages in the artillery's officer corps. According to his great admirer and former aide-de-camp, Paul Grabbe, Ermolov not only loathed Arakcheev and Lev Iashvili with particular virulence, but also infected everyone around him with equally black-and-white feelings, which did not benefit either the artillery's efficient management or the careers of Ermolov's own clients.[5]

Aleksei Ermolov was not just a thoroughly skilful and professional artillerist but also an exceptionally intelligent and resolute commander. Above all, he had great charisma. His appearance helped. A big man with a huge head, wide shoulders and a mane of hair, he struck one young officer on first acquaintance as a 'true Hercules'. First impressions were reinforced by the friendly and informal way he treated his subordinates. Ermolov was a master of the memorable phrase or action. When his mare foaled on the eve of the 1812 campaign he had the newborn animal cooked and fed to his young officers, as a warning of what they would have to put up with during the forthcoming campaign. With the possible exception of Kutuzov, no other Russian senior general so caught the imagination of younger officers at the time or of subsequent nationalist legend.[6]

Ermolov owed his appeal not just to his charisma but also to his opinions. Coming from a well-off family of the provincial gentry and well educated in Moscow, he was never closely associated with Petersburg or the imperial court. He shared the conviction of most of his class that Russian soldiers were best commanded by gentlemen and that promotion from the ranks was at best an undesirable wartime necessity. In Ermolov's day, however, Germans were far more serious rivals to Russian nobles than commoners promoted from the ranks, and Ermolov was famous and popular for his witticisms at their expense. This made him an uncomfortable bedfellow for Barclay de Tolly and a ferocious enemy of Barclay's German aides. Two of the latter, Ludwig von Wolzogen and Vladimir von Löwenstern, wrote memoirs in which they chronicled Ermolov's ruthless intrigues against them.[7]

More importantly, Ermolov was at the heart of the opposition to Barclay's strategy in July and August 1812. Alexander had invited the chiefs of staff of both Bagration and Barclay to write to him directly. Though initially Bagration was very suspicious of his chief of staff as a result, in fact Emmanuel de Saint-Priest's letters to the emperor strongly supported his commander. Ermolov on the contrary used his direct line to Alexander to undermine Barclay. To do him justice, he acted in this way out of a genuine – albeit misguided – conviction, shared by almost all the senior generals, that Barclay's strategy was endangering the army and the state.[8]

Though in the short run Alexander used Ermolov and valued his military skill, it is very unlikely that he ever trusted him. On one occasion he called him 'black as the devil but armed with as many skills'. With his charisma, his Russian patriotic credentials and his many admirers in the officer corps Ermolov was the perfect focus for gentry feeling against the court. On 30 July 1812, as indignation against Barclay reached its height, Ermolov wrote to Bagration that the army commanders would need to account for their actions not just to the emperor but also to the Russian fatherland. To a Romanov autocrat this was very dangerous language. Not coincidentally, when young Russian officers attempted to overthrow the absolute monarchy in December 1825 it was widely believed that Aleksei Ermolov was a source of inspiration and even possible future leadership.[9]

A quieter presence at headquarters but also a formidable one was the First Army's intendant-general, Georg Kankrin. Aged 38 when the war began, Kankrin was a native of the small town of Hanau in Hesse. His father had been lured to Russia, partly by the high salary offered for his skills as an expert in technology and mining, and partly because his sharp tongue had ruined his prospects in Germany. After a German youth which included first-rate university studies and writing a romantic novel, young Georg Kankrin found it very difficult to adapt to life in Russia. He hibernated for a number of years, too poor to buy tobacco and forced to mend his own boots in order to save money. Eventually, his writings on military administration brought him to the attention of Barclay de Tolly and won him a key position in the war ministry's victualling department, where he proved a great success. As a result, Barclay brought Kankrin with him when appointed to command First Army. During the next two years Kankrin overcame the immense challenge of feeding and equipping Russia's armies as they marched first across the empire and then through Germany and France. He proved extremely efficient and hard-working, as well as honest and intelligent. On the strength of his achievement in 1812–14 he subsequently served for twenty-one years as minister of finance.[10]

Between 26 April when he arrived in Vilna and 19 July when he departed for Moscow Alexander lived alongside Barclay de Tolly near First Army headquarters. A curious duumvirate ran Russian strategy and even to some extent tactics. In some ways Barclay benefited from this. He and the emperor shared the view that strategic withdrawal was essential but could not be too openly advocated for fear of undermining morale and alienating public opinion. They believed that Russians, both inside and outside the army, had become inured to easy victories over inferior opponents and were unrealistic about what it meant to face Napoleon's immense power. Through Alexander, Barclay could exercise a degree of control over Tormasov and Bagration. Since he was positioned with First Army the emperor naturally tended to view operations from its perspective. In addition, though Alexander had no great opinion of any of his leading generals, he trusted Barclay's strategic insight and military skill much more than he did Tormasov, let alone Bagration. Almost certainly Bagration had been the lover of Alexander's sister, the Grand Duchess Catherine. To her the emperor wrote in 1812 that Bagration had always totally lacked any skill or indeed conception when it came to strategy.[11]

If Alexander's presence allowed Barclay some influence over Second and Third armies, the price he paid was the emperor's interference in the affairs of his own First Army. First Army's corps commanders sent reports in duplicate to Alexander and Barclay. At the beginning of the campaign they sometimes received orders from both men, too. Eight days after the war began Lieutenant-General Karl Baggohufvudt, the huge and jovial commander of Second Corps, wrote to Barclay that 'I just received your orders of June 18th: since they are in contradiction with His Majesty's orders what are we to do?' On 30 June Barclay wrote to the emperor that he was unable to give instructions to Count Peter Wittgenstein, who commanded First Corps on the army's vulnerable right flank, 'because I don't know what planned deployment Your Imperial Majesty intends for the future'. When Lieutenant-General Count Shuvalov, the commander of Fourth Corps, suddenly fell ill Alexander replaced him on 1 July with Count Aleksandr Ostermann-Tolstoy, claiming that there was no time to consult Barclay on this appointment.[12]

This degree of confusion was obviously dangerous and Alexander subsequently usually refrained from undermining Barclay's control over his subordinates. The fact that both the emperor and Barclay had agreed on an initial retreat to the camp at Drissa also helped to reduce misunderstanding. Nevertheless tensions remained, not least because Alexander had been accompanied to Vilna by a gaggle of underemployed senior generals, courtiers and relatives who attempted to press their own ideas about how best to combat Napoleon on both the emperor and Barclay.

Among this gaggle the most competent but also in the long run probably the most destructive person was Levin von Bennigsen. Since

Tilsit Bennigsen had been living in retirement and semi-disgrace on his estate at Zakrent very close to Vilna. When Alexander arrived in Vilna in April 1812 he invited the general back into his suite. In some ways bringing Bennigsen back into active service made sense and was part of Alexander's policy of mobilizing all resources and all talents at this time of extreme emergency.

Bennigsen was undoubtedly a talented soldier. In the eyes of some observers he was indeed the most skilful tactician among the senior Russian generals. On the other hand, he was a born intriguer and a man of great pride and ambition. He himself confessed in his memoirs to 'ambition and a certain pride which cannot, indeed ought not, ever to be absent from a soldier'. He also admitted that this pride made him 'feel repugnance at the thought of serving in a subordinate position having once been commander-in-chief against Napoleon'. He did not forget that Barclay had once upon a time been a mere major-general in his army. He was also much inclined to remind people that in 1806–7 he had held his ground for six months against Napoleon though out-numbered two to one. In the early stages of the campaign Bennigsen was merely a minor nuisance. In time, however, he was to contribute greatly to the conflicts and jealousies that wracked the Russian high command.[13]

When news arrived in Vilna late on 24 June that Napoleon's advance guard had crossed the Russian border earlier that day Alexander was actually attending a ball in Bennigsen's country house at Zakrent. The roof of a temporary ballroom erected for the occasion had collapsed and the guests danced beneath the stars. The emperor was not surprised by the timing of the invasion or by the place where Napoleon had chosen to cross the river Neman and enter the Russian Empire. Russian intelligence and French deserters had given ample warning of the attack in the previous two days. Russian intelligence also had an accurate sense of enemy numbers. Alexander and Barclay had long since agreed on the need for a strategic withdrawal to the camp at Drissa in the face of this overwhelming enemy force. Orders went out immediately to the Russian commanders to execute this planned move. Manifestos had already been printed in advance to prepare both the army and Alexander's subjects for the forthcoming struggle.

In the two weeks between the French invasion and First Army's arrival in Drissa most of Barclay's units retreated in good order and without significant losses. From the perspective of the high command, things mostly went according to plan. As is always true in war, matters did not look so orderly and well managed to the officers and men at ground level. Though most stores were carried away or burned, inevitably some fell into enemy hands, though not remotely enough to satisfy the enormous demands of Napoleon's horses and men. Barclay's attempt to requisition local carts for his army's 'mobile food magazine' was delayed by the foot-dragging of local – often Polish – officials and many of these carts were lost to Napoleon.[14]

For troops who had been in quarters for weeks the sudden need for forced marches could be quite a shock. Even the Guards, which had least far to march, suffered initially. On 30 June Captain Pavel Pushchin of the Semenovskys wrote in his diary that they had broken camp and marched for eleven hours in pouring rain. As a result, forty of the regiment's Guardsmen had fallen ill and one had died. Further long marches followed amidst intermittent downpours and extreme heat. To Pushchin's great indignation three Polish soldiers in his company deserted. Especially in the lancer regiments, mostly recruited from Poles, desertion rates were far higher than this. The basic point, however, is that, in comparison to the devastating losses of horses and men in Napoleon's ranks during these days, the losses on the Russian side were pinpricks.[15]

Of Barclay's units the ones most at risk in these first two weeks stood on his left flank where they were in danger of being cut off from the rest of First Army by Napoleon's advance. The biggest single error made by the Russian high command in the war's first days was Fourth Corps's failure quickly to notify its advance guard deployed close to the river Neman that the French had crossed the river to their north. As a result, the 4,000 men commanded by Major-General Ivan Dorokhov were very nearly overwhelmed and only escaped by marching southward to join up with Bagration's Second Army.

Dorokhov's detachment comprised one hussar, two Cossack and two jaeger regiments, including the excellent 1st Jaegers. An officer of this regiment, Major Mikhail Petrov, wrote in his memoirs that the 1st Jaegers only escaped by dint of uninterrupted days and nights of forced marches which left some men dead and others near senseless from exhaustion. Petrov recalled that the officers dismounted, piled the men's equipment on their horses and helped to carry the muskets of their soldiers. For the first but by no means the last time in the campaigns of 1812–14 Russian light infantry displayed phenomenal endurance as they kept up with light cavalry and horse artillery while serving in advance and rearguards.[16]

Lieutenant-General Dmitrii Dokhturov's Sixth Corps was much larger than Dorokhov's detachment and therefore less likely to be over-whelmed. Nevertheless Dokhturov did well by not just avoiding Napoleon's clutches but also cutting across the advancing French army and rejoining First Army before Drissa. Among Dokhturov's officers was young Nikolai Mitarevsky, an artillery lieutenant in the Twelfth Light Battery. He recalled that on the eve of the war it had never occurred to any of the officers that they would retreat. All expected to advance in time-honoured style to meet the invader and when this did not happen rumours quickly spread about the unstoppable strength of Napoleon's army.

Mitarevsky's battery had long been posted far in the Russian interior and it took officers and men some time to learn how to survive on campaign. Initially they went hungry when their transport carts temporarily vanished but they quickly learned to carry enough food to last men and horses festooned on their guns and caissons. Though the horses had to eat grass for part of the two-week retreat this was a small hardship since they began the campaign in fine condition and the battery was equipped with sickles to cut the long grass. Most of the population had fled into the forests but Sixth Corps had little difficulty in either finding sufficient food to requisition or ensuring that nothing was left for the French.

Though rumours abounded that the enemy was nearby, the closest Mitarevsky's battery came to action was when a large herd of cattle in a forest was mistaken for French cavalry. The worst actual enemy assault on the column came when the Poles captured two straggling regimental priests, tied their beards together, fed them an emetic, and returned them to Dokhturov's furious soldiers, for whom Orthodoxy and suspicion of Poles were much of what it meant to be a Russian. Sixth Corps eluded the French partly by dint of hard marching. In addition, however, it was expertly shielded and shepherded by Peter von der Pahlen's cavalry.[17]

In a retreat of this sort a strong cavalry arm was essential. Barclay was weakened by the fact that Napoleon's advance had cut off General Matvei Platov's independent Cossack detachment from First Army and forced it to move southwards to join up with Bagration. Platov's force was made up of nine Cossack regiments, all but two of them from the Don region. It also included four 'native' regiments of irregular cavalry, of which two were Crimean Tatar, one was Kalmyk and one was Bashkir.

No one needed to fear for the safety of Platov's regiments. Napoleon's whole army could have chased these Cossacks all year without the least chance of catching them. But the temporary loss of almost all its irregular cavalry put Barclay's regular cavalry regiments under some strain. Fedor Uvarov reported that in the absence of the Cossacks he had been forced to use regular line and even Guards cavalry regiments for outpost duty. Not merely did this exhaust their horses, it also involved them in work for which they had often not been fully trained. One result of this was that Uvarov could not harass the enemy or pick up anything like the normal number of prisoners, who were important as a source of intelligence about the enemy's size and movements.[18]

Even without the Cossacks, however, the Russian cavalry usually came out on top in its skirmishes with the French. The French cavalry had very little success in impeding or embarrassing Barclay's men in their planned retreat to Drissa. In other ways, too, the Russian high command had reason to be satisfied. Napoleon had yearned for a decisive battle in the first days of the war. His overriding strategic purpose was not the conquest of territory but the destruction of the Russian army. Correctly, he believed that if he could annihilate the armies of Barclay and Bagration in a second Austerlitz then Alexander would have little option but to make peace on French terms. The Russians had encouraged his hopes of an early decisive battle by 'turning' a key French agent in Lithuania and passing disinformation through him that they intended to fight for Vilna. Caulaincourt recalls that 'Napoleon was amazed that they had yielded Vilna without a struggle, and had taken their decision in time to escape him. It was truly heartbreaking for him to have to give up all hope of a great battle before Vilna.'[19]

The Russian high command also learned quickly that Napoleon's army was paying a heavy price for his determination to press the retreating enemy and force it to battle. Many of Napoleon's men and, more importantly, his horses had been poorly fed in the weeks before the invasion. In all circumstances his huge army, concentrated in anticipation of an early decisive battle, would have found it impossible to feed itself adequately in impoverished Lithuania. Speeding forward in an attempt to force Barclay to battle across terrain eaten out and scorched by the Russians made matters worse. Torrential rain completed a picture of misery. After only two weeks of campaigning Napoleon wrote to his war minister in Paris that there was no point trying to raise new cavalry regiments since all the horses available in France and Germany would barely suffice to remount his existing cavalry and make up for the enormous losses he had already suffered in Russia. Deserters and prisoners of war informed the Russians of hunger and disease in the French ranks, and above all of the devastating loss of horses. So too did the military intelligence officers who were sent on supposedly diplomatic missions to French headquarters under flag of truce.[20]

Much the best-known mission was General Balashev's visit to Napoleon's headquarters immediately after the war's outbreak carrying a letter to the French emperor from Alexander. Balashev left Vilna on 26 June shortly before its evacuation by the Russians and found himself back in the city, now occupied by the French, four days later. On 31 June he met Napoleon in the very room where Alexander had given him his instructions only five days before. Part of this mission's purpose was to put the French clearly in the wrong before European public opinion by showing Alexander's commitment to peace despite Napoleon's aggression. Less well known is that Balashev was accompanied by a young intelligence officer, Mikhail Orlov, who kept his eyes and ears open during the days he spent behind the French lines. When Orlov returned to Russian headquarters, Alexander spent an hour with him alone and was so pleased by the information he received about enemy movements and losses that he promoted Orlov and made him his own aide-de-camp on the spot. Few lieutenants, to put it mildly, could expect such attention from their sovereign, which illustrates the importance Alexander attached to the information Orlov provided.[21]

Paul Grabbe, formerly the Russian military attaché in Munich, was dispatched on a similar mission, ostensibly in response to an enquiry by Marshal Berthier as to the whereabouts of General Lauriston, Napoleon's ambassador to Alexander. Penetrating well behind the French front lines, Grabbe was able to confirm the 'carelessness' and 'disorder' which reigned amongst the French cavalry, reporting that the 'exhausted' horses were being left without any care. Partly from his own eyes and partly through conversations, he was also able to inform Barclay that the French had no intention of attacking the camp at Drissa and were in fact advancing well to its south.[22]

The information provided by Grabbe confirmed all Barclay's doubts about the strategic value of the camp at Drissa. Already on 7 July he had written to Alexander that the army was retreating towards Drissa with excessive and unnecessary speed. This was having a bad effect on the troops' morale and was causing them to believe that the situation was much more dangerous than was actually the case. Two days later, when the first units of Barclay's army were arriving at the camp, Barclay wrote to the emperor that Grabbe's information provided clear evidence that Napoleon's main forces were advancing well to the south of Drissa, splitting First and Second armies and pushing towards the Russian heartland: 'It seems clear to me that the enemy will not attempt any attack against us in our camp at Drissa and we will have to go and find him.'[23]

When Alexander and his senior generals arrived in Drissa the camp's uselessness quickly became evident. If First Army sat in Drissa Napoleon could turn almost all his army against Bagration, perhaps annihilating him and certainly driving him far to the south and away from the key theatre of operations. The gateway to Moscow would then be wide open, with First Army far off to the north-west. Still worse, Napoleon might himself move northwards into the rear of Drissa, cutting the Russian communications, encircling the camp and virtually ending the war by forcing First Army's surrender.

In addition to these strategic dangers, the camp was also shown to have many tactical weaknesses. Above all, it could easily be surrounded or even taken from the rear. Alexander, Barclay and even Pfühl were seeing Drissa for the first time. Even Wolzogen, who chose the spot, had only spent thirty-six hours in Drissa. As the Russian engineering corps was quick to point out, none of their officers had played any part either in choosing the camp or in planning and building its fortifications. They had been too overstretched trying to get the fortresses of Riga, Dünaburg, Bobruisk and Kiev ready for war.[24]

Faced with a storm of objections from almost all his chief military advisers, Alexander agreed that the army must abandon Drissa and retreat eastwards to reach Vitebsk before Napoleon. There is no record of the emperor's innermost thoughts when he made this decision. Whatever may have been his doubts about the camp, he was undoubtedly very unhappy that the whole line of defence along the river Dvina was being abandoned within three weeks of the war's start, threatening all efforts to organize reserve armies or a second line of defence in the rear in good time.[25]

On 17 July First Army abandoned Drissa and retreated towards Vitebsk, hoping to reach this city before Napoleon. Two days later Alexander departed for Moscow. The emperor had been urged to take this step in a joint letter signed by three of his most senior advisers, Aleksei Arakcheev, Aleksandr Balashev and Aleksandr Shishkov. Above all, they argued that Alexander's presence in the two capitals was essential in order to inspire Russian society and mobilize all its resources for war. Before leaving the army the emperor had a one-hour conversation with Barclay. His last words to his commander before he departed were overheard by Vladimir Löwenstern, Barclay's aide-de-camp: 'I entrust my army to you. Don't forget that it is the only army I have. Keep this thought always in mind.' Two days earlier Alexander had written in similar fashion to Bagration:

Don't forget that we are still opposed by superior numbers at every point and for this reason we need to be cautious and not deprive ourselves of the means to carry on an effective campaign by risking all on one day. Our entire goal must be directed towards gaining time and drawing out the war as long as possible. Only by this means can we have the chance of defeating so strong an enemy who has mobilised the military resources of all Europe.[26]

Bagration was much more in need of such advice than Barclay. His system of war is well summed up in a number of his letters and circulars from the summer of 1812. 'Russians ought not to run away,' he wrote; 'we are becoming worse than the Prussians.' He urged his officers 'to instil into our soldiers that the enemy's troops are nothing more than scum drawn from every corner of the earth, whereas we are Russians and Christian believers (*edinovernye*). They don't know how to fight bravely and above all they fear our bayonets. So we must attack them.' To be sure, this was propaganda designed to raise morale, but even in private Bagration stressed aggression, moral superiority and offensive spirit. At the beginning of the war he urged Alexander to allow him to launch his army on a diversionary raid towards Warsaw, which in Bagration's view would be the most effective way of drawing French troops away from First Army. He conceded that in the end superior enemy forces would concentrate against him and force him to withdraw, and planned then to move southwards to link up with Tormasov's Third Army and defend the approaches to Volhynia.[27]

Correctly, Alexander dismissed this proposal, which would have given Napoleon a golden opportunity to surround and destroy Second Army and which even in the most optimistic scenario would have resulted in Bagration's force moving far to the south and away from the decisive theatre. Instead the emperor urged on Bagration his own strategy: while First Army retreated in the face of superior numbers, Second Army and Platov's Cossacks must harass Napoleon's flanks and rear.

In pressing this strategy Alexander was sticking to the basic principles which had guided Barclay's thinking from early 1810 and which in the end were to bring victory in 1812. Whichever Russian army was threatened by Napoleon's main body must withdraw and refuse battle, while the other Russian armies must strike into the ever-lengthening enemy flanks and rear. But this strategy was only fully realizable by the autumn of 1812 when Napoleon's armies had been hugely depleted and their immensely long flanks were vulnerable to the Russian armies brought in from Finland and the Balkans. Launching Bagration into the flank of Napoleon's main body in June 1812 was almost as sure a recipe for disaster as allowing him to mount a diversion into the Duchy of Warsaw.

In time sense prevailed and Bagration was ordered to retreat and to attempt to join up with First Army. By then, however, precious time had been wasted and Davout's advancing columns were cutting across Bagration's route to join Barclay. In these first weeks of the war Barclay's First Army executed a planned and for most units safe withdrawal to Drissa. By contrast, the movements of Bagration's Second Army had to be improvised and were more dangerous. For the next six weeks the Russians' main aim was to unite their two main armies. Napoleon's key goal was to stop them from doing so, to force Bagration southwards and, if possible, to crush Second Army between Davout's corps to the north and Jérôme Bonaparte's forces advancing from the west.

In the end the Russians won this competition. Jérôme's troops, mostly Westphalians, had been held back well behind Napoleon's first echelon, partly in the hope that Bagration would advance to attack them and thrust his head into a sack. Even after Bagration wasted a number of days before retreating, Jérôme still had ground to make up if he was to catch them. The Russians were on the whole superior troops and quicker on the march than Jérôme's Westphalians. They were marching towards their own supply magazines and across still unravaged countryside. By contrast, Jérôme's soldiers were advancing away from their supplies and into a region which the Russians had already stripped.

In addition, Jérôme was up against the formidable cavalry of Bagration's rearguard. When Napoleon's advance forced Platov to escape to the south-east he joined up with Second Army. On three successive days between 8 and 10 July near the village of Mir Platov ambushed and routed Jérôme's advancing cavalry. The biggest victory came on the last day, when six regiments of Polish lancers were destroyed by a combination of Platov's Cossacks and Major-General Ilarion Vasil-chikov's regular cavalry. This was the first time in the war that the French had encountered the full force of combined Russian regular and irregular light cavalry. It was also the first time they met Vasilchikov, one of the best Russian light cavalry generals. The superiority of the Russian light cavalry, established at the start of the 1812 campaign, was to grow ever more pronounced over the next two years of war. The Russian victory at Mir ensured that henceforth Jérôme's advance guard kept a healthy distance behind Bagration.

Davout's corps proved a tougher nut. They blocked Bagration's efforts to push his way through to First Army via Minsk, forcing him to make a big detour to the south-east. At Saltanovka on 23 July Davout's men defeated another attempt by Bagration to link up with Barclay, this time via Mogilev. Only on 3 August, having crossed the Dnieper, did Second Army finally join First Army near Smolensk. For the whole of July both Barclay and Bagration had been attempting to bring their two armies together. Each blamed the other for their failure to do so. In retrospect, however, it is possible to see that not merely was the failure to unite neither general's fault, it also worked out to the Russians' advantage.

This was partly because the attempt to cut off Bagration exhausted and depleted Napoleon's army much more than the retreating Russians. Even by the time Davout reached Mogilev the result of hastening forward to catch Bagration through a ravaged countryside had cost him 30,000 of the 100,000 men with whom he had crossed the Neman. After Mogilev he gave up his attempt to pursue Second Army for fear of wrecking his corps. In addition, the fact that the Russian armies were split provided Barclay with a perfect reason to retreat and not to risk facing Napoleon in a pitched battle. Had the two armies been joined and the charismatic and very popular Bagration been on hand to lead the call to battle this would have been far more difficult. If the two Russian armies had fought Napoleon in early July the odds would have been worse than two to one. By early August they were closer to three to two. In that sense the strategy planned by Barclay and Alexander to wear down Napoleon had proved a triumphant success. But there was an element of good fortune in their ability to pursue this strategy as long as they did.

After abandoning Drissa and bidding farewell to Alexander, Barclay de Tolly was in fact planning to make a stand in front of Vitebsk. Partly this was to sustain his troops' morale. When the army had reached Drissa the soldiers had been served up a bombastic proclamation promising that the time for retreating was over and that Russian courage would bury Napoleon and his army on the banks of the Dvina. When a few days later the retreat was renewed there was inevitable muttering. Ivan Radozhitsky, a young artillery officer in Fourth Corps, overheard grumbling among his gunners at the 'unheard-of' retreat of Russian troops and the abandonment of huge swaths of the empire without a fight. 'Obviously the villain [i.e. Napoleon] must be very strong: just look at how much we are giving him for free, almost the whole of old Poland.'[28]

Barclay's main reason for risking a battle at Vitebsk, however, was to distract Napoleon's attention and allow Bagration to advance through Mogilev and unite with First Army. Barclay's troops arrived at Vitebsk on 23 July. To gain time for them to gather their breath and for Bagration to arrive he detached Count Aleksandr Ostermann-Tolstoy's Fourth Corps down the main road leading into Vitebsk from the west in order to slow down Napoleon's advancing columns. On 25 July at Ostrovno, roughly 20 kilometres from Vitebsk, there occurred the first major clash between Napoleon's forces and First Army.

Aleksandr Ostermann-Tolstoy was immensely wealthy and had some of the eccentricities worthy of a Russian magnate of this era. Despite his name, he was a purely Russian type: adding the prefix 'Ostermann' to his own proud surname of Tolstoy had been an unwilling concession to rich bachelor uncles who had left him their great fortunes. Ostermann-Tolstoy was a handsome man, thin-faced and with an eagle's nose. He looked the pensive, Romantic hero. On his estate in Kaluga province Tolstoy lived with a pet bear decked out in fantastic dress. More modest when on campaign, he nevertheless liked when possible to be accompanied by his pet eagle and his white crow. In some ways Ostermann-Tolstoy was an admirable man. He was a great patriot, who had loathed what he saw as Russia's humiliation at Tilsit. Well educated, fluent in French and German and a lover of Russian literature, he was enormously and inspiringly brave, even by the very high standard of the Russian army. He was also careful of his men's food, health and welfare. He shared their love for buckwheat *kasha* and was physically as tough as the toughest of his veteran grenadiers. Ostermann-Tolstoy was in fact an inspiring colonel of a regiment and an acceptable commander of a division so long as he was operating under the noses of more senior generals. But he was not a man one could safely trust with a larger detached force.[29]

Fourth Corps fought the battle at Ostrovno in a manner that rather reflected Ostermann-Tolstoy's character, though to be fair it also reflected the inexperience of many of its units and the Russian soldiers' longing finally to get to grips with the enemy. Barclay sent forward his aide-de-camp, Vladimir Löwenstern, to keep an eye on Ostermann-Tolstoy. Subsequently Löwenstern recalled that the corps commander showed exceptional courage but also exposed his troops to unnecessary losses. The same point was made by Gavril Meshetich, a young artillery officer serving in the Second Heavy Battery of Fourth Corps.

According to Meshetich, Ostermann-Tolstoy failed to take proper precautions despite the fact that he had been warned that the French were nearby. As a result his advance guard was ambushed and lost six guns. Subsequently he did not use the cover available on either side of the main road to shelter his infantry from enemy artillery fire. He also attempted to drive back enemy skirmishers with a massed bayonet charge, a tactic much used by the Russians in 1805 and which generally proved both costly and ineffective. Ostermann-Tolstoy could not, however, be blamed for the small-scale debacle which occurred on his left flank where the Ingermanland Dragoon Regiment had been posted in a wood to keep an eye on the French. At last given the opportunity to have a go at the enemy, the Russian dragoons stormed out of the forest, smashed through the nearest enemy cavalry and were then overwhelmed by superior French numbers, losing 30 per cent of their men. One result of these losses was that the regiment was kept out of the front line and relegated to military police duties for much of the rest of 1812. To fill the shoes of the officers lost at Ostrovno, five non-noble NCOs were promoted, one of the earliest examples of what was to become a common occurrence in 1812–14.[30]

It would be wrong just to dwell on Russian failings at Ostrovno, however. Fourth Corps fulfilled its task by delaying the French and inflicting heavy casualties despite facing increasingly superior numbers. Though not very skilful, Ostermann-Tolstoy was nevertheless an inspiring commander. Ostrovno was young Ivan Radozhitsky's first battle, as was true for very many of Fourth Corps's soldiers. He recalled scenes of growing desolation and potential panic as enemy pressure mounted and men's bodies were eviscerated and torn limb from limb by French cannon balls. In the thick of the fire Ostermann-Tolstoy sat unmoved on his horse, sniffing his tobacco. To messengers of doom requesting permission to retreat or warning that more and more Russian guns were being put out of action, Ostermann-Tolstoy responded by his own example of calm and by orders to 'stand and die'. Radozhitsky commented that 'this unshakeable strength of our commander at a time when everyone around him was being struck down was truly part of the character of a Russian infuriated by the sufferings being inflicted on his country. Looking at him, we ourselves grew strong and went to our posts to die.'[31]

That evening Fourth Corps retired 7 kilometres towards Kakuviachino where responsibility for delaying the French was handed over to Lieutenant-General Petr Konovnitsyn, the commander of 3rd Infantry Division. Konovnitsyn was as courageous as Ostermann-Tolstoy but a much more skilful rearguard commander. His men kept the French at bay for most of 26 July. That night, however, Bagration's aide-de-camp, Prince Aleksandr Menshikov, arrived at Barclay's headquarters with news that transformed the situation. At Saltanovka on 23 July Davout had blocked Bagration's attempts to march northwards via Mogilev to join up with Barclay. As a result, Second Army was being forced to march still further eastwards and there was no chance of any link-up between the two Russian armies in the immediate future.

Even after receiving this news Barclay still wanted to fight at Vitebsk but he was dissuaded by Ermolov and the other senior generals. As Barclay later acknowledged, Ermolov's advice was correct. The position at Vitebsk had its weaknesses and the Russians would have been outnumbered by more than two to one. Moreover, even if they had beaten off Napoleon's attacks for a day this would have served no purpose. In fact it would merely have widened the distance between First and Second armies and allowed Napoleon to push between them and take Smolensk. Orders therefore went out for First Army to retreat. With Napoleon's entire army deployed under the Russians' noses, slipping away unscathed would be no easy matter, however.[32]

First Army's retreat began at four in the afternoon of 27 July. All that day the Russian rearguard commanded by Peter Pahlen kept the French at bay, manoeuvring with skill and calmly giving ground when necessary but mounting a number of sharp counter-attacks to deter any attempt to press too hard. Barclay de Tolly was not at all inclined to excessive praise of subordinates but in his reports to Alexander he stressed Pahlen's great achievement in disengaging First Army from Napoleon and covering its tracks during the retreat from Vitebsk to Smolensk. French sources are more inclined to argue that Napoleon missed a great opportunity on 27 July by taking it for granted that the Russians would stand and fight on the following day and not pressing Pahlen very hard. That night the Cossacks kept all the bonfires burning in the Russian bivouacs, which convinced the French that Barclay was still in position and awaiting battle. When they woke the next morning to discover that the Russians had gone there was much dismay, increased by the fact that Pahlen covered Barclay's tracks with such skill that for a time Napoleon had no idea in which direction his enemy had retreated.[33]

The Duc de Fezensac, who was serving as aide-de-camp to Marshal Berthier, recalls in his memoirs that the wiser and more experienced French officers began to feel uneasy at Vitebsk: 'They were struck by the admirable order in which the Russian army had made its retreat, always covered by its numerous Cossacks, and without abandoning a single cannon, cart or sick man.' The Count de Segur was on Napoleon's staff and recalls an inspection of Barclay's camp on the day after the Russians had departed: 'nothing left behind, not one weapon, nor a single valuable; no trace, nothing in short, in this sudden nocturnal march, which could demonstrate, beyond the bounds of the camp, the route which the Russians had taken; there appeared more order in their defeat than in our victory!'[34]

After abandoning Vitebsk Barclay's army headed for Smolensk. Initially there were fears that the French might get there first and Preradovich's detachment of Guards cavalry and jaegers covered

80 kilometres in thirty-eight hours in order to forestall them. In fact this was something of a false alarm since Napoleon's troops were exhausted and needed a rest. On 2 August Barclay and Bagration met in Smolensk and the two main Russian armies were united at last.

Both generals did their best to put past grievances behind them and act in a united fashion. Barclay went to meet Bagration outside his headquarters in full uniform, hat in hand. He took Bagration round the regiments of First Army, showing him to the soldiers and making great show of the two commanders' unity and friendship. Meanwhile Bagration conceded the overall command to Barclay. Since he was marginally senior, came from the ancient royal family of Georgia and had married into the heart of the Russian aristocracy, by the standards of the time this represented great self-sacrifice. But unity and subordination were always conditional. In the end, as Barclay well understood, Bagration would only go along with his plans if he chose to do so.

In reality, despite goodwill on both sides, unity could not last. The fiery Georgian and the cool and cerebral 'German' were simply too different in temperament and this fed directly into contrasting views on what strategy to adopt. Bagration, supported by almost all the leading generals, was for an immediate, decisive offensive. Quite apart from all the military reasons which inspired them to support this strategy, it is clear from many officers' memoirs that once they reached Smolensk the army became acutely aware that they were now defending Russian national soil.

Luka Simansky, for example, was a lieutenant in the Izmailovsky Guards. In the first weeks of the war his diary shows little emotion and is largely a record of everyday conversations and minor pleasures and frustrations. Only when Simansky gets to the Russian city of Smolensk, views the miracle-working icon of the Mother of God and writes of its saving grace in earlier times of national emergency do strong emotions emerge. For Ivan Paskevich, the commander of the 26th Division in Bagration's army, nature rather than anything man-made provided the first great reminder that this was a 'national' war: 'now we were fighting in old Russia, as every birch-tree standing by the side of the road reminded us'.[35]

In many ways the most cogent justification for Bagration's line was set out in a letter from Ermolov to Alexander. He argued that the armies would find it hard to remain united and static at Smolensk for long.

Since it had never been envisaged that they would concentrate here, few supplies had been gathered and they would be hard pressed to feed themselves. Smolensk was in any case not a strong defensive position. The slightest threat to the army's communications back to Moscow would force a further retreat. Now was the time to strike while Napoleon's army was dispersed. The enemy's inactivity must be caused by weakness, having had to make many detachments to fend off threats from Wittgenstein and Tormasov on the northern and southern flanks.

Ermolov stated that the main obstacle to an offensive was Barclay: 'The commander-in-chief . . . as far as possible will avoid a major battle and will not agree to one unless it is absolutely and unavoidably necessary.' Alexander by now knew from many sources how deeply unpopular Barclay's strategy was among the generals and soldiers alike. An expert at avoiding responsibility for unpopular policies, the emperor cannot have been pleased to read Ermolov's comment that Barclay 'did not hide from me Your Majesty's will in this matter'.[36]

In fact, by the time the two armies had united at Smolensk Alexander's position had changed radically and he himself was putting Barclay under heavy pressure to advance against Napoleon. Probably the emperor was sincere in stating that he had never expected retreat to reach Smolensk before risking a battle but he will also have been aware of the political risks if Barclay continued to retreat without fighting. On 9 August he wrote to the commander-in-chief that 'I now hope that with the help of the Supreme Being you will be able to take the offensive and thereby stop the invasion of our provinces. I have placed the safety of Russia in your hands, general, and I like to hope that you will justify all my confidence in you.' Two days later Alexander repeated his calls for an attack, adding without any apparent sense of irony that 'you are free to act without any impediment or interference'. Under great pressure to attack from his own generals and Bagration, Barclay was in no position to ignore his master also. In any case he was the captive of his own earlier promise to Alexander that he would attack once the armies joined.[37]

Barclay was therefore forced to agree that the army would go over to the offensive but it is clear from both his words and his actions that he had strong doubts about the wisdom of this policy. In part this reflected his fear that Napoleon would take the opportunity to sweep round the flanks of the advancing Russians and cut them off from their communications back to Moscow. The Russian cavalry had lost contact with Napoleon's forces and Barclay would be advancing without a clear idea where the enemy was concentrated or definite knowledge about their numbers. In addition, Barclay had some concerns about the Russian army's own quality when compared to its enemy.

He wrote to Alexander that 'the simple soldier of Your Imperial Majesty's army is without doubt the best in the world' but that this was not true of the officers. In particular, the junior officers were usually too young and inexperienced. This was a little unfair since any criticism of the army's subalterns needed to be qualified by recognition of their great courage, their loyalty to their comrades and regiments, and their impatience to get to grips with the French. Much more solidly based were doubts about the Russian army's high command. Barclay would also have been less than human had he not experienced some fears about facing the greatest commander of the era.[38]

Moreover, it was one thing to take up a strong defensive position and invite Napoleon to attack, as Bennigsen had done successfully at Eylau and the Archduke Charles at Aspern, and as Wellington was to do at Waterloo. It was quite another to attempt to outmanoeuvre Napoleon and defeat him on the offensive. So long as Napoleon was present in person, his authority over his commanders, the power of his reputation, and his exceptional military instincts were likely to give the French victory in such a war. His corps' movements would be better coordinated, opportunities more quickly spotted, and any advantage more ruthlessly exploited. If this was true in all cases, it was doubly so in present circumstances when the Russians were heavily outnumbered and were operating with two independent armies whose commanders had very different perceptions and instincts.

Above all, Barclay remained faithful to the strategy on which he and Alexander had agreed before the war started. It was far easier to express this honestly to outsiders than to his own increasingly hostile and frustrated generals. On 11 August he wrote to Admiral Chichagov, whose Army of the Danube was marching northwards towards Napoleon's rear, that 'the enemy's desire is to finish this war by decisive battles and we on the contrary have to try to avoid such battles because we have no army of any sort in reserve which could sustain us in the event of a defeat. Therefore our main goal must be to gain as much time as possible which will allow our militia and the troops being formed in the interior to be organized and made ready.' Until that happened First and Second armies must not take any risks which might lead to their destruction.

Subsequently Barclay was to justify his strategy in very similar terms to Kutuzov, stating that he had sought to avoid decisive battles because if First and Second armies were destroyed no other forces yet existed in the rear to continue the war. Instead, he had attempted with considerable success 'to stop the enemy's rapid advance only by limited engagements, by which his forces were diminished more and more every day'. As he wrote to Alexander at the end of August, 'had I been guided by a foolish and blind ambition, Your Imperial Majesty would perhaps have received many dispatches telling of battles fought but the enemy would be at the walls of Moscow without it being possible to find any forces to resist him'.[39]

As the Russian official history of the war subsequently recognized, though Barclay was almost in a minority of one at the time, in fact he was right and his opponents were wrong. Among other things, they greatly underestimated the strength of Napoleon's forces and they exaggerated the extent to which they were dispersed. But Barclay's 'offensive', crippled by his doubts, brought him only ridicule at the time. Even his loyal aide-de-camp, Vladimir Löwenstern, wrote that 'it was the first time that I wasn't entirely happy with his performance'.[40]

As agreed with Bagration at the council of war of the previous day, on 7 August Barclay advanced to the north of the river Dnieper towards Rudnia and Vitebsk. But he did so with the proviso that he would not initially go more than three marches from Smolensk. No serious offensive was possible with such equivocation and uncertainty. When Barclay was informed in the night of 8 August that a large enemy force had been discovered to his north at Poreche he immediately believed that this was the outflanking movement he had feared. As a result he shifted his line of march northwards to meet the threat, only to discover that the 'large enemy force' was little more than a figment of his scouts' imagination. Bagration complained that 'mere rumours shouldn't be allowed to alter operations'. Officers and men grumbled as uncertainty reigned and the troops marched and counter-marched.[41]

Moving ahead of Barclay down the road to Rudnia, Platov routed a large force of French cavalry near the village of Molevo-Bolota, capturing General Sebastiani's headquarters and much of his correspondence in the process. When these documents seemed to show that the French had been tipped off about the offensive an ugly wave of xenophobia and spy-mania spread in the Russian army. A number of officers at headquarters who were not ethnic Russians, including even some officers such as Löwenstern who were the emperor's subjects, were escorted to the rear under suspicion of treason. Bagration wrote to Arakcheev: 'I just cannot work with the minister [i.e. Barclay]. For God's sake send me anywhere you like, even to command a regiment in Moldavia or the Caucasus but I just cannot stand it here. The whole of head-quarters is packed with Germans so it is impossible for a Russian to live there.'[42]

While the Russians were dithering and arguing Napoleon struck. He concentrated his army near Rasasna south of the river Dnieper and on 14 August marched on Smolensk via Krasnyi. The only Russian forces in his way were the 7,200 men commanded by Dmitrii Neverovsky, whose core were the regiments of his own 27th Division. These regiments had been formed just before the war, mostly from new recruits and soldiers from the disbanded garrison regiments. Given time and efficient training, most of the recruits and garrison soldiers could be turned into good troops. The big problem was finding good officers to train and lead them. Most of the officers were initially drawn from the former garrison regiments but they quickly proved useless. In the Odessa Regiment, for example, within a few weeks only one of the initial twenty-two former garrison officers was considered fit for front-line service. Desperate measures were sometimes required to find officers. Dmitrii Dushenkovich, for instance, was commissioned as an ensign into the newly formed Simbirsk Regiment aged only 15, after a crash course as a cadet in the Noble Regiment.[43]

Neverovsky's force was buttressed by two experienced regiments of line infantry and included one dragoon regiment, some Cossacks and fourteen guns. Nevertheless it should have been very easy meat for the far larger enemy advance guard under Marshal Murat which it faced on 14 August. In fact Neverovsky lost some guns and possibly as many as 1,400 men, but the bulk of his force escaped, despite between thirty and forty assaults by Murat's cavalry.

Napoleon's secretary, Baron Fain, had the following to say about the affair at Krasnyi:

our cavalry dashes forward, it attacks the Russians in more than forty consecutive charges: many times our squadrons penetrate into the square; ... but the very inexperience of the Russian peasants who make up this body gives them a strength of inertia which takes the place of resistance. The élan of the horsemen is deadened in this mob which packs together, presses against each other, and closes up all its gaps. Ultimately the most brilliant valour is exhausted in striking a compact mass which we chop up but cannot break.[44]

Fighting in what to many of them seemed to be Europe's semi-savage periphery, many of the French have left descriptions of the 1812 campaign that have a ring of cultural arrogance more familiar from European descriptions of colonial warfare. Not surprisingly, Russian descriptions of the battle at Krasnyi are rather different from Fain's account.

Dmitrii Dushenkovich experienced his first battle before his sixteenth birthday. He wrote in his memoirs:

Anyone who has been through the experience of a first hot, dangerous and noisy battle can imagine the feelings of a soldier of my age. Everything seemed incomprehensible to me. I felt that I was alive, saw everything that was going on around me, but simply could not comprehend how this awful, indescribable chaos was going to end. To this day I can still vividly recall Neverovsky riding around the square every time the cavalry approached with his sword drawn and repeating in a voice which seemed to exude confidence in his troops: 'Lads! Remember what you were taught in Moscow. Follow your orders and no cavalry will defeat you. Don't hurry with your volleys. Shoot straight at the enemy and don't anyone dare to start firing before my word of command.'[45]

After retreating over 20 kilometres under intense pressure Neverovsky's men were relieved by Major-General Ivan Paskevich's 26th Division, which Bagration had rushed forward to rescue them. Paskevich wrote that 'on that day our infantry covered itself in glory'. He also recognized Neverovsky's excellent leadership. He pointed out, however, that if Murat had shown minimal professional competence the Russians would never have escaped. It was true that the double line of trees on either side of the highway down which Neverovsky retreated had impeded the French attacks. That was no excuse, however, for complete failure to coordinate the cavalry attacks and use his overwhelming superiority in numbers to slow the Russians' march. It was also elementary tactics that cavalry attacking disciplined infantry in square needed the help of horse artillery. 'To the shame of the French one has to note that though they brought up 19,000 cavalry and a whole division of infantry they only deployed one battery of artillery.' Whether this omission occurred through sheer incompetence or whether Murat wanted all the glory for his horsemen Paskevich could not guess.[46]

Maybe Paskevich was a little unfair. French sources claimed that their artillery had been stopped by a broken bridge. Nor was the fight at Krasnyi in itself very significant. The fate of Neverovsky's 7,000 men would hardly decide the campaign one way or another. Neverovsky's action did not even seriously slow down the French advance. But what happened at Krasnyi was to prove symptomatic. During August 1812, in and around Smolensk, Napoleon was to have a number of opportunities seriously to weaken the Russian army and possibly even to decide the campaign. These chances were lost because of failures in executing his plans, above all by his senior generals.

When he heard of Neverovsky's plight and the threat to Smolensk Bagration ordered Nikolai Raevsky's corps (which included Paskevich's division) back to the city at top speed. By the late afternoon of 15 August when Napoleon's army approached Smolensk, Raevsky and Neverovsky were deployed behind its walls. Even together, however, their force probably only added up to 15,000 men and if Napoleon had pushed hard from dawn on 16 August Smolensk might well have fallen. Instead he delayed throughout that day, allowing both Bagration and Barclay's armies to arrive.

That night First Army took over responsibility for Smolensk's defence, with Second Army moving out to defend the Russian left and the road to Moscow from any French outflanking movement. By the morning of 17 August 30,000 men of Barclay's army were strongly posted in the suburbs and behind the walls of Smolensk. Had Napoleon chosen to dislodge them, at little cost, it was within his power to do so by an outflanking movement, since he well outnumbered the Russians, there were many fords across the Dnieper and any serious threat to their communications back to Moscow would have forced Barclay to abandon the city. Instead he chose a head-on assault, losing heavily in the process.

Ever since 1812 historians have puzzled as to why Napoleon acted in this fashion. The most plausible explanation is that he did not want to dislodge the Russians but rather to destroy their army in a battle for the city. Perhaps he believed that if he gave them the chance to fight for Smolensk they would not dare simply to abandon so famous a Russian city. If so, Napoleon's calculation proved wrong, because after a day's ferocious fighting on 17 August Barclay once again ordered his army to retreat. It is worth remembering, however, that Barclay did this against the strong and universal opposition of Bagration and all of First Army's senior generals. He faced furious accusations of incompetence and even treason. Predictably, the Grand Duke Constantine's was the loudest and most hysterical voice, screaming out within earshot of junior officers and men that 'it isn't Russian blood that flows in those who command us'. Barclay de Tolly also knew that his decision to retreat would anger Alexander and probably wreck his standing with the emperor. It took great resolution, unselfishness and moral courage for Barclay to act in the way he did. Perhaps Napoleon cannot be blamed for failing to predict this.[47]

The Russian generals' opposition to abandoning Smolensk was all the stronger because they had defended it successfully against great odds and with heavy losses throughout 17 August. In the battle for Smolensk, 11,000 Russians died or were wounded. Nevertheless, nowhere had the French broken through the walls and into the city. Though Smolensk's defences were medieval they did sometimes provide good cover for Russian artillery and skirmishers. In some cases, too, attacking French columns could be hit by Russian batteries firing from across the river Dnieper.

The Russian infantry fought with great courage and grim determination. Ivan Liprandi was a senior staff officer in Dmitrii Dokhturov's Sixth Corps. His accounts of the 1812 campaign are among the most thoughtful and accurate from the Russian side. He remembered that at Smolensk it was difficult for the officers to stop their men from launching wasteful counter-attacks against the French at every opportunity. Volunteers for dangerous tasks were plentiful. Many soldiers refused to go off to the rear to have their wounds seen to. The sight of the city in flames and of the wretched remnants of the civilian population was an additional incentive to fight to the death. So too was the sense, absorbed with their mother's milk, that Smolensk was from ancient times Orthodox Russia's citadel against invasion from the 'Latin' West. In previous centuries the city had at times been a prize contested between the

Russians and the Poles. One officer remembered that, although the soldiers sometimes took French prisoners, on 17 August they always killed the Poles.[48]

The Russian troops in the city had been commanded by Dmitrii Dokhturov and on the night of 18 August he very unwillingly obeyed Barclay's order to evacuate Smolensk and pull back to the city's northern suburbs across the river Dnieper. That day Barclay allowed his exhausted soldiers a rest. On the night of 18–19 August he ordered them to retreat towards the main road which led back through Solovevo and Dorogobuzh into the Great Russian heartland and ultimately to Moscow.

The initial stages of this retreat presented serious difficulties. After it left Smolensk the main road to Moscow passed along the east bank of the Dnieper in full view and easy artillery range of the west bank. The river was also easily fordable in a number of places during the summer. Barclay did not want his retreating column, spread out as it would be for miles, to offer a perfect opportunity for the French to attack it on the march. So he decided to move his men in the night of 18–19 August down side roads which would lead them out onto the main Moscow road at a safe distance from Smolensk and the French. First Army would be divided into two halves. Dmitrii Dokhturov would lead the smaller half of the army on the longer detour which would take a night and a day before ultimately bringing them out on the Moscow road, not far from Solovevo. This part of the operation went without a hitch but it did mean that when disaster threatened the other half of First Army on 19 August Dokhturov was far away and unable to help.

The other column, commanded by Lieutenant-General Nikolai Tuchkov, was to make a shorter detour, coming out on to the Moscow road closer to Smolensk and just to the west of the village of Lubino. It adds something to the confusion of what is already a rather confusing story that the advance guard of Tuchkov's column was commanded by his younger brother, Major-General Pavel Tuchkov. The younger Tuchkov was given the task of leading the march down the side roads to Lubino and the Moscow road, where he was supposed to link up with Lieutenant-General Prince Andrei Gorchakov's division of Bagration's Second Army. It had been agreed that Gorchakov and Second Army would guard the Moscow road until First Army's column had emerged safely down the back lanes and onto the main highway near Lubino.

Everything went wrong, partly because of poor coordination between the First and Second armies and partly because of the difficulty of moving down country lanes at night. In principle, these roads should have been reconnoitred in advance by staff officers who should then have guided the columns to their correct destinations. The army's movements were these staff officers' responsibility. Any movement at night of large bodies of men requires very careful arrangements, especially if tired troops are to march through forests and down country lanes. The historian of the general staff claims, not altogether implausibly, that there were simply too few staff officers available for all the tasks in hand in the immediate aftermath of the evacuation of Smolensk. Some had been sent ahead to look for quarters for the following night and others had been dispatched to find possible battlefields on the road to Moscow where the army might make a stand. It is certainly evident from staff officers' memoirs that their corps was seriously overstretched in the first half of the 1812 campaign with very responsible jobs sometimes being allocated to junior and inexperienced officers. That was no doubt the inevitable price of having to build the general staff corps at such speed in the years just before the war.[49]

Whatever the reasons, the result was confusion. Only one-third of Nikolai Tuchkov's column – mostly made up of his own Third Corps – set off at the right time and took the correct road. Even they faced many obstacles in trying to get artillery and thousands of cavalry down lanes and over bridges designed to carry peasant carts. Next to move was Ostermann-Tolstoy's Fourth Corps, but they started late, lost track of Tuchkov's men and completely lost their way, splitting up into separate groups and wandering around through the night down a number of country lanes.

This threw into confusion the final third of the column, Karl Baggohufvudt's Second Corps. The last elements of Second Corps, commanded by Prince Eugen of Württemberg, could only set off far behind schedule at one in the morning of 19 August. Since Second Corps was following Ostermann-Tolstoy they inevitably got lost too and wandered in their own circle. At roughly six o'clock in the morning of 19 August Prince Eugen and his men found themselves near the village of Gedeonovo less than 2 kilometres from the Smolensk suburbs and in full view of Marshal Ney's corps, whose bands they could hear playing rousing music to get the men from their bivouacs.

Disaster loomed. Ney's corps far outnumbered the three infantry regiments and handful of cavalry and guns which Eugen commanded. Most of the rest of Fourth and Second corps were still wandering around in the forests and would be routed and cut off from the Moscow road should Ney advance and push Eugen aside. Fortunately, Barclay himself turned up – completely by accident – at the point of crisis and began making arrangements to block any advance by Ney.

The commander-in-chief will not have been overjoyed to find that his army's fate rested in the hands of by far its youngest and least experienced division commander. The 24-year-old Eugen held his rank because he was Empress Marie's favourite nephew and Alexander's first cousin. Barclay disliked aristocratic amateurs and was suspicious of Eugen's relatives and friends at court. No doubt the decent but rather solemn Barclay saw the lively young prince, whose pastimes included writing plays and operas, as a terrible dilettante. In fact, however, Eugen was to prove one of Russia's best generals in 1812–14. He had received a thorough military education, had seen a little of war in 1807 and against the Turks, and was to prove himself a courageous, resolute and intelligent commander in the campaigns of 1812–14. The battle outside Smolensk on 19 July was to be his first real test and he passed it well.

Luckily for Eugen, Ney was as surprised to see the Russians as they were to see him. It took him three hours to begin his attack. Even then, Eugen recalled, large numbers of French troops never moved from their camp. During these three hours Eugen could post his three regiments in good positions behind breastworks and bushes in the woods. Russian infantry of the line did not always perform well in a light infantry role but on the morning of 19 August the men of the Tobolsk, Wilmanstrand and Beloozero regiments fought like heroes, beating off repeated French attacks for just long enough for reinforcements to hurry through the forest to the sound of the guns. When Barclay finally ordered a retreat, Eugen was able to put together a rearguard which held off the French while Second and Fourth corps were led through the forest paths to the Moscow road.[50]

Unfortunately, however, confusion on the Moscow road very nearly allowed the French to get first to Lubino, block the paths out of the forest, and undermine everything Eugen and his men had achieved. Barclay had just made what arrangements he could to deal with the emergency facing Eugen, when he was informed that Second Army had retreated eastwards along the Moscow road without waiting for First Army, leaving the vital crossroads near Lubino open for the French to seize. Friedrich von Schubert was alone with Barclay when the message was delivered and he recalled that the commander-in-chief, normally so self-controlled and calm in crisis, said out aloud: 'Everything is lost.' Barclay can be forgiven his temporary loss of composure because this was one of the most dangerous moments for the Russians in the 1812 campaign.[51]

The situation was partly saved by Pavel Tuchkov. After a long and exhausting night-time march through the forests he moved onto the Moscow road near to Lubino at about eight o'clock in the morning. Tuchkov was astonished to find no one there from Second Army save a few Cossacks. Though his orders had been to turn eastwards on the high road and head for Solovevo, this had presumed that Gorchakov's troops would be on the road to block any French advance and guarantee the rest of First Army a safe retreat. To make matters worse, Cossacks reported that Junot's Westphalian corps was preparing to ford the Dnieper at Prudishchevo, which would allow them to move onto the road from the south against minimal opposition.

Pavel Tuchkov kept his head and showed praiseworthy initiative. Ignoring his orders, he turned his 3,000 men right rather than left onto the Moscow road and took up a good defensive position as far to the west of Lubino as possible, behind the river Kolodnia. Here his men hung on against growing French pressure for five hours, reinforced by two fine Grenadier regiments rushed forward to his assistance by his elder brother. In mid-afternoon Pavel Tuchkov fell back to a new position behind the river Strogan, which was the last defensible position if the army's exit routes from the forests onto the Moscow road were to be kept open. Ferocious fighting continued until the evening but Tuchkov held out, supported by a growing stream of reinforcements organized by Aleksei Ermolov.

As at Krasnyi, the Russian generals had kept their heads and the Russian infantry had shown great steadiness and courage in emergency. Unlike at Krasnyi, the cavalry and artillery had also contributed to the victory. In particular, Count Vasili Orlov-Denisov's cavalry had protected Tuchkov's vulnerable left flank against strong pressure from French cavalry and infantry, using the terrain with great skill and timing their counter-attacks to perfection.

Nevertheless, no amount of Russian skill and courage could have saved Tuchkov had the French used all their available troops intelligently. Having crossed the Dnieper at the ford near Prudishchevo, for most of the day General Junot's corps stood motionless behind the Russian left flank and rear, with Tuchkov at their mercy. French sources later explained this failure by Junot's incipient mental illness but it also made clear that the French army's reputation for rapid and decisive exploitation of opportunities on the battlefield only applied when Napoleon was present. But the emperor had no reason to expect a serious battle on 19 August and had remained in Smolensk. His absence rescued the Russians from disaster, as their commanders well understood. Aleksei Ermolov wrote to Alexander that 'we ought to have perished'. Barclay told Bennigsen that one chance in a hundred had saved First Army.[52]

As the Russian armies retreated eastwards the initiative lay with Napoleon. Either he could pursue them or he could end his campaign at Smolensk, and seek to turn Lithuania and Belorussia into a formidable base from which to launch a second, decisive strike in 1813. Both at the time and subsequently there has been much debate about the relative advantages and dangers of these two options.

In favour of stopping at Smolensk were the dangers of extending French communications still further eastwards. Not merely were the lines of communication already very long but by mid-August they were facing a growing threat on both flanks, especially in the south where Admiral Chichagov's formidable Army of the Danube was approaching the theatre of operations. In addition, two months of war had not only greatly reduced French numbers, they had also seriously weakened discipline and morale. With sick, deserters and marauders scattered across Lithuania and Belorussia in their tens of thousands was it not more sensible to consolidate one's base, restore order to one's army and not risk even more pressure on its fragile discipline?

There were also powerful political reasons for stopping in Smolensk. Given satisfied elites and effective administration, Lithuania and Belorussia could have become key allies in a war against Russia. The Russian leaders had always feared that by abandoning the western provinces they would allow Napoleon to consolidate his power there and mobilize Polish resources against them. One of the calculations on which Napoleon had based his invasion was that the Russian elites would never fight to the death to preserve their empire's Polish provinces. If he conquered and organized these provinces, how much pain would the Russians be willing to endure in the hope of getting them back?

For Napoleon, 1812 was a cabinet war fought for strictly limited political purposes. At the absolute maximum he would have annexed Lithuania and part of Belorussia and Ukraine, forced Russia back into the Continental System, and – possibly – coerced the Russians into helping him to challenge British power in Asia. Having experienced the problems of campaigning in Russia he might have settled for less, even in the event of victory. Already embroiled in one national war in Spain, the last thing he wanted was to ignite another in Russia. From the start there had been strong signs that Alexander and his generals were trying to incite a national war against him. As he approached Smolensk these signs became more ominous. The further he penetrated into Great Russia the likelier a national war became.

Napoleon was a man of order who had put the lid on the French Revolution and married the daughter of the Habsburg emperor. He had no desire to launch a serf insurrection in Russia. But the threat might be a useful form of political leverage. It was much more likely to work with the French army poised menacingly on Great Russia's borders than if it actually invaded the Russian heartland. With their churches desecrated, their women raped and their farms destroyed the Russian peasants were unlikely to listen to French promises.

All these points were fully comprehensible at the time. To them one might add other points with the wisdom of hindsight. The restoration of a powerful Polish state was crucial if French hegemony in Europe was to survive. A restored Poland would be a far more reliable ally of France than the Habsburg, Romanov or Hohenzollern monarchies could ever be. It was also well within Napoleon's means to make Poland's restoration fully acceptable to Austria, by restoring the Illyrian provinces he had annexed from it in 1809. Standing even further back from events and looking at the last three centuries of Russian history, it is true to say that whereas simple military assaults on Russia tend to break against the country's immense scale and resources, the Russian Empire has been vulnerable to a combination of military and political pressures. This proved true both in the First World War and in the Cold War, both of which Russia lost in large part because of the revolt of non-Russians but also of the Russians themselves against the price of empire and the nature of the regimes required to secure it. In the early nineteenth century military pressure combined with exploiting the Romanov empire's political weaknesses might have worked when geared to strictly limited war aims.

Even leaving aside the fact that Napoleon could not see into the future, there were, however, powerful arguments against stopping in Smolensk. Napoleon was very unwilling to spend more than one campaigning season away from Paris. As we have seen, Chernyshev had pointed this out before 1812 and linked it to the nature of the Bonapartist regime and the challenges it faced. After noting a number of these challenges (the economy, the Pope, Spain, the elites) the leading contemporary French expert on Napoleon concludes that 'Chernyshev was correct when he reported to his government that Napoleon would take a major domestic risk if the war against Russia was prolonged'. If this judgement can be made now in calm retrospect, how much greater must Napoleon's feeling of insecurity have been in 1812? He had seen the enormous instability of French politics in the 1790s. He understood how very conditional was the French elite's loyalty to him. He knew how much his throne owed to victory and to chance.[53]

He also knew that consolidating a secure base in the western borderlands would be difficult. Lithuania and Belorussia found it hard to feed armies even in peacetime, and especially in winter and spring. The Russian First Army was far smaller than Napoleon's forces and by no means all of it had wintered in the western borderlands in 1811–12. Even so it had been forced to quarter itself across a huge area to secure adequate supplies. This was particularly true of the cavalry. The five regiments of Baron Korff's Second Cavalry Corps had been quartered all the way from the Prussian frontier to central Ukraine in order to feed their horses.[54]

Matters were hardly likely to be better in the winter of 1812 after a year in which the region had been plundered by two armies. The Russian light cavalry was superior to the French even in the early summer of 1812. As Napoleon had discovered in 1806–7, however, the Cossacks revealed their true potential in winter, when they could operate in conditions which destroyed regular light cavalry. With the full manpower of the Cossack regions now being mobilized by the Russians, the French would face huge difficulties in securing their base or feeding their horses and even their men in the winter of 1812.

Of course, if Napoleon had stopped at Smolensk his entire army would not have been destroyed, as happened after his botched invasion of the Russian heartland. But the destruction of Napoleon's army was by no means inevitable just because he advanced from Smolensk. Other factors – and mistakes – intervened.

In August 1812 Napoleon would have preferred not to be sitting in Smolensk with an undefeated Russian army still in the field. His strategy had been rooted in the correct belief that if he could destroy First and Second armies Russia would lose any hope of ultimate victory. He had chased the Russians all the way to Smolensk in pursuit of this strategy but they had frustrated him. One political calculation made by Napoleon was correct: the Russians could not surrender Moscow without a fight. Moscow was two weeks' march from Smolensk. Since he had come this far in pursuit of a battle, it might well seem foolish to give up now with the prize so nearly in his grasp. Operating in the rich Moscow region in the midst of the harvest season, he would have no serious problems feeding his men and horses so long as they kept on the move. No doubt to advance was a gamble, but Napoleon was a great gambler. He was also right to believe that in August 1812 stopping in Smolensk was by no means a safe bet. So he decided to push on towards Moscow.

6

Borodino and the Fall of Moscow

As Napoleon's main body advanced into central Russia in the second half of August 1812 the situation on its northern and southern flanks began to turn against the French. In part this reflected the enormous area across which Napoleon's armies were now being forced to operate. In the north, Marshal MacDonald, the descendant of a Scottish Jacobite émigré, had been given the task of covering Napoleon's left flank, clearing Courland and capturing Riga. In the south, the Austrians and Saxons were facing General Aleksandr Tormasov's Third Army on the borders of Ukraine. More than 1,000 kilometres separated these forces. The distance between Napoleon's spearhead beyond Smolensk and his bases in East Prussia and Poland was even greater. Inevitably, as distance and sickness took their toll, his forces began to thin out. Napoleon could not be strong everywhere.

Marshal MacDonald's Tenth Corps comprised 32,500 men. Almost two-thirds of these troops were Prussians and in the early stages of the campaign they fought hard. Their commander, Lieutenant-General von Gräwert, stressed the need to restore Prussian military pride and regain the respect of the French for the army of Frederick the Great. Near the main estate of the Pahlen family at Gross Eckau on 19 July 1812 the Prussians defeated a Russian attempt to check their advance. Within a month of the war's commencement the Prussians were in the vicinity of Riga, a huge Russian supply base, the largest city in the Baltic provinces and the key to the river Dvina.

Riga was not a strong fortress. Uniquely, the costs of its upkeep were borne not by the Russian state but by the Riga municipal government. In the century that had passed since the city was last seriously threatened its defences had been allowed to deteriorate. Only in June 1810 did the state take back responsibility for the city's fortifications. During the next two years much was done to prepare Riga for a siege, but major weaknesses remained. Many of the key fortifications were out of date. The citadel was very cramped and hemmed in by residential areas. Riga's suburbs had also grown greatly during the eighteenth century, occupying much of what had been open ground in front of the city's outer walls.

The 19,000-strong garrison of Riga was commanded by Lieutenant-General Magnus von Essen. Most of these men came from reserve battalions and many were poorly trained. Sickness was rife in the garrison even before the siege began. Immediately on hearing that Napoleon had crossed the Neman Essen declared Riga to be in a state of siege: every household was ordered to store four months' supply of food and any civilian departing the town was required to leave behind two able-bodied citizens in his household to help defend the city. In the fourth week of July, as the enemy approached Riga, Essen ordered that its western and southern suburbs be burned to the ground, in order to give the garrison a free field of fire beyond the walls. More than 750 buildings were destroyed, at an estimated cost of 17 million rubles. Nevertheless, it was generally agreed that Riga could not hope to hold out for more than two months against a serious siege.

If Napoleon had stopped in Vitebsk or Smolensk and dispatched part of his main army to help MacDonald, Riga would certainly have fallen. Without additional help, however, the French commander could not hope to take the city. A complete blockade line would have needed to stretch around Riga for more than 50 kilometres on both sides of the river Dvina. MacDonald's 32,500 men on their own could never man such a line. In addition, Russian gunboats controlled the river and the British navy dominated the Baltic Sea and raided MacDonald's communications along the coast. The French siege artillery, initially sent to Dünaburg, did finally arrive near Riga, but by the time it could be deployed for a serious siege the balance of forces on Napoleon's northern flank was beginning to turn against the French.

Above all, this was because of the intervention of the Russian army in Finland. In the last week of August Alexander travelled to Åbo in Finland to meet the Swedish crown prince, Jean-Baptiste Bernadotte. The two leaders confirmed their alliance as well as arrangements for future military collaboration in northern Germany and Denmark. Of more immediate importance was the fact that Bernadotte released Alexander from his promise to use the Russian troops in Finland for a joint

Russo-Swedish landing in Denmark in 1812 and urged him to send them to Riga instead. As a result, the Russian navy transported the bulk of the 21,000-strong Finland Corps to the Baltic provinces. Commanded by Count Fabian von Steinhel, these were mostly battle-hardened troops. By the second half of September their arrival in Riga was promising to end the stalemate on the northern front.[1]

Though Riga was Marshal MacDonald's main preoccupation, he was also forced to keep one eye over his right shoulder towards Dünaburg and Polotsk. This was the area in which Lieutenant-General Count Peter von Wittgenstein's First Russian Corps was operating. When Barclay's army abandoned the camp at Drissa and headed for Vitebsk Wittgenstein's corps was detached to block the roads leading north-westwards to Pskov, Novgorod and ultimately Petersburg. Wittgenstein's main opponent was Marshal Oudinot, whose orders were to advance over the river Dvina and drive the Russians back on Pskov. In principle, this task should not have been beyond Oudinot, whose corps was more than 40,000-strong when it entered Russian territory. By contrast, Wittgenstein had only 23,000 men in First Corps and, though his forces were reinforced by two other small detachments, he was also responsible for containing any attempt by MacDonald's right-wing division to advance from Dünaburg.[2]

In fact, however, Oudinot was to prove a complete failure as the commander of an independent force, allowing himself to be dominated and overawed by Wittgenstein. Russian light cavalry raided constantly over the Dvina, disrupting French communications and supplies. When Oudinot advanced on Wittgenstein's army in late July he allowed himself to be surprised and routed by the Russians in three days of battle at Kliastitsy and Golovshchina between 30 July and 1 August. One reason for his defeat was his failure to concentrate all his forces on the battlefield. According to the Russian account, he had more than 8,000 men in the neighbourhood of Kliastitsy who never got into action.

In addition, however, the Russian troops fought exceptionally well. The core of Wittgenstein's little army had recent experience of fighting in Finland's forests during the war of 1808–9. Not only Wittgenstein's jaegers but also some of his infantry proved very adept at skirmishing in the similar terrain of north-western Russia. Perhaps it was their example that inspired the many reserve battalions and new regiments formed from garrison troops in Wittgenstein's divisions to perform much better than anyone had the right to expect right from the start of the campaign. Wittgenstein immediately took the offensive, won battles and imposed his will on the enemy; as a result, his soldiers' morale was high and no one carped at his German origins.[3]

It probably helped Wittgenstein that, unlike Barclay de Tolly, he came from an aristocratic, albeit rather impoverished, family. Born in Russia and the son of a general in Russian service, he moved much more assuredly in Russian aristocratic circles than was the case with the awkward Barclay. In addition, Peter Wittgenstein was a cavalryman and something of a *beau sabreur*. A fine horseman, bold, generous and often chivalrous, Wittgenstein's values were very much those of the Russian military aristocracy. In addition, he was personally modest and kindly, as well as very generous in recognizing and reporting his subordinates' achievements. Combined with a string of victories, these qualities ensured that great harmony reigned at Wittgenstein's headquarters in 1812.[4]

Harmony at headquarters was combined with professional skill. Wittgenstein's chief of staff was Friedrich d'Auvray, an intelligent, loyal and excellently educated staff officer of French origin who was born in Dresden and began his military career in the Polish army. The commander of First Corps's artillery was the Georgian, Prince Lev Iashvili. His deputy was the 24-year-old Ivan Sukhozhanet, the son of a Polish officer. Both men had performed well in the East Prussian campaign of 1806–7.[5]

The pick of the bunch, however, was the 27-year-old quartermaster-general of Wittgenstein's corps, Colonel Johann von Diebitsch. He was the son of a senior Prussian staff officer who had transferred to the Russian service in 1798. The young Diebitsch had begun his military service in the Semenovsky Guards regiment, from which Petr Mikhailovich Volkonsky – another former Semenovsky officer – had plucked him for the general staff. Diminutive, pop-eyed and ugly, Diebitsch's appearance had so appalled the Semenovskys' colonel that he had tried to keep the young officer away from service at court and on the parade ground. Diebitsch was known by his many friends as 'the samovar' because when he became excited he boiled over, with words spilling out in almost incomprehensible fashion. For all his oddities, Diebitsch was probably the ablest staff officer in the Russian army in 1812–14. He also showed energy, initiative and judgement on the occasions when called upon to command detachments. Though ambitious and determined, Diebitsch was also very loyal to the army and the cause which he served. By 1814, aged only 28, he was a lieutenant-general, having skyrocketed past his former peers in the Semenovskys. Nevertheless, to his credit and theirs, he remained on good terms with his old comrades.[6]

After Kliastitsy Oudinot complained to Napoleon that he was faced by far superior Russian numbers. Often in 1812–14 the emperor was to torment his subordinates by underestimating the size of the enemy forces they faced. On this occasion, however, his sour response to Oudinot was accurate and justified:

> You are not pursuing Wittgenstein ... and you are allowing this general the freedom to attack the Duke of Tarento [i.e. MacDonald] or to cross the Dvina to raid our rear. You have the most exaggerated notions of Wittgenstein's strength: he has only two or at most three divisions of the line, six reserve battalions under Prince Repnin and some militia who aren't worth counting. You must not allow yourself to be hoodwinked so easily. The Russians are announcing everywhere that they have scored a great victory over you.[7]

Despite this criticism, Napoleon reinforced Oudinot by all the infantry and artillery of Gouvion Saint-Cyr's Sixth (Bavarian) Corps. Marching in the wake of the first echelon of Napoleon's army, Sixth Corps was 25,000-strong when it crossed the Neman but had only 13,000 men left by the time they joined Oudinot at Polotsk just five weeks later. It is true that the Bavarian cavalry had been detached to join Napoleon's main body, but most of the losses were due to sickness, straggling and desertion. During this period the Bavarians had not fired a shot in anger.

Although Wittgenstein knew that with the arrival of Saint-Cyr's corps he was heavily outnumbered, he was determined to retain the initiative and impose his will on the enemy. With this goal in mind he attacked the joint forces of Oudinot and Saint-Cyr at Polotsk on 17 August. Unfortunately for Wittgenstein, although on the battle's first day he succeeded in pushing the French back into the town of Polotsk, Oudinot himself was wounded and command passed to the far more competent Saint-Cyr. The next day the new French commander concentrated much of his artillery and two fresh infantry divisions for a counter-attack on the Russian centre. With a sleight of hand rather familiar in descriptions of battles at this time, Saint-Cyr claimed that his army was substantially outnumbered. He wrote in his memoirs that one-quarter of the 31,000-

strong French force was absent 'foraging', whereas Wittgenstein had more than 30,000 soldiers to hand. In reality, as Wittgenstein reported to Alexander, constant battles, combined with the need to need to keep an eye on MacDonald, meant that his available strike force was reduced to barely 18,000 men.[8]

Surprise combined with overwhelming numbers meant that the Russians were forced to retreat but they did so with great steadiness and courage. The Estland Regiment, for example, had been formed in 1811 from the soldiers of garrison units. The battle of Polotsk was its first serious action. As part of Major-General Gothard Helfreich's 14th Division, the men of the Estland Regiment stood right in the path of the French counter-attack. Despite this and despite losing fourteen officers and more than 400 men, the Estland Regiment held off repeated enemy attacks during 18 August, skirmished effectively in the woods, and finally won their way to safety. The regiment's commanding officer, Colonel Karl Ulrikhin, was wounded twice and subsequently forced to retire from the army as a result. But he stayed with his men throughout the retreat, leading a number of counter-attacks to keep the enemy at a safe distance. Forty-three men of the Estland Regiment won military medals for their performance on 18 July and the regiment itself was awarded a standard to mark its exploits.[9]

One might perhaps take a regimental history's account of its own soldiers' courage with a pinch of salt, but in this case the Russian story is supported by Saint-Cyr himself, who wrote that

the Russians showed in this battle a sustained courage and an individual boldness of which one finds very few equivalents in the armies of other nations. Surprised, fragmented, with their battalions isolated as much as actually attacked (for we had penetrated through their lines), they nevertheless were not disconcerted and continued to fight as they retreated, which they did very slowly, facing about in all directions with a courage and a steadiness which is, I repeat, particular to the soldiers of this nation. They performed prodigies of valour but they could not beat back the simultaneous attack of four concentrated and ordered divisions.[10]

Technically the battle of Polotsk was a defeat for Wittgenstein but in fact it helped him to achieve his strategic goal, which was so to weaken and impress the enemy that they would refrain from advancing down the roads to Pskov, Novgorod and Petersburg. After the battle, Wittgenstein fell back roughly 40 kilometres to a fortified position near Sivoshin, where the French left him in peace for the next two months. During that time stalemate reigned in the north-west, with the war degenerating into raids and a competition between the two armies to feed themselves and rebuild their strength. To an extent, what happened next was precisely what Pfühl had planned at Drissa. Weakened by the advance across the western borderlands, Saint-Cyr lacked the numbers either to attack Wittgenstein behind his entrenchments or to move past his flank. Pinned down in a static position in a poor and devastated countryside, sickness and hunger melted away the French army.

Meanwhile Wittgenstein's corps was abundantly supplied by the Russian administration and population in its rear, which in this case meant the province of Pskov. As Wittgenstein recognized with his customary generosity, the true hero here was Pskov's governor, Prince Petr Shakhovskoy. In mid-August Wittgenstein wrote to Alexander that 'from the first moment when First Corps stood on the river Dvina, it received all its victuals from Pskov province. Thanks to the untiring efforts, the efficiency and the care of the governor, Prince Shakhovskoy, these victuals were supplied all the time and with excellent efficiency so that the troops were provided with everything they needed and suffered not the slightest lack of anything.' Shakhovskoy mobilized thousands of carts from his province to transport food to Wittgenstein. The governor's efforts continued throughout the 1812 campaign, by the end of which it was reckoned that Pskov province alone had voluntarily contributed 14 million rubles to the war effort. This voluntary contribution from just one (out of more than fifty) provinces, amounted to one-third of the war ministry's total budget for feeding the entire army in 1811.[11]

By September Napoleon was facing growing danger on his northern flank as Steinhel's men approached Riga and the hungry and exhausted corps of Oudinot and Saint-Cyr melted away in front of Wittgenstein. Meanwhile an even greater danger was looming to the south where Admiral Chichagov's Army of the Danube was about to link up with Tormasov's Third Army near Lutsk in north-west Ukraine.

In the first weeks of his campaign Napoleon had underestimated the size of Tormasov's army. Though Tormasov's 45,000 men had to be quite widely dispersed to guard Ukraine's northern border, nevertheless they far outmatched the 19,000 Saxons of General Reynier's corps who were initially given the task of protecting Napoleon's southern flank. Urged on by Alexander and Bagration, Tormasov advanced northwards and on 27 July destroyed a Saxon detachment at Kobrin, taking more than 2,000 prisoners. Tormasov was more a military administrator and diplomat than an aggressive commander in the field. He was widely criticized after Kobrin for failing to press his advantage and destroy the rest of Reynier's corps. Napoleon was given time to send Prince Schwarzenberg southwards with the whole of the Austrian corps to rescue Reynier. In the face of overwhelming numbers, Tormasov was forced to move back to a strong defensive position on the river Styr.

Though this seemed at the time to be a disappointing aftermath to the victory at Kobrin, in fact Tormasov had achieved his main objective. It was premature in July 1812 to think that one or other of the Russian flanking armies could drive deep into Napoleon's rear. Meanwhile, however, the victory at Kobrin had not only boosted Russian morale but had also drawn 30,000 Austrian troops out of the main theatre of operations and well to the south.

So long as the Russo-Austrian border remained neutralized and his left flank was thereby secured, Tormasov could hold his position behind the fast-flowing river Styr without difficulty. The south bank of the river where the Russians stood was wooded and was higher than the north bank. The Russians could hide their own forces and see exactly what their enemies were doing. With fertile Volhynia at their back, they could feed themselves more easily than was the case with their enemies. The Austrians and Saxons were much better off than Oudinot and Saint-Cyr's corps in the barren Russian north-west. Even so they suffered from hunger and from raids by Third Army's light cavalry. Meanwhile Tormasov's men enjoyed a good rest.[12]

The stalemate on the river Styr could only be ended by the arrival of Chichagov's Army of the Danube. Though in all circumstances Chichagov would have to leave part of his army behind to guard the Ottoman frontier, potentially he could bring more than 50,000 troops northwards to join Tormasov. These tough, battle-hardened soldiers were among the best in the Russian army.[13]

Chichagov's army could not move northwards until peace was sealed with the Turks. The peace treaty was signed on 28 May by Kutuzov before Chichagov arrived to take over command of the Army of the Danube. Seven nervous weeks then passed before Alexander received news that the sultan had finally ratified the treaty. During this time, fearing that the Ottomans would refuse to ratify, Chichagov floated a plan to advance on Constantinople, incite insurrection among the sultan's Christian subjects, and resurrect a great Byzantino-Slav empire. Such plans were doubly dangerous: it was difficult to control a viceroy so far from Petersburg and Alexander himself could be carried away by grandiose dreams. Fortunately, the Ottomans did in the end ratify the treaty and sanity returned to Russian planning.[14]

After hearing that the Turks had ratified the peace, Alexander wrote to Chichagov: 'Let us adjourn our projects aimed at the Porte and employ all our forces against the great enemy by whom we are faced.' Thoughts of Constantinople would merely draw Chichagov away from 'the true centre of action – which is Napoleon's rear'. Nevertheless these thoughts were being postponed, not abandoned: 'Once our war against Napoleon goes well, we can return to your plan against the Turks immediately, and then proclaim either the empire of the Slavs or that of the Greeks. But to occupy ourselves with this at a moment when we already face such difficulties and so numerous an enemy seems to me risky and unwise.' Alexander knew that this risked alienating Russia's Balkan clients but in present circumstances they must be told that Russia's survival had to be the top priority for all Slavs: 'You can tell them secretly that all this is only temporary, and that as soon as we have finished with Napoleon we will retrace our steps and will then create the Slav empire.' Meanwhile Chichagov's thirst for glory was assuaged by the promise of supreme command over both his own and Tormasov's armies.[15]

Throughout the spring and early summer of 1812 all plans to use Chichagov's army were greatly affected by fear and uncertainty as to what role Austria would play in the war. As we have seen, it was news of the Franco-Austrian treaty which ended Russian thoughts about a pre-emptive strike into the Duchy of Warsaw. In the very same letter of 19 April in which he informed Barclay of the Franco-Austrian alliance and told him that this ruled out a Russian offensive, the emperor also outlined his plans for neutralizing the Austrian threat:

We must adopt a great plan capable of paralysing the efforts of the Austrians against us. We must give assistance to the Slav nations and launch them against the Austrians, while seeking to link them to discontented elements in Hungary. We need a man of intelligence (*un homme de tête*) to direct this important operation and I have chosen Admiral Chichagov, who supports this plan enthusiastically. His ability and energy make me hope that he will succeed in this crucial commission. I am preparing all the necessary instructions for him.[16]

These instructions were issued on 21 April. They started by warning Chichagov that 'the treacherous behaviour of Austria, which has allied with France, forces Russia to use all available means to defeat the harmful plans of these two powers'. Chichagov must use his army to incite and support a massive Slav insurrection in the Balkans which would threaten Austria, undermine her strength, and also destroy Napoleon's position on the Adriatic. Believing that revolt could break out all the way to Illyria and Dalmatia, Alexander instructed Chichagov to link up with British naval and financial power in the Adriatic in order to support and subsidize insurrection as far afield as the Tyrol and Switzerland. Encouraging revolt in Napoleon's rear was a key part of Alexander's grand strategy in 1812–14. In the end it was to score important successes by mobilizing opposition to Napoleon in Germany and in France itself. The plan for a great Slav insurrection was one of this grand strategy's earliest, most spectacular and least realistic elements.[17]

This plan was to a great extent the result of panic and anger on learning of the Franco-Austrian alliance but it also reflected the deep-seated views of Nikolai Rumiantsev. Even with Napoleon approaching Smolensk, Rumiantsev's eyes remained turned towards the south and the spoils which Russia could obtain from the declining Ottoman Empire. He wrote to Alexander on 17 July that 'I have always believed that the British Cabinet sees its interest to lie in the weakening of your empire: together with the Cabinet of Vienna, it wishes that because of serious threats to your own territories Your Majesty should allow to slip from your hands the huge advantages which the war with Turkey offered you'. As regards Austria, 'I believe that Your Majesty's interests require that no mercy be shown to the court of Vienna. Only by maximizing her difficulties, will you be able to drive her to a separate peace with Your Majesty, and this will not be achieved immediately.' As part of his grand strategy Alexander must appeal to the Slavs, stressing that 'the very same Emperor Napoleon who has subjected the Germans, now proposes to enslave the Slav peoples. To this end he makes war with no justification against Your Majesty to stop you from giving protection to them [i.e. the Slavs] and because Providence has made you the sovereign of this great nation of Slavs, of which all the other tribes are but branches (*souches*).' Alexander must stress in his proclamation that Chichagov was advancing towards the Adriatic through the lands of the South Slavs in order to provide Russian leadership in their struggle for freedom.[18]

Fortunately for Russia, Rumiantsev's plans were aborted. The Russian military attaché in Vienna, Theodor Tuyll van Serooskerken, wrote to Barclay that given Napoleon's overwhelming numbers it was madness to divert so many troops and so much money to a peripheral and risky enterprise. Above all, however, it was fear of Austrian reactions which doomed Chichagov's plans. Quiet conversations between Russian and Austrian diplomats revealed that Vienna's contribution to the war would be strictly limited unless Russia provoked additional action. In no circumstances would Schwarzenberg's corps be increased to more than 30,000 men and the Russo-Austrian border would be neutralized. Subsequently Schwarzenberg kept to this promise by moving northwards into the Duchy of Warsaw and crossing into Russia over the Polish border. By July Alexander was increasingly convinced that Vienna would keep its promises, which made Chichagov's planned advance to the Adriatic not only unnecessary but also politically very dangerous.[19]

By late July therefore all political complications had been cleared aside and the Army of the Danube was on the march to join Tormasov. It was to take Chichagov's men fifty-two days to cover the distance from Bucharest to the river Styr. Only after the Army of the Danube began to join Tormasov's men on 14 September could a decisive move against Napoleon's communications begin.[20]

On that very day Napoleon's advance guard entered Moscow. In retrospect the fact that the threat from Chichagov took time to emerge was all to the Russians' good. It encouraged Napoleon to plunge ever further into Russia. This was not how the overwhelming majority of Russian generals saw things at the time, however. As they retreated from Smolensk towards Moscow most of them became ever more desperate to protect Russia's ancient capital.

Exceptionally, though Barclay would defend Moscow if he could, he made it clear to his aide-de-camp that this was not his top priority: 'He would regard Moscow just like any other place on the map of the empire and he would make no more extra movement for the sake of this town than he would for any other, because it was necessary to save the empire and Europe and not to protect towns and provinces.' Inevitably Barclay's opinion spread around and contributed to the unpopularity of a 'German' who was willing to sacrifice Russia's heart for the sake of Europe. Though at one level Barclay's cold and honest military rationality was admirable, one can understand the exasperation of Alexander, whose difficult job it was to manage morale and politics on the home front. As he once wrote to Barclay, the long retreat was bound to be unpopular but one should avoid doing or saying things which might increase public exasperation.[21]

In the nineteen days between the evacuation of Smolensk and the battle of Borodino Barclay's popularity reached its lowest point among the troops. The soldiers had been told they would bury Napoleon on the river Dvina and then that they would fight to the death first for Vitebsk and then for Smolensk. Each promise had been broken and the hated retreat had continued. After Smolensk the same pattern continued, with the soldiers first being ordered to dig fortifications on a chosen battlefield and then retreating yet again when either Barclay or Bagration considered the position unsuitable. They nicknamed their commander-in-chief 'Nothing but Chatter' (*Boltai da Tol'ko*) as a pun on Barclay de Tolly. The historian of the Chevaliers Gardes wrote that Barclay misunderstood the nature of the Russian soldier, who would have accepted the unvarnished truth but grumbled at broken promises. The comment is probably true but glosses over the fact that Kutuzov subsequently spoke and acted in a fashion very similar to Barclay.[22]

Along with the grumbling went a decline in discipline in some units. On Alexander's urging, Barclay ordered the execution of some marauders at Smolensk. According to a young artillery officer, Nikolai Konshin, one of these so-called 'marauders' was a wholly innocent orderly from his battery, who had been sent off to find some cream for the officers. Bitterness against Barclay increased in the ranks but despite the executions marauding continued, with Kutuzov writing to Alexander that the military police picked up almost two thousand stragglers within days of his arrival to take over command of the army. Perhaps one should take the new commander-in-chief's gloomy comments with a pinch of salt, however, since he had an obvious interest in painting his new command in a bad light when reporting to the emperor. A few days later he wrote to his wife that the troops' morale was excellent.[23]

In reality some degree of disorder was inevitable among soldiers who had retreated so far and had been ordered to destroy all food and shelter along the way to deny it to the French. Once encouraged, the habit of destruction is hard to contain. The sight of burning Russian towns and miserable civilian refugees also had its impact on morale. In most other armies in a similar situation, the deterioration of discipline would have been worse. As General Langeron wrote in his memoirs, with only a little exaggeration, 'an army which during a retreat of 1,200 versts from the Neman to Moscow sustains two major battles and loses not a single gun or caisson, nor even a cart or a wounded man, is not an army to disdain'. Perhaps the most important point was that the soldiers longed for battle. Once given the opportunity to take out their anger and frustration on the French, most problems of morale and discipline would disappear.[24]

In the ranks of the retreating Russian army was Lieutenant-Colonel Karl von Clausewitz, who was to become the most famous military thinker of the nineteenth century. A passionate Prussian patriot, he could not stomach his king's alliance with Napoleon and had resigned his commission in order to join the Russian army. Unable to speak Russian, at sea amidst the battles within the Russian high command and sometimes engulfed in an atmosphere of xenophobia and suspicion, he experienced these weeks as a time of great personal trial. Perhaps this is one reason why he is anything but generous in his comments on the Russian retreat:

As, with the exception of the halt at Smolensk, the retreat from Vitebsk to Moscow was in fact an uninterrupted movement, and from Smolensk the point of direction lay always tolerably straight to the rear, the entire retreat was a very simple operation ... When an army always gives way and retires continually in a direct line, it is very difficult for the pursuer to outflank it or press it away from its course: in this instance, also, the roads are few, and ravines rare; the seat of war, therefore, admitted of few geographical combinations ... in a retreat this simplicity greatly economises the powers of men and horses. Here were no long arranged rendezvous, no marches to and fro, no long circuits, no alarms; in short, little or no outlay of tactical skill and expenditure of strength.[25]

The other great military thinker of the era, Antoine de Jomini, also took part in the 1812 campaign, in his case on the French side. He was far more appreciative of the Russian achievement. He wrote that 'retreats are certainly the most difficult operations in war'. Above all, they put a tremendous strain on the troops' discipline and morale. In his opinion, the Russian army was far superior to any other in Europe when it came to managing such retreats. 'The firmness which it has displayed in all retreats is due in equal degrees to the national character, the natural instincts of the soldiers, and the excellent disciplinary institutions.' To be sure, the Russians had enjoyed a number of advantages, such as the great superiority of their light cavalry and the fact that the two key French commanders, marshals Murat and Davout, were at each other's throats. Nevertheless, the ordered retreat by the Russians 'was highly deserving of praise, not only for the talent displayed by the generals who directed its first stages but also for the admirable fortitude and soldierly bearing of the troops who performed it'.[26]

As one might expect, the reminiscences of Russian generals who fought in the rearguards agree with Jomini rather than Clausewitz. Eugen of Württemberg criticized Clausewitz for prejudice and misjudgements where the Russian army was concerned. He commented that 'our retreat was one of the finest examples of military order and discipline. We left behind to the enemy no stragglers, no stores and no carts: the troops were not tired by forced marches and the very well-led rearguards (especially under Konovnitsyn) only fought small-scale and usually victorious actions.' The commanders picked good positions in order to exhaust and delay the enemy, forcing him to bring forward more artillery and deploy his infantry. They only retreated once the enemy had advanced in great strength, inflicting casualties as they retired. 'In general the withdrawals were carried out by horse artillery moving back in echelon, covered by numerous cavalry in open ground and by light infantry in broken terrain . . . Any attempt to move around the position would be reported quickly and unfailingly by the Cossacks.'[27]

During these weeks the French advance guard was usually led by Joachim Murat, the King of Naples. The commander of the Russian rearguard was Petr Konovnitsyn. A Russian officer remembers,

as a total contrast to the elegant outfit of Murat one had the modest general, riding a humble little horse . . . in front of the Russian ranks. He wore a simple grey coat, rather worn, and held together a bit carelessly by a scarf. Underneath his uniform hat you could glimpse his nightcap. His face was calm and his years, some way beyond middle age, suggested a cold man. But beneath this appearance of coolness there existed much warmth and life. There was a great deal of courage beneath the grey coat. Under the nightcap lived a sensible, energetic and efficient mind.[28]

Petr Konovnitsyn was one of the most attractive senior Russian generals in 1812. Modest and generous, he was less of an egoist and far less concerned with fame and reward than many of his peers. Extremely courageous but also very religious, in battle he was always in the thick of the action. The same was true at parties, where he played the violin badly but with fine gusto. Even so, Konovnitsyn was above all a calm man, who in moments of stress puffed away at his pipe, invoked the intercession of the Virgin Mary and seldom lost his temper. He controlled wayward subordinates more by irony than by anger.

Konovnitsyn also earned his subordinates' respect by professional skill. As a rearguard commander he knew exactly how to use his cavalry, infantry and artillery in combination and to best effect. Picking positions to bring advancing French columns under a crossfire was one trick. Trying to ensure that his own night-time bivouacs were close to fresh water and that the enemy was forced to thirst was another. In the intense heat of August 1812 water became a major issue. Thousands of men and horses marching down unpaved roads raised a vast dust storm. With faces blackened by the dust, throats parched and eyes half-closed, the men in the ranks stumbled onwards day after day. In these circumstances, which side had better access to water mattered greatly.[29]

On 29 August at Tsarevo-Zaimishche the army was joined by its new commander-in-chief, Mikhail Kutuzov. Young Lieutenant Radozhitsky recalled that morale soared:

The moment of joy was indescribable: this commander's name produced a universal rebirth of morale among the soldiers ... immediately they came up with a ditty: 'Kutuzov has come to beat the French' ... the veterans recalled his campaigns in Catherine's time, his many past exploits such as the battle near Krems and the recent destruction of the Turkish army on the Danube: for many men all this was still a fresh memory. They remembered also his miraculous wound from a musket ball which passed through both sides of his temple. It was said that Napoleon himself long since had called Kutuzov the old fox and that Suvorov had said that 'Kutuzov ... can never be tricked'. Such tales flying from mouth to mouth still further strengthened the soldiers' hope for their new commander, a man with a Russian name, mind and heart, from a well-known aristocratic family, and famous for many exploits.[30]

Ever since First and Second armies had joined before Smolensk the Russians had been in dire need of a supreme commander. Lack of such a commander had resulted in confusion and near catastrophe as the Russian troops withdrew from the city. In fact, however, Alexander had decided to appoint an overall commander-in-chief even before hearing of events at Smolensk. There were very few possible candidates. The supreme commander had to be unequivocally senior to all his subordinate generals, otherwise some would resign in a huff and others would drag their feet when obeying his commands. With Napoleon advancing towards Moscow and Russian national feeling outraged, it was also essential that the new commander be a Russian. Of course, he also needed to be a soldier of sufficient wit and experience to take on the greatest general of the age. Though a number of candidates were in principle discussed by the six grandees to whom Alexander delegated the initial selection, in reality – as the emperor recognized – there was little choice but Kutuzov.[31]

It was no secret within the Russian elites that Alexander did not admire Kutuzov. Captain Pavel Pushchin of the Semenovskys wrote in his diary that new supremo had been 'summoned to command the field army by the will of the people, almost against the wishes of the sovereign'. Alexander himself wrote to his sister that there had been no alternative to Kutuzov. Barclay had performed poorly at Smolensk and had lost all credit in the army and in Petersburg. Kutuzov was the loudly expressed choice of the Petersburg and Moscow nobilities, both of which had chosen him to command their militias. The emperor commented that of the various candidates, all of them in his opinion unfit to command, 'I could not do otherwise ... than fix my choice on him for whom overwhelming support was expressed'. In another letter to his sister he added that 'the choice fell on Kutuzov as being senior to all the rest, which allows Bennigsen to serve under him, for they are good friends as well'. Alexander did not say but probably believed that in the circumstances of 1812 it would be dangerous to ignore society's wishes: in addition, if disaster befell the army, it might even be convenient that its commander was known to be the choice of public opinion rather than of the monarch.[32]

Mikhail Kutuzov became a Russian patriotic icon after 1812, thanks partly to Leo Tolstoy. Stalinist historiography then raised him to the level of a military genius, superior to Napoleon. Of course all this is nonsense, but it is important not to react too far in the other direction by ignoring Kutuzov's talents. The new commander-in-chief was a charismatic leader who knew how to win his men's confidence and affection. He was a sly and far-sighted politician and negotiator. But he was also a skilful, courageous and experienced soldier. His trapping and destruction of the main Ottoman army in the winter of 1811–12 had shown up the previous efforts of Russian commanders in 1806–11. In 1805 he had extricated the Russian army with skill and composure from the very dangerous position in which it had been placed by the Austrian capitulation at Ulm. Had Alexander listened to his advice before Austerlitz, catastrophe would have been avoided and the 1805 campaign might have ended in victory.[33]

The main problem with Kutuzov was his age. In 1812 he was 65 years old and his life had been anything but restful. Though he could still ride, he preferred his carriage. There was no chance of his riding around a battlefield to act as his own troubleshooter in the style of a Wellington. The 1812 campaign entailed enormous strains, physical and mental, and at times Kutuzov's energy was suspect. On occasion he seemed to have an old man's aversion to risk and great exertion. In time it also became clear that Kutuzov did not share Alexander's views on Russia's grand strategy and the liberation of Europe. This did not matter in the first half of the 1812 campaign but it became important during Napoleon's retreat from Moscow.

Though the appointment of Kutuzov was certainly a great improvement it did not solve all problems in the Russian command structure and indeed created some new ones. Barclay de Tolly reacted loyally to Kutuzov's appointment and understood its necessity, but the enormous criticism to which he had been subjected made him very sensitive to slights from his new commander, and these were not slow in coming, above all from the new chief of staff, Levin von Bennigsen. Meanwhile, though Barclay's replacement by Kutuzov was a major concession to Russian sentiment it did not at all satisfy the leaders of the 'Russian party' at headquarters, Petr Bagration and Aleksei Ermolov. Perhaps Bagration himself dreamed of the supreme command, though this is hard to believe given that he knew how little favour he enjoyed with Alexander. Certainly, neither general thought highly of Kutuzov's ability. As for the new commander-in-chief, he respected Bagration as a battlefield commander. Rather like Barclay, he appreciated Ermolov's talent but had justified doubts about his loyalty.[34]

The problems were structural as much as personal, however. It would have been rational for the new commander-in-chief to suppress First and Second armies and to subordinate their seven infantry and four cavalry corps directly to himself and to his chief of staff, Bennigsen. To have done this, however, would have meant public demotion and humiliation for Barclay, Bagration and their staffs. This was contrary to the modus vivendi of the tsarist elite. It would also have required the emperor's assent, since he had appointed both generals and created their armies. The survival of both armies produced a cumbersome command structure, however. It also made conflict inevitable between the staffs of the supreme commander and those of Barclay and Bagration. In particular, Barclay soon found that general headquarters was poaching some of his staff officers and giving direct orders to some of his units.

In this case too, structures and personalities intertwined. The new chief of staff, Bennigsen, had only been persuaded to take the job with difficulty and after Kutuzov stressed the emperor's desire that he should do so. In traditional style, Alexander may have wanted to use Bennigsen to keep tabs on Kutuzov. He undoubtedly had more faith in Bennigsen's ability, as well as in his energy. To do Alexander justice, Kutuzov and Bennigsen had been firm friends for many years before 1812 so the emperor did not anticipate that they would become deadly enemies in the course of that year. Kutuzov was always suspicious of any subordinate who might seek to steal his laurels. Bennigsen on the other hand was intensely proud and firmly convinced that he was a far more skilful general than Kutuzov, let alone Barclay. In time-honoured fashion, feeling himself rather isolated, Kutuzov increasingly leaned on the advice and support of Karl von Toll, his old protégé. For Bennigsen it was intolerable that anyone else's advice should be preferred to that of the chief of staff but to be sidelined in favour of a mere bumptious colonel was a source of fury.[35]

Ever since the army had evacuated Smolensk, a relay of staff officers had been sent back down the road to Moscow to find good positions on which the army could fight Napoleon. It was unthinkable to almost all senior officers to give up Russia's ancient capital without a battle. Clausewitz describes well the difficulties these staff officers faced:

Russia is very poor in positions. Where the great morasses prevail [i.e. in much of Belorussia], the country is so wooded that one has trouble to find room for a considerable number of troops. Where the forests are thinner, as between Smolensk and Moscow, the ground is level – without any decided mountain ridges – without any deep hollows; the fields are without enclosures, therefore everywhere easy to be passed; the villages of wood, and ill adapted for defence. To this it must be added, that even in such a country the prospect is seldom unimpeded, as small tracts of wood constantly interpose. There is therefore little choice of positions. If a commander, then, wishes to fight without loss of time, as was Kutuzov's case, it is evident that he must put up with what he can get.[36]

What Kutuzov got was a position near the village of Borodino, 124 kilometres from Moscow. For the Russian staff officers who initially viewed this position from the main highway – the so-called New Smolensk Road – first impressions were very good. Troops standing on either side of the highway would have their right flank secured by the river Moskva and their front protected by the steep banks of the river Kolocha. Problems became much greater when one looked carefully at the left flank of this position, south of the main road. Initially the Russian army took up position on a line which ran from Maslovo north of the road, through Borodino on the highroad itself and down to the hill at Shevardino on the left flank. The centre of the position could be strengthened by the mound just to the south-east of Borodino which became the famous Raevsky Redoubt. Meanwhile the left could be anchored at Shevardino, which Bagration began to fortify.

Closer inspection soon revealed to Bagration that the position on the left assigned to his army was very vulnerable. A ravine in his rear impeded communications. More important, another road – the so-called Old Smolensk Road – cut in sharply behind his line from the west, joining with the main highway to the rear of the Russian position. An enemy pushing down this road could easily roll up Bagration's flank and block the army's line of retreat to Moscow. Faced by this danger, Bagration's army began to withdraw to a new position which abandoned Shevardino and turned sharply southwards from Borodino in a straight line to the village of Utitsa on the Old Smolensk Road. On 5 September Bagration's troops at Shevardino fought off fierce French attacks in order to cover the redeployment to this new line, losing 5,000–6,000 men and inflicting perhaps slightly fewer casualties on the enemy.[37]

The new line was certainly safer because it blocked the Old Smolensk Road. To do this, however, it had been forced to abandon the strong position at Shevardino and instead to stretch across terrain between Borodino and Utitsa which offered no help to the troops that were defending it. In addition, by turning sharply southwards near Borodino and the Raevsky Redoubt the Russian line now became a sort of salient with all the troops between Borodino and the left of Bagration's line beyond the village of Semenovskoe vulnerable to French artillery crossfire.

During the battle of Borodino on 7 September the great majority of the Russian army was packed into this small salient. This included five of the seven Russian infantry corps, which alone added up to 70,000 men. In addition, there were more than 10,000 cavalry in the 'salient'. Even the other two Russian infantry corps – Baggohufvudt's Second and Tuchkov's Third – detached half of their men to defend this area. The Russian deployment was not just on a very narrow front but also extremely dense. The infantry divisions were drawn up in three lines. In front were the jaegers. Behind them came two lines of infantry, deployed in so-called 'Battalion Columns'. These columns had a frontage of one company and a depth of four. Not far to the rear of the infantry divisions stood the cavalry, with the army's reserve units deployed behind them but still often within range of Napoleon's heavy artillery, to which the six or even sometimes seven lines of Russian troops offered a fine target.[38]

To explain what all this means to an English-language readership it is perhaps useful to make comparisons with the familiar landscape of Waterloo. Napoleon brought 246 guns to Waterloo, some of which had to be deployed even at the very start of the battle on his right against the Prussians. The so-called 'Grand Battery' which pounded Wellington's infantry squares in the afternoon of 18 June 1815 consisted of 80 guns. Napoleon's artillery was ranged face-to-face with Wellington's army. Almost all the fighting was confined to a line running roughly 3,500 metres east from the chateau of Hougoumont, into which Wellington packed his 73,000 men. Waterloo was indeed probably the most densely packed of the major battlefields of the Napoleonic Wars – with the exception of Borodino. The British commander partly shielded his men behind a reverse slope, though he was also helped by the fact that mud reduced the number of ricochets and therefore the killing power of Napoleon's guns.[39]

At Borodino Napoleon deployed 587 guns. The great majority of them were targeted against the Russian troops defending the line from just north of the Raevsky Redoubt to the three field fortifications which Bagration's men constructed beyond Semenovskoe, and which have gone down in history as the Bagration *flèches* – arrow-shaped earth-works, open to the rear, whose crumbling earthen breastworks offered little cover to defenders. When the *flèches* fell the Russian line bent southwards still more sharply around Semenovskoe itself. The distance from the Raevsky Redoubt to Semenovskoe is only 1,700 metres. The *flèches* were a few hundred metres beyond the village. More than 90,000 Russian troops were packed into this area. From Barclay's report after the battle it is clear that his lines within the salient were not just being subjected to cross-fire. French batteries near Borodino were also some-times on the flank of Russian lines and able to inflict maximum casualties by shooting right along them.[40]

It is true that Wellington was more skilful than either Russian or Prussian generals in using reverse slopes and other natural obstacles to shield his troops. But Barclay did on a number of occasions order his generals to keep their men under cover, only to be told that there was none available. When one walks around the position held by the Russian army on this still unspoiled battlefield it is easy to confirm the generals' claim. Contrary to tradition, some Russian commanders also told their men to lie down to avoid the bombardment, though not all units obeyed. The Russians can fairly be criticized for bunching their troops too tightly and not keeping at least their reserves and part of their cavalry beyond the range of Napoleon's guns. On the other hand the bone-hard stony ground did them no favours when it came to ricochets. Russian villages constructed of wood also gave no help to defenders and instead threatened them by bursting into flames. For that reason the Russians destroyed the village of Semenovskoe before the battle began. The contrast with the enormous assistance which the stone buildings at Hougoumont and La Haye Sainte gave to Wellington is obvious.[41]

The dense Russian deployment was designed to force Napoleon to fight a battle of attrition. The cramped battlefield would give his units little room to manoeuvre or to exploit tactical successes. It would in the most literal sense cramp Napoleon's own genius. The price to be paid, as the Russian commanders knew, was very high casualties. In addition, committing oneself to a battle of attrition more or less precluded any chance of a striking Russian victory. With Napoleon present in person and his army considerably outnumbering the Russians as regards trained troops, such a victory was in any case unlikely. In many ways therefore the battle of Borodino was a microcosm of the 1812 campaign as a whole, during which the Russian high command had forced Napoleon to fight the kind of war that suited them but not him.

History had accustomed Russian troops to fighting on terrain that gave them few natural advantages. By tradition therefore they were more inclined than most European armies to build field fortifications to strengthen a position. This they did at Borodino but with only limited success. The strongest and most professionally constructed fortifications were on the far north of the Russian line, beyond the village of Gorki. No fighting occurred in this area, so the fortifications were largely wasted. The two fortifications which did play a significant role in the battle were the much weaker Bagration *flèches* and the Raevsky Redoubt. Though the redoubt in particular was a key element in the Russian line of defence, one has to be very cautious in taking French descriptions of these supposedly formidable fortifications at face value.[42]

Neither the *flèches* nor the Raevsky Redoubt were built by engineer officers. All the small cadre of army engineers were assigned on other tasks as were most of the pioneer companies, which in any case even in principle were only 500 strong. The Moscow militiamen who did most of the construction work on the Raevsky Redoubt had no clue about how to build fortifications and were impeded by the stony ground and lack of implements. Matters were not helped by an argument between Toll and Bennigsen about how best to construct fortifications on the mound. Karl Oppermann, the army's senior and most authoritative engineer, devoted most of his attention to fortresses in 1812 and had not yet rejoined the main army in time for the battle. In addition, however, there were delays in finding spades and pickaxes for the militiamen. Work therefore began in the late afternoon of 6 September and continued through the night. Ensign Dementii Bogdanov and his small command of pioneers only arrived to help with the construction of the redoubt shortly before midnight. It was far from completed when the battle began on the morning of 7 September.[43]

As a result, according to the official history of the military engineering corps, there were all sorts of elementary mistakes even in the redoubt, let alone the *flèches*. The mound on which the Raevsky Redoubt was constructed is in any case small and low. In the end eighteen guns with one battalion of infantry as a covering force was all that could be squashed into the position. When one walks over the mound, it seems remarkable that the Russians managed to pack in even this many men. The slope up to the front of the redoubt was very gentle, the slope in its rear only a little less so. The militiamen had done their best to make up for these weaknesses but with limited success. One problem was that 'the counter-escarpment was much lower than the escarpment, and the ditch in front of the redoubt was completely inadequate'. Of course, the militiamen had no idea how to use fascines, gabions and other elements of the pioneer's art. Through lack of time, embrasures were only constructed for ten guns. One result of this was that the artillery within the redoubt could not cover part of the approaches. The area in front of the redoubt was swept by the fire of Russian batteries of First Army to the north and Second Army to the south but almost all these guns were deployed in the open and subjected to devastating enemy counter-battery fire. All of this, together with the massive artillery bombardment which it suffered on 7 September, helps to explain how the redoubt could finally be stormed by cavalry.[44]

The officer who initially oversaw the construction of the Raevsky Redoubt was Lieutenant Ivan Liprandi, the senior quartermaster of Dmitrii Dokhturov's Sixth Corps. That a mere lieutenant should be the second senior staff officer in a corps indicates the shortage of senior staff officers. That he should also be doing a job which belonged properly to a military engineer was due not just to the scarcity of engineer officers but also to the fact that First Army's engineers had been committed to building the much more formidable fortifications on the army's right flank north of Gorki. While so much effort went into fortifying the northern flank on 4, 5 and 6 September nothing was done until almost the eve of battle at the Raevsky Redoubt. This says a great deal about the priorities of the Russian high command and where they expected the most important fighting to take place.[45]

Even more striking was Kutuzov's initial deployment of the Russian army. Of the five infantry corps placed in the front line, two – Baggohufvudt's Second and Ostermann-Tolstoy's Fourth – were positioned north of Gorki, as was one regular cavalry corps and Platov's Cossacks. Dokhturov's Sixth Corps stood opposite Borodino and between the village of Gorki and the Raevsky Redoubt. The entire line south of the redoubt as far as the *flèches* was manned by the two corps of Bagration's Second Army: Nikolai Raevsky's Seventh Corps stood next to the redoubt and Mikhail Borozdin's Eighth Corps held the left of the line at and beyond the village of Semenovskoe. The two remaining corps of First Army, Nikolai Tuchkov's Third and the Fifth (Guards) Corps formed the overall reserve. The army's deployment as well as its fortifications thus reflected Kutuzov's overriding concern for his right flank and for the New Smolensk Road, which was his line of communications and supply to his base at Moscow.

In the two days before the battle, many of Kutuzov's senior generals pointed out the vulnerability of the Russian left flank. Napoleon's attack on Shevardino seemed to presage an assault on this section of Kutuzov's line. Even quite junior officers were aware that the enemy was likely to strike in the south. Kutuzov made some changes to counter this danger. Above all, he moved Nikolai Tuchkov's corps out of the reserve and onto the Old Smolensk Road to block any attempt to outflank the Russian left. But despite pleas from, among others, Barclay de Tolly, he insisted on keeping the corps of Baggohufvudt and Ostermann on his right flank beyond Gorki.[46]

An uncharitable explanation for this might be mere stubbornness, for which Kutuzov's chief adviser, Karl von Toll, was noted. Given antagonisms within the high command, to change the army's deployment on the advice of rival generals might smack of humiliation. More probably, Kutuzov and Toll were unwilling to weaken the force guarding their vital line of communication until absolutely convinced that Napoleon did not intend to strike in this direction. The price of defensive tactics is that troops must be deployed on the basis of assumptions and fears about where the enemy will strike. Given Napoleon's reputation for surprise and daring this might result in many units being wasted far from the battlefield. Once again a comparison with Waterloo may be useful. Deeply concerned by what proved to be a non-existent threat to his communications with the sea, Wellington kept 17,000 men under Prince Frederick of the Netherlands inactive at Hal for the duration, many kilometres from the battlefield. At least the 23,000 men of Ostermann and Baggohufvudt did join the battle of Borodino, albeit dangerously late.

Nevertheless the mis-deployment of Second and Fourth Corps had serious consequences. In their absence, Kutuzov was forced to send most of the army's supposed reserve into the front line by early on 7 September, contrary to all normal practice and much to Barclay's indignation. The fact that the Guards were moved without Barclay even being informed speaks to the confusion and divisions in the Russian command structure. In the end the two right-wing corps did act as a substitute reserve, but it took desperate appeals from Bagration to shift Baggohufvudt's men and two hours for them to arrive on the army's threatened southern wing. Ostermann's Fourth Corps moved even later. By the time all these reinforcements were on the spot, enormous losses had been suffered by Bagration's outnumbered Second Army.[47]

Disputes about exactly how many men each side brought to Borodino have rumbled on ever since 1812, partly out of a rather childish effort by historians to boost their side's prowess by proving it to have been outnumbered. The Russians certainly had more men but only if one counts the 31,000 militiamen from Moscow and Smolensk who were mostly armed with pikes and axes and had no military training. The militia was not totally useless, because it fulfilled auxiliary tasks such as collecting the wounded and acting as military police. But these militia units could not and in fact did not take any part in the fighting. If one discounts the militia entirely, Napoleon probably had a slight numerical edge: perhaps 130,000 of his soldiers faced somewhat less than 125,000 Russians. Certainly Napoleon had the edge if one discounts the 8,600 Cossacks in the Russian army. Though far more useful than the militia, most Cossack units could not be expected to stand against regular cavalry, let alone infantry, on a battlefield.[48]

As regards the quality of the two armies' regular units, even men who had started the campaign as rookies could now almost be seen as experienced troops. Weaklings had long since fallen out of the ranks during ten weeks of gruelling marches and battles. The one exception to this were the 13,500 men of the fourth (i.e. Recruit Depot) battalions commanded by General Mikhail Miloradovich, who joined Kutuzov one week before the battle and were dispersed among the regiments of First and Second armies. These men had been adequately trained but, as usual in the peacetime army, target practice had been constrained by shortage of lead and none of them had ever previously fired a shot in anger. On the other hand, the elite units of both armies were present in strength. In the Russian case this meant the regiments of Guards and Grenadiers. In Napoleon's it included the Guards, Davout's

First Corps, and many excellent German and French heavy cavalry regiments.[49]

The two armies prepared for battle in ways that reflected their rather different natures, but both were highly motivated and itching to fight after weeks of frustrating marches. As the decisive battle loomed, postponed so often and for so many weeks, both sides knew that they were fighting for very high stakes.

Kutuzov ordered the famous Icon of the Smolensk Mother of God, which had been evacuated from the city, to be carried down the line of his army. Segur recalls that the religious procession was visible from Napoleon's headquarters: they could see how 'Kutuzov, surrounded with every species of religious and military pomp, took his station in the midst of it. He had made his popes and archimandrites dress themselves in those splendid and majestic insignia, which they had inherited from the Greeks. They marched before him, carrying the venerated symbols of their religion.' Kutuzov was a master of speaking to his soldiers in terms they understood but after watching Smolensk and many other Russian towns burn, they barely needed his appeals to defend their native land and its faith to the last.[50]

By contrast the French army of 1812 was entirely secular, having preserved many of the republican norms of the 1790s. Moreover, the force which fought at Borodino included tens of thousands of Poles, Germans and Italians. Napoleon's order of the day, read out to his troops by their commanders, therefore spoke neither of religion nor patriotism. It appealed to the pride and confidence they should derive from their past victories and invoked the glory they would obtain in the eyes of posterity by having triumphed in a battle 'under the walls of Moscow'. More prosaically, but very much to the point, it stressed the necessity of victory: 'It will give you abundance, good winter quarters and a rapid return to your homeland.'[51]

Well into the afternoon of 6 September, while Napoleon was reviewing the Russian position from near Borodino, Marshal Davout approached him with a proposal to abandon plans for a frontal assault on Bagration's army and instead to authorize a flanking movement by 40,000 men of his and Poniatowski's corps down the Old Smolensk Road in order to envelop and roll up the Russian left flank. In principle this was a good idea. Napoleon needed a decisive victory and there had to be doubts whether this could be achieved by a frontal assault. The toughness and stubbornness of Russian troops were legendary. A flanking movement might bring on a battle of manoeuvre rather than attrition, which could only work to Napoleon's advantage.

Nevertheless the emperor was right to reject Davout's suggestion. Given the quality of their light cavalry the Russians were unlikely to be surprised by a flanking movement but in any case a threat to his flank might simply inspire Kutuzov to decamp which after so long a pursuit Napoleon dreaded. To redeploy Davout's corps for such a movement would by now require large-scale movements in the dark through the forests on the French right, which was a recipe for chaos. Moreover, the Russian strategy of whittling down Napoleon's army now bore fruit. Earlier in the campaign he could easily have spared 40,000 men for such a movement but by now his margin for risk and error was much more tight.[52]

Soon after first light on 7 September the battle of Borodino began. At about six in the morning the Russian Guards Jaeger Regiment was driven out of the village of Borodino and back across the river Kolocha, with heavy losses. The French attacked under cover of a mist and in over-whelming numbers. Either the regiment should not have been left in so exposed and isolated a spot or it had failed to take proper precautions. Barclay believed the former to be true and had urged the Jaegers' with-drawal on Kutuzov. But army gossip often blamed the regiment's com-manders for the defeat. The French units which had taken Borodino pursued the Guards Jaegers over the river Kolocha and were then ambushed and driven back with heavy losses, so in tactical terms the battle was a draw. Its broader significance was that it enabled the French artillery pounding the Raevsky Redoubt to be brought forward and given excellent positions to enfilade the Russian lines. This initial blow towards the northern end of the Russian line may also have persuaded Kutuzov that Napoleon might strike his right wing after all. If so, it can only have increased his hesitation about sending Ostermann and Baggohufvudt southwards.[53]

Shortly after the attack on Borodino the vastly bigger assault on the Bagration *flèches* began. Though initially the assault was made by Davout's men, quite soon Marshal Ney threw his corps into the battle as well. Russian sources claim that by the end of the fight 400 enemy guns supported the advance on the *flèches*. This sounds exaggerated but there is no question that the three divisions of Borozdin's Eighth Corps, the only Russian infantry initially deployed in this area, were heavily outnumbered and subjected to an immense bombardment. The three *flèches* – their earthen walls soon shattered by the French bombardment – were held by Count Mikhail Vorontsov's Second Combined Grenadier Division, which was annihilated in the course of the fighting and subsequently disbanded. Vorontsov himself was severely wounded. So too were most of the other generals of Second Army, who showed outstanding courage and self-sacrifice. Within three hours Petr Bagration, his chief of staff Emmanuel de Saint-Priest, and Mikhail Borozdin were all out of action.[54]

Both the French and the Russian armies used basically similar tactics. Attacks were mounted behind a cloud of skirmishers and with strong artillery support but the bulk of the infantry was deployed in columns. As Jomini pointed out in his theoretical writings, if the attacking force was sufficiently numerous and determined it was unlikely to be stopped by the musketry of enemy infantry themselves largely deployed in column. Having broken into the front line, however, the attacker would then be very vulnerable to immediate counter-attack by fresh enemy forces as yet untouched by the fighting and already deployed for a counter-strike in battalion columns. If both sides were equally motivated, attack would follow counter-attack and the pendulum would swing between the two sides until the first one to exhaust its reserves was defeated and withdrew. Great efforts have been expended by Russian historians to discover how many times waves of French infantry assaulted the *flèches* but this is almost impossible to establish and not that important. For all their immense courage the outnumbered Russians were finally forced to withdraw over the Semenovsky stream and redeploy on either side of the village of Semenovskoe.[55]

In the course of the ferocious battle for the *flèches* Bagration drew in reinforcements from both his right and his left. On the right this meant that some of the infantry of Nikolai Raevsky's Seventh Corps, positioned just to the left of the Raevsky Redoubt, redeployed southwards towards Semenovskoe. Meanwhile on the far left of the Russian line Nikolai Tuchkov was forced to send one of his two infantry divisions under Petr Konovnitsyn to help Bagration.

As a result, Tuchkov was hard pressed when Prince Poniatowski's Polish corps began its advance down the Old Smolensk Road towards the village of Utitsa. Fortunately for the Russians, Poniatowski had been forced to make a big detour to avoid getting lost in the forests, which suggests what kind of fate would have awaited Davout's much larger force had he attempted his proposed flank attack. When Poniatowski did advance, his 10,000 men forced the outnumbered Tuchkov to fall back to a stronger position anchored by a hill just to the east of Utitsa.

For the rest of the day fierce but ultimately indecisive fighting continued around Utitsa and the Old Smolensk Road. The Poles were reinforced by most of Junot's Westphalian corps. On the other side, Karl Baggohufvudt's Second Corps arrived to rescue Tuchkov. Meanwhile in the Utitsa forest between the Old Smolensk Road and the open ground where the *flèches* had been constructed Prince Ivan Shakhovskoy's jaeger regiments put up a tremendous fight, tying down a larger enemy force and, in the words of a German historian, showing 'not only their courageous endurance but also a skill which Russian light infantry did not always and everywhere display'.[56]

Once Baggohufvudt arrived, the battle on the Russian far left became something of a sideshow. Given the relatively even balance of forces in the area, it was very unlikely that Poniatowski would succeed in pushing far down the Old Smolensk Road and into the Russian rear. Much more dangerous was the situation around the Raevsky Redoubt. If the French broke through here they would split the Russian line in two. They would also be within easy striking distance of the New Smolensk Road, Kutuzov's key line of communication to the rear.

For more than two hours after the fall of Borodino the enemy's artillery and skirmishers poured fire on the defenders of the Raevsky Redoubt, but no mass attack was made by the infantry of Eugène de Beauharnais, who commanded the left wing of Napoleon's army. When the order for the attack did finally come, its weight was too great for the redoubt's defenders, who were driven off the mound. One problem for the Russians was that their artillery in the redoubt was running short of ammunition. In addition, the advancing columns were concealed by the dense clouds of smoke which clung around the redoubt in the still morning air. Panic resulted when the French infantry suddenly emerged out of the smoke and swarmed over the redoubt. Precise timings for the various episodes during the battle of Borodino are very difficult to establish. The one certainty as regards the attack on the redoubt is that it occurred shortly after Petr Bagration was wounded and after part of

Nikolai Raevsky's corps had left the area of the redoubt to go to his aid.[57]

On hearing the news that Bagration was a casualty, Kutuzov sent Aleksei Ermolov down to Second Army to help its remaining commanders and report back on the situation. Together with Ermolov rode Major-General Count Aleksandr Kutaisov, the overall commander of the artillery. Kutaisov was an able young artillerist, passionately committed to his profession. He was also handsome, kindly, charming and cultured, which helped to make him one of the most popular figures in the army. In this there was some irony since his grandfather, the first Count Kutaisov, was a universally loathed and barely literate former Turkish prisoner of war whom Paul I had made his close confidant and a count, partly to spite the Russian aristocracy.[58]

As Ermolov and Kutaisov were riding past the Raevsky Redoubt on their way to Second Army they saw the Russian troops in the neighbourhood in full flight. It was crucial for the Russians to counter-attack immediately before the enemy could consolidate its hold on the redoubt.

Aleksei Ermolov was just the right man for such an emergency. He immediately took command of the troops which remained in his vicinity and led them in a successful counter-attack. When Ermolov's men – mostly from the Ufa Regiment of Dokhturov's Sixth Corps – fought their way back into the redoubt they found other units from Sixth Corps, led by Barclay's aide-de-camp Vladimir Löwenstern, storming into the position from the other side of the hill. Meanwhile Ivan Paskevich had rallied the remnants of his own 26th Division and advanced in support of Löwenstern and Ermolov to the left of the redoubt. The Russian counter-attack succeeded because the Russian officers on the spot acted immediately, resolutely and on their own initiative, without waiting for orders. In addition, General Morand's division, which had spearheaded the assault, had moved ahead of Eugène de Beauharnais's other divisions and was isolated.[59]

For the Russians the most important casualty of the counter-attack was Aleksandr Kutaisov, who was killed in the retaking of the redoubt. His body was never found. No doubt the army's chief of artillery should not have risked his life in this way, and subsequently Kutaisov's death was used to explain mistakes in the way in which the Russian artillery was handled during the battle. Explanations were certainly in order. The Russians had 624 guns on the battlefield and, in particular, had many more heavy twelve-pounders than the French. Nevertheless they fired only the same number of rounds. Problems occurred with the re-supply of ammunition to batteries. Much worse, though individual batteries fought with great skill and courage, the Russians failed to concentrate their artillery fire. In key areas of the battlefield the Russian batteries were heavily outnumbered and smothered by enemy fire. After they were destroyed or forced to retire, the new batteries brought up from the reserve in ones and twos often then suffered a similar fate. According to Ivan Liprandi, this failing had little to do with Kutaisov's death. In his view, the Russians always failed to concentrate their artillery in 1812, though by 1813 they had learned their lesson and sometimes did better.[60]

In normal circumstances the repulse of Morand's division should have been followed by a renewed attack by the rest of Eugène's corps. In fact, however, hours passed before the next major attack, which was launched after three o'clock in the afternoon. The delay proved crucial. More than half of Paskevich's 26th Division were casualties and Barclay sent the division to the rear to rest and reorganize itself. He was able to do this because in the meantime the whole of Aleksandr Ostermann-Tolstoy's Fourth Corps had arrived and could be used to plug the gap between the Raevsky Redoubt and the Russian troops involved in the ferocious battle around the village of Semenovskoe. The 'lull' around the redoubt was strictly relative. Ostermann-Tolstoy's men were subjected to a devastating artillery barrage. But the full-scale infantry attack which might have broken through the weakened Russian defences near the redoubt in the late morning never occurred.[61]

The reason for this delay was that Eugène was distracted by a Russian cavalry raid which came in from the north and threatened his rear. The raid was initiated by Matvei Platov, whose Cossack corps stood on the far right of the Russian line. Early in the morning of 7 September his patrols reported that there were no French troops in front of them and that it was possible for cavalry to ford the river Kolocha and work their way southwards behind the French lines. As a result, not only Platov's Cossacks but also Fedor Uvarov's First Cavalry Corps were ordered off to harass Eugène. In reality a few thousand cavalry, unsupported by infantry and with just two batteries of horse artillery, were unlikely to achieve much. Platov's Cossacks raided Eugene's baggage train while Uvarov's regulars made a number of not very determined attacks on his infantry. At the time Kutuzov saw the attack as a failure and was annoyed by Uvarov's lacklustre performance. It was only much later that the Russians came to understand what a difference the raid had made.

Meanwhile throughout the late morning and early afternoon fierce fighting continued in and around the village of Semenovskoe, towards the Russian left. In the village and to its right were the remnants of Bagration's Second Army and Prince Grigorii Cantacuzene's small brigade of Grenadiers which had come up from the reserve to help them. To the left of the village stood Petr Konovnitsyn's infantry division and three Guards regiments, the Izmailovskys, the Lithuania (Litovsky) Guards and the Finland Regiment. Some way behind the infantry were the six dragoon and hussar regiments of Karl Sievers's Fourth Cavalry Corps but by the end of the day most of the Russian heavy cavalry had also been committed to the battle near Semenovskoe.

All the Russian infantry near Semenovskoe were subjected to repeated attacks and devastating artillery fire. Casualties were immense. The Guards were worst placed since there was no cover to the left of the village. On the contrary, the area where they stood was dominated by the other bank of the Semenovsky stream on which Davout and Ney brought forward and deployed many batteries. The range was so short that at times the French guns were firing canister into the ranks of the Russian Guards. The latter were under repeated attack from a mass of French cavalry so they were forced to remain in squares, the juiciest of all targets for artillery. As at Waterloo, the attacks of the enemy cavalry became a welcome respite from the artillery fire. The Guards also had to deploy many skirmishers against the French infantry attempting to break out from the forest to their left. Nevertheless the three regiments held firm against all these threats. They kept the French cavalry and infantry at bay, and their steadiness was the rock around which the Russian defence coalesced.

In all, the Izmailovskys and Lithuania Guards suffered more than 1,600 casualties. In the Lithuania Regiment, for example, all the majors and colonels were killed or wounded, some of them remaining in the ranks despite multiple wounds. Casualties were also very heavy in the Guards artillery batteries which moved forward in the regiments' support and were smothered by the more numerous French guns. Among these casualties, for example, was the 17-year-old ensign Avram Norov, who lost a leg at Borodino but nevertheless later made a brilliant career, ending as minister of education. His battery commander 'could not hold back his sorrow at seeing Norov, who was a handsome and fine young man – indeed really only a boy – disfigured for life. But Norov responded with his usual slight stammer. "Well, brother, but there's nothing to be done! God is merciful and I will recover and then get back to the battle on crutches." ' Kutuzov reported to Alexander that the Guards regiments 'in this battle covered themselves in glory under the eyes of the whole army'. Borodino was in fact the day in the Napoleonic Wars when the Russian Guards came of age as ever-reliable elite troops whose commitment could turn the fate of a battle.[62]

The Russians were ultimately forced to abandon Semenovskoe and retreat a few hundred metres to the east but they kept their discipline, continuing to present a firm front to the enemy. The French cavalry attacked the squares but could not break them. When they tried to break out to the rear of the Russian line they found that they had little room to manoeuvre and were counter-attacked by the Russian cuirassiers and by Sievers's Fourth Cavalry Corps, both of which more than held their own. By mid-afternoon it was clear that Davout's and Ney's corps were played out. If Napoleon was to break through the Russian line beyond Semenovskoe he would have to commit fresh troops. All that remained were his Guards. One of the Guards infantry divisions had been left behind at Gzhatsk but the other two were on hand and roughly 10,000 strong. Ney and Davout appealed to Napoleon for their release.

Ever since September 1812 a debate has raged as to whether the emperor's refusal to commit his reserve cost him a decisive victory at Borodino and thereby his chances of winning the campaign of 1812. There can be no definite answer to this. The Russians themselves disagreed about the probable result if Napoleon had sent forward his Guards. The best of the nineteenth-century Russian historians, General Bogdanovich, believed that he would have secured a decisive victory and thereby seriously damaged Russian morale. On the other hand, Eugen of Württemberg wrote that the introduction of the Guards would have turned an almost drawn battle into an unequivocal French victory but that Kutuzov's army would still have got away down the New Smolensk Road and the ultimate strategic outcome of the battle would therefore not have been altered.[63]

My own hunch is that Eugen was probably right. On the Russian side, the six battalions of the Preobrazhensky and Semenovsky Guards were still in reserve and had together suffered only 300 casualties from artillery fire. The Second Guards Infantry Brigade had already shown the Guards regiments' powers of resistance and the First Guards Brigade was not likely to do worse. As at Semenovskoe, other units would have formed around the Guards. Ivan Paskevich's division, for example, had been sent to the rear to re-form and was quite capable of renewing the struggle in emergency, as were a number of artillery batteries also withdrawn from the front line to rest and restock with ammunition. A combination of Russian stubbornness, the bushes and broken country behind the Russian lines, and the distance to the main highway probably meant that the Russians would be able to delay the French advance for long enough to allow the army to slip away. Given time, Kutuzov could also bring four untouched jaeger regiments and some artillery batteries down from beyond Borodino to form a rearguard. Barclay still believed that his army had a lot of fight left in it and was expecting the battle to be renewed on the next day.[64]

The whole debate is of course theoretical since Napoleon refused to risk his Guards. The smoke and dust thrown up by the battle made it impossible to see what was going on behind the Russian lines. The Russians had fought with immense stubbornness, which showed no sign of abating. The commander of the Guards, Marshal Bessières, whom Napoleon sent forward to spy out the land, reported that Russian resistance was still strong. With the possibility of another battle before Moscow and given the insecurity of his position deep in central Russia it is not surprising that Napoleon wished to retain his ultimate strategic reserve. The fact that the Guards were still intact was indeed to prove a major asset during the retreat from Moscow.[65]

Given the emperor's refusal to commit his Guards to the battle at Semenovskoe, his final chance of victory was to be Eugène de Beauharnais's second assault on the Raevsky Redoubt, which was launched not long after three o'clock. By now the redoubt was a near ruin. It was defended by Petr Likhachev's 24th Division of Sixth Corps, with Ostermann-Tolstoy's Fourth Corps in support to the left. The attack was spearheaded by heavy cavalry, which was an unorthodox way to take a field fortification. The hand-to-hand fighting in the confined space of the redoubt was grim. Dead and wounded men piled up in mounds. Likhachev himself was captured but most of the Russian defenders were slaughtered, though some of the guns were withdrawn in time. On this occasion enough of Eugène's remaining 20,000 infantry came up to consolidate their hold on the redoubt.[66]

Barclay de Tolly had been in the thick of the fighting all day, calmly re-forming and redeploying his regiments to meet one emergency after another. Dressed in full uniform and wearing all his decorations, he seemed to be – and indeed was – courting death. Most of his aides were killed or wounded. The example he showed of courage, coolness and competence at moments of extreme stress and danger won him renewed respect. Now once again, but for the last time on 7 September, he rallied his infantry and artillery a kilometre or so to the east in a good defensive position on rising ground and drew on his cavalry to stop the enemy from exploiting their capture of the redoubt. Napoleon's own cavalry had suffered heavy casualties in storming the Raevsky Redoubt. Their horses were also in a much worse state than those of their Russian opponents. On the other hand, Napoleon's regular cavalry outnumbered the Russians by a wide margin. Barclay was forced even to commit his ultimate reserve, the Chevaliers Gardes and the Horse Guards, but these elite troops drove back the enemy cavalry and his lines held. When Napoleon once again refused to commit his Guards to exploit the fall of the redoubt the battle of Borodino was over.

That night Lieutenant Luka Simansky of the Izmailovsky Guards recalled the day's events in his diary. The Smolensk Icon of the Mother of God was positioned close behind the Izmailovskys' bivouac and before loading their muskets the regiment had turned to pray to it. In their squares near Semenovskoe the regiment was deluged by round-shot and canister. In comparison the attacks of the enemy cavalry were relaxing. No Russian artillery seemed to be anywhere in sight. All the senior officers of the Izmailovskys fell. A staff captain commanded the battalion and a mere ensign its skirmishers. By some miracle Simansky himself was untouched. When his orderly saw him returning unscathed from the fray he burst into tears of joy. Simansky ended his entry by writing: 'I thought of my family and of the fact that I had remained calm and not budged one step from my post; of how I had cheered up my men and how I had prayed and given thanks to God as every cannon ball flew past me. The Almighty heard my prayer and spared me. Pray God that in His mercy he will also save dying Russia, which has already been punished for her sins sufficiently.'[67]

Kutuzov had spent the day at his command post on the right wing, near the village of Gorki. He had positioned his corps before the battle and played some role on 7 September as regards the release of the reserves. On the whole, however, he left Barclay and Bagration to conduct the fighting. When Bagration was wounded he sent Dmitrii Dokhturov to replace him but himself never budged from the hill at Gorki. This made good sense. Barclay, Bagration and Dokhturov were fully competent to run a defensive battle of this sort in which no grand manoeuvres were attempted by the Russians. They were also much younger and more mobile than Kutuzov. Moreover, he was irreplaceable. Had Kutuzov been killed the army's morale and cohesion would have collapsed. No other commander could have drawn anything approaching the same degree of trust and obedience. As Ivan Radozhitsky put it, 'only Field-Marshal Prince Kutuzov, a true son of Russia, nourished at her breast, could have abandoned without a fight the empire's ancient capital'.[68]

In the immediate aftermath of the fighting, abandoning Moscow seems to have been far from Kutuzov's mind. On the contrary, he told his subordinates that he intended to attack the next day. Only the news that Napoleon had not committed his Guards and that Russian losses were enormous persuaded him to change his mind. In all, the most recent Russian estimates suggest that they lost between 45,000 and 50,000 men at Shevardino and Borodino, as against perhaps 35,000 French casualties. In particular, Bagration's Second Army had been nearly destroyed. Even some weeks later, after stragglers had returned to the ranks, Second Army was reckoned to have lost more than 16,000 men on 7 September, and this was on top of the 5,000 lost at Shevardino two days before. As serious, casualties among the army's senior officers had been crippling.[69]

Kutuzov therefore ordered a retreat. For almost the only time during the campaign the Russian rearguard performed poorly. This was blamed on its commander, Matvei Platov, and was seen by regular officers as confirmation of their long-held view that Cossack generals were not competent to command infantry and artillery. The basic problem was that Platov's rearguard did not impose delays on the French or keep them at a sufficiently respectful distance from the main body of the retreating Russian army, as Konovnitsyn had always done with great skill. As a result, the already exhausted troops did not get the rest they needed. The army's precipitate departure from Mozhaisk meant that thousands of wounded were left behind, in sharp contrast to what had happened previously during the retreat. When Kutuzov reinforced the rearguard and replaced Platov by Mikhail Miloradovich matters improved greatly but the episode fed growing tensions between the regular and Cossack leaders.[70]

The basic point, however, was that the Russians were running out of space. Six days after the battle of Borodino, Kutuzov's army was on the outskirts of Moscow. The great question now was whether or not to fight for the city. Kutuzov would find it harder than Barclay to abandon Moscow. Both generals were patriots who had risked their lives on many battlefields, but the Russia for which they fought was not quite the same. Barclay had great loyalty and admiration for the Russian soldier but he was a Protestant Balt brought up in Petersburg. For him, Russia meant above all else the emperor, the army and the state. For reasons both of sentiment and interest these were very much part of Kutuzov's Russia too, but not all of it. For any member of the old Russian aristocracy who had not lost his roots there was also another Russia, an Orthodox land which had existed before the Romanovs and before the empire and whose capital was Moscow.

Kutuzov's last words to Alexander on leaving Petersburg to assume the supreme command were that he would rather perish than abandon Moscow. Shortly after arriving at headquarters he wrote to Rostopchin, Moscow's governor-general, that 'the question remains undecided as to which is more important – to lose the army or to lose Moscow. In my opinion the loss of Moscow entails the loss of Russia itself.' When the council of war met at Fili on 13 September, however, Kutuzov understood that actually this was no longer the question. If he stood and fought, there was every probability that both the army and the capital would be lost. No doubt the commander-in-chief had already made his decision to abandon the city before the council met at four o'clock that afternoon. But such a momentous step could not be taken without consulting his senior generals. Moreover, Kutuzov was anxious to share some of the responsibility for a decision which was bound to cause huge anger and condemnation.[71]

The main protagonists at the council of war were Bennigsen and Barclay. The former had chosen the ground on which the army was preparing to fight outside Moscow. In time-honoured fashion pride alone would have forbidden him to admit that he had made a mistake. From his subsequent correspondence with Alexander it was also clear that he was anxious to thrust responsibility for the city's loss onto Kutuzov and Barclay. At the council of war Barclay set out the reasons why the Russian army would certainly be defeated if it stood on the defensive in this position. Not only would they be greatly outnumbered but their position was divided up by ravines, which would make it very difficult to coordinate resistance. A lost battle would entail a rushed retreat through Moscow, which could easily result in the army's disintegration. The only possibility was to attack Napoleon's army but the huge loss of officers at Borodino made a battle of manoeuvre immensely risky. Toll and Ermolov shared Barclay's view, though Ermolov lacked the moral courage to speak up and take responsibility in front of his seniors. On the contrary, Barclay showed not just moral courage but also some generosity of spirit by speaking up decisively and thereby sharing the burden of responsibility of a man who had superseded him in command.[72]

There remained the difficult task of getting an exhausted and somewhat demoralized army with all its baggage and some of its wounded through the streets of a great city. With the enemy on their heels this could be an extremely dangerous enterprise. Matters were not helped by the fact that the news that Moscow was to be abandoned had broken on the civilian population very late. As the army passed through Moscow on 14 September a mass civilian exodus was still under way. One staff officer described the scene as 'not the passage of an army but the relocation of whole tribes from one corner of the earth to another'. Barclay did his usual indefatigable best to impose some order on this chaos. Officers were posted at key intersections to direct the troops. Cavalry rode down the sides of the columns to stop desertion and plundering. Barclay himself oversaw arrangements.[73]

The true hero of the occasion, however, was Miloradovich, who was now commanding the Russian rearguard. His opposite number in the French advance guard was usually Joachim Murat, and the two men had much in common. Both generals were showmen who loved splendid clothes and the grand gesture. It would be an understatement to say that neither man was an intellectual but Miloradovich was not only honourable and generous but on occasion surprisingly modest and shrewd. He certainly summed up the essence of the present danger and with some *bravura* sent his aide-de-camp to Murat to suggest a one-day truce so that the Russians could depart, leaving the city intact. In the event that this request was refused, Miloradovich threatened to fight in the streets and turn Moscow into a ruin. Even more than most of the French generals, Murat was longing for comfortable quarters, peace and a return home. Perhaps lulled by Napoleon's own illusions, he saw the fall of Moscow as a prelude to peace. All this disposed him not just to accept Miloradovich's offer of a truce but also subsequently to extend it for a further twelve hours. As a result of Miloradovich's cheeky initiative, the Russian army emerged from Moscow almost unscathed.[74]

In principle Kutuzov might have retreated out of Moscow in a number of directions. Had he turned north-west, for instance, he could have blocked the road to Tver and Petersburg, whose population was bound to be in an uproar at the news of Moscow's fall. In fact he retreated south-eastwards down the road to Riazan. This was in many ways the safest exit from Moscow in the face of an enemy who was entering the city from the west. On 17 September, however, after crossing the river Moskva at Borovsk, Kutuzov turned sharply westwards. Marching rapidly he crossed the roads to Kashira and Tula before turning southwards down the Old Kaluga Road which led out from Moscow to the south-west.

Meanwhile on 15 September Napoleon entered Moscow and set up his headquarters in the Kremlin. That very day fires started in many parts of the city. Moscow burned for six days. Three-quarters of its buildings were destroyed. In all, during the summer and autumn of 1812, 270 million rubles' worth of private property was destroyed in the city and province of Moscow, an astronomical sum for that era. The overwhelming majority of the civilian population had already fled but those who remained were driven from their homes, made destitute and sometimes killed. Of the more than 30,000 wounded soldiers who had been in Moscow, all but 6,000 were evacuated in time, thanks above all to the efforts of James Wylie, the efficient head of the army's medical services. But very many of those who were left behind died in the flames. When the Russians recaptured Moscow they found and burned 12,000 corpses.[75]

Even before the fire began the Russians had also been forced to abandon vast stocks of military materials in the city, including more than 70,000 muskets, though admittedly half of these were in need of repair. Moscow had been the rear base for Kutuzov's army and by the time the news came that the city was to be abandoned it was very difficult to evacuate all military stores. Finding sufficient carts at this last moment was impossible, so most weapons, equipment and other military goods were evacuated on twenty-three barges. The first three escaped but the fourth, overloaded by the artillery department, got stuck in the river Moskva and blocked the passage of the remaining nineteen. These barges carried almost 5 million rubles' worth of weapons, clothing and equipment, all of which had to be burned in order to keep it out of Napoleon's hands.[76]

Who or what caused the fire has always been a source of dispute. The one certain point is that neither Alexander nor Napoleon ordered the city to be burned. Rostopchin said before the city's fall that the French would only conquer its ashes. He evacuated the 2,000 men of Moscow's fire brigade and all its equipment. Cossack detachments from Kutuzov's army burned one at least of the city's quarters, following a scorched-earth policy of destroying all houses which the Russians had pursued ever since Napoleon passed Smolensk and invaded the Russian heartland. Kutuzov also ordered that the many remaining military stores should be set alight. Although French carelessness and plundering may have contributed to the city's destruction, it was undoubtedly the Russians who were most responsible for what happened. What mattered at the time, however, was the perception that Napoleon was to blame and that the city's destruction was a huge sacrifice to Russian patriotism and Europe's liberation.[77]

Maybe the fire helped to distract French attention from Kutuzov's flank march from the Riazan to the Kaluga road. In normal circumstances this would have been a risky undertaking since it took the Russian columns right across the front of Napoleon's army in Moscow. In fact, however, a combination of French exhaustion and the Cossack rearguard's skill meant that it was some time before Napoleon even realized that his enemy was no longer en route to Riazan.

Once installed in his camp near Tarutino on the Old Kaluga Road, Kutuzov was in a strong position. He could cover the arms works and stores at Briansk and above all the crucial arms factories and workshops at Tula. At the news of Moscow's fall many artisans in the Tula arms works fled back to their native villages. Major-General Voronov, the commandant of the Tula arms works, reported that if he was forced to evacuate Tula it would be six months before production could resume, which would have been a disaster for the Russian war effort. The field-marshal was able to reassure him that Tula was now covered by the Russian army and in no immediate danger.[78]

At Tarutino Kutuzov was excellently positioned to send out raiding parties to harass the long French lines of communication stretching westwards from Moscow all the way back to Smolensk. He was also best placed for communication with Tormasov and Chichagov. Since his food supplies and reinforcements were mostly coming up through Kaluga from the fertile and populous southern provinces, his new deployment gave him every opportunity to feed his men and horses and rebuild their strength. To understand how this was done, however, means we must turn aside from military operations for a moment and look instead at the mobilization of Russia's home front.

7

The Home Front in 1812

Napoleon's plan had been to wage a limited 'cabinet' war against Alexander I. The French emperor might contemplate wiping Prussia off the map but he believed that it was neither in his power nor in his interests to destroy the Russian Empire. Instead he hoped to weaken Russia, force her back into the Continental System, and make her accept French domination of Europe. Far from desiring to drive Alexander off his throne or throw Russian society into revolution and chaos, Napoleon looked to the tsar to agree peace conditions and then enforce them on Russian society. Partly for this reason, he stressed his personal respect for Alexander during the 1812 campaign and made clear his view that the true initiator of the war was Britain and her stooges in the Petersburg elite.

Alexander and his advisers well understood Napoleon's aims and tactics. In this as in every other way, they sought to impose on him the kind of war he least wanted to fight. In political terms this meant a Spanish-style national war to the death, in which the emperor would refuse all negotiations and would seek to mobilize Russian society behind the war effort by appeals to patriotic, religious and xenophobic sentiment. In his memorandum of April 1812 Petr Chuikevich stressed that Russia's key strengths must include 'the resoluteness of its monarch and the loyalty to him of his people, who must be armed and inspired, as in Spain, with the help of the clergy'. In addition, in a national war fought on the nation's soil Russian society would willingly provide the resources and make the sacrifices which victory over Napoleon's immense empire would require.[1]

The best source on Alexander's own views about the war's domestic political context is the record of a long conversation he had in Helsingfors (Helsinki) in August 1812 while on the way to his meeting with

Bernadotte. The emperor noted that for the past century all Russia's wars had been fought abroad and had seemed to most Russians to be far removed from their own immediate interests and concerns. The landowners had resented the conscription of their peasants and all setbacks resulted in relentless criticism of the government and its military commanders.

In present circumstances it was necessary to persuade the people that the government did not seek war and that it was arming only in order to defend the state. It was vital strongly to interest the people in the war, by waging it for the first time in over a hundred years on the territory of their motherland (*rodina*). This was the only way to make this a truly people's war and to unite society around the government, of its own freewill and conviction, and in the cause of its own defence.

Alexander added that the united resolution shown by Russian society since Napoleon's invasion showed that his calculation had proved correct. He added that, as for himself, he would never make peace so long as a single enemy soldier remained on Russian soil, even if that meant standing firm on the line of the river Volga after being defeated in battle and losing Petersburg and Moscow. The Finnish official to whom Alexander was speaking recorded in his memoirs that the intelligence, clarity and resolution with which the emperor spoke was impressive and inspiring.[2]

From the moment Napoleon crossed the frontier Alexander proclaimed the national character of the war. After the line of defence on the river Dvina was breached and the French approached Smolensk and the borders of Great Russia, this call was redoubled. In early August Barclay de Tolly wrote to the governor of Smolensk, Baron Casimir von Asch, that he knew that the loyal population of the province would rise up to defend 'the Holy Faith and the frontiers of the Fatherland', and that in the end Russia would triumph over the 'perfidious' French as it had in the past over the Tatars.

In the name of the Fatherland call upon the population of all areas close to the enemy to take up arms and attack isolated enemy units, wherever they are seen. In addition I have myself issued a special appeal to all Russians in areas occupied by the French to make sure that not a single enemy soldier can hide himself from our vengeance for the insults committed against our religion and our Fatherland,

and when their army has been defeated by our troops then the fleeing enemy must everywhere meet ruin and death at the hands of the population.[3]

When Alexander left the army on 19 July and set off to Moscow to mobilize the home front for war, his immediate priority was to create a militia as a second line of defence against the invaders. Aleksandr Shishkov drafted the imperial manifesto appealing for the support of all estates of the realm for the new militia. The manifesto harked back to the so-called Time of Troubles exactly two hundred years before, when Russian society had risen up against an attempt to put a Polish prince on the throne and had ended a period of Russian powerlessness and humiliation by electing the first Romanov tsar and rebuilding a strong state.

The enemy has crossed our frontiers and is continuing to carry his arms into Russia, seeking to shake the foundations of this great power by his might and his seductions ... With slyness in his heart and flattery on his tongue he brings us ever-lasting chains and fetters ... We now appeal to all our loyal subjects, to all estates and conditions both spiritual and temporal, to rise up with us in a united and universal stand against the enemy's schemes and endeavours.

After appealing to the nobility – 'at all times the saviours of the Fatherland' – and the clergy, the manifesto turned to the Russian people. 'Brave descendants of courageous Slavs! You always smashed the teeth of the lions and tigers who sought to attack you. Let everyone unite: with the Cross in your hearts and weapons in your hands no human force will defeat you.'[4]

In the Soviet era it was an article of faith for Russian historians that the 'patriotic masses' were the key to resistance against Napoleon's invasion. By far the greatest contribution of the 'masses' – which in this era really meant the peasantry – to the Russian war effort was their service in the armed forces and the militia. From 1812 to 1814 roughly one million men were drafted, more than two-thirds of them into the regular army. No peasant volunteered for the army. In the first place, it would have taken a saintly degree of patriotism to volunteer for twenty-five years' service with minimal prospects of promotion to senior NCO, let alone into the officer corps. In any case peasants were not allowed to volunteer. Their bodies belonged to the state and to the landlords, not to themselves.

Nor were peasants allowed to volunteer for the militia. The latter was formed only from privately owned serfs, not from the state peasantry. It was entirely up to the landlord which peasants were assigned to serve. In principle, service in the militia was a less awful prospect than service in the regular army because the emperor had promised that militiamen would be released at the end of the war. The promise had to be renewed on many occasions and the militiamen were allowed to keep their beards and to dress in everyday peasant clothes, in order to underline the point that they were not soldiers. Nevertheless, no one could easily forget that at the end of the 1806–7 war the great majority of militiamen had in fact been transferred to the regular army.

In March 1813 John Quincy Adams was told by his landlord that none of the Petersburg militia would ever return home. Many had already perished. 'The rest have been, or will be, incorporated in the regiments [i.e. of the regular army]. Not one of them will ever come back.' In fact this was too pessimistic. Alexander kept his promise and the militia was disbanded and the men sent home at the end of the war. Losses had been immense, however, above all due to disease, exhaustion and the sheer shock of wartime military service for many peasants. Of the more than 13,000 men mobilized into the Tver militia in 1812, for example, only 4,200 returned home in 1814 and this was by no means exceptional.[5]

In Soviet times great stress was also laid on so-called 'partisan warfare' in 1812. The partisans of the Napoleonic era were portrayed as the ancestors of the partisan movement behind German lines in 1941–5 and as key heroes of a 'people's war'. The incautious Western reader thereby gets the impression that something akin to the French *maquis* played a major role in harrying Napoleon's communications in 1812. In fact this is to misunderstand the meaning of the word 'partisan' in the Napoleonic era. The Russian partisan units which struck deep into the French rear in 1812 were commanded by officers of the regular army. The core of these units were usually squadrons of regular light cavalry detached from the main Russian armies. Around them were grouped Cossack regiments. Sometimes armed civilians joined these detachments but the most important role of the civilian population was to provide local guides and intelligence on French movements and whereabouts. Partisan raids began even before Napoleon advanced beyond Smolensk and they were to continue in 1813–14. In strategic terms the most important partisan raids actually occurred in early 1813. Led most famously by Aleksandr Chernyshev, these penetrated deep into Prussia and played a major role in bringing Prussia into the Russian camp.[6]

A much more genuine 'people's war' was waged by the peasantry of provinces close to Napoleon's line of advance in 1812. When the French army occupied Moscow it was forced to send out ever larger foraging parties to secure food and, above all, fodder for the horses. The resistance these parties encountered in the villages was a major nuisance to Napoleon and rammed home the point that if he tried to sit in Moscow through the winter his army would be without horses and thereby immobilized when the 1813 campaign began. Much of this peasant resistance was not completely spontaneous. The local noble militia commanders and officials organized cordons of 'home guards' to beat off French foraging parties and marauders. But in many cases the peasants organized resistance by themselves.

There are numerous reports of peasant ambushes of foraging parties, some of which developed into running battles that lasted a number of days. In early November 1812 Kutuzov reported to Alexander that in the great majority of cases the peasants of Moscow and Kaluga provinces had rejected all overtures from the French, had hidden their families and children in the forests, and had then defended their villages against foraging parties. 'Quite often even the women' had helped to trap and destroy the enemy. There is no reason to doubt accounts that the Russian peasants were infuriated by the way in which the French turned churches into stables, storehouses and dormitories. Even more obvious is the elemental small-scale patriotism involved in defending one's home and family against alien plunderers.[7]

As regards spontaneous action by the peasantry, however, the most important issue was not what the masses did but what they did not do. The government's appeals to the population, with their references to enemy slyness and seduction, reflect the elite's worries about potential peasant insurrection. In fact this did not occur. In part this was because Napoleon did not try to launch a peasant war against serfdom. Until the French army reached Smolensk this would have been unthinkable because in Lithuania and most of Belorussia the landlords were Polish and therefore Napoleon's potential allies. Beyond Smolensk, the French might have tried to incite insurrection but they only stayed in Great Russia for two months and in any case Napoleon's strategy was to defeat the Russian army and then agree peace terms with Alexander. By the time he realized that the Russian emperor would not negotiate it was far too late to adopt an alternative strategy. In any case, though an appeal to the peasantry to throw off serfdom might well have increased the chaos in the Moscow area, the behaviour of Napoleon's army made it unthinkable that Russian peasants would trust him or look to him for leadership. In the Russian heartland there were no alternative indigenous potential leaders or shapers of social revolution.

On the other hand, even without Napoleon's incitement there was a good deal of anarchy in the Moscow region in the autumn of 1812. There were three times more peasant disturbances than in an average pre-war year and most of these disturbances occurred in the areas close to military operations, where the state's authority had been weakened. The effects of shaken authority were apparent to all. One week after the fall of Moscow Prince Dmitrii Volkonsky recorded in his diary that a drunken NCO had insulted him in an inn, which was not at all a normal experience for a Russian lieutenant-general. He added, 'The people are ready for disturbances, assuming that everyone in authority has fled in the face of the enemy.' In some cases these 'disturbances' were serious, though always very localized, and they required the detachment of small regular units from the field army.[8]

The worst peasant disturbances occurred in and around Vitebsk province, which was the area of operations of Peter Wittgenstein's First Corps. A number of landowners were murdered or assaulted in the summer and autumn of 1812, sometimes by crowds of 300 peasants or more. On one notorious occasion a troop of forty dragoons was routed by the rioters, two dragoons were killed, twelve taken prisoner and their officer badly beaten up. The civil authorities could not cope with this level of trouble and appealed to Wittgenstein for help. In the short run he refused, saying that he had too few cavalry and only one regiment of Cossacks. These had to concentrate on the autumn counter-offensive to drive the French out of Polotsk. Wittgenstein added that the disturbances had been caused by the French incursion into the region and would quickly cease once the enemy was ejected, which in fact occurred soon after.[9]

In time, however, Wittgenstein was able, for example, to deploy a squadron of Bashkirs on one particularly troublesome estate. This underlines a general point. In some areas close to the war authority briefly tottered, though it never collapsed in any large area unoccupied by the French. But the Russian Empire was enormous and the government could draw on resources from regions untouched by crisis. On 21 November, for example, Alexander wrote to the war minister, Prince Aleksei Gorchakov, that there were no fewer than twenty-nine irregular cavalry regiments, twenty of them Bashkir, en route from the Urals and western Siberia. These might often be of limited use against the French but they were more than adequate to overawe the peasants of Vitebsk.[10]

For the government, the loyalty of the peasantry was closely connected to the issue of order in the towns, and especially in Moscow. Only one-third of the city's population were full-time, deeply rooted urban residents. Nobles and their horde of household serfs migrated to their estates in the late spring and returned as winter approached. In addition, many peasant workmen and artisans worked for part of their lives in the city but retained their links to their villages. The household serfs, concentrated in large numbers and with their ears open to their masters' gossip, were of particular concern to the authorities. Calm and order in Moscow was the responsibility of Fedor Rostopchin. In the empire as a whole it was the responsibility of the minister of police, Aleksandr Balashev. Rostopchin employed all his wiles to divert and pacify Moscow's masses, but his letters to Balashev suggest confidence in public order and the masses' loyalty in the late spring and early summer of 1812. Only at the last, after the authorities had evacuated the city and during the French occupation, did anarchy take hold in Moscow. Servants looted their masters' homes, respectable women turned to prostitution in order to survive and the general mayhem was increased because gaols emptied and prisoners roamed the streets in search of easy pickings. As in the countryside, however, this was anarchy pure and simple, without any of the leadership or ideology to fuel social revolution.[11]

The government had no reason to fear for the loyalty of the urban elites. Russian merchants were usually deeply conservative and Orthodox in their mentalities, and contributed generously to the war effort. Moscow showed the lead here. When Alexander visited the city in late July to appeal for support for the militia, the city's merchants instantly pledged 2.5 million rubles, over and above their other existing contributions to the war effort. Even less need the government fear the Church, which was its main ideological ally in mobilizing mass resistance to the invader. In the war of 1806–7 the Orthodox Church had issued an anathema against Napoleon which caused some embarrassment after Tilsit. Now, however, the clergy could denounce the Antichrist with full gusto. On 27 July the Synod issued a blistering manifesto, warning that the same evil tribe which had brought down God's wrath on the human race by overthrowing their legitimate king and Church were now directly threatening Russia. It was therefore the duty of every priest to inspire unity, obedience and courage among the population in defence of the Orthodox religion, monarch and Fatherland.[12]

Given the nature of Russian society and government in this era, it was inevitably the support of the nobility which was most crucial to the war effort. Nobles controlled most of the resources which the state needed for its war and often could not afford to pay for: surpluses of food and fodder, horses, manpower. Nobles would have to provide the great majority of the officers for the militia and the enormously expanded army. Even in peacetime the crown depended on the nobility to help it govern Russia. Below the level of the provincial capital, elected noble marshals, police captains and court officials were the administration's bedrock. In wartime their jobs became even more essential and far more burdensome. One of their key traditional tasks was managing the system of conscription. In 1812–14 they had to handle ten times more conscripts than would normally have been the case. Nobles also needed to volunteer for new jobs. Transport columns of food, fodder and equipment had to be escorted from deep in the Russian interior to the armies. So too did thousands of horses. The hugely overworked officers of the internal security troops needed noble volunteers to assume some of the burden of escorting parties of new recruits to the army and prisoners of war away from it.

It is true that in this emergency the crown had the right to require the nobles' assistance. A hundred years before, in the reign of Peter the Great, male nobles were forced to serve as officers for as long as their health permitted. After Peter's death compulsory service was first reduced in length and then in 1762 abolished. Catherine II subsequently confirmed the nobles' freedom from compulsory service to the state but the charter she issued to the nobility made an exception for emergencies.

Since the title and dignity of noble status from ancient times, now and in the future is won by service and labour useful to the empire and to the throne, and since the existence of the Russian nobility depends on the security of the father-land and the throne: for these reasons at any time when the Russian autocracy needs and requires the nobility to serve for the common good then every noble-man is bound at the first summons of the autocratic power to spare neither his labour nor his very life for the service of the state.[13]

Though no one could deny that the present situation was precisely the kind of emergency envisaged by Catherine II, her grandson with his usual tact 'invited' the nobility to contribute to the war effort and expressed his conviction that noble patriotism would respond to his call with enthusiasm. But the provincial governors often referred to these 'requests' as the emperor's commands. When it came to sharing out the financial burden of providing supplies for the army or to finding officers for the militia the marshals of the nobility also assumed that all nobles had the obligation to serve the state at this time of crisis. Though they usually called first for volunteers, they had no doubt of their right to assign nobles to the militia when this was necessary. Many nobles volunteered for the army or the militia out of patriotism and on their own initiative. Others responded loyally to the noble marshals' call. But there were also many examples of nobles who evaded service. Faced with evasion, provincial governors and noble marshals harangued and blustered but actually did very little to punish evaders. Probably the only effective response would have been imprisonment, confiscation of property and even execution, but none of these seems to have been even threatened.[14]

This says something fundamental about the Russia of Alexander I. Alexander's regime was in some ways formidable and devastating in the demands it imposed on the Russian masses, especially in wartime. But this was not the Russia of Peter the Great, let alone of Stalin. It was not possible to control the elites through terror. Nobles could not openly oppose Alexander's policies but they could drag their feet and subvert the execution of policy: their sabotage of attempts to increase tax revenue from noble estates in the months before the war illustrates this facet of their power. Noble sentiment therefore had to be taken into account and the elites needed to be wooed as well as constrained. Indeed, faced by Hitler's invasion even Stalin's regime realized that terror was not enough and that Russian patriotism must be mobilized. Alexander needed no reminding on this score, still less on the need to achieve harmony with the nobility in order to stabilize the home front and ensure commitment to the war. In late August he told one of his wife's ladies-in-waiting that so long as Russians remained committed to victory and 'so long as morale doesn't collapse, all will go well'.[15]

The diary of Major-General Prince Vasili Viazemsky illustrates why Alexander did need to worry about noble 'morale'. The Viazemskys were an ancient princely family but only a few of them were still rich and prominent by the reign of Alexander I. Vasili Viazemsky owned fewer than a hundred serfs and was definitely not in this group. His career had been spent far from Petersburg and the Guards, in ordinary jaeger regiments. Though well educated, his concerns and opinions were those of the middling provincial gentry. When the war began, Viazemsky was commanding a brigade of jaegers in Tormasov's Third Army, guarding the approaches to the Ukraine.

Like almost all his peers, Viazemsky was baffled and dismayed by the retreat of the Russian army in the face of Napoleon's invasion. By early September, as news arrived that Napoleon was approaching the Russian heartland, bafflement turned to anger.

One's heart trembles at Russia's condition. It is no wonder that there are intrigues in the armies. They are full of foreigners and are commanded by parvenus. Who is the emperor's adviser at court? Count Arakcheev. When did he ever fight in a war? What victory made him famous? What did he ever contribute to his fatherland? And it is he who is close to the emperor at this critical moment. The whole army and the whole people condemn the retreat of our armies from Vilna to Smolensk. Either the whole army and the entire people are idiots or the person who gave orders for this retreat is an idiot.

In Viazemsky's view his personal prospects and those of his country were intertwined and gloomy. Russia faced defeat and the loss of its glory. It would be reduced in size and population, its long and weak borders thereby becoming even more difficult to defend. A new system of administration would be needed and would be a source of much confusion. 'Religion has been weakened by enlightenment and what therefore will be left to us as regards the control of our ungovernable, tempestuous and hungry masses?' With new demands now being imposed on noble estates to support the militia, 'my own position will be really good. Every tenth man taken as a militia recruit from my estate and I have to feed the people they leave behind: I don't have a kopek,

I have many debts, I have nothing to support my children and no secure future in my career.'[16]

In the summer of 1812 Alexander worried that the morale of Russia's elites might collapse and they in turn harboured doubts about his strategy and the strength of his commitment to victory. Nevertheless the alliance between crown and nobility held firm. This was hugely important as regards the army's supply during the 1812 campaign.

On the eve of the war Alexander appealed to Russian society to help provide food and transport for the army. In response, Moscow's nobles and merchants donated a million rubles in one day. In far-off Saratov on the banks of the Volga the governor, Aleksei Panchulidzev, received Alexander's appeal and a 'request' from the minister of police that Saratov province contribute 2,000 oxen and 1,000 carts to help with the army's transport and an additional 1,000 cattle for its food. The nobles and town corporations of the province agreed but added an extra 500 cattle to this list on their own initiative. They reckoned that in Saratov a cart with two oxen would cost 230 rubles, of which the cart itself accounted for only 50. Beef cattle would cost 65 rubles a head. In addition, however, 270 workers would have to be hired for six months to get the carts and animals to the army. Their pay was 30 rubles a month, which came to 48,600 rubles in all. Even before the war had begun, Saratov had therefore committed more than 400,000 rubles to the army's upkeep.[17]

During the 1812 campaign the field armies spent extremely little on food. Total expenditure by the Russian field armies was only 19 million rubles in 1812, most of which was the troops' pay. In the initial stage of the campaign the army was partly fed from the magazines established in the western borderlands in the two previous years. Food and fodder sufficient to feed an army of 200,000 men and their horses for six months had been stored. These preparations were only partly successful, however, since there were too few small magazines (*etapy*) at intervals along the roads down which the army retreated. In any case, the stores had often been positioned to support a Russian advance into the Duchy of Warsaw. One Soviet source suggests that 40 per cent of the food stored in magazines was lost to the French or, much more often, burned, though the intendant-general, Georg Kankrin, had always denied this.[18]

From the start of the campaign food was requisitioned by the army's intendancy or even just taken from the civilian population by the regiments in return for receipts. This made good sense. Any food not taken by the Russians would be seized by the French. The system of handing out receipts was supposed to ensure that requisition was conducted in orderly fashion and did not become mere plunder. It was also designed so that the government could compensate the population later for the food supplied. The Russian government did actually do this, after the war setting up special commissions to collect the receipts and offset them against future taxes. In a way, therefore, when it worked properly the system of requisitioning and providing receipts was a sort of forced loan, which allowed the state to defer wartime expenditure until its finances returned to peacetime order.[19]

How Russian troops were supposed to feed themselves when on campaign was set out in great detail in the new law on field armies issued early in 1812. The basic principle was that the army must requisition all the food it needed from the local population. The catch was that the new law was designed to cover Russian armies operating abroad. Two months later, however, in late March 1812 the scope of this law was extended to campaigns in the Russian interior as well. Provinces declared to be in a state of war would come under the authority of the army's commander-in-chief and of his intendant-general, to whom all civil officials were subordinated. As one might expect of a law designed for the administration of conquered territory, the powers given to the military authorities were sweeping. The supplementary law only envisaged border regions coming within its scope but by September 1812 a swath of provinces reaching as far as Kaluga to the south of Moscow had been declared to be in a state of war. In these provinces much of the business of feeding the army, caring for its sick, and even levying winter clothing for the coming campaign was dumped on the shoulders of the provincial governors.[20]

Between them the army's intendants, the provincial governors and the nobility ensured that Russian troops seldom went hungry in the first half of the 1812 campaign. This was not too difficult in the prosperous Russian heartland of the empire during and just after the harvest season. It helped that a network of magazines existed in the Russian countryside as a guarantee against harvest failure and famine. On a number of occasions the nobles agreed to feed the army from these magazines which they would then refill at their own expense. Voluntary contributions of food, fodder, horses, transport, equipment and clothing were very numerous. As one might expect, the biggest donations came from nearby provinces which felt the enemy threat and could most easily transport supplies to the army. Probably no other province quite matched the scale of Pskov's contribution to Wittgenstein's corps but Smolensk and Moscow were not far behind, and Kaluga's governor, Pavel Kaverin, proved immensely efficient and hard-working in channelling supplies to Kutuzov's army in the camp at Tarutino. One rather sober contemporary historian puts the voluntary contributions to the war from Russian society in 1812 at 100 million rubles, the great majority of which was provided by the nobles. Accurate estimates are very difficult, however, since so much of this contribution came in kind.[21]

At the same time as they were helping to feed the army, the provincial governors and nobles were also being asked to help with the creation of new military units which would form a second line of defence behind Barclay's and Bagration's armies. The first requests for assistance went out from Alexander in Vilna in early June, in other words before Napoleon had crossed the Russian border.

Part of this new military reserve was to be the recruits currently assembled in the ten so-called 'second-line' recruit depots. Major-General Andreas Kleinmichel was given the task of forming six new regiments – in other words somewhat fewer than 14,000 men – from these conscripts. With Napoleon now advancing through Belorussia, Kleinmichel was ordered to concentrate and train his six regiments well to the rear, in the area between Tver and Moscow. He was given an excellent cadre of officers and veteran troops to help him in this task. They included all the training cadres from the second-line recruit depots and all the officers and NCOs left behind to evacuate stores and close down the twenty-four first-line depots. In addition, he was sent two battalions of the Moscow garrison regiment and two fine battalions of marines from Petersburg. In time Kleinmichel had enough officers to be able to dispatch some of them to help Prince Dmitrii Lobanov-Rostovsky, who was struggling to form twelve new regiments in the central Russian provinces.[22]

Alexander's orders to create these twelve regiments were drafted on 25 May in Vilna. The great novelty was that these regiments were supposed to be created and paid for by the efforts of provincial society. The state would supply recruits and muskets but it was hoped that nobles who had previously served in the army would come out of retirement and provide all the officers. A province's nobles were expected to pay for their regiment's uniforms, equipment and food. The town corporations must pay for their transport. The twelve regiments would be formed in six provinces: Kostroma, Vladimir and Iaroslavl to the north, and Riazan, Tambov and Voronezh to the south. Each of these six provinces was supposed to officer and equip one regiment. Nine other provinces were to share responsibility for the formation of the six remaining regiments.[23]

As usual when receiving orders of this sort, the governor's first move was to discuss the matter with his province's marshal of the nobility. The district noble marshals were summoned to the provincial capital to organize the new decree's execution. Given the size of Russian provinces, it was seldom possible to arrange the governor's crucial meeting with the district marshals within less than eight days. Both the nobles and the town corporations immediately accepted the task set by the monarch. Alexander had suggested that the three southern provinces – Riazan, Tambov and Voronezh – coordinate their efforts to form their regiments. Their governors reckoned that it would cost 188,000 rubles to feed, clothe and equip each regiment and a further 28,000 rubles to build its transport wagons. Prices differed greatly across Russia's regions, however. The Kostroma noble marshals believed that in their province 290,000 rubles would be needed. The marshals agreed to divide the required sum equally among all the province's serfowners.[24]

Raising the money was relatively simple. Acquiring the uniforms, equipment and wagons was far more complicated. The governors and noble marshals had little experience of forming regiments and these weeks of dire emergency as Napoleon advanced into Russia were not the easiest time to learn. All the provinces agreed that most of the equipment and materials would have to come from Moscow. Since a single regiment required, for example, 2,900 metres of dark-green cloth and almost 4,500 pairs of boots, a great deal of transport had to be arranged. The three southern provinces opted to have the uniforms tailored in Moscow because they did not have sufficient workers competent to do the job in time themselves. The result was that, for example, 1,620 uniforms for the Riazan regiment never left Moscow and were destroyed in the fire. The northern provinces were much less purely agricultural, however, and Governor Nikolai Pasynkov was convinced that the tailors of Kostroma could handle the task for themselves.[25]

All the provinces baulked at the need to construct ammunition and provisions wagons on the models supplied by the army, though in Kostroma Governor Pasynkov told the local artisans to construct an approximation to the model. Much more common was the wail from the governor of Penza, deep into the agricultural region south-east of Moscow: 'For all my desire and zeal to help with the actual construction of the ammunition and provisions wagons, it is totally impossible for me to do so because we completely lack artisans who could do such work.' Very soon the governors were relieved to hear that they need only provide the money for the wagons, which would be built in Moscow under the supervision of the city's commandant, Lieutenant-General Hesse. Unfortunately, however, Alexander and Balashev had neglected to forewarn Hesse, who reacted to the governors' joyous thanks for his help with bafflement. It was to avoid messes like this in the future that on 29 June Alexander made Aleksei Arakcheev his chief assistant for military administration. Arakcheev never had much influence on strategy or operations but for the rest of the war he was to be a very effective overlord of all matters concerning the mobilization, training and equipment of Russia's reserve and militia forces.[26]

The desperate efforts required to form the new regiments tell one much about Russian provincial life in Alexander's reign. In Riazan, the local merchants tried to charge exorbitant sums to feed the regiments forming around the town. Perhaps because they would have to pay for half of this food anyway, the nobility offered to provide it all for free. The provincial marshal, retired Major-General Lev Izmailov, who had a vicious reputation for mistreating his serfs, took a large proportion of this burden on himself. More difficult was medical help for the new regiments. There only appear to have been two doctors available in Riazan in 1812. One of them, young Dr Gernet, behaved heroically, adding care for the regiments' sick to his usual job, volunteering to accompany them when they went on campaign, and even paying for some of their medicines out of his own pocket. Dr Moltiansky on the other hand did everything possible to avoid helping the soldiers even when they were in Riazan and flatly refused to accompany them on campaign. In the end Governor Bukharin forced him to do so by threatening to exile him from the province and thereby destroy his practice.[27]

The most difficult task of all was to find enough officers for the new regiments. Alexander clearly overestimated nobles' willingness to return to service, and failed to offer sufficient incentives for them to do so. The governor of Voronezh province reported to Lobanov in early July that although he had summoned an emergency assembly of the province's nobles not one of those present had volunteered to return to military service. In Riazan, 'the number of men wanting to become officers was very small, even among the very numerous nobility of the province'. Returning to military service contradicted the basic pattern of life for Russian nobles, by which young men served for a number of years as bachelor officers and then retired to the provinces to marry, run their estates, or take up elected jobs in the local administration. In time the number of volunteers grew, and it may have helped that the emperor now allowed ex-officers to return at the rank to which they had been promoted on retirement, rather than the one last held when in their regiments. In some cases, however, dire poverty seems to have been the main motive for nobles to return to military service.[28]

Lobanov did not help his own cause by interpreting Alexander's decree in typically nit-picking and infuriating fashion. Among the governors, Prince Aleksei Dolgorukov of Simbirsk seems to have been the most enthusiastic about trying to mobilize volunteers to return to military service. By mid-August he had sent forty-two would-be officers to join Lobanov's regiments. By Dolgorukov's own recognition one of these men, retired Sub-Lieutenant Ianchevsky, was a marginal case, since he had at one point been censured for drunkenness. The governor wrote to Lobanov that he was submitting Ianchevsky's case to him for decision, since the man was very repentant and wanted to redeem himself on the battlefield. Lobanov believed in fulfilling imperial orders down to the last comma, however, and promptly issued an official reprimand against Dolgorukov since the emperor's decree inviting ex-officers to return to service had required them to have good records.[29]

Even by mid-September Lobanov's regiments had less than half their full complement of officers, and of the 285 men assigned to regiments only 204 were nobles returning to service, most of the rest coming from that thoroughly dubious source, the internal security troops. The urgent need for the 227 spare officers dispatched by Andreas Kleinmichel is clear. On the other hand Lobanov had been sent twelve excellent officers from the Petersburg cadet corps, as well as an almost complete battalion of trainee NCOs from one of the grenadier training units. He had also been promised officers, NCOs and the best unmarried veterans from the units patrolling the frontier in south-western Siberia, who had already set out on their long trek to join his command.[30]

Lobanov's battle with Prince Dolgorukov was by no means the only fight which enlivened the formation of the twelve regiments. One of Lobanov's two assistants, Major-General Rusanov, was so infuriated by his boss's behaviour that he denounced him directly to the emperor, much to Arakcheev's rage. There were also conflicts between the military officers overseeing the regiments' formation and the provincial marshals, since the officers were interested only in getting the units ready at top speed whereas the marshals were also concerned at the price of the uniforms and equipment, for which they were going to have to pay. For all the arguments and difficulties, however, the new regiments proved a success. Six of them, together with three of Kleinmichel's regiments, reinforced Kutuzov's army while the latter was in camp at Tarutino. The field-marshal reported to Alexander that despite the 'very short' time available to train them 'they were extremely well formed and most of the men also shoot well'.[31]

Whatever the quality of Lobanov and Kleinmichel's troops, 40,000 reinforcements were far too few to turn the war in Russia's favour. Even as the two generals were struggling to form their eighteen regiments, Alexander ordered a massive new recruit levy – the 83rd – designed to net well over 150,000 conscripts. It would take months to assemble and train these men, however. To provide a second line of defence in the interim Alexander appealed to his nobles to mobilize and officer a temporary wartime militia from their serfs. In fact, with French troops already threatening their province the nobility of Smolensk was beginning to organize a 'home guard' even before the emperor's appeal. But the drive to mobilize the militia was really launched when Alexander travelled to Moscow in late July. There he met a strong patriotic response to his appeal from the Moscow nobility. On 30 July a manifesto was issued, calling for a militia to be mobilized in sixteen provinces.[32]

In all, some 230,000 men served in the militia. Almost all of them were private serfs, just as their officers were in the great majority of cases nobles from the militia's own province. No state or crown peasants joined the militia. This made good sense. It was vital not to drain the pool of recruits for the regular army since the army would always be the core of Russian military power and the key to victory. In addition, finding enough officers for the militia was bound to be difficult. Nobles might well feel some obligation to serve in militia forces volunteered and formed by their own province's noble assemblies, though many did in fact do everything possible to avoid this obligation. Finding suitable men to officer a militia drawn from state and crown peasants would be impossible.[33]

The militiaman was to keep his civilian clothes. He needed a cloak (*kaftan*) which had to be voluminous enough for him to wear a fur jacket underneath it. His two pairs of boots also had to be wide enough to accommodate feet wrapped in socks and leggings against the winter cold. He would also need two Russian shirts with slanted collars, some handkerchiefs and puttees, and a cap which could be tied under his beard and keep his head warm in winter.[34]

Both the peasant militiamen and the state liked this arrangement. For the militiaman it implied recognition that he was not a soldier and would return home at the end of the war. Meanwhile the state was freed from the obligation to provide militiamen with uniforms, which in present circumstances it was totally incapable of doing. As the minister of the interior reported in mid-July, there was already a 340,000-metre deficit on existing military orders for uniform cloth. It was totally inconceivable to meet the projected additional wartime requirement for 2.4 million metres. Not merely, wrote the minister, were there too few factories but Russia even lacked the sheep to provide this amount of wool. In fact, apart from the Guards, Dmitrii Lobanov-Rostovsky's men were the last Russian recruits in 1812–14 to be supplied with the dark-green uniforms traditional in the Russian infantry. All subsequent conscripts had to struggle along in shoddy, grey 'recruit dress', made from inferior 'peasant cloth' and ill-suited to the rigours of a campaign.[35]

The new militia was divided into three districts. The eight provinces of the first district were in principle committed to the defence of Moscow. The two provinces (St Petersburg and Novgorod) which made up the second district were given the task of defending the emperor's capital. Both these districts were to be mobilized immediately. The third district of six provinces was not to be mobilized until after the harvest, and even then in stages. The third district's commander was Lieutenant-General Count Petr Tolstoy, previously the ambassador in Paris. Tolstoy was far happier fighting Napoleon than paying court to him. As he explained, if only someone would give him enough artillery to cover his attacks, he would launch his columns of militia armed with pikes against the enemy in a Russian version of France's own *levée en masse* of 1793.[36]

Much the most effective militia in 1812 were the regiments formed by St Petersburg and Novgorod. With Wittgenstein keeping the French at bay, they had a short time to train before being committed to action. The capital's garrison provided officers and NCOs with long experience of training recruits. With the St Petersburg Arsenal at their service, all these militiamen received muskets. After five days and nights of training, Alexander I reviewed the Petersburg militia in the presence of the British ambassador, Lord Cathcart. Watching the new recruits perform their basic drill with remarkable skill, the ambassador commented to Alexander that 'these men have sprouted out of the earth'. In the autumn 1812 campaign the Petersburg and Novgorod militias were to fight alongside Wittgenstein's regulars in a number of battles, performing better than anyone had a right to expect.[37]

The operations of the second militia district in 1812 were exceptional. Unlike their Prussian equivalent – the Landwehr – in 1813–15, the Russian militia was never integrated into brigades and divisions with units of the regular army. In the great majority of cases it remained an auxiliary corps rather than a part of the field army. In the early autumn of 1812 most militiamen were employed to man cordons and block roads in order to stop enemy foraging parties and marauders breaking out of the area around Moscow. When Napoleon retreated some militia units were used to police reconquered territory and help with the restoration of order, administration and communications. Others escorted prisoners of war. In 1813 most of the militia was used to blockade Danzig, Dresden and a number of other fortresses in the allied rear with large enemy garrisons of regular troops. None of this work was particularly heroic or romantic, though it took a heavy toll in lives. Nevertheless, the militia's role was very important because it freed tens of thousands of Russian regular soldiers for service in the field.[38]

A crucial problem for the militia in 1812 was lack of firearms. By the end of July Russia was facing an acute shortage of muskets. By now almost 350,000 of the 371,000 muskets held in store in the eighteen months before the war had been distributed. Current production of muskets depended almost entirely on state and private manufacturers in Tula. Between May and December 1812 Tula produced 127,000 muskets, at an average of just under 16,000 a month. After the fall of

Moscow, however, many artisans fled from Tula back to their villages, which seriously affected production for many weeks and infuriated Alexander. Subsequently much effort had to be directed into manufacturing pistols for the cavalry reserves and for a time the main source of Russian muskets was the 101,000 imported from Britain and the many thousands captured from the French. Correctly, Kutuzov put top priority on arming the new recruits destined for the field army. The militia came at the back of the queue for firearms. The leftovers it received were usually of wretched quality and most militiamen in December 1812 were still armed with pikes.[39]

All of this was a big disappointment to Kutuzov. On appointment as commander-in-chief, one of his first concerns was to learn what reserve forces stood behind the armies in the field. The truth was discouraging. The last remnant of what had initially been seen as a second line of defence were Miloradovich's battalions, most of which joined Kutuzov before Borodino. All that now remained were Lobanov and Kleinmichel's regiments, and the militia. Even if Lobanov could arrive in time to defend Moscow, Alexander forbade Kutuzov to use his regiments. In the emperor's opinion the men were insufficiently trained and, more importantly, it was crucial to retain a cadre around which the horde of new recruits could be formed into an effective army. Part of the Moscow and Smolensk militias did arrive in time to defend the city. After Borodino Kutuzov incorporated some of them into his regiments in order to make up for his enormous losses. With so many untrained and sometimes even unarmed men in the ranks, however, it is not at all surprising that he and Barclay rejected the idea of risking a battle on the outskirts of Moscow.[40]

As a result, the city was lost. Thanks to Miloradovich and Barclay, the army did not disintegrate as it retreated through Moscow but in the following days it came closer to doing so than on any previous occasion. For the first time Kutuzov was not greeted with cheers as he rode past his marching regiments. To exhaustion and enormous losses were now added the shame and despair of abandoning Moscow without a fight. As always, a thin line could divide official requisitioning from arbitrary theft. Discipline suffered and many soldiers began to plunder the countryside. The Cossacks took the lead here but they were by no means alone. An impromptu market for plunder – officially taken from the French – was established near the camp at Tarutino.[41]

Even a few junior officers joined in the plundering. Most felt deep gloom and a sense of betrayal at Moscow's abandonment. Lieutenant Radozhitsky recalls that 'superstitious people, unable to comprehend what was going on in front of their eyes, thought that Moscow's fall meant the collapse of Russia, the triumph of the Antichrist and soon after a terrible judgement and the end of the world'. Far away with Tormasov's army a despairing Major-General Prince Viazemsky asked God why he had allowed Moscow to fall: 'This is to punish a nation that so loves thee!' But Viazemsky had no lack of mundane villains on whom to blame disaster. They included 'allowing foreigners to take root, enlightenment . . . Arakcheev and Kleinmichel and the degenerates of the court'. If this already came very close to blaming the emperor, the Grand Duchess Catherine was even more explicit in her letters to her brother. She told him that he was widely condemned for poor direction of the war and for dishonouring Russia by abandoning Moscow without a fight.[42]

Although the despair was fierce, it was also rather brief. Within a few days moods were changing. A staff officer wrote that the sight of Moscow on fire, though initially contributing to the gloom, soon transformed it into anger: 'In the place of despondency came courage and a thirst for revenge: at that time no one doubted that the French had deliberately set fire to it.' The view began to spread that all was far from lost and that, as young Lieutenant Aleksandr Chicherin of the Semenovskys put it, the barbarians who had invaded his country would be made to pay for their 'impertinence'. Barclay de Tolly contributed to the change of mood by visiting every unit in his army to explain why the Russians now had the upper hand and would win the campaign. Lieutenant Meshetich recalled how Barclay explained to the men of his battery that he had operated according to a plan and that 'the long retreat had denied any successes to the enemy and would lead to his ruin, since he had fallen into a trap which had been prepared for him and would cause his destruction'.[43]

At Tarutino the army resumed some elements of its normal life. Kutuzov insisted that religious services should be compulsory every Sunday and feast day, and he set an example by attending them all himself. That other great institution of Russian life, the bath-house, also came to the rescue as regiments got down to constructing *banias* for themselves. The fierce disciplinary code of the army also made its mark, on this occasion usefully. On 21 October, for example, Kutuzov confirmed a court martial's death sentence on Ensign Tishchenko, who had turned his platoon of jaegers into a robber band, robbing and even killing the local population. The death sentence on eleven of his jaegers was reduced to running the gauntlet three times between 1,000 men.[44]

Perhaps as much as anything, however, the change of mood was owed to the fact that after months of movement and exhaustion, the army finally had a few weeks rest in the camp at Tarutino. The position and fortifications of the camp were not particularly strong but the French army had shot its bolt and left the Russians in peace. Just after the harvest in fertile central Russia the army could remain sedentary for a few weeks without going hungry. Abundant supplies came up through Kaluga from the rich agricultural provinces to the south. Reinforcements moved up too. Lieutenant Chicherin of the Semenovskys arrived in Tarutino soaked to the skin, penniless and without any change of clothes, since all his baggage had been lost in Moscow. But his family came to the rescue, bringing him among other things a tent so palatial that it was temporarily borrowed by Kutuzov himself. He recalls that the weather was perfect and that the officers indulged in conversations, music and reading – all enjoyed with the special flavour of a wartime camp. Only one point truly worried them and that was the fear that their emperor might make peace with the French. One of the officers commented that if that happened he would emigrate and fight Napoleon in Spain.[45]

The decision on war or peace rested with the emperor in Petersburg. In all reason there was no cause to expect him to make peace. Frederick William III had fought on after the fall of Berlin and Francis II had refused to make peace after the fall of Vienna both in 1805 and 1809, though in the latter case the Austrians were fighting without allies. Moscow was not even Alexander's real capital. In addition, to make peace after Moscow's fall, in the teeth of elite opposition, was to put his life and throne at risk, as the emperor well knew. Underlying many of the tensions of 1812, however, was the fact that neither Alexander nor the Russian elites fully trusted the other to keep their nerve or preserve their commitment to victory amidst the great strains of Napoleon's invasion.[46]

After leaving the army on 19 July Alexander had paused briefly in Smolensk to consult with his provincial governor and generals before pressing on to Moscow. He arrived in the city late in the evening of 23 July. The next day provided one of the most striking images and memories of 1812 and was immortalized by Leo Tolstoy. At nine in the morning of a bright summer day, when Alexander emerged onto the 'Red Steps' outside his Kremlin palace in order to make his way to the Uspensky cathedral he was greeted by an immense crowd, packed so tightly that his adjutants-general had a great battle to force a path through to the church. One of these generals, Evgraf Komarovsky, wrote, 'I never saw such enthusiasm among the people as at that time.' The emperor was greeted with the ringing of the bells of all the Kremlin churches and wave after wave of cheers from the crowd. The ordinary people pressed forward to touch him and implored him to lead them against the enemy. This was the union of tsar and people, the core political myth of imperial Russia, in its fullest and most perfect form. Even more than in normal times, at this moment of threat and uncertainty, for most ordinary Russians the monarch was the supreme focus for their loyalty and a vital part of their identity.[47]

The next day Alexander met the nobles and merchants of Moscow, who greeted him with promises of massive support in men and money for the new militia. The emperor was moved, subsequently commenting that he felt unworthy to lead such a people. Delighted by Rostopchin's achievement in mobilizing this vast show of loyalty and support, Alexander kissed him on both cheeks on his departure. Aleksei Arakcheev congratulated Rostopchin on this unique mark of imperial approval. 'I who have served him since the day he began his reign have never received this.' Aleksandr Balashev, the minister of police, overheard this remark and subsequently muttered to Rostopchin, 'You may be very sure that Arakcheev will never forgive or forget that kiss.' Amidst all the patriotic enthusiasm normal political life continued in other ways too. When Alexander was leaving Rostopchin asked him for instructions as to future policy but the emperor responded that he had full confidence in his governor-general, who must act according to circumstances and his own judgement. In the midst of war's chaos this was fair enough but it did mean that Rostopchin ultimately bore sole responsibility for the fire which destroyed the city.[48]

Except for a brief expedition to Finland to meet Bernadotte, Alexander spent the rest of the summer and autumn in Petersburg. When he returned from Finland on 3 September he found waiting for him Sir

Robert Wilson, a British officer who had been attached to the Russian army in 1806–7 and who had just arrived in Petersburg from Barclay de Tolly's headquarters. Wilson spoke to Alexander about dissension among his generals and their opposition to Barclay, which came as no surprise to the emperor. Far more shocking was his generals' request that he rid himself of Rumiantsev or, as Wilson put it, if his generals 'were but assured that His Majesty would no longer give his confidence to advisers whose policy they mistrusted, they would testify their allegiance by exertions and sacrifices which would add splendour to the crown, and security to the throne under every adversity'.[49]

Fine rhetoric aside, this was a demand by his generals to impose their will on the monarch. It was certainly not made more palatable to Alexander by being conveyed through the agent of a foreign power. Wilson recorded that 'during this exposition the Emperor's colour occasionally visited and left his cheek'. Alexander took some time to regain his composure, though he handled Wilson's démarche with skill and patience. Calling Wilson 'the rebels' ambassador', he reacted calmly to his generals' request, saying that he knew and trusted these officers: 'I have no fears of their having any unavowed designs against my authority.'[50]

Alexander insisted, however, that his generals were wrong to believe that Rumiantsev had ever advised submission to Napoleon. He could not dump a loyal servant 'without cause', especially as 'I have a great respect for him, since he is almost the only one who never asked me in his life for anything on his own account, whereas everyone else has always been seeking honours, wealth, or some private object for himself and connections'. Above all, there was a vital principle involved. The emperor must not be seen to give way to such pressure, which would set a very dangerous precedent. Meanwhile, however, Wilson must 'carry back to the army pledges of my determination to continue the war against Napoleon whilst a Frenchman is in arms on this side of the frontier. I will not desert my engagements, come what may. I will abide the worst. I am ready to remove my family into the interior, and undergo every sacrifice; but I must not give way on the point of choosing my own ministers.'[51]

During the summer Alexander lived in the small palace – really little more than a villa – on Kamennyi Ostrov, a small island in one of the branches of the river Neva in Petersburg's northern suburbs. There were no guards in sight and Alexander lived in great simplicity. It was here that he learned the news of Moscow's fall, all the more shocking because of Kutuzov's previous claims to have held the French at Borodino. His wife's lady-in-waiting, Roxandra Stourdzha, recalled that rumours flew round Petersburg. Riots among the plebs were feared and widely expected. 'The nobility loudly blamed Alexander for the state's misfortunes, and in conversations it was a rare person who tried to defend and justify him.' September the twenty-seventh was the anniversary of the emperor's coronation. For once Alexander bowed to his advisers' fears for his safety and travelled to the Kazan cathedral in a carriage, rather than on horseback as usual. When the imperial party went up the stairs into the cathedral they were greeted by absolute silence. Roxandra Stourdzha was no faint-heart but she remembered that she heard the echo of every step and her knees trembled.[52]

A foolish letter from his sister Catherine attacking his performance drove Alexander over the edge, his reply illustrating just how strained his feelings were at this critical time. After pointing out to Catherine that it hardly made sense to criticize him both for undermining his generals by his presence with the army and for not taking over command and saving Moscow, he wrote that if his abilities were not sufficient for the role which fate had given him, that was not his fault. Nor was the poor quality of so many of his military and civilian lieutenants.

With such poor backing as I have, lacking adequate means in all areas, and guiding such a vast machinery in a time of terrible crisis and against an infernal opponent who combines the most awful evil with the most transcendent talent, and is backed by the whole power of Europe and by a group of talented lieutenants who have been honed by twenty years of war and revolution – in common justice is it surprising if I meet with reverses?

But the sting of Alexander's letter was in the tail, where he wrote that he had been warned that enemy agents would even seek to turn his family against him, with Catherine herself as their first choice. Even the very self-confident grand duchess was shocked by this response and Alexander subsequently relented by adding, 'If you find me too touchy, begin by putting yourself in the cruel position where I am.'[53]

At a time when his own blood relations were proving worse than useless, Alexander did get loyal support from his wife, the sensitive and beautiful Empress Elizabeth. She remained calm and confident throughout these weeks, writing to her mother that 'in truth we are prepared for everything except negotiations. The further Napoleon advances the less he should believe that any peace is possible. That is the unanimous view of the emperor and all classes of the population . . . each step he advances in this immense Russia brings him closer to the abyss. Let us see how he copes with the winter.' She added that peace would be the beginning of Russia's destruction but fortunately it was impossible: 'The emperor does not even conceive of the idea and even if he did want to do this, he would not be able to.'[54]

If Alexander drew comfort from his wife and from walking in the groves on Kamennyi Ostrov, his main solace was religion. The emperor had been brought up in Catherine II's court on a combination of Enlightenment rationalism and aristocratic hedonism. The Orthodox clergy who tutored him in their religion left little mark. But the sensitive and idealistic sides of his personality increasingly inclined him towards seeking answers to life's problems in Christianity. He had in fact been reading the Bible for some time before Napoleon's invasion but amidst the tremendous strains of 1812 his religious sense grew much stronger. Alexander would read the Bible every day, underlining in pencil the parts he found most relevant. To his old friend and fellow-convert to Christian belief, Prince Aleksandr Golitsyn, he wrote even in early July 1812 that 'in moments such as those in which we find ourselves, I believe that even the most hardened person feels a return towards his creator . . . I surrender myself to this feeling, which is so habitual for me and I do so with a warmth, an abandon, much greater than in the past! I find there my only consolation, my sole support. It is this sentiment alone that sustains me.'[55]

It was in this mood that Alexander heard the news of Moscow's loss and the city's subsequent destruction by fire. By the time Kutuzov's own messenger, Colonel Alexandre Michaud de Beauretour, came with this news, the emperor was well prepared to meet him and send a firm message back to his army. Amidst much emotion on both sides, Alexander and Michaud reassured themselves on the points that concerned them most. The emperor was promised by Michaud that the abandonment of Moscow had not undermined the army's morale or its total commitment to victory. Michaud, and through him the army, in return received the pledge they wanted to hear. Far from undermining the emperor's confidence or will, the loss of Moscow had hardened his determination to achieve total victory. Alexander ended the conversation with the words:

'I will make use of every last resource of my empire; it possesses even more than my enemies yet think. But even if Divine Providence decrees that my dynasty should cease to reign on the throne of my ancestors, then after having exhausted all the means in my power I will grow my beard down to here' (he pointed his hand to his chest) 'and will go off and eat potatoes with the very last of my peasants rather than sign a peace which would shame my fatherland and that dear nation whose sacrifices for me I know how to appreciate ... Napoleon or me, I or him, we cannot both rule at the same time; I have learned to understand him and he will not deceive me.'[56]

This was fine theatre and fighting words, which in the circumstances was just what was required. But there is no reason to doubt Alexander's sincerity or commitment when he said them. They spelled the ruin of Napoleon's strategy and pointed to the destruction of his army.

8

The Advance from Moscow

Even as Kutuzov was preparing to fight Napoleon at Borodino, Alexander I was concocting a plan for a counter-offensive which would drive the French out of Russia and destroy the *Grande Armée*. Kutuzov's initial report to the emperor on the battle of Borodino had stated that 'despite their superior forces, nowhere had the enemy gained a single yard of land'. Immediately after receiving this report, Alexander dispatched Aleksandr Chernyshev to the field-marshal's headquarters with detailed plans for a coordinated counter-offensive by all the Russian armies. Alexander wrote to Kutuzov that he hoped that the field-marshal's skill and his troops' courage at Borodino had now put a final stop to the French advance into Russia. He also encouraged Kutuzov to discuss all details about the operation with Chernyshev, who was fully informed about Alexander's aims and in whom he had full confidence. The emperor was careful to state that it was up to the commander-in-chief whether to accept the plan or to make alternative proposals of his own but no Russian general was likely openly to flout the monarch's wishes.[1]

The gist of Alexander's plan was that the Russian armies in the north (Wittgenstein and Steinhel) and the south (Chichagov) should simultaneously advance deep into Napoleon's rear in Belorussia. They must defeat and drive off the enemy forces guarding Napoleon's communications. In Chichagov's case this meant Prince's Schwarzenberg's Austrians and General Reynier's Saxon corps, which were to be thrust back into the Duchy of Warsaw. Alexander wrote to Kutuzov that 'as you will see from this plan, it is proposed that the main operations will be carried out by Admiral Chichagov's army', which would be reinforced both by Tormasov's Third Army and by a small corps commanded by

Lieutenant-General Friedrich Oertel, currently guarding the supply base at Mozyr.

Nevertheless, Peter Wittgenstein's role was also crucial. Aided by Count Steinhel, he was to advance southwards, take Polotsk, and drive the defeated corps of Oudinot and Saint-Cyr north-westwards into Lithuania and away from Napoleon's line of retreat across Belorussia. As a result, the combined forces of Chichagov and Wittgenstein would control the whole area through which Napoleon's main army would have to retreat, with Kutuzov's forces in close pursuit. The enemy was already 'exhausted', having been drawn deep into Russia and having suffered heavy losses. It now faced still heavier losses and a very difficult retreat. If the plan was properly executed, 'not even the smallest part of the main enemy army . . . can escape over our borders without defeat and ultimately total annihilation'.[2]

The key figure behind the plan was Alexander himself, though no doubt he discussed it with young Colonel Chernyshev and other more senior military figures in his entourage, including Petr Mikhailovich Volkonsky. To some extent this new plan inherited aspects of pre-war thinking about military operations. Drawn forward deep into Russia and then blocked by the main Russian army, Napoleon was to be defeated by other Russian armies thrusting far into his flanks and rear. In broad outline Alexander's plan made sense and was the best way to deploy Russian forces in this theatre of operations and exploit Napoleon's mistakes.

The emperor's plan was, however, very ambitious. A number of armies initially hundreds of kilometres apart were expected to coordinate their operations and arrive simultaneously in central Belorussia. Communications between these armies would be difficult. To the mud, snow and cold which impeded all movements in a Russian autumn and winter one needed to add the fact that Wittgenstein and Chichagov were separated by a swath of land in which no less than five full enemy corps and a number of smaller detachments were operating. At the very moment when Alexander was sending Chernyshev to Kutuzov, an additional 36,000 French reinforcements under Marshal Victor were entering Belorussia from the west. They reached Minsk on 15 September and Smolensk twelve days later.

Alexander's plan assumed that his armies would defeat all these enemy forces and drive them out of Belorussia, though at the time he was concocting his plan the Russians were not yet numerically superior to their foes. Advancing into Belorussia in the middle of winter the Russian columns would certainly suffer heavy losses from sickness and exhaustion. Alexander instructed Wittgenstein and Chichagov to fortify the defiles and obstacles through which Napoleon's army would have to retreat, but would they have the time or the manpower to do this? As the emperor himself acknowledged, the enemy could head for Minsk or Vilna and had the choice of at least three highways down which to make his escape. In the event, Alexander's plan about two-thirds succeeded, which was more than one might have expected in the circumstances. In the second half of November, however, as Napoleon approached the river Berezina it appeared briefly as if the plan might succeed completely and might result in the total destruction of the French army and even in the capture of Napoleon himself. Because this did not happen, Russian accounts of the autumn campaign have always tended to combine triumph at the French debacle with regret that it was not even more complete.

Chernyshev himself had to do a big detour to the east of Moscow before finally reaching Kutuzov's headquarters south of the city on 20 September. There he had discussions with Kutuzov and Bennigsen which showed his intimate knowledge of Alexander's thinking and filled in many of the gaps in the emperor's written proposals. On 22 September Chernyshev reported to Alexander that he had shown the necessary tact in urging the emperor's ideas on the commander-in-chief and that both Kutuzov and Bennigsen had warmly endorsed the plan. He added that the fall of Moscow had not fundamentally changed 'the enemy's poor situation' and that Napoleon would not be able to sustain himself in the Moscow region for long. There was every chance of destroying him 'so long as the people here don't again make serious mistakes before our armies have united in his rear'.[3]

Immediately afterwards Chernyshev set off for Chichagov's headquarters in north-west Ukraine in order to inform the admiral of Alexander's plan. In the autumn and winter of 1812 the dashing young colonel was to add to the laurels he had won in Paris and fully to justify Alexander's confidence. In mid-October he led a large partisan raiding party of seven regular light cavalry squadrons, three Cossack regiments and one Kalmyk unit deep into the Duchy of Warsaw, destroying magazines, disrupting conscription and forcing Schwarzenberg to divert much of the Austrian cavalry back to the Duchy in order to track him down. Subsequently, Chernyshev took a Cossack regiment right through the French rear and linked up with Wittgenstein, bringing the latter his first clear sense of Chichagov's movements and intentions. By happy accident, during this journey Chernyshev liberated Ferdinand Winzengerode and his aide-de-camp, Captain Lev Naryshkin, who had been captured in Moscow and were en route back to France. Since Winzengerode was one of Alexander's favourite generals and Naryshkin was the son of the emperor's mistress this was a great coup for Chernyshev. Wittgenstein praised Chernyshev's achievements in glowing terms and Alexander promoted his 26-year-old aide-de-camp to the rank of major-general.[4]

While Chernyshev was carrying Alexander's plans for a counter-offensive first to Kutuzov and then to Chichagov, a vicious 'people's war', reminiscent of events in Spain, had spread across the Moscow region. Eugen of Württemberg wrote that the Russian peasants, usually so friendly, hospitable and patient, had been turned into 'veritable tigers' by the depredations of French foraging parties and marauders. Sir Robert Wilson recalls that enemy soldiers who fell into the peasants' hands suffered 'every imaginable previous mode of torture'. The narratives of torture, mutilation and burial alive might be put down to foreign prejudice, were they not confirmed by many Russian sources too. In military terms the main significance of this 'people's war' was that it made it even more difficult for the French to forage. Any large and static army had trouble feeding its horses in this era. Napoleon's cavalry had suffered badly at Borodino, but it was the weeks spent in Moscow with ever-diminishing supplies of forage that destroyed most of his mounted regiments and devastated his artillery horses. Foraging expeditions had to travel ever greater distances with larger and larger escorts. Even so they often returned empty-handed, having lost men to ambushes and exhausted their horses without reward.[5]

In the classic style of guerrilla war, the peasants and the army's partisan units helped each other. The partisan commanders often distributed arms to the peasantry and came to their assistance when large enemy requisition parties were spotted. The peasants in turn provided the intelligence, local guides and extra manpower which enabled the cavalry to track down and ambush enemy detachments and to evade capture by superior forces. Partisan units operated along all the roads leading out from Moscow. Already by mid-October they were willing to take on quite large enemy detachments. On 20 October, for example, Denis Davydov's partisans attacked an enemy transport column near Viazma which was escorted by no less than three regiments, capturing most of the wagons and five hundred men. During the weeks that Napoleon spent in Moscow his communications with Smolensk and Paris were harried but never cut. Had he chosen to spend the winter in the city, however, it would have been a very different matter.[6]

Denis Davydov was one of the first partisans, having persuaded a doubtful Kutuzov on the eve of Borodino to detach him with a small band of cavalry and Cossacks to raid enemy communications. Davydov's success in the following weeks won him reinforcements and helped to legitimize the whole idea of partisan warfare, which was new to Russian generals. Karl von Toll in particular urged this new form of war on Kutuzov and the commander-in-chief quickly grasped its potential. Davydov captured or destroyed enemy supply columns, routed detachments sent to gather food, liberated many hundreds of Russian prisoners of war and gathered useful intelligence. He also punished traitors and collaborators, whom he describes as a very small minority. Davydov's weapons were speed, surprise, daring and excellent local sources of information. His bands struck out of nowhere, dispersed and then regrouped secretly for further attacks.

Davydov was not only one of the most successful of the partisans but also the most famous and romantic. A well-known poet, he was immortalized by his friend Aleksandr Pushkin thus: 'Hussar-poet, you've sung of bivouacs / Of the licence of devil-may-care carousals / Of the fearful charm of battle / And of the curls of your moustache.' Well after his death, Davydov became more famous than ever as the figure on whom Tolstoy based his character Denisov, the charming and generous hussar who loses his heart to Natasha Rostov and in whose band of partisans her brother Petia loses his life in the autumn of 1812.[7]

The most notorious partisan commander was Captain Alexander Figner, who commanded an artillery battery at the battle of Borodino. The fall of Moscow left Figner lost in gloom and determined to revenge himself on the French for his country's humiliation. The battery's second-in-command described him as 'good-looking, of medium height: he was a true son of the North, muscular, round-faced, pale and with light-brown hair. His big, bright eyes were full of liveliness and he had a powerful voice. Figner was eloquent, full of common sense, tireless in all his enterprises and with a fiery imagination. He despised danger, never lost his head and was totally fearless.' Speaking German, French, Italian and a number of other foreign languages fluently, Figner was also an excellent actor. On a number of occasions he went into enemy camps in and around Moscow to gather intelligence, easily passing himself off as an officer of Napoleon's multi-national army.[8]

Like many guerrilla commanders in history, however, there was a dark side to the brilliant, cunning and ruthless Figner. In September and October 1812 even Davydov was sometimes disinclined to take prisoners, since these put an intolerable strain on small and fast-moving partisan bands.[9] Alexander Figner, however, twisted even this practice. One fellow-officer recalls that 'his favourite and most frequent amusement was first to inspire captured officers' trust and cheerfulness by his reassuring conversation, and then suddenly to shoot them with his pistol and watch their agonies before they died. He did this well away from the army, which only heard dark rumours which it either disbelieved or forgot amidst the pressures of military operations.' In the midst of the awful cruelties and extreme emotions of autumn 1812 senior officers were sometimes willing to turn a blind eye to the nastier side of partisan warfare. By 1813, however, with the war no longer on Russian soil, few officers still harboured any great hatred for their enemy. When Figner drowned in the river Elbe trying to escape from the French few of his fellow-officers shed any tears.[10]

The many partisan units operating around Moscow overlapped with larger detachments watching the main roads leading out of the city. Some of these detachments also waged partisan war. Their main role, however, was to defend the provinces around Moscow from enemy raiding parties and to provide early warning should Napoleon make any major move out of the city. Of these detachments, the most important was commanded by Major-General Baron Ferdinand von Winzengerode, whose task it was to watch the highroad leading to Tver and thence to Petersburg. Most of Winzengerode's troops were Cossacks and militia but some regular cavalry were cut off from Kutuzov's army during the retreat through Moscow and escaped out of the city to the north, joining Winzengerode's men. Of these reinforcements, the best were the excellent soldiers of the Cossack Life Guard Regiment.

Ferdinand von Winzengerode could best be described as a full-time anti-Bonapartist. His father had been aide-de-camp to the Duke of Brunswick, of all the German dynasties the one most noted for its unwavering hatred of Napoleon. Winzengerode himself transferred on a number of occasions between the Russian and Austrian armies, depending on which service offered the better opportunity to fight the French. Logically enough, having fought with the Austrians in 1809, he moved back to the Russian army early in 1812. In 1812 he was one of a number of political refugees whom hatred of Napoleon had washed up on Russia's shores. Had circumstances turned out just a little differently, he could easily have been serving alongside many of his compatriots in the King's German Legion in Spain, under Wellington's command.

The peppery, pipe-smoking, impetuous Winzengerode was a loyal friend and patron. His excellent French cook and his penchant for whist were much appreciated by his staff. So too were his decency and fairness. In the autumn of 1812, for example, he was outraged when the steward on one of the estates of Aleksandr Balashev, the minister of police, tried to use his master's position to evade requisitioning for the army's needs. Winzengerode promptly slapped a double requisition on Balashev and ignored the complaints of Aleksei Arakcheev, who was up to similar tricks as regards his own estates in Novgorod. The problem, however, was that Winzengerode was a decent man but a poor general. When the French were on the point of evacuating Moscow, Winzengerode bungled an attempt to parley with them and was captured. Napoleon was initially intent on shooting him as a traitor but was dissuaded by his horrified generals. Kutuzov rightly called Winzengerode's capture an act of barely credible carelessness. Though Alexander was overjoyed by Chernyshev's rescue of Winzengerode, the Russian war effort would actually have benefited had Winzengerode been sitting quietly in French captivity in 1813–14 rather than commanding Russian armies.[11]

The most competent of Winzengerode's subordinates was the 31-year-old Colonel Alexander von Benckendorff. In 1812–14 Benckendorff had a 'good war' and this was to be the foundation for a brilliant subsequent career. The young Benckendorff started life with many advantages. His mother was the close friend of the Empress Marie, whom she accompanied to Russia as lady-in-waiting after the young Württemberg princess married the Grand Duke Paul. Juliana Benckendorff died in Marie Feodorovna's arms in 1797, bequeathing to the empress the care of her young children. Alexander thereby became a core member of Marie's circle. His sister Dorothea married Christoph Lieven, who was a key protégé of Empress Marie but also close to Alexander I and a source of patronage in his own right.

The Empress Marie sent Alexander von Benckendorff to an excellent school but for a time it seemed that her investment had been in vain. The handsome, charming and pleasure-loving young man proved neither a good scholar nor a particularly virtuous officer. Like Chernyshev and Nesselrode, he served in the Russian mission in Paris in the years after Tilsit. His main achievement in Paris, however, was to fall for a famous French actress and femme fatale, a former mistress of Napoleon, whom he smuggled back to Russia with him after quitting diplomatic life under a cloud. He subsequently redeemed himself by abandoning his actress and volunteering to fight against the Turks, after which Marie paid off his debts. But it was the courage and skill he showed in 1812 which really brought him back into favour.[12]

As one of Alexander I's aides-de-camp, Benckendorff started the war by carrying out a number of important and dangerous missions to Bagration's headquarters. Serving under Winzengerode in the autumn of 1812, he was responsible for protecting a key road and its surrounding territory from French incursions and for launching raids against the main enemy line of communications down the highway from Moscow to Smolensk. In his memoirs, Benckendorff recalls that one of his most difficult tasks was to rescue French prisoners from the clutches of the peasants, in which he did not always succeed. Some of the cruelties perpetrated against the wretched prisoners of war made him think he was living 'in the midst of a desolation which seemed to witness the abandonment of God and the rule on earth of the devil'. He adds, however, both that the peasants had every reason to be enraged by French behaviour and that the people showed great loyalty to their religion, their country and their emperor. In this context the orders he at one point received from a nervous Petersburg to disarm peasants and punish disorder were nonsensical, as he reported to Alexander I. Benckendorff told the emperor that he could hardly disarm men to whom he himself had given weapons. Nor could he allow to be called traitors a people 'who were sacrificing their lives for the defence of their churches, their independence, and of their wives and their homes. Rather the word traitor fitted those who at such a sacred moment for Russia dared to tell false tales about the country's purest and most zealous defenders.'[13]

Napoleon had entered Moscow on 15 September, and left the city on 19 October. During that period the relative strength of the rival armies changed in ways that had a decisive impact on the autumn campaign. While in Moscow Napoleon was reinforced by substantial numbers of infantry, which brought his overall numbers back over 100,000 and filled most of the gaps left by Borodino. Some of these infantry units were of good quality. They included, for example, the First Guards division, which had not been present at Borodino. By definition, infantry which had marched all the way from central and western Europe to Moscow was relatively tough. The core of Napoleon's army was his Guards. Very few of these excellent troops had seen any action since the beginning of the campaign, as Kutuzov knew.

The Russian infantry was weaker than Napoleon's in both numbers and quality. On 5 October Kutuzov had 63,000 officers and men in the ranks of his infantry regiments. Of these men, 15,000 were Moscow militiamen and 7,500 were new recruits. In addition, almost 11,000 men from Lobanov-Rostovsky's new units were with Kutuzov's army but had not yet been assigned to his regiments. These men were much better armed and trained than militia but none of them had ever been in action. The Russian commander-in-chief had good reason to avoid pitched battles with Napoleon, in which infantry always played the key role. In particular, he was right to worry about his regiments' ability to carry out complicated manoeuvres. If he had to fight Napoleon, it would be wise to do so in a strong defensive position. The Russian army traditionally fought with a higher ratio of artillery to infantry than was the case elsewhere in Europe. Given his infantry's rawness, Kutuzov was unlikely to break with this tradition. His army therefore set off on the autumn campaign with a vast train of 620 guns, which soon far outnumbered Napoleon's artillery and had inevitable consequences as regards its speed, manoeuvrability and supply.[14]

The situation as regards cavalry was totally reversed. Napoleon had too few horsemen and, much more importantly, far too few viable horses. Even before he left Moscow some of his cavalry were dismounted. During these six weeks Kutuzov's regular cavalry had received just 150 recruits and no reinforcements from the militia. This made good sense since useful cavalrymen could not be trained in a hurry. But many new horses had arrived for his 10,000 regular cavalrymen, often donated by the nobility of the neighbouring provinces.[15]

Above all, Kutuzov's army was reinforced by twenty-six regiments of Don Cossacks, a total of 15,000 new irregular cavalry. The total mobilization of the Don Cossack reserves was a great success, for which the Cossack ataman, Matvei Platov, was made a count. Sometimes these new Cossack regiments are described as militia but this is misleading. Ordinary Russian militiamen in 1812 had no previous military experience. All able-bodied Cossacks had served in the army, however, and were expected to bring their own weapons as and when they were recalled to service. The twenty-six new Cossack regiments were therefore well armed, and packed with veterans. In normal circumstances such an enormous number of irregular cavalry might have been excessive but in the conditions of the autumn and winter campaign of 1812 their impact was to be devastating. Back in April 1812 Colonel Chuikevich's memorandum had stressed the damage that Russian cavalry would do to a retreating enemy. Kutuzov was a shrewd and experienced campaigner. He knew that his cavalry would confine the enemy to the road on which they were retreating, force them to march at great speed, and deny them any chance of foraging away from their column. It took little imagination to realize what this would imply for an army marching into the Russian winter. Kutuzov therefore allowed his Cossacks, hunger, the weather and French indiscipline to do his work for him. Quite rightly, he was in no hurry to commit his infantry to battle.[16]

Obviously Napoleon made a fatal mistake in dwelling almost six weeks in Moscow while his cavalry withered, reinforcements poured in to Kutuzov and winter approached. Had he rested his troops in Moscow even for a fortnight, he could still have made it safely back to Smolensk long before the first snows or the arrival of Kutuzov's Cossack regiments from the Don. Instead he hung on, awaiting Alexander's response to his hints about peace. Perhaps the only thing one can say in Napoleon's defence is that most European statesmen and much of the Russian elite shared some of his doubts about Alexander's strength of will. Inevitably, however, Napoleon's peace feelers themselves fed Russian confidence and gave them every opportunity to encourage him to stay in Moscow while awaiting some response from Alexander. The basic point, however, was that Napoleon had failed to destroy the Russian army and had completely miscalculated the effect of Moscow's fall on both Alexander and the Russian elites. Having made this mistake he was too stubborn to listen to wise advice, to cut his losses, and to retreat in time.

Subsequently Kutuzov was to have a revealing discussion with a captured senior official of the French commissariat, the Viscount de Puybusque. Puybusque wrote that the Russian commander had asked him 'through what form of blindness had he [Napoleon] failed to spot a trap which was visible to the whole world? In particular, the field-marshal was astonished at the ease with which all the ruses employed to keep him in Moscow had succeeded and at his absurd cheek (*prétention*) in offering peace when he no longer possessed the means to make war.' The Russians had been only too happy to encourage the hopes of Napoleon's envoy, General Lauriston, that Alexander would respond to Napoleon's advances or the even sillier faith placed in the possible disloyalty of the Cossacks. 'Of course,' added Kutuzov, 'we did everything possible to drag out the conversations. In politics if someone offers you an advantage, you don't reject it.'[17]

By mid-October even Napoleon acknowledged that Alexander had duped him and that he must retreat. His departure from Moscow was hastened, however, by an attack by Kutuzov's army on Marshal Murat's detachment, which was watching the Russian camp at Tarutino. Left to his own devices, Kutuzov is unlikely to have ordered the attack. He was happy for Napoleon to stay in Moscow for as long as possible. In addition, as he told Miloradovich, 'we are not yet up to complicated movements and manoeuvres'. But the commander-in-chief was under pressure from Alexander to take the offensive and liberate Moscow. Kutuzov's generals were also raring for action, with Bennigsen stressing the need to inflict a heavy blow on Napoleon before the arrival of Marshal Victor's reinforcements from Smolensk. Above all, Russian reconnaissance showed that Marshal Murat's corps was vulnerable. Murat was heavily outnumbered and might be crushed long before reinforcements could arrive. Especially on its eastern flank, his camp could easily be stormed by a surprise attack from the nearby forest. French outposts and patrols were slack, which made the idea of a surprise attack all the more enticing.[18]

The initial plan was to attack early in the morning of 17 October. Kutuzov's orders had to be passed to the troops through Aleksei Ermolov, as chief of staff of the now combined First and Second armies. On the evening of 16 October, however, Ermolov had gone to a fellow-general's headquarters for dinner and was not to be found, so the attack had to be postponed. Ermolov's memoirs are silent on this subject and this is by no means the only occasion where they have to be read with a critical eye. Conceivably Ermolov proved non-cooperative because he believed that the attack was Bennigsen's brainchild and would not bring him any personal credit, but perhaps this is too harsh. Kutuzov was more angry about the bungling on 16 October than at any other time during the campaign.[19]

The mess which occurred on the evening of 16 October reflected the confusion in the army's structure of command. Kutuzov by now deeply distrusted his chief of staff, Levin von Bennigsen, but he could not yet get rid of him. Instead he brought Petr Konovnitsyn into his headquarters, officially as duty-general but in reality as a substitute for Bennigsen. Inevitably this caused still further enmity between Kutuzov and his chief of staff. Moreover, for all his virtues as a front-line commander, Konovnitsyn had neither the training nor the aptitude for staff work.

By mid-October Kutuzov and Bennigsen had between them succeeded in humiliating Barclay de Tolly sufficiently to make him resign.[20] Logically at this point the whole headquarters of combined First and Second armies should have been dismantled and orders passed straight down from Kutuzov to the corps commanders. Since the army's overall structure had been decreed by the emperor, however, only he could authorize such a change. Meanwhile Ermolov resented both the fact that Konovnitsyn had been inserted into the chain of command and that his inefficiency created additional bother for himself. The army's high command was therefore a maze of overlapping jurisdictions poisoned by personal rivalries among its senior officers. Nikolai Raevsky, the commander of Sixth Corps, wrote at the time that he kept as far as possible from headquarters since it was a viper's nest of intrigue, envy, egoism and calumny.[21]

Postponed for one day, the attack went ahead early in the morning of 18 October. The plan was for Count Vasili Orlov-Denisov's cavalry to attack out of the forests on the right of the Russian line, crush Murat's left flank and storm into his rear. On Orlov-Denisov's left he would be supported by a column of two corps, commanded by General Baggohufvudt. Next to Baggohufvudt would advance another column, made up of Aleksandr Ostermann-Tolstoy's Fourth Corps. Once these columns had attacked, the two corps commanded by Mikhail Miloradovich would move up to their support from the western (i.e. left) end of the Russian line. Behind Miloradovich stood the Guards and cuirassiers in reserve. The main problem with this plan was that it entailed all these columns marching through the forests at night in order to take up their positions for a dawn attack. In addition, in order to achieve surprise, the columns must make no noise and strike at first light. Overall responsibility for planning and executing the army's movements lay with Karl von Toll and the quartermaster-general's staff.[22]

Orlov-Denisov's column made its way successfully through the forests to its jumping-off point in the east. Since most of his men were Cossacks their ability to find their way was to be expected. The infantry columns of Baggohufvudt and Ostermann-Tolstoy were less successful. When dawn came Ostermann's column was nowhere to be seen and only part of Baggohufvudt's men were in place. When Karl von Toll arrived on the scene and found the columns in confusion he exploded into one of his rages, with Baggohufvudt and the nearest divisional commander, Eugen of Württemberg, as his targets. Karl Baggohufvudt was so infuriated by the insults being rained down not just on him but also on the emperor's first cousin that he resigned his command and took himself off to the Fourth Jaegers, of which he was colonel-in-chief, vowing to die at their head.

Although the neighbouring columns were not yet in place, Orlov-Denisov could not delay his attack for fear of being spotted once daylight had arrived and the French had finally woken up. He therefore launched his Cossacks against the enemy's eastern flank, which disintegrated and fled in all directions. To Orlov-Denisov's left matters went less well for the Russians. Storming out of the forest with the only two jaeger regiments on the spot, Baggohufvudt was immediately killed by a cannon ball. Although the French were initially thrown into confusion by the attack, Murat rallied them and they showed their usual courage and fighting spirit on the battlefield. Eugen of Württemberg and Toll rearranged their troops for a renewed and more coordinated assault, which in the end pushed back the enemy. Further back in the forest was Bennigsen, to whom Kutuzov had devolved overall command of the operation. He too was doing his best to impose order and coordination on the advancing infantry brigades, but his efforts cut across Eugen's. Meanwhile the confusion confirmed Kutuzov's doubts about his army's ability to manoeuvre. He refused to allow even Miloradovich's corps, let alone the Guards, to attack, despite the fact that the French were badly outnumbered and would almost certainly have been routed.[23]

Perhaps the most extraordinary point amidst all this chaos is that the Russians did actually win the battle of Tarutino. Murat was driven off the battlefield with a loss of 3,000 men and many cannon, standards and other booty. This was small consolation for most of the Russian generals, and above all for Bennigsen and Toll who had masterminded the operation. Given Murat's carelessness and Russian numbers, the surprise attack should have destroyed much of his detachment. Bennigsen saw Kutuzov's refusal to commit Miloradovich's troops as deliberate sabotage born of the field-marshal's envy of any rival who might steal his glory. Though the battle of Tarutino spread the poison at headquarters, its impact on the junior officers and men was the exact opposite. They rejoiced in the fact that for the first time in 1812 the main army had attacked and defeated the enemy. Kutuzov made sure that all the trophies captured on 18 October were laid out for his men to see. He organized a Te Deum to celebrate the victory, which he reported in glowing terms to Alexander. Whatever his limitations as a tactician, Kutuzov was a master when it came to public relations and his troops' morale.[24]

Napoleon heard the news of Murat's defeat while inspecting troops near the Kremlin. The emperor was always acutely sensitive to anything that reflected on his own prestige and his army's victorious reputation. Now not merely would he be retreating from Moscow but would be doing so after a defeat. On the next day, 19 October, he left the city with his army's main body, leaving a substantial rearguard behind to complete the evacuation and blow up the Kremlin. During the month of October he had contemplated a number of possible moves after leaving Moscow. The most conservative would be to retreat the way he had come, down the highway to Smolensk. This was the quickest way to get back to his supply bases at Smolensk, Minsk and Vilna and took him down Russia's best road, which was a major consideration given the vast and motley baggage train he was dragging along in his wake. But the area along the road had been devastated and his army would find little food or quarters.[25]

The obvious alternative was to move on Kaluga, Kutuzov's main supply base one week's march to the south-west of Moscow. Napoleon even contemplated then turning towards the great armaments centre at

Tula, at least an additional three days' march to the south-east. Capturing Tula would badly damage the whole Russian war effort. Taking Kaluga might net some supplies for Napoleon and would disrupt any subsequent Russian pursuit of his army. It would also conveniently hide the fact that the French were retreating. From Kaluga, Napoleon could withdraw down the relatively good road which led through Iukhnov to Smolensk and Belorussia.

With November and winter only two weeks away Napoleon could not afford detours and delays. There were strict limits to how much food he could carry with him from Moscow. As always, the biggest problem was the enormously bulky fodder for the horses. Every day of extra marching brought hunger, winter and disintegration that much closer. To be sure, he could feed and quarter his army more easily along the Kaluga–Smolensk road than on the Moscow–Smolensk highway but the advantages of this should not be exaggerated. To survive, his army would need to forage well away from the road and the overwhelmingly superior Russian light cavalry would make this impossible. The French army was never likely to match the steady discipline of Russian rearguards. In addition, by late October 1812 the state of Napoleon's horses meant that his rearguards would lack two crucial components: sufficient cavalry and fast-moving artillery. While facing Russian light cavalry and horse artillery in overwhelming numbers, there was no chance of the French maintaining a steady, methodical retreat. Speed was the only option and rapid retreats turned easily into rout.

The basic point was that by mid-October Napoleon had no safe options. Unless he was very lucky or the Russians blundered terribly his army was going to suffer great losses during its retreat. The key to minimizing these losses would be discipline. If the men abandoned their units and disobeyed their officers, disaster would be inevitable. Every scrap of food in Moscow had to be collected and a system of fair distribution established down the hierarchy of command. Not merely would this ensure that everyone got their share, it was also a vital method of maintaining control and discipline. Superfluous baggage, civilians and plunder had to be reduced to a minimum. Elementary precautions – such as shoeing the horses against winter ice – needed to be taken in time.

Just to list what needed to be done more or less describes what did not happen. The fire of Moscow had encouraged all the army's worst plundering instincts but ever since Napoleon's first great campaign in Italy in 1796–7 his troops had plundered on a grand scale wherever they went. Segur comments that the army leaving Moscow 'resembled a horde of Tatars after a successful invasion', but the emperor could not 'deprive his soldiers of this fruit of so many toils'. While carts bulged with plunder, some food supplies were burned before leaving Moscow. Finding enough to eat quickly became a matter of every man for himself in many units, Fezensac commenting that the system of distribution was uneven and chaotic. Caulaincourt is even more scathing about the near total and entirely avoidable failure to provide winter horseshoes, which in his opinion killed many more horses than even hunger. Sir Robert Wilson's comment that 'never was a retreat so wretchedly conducted' might seem the biased view of an enemy were it not confirmed by Caulaincourt: 'The habit of victory cost us even dearer in retreat. The glorious habit of always marching forwards made us veritable school-boys when it came to retreating. Never was a retreat worse organized.'[26]

Napoleon marched out of Moscow on 19 October down the Old Kaluga Road which led towards Kutuzov's headquarters at Tarutino. About halfway to Tarutino he swung to the west down the side roads which brought him out on to the New Kaluga Road near Fominskoe. His goal was to get ahead of Kutuzov on the road to Kaluga. The emperor's movements were shielded by Murat's advance guard. The presence of enemy troops near Fominskoe was quickly discovered by the Russians and Kutuzov sent Dmitrii Dokhturov's Sixth Corps to attack them. Just in time, in the evening of 22 October, Russian partisans warned Dokhturov that the enemy force at Fominskoe was not an isolated detachment but Napoleon's main army, including the Guards and the emperor himself. Armed with this information Kutuzov was able both to stop what would have been a disastrous attack on over-whelmingly superior enemy forces and to send Dokhturov scurrying southwards to block the New Kaluga Road at the small town of Malo-iaroslavets, thereby denying Napoleon the chance to take Kaluga. Kutu-zov himself marched cross-country from Tarutino to Maloiaroslavets to support Dokhturov.[27]

Napoleon's advance guard on the New Kaluga Road was the largely Italian corps commanded by his stepson, Eugène de Beauharnais. The first units of this corps crossed the river Luzha in the evening of 23 October and entered Maloiaroslavets, a town with 1,600 inhabitants, from the north. At dawn the next day the first regiments of Dokhturov's corps arrived from the south and drove the enemy out of most of the town.

All that day the battle swung back and forth in the streets of Maloiaroslavets as one assault succeeded another. Some 32,000 Russian troops fought 24,000 Italians. If Eugène's men had not succeeded in barricading themselves behind the stout walls of the Chernoostrov Nicholas monastery in the centre of the town it is possible that the Russians would have driven them out of Maloiaroslavets and back over the river. The Russians had the advantage of attacking downhill towards the river valley. Eugène's Italians fought with immense courage and pride. So too did the Russian regiments, their ranks filled with new recruits and militiamen. At the forefront of Dokhturov's attacks was, for instance, the 6th Jaeger Regiment. This was a fine unit whose inspiring colonel-in-chief, Prince Petr Bagration, had led it through Suvorov's Italian campaign of 1799 and many rearguard actions in 1805. At Maloiaroslavets, however, 60 per cent of its men were new recruits or militia.

By the end of the day the largely wooden town of Maloiaroslavets had burned to the ground. With it burned hundreds of wounded Russian and Italian soldiers, who had been unable to drag themselves away from the flames. The narrow streets of the town were an appalling sight, with bodies pulped into sickening mounds of blood and flesh by the infantry and guns which had fought their way up and down the steep sides of the valley. In tactical terms the battle was more or less a draw. Napoleon's troops held the town itself, while the Russians ended the day deployed in a strong position just south of the town but blocking the road to Kaluga. Casualties were roughly equal too, both sides having lost some 7,000 men.[28]

To the fury of most of his generals, Kutuzov decided on the following day to fall back towards Kaluga. He subsequently claimed that he had done so because Prince Poniatowski's Polish corps was advancing through the small town of Medyn to his left and threatening his communications with Kaluga. Meanwhile, after wavering for two days, Napoleon himself decided to retreat up the road which led through Borovsk to the Moscow–Smolensk highway at Mozhaisk. He took this decision despite the fact that Kutuzov's retreat meant that he could have marched along the road that led out westwards from Maloiaroslavets through Medyn and thence to Iukhnov and Smolensk. Perhaps he believed that it would be both quicker and safer to march down the highway rather than to entrust his army and its baggage to unknown country roads infested by swarms of Cossacks and with Kutuzov's army hovering menacingly nearby. Whatever the reasoning behind his move, the attempt to march on Kaluga had proved a disaster. The army had eaten nine days of its food supply and come nine days closer to winter without achieving anything or getting away from the Moscow region and back towards its base at Smolensk.[29]

With the French retreat from Maloiaroslavets the second stage of the autumn campaign had begun. Kutuzov was happy to wear down the enemy with his Cossacks, relying on nature and French indiscipline to do its work. Quite rightly, he retained a healthy respect for French courage and élan on the battlefield. Despite pleas even from Konovnitsyn and Toll, his most devoted subordinates, he was unwilling to commit his infantry to pitched battles, at least until the enemy was further weakened.

Along with the good military reasons for this strategy, politics probably also played a role. Stung by Sir Robert Wilson's complaints about his retreat after the battle of Maloiaroslavets, Kutuzov retorted:

I don't care for your objections. I prefer giving my enemy a 'pont d'or' [golden bridge], as you call it, to receiving a 'coup de collier' [blow born of desperation]: besides, I will say again, as I have told you before, that I am by no means sure that the total destruction of the Emperor Napoleon and his army would be of such benefit to the world; his succession would not fall to Russia or any other continental power, but to that which commands the sea, and whose domination would then be intolerable.[30]

Kutuzov was not personally close to Nikolai Rumiantsev but their views on foreign policy and Russian interests did to some extent overlap, as one might indeed expect of Russian aristocrats brought up in Catherine II's reign and deeply involved in her expansion southwards against the Ottomans. Like Rumiantsev, he was no lover of England, once commenting to Bennigsen that it would not worry him if the English sank to the bottom of the sea. How much these views influenced Kutuzov's strategy in the autumn and winter of 1812 it is difficult to say. The field-marshal was a shrewd and slippery politician who seldom exposed his innermost thoughts to anyone. He would certainly be slow to admit to any Russian that his strategy was driven by political motives, since this was to stray into a sphere which belonged to the emperor and not to any military commander. Probably the safest conclusion is that Kutuzov's political views were an additional reason not to risk his army in an attempt to capture Napoleon or annihilate his army.[31]

Alexander was kept aware of Kutuzov's unwillingness to confront the retreating enemy, not least by Wilson. The emperor had encouraged the Englishman to write to him, employing this foreigner as an additional, 'unaffiliated' source of information on his generals, while secretly intercepting and deciphering Wilson's correspondence with the British government to make sure that his British 'agent' was not trying to pull the wool over his eyes. Wilson was one of a number of people who begged the emperor to return to headquarters and take over command himself. Another officer who did so was Colonel Michaud de Beauretour, who came to Petersburg on 27 October with news of the victory over Murat at Tarutino.[32]

Alexander responded to Michaud that

all human beings are ambitious for fame (*chestoliubivye*) and I admit openly that I am no less ambitious than others. If I listened only to this feeling, then I would get into your carriage and set off for the army. Given the unfavourable position into which we have lured the enemy, our army's excellent spirit, the empire's inexhaustible resources, the large reserve forces which I have made ready, and the orders sent by me to the Army of Moldavia [i.e. Chichagov's army] – I am very confident that we cannot be denied victory and that all that remains to us, as they say, is to put on the laurels. I know that if I was with the army, then I would gather all the glory and that I would take my place in history. But when I think how inexperienced I am in military matters in comparison to our enemy and that, for all my goodwill, I could make a mistake which would cost the precious blood of my children, then despite my ambition for fame I am very ready to sacrifice my glory for the good of the army.[33]

To some extent, as usual, this was Alexander striking a pose. Other factors were also important in his decision to stay away from headquarters and leave Kutuzov in command. The field-marshal's enormous popularity as the reality of victory sank in to Russian consciousness was one such factor. But there is good reason to believe Alexander's lack of confidence in his own military abilities, a lack of confidence which had haunted this sensitive and proud man since the humiliation of Austerlitz. Though the emperor had more faith in Bennigsen's ability and shared his views on strategy, he nevertheless allowed Kutuzov to remove the chief of staff from headquarters, recognizing that in present circumstances he had no alternative but to put his faith in his commander-in-chief and had no interest in allowing the army's high command to be undermined by personal hatreds.[34]

Kutuzov's retreat after Maloiaroslavets had left his main body three days' march behind the enemy as it headed for Mozhaisk and the Moscow–Smolensk highway. Aleksei Ermolov reported on 28 October that Napoleon was retreating at such speed that it was impossible for Russian regular troops to keep up without exhausting themselves. Other reports confirmed this, while adding that this speed was destroying the French army. Two days later Matvei Platov, in command of the Cossacks swarming around the enemy's column, wrote that 'the enemy army is fleeing like no other army has ever retreated in history. It is abandoning its baggage, its sick and its wounded. It leaves behind horrible sights in its wake: at every step one sees the dying or the dead.' Platov added that the Cossacks were stopping the enemy from foraging and Napoleon's troops were running very short of food and fodder. Nor could the enemy rearguards hold for any length of time against the light cavalry which moved around their flanks and the concentrated fire of the Russian horse artillery.[35]

By 29 October Napoleon's headquarters were at Gzhatsk, back on the highway and 230 kilometres from Smolensk. After rejoining the Moscow–Smolensk road at Mozhaisk, his army passed the battlefield of Borodino and the Kolotskoe monastery, which had been turned into a hospital. Many hundreds of wounded men remained there, who should have been evacuated well before the army's arrival. Instead Napoleon now tried to load them onto the carts of his baggage train, many of whose drivers took the first opportunity to tip them off into the ditches beside the road.[36]

The battlefield itself was a terrible sight. None of the bodies had been buried. Scores of thousands of corpses lay out in the fields or in great mounds around the Raevsky battery and other points where the fighting had been most fierce.

For fifty-two days they had lain as victims of the elements and the changing weather. Few still had a human look. Well before the frosts had arrived, maggots and putrefaction had made their mark. Other enemies had also appeared. Packs of wolves had come from every corner of Smolensk province. Birds of prey had flown from the nearby fields. Often the beasts of the forest and those of the air fought over the right to tear apart the corpses. The birds picked out the eyes, the wolves cleaned the bones of their flesh.[37]

As Napoleon's army turned towards Smolensk along the highway, the closest Russian forces remained Matvei Platov's Cossacks. Their orders were to harass the enemy day and night, allowing him little sleep and no chance to forage. By 1 November Miloradovich's advance guard of Kutuzov's army was also approaching. It was made up of two infantry corps and 3,500 regular cavalry. Kutuzov's main body was still some way to the south, marching along country roads parallel to the highway. This line of march made clear Kutuzov's intention not to fight a pitched battle with Napoleon. Food supply was also an incentive to keep well away from the highway and march through districts untouched by war.

Once Kutuzov's army began to pursue Napoleon, problems of supply were inevitable. The army was moving away from its bases and into an impoverished war zone. Even in Smolensk province, let alone Belorussia and Lithuania, there was every likelihood that food would be impossible to find and that the army would have to feed itself from its own wagons. It required 850 carts to carry a day's food and forage for an army of 120,000 men and 40,000 horses. To sustain itself for a long period would therefore require many thousands of carts. Even if they could be found, this would not necessarily solve the problem. The horses and drivers of the supply train had to feed themselves as well. In a vicious circle very familiar to pre-modern generals the army's supply train could end up by eating all the food it was attempting to deliver. The longer it spent on the march, the likelier this was to happen. Moving thousands of carts along side roads in a Russian autumn was bound to be a very slow business, especially if they were travelling in the rear of a huge artillery train. These realities go a long way to explaining Kutuzov's predicament in the autumn and winter of 1812.[38]

When the campaign began the men carried three days' rations, and seven more days of 'biscuit' – in other words the dried black bread which was the staple of Russian regiments on the march – were in the regimental carts. This was what the regulations required and Kutuzov insisted that they were fully complied with. Large extra supplies were in the army's wagon train to the rear of the marching columns. On

17 October the army's chief victualling officer reported that he had sufficient biscuit to feed 120,000 men for twenty days – in other words until 6 November – and 20,000 quarters of oats for the horses.[39]

Well before the start of the autumn campaign Kutuzov had attempted to create a large mobile magazine to support the army's advance. On 27 September orders had gone out to twelve provincial governors to form mobile magazines and send them to the army immediately, stressing that 'extreme speed' was crucial. Each magazine was to consist of 408 two-horse carts packed in equal measure with biscuit and groats for the soldiers and oats for their horses. The provincial nobility was to provide most of the food and the carts, as well as the 'inspectors' who were to organize and lead the magazines. The governors went through the inevitable process of summoning the noble marshals. As one of them reported to headquarters, 'without the full cooperation of the marshals of the nobility nothing effective can be done'.[40]

With few exceptions the marshals did everything possible and the nobles volunteered the food and transport needed but the enemy was time and distance. Napoleon would have had to stay in Moscow for an extra month at least for mobile magazines from far-off Penza, Simbirsk and Saratov to arrive in time for the autumn campaign. In fact, however, the autumn campaign started even before the mobile magazines from less distant provinces could arrive. The first half of the Riazan mobile magazine, for instance, set off on 29 October, the first echelon of the Tambov mobile magazine on 7 November. Even these mobile magazines had a considerable journey to the army. Moreover they soon found themselves marching in its wake, behind its vast artillery train and through areas eaten out by the men and horses which had already passed. Soon the supply train began to eat its own food in order to stop men and horses from starving. Stuck in the rear with the supply train was also much of the winter clothing which Kutuzov had ordered the governors of nearby provinces to requisition for the army.[41]

In principle the mobile magazines should have been directed along march-routes which would intersect the advance of Kutuzov's columns. Kutuzov did actually order the intendant-general of the combined First and Second armies, Vasili Lanskoy, to send all supplies from Tula towards the army's line of march through the southern districts of Smolensk province. Just possibly if Barclay de Tolly and Georg Kankrin had been masterminding supply operations rather than Kutuzov,

Konovnitsyn and Lanskoy the arrangements might have been more efficient but the task was difficult. Until the last week of October no one could know along which route Napoleon would retreat or Kutuzov would pursue him. Mobile magazines wrongly directed could fall into enemy hands. Once the campaign had begun the armies never stopped moving. Together with the distances involved, the pre-modern communications and the total inexperience of the noble inspectors who led the mobile magazines, this made coordination of army and supply column movements very hard.[42]

By 5 November Kutuzov acknowledged that 'the rapid movement of the army in pursuit of the fleeing enemy means that the transport with food for the troops is falling behind and therefore the army is beginning to suffer a shortage of victuals'. As a result he issued detailed orders on where and how much to requisition from the local population, threatening anyone failing to cooperate with field courts martial. The problem, however, was that as the army approached Smolensk in mid-November it was entering an area ravaged by war and previously occupied by the enemy, where part of the population had fled to the forests, very many farms had been destroyed and there was no friendly local administration to help levy supplies. When they reached the area around the city of Smolensk many of Kutuzov's troops began to go hungry for the first time in the campaign.[43]

The only major clash between regular Russian troops and Napoleon's retreating army occurred at Viazma on 3 November. The various corps of Napoleon's army retreating down the Smolensk highway were strung out over 50 kilometres. Miloradovich therefore attempted to cut off the French rearguard, commanded by Marshal Davout. The attempt failed, above all because Miloradovich was tightly constrained by Kutuzov's cautious orders and the field-marshal refused to move up in his support with the army's main body. The corps of Eugène de Beauharnais, Poniatowski and Ney were still close enough to help Davout, and together they well outnumbered Miloradovich's force. Most of Davout's corps therefore escaped but since the day ended with the Russians storming into Viazma and driving the enemy off the battlefield the Russian soldiers saw themselves as clear victors, which was good for their morale.

The battle of Viazma showed that there was still plenty of fight left in many of Napoleon's troops but it also revealed his army's growing weakness. For the first time in 1812, a clash between Kutuzov and

Napoleon's infantry resulted in much heavier French than Russian losses. Lieutenant Ivan Radozhitsky's battery was part of Miloradovich's force and fought at Viazma. He wrote that 'our superiority was clear: the enemy had almost no cavalry and in contrast to previous occasions his artillery was weak and ineffective . . . we rejoiced in our glorious victory, and in addition saw our superiority over the terrible enemy'. Eugen of Württemberg wrote that at any time after the battle of Viazma a determined attack by the whole Russian army would have destroyed Napoleon's force. But Kutuzov preferred to leave the job to the winter, which put in its first appearance three days after the battle.[44]

Subsequently Napoleon himself and some of his admirers were much inclined to blame the unusually cold winter for the destruction of his army. This is mostly nonsense. Only in December, after most of the French army had already perished, did the winter become unusually and ferociously cold. October had been exceptionally warm, maybe lulling Napoleon into a false sense of security. As sometimes happens in Russia, winter then came suddenly. By 6 November Napoleon's men were marching through heavy snow. All the Russian sources say, however, that November 1812 was cold but seldom exceptionally so for this time of year. The main 'trick' played on Napoleon in this month by the weather was in fact the milder spell in the second half of November, which thawed the ice on the river Berezina and thereby created a major obstacle to his retreat. The basic point, however, is that Russian Novembers are cold, especially for exhausted men who sleep in the open, without even a tent, with very inadequate clothing, and with little food.[45]

Ivan Radozhitsky's battery pursued the enemy down the Smolensk highway from Viazma to Dorogobuzh. He wrote that a mass of prisoners were taken and led away under Cossack escort but they still included very few officers. Dead and dying men littered the road in large numbers. For the Russian troops the sight of French soldiers eating often semi-raw horsemeat was deeply disgusting. Radozhitsky recalls one particularly awful scene of a French soldier frozen in death at the very moment he was trying to rip the liver out of a fallen horse. The Russian soldiers had no love for their enemy but even so pity often became the dominant feeling amidst such dreadful scenes. Things were not easy for the Russians themselves, however, let alone for their horses. Radozhitsky writes that there was no hay, his battery had exhausted its supply of oats and the exhausted animals were surviving on whatever scraps of straw could be scrounged. His soldiers did at least have fur jackets and felt boots, which had been distributed to his battery at the camp in Tarutino before the campaign began, but they had nothing to eat save biscuit and a very thin gruel. A growing number of sick and exhausted men dropped out of the ranks and by the time it turned off the highway and joined Kutuzov's main body on 11 November very few infantry companies had more than eighty men. Nevertheless, buoyed by victory, their morale was excellent.[46]

Napoleon himself arrived in Smolensk on 9 November and left five days later. For the soldiers retreating down the highway the city offered the hope of warmth, food and security. In different circumstances it might have been just that. Its stores contained plentiful food and until recently the fresh corps of Marshal Victor, 30,000 strong, had been located in Smolensk. The advance of Peter Wittgenstein had forced Victor to march to the support of Saint-Cyr and Oudinot, however, leaving the city with a feeble garrison, far too weak to protect the food-stores or impose order on the arriving horde of desperate soldiers from Moscow. Even the day before the main body of the *Grande Armée* arrived a senior commissariat officer in Smolensk was predicting disaster. Marauders were already trying to storm the magazines and he had almost no troops to stop them. Subsequently he wrote that the 'regiments' entering the city looked like convicts or lunatics and had lost all traces of discipline. The Guards took far more than their share, whereas those corps which arrived last received a pittance. Amidst the chaos, food which could have lasted a week was devoured in a day. Stores of food and spirits were stormed and looted, with his own men overwhelmed and often deserting in droves.[47]

Napoleon's advance guard left Smolensk on 12 November and began the retreat westwards. His army's immediate goal was to cross the river Dnieper at Orsha.

The emperor's lack of cavalry made reconnaissance impossible and meant that he did not know Kutuzov's whereabouts. In fact Napoleon's delay in Smolensk, however essential, had enabled the main Russian enemy to catch up and move around the city to the south. By 12 November it was within Kutuzov's power to place his whole army across the road to Orsha and force Napoleon to fight his way back to the Dnieper. Most Russian generals longed for Kutuzov to do this. They included Karl von Toll, who later said that if Kutuzov had acted in this way the great majority of the enemy army would have been destroyed, though no doubt Napoleon himself and a picked escort would have sneaked away.[48]

Kutuzov, however, remained true to his system of offering Napoleon a 'golden bridge'. He refused to commit the bulk of his army to battle, and certainly not until he was sure that Napoleon and his Guards were safely out of the way. The last thing he wanted was to wreck the core of the Russian army in the life-and-death struggle that the French Guards would undoubtedly wage to save their emperor and themselves. Kutuzov's caution inevitably affected his subordinates. Vladimir Löwenstern recalls how Baron Korff, the commander of much of the main army's cavalry, cited Kutuzov's words about a 'golden bridge' as a reason not to allow his corps to become too closely engaged with the French. Miloradovich was more direct. His subordinate, Eugen of Württemberg, was furious at being ordered to let the enemy pass, as he had also been told to do once before at Viazma. Miloradovich responded that 'the field-marshal has forbidden us to get involved in a battle'. He added: 'The old man's view is this: if we incite the enemy to desperation, that will cost us useless blood: but if we let him run and give him a decent escort he will destroy himself in the course of a few days. You know: people cannot live on air, snow doesn't make a very homely bivouac and without horses he cannot move his food, munitions or guns.'[49]

Kutuzov's strategy is the key to understanding what happened in the so-called battle at Krasnyi between 15 and 18 November. In reality this was less a battle than an uncoordinated succession of clashes as Napoleon's corps passed one after the other around the Russians on the same ground where Neverovsky's detachment had held off Murat three months before. Napoleon sent his corps out of Smolensk at one-day intervals, which could have had serious consequences if Kutuzov had made a serious effort to intercept the retreat. Instead the Russian commander-in-chief watched happily as the French Guards and the remnants of the Polish and Westphalian corps brushed past him down the road from Smolensk to Orsha. By the evening of 15 November they had reached the village of Krasnyi. They were followed by the corps of Beauharnais and Davout: any thought Kutuzov might have had of intervening to block their retreat ended when Napoleon threatened to move back with part of his Guard to their rescue. Eugène and Davout therefore both escaped though only after losing hordes of men and almost all their remaining baggage and guns as they struggled down the highroad and cross country under fire from Miloradovich's infantry and guns, and harassed by his cavalry. Most of the senior officers and staffs survived but as fighting units the corps of Eugène and Davout no longer existed after Krasnyi.

There remained only Michel Ney's rearguard, which Napoleon was forced to abandon to its fate. Ney evacuated Smolensk on 17 November with roughly 15,000 men, of whom almost half were still in the ranks and ready for battle. By now Miloradovich's corps was deployed across the road westward. After a number of desperate efforts to break through the Russian lines on 18 November failed, Ney's corps disintegrated, with the overwhelming majority of its men killed or captured. Thanks to Ney's courageous and inspiring leadership a hard core of 800 men evaded the Russians by taking to the woods, crossing the river Dnieper and rejoining Napoleon at Orsha on 20 November.[50]

Once Napoleon's army had passed Kutuzov and crossed the river Dnieper at Orsha the Russian main army ceased to play an active fighting role in the 1812 campaign. Even had Kutuzov wished to catch up with Napoleon, there was no way that he could match the speed of the French retreat without wrecking his army. The old field-marshal was very happy with this situation. He regarded the 'battle' of Krasnyi as a triumph and as a vindication of his strategy. Well over 20,000 prisoners and 200 guns had fallen into Russian hands, and a further 10,000 enemy troops had been killed, at a minimal cost in his own soldiers' lives. Captain Pushchin of the Semenovskys recalled that when Kutuzov visited the regiment to tell them the results of the battle 'his face shone with happiness'. Pushchin added that after hearing Kutuzov's account of guns, flags and prisoners taken, 'the universal joy was immeasurable and we even cried a bit from happiness. A huge cheer thundered out which moved our old general.'[51]

Many Russian commanders on the other hand were deeply dissatisfied with the results of the battle, among them Prince Eugen of Württemberg. He recalled that he met Kutuzov for the first time since the camp at Tarutino in a little village between Krasnyi and Orsha. The commander-in-chief knew of Eugen's unhappiness and tried to justify his strategy, saying: 'You don't realize that circumstances will in and of themselves achieve more than our troops. And we ourselves must not arrive on our borders as emaciated tramps.'[52]

Kutuzov's concern for his troops was well justified. Although in the first half of the campaign the main body suffered less than Milora-dovich's advance guard, by mid-November it too was under great strain. Forced to move themselves, their baggage and artillery down country roads in deep snow, the men were becoming exhausted. Many of them did not have adequate winter clothing, since some provinces' wagons with fur coats and felt boots only arrived when the army reached Vilna. Food supplies were facing an emergency, with mobile magazines well in the rear and requisitioning becoming more and more difficult as they advanced through Smolensk province. Their next destination, Belorussia, fought over and plundered for six months, was unlikely to prove easier in this respect. Worst of all were medical services, which had almost collapsed under the strain of constant movement and enormous numbers of sick and wounded. The army's medical officials and doctors were scattered along the army's line of march, attempting desperately to set up temporary hospitals and procure medicines in a desert where no civilian authorities existed to help them and most buildings suitable as hospitals had been ruined.[53]

It may well be, however, that when Kutuzov spoke to Eugen he was thinking of more than just his army's immediate material needs. He did not believe that Russian interests could simply be reduced to the defeat of the French Empire. Britain and Austria were at least as 'natural' rivals as France. Moreover, even if the Russians captured Napoleon himself, which was possible though unlikely, this was no guarantee of peace and stability in Europe. It took no foresight to realize that if French dominion collapsed, the other European states would be in sharp competition to inherit the spoils. Nor was it easy to predict what kind of regime might replace Napoleon in France. From French prisoners Kutuzov had heard of the attempted coup by General Malet, aimed at replacing the Bona-partes by a republic. If the 1790s were anything to go by, a French republic might be anything but pacific or stable. In a very uncertain world, the one clear point was that the defence of Russian interests rested with its army, for whose survival Kutuzov was responsible.[54]

By early November another factor was also becoming important for Kutuzov. He had always known that, in accordance with Alexander's plan, Admiral Chichagov's army was supposed to be heading for Minsk and the river Berezina to block Napoleon's retreat. An old soldier like Kutuzov also knew, however, that grandiose plans which looked brilliant on paper had a way of going wrong when faced with war's reality. This was what Clausewitz meant when in his great work on war he wrote of 'friction', and never was there more of it than in the winter of 1812. Throughout October and in the first days of November Kutuzov had no clear idea of Chichagov's movements but was frustrated by their seeming slowness. On the very day that Napoleon left Smolensk, however, the commander-in-chief received a letter from Chichagov written in Pruzhany twelve days before. This letter detailed how successful Chichagov's recent advance had been and stated that the admiral expected to be in Minsk by 19 November. One key point about Minsk was that it was Napoleon's main food magazine in Belorussia. Another was that it was only 75 kilometres from Borisov and the vital bridge over which Napoleon's army would try to cross the river Berezina.[55]

Kutuzov responded that 'I received your report of 20 October [1 November NS] with immense satisfaction. From it I see that you hope to be in Minsk around 7 November [19 November NS]. This advance by you will have decisive consequences in present circumstances.' Kutuzov wrote to Wittgenstein that by 19 November Chichagov should be only 75 kilometres from the Berezina with 45,000 troops. Subsequently he wrote to Chichagov that even 'if General Wittgenstein is pinned down by Victor and Saint-Cyr and won't be able to help you to defeat the enemy, you should be strong enough together with the forces of Lieutenant-General Oertel and Major-General Lüders to destroy the fleeing enemy army, which has almost no artillery or cavalry, and is being pressed from behind by me'. To Aleksei Ermolov, whom Kutuzov appointed to command his advance guard, Kutuzov was – so it is reported – more blunt. 'Look, brother Aleksei Petrovich, don't get too carried away and take care of our Guards regiments. We have done our bit and now it's Chichagov's turn.'[56]

At one level Kutuzov's attitude is a perfect example of the selfishness and lack of collective loyalty which dogged the Russian high command. The commander-in-chief knew that Chichagov stood much higher in Alexander's esteem than he did himself and he resented the fact that the admiral had been sent to replace him as commander-in-chief of the Army of the Danube. On the other hand, some allowance should be made for the exhaustion of both the old and by now distinctly decrepit Kutuzov and his army. Clausewitz comments that we must consider the scale of operations. In November and December, in the ice and snow of Russia, after an arduous campaign, either by side roads little beaten, or on the main road utterly devastated, under great difficulties of subsistence . . . Let us reflect on the winter in all its inhospitality, on shattered powers, physical and moral, an army led from bivouac to bivouac, suffering from privation, decimated by sickness, its path strewn with dead, dying, and exhausted bodies, – [the reader] will comprehend with what difficulty each motion was accomplished, and how nothing but the strongest impulses could overcome the inertia of the mass.[57]

None of this was of much consolation to Pavel Chichagov, onto whom Kutuzov had offloaded the emperor's high expectations of destroying the French army and even capturing Napoleon. The admiral's campaign had got off to a good start. Though he had needed to leave substantial garrisons behind to watch the Ottomans, the men who marched northwards with him were the veterans of many campaigns and were fine troops. On 19 September they joined Tormasov's army on the river Styr.

Tormasov's regiments contained fewer veterans than Chichagov's but they had gained experience in 1812 while suffering far fewer casualties than the armies of Bagration and Barclay. There were no new recruits, let alone militia, in either army by September 1812. On 29 September Aleksandr Chernyshev arrived at their headquarters with orders for Chichagov to take over command of both armies and for Tormasov to join Kutuzov. He also brought Alexander's plan, which required Chichagov to push the Austrian and Saxon corps westwards into the Duchy of Warsaw and himself then advance to Minsk and the river Berezina in order to block Napoleon's retreat.

After uniting with Tormasov, Chichagov initially had 60,000 men available for the campaign, though if Alexander's plan was properly executed he would be joined in Belorussia by General Oertel's 15,000 troops, currently in Mozyr, and by 3,500 men under Major-General Lüders, who had fought the Ottomans in Serbia during the recent war. When Chichagov advanced in late September, the Austrian and Saxon corps retreated westwards into the Duchy of Warsaw. With his headquarters in Brest, Chichagov then spent two weeks gathering supplies for his advance towards Minsk and the Berezina. Since he would be marching 500 kilometres into a devastated war zone this made good sense, though his delay caused some grumbling. But the delay meant that Chichagov could only arrive on the Berezina just before Napoleon. He would have no time to get to know the unfamiliar terrain he was supposed to defend. It would not be possible to carry out Alexander's instructions to fortify the key choke-points and defiles through which Napoleon's army might pass.

In the last week of October Chichagov set off for Belorussia, leaving almost half his army – 27,000 men under Fabian von der Osten-Sacken – to hold off Schwarzenberg and Reynier. Since together the Austrians and Saxons numbered 38,000 men and were expecting reinforcements this was to ask a great deal of Sacken. In fact, however, the Russian general fulfilled his mission to perfection, though he complained – in this case correctly – that his army's achievements were forgotten since he could not hope for brilliant victories against so superior an enemy and in any case all Russian eyes were turned on the fate of Napoleon and his army.

When Schwarzenberg set off in pursuit of Chichagov in accordance with Napoleon's instructions, Sacken's surprise attack on Reynier's Saxons forced him to turn back to their rescue. Subsequently, Sacken succeeded in slipping away from Schwarzenberg's attempts to catch him, and in pinning down the Austrian and Saxon corps for the rest of the campaign. Sacken preserved his own little army amidst a flurry of manoeuvres and rearguard actions, and it provided some of the best and freshest regiments for the 1813 campaign. Above all, by drawing both Schwarzenberg and Reynier well away from Minsk and the Berezina he made it possible for Chichagov to advance into central Belorussia and threaten the survival of Napoleon and his army.[58]

Chichagov moved swiftly. His advance guard was commanded by yet another French émigré, Count Charles de Lambert, who had joined the Russian army in 1793. Lambert's force comprised some 8,000 men, mostly cavalry, its four jaeger regiments being commanded by Prince Vasili Viazemsky, whose diary as we have seen breathed such distrust for the foreigners and parvenus who were wrecking Russia. The main uncertainty for the Russian commanders was the whereabouts of Marshal Victor's corps. Vasili Viazemsky, one of nature's pessimists, was convinced that the Russian advance could not succeed since the enemy had at least as many men in central Belorussia as Chichagov. In fact Napoleon had ordered Victor to send one of his divisions to reinforce the garrison of Minsk but by the time the order arrived Victor's whole corps had already moved northwards to stop Wittgenstein. With Victor deflected northwards and the Austrians and Saxons far off to the west, the defence of the southern approaches to Belorussia was left to General Jan Dombrowski and no more than 6,000 combat-worthy soldiers.

Dombrowski could not have stopped Lambert but he might well have slowed him down. Instead he and his fellow Polish generals made a number of crucial mistakes. The force sent to guard the key crossing over the river Neman allowed itself to be surrounded and captured south of the river, leaving the bridge to fall intact into Lambert's hands. So too did the immense stores of food and fodder in Minsk, which had been designed to sustain the *Grande Armée* for a month. From Minsk, Lambert raced for Borisov and the vital bridge over the river Berezina. In what was probably the outstanding achievement of Russian light infantry in 1812, Viazemsky's four jaeger regiments covered the last 55 kilometres to Borisov in twenty-four hours, and then stormed the fortifications protecting the bridge at dawn on 21 November before the 5,500 enemy troops in the neighbourhood of Borisov could concentrate to defend the river crossing. At least half of Lambert's 3,200 jaegers were killed or wounded, including Vasili Viazemsky. After the war a gallery was constructed in the Winter Palace in which were hung the portraits of all Russia's generals in 1812–14. Viazemsky was one of the few names missing. No doubt he would have considered this the final trick played by the Petersburg courtiers in death as in life on a general from Chichagov's 'Forgotten Army' who had no 'protectors'.[59]

Lambert's capture of the bridge at Borisov was for the Russians the high point of the winter 1812 campaign. Hopes soared and Alexander's dream of capturing Napoleon at the Berezina looked as if it might become reality. In a move he was later to regret, Chichagov issued the following proclamation to his troops:

Napoleon's army is in flight. The person who is the cause of all Europe's miseries is in its ranks. We are across his line of retreat. It may easily be that it will please the Almighty to end his punishment of the human race by delivering him to us. For that reason I want this man's features to be known to everyone: he is small in height, stocky, pale, with a short and fat neck, a big head and black hair. To avoid any uncertainty, catch and deliver to me all undersized prisoners. I say nothing about rewards for this particular prisoner. The well-known generosity of our monarch guarantees them.[60]

At just the moment that Russian hopes were at their highest, Chichagov's prospects began to unravel. Kutuzov's estimate was that the admiral could bring 45,000 troops to the Berezina, but this depended on Lieutenant-General Oertel, who commanded the garrison at Mozyr, obeying his orders to march his 15,000 men to Borisov. Oertel, however, was a tidy and meticulous administrator, much of whose career had been spent as head of first the Moscow and then the Petersburg police. Training the recruits who formed part of the Mozyr garrison and securing the neighbourhood against Polish insurgents was well within his competence but his imagination quailed at the thought of abandoning his local responsibilities and marching against Napoleon. Oertel found every possible excuse for delay, citing broken bridges, the dangers of local rebellion if he departed, the need to protect his magazines and even cattle plague. By the time Chichagov could replace him it was too late to get his troops to the Berezina. As the admiral reported to Alexander, this left him with just 32,000 men. Half of these soldiers were cavalry, who would be of little use in the defence of a river crossing or in fighting in the woods and swamps on the west bank of the Berezina.[61]

If Chichagov was to stop Napoleon, therefore, he would need help, and its likeliest source was Peter Wittgenstein. Before the autumn campaign Wittgenstein's corps had been reinforced up to a strength of 40,000 men, though 9,000 of these were militia. Marching southwards to join Wittgenstein from Riga were also 10,000 regulars under Count Steinhel. Together on 16–18 October Wittgenstein and Steinhel defeated Marshal Saint-Cyr and recaptured the town of Polotsk and its bridge over the river Dvina. The victory owed much more to superior numbers and the courage of the Russian soldiers than to skilful leadership. Steinhel and Wittgenstein were advancing on opposite sides of the Dvina and coordination was poor. If Wittgenstein had possessed a pontoon train he could have crossed the Dvina beyond Saint-Cyr's right flank and driven him off to the west, in other words away from Napoleon's line of retreat. This was the goal set out in Alexander's plan for the autumn campaign. Instead, however, the Russian commander was forced into a more pedestrian and costly direct assault on Polotsk.

Even so, victory at Polotsk brought important results. General Wrede, who commanded Saint-Cyr's Bavarian troops, did retreat due west towards Lithuania and effectively removed his men from any further participation in the war, though Wittgenstein could never be quite sure that Wrede would not re-emerge at some point to endanger his right flank. In his report to Alexander on the battle, Wittgenstein claimed correctly that he had weakened the corps of both Oudinot and Saint-Cyr to such an extent that they were no longer capable of serious resistance unless reinforced. Marshal Victor had therefore been forced to abandon Smolensk and march his entire corps to their assistance at top speed. Wittgenstein had every reason to take pride in this achievement. Three French corps, each of them initially as strong as his own, had by now been drawn away from the crucial theatre of operation in central Belorussia thanks to his efforts.[62]

Wittgenstein advanced south from Polotsk and defeated marshals Saint-Cyr and Victor at the battle of Chashniki on the river Ulla on 31 October. According to Saint-Cyr, the Russians owed their victory to their superior artillery and to Marshal Victor's failure to concentrate much of his corps on the battlefield. As usual, in Napoleon's absence his marshals fought each other and Oudinot's return from convalescence did nothing to improve coordinated leadership in the small army facing Wittgenstein. An angry Napoleon then gave Victor categorical orders to attack Wittgenstein and drive him right back over the river Dvina and away from the *Grande Armée*'s line of retreat, to which he was becoming dangerously close. Victor attacked towards Smoliany further east on the Ulla on 13–14 November but failed to dislodge Wittgenstein's men from their position, despite bitter fighting.[63]

For the first three weeks of November 1812 Wittgenstein was content to hold the line of the river Ulla and beat off any French attacks. Prince Petr Shakhovskoy, the governor of Pskov, mobilized thousands of carts and formed six mobile magazines to provide supplies for Wittgenstein's men. Thanks to him, the Russians were far better fed than their enemies. They were also much warmer, since Wittgenstein's corps had been sent 30,000 fur jackets in September from the provinces in his rear. With every day they stood still, the relative strength of the two armies shifted in Wittgenstein's favour. Though only one and a half day's march from the main Orsha–Borisov highway, Wittgenstein made no attempt to advance any further across Napoleon's lines of communication. His caution was justified. In the first half of November he had no information about either the position of the other Russian forces or the state of Napoleon's army. Not only Wittgenstein but also the emperor and Kutuzov feared for the safety of his corps if it found itself under attack from both Napoleon and Victor, with neither Chichagov's nor Kutuzov's army in the neighbourhood to help. Only when Victor retreated on 22 November did Wittgenstein move forward in his wake. He would therefore be in a position to interfere with the French crossing of the Berezina, but unlike Chichagov he would not be directly in their path.[64]

He would nevertheless be much closer than Kutuzov's main army. After the 'battle' of Krasnyi Kutuzov's main concern was to rest and feed his troops. For that reason he marched south-west from Krasnyi to the small town of Kopys, the next crossing over the river Dnieper south of Orsha. There he rested his main body and succeeded in requisitioning a significant amount of food from the neighbouring districts to his south. He also parked many of his batteries, since it was obviously no longer necessary to drag along all these guns. Kutuzov did send forward an advance guard of two infantry and one cavalry corps under Miloradovich but unless Chichagov could block Napoleon on the Berezina for four days or more there was no chance of Miloradovich's men arriving in time to dispute the crossing. As they struggled across the Dnieper and into Belorussia Miloradovich's troops suffered badly. The historian of the 5th Jaeger Regiment wrote that 'from Kopys on we found no civilians anywhere: the villages were empty, there weren't even the proverbial cats or dogs. The barns and stores were also empty: there was no grain, no groats and not even a scrap of straw.'[65]

Ahead of Miloradovich were Platov's Cossacks and Aleksei Ermolov's so-called 'flying column', made up of two cuirassier and three infantry regiments of the line, some Cossacks, and the two light infantry regiments of the Guards, in other words the Guards Jaegers and the Finland Guards. The flying column set off for Orsha on 19 November but was delayed for a day and a half because Napoleon had burned the bridge over the Dnieper. Ermolov's Cossacks swam the river but his heavy cavalry horses had to be tied down on rafts to make the crossing. Only the exhaustion of the regular light cavalry could explain using Russian cuirassiers in such a role. All the baggage had to be left behind on the east bank of the Dnieper. Kutuzov ordered Ermolov not to exhaust his men and to wait for Miloradovich at Tolochin before pressing on in pursuit of Napoleon. But Ermolov knew that speed was of the essence if Napoleon was to be stopped on the Berezina, and he ignored both orders.[66]

By dint of heroic efforts Ermolov arrived at Borisov on 27 November, the very day that Napoleon and his Guards had crossed the Berezina 18 kilometres to the north near the village of Studenka. The Russian troops paid a high price for this speed. The Cossacks could usually forage off the road and turn up something to eat and the artillery carried some emergency rations in their caissons but life for the infantry was very hard. The Guards Jaegers had slept with a roof over their heads for one night in the last month. In their week-long march from the Dnieper to the Berezina they only twice received any biscuit. At every bivouac the men rootled for potatoes. Even they were hard to find and amidst the rush and exhaustion were often eaten raw.[67]

As for the Finland Guards, they did still have a little groats in their knapsacks but their kettles were with the regimental baggage and raw groats were inedible. The men survived by cutting the bark off the trees and turning it into impromptu cooking vessels. After stuffing the groats into the bark and heating this concoction up over a spluttering fire coaxed from damp wood, the Guardsmen wolfed down the whole 'meal', bark and all. Their reward for all these efforts was to arrive at the Berezina one day too late. The next morning the two Guards regiments crossed the river and were deployed in reserve behind Chichagov's army, which was fighting Napoleon in the forests near the village of Brili. They spent the next two days up to their knees in snow and with no food at all. Not surprisingly, men fell ill in droves. Nevertheless the troops' morale remained high. These Guardsmen were fine soldiers. Their spirits were buoyed by the fact that they were advancing and were clearly winning the war. Ermolov himself was an inspiring leader on the battle-field, just the man to get the last ounce of effort from Russian soldiers in an emergency.[68]

When he first arrived near Borisov on 22 November Chichagov had moved his headquarters and all his baggage across the river and into the town, which was on the east bank of the Berezina. Count Lambert had been wounded in the capture of the bridge, so Chichagov appointed Count Paul von der Pahlen to replace him. The next day Pahlen was sent forward down the main road. With Napoleon's main body now linking up with Oudinot and Victor, and heading for Borisov, this was a dangerous move. Neither Chichagov nor Pahlen showed proper caution. Pahlen's men were overwhelmed by Napoleon's advance guard and fled back into Borisov. Chichagov and his staff decamped at speed back over the Berezina, leaving much of the army's baggage behind. Subsequently this debacle was used by Chichagov's enemies as a stick to beat him, but it was not actually very significant. Though much of Pahlen's advance guard was cut off, almost all of it succeeded in making its way back across the Berezina by finding fords. Four days later Borisov and most of Chichagov's baggage was recaptured by Wittgenstein. Above all, the Russians succeeded in burning the crucial bridge at Borisov so the river was still an obstacle for Napoleon.

Back on the west bank of the Berezina, Chichagov faced a difficult dilemma. It was impossible to coordinate operations even with Wittgenstein on the other side of the river, let alone with Kutuzov, who was still far away near the Dnieper. The defence of the Berezina line therefore rested in the admiral's hands alone. Chichagov had, at most, 32,000 men, of whom only half were infantry. If he could be sure that Napoleon was heading north-west for Vilna, all Chichagov needed to cover was the 20 kilometres between Borisov and the ford at Veselovo, opposite the village of Zembin. The problem was that Napoleon might cross the river south of Borisov and head westwards for Minsk, or even march via Igumen for Bobruisk, well to the south. These possibilities hugely extended the river front which Chichagov had to cover, up to 100 kilometres or more. Napoleon pretended to be making preparations to head for Minsk by building a bridge at Ukholoda, 12 kilometres south of Borisov. In fact, however, he crossed at Studenka, 18 kilometres north of Borisov, and headed for Vilna.[69]

As often happens in war, amidst all the strains and the conflicting intelligence Chichagov believed the evidence that best fitted his own assumptions and fears. The admiral's greatest worry was that Napoleon was heading for Minsk to recapture the huge store there on which Chichagov's own army now depended. At Minsk he could link up with Schwarzenberg, whom Chichagov believed to be advancing towards the Berezina into the rear of the Russian forces. To do Chichagov justice, most of the other senior Russian commanders believed both that Napoleon would head for Minsk or Bobruisk, and that this would be the most dangerous move from the Russian perspective. On 22 November, for instance, Kutuzov had written to Chichagov warning him that if Napoleon could not cross the Berezina he might well head south. Clausewitz, now at Wittgenstein's headquarters, recalls that 'every man was possessed with the idea, that the enemy would take the direction of Bobruisk'.[70]

Perhaps the most striking evidence comes from Ermolov's memoirs. When he finally reached Chichagov's headquarters on 29 November, the admiral was still trying to send Platov's Cossacks around Napoleon's flank and into his rear in order to destroy the bridges and causeways that crossed the swamps at Zembin and opened the way to Vilna. Ermolov responded that this was unwise: 'If Napoleon found it impossible to pass through Zembin, his only possibility was to seize the road to Minsk, where he would find abundant stores of every kind (which supplied our own army and other forces) and be able to rest his army, having drawn reinforcements from Lithuania and restored order there.' If the highly intelligent Ermolov, who had been an eyewitness to the disintegration of Napoleon's army for the last month, thought this way, then it is hardly surprising that Wittgenstein and Chichagov did so too.[71]

Hoodwinked by Napoleon, Chichagov took most of his army southwards on 25 November to Shabashevichi to cover the road to Minsk. He left Count Langeron with one weak infantry division in Borisov, but ordered Major-General Chaplitz to abandon his position opposite Studenka and bring his detachment to join Langeron. By the time he received these orders Chaplitz's scouts had already provided him with clear indications that Napoleon was preparing bridges for a crossing at Studenka. Nevertheless in the face of categorical orders from both Chichagov and Langeron he marched south, to the joy of French observers on the opposite side of the river. He also failed to destroy the bridges and causeways through the swamps near Zembin. The narrow defile at Zembin was in fact the best defensive position available to any Russian force which was trying to stop Napoleon breaking out to Vilna. If the bridges and causeways had been destroyed, a single division at Zembin might have held up the whole French army. Even if Chaplitz had destroyed the causeway and bridges and then departed, rebuilding them would have delayed Napoleon's escape for at least a day.[72]

On the morning of 26 November French cavalry swam across the Berezina at Studenka and 400 light infantry crossed on rafts. The building of the two bridges began. On the opposite shore Napoleon was faced by a puny force of two jaeger regiments, a smattering of cavalry and one horse artillery battery positioned near the village of Brili. The battery's commander was Captain Ivan Arnoldi, one of the best young artillery officers in the Russian army, who already had a fine war record in 1806–7 and was to retire as a full general. In his memoirs Arnoldi states that even if the Russian forces opposite Studenka had been much stronger, they still could not have stopped Napoleon crossing the river. The east bank was higher than the west and it was possible to deploy all Napoleon's batteries in a commanding position. The west bank, on the contrary, was low-lying, very swampy and forested: it was impossible to deploy more than a very few guns there within range of the river and the bridges.[73]

On the other hand, if thousands of Russian infantry had been present they might have been able to keep Napoleon pinned in the bridgehead and away from the road from Borisov to Zembin, and they certainly could have blocked the defile at Zembin. The tiny Russian force present on 26 November had no chance of doing either of these things. Commanded by Marshal Oudinot, the French forced their way out of the bridgehead and then turned south down the road towards the village of Stakhovo. By the time Chaplitz had returned with his whole detachment he was outnumbered. Chichagov and the core of his army did not reach the area until the evening of 27 November and only went into action the next day. By then, however, all but Napoleon's rearguard had already crossed the Berezina. Though there was fierce fighting near Stakhovo from 26 to 28 November there was never any likelihood that the Russian forces would break through the enemy line and regain control of the road to Zembin. Napoleon had more infantry than the Russians on the west bank, the terrain favoured the defensive and his troops fought with the desperate courage that their perilous situation required.[74]

Meanwhile there was also fierce fighting on the east bank of the Berezina as Peter Wittgenstein's corps came into action against Marshal Victor's rearguard. Wittgenstein showed little initiative during these crucial days, though his troops were much less exhausted than Kutuzov's men. It was hard to recognize the daring general of the summer months. Perhaps Wittgenstein was unenthusiastic about coming under Chichagov's command, or was made cautious by the fact that Napoleon was present in person. He followed Victor down the road to Borisov, claiming – perhaps correctly – that the country paths leading directly into Napoleon's rear at Studenka were impassable. Having reached Borisov on 27 November, Wittgenstein did then turn to the north towards Studenka to interrupt Napoleon's crossing of the Berezina. More by luck than good design, this move cut off General Partouneaux, whose division was forced to surrender. Seven thousand men went into captivity, though of these half were by now stragglers rather than fighting soldiers. During the whole of 28 November Wittgenstein fought the rest of Victor's corps which was forming a rearguard around the bridgehead at Studenka, but he got only 14,000 of his men into action. Though the Russian artillery did dreadful damage to the hordes of people trying to cross the river, the Russians could not break through the outnumbered but courageous enemy rearguard, which held them at bay all day and then made its escape safely over the bridges.[75]

They left behind a vision of desolation. Ermolov recalled the scene on the east bank of the Berezina after the end of the battle:

Near the bridges, which were partially destroyed, guns and transport wagons had fallen into the river. Crowds of people, including many women, children and infants, had moved down to the ice-covered river. Nobody could escape from the terrible frost. No one could ever witness a more terrible sight. The people who ended their miseries there and then by dying were the lucky ones. Those who remained alive envied them. Much less fortunate, they had preserved their lives only subsequently to die of the cruel cold, amidst terrible suffering . . . The river was covered with ice which was as transparent as glass: there were many dead bodies visible beneath it across the whole width of the river. The enemy had abandoned huge numbers of guns and wagons. The treasures of ransacked Moscow had also not succeeded in getting across the river.[76]

At one level the crossing of the Berezina was a disaster for Napoleon. He had lost somewhere between 25,000 and 40,000 men, and almost all his artillery and baggage. Even his Old Guard was now down to 2,000 men. His last viable corps, commanded by marshals Victor and Oudinot, were now barely capable of further action. Had Napoleon held the bridge at Borisov or had the Berezina been firmly frozen the great majority of these casualties would have been avoided.

Nevertheless he had every reason for satisfaction on 29 November. Outnumbered, surrounded and faced with the threat of total destruction, he had escaped. Above all, this was thanks to the splendid courage of his remaining troops and the resolution of their commanders. It is also true that even at the Berezina Napoleon possessed some advantages. His forces were concentrated, they were in the middle of the Russians and they were directed by a single will. Nature as well as human failures made coordination between the Russian armies difficult. When one looks at the perceptions and actions of the individual Russian commanders, it is almost always possible to see some logic to their behaviour and to sympathize with their dilemmas. Nevertheless, taken as a whole, the miscalculations, lack of resolution and the selfishness of the Russian senior generals had allowed more of Napoleon's army to escape than should have been the case.

For many Russians, and above all for Alexander, the chief cause of discontent was that Napoleon himself had escaped. This feeling, though natural, was misplaced. It was always in Napoleon's power to ride up the east bank of the Berezina and then cut across country towards Vilna. At Studenka he still had more than sufficient well-horsed cavalry to provide him with a strong escort. On his route to Vilna he would have had to be very unlucky to encounter a Cossack detachment sufficiently large and determined to challenge such an escort.

Much less probable and more annoying was the escape of many thousands of Napoleon's troops. At first blush this might not seem a serious matter. More than half the men who escaped over the Berezina died or were taken prisoner amidst the fearful cold of the next three weeks. Fewer than 20,000 men survived to serve again in Napoleon's armies. But 2,500 officers just from the Guards and the corps of Davout, Ney and Eugène escaped back over the Russian frontier. They included most of the senior commanders and many of their staff officers. Had they been captured at the Berezina it would have been very difficult for Napoleon to rebuild a new *Grande Armée* in time to defend Germany in the spring of 1813. The huge Russian sacrifices of the next year's campaign might thereby have been avoided. Moreover, had Napoleon's army been captured at the Berezina, the Russians could have gone into winter quarters, without the heavy losses incurred in the pursuit of the enemy across Lithuania in December 1812.[77]

After the drama on the Berezina, the last weeks of the 1812 campaign are an anticlimax, though this is a poor word to describe seventeen days of immense suffering. Everything that French apologists say about the weather in December 1812 is true. Even by the standards of a Russian December, it was exceptionally cold. This caused the final disintegration of most French units. On 5 December Napoleon himself left the army

Alexander I

The Commanders

Mikhail Barclay de Tolly

Mikhail Kutuzov

Levin von Bennigsen

Peter von Wittgenstein

Diplomacy and Intelligence

Petr Rumiantsev

Karl von Nesselrode

Aleksandr Chernyshev

Christoph von Lieven

The Statesmen

Mikhail Speransky

Aleksei Arakcheev

Dmitrii Gurev

Fedor Rostopchin

Heroes of 1812

Petr Bagration

Mikhail Miloradovich

Matvei Platov

Eugen of Württemberg

Headquarters

Petr Volkonsky

Aleksei Ermolov

Karl von Toll

Johann von Diebitsch

Army of Silesia

Alexandre de Langeron

Fabian von der Osten-Sacken

Ilarion Vasilchikov

Johann von Lieven

Organising the Rear

Aleksei Gorchakov

Dmitrii Lobanov-Rostovsky

Georg Kankrin

Andrei Kologrivov

Private: Preobrazhensky Guards Regiment   Private: Finland Guards Regiment

Private: Riazan Infantry Regiment

Lieutenant: field artillery of the line –
heavy battery

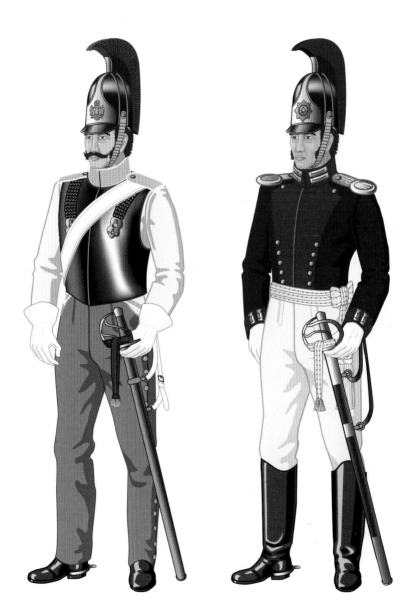

Private: Ekaterinoslav Cuirassier Regiment   Lieutenant: Guards Dragoon Regiment

Private: Sumi Hussar Regiment

Private: Lithuania Lancer Regiment

Napoleon awards Grenadier Lazarev the Légion d'honneur at Tilsit

Borodino: the Raevsky Redoubt after the battle

Spring 1813: the Cossacks in Hamburg

Fère-Champenoise: the Cossack Life Guard Regiment attacks French infantry

and headed for Paris, leaving Murat in charge. By then nothing and no one could have rallied the French army east of the Russian border and Napoleon was right to depart. On 11 December Vilna fell to the Russians. Three days later Matvei Platov's Cossacks captured Kovno, Michel Ney led his indomitable rearguard back across the river Neman and the 1812 campaign was over.

During these weeks the Russian army also suffered grievously. On 19 December Kutuzov reported to Alexander that the army's losses had been so enormous that he was obliged to hide them not just from the enemy but even from his own officers. Of the 97,000 men whom Kutuzov had commanded at Tarutino before the beginning of the campaign, 48,000 – in other words almost half – were in hospital. Only 42,000 soldiers were still in the ranks. The position of Chichagov and Wittgenstein's armies was better but not good. The admiral had 17,000 men in the ranks, plus 7,000 more who had finally arrived from Oertel's corps. Peter Wittgenstein still commanded 35,000 men, which reflected the fact that his men had been better fed and clothed than the rest of the army and had also marched less far. But most Russian regiments by now were hungry and exhausted, with their uniforms in tatters and dressed in any clothes they could find to keep out the cold. One young staff officer described himself as wearing a soldier's overcoat, with sleeves badly charred by bivouac fires, boots whose soles were coming off, headgear which combined a soldier's forage cap and a woollen civilian hood, and a tunic with no buttons but held together by a French sword-belt.[78]

As they advanced into freezing, barren and devastated Lithuania cold and hunger hit Kutuzov's troops hard. So too did another enemy: typhus. The disease was rampant among the prisoners of war whom the Russians were capturing in droves and it spread quickly. 'Its distinguishing features were: exhaustion, loss of appetite, nausea, total weakening of the muscular system, dry heat of the skin and an unbearable thirst.' Against the disease the regimental doctors used quinine, camphor and emetics so long as their medicines lasted. As the intendant-general, Georg Kankrin, subsequently admitted, however, of all the backup services provided by the Russian commissariat medical help was the weakest. That owed something to the new and confused administration of hospitals, and more to the shortage of trained doctors and hospital administrators. So long as the army was operating in the Great Russian provinces it could hand over care of its sick and wounded to the governors, but once it moved into Belorussian and Lithuanian districts formerly occupied by Napoleon no civilian institutions existed. Many Russian doctors and officials themselves fell ill. The rest were scattered along the army's line of advance, desperately trying to establish hospitals in a wilderness.[79]

Kankrin wrote that his officials,

themselves barely alive, were forced almost every other day to establish hospitals in ruined areas, in the midst of extreme cold and deprived of almost any help. There was a complete shortage of experienced officials. We took anyone who fell into our hands, grateful for being able to find any officials for this job. The man chosen was given the regulations, some money, open orders to the local administration requiring them to assist him, and a small staff. This was all the help one got in setting up a hospital, together whenever possible with some biscuit and groats, a few beef-cattle and some spirits.

Nevertheless, wrote Kankrin, the majority of the men in hospital did recover and rejoin the army, 'which on the one hand shows the toughness of Russian soldiers but also shows that they were given some care'.[80]

On 13 December Kutuzov reported to Alexander that unless his army got a rest it might disappear entirely and have to be rebuilt from scratch. Any commander would dread such a possibility, but a Russian general had more reason than most to protect the professional and veteran cadre around which the army was built. Men with the education and willingness to serve as officers were not that plentiful. Highly skilled cadres who could serve in the engineers, artillery or staffs were much rarer still. Above all, the emperor's army was not the nation in arms. Its strength lay in the great loyalty of its veterans to their comrades and regiments. Destroy these men and these loyalties, and the army would become worse than a mere militia. The inner force which made this army so formidable and resilient would be undermined. In the winter of 1812 this came too close to happening for Kutuzov's comfort. In fact the army's core survived, large numbers of veterans subsequently returned from hospital, and around this cadre a fine new army was rebuilt in 1813. But it was not really until the summer of 1813 that it recovered from the awful strains of the 1812 campaign and regained its full potential.[81]

9

1813: The Spring Campaign

Alexander I arrived in Vilna on 22 December 1812. This time he brought with him a smaller entourage than the gaggle of bored and squabbling courtiers who had been such a nuisance in the first weeks of the 1812 campaign. Three men whom he summoned to Vilna were to be his closest assistants for the rest of the war. Prince Petr Mikhailovich Volkonsky became Alexander's right-hand man as regards military operations; Aleksei Arakcheev remained in charge of all matters concerning the mobilization of the home front, the militia and the provision of reinforcements to the field army. Karl Nesselrode became Alexander's chief diplomatic adviser. In fact if not in name Nesselrode acted as deputy minister of foreign affairs. The true foreign minister was Alexander himself. The emperor intervened frequently in military matters but he lacked the confidence to take over command or play the leading role in military operations himself. Where diplomacy was concerned, however, Alexander was unequivocally in charge and in 1813 on the whole remarkably skilful and effective.

Though Nikolai Rumiantsev remained foreign minister in name, he was completely excluded from the making of foreign policy. Alexander claimed to have left him behind in Petersburg to preserve his health. It was indeed true that Rumiantsev had suffered a minor stroke while on campaign with Alexander in 1812. For the emperor this was just a good excuse to escape from his foreign minister in 1813. The last thing Alexander wanted was an 'Old Russian' foreign minister, distrusted by all Russia's current allies and critical of the emperor's policy, looking over his shoulder. In Rumiantsev's opinion Alexander's crusade against Napoleon was wrong-headed. As he said to John Quincy Adams, Napoleon was by no means the only issue in Russian foreign relations. By concentrating so exclusively on Napoleon's defeat, Alexander was downgrading Russian policy towards the Ottoman Empire and Persia, and even allowing historical Russian interests to be sacrificed to a desire to placate the Austrians and the British. Rumiantsev on occasion even upbraided Alexander in thinly camouflaged terms for forgetting his ancestors' proud legacy.

The foreign minister also feared anarchy as a result of the efforts being made to incite mass risings against Napoleon, especially in Germany. In Rumiantsev's words, this was 'in essence a return of Jacobinism. Napoleon might be considered the Don Quixote of monarchy. He had, to be sure, overthrown many monarchs, but he had nothing against monarchy. By affecting to make his person the only object of hostility, and by setting the populace to work to run him down, there would be a foundation laid for many future and formidable disorders.' Alexander could afford to ignore Rumiantsev, both far away and sidelined, though when Metternich made precisely the same points two months later he was forced to pay far more attention.[1]

Decorations and fireworks greeted Alexander's arrival in Vilna. The day after his arrival was his birthday and Kutuzov hosted a great ball in his honour. Captured French standards were thrown down at Alexander's feet in the ballroom. Further celebrations and parades followed. The price of luxuries in Vilna became exorbitant. Even Lieutenant Chicherin, an aristocratic Guards officer, could not afford to have a new uniform tailored with the appropriate gold braid. The glitter and congratulations could not conceal even from the emperor the terrible suffering in Vilna at that time. Forty thousand frozen corpses lay in the city and its suburbs awaiting the spring thaw when they could be burned or buried. Starving and typhus-ridden scarecrows roamed the streets, collapsing and dying across the doorways of Vilna's citizens. The Guards artillery was used to transport the corpses to the frozen walls and hillocks of bodies awaiting disposal outside the town. A third of the soldiers involved fell ill with typhus themselves. Worst of all were the scenes in the hospitals. To his credit, Alexander visited the French hospitals, but there was not much the overstretched Russian medical services could do to help. The emperor recalled a visit 'in the evening. One single lamp lighted the high vaulted room, in which they had heaped up the piles of corpses as high as the walls. I cannot express the horror I felt, when in the midst of these inanimate bodies, I suddenly saw living beings.'[2]

On the surface all was harmony between a grateful emperor and his devoted commander-in-chief. Alexander awarded Kutuzov the Grand Cross of the Order of St George, the rarest and most prized of honours any Russian monarch could bestow. In reality, however, the emperor was dissatisfied with Kutuzov's pursuit of Napoleon and determined to assert control over military operations. Petr Konovnitsyn, the army's chief of staff, went on extended sick leave. In his place Alexander appointed Petr Volkonsky. Kutuzov would continue to command and to play the leading role in strategic planning but he would do so under the close eye of the emperor and his most trusted lieutenant. In terms of administrative efficiency Volkonsky's arrival was of great benefit. Both Kutuzov and Konovnitsyn were lazy and inefficient administrators. Key documents went unsigned and unattended for days. Serge Maevsky, a staff officer in Kutuzov's headquarters, commented that

it seemed to me that the field-marshal was extremely unhappy about this appointment because now the tsar's witness could pass on a true picture of the field-marshal. In addition he worked with us when he felt like it but he was forced to work with Volkonsky even when he didn't want to. Volkonsky was very hard-working and exhausted the old man by numerous discussions of problems. It is true that our business flew along. That isn't to be wondered at: in one day Volkonsky would decide matters that before him had piled up for months.[3]

Kutuzov was determined that his exhausted troops should have some rest before embarking on a new campaign across Russia's borders. The emperor was very unwilling to heed such advice. In his view, not a moment was to be lost at this crucial time while Napoleon was at his weakest, revolt against his empire was bubbling in Europe, and Russian prestige was sky-high. The army must press forward into Germany in order to control as much territory as possible and encourage Prussia and Austria to join the Russian cause. Just before leaving Petersburg Alexander had told one of his wife's ladies-in-waiting that the only true and lasting peace would be one signed in Paris. On arriving in Vilna he told his assembled generals that their victories would liberate not just Russia but Europe.[4]

Kutuzov had no enthusiasm for this vision. The tired old commander felt that he had done his duty in liberating Russia. Liberating Europe was not Russia's concern. Kutuzov was not alone in believing this. How many officers shared his view no one can say: the army did not conduct polls and, on the surface at least, the emperor's word was law. But particularly towards the end of the spring campaign, as exhaustion grew and fortune turned against the allies, foreign observers commented on the lack of enthusiasm for the war at headquarters and among many of the Russian generals. This was less evident at regimental level, where officers and men were bound up in a culture of discipline, courage and mutual loyalty. Once the summer armistice allowed the army to rest and fortune turned the allies' way again in the autumn, much less was heard of defeatism and exhaustion among the generals. But the spirit of the 1813 campaign for the Russian officers was always rather different to the defence of their homeland in 1812.[5]

To an extent, this was now a campaign like so many in the past for personal glory, honour and promotion. The presence of the emperor with the army meant that rewards showered down on officers who distinguished themselves, a big incentive in a society where rank, medals and imperial benevolence counted for so much. In the officers' memoirs about 1813 and 1814 one sometimes gets the sense too that they were 'military tourists' as they passed through one exotic foreign territory after another, accumulating adventures and impressions as they went. Seducing first Polish, then German and finally French women was a joyful element in this tourism for some of the officers, particularly the aristocratic young Guardsmen. In a way it seemed as much an affirmation of the officers' manhood, tactical skill and all-conquering spirit as defeating Napoleon on the battlefield.[6]

Admiral Shishkov was too old and too virtuous for such adventures. He was also a dyed-in-the-wool isolationist. Shortly after returning to Vilna with Alexander, he questioned Kutuzov as to why Russia was advancing into Europe. Both men agreed that after the devastation he had suffered in 1812 Napoleon was unlikely to attack Russia again and, 'sitting in his Paris what harm can he do us?' When asked by Shishkov why he had not used all his present prestige to press this view on Alexander, Kutuzov answered that he had done so but 'in the first place he looks on things from a different perspective whose validity I cannot altogether reject, and in the second place, I tell you frankly and honestly, when he cannot deny my arguments then he embraces and kisses me. At that point I begin to cry and agree with him.' Shishkov himself suggested that at the most Russia should act as Paul I had done in 1798–9, sending an auxiliary corps to help the Austrians but leaving the main efforts for Europe's liberation to the Germans themselves, supported by British paymasters. Subsequently Kutuzov was to take up this idea, encouraging Karl von Toll to present a plan in late January 1813 whereby the main burden of the war could be passed on to the Austrians, British and Prussians while Russia, 'because its home provinces are so very distant, will cease to play the leading military role in this war and will become the auxiliary of a Europe mobilized in its entirety against French tyranny'.[7]

Alexander rejected Shishkov's and Toll's arguments for a limited Russian commitment, and was right to do so: in spring 1813 only full-scale Russian participation in the war in Germany could inspire Prussia and Austria to join in, or provide any realistic hope of victory even should they do so. The emperor was also right to doubt Shishkov's and Kutuzov's view that Napoleon was no longer a serious threat to Russian security. Given Napoleon's personality and his record, it was optimistic to imagine that he would simply accept a devastating defeat at Russian hands and seek no revenge. Even leaving personal considerations aside, Napoleon believed that the legitimacy of his new dynasty required military victory and glory. In addition, since France's war with Britain was continuing, so too was the geopolitical logic that had driven Napoleon to confront Russia in 1812. Getting rid of the last independent continental great power and consolidating French dominion in Europe while Napoleon himself was still an active and inspirational leader remained a credible strategy. Just conceivably, his experience in 1812 might persuade Napoleon to leave Russia in peace. More probably it might teach him to attack it in more intelligent fashion, making full use of the Polish factor and of Russia's political and financial weaknesses. Of course all predictions about what Napoleon might do in the future were uncertain. What was beyond question was that his empire was much stronger than Russia. In peacetime it would not be possible to sustain for long the level of military expenditure which security against Napoleon would require. For that reason too it made good sense to try to end the Napoleonic threat now, while he was weakened, while Russia's resources were mobilized, and while there was a strong chance of drawing Austria and Prussia into the struggle.

The best source on Alexander's policy at this time is provided by a memorandum submitted to him by Karl Nesselrode, his chief diplomatic adviser, early in February 1813. Tactfully, the memorandum started by repeating the emperor's own words to its author. Alexander had stated that his overriding aim was to create a lasting peace in Europe, and one which would be proof against Napoleon's power and ambition.

The most complete way in which this goal could be achieved would undoubtedly be for France to be pushed back within its natural borders; that all the territories not situated between the Rhine, the Scheldt, the Pyrenees and the Alps would cease to be either integral parts of the French Empire or its dependants. This is of course the maximum we could want but it could not be achieved without the cooperation of Austria and Prussia.

Nesselrode acknowledged that not even Prussian participation in the war was yet certain and that Austria might possibly remain Napoleon's ally. If Prussia joined Russia but Austria was hostile, the most the allies could achieve would be to hold the line of the Elbe and make it Prussia's permanent frontier. Nesselrode was confident that Prussia would ally itself to Russia soon but even if it did not there was every reason for Russia to push on now and occupy the Duchy of Warsaw, which was both vital for its security and no doubt a pawn in any future peace negotiations.[8]

Nesselrode's memorandum illustrated how very much the nature of Russia's war had changed. Once the 1812 campaign had begun diplomacy was of secondary importance during the rest of that year. In the spring 1813 campaign, by contrast, Russia's objectives could not be achieved by military means alone. Success required bringing in Austria and Prussia, and this in turn could only be achieved by a combination of diplomatic and military policies. As was typical of Nesselrode, the tone of his memorandum was coolly realistic. There was, for instance, no mention of pursuing Napoleon to Paris or overthrowing his regime. Such goals would have seemed wholly unrealizable in February 1813 and would have alienated even the Prussians, let alone the Austrians.

Also realistic was Nesselrode's understanding of power. Some of Alexander's advisers dreamed of instigating a European – and in particular German – revolt against Napoleonic tyranny. The leader of this group was Baron Heinrich vom Stein, the former Prussian chief minister who had joined Alexander's entourage in 1812. On the contrary, Nesselrode's memorandum said nothing about popular revolts or public opinion. For him, it was states and governments which counted. On the whole the events of 1813–14 bore him out. However much public opinion in the

Confederation of the Rhine had turned against Napoleon, the princes stuck by him and the great majority of their soldiers fought loyally on his behalf until very near the end. In 1813 Napoleon was defeated, not by rebellions or nationalist movements, but because for the first time Russia, Prussia and Austria fought together and because, unlike in 1805 and 1806, Russian armies were already in central Europe when the campaign began.

But Nesselrode argued that only states and governments really mattered in international relations, partly because he strongly believed that this ought to be the case. Like Metternich, whom he admired, Nesselrode longed for stability and order amidst the never-ending turbulence of the Revolutionary and Napoleonic eras. Both men feared that any form of autonomous politics 'from below' – whether led by Jacobin demagogues or by patriotic Prussian generals – would throw Europe into further chaos. Ironically, however, in the winter of 1812–13 it was to be a Prussian general acting without his king's sanction who was to begin the process which culminated in the Russo-Prussian alliance against Napoleon, thereby achieving Nesselrode and Alexander's first great diplomatic triumph in 1813.

Lieutenant-General Hans David von Yorck, the commander of the Prussian corps on the left flank of Napoleon's forces, was a very difficult man even by comparison with senior Russian generals of the era. Arrogant, prickly and hypercritical, he was a nightmare as a subordinate. The other Prussian corps commander in the east, Lieutenant-General Friedrich Wilhelm von Bülow, in fact told the Russians that Yorck's actions sprang less from patriotism than from personal enmity towards his French commander, Marshal MacDonald.[9]

This was unfair because there was no reason to doubt Yorck's commitment to restoring Prussian independence, pride and status. In November and December 1812 the governor-general of Riga, Marquis Philippe Paulucci, attempted to win over Yorck to the Russian side by playing on these themes. The fact that Yorck responded to his letters raised Paulucci's hopes. Initially he ascribed the Prussian general's caution to Yorck's need to seek guidance from his king. By late December, however, Paulucci was beginning to fear that Yorck was just playing for time. The collapse of the *Grande Armée* had left Napoleon's forces in southern Latvia isolated. Orders for their retreat came very late. Paulucci began to fear that Yorck was merely hoodwinking the Russians in order to get his corps back to Prussia in one piece. A threatening note had entered Paulucci's communications to Yorck by 22 December.[10]

Russian threats only became meaningful, however, when Wittgenstein's advance guard under Major-General Johann von Diebitsch cut across Yorck's line of retreat near Kotliniani. Even then Yorck could have fought his way through Diebitsch's weak force had he so wished. The thought of shedding Prussian and Russian blood on behalf of Napoleon's fading cause must have been a deterrent to Yorck. More importantly, Diebitsch's presence gave Yorck the excuse he needed to pretend that his hand had been forced. He sat down to discuss terms with Diebitsch, using as a basis the offer made by Paulucci for the neutralization of the Prussian corps. No doubt it helped negotiations that Diebitsch himself was a German and the son of a former Prussian officer.

On 30 December 1812 Yorck and Diebitsch signed the so-called convention of Tauroggen. The Prussian corps was declared neutral and deployed out of the way of Russian operations. If the King of Prussia denounced the agreement, the Prussian troops could retire behind the French lines but could not take up arms against Russia again for two months.[11] In military terms the convention resulted in East Prussia and all the other Prussian territory east of the Vistula falling immediately to the Russians. The number of soldiers actually present in Yorck's corps by December 1812 was barely 20,000, but the enormous losses sustained by the main French and Russian forces meant that this number of combat-ready troops could make a substantial difference in the winter of 1812–13. If Yorck's corps had remained with MacDonald and resisted the Russian advance it would have been difficult for Wittgenstein's exhausted and overstretched corps to force its way past them into East Prussia. Once Murat heard of Yorck's defection, however, he quickly retired behind the Vistula, leaving the well-garrisoned fortress-port of Danzig as France's only remaining outpost in Prussia's eastern lands.[12]

The business of mobilizing all East Prussia's resources for war got under way immediately. A Russian governor-general would have trodden on many toes, as Paulucci did to a truly crass degree in Russian-occupied Memel, by absolving local officials of their oath to the king and talking about possible Russian annexation.[13] Alexander therefore appointed Baron vom Stein, who had been his chief adviser on German affairs since June 1812. The Russians needed to mobilize East Prussia's resources immediately but they also had to avoid alienating the Prussians by disorderly requisitioning or by seeming to covet Prussian territory. As Russian forces began to cross the Prussian border, Kutuzov issued a proclamation declaring that Alexander's only aim in advancing across the Russian frontier was 'peace and independence' for all the European nations, which he invited to join him in the task of liberation. He added: 'This invitation is directed firstly and above all to Prussia. The emperor intends to end the misfortunes which shackle her, to bear witness to the friendship which he still preserves for the king, and to restore to the monarchy of Frederick its territory and prestige.'[14]

Feeding the advancing Russians was not too great a problem because their numbers were not huge, they did not need to concentrate for battle, and the local population and officials in East Prussia loathed the French even more than was the case elsewhere in Prussia and greeted the Russian forces as an army of liberation.[15] Kutuzov demanded excellent behaviour from his troops towards the civilian population and, despite their exhaustion, the Russian soldiers responded well and retained their discipline.[16]

Politically much more delicate was the decision to summon the provincial estates without the king's consent, and to call up 33,000 men for the army and militia. Fortunately, while this was in train Stein received a coded message from the Prussian chancellor, Prince Karl August von Hardenberg which had been slipped through the French lines. This conveyed Frederick William's support and announced that a treaty of alliance with Russia would soon be signed. This was the crucial breakthrough. For all the enthusiasm of the East Prussian estates, the province had less than a million inhabitants. To have any chance of defeating Napoleon the resources of the whole kingdom needed to be mobilized. Only Frederick William could do this.[17]

The king received the news of the convention of Tauroggen on 2 January 1813 while taking his afternoon walk in his garden in Potsdam. Frederick William detested Napoleon and feared that the French emperor intended to carve up Prussia. He liked and admired Alexander, and he distrusted Russian ambitions much less than those of Napoleon. On the other hand Frederick William was a great pessimist: as Stein put it, 'he lacks confidence both in himself and in his people. He believes that Russia will draw him into the abyss.' The king also quite simply hated having to make decisions. His natural inclination was to ask for advice and to vacillate. In particular, he thoroughly disliked the idea of further wars. This was partly out of honourable concern for his people's welfare, but it also reflected his own entirely disastrous experience of defeat and frustration in 1792–4 and 1806–7.[18]

To do the king justice, he had good reason for nervousness and equivocation in January 1813. When he heard the news of Tauroggen the Russian armies were still hundreds of kilometres away in Poland and Lithuania. French garrisons on the contrary were scattered across Prussia, including a large one in Berlin. This dictated that Frederick William's first public reaction must be to denounce the convention and to send messages to Napoleon pledging his continued loyalty. The king took advantage of Napoleon's request to contribute more troops to the *Grande Armée* by levying extra recruits and expanding his army. On 22 January he himself, his family and the Guards regiments decamped from Potsdam and Berlin to the Silesian capital, Breslau. By so doing he achieved independence from the French and secured himself against kidnap. Since Breslau was right in the path of Russian armies advancing through Poland the king could put forward the half-plausible excuse that he was preparing Silesia's defence.

Ideally Frederick William would have preferred an alliance with Austria to secure Germany as a neutral zone and stop the French and Russians fighting on his territory. A Prusso-Austrian alliance could also attempt to mediate a continental peace settlement which would restore to Vienna and Berlin much of the territory they had lost in 1805–9. With this goal in mind, the king's trusted military adviser, Colonel Karl von dem Knesebeck, was sent to Vienna. He arrived on 12 January and stayed for no less than eighteen days.

At one level Knesebeck's mission was a failure. The Austrians made it clear that they could not abandon the French alliance overnight and attempt immediately to impose mediation on the warring sides. The emperor's honour and the completely unready state of their armies dictated a longer period of disengagement from the alliance with Paris. The basic point was that the Austrians had much more time for manoeuvre than the Prussians: Russian troops were not crossing the Austrian border, nor were Austrian generals threatening disobedience unless their sovereign changed his foreign policy.

On another level, however, Knesebeck's mission was of great service.

Both Metternich and Francis II promised categorically that they would reject Napoleon's efforts to buy Austrian support against Prussia by offering her Silesia. They stressed that the two Germanic great powers must on the contrary both be restored to their pre-1805 dimensions in order to hold their own against France and Russia, thereby securing the independence of central Europe and the overall European balance of power. Far from opposing the Russo-Prussian alliance, the Austrians hinted that it seemed Prussia's best option in the circumstances. Meanwhile, once ready, Vienna would put forward its own ideas for peace. Knesebeck concluded optimistically, and in a sense that went to the core of Russo-Prussian strategy in the spring and summer of 1813, 'sooner or later Austria will go to war with France because the peace terms which she wants to achieve by mediation are unobtainable without war'.[19]

After reporting to Frederick William at Breslau, Knesebeck was sent on to Alexander's headquarters. Before he would commit himself to Russia, the king needed reassurance on a number of points. Most basically, the Russians had to commit themselves to an advance which would liberate all of Prussian territory and allow the mobilization of its resources. Unless this was achieved it would be useless and suicidal for Frederick William to fight on Russia's side since victory would be impossible and Prussia would become the inevitable target of Napoleon's wrath. The king also sought confirmation that Russia would guarantee Prussian territory and her status as a great power.

Inevitably these complicated diplomatic manoeuvres took time and in the winter of 1812–13 time was of the essence. To some extent the spring 1813 campaign was a race between Napoleon and his enemies as to who could mobilize reinforcements and get them to the German theatre of operations most quickly. In this competition Napoleon had all the advantages. He arrived back in Paris on 18 December 1812 and began immediately to form a new *Grande Armée*. Even the mobilization of East Prussian manpower could not begin before early February 1813 and it was to be yet another month before Berlin and the heart of the Prussian kingdom fell to the allies. The Russian situation was of course different. There the levy of new recruits was already under way in the late autumn. But Russia's immense size meant that it would take far longer to concentrate recruits in depots and deployment areas than was the case in France. Even after they had gathered in their training camps in the Russian interior they still faced marches of 2,000 kilometres or more to reach the Saxon and Silesian battlefields. There was never any doubt that Napoleon was going to win the race to get reinforcements to the field armies. The only issues were how wide the gap was going to be and whether Napoleon would be able to use it to achieve a decisive victory.

Frederick William's diplomacy also delayed Russian military operations. Until the king allied himself with Russia the 40,000 men of Yorck and Bülow's corps could not go into action against the French. In their absence, in January 1813 the Russian forces in the northern theatre were too weak to advance into the Prussian heartland. The two main Russian concentrations were Wittgenstein's corps in East Prussia and the much-diminished core of Chichagov's army near Thorn and Bromberg in north-west Poland. Both these Russian forces had been greatly weakened by months of ceaseless campaigning. In addition, very many of their troops had to be detached to besiege or blockade French fortresses. In Wittgenstein's case this above all meant Danzig, to which he had to send 13,000 good troops under Lieutenant-General von Loewis. Since Loewis's men were much outnumbered by the French garrison and had to beat off a number of sorties this was not a man too many, but without Loewis Wittgenstein had only 25,000 soldiers at his disposal.

Meanwhile on 4 February Mikhail Barclay de Tolly re-emerged to replace Chichagov as commander of the army besieging Thorn. Almost all Barclay's troops were committed to the siege since Thorn was a major fortress commanding a key crossing of the Vistula and blocking all use of the river for transporting supplies. The only men Barclay could spare in the short run for an advance were Mikhail Vorontsov's 5,000-strong detachment. Napoleon is often condemned for leaving so many good troops behind as garrisons for the Polish and Prussian fortresses, and, later in 1813 when these fortresses were blockaded by Russian militia and recruits this mistake became clear. In January and February 1813, however, matters were not so obvious. The detachment of so many front-line Russian troops to watch French fortresses offered the new French commander in the east, Eugène de Beauharnais, an opportunity to block the Russian advance into the Prussian heartland.

On 22 January 1813 Aleksandr Chernyshev wrote to Kutuzov suggesting the formation of three 'flying detachments' which would raid deep into the French rear up to and beyond the river Oder. These raiding parties 'will both have an impact on the indecisive Berlin cabinet and cover the main army in its quarters, since the latter after its glorious but difficult campaign absolutely must get some rest having reached the Vistula'. Chernyshev told Kutuzov that reconnaissance showed that many routes to the Oder and Berlin were open. The French losses, especially of cavalry, had been huge and the garrisons in their rear were too small and too immobile to cope with Russian raiders. He added that 'all the information I have received' argued that only when Russian troops reached the Oder 'will this force Prussia to declare itself decisively in our favour'. There was not a moment to be lost: the French must be harried while they were still shaken and bewildered; they must not be given the opportunity to regain their senses, reinforce or reorganize themselves.[20]

Kutuzov and Wittgenstein took up Chernyshev's suggestion and three flying columns were dispatched. The most northerly column was commanded by Colonel Friedrich von Tettenborn, a former Austrian officer and a German patriot who dreamed of raising the population of northwest Germany against Napoleon. Shortly after Tettenborn had crossed the Oder north of Kustrin, a second raiding party under Alexander Benckendorff got across south of that town. Both then carried out a number of attacks on French units and supplies in the Berlin region. Meanwhile Chernyshev himself began his operations further to the east, in the rear of Eugène's headquarters in Posen, in the hope of causing such chaos that the viceroy would abandon this key position and fall back on the Oder. Together the three raiding parties numbered fewer than 6,000 men. Most were Cossacks but they included some squadrons of regular cavalry since, in Chernyshev's opinion, 'however good Cossack units are, they act with much more confidence if they see regular cavalry in support behind them'. None of the three parties contained infantry and only Chernyshev had horse artillery, though even in his case this only amounted to two guns.[21]

The Russians were greatly helped by the small numbers, low quality and poor morale of the enemy cavalry. Whatever enemy horsemen they encountered they destroyed. Chernyshev annihilated 2,000 Lithuanian lancers near Zirche on the river Warthe behind Posen, whom he bamboozled and attacked simultaneously from front and rear. A few days later Wittgenstein reported to Kutuzov that Benckendorff, operating along the road from Frankfurt on the Oder to Berlin, had ambushed and 'destroyed almost the last unit of enemy cavalry, which even without this was very weak'. The Russian cavalry caused confusion along the French lines of communication, attacking infantry and recruit parties, destroying supplies, and intercepting correspondence. Inevitably this increased the already existing fear and confusion among French commanders. The extraordinary mobility of the Russian horsemen meant that their numbers were greatly exaggerated. Because they captured so many French couriers, the Russians on the other hand were very well informed about French deployments, numbers, morale and plans.[22]

Eugène decided to pull back and defend the line of the river Oder, a decision for which he was castigated by Napoleon at the time and by a number of subsequent historians.[23] They were correct to suggest that it made no sense to string troops along the line of the Oder, especially at a time when vastly superior Russian cavalry could so effectively impede communication and cooperation between them. Eugène believed that the ice on the rivers was now melting, which would make the Oder defensible. In fact, however, even Chernyshev, well informed about where the ice remained strongest, just succeeded in getting across the Oder in time. He commented that the ice was very thin and the operation extremely risky but his troops' morale by this time was so high that they were convinced that they could achieve wonders.[24]

Once all three raiding parties were across the river they harassed Marshal Pierre Augereau's garrison in Berlin ceaselessly, at one point actually breaking right into the city centre. By now the Russians had captured so many French couriers that the enemy's intentions were an open book to them. Wittgenstein was told that the French would abandon Berlin and retire behind the Elbe the moment any body of Russian infantry approached. Armed with this information, Wittgenstein hurried forward his corps's advance guard – only 5,000 strong – under Prince Repnin-Volkonsky. Benckendorff rebuilt a bridge over the Oder for Repnin's men and the Russian forces entered Berlin on 4 March to a tremendous reception. Wittgenstein reported to Kutuzov in triumphant mood that very day: 'The victorious standards of His Imperial Majesty are flying over Berlin.'[25]

The liberation of Berlin and the retreat of the French behind the Elbe were very important. The capital's recapture raised morale and the resources of all of Prussia could now be mobilized for the allied cause. Large French forces were being gathered by Napoleon and had Eugène been able to hang on for just a few more weeks the 1813 campaign would have started on the Oder, within range of rebellious Poland and Napoleon's fortresses on the Vistula. That in itself would have reduced the chances of Austrian intervention. Instead the campaign began well to the west of the Elbe, gaining for the allies a number of precious weeks in which Russian reinforcements could approach and Austria could gird itself for battle.

A number of factors explain the French retreat. Among them should not be forgotten the outstanding performance of the Russian light cavalry and Cossacks. In his journal Chernyshev commented that in previous wars 'partisan' units had raided behind enemy lines to capture supply trains and take prisoners in order to gather intelligence. They had also attacked small enemy units. He added that in the 1813 campaign his own partisans did much more than this. For considerable periods they had cut enemy operational lines and stopped all movement and communication. Operating sometimes hundreds of kilometres ahead of the main Russian forces, they had created a complete fog around enemy commanders and in some cases had actually forced fundamental changes in enemy plans. With typical modesty, Chernyshev concluded that the commander of a 'flying detachment' needed great energy, presence of mind, prudence and ability to grasp situations quickly. Chernyshev had a penchant for self-advertisement and self-promotion worthy of Nelson. To do him justice, he also had Nelson's boldness, tactical skill, strategic insight and capacity for leadership.[26]

Just five days before the fall of Berlin Frederick William finally buried his doubts and consented to the treaty of alliance with Russia. An officer on Kutuzov's staff wrote that 'in our negotiations with them [i.e. the Prussians] the news we often received about the successes of our advance guards which were already approaching the Elbe gave us great weight'. Nevertheless, negotiations were difficult almost to the end. The main reason for this was disagreement on the fate of Poland. Prussia had been a key beneficiary of the Polish partitions. It wanted back the Polish lands which Napoleon had forced it to concede at Tilsit, and argued that without this territory Prussia could not possess the strength or security essential for a great power. On the other hand, the events of 1812 had further confirmed Alexander in his belief that the only way to square the demands of Polish nationhood and Russian security was to unite as many Poles as possible in an autonomous kingdom whose ruler would also be the Russian monarch. At a time when Russia was expending huge amounts of blood and money to restore large territories to Austria and Prussia, and when Britain had made a clean sweep of the French and Dutch colonial empires, the emperor no doubt also felt that his empire should have some reward for his efforts.[27]

Baron vom Stein helped to smooth over the difficulties by travelling to Breslau to win over Frederick William. Stein himself disliked Alexander's plans for Poland, which he thought were dangerous for Russian internal stability and a threat to Austrian and Prussian security. He also wondered whether the Poles, 'with their serfs and their Jews', were capable of self-government. But Stein knew that on this issue Alexander was adamant and he helped to broker a Russo-Prussian compromise.

Russia would guarantee all existing Prussian possessions and it would ensure that East Prussia and Silesia were linked by a substantial and strategically defensible band of territory taken from the Duchy of Warsaw. The Russians also promised that they would commit all their strength to the war in Germany and would not make peace until Prussia was restored to the same level of power, territory and population as it had possessed before 1806. Article I of the Treaty of Kalicz's secret clauses promised that Prussia would be fully compensated in northern Germany for any Polish territory it lost to Russia in the east. Unlike Napoleon, the Russians could not bribe the Prussians with Hanoverian territory, since this belonged to their ally, the British king. The only likely source of compensation was therefore Saxony, whose weakening or dismemberment would go down badly in Vienna. The Treaty of Kalicz therefore in part remained strictly secret and was storing up problems for the future.

For the moment, however, it was a satisfactory basis for Russo-Prussian cooperation. The main thrust of the treaty was its commitment to restoring Prussia as a great power, above all so it could check France but also perhaps in order to balance Austrian power in Germany. On this all-important issue the Russians were just as committed as the Prussians. In addition, although the preamble to the treaty contained its share of sanctimonious hypocrisy, its call for 'the repose and well-being of peoples exhausted by so many disturbances and so many sacrifices' was genuine and heartfelt. Add this to the friendship which existed between Alexander and Frederick William and there are the ingredients of a strong and lasting bond between the two states. Indeed in one form or another the Russo-Prussian alliance of February 1813 was to survive until the 1890s, forming one of the most stable and enduring elements in European diplomacy.[28]

Article VII of the treaty bound both Prussia and Russia to give top priority to bringing Austria into their alliance. This priority was to dominate not just allied diplomacy but even to some extent military strategy in the next three months. Austria, however, was intent on playing hard to get, and with good reason. The Austrians believed that they had borne the biggest share of fighting the French since 1793 and that they had been let down by the Prussians and Russians on a number of occasions and taken for granted by the British. This time they would exploit all the potential leverage of their position and not be rushed into anything.

Numerous defeats bred pessimism and aversion to risk among some Austrians, above all in Francis II, on whom in the last resort all decisions on war and peace depended. Suspicion of Russia ran deep, with traditional fears of Russian power and unpredictability exacerbated by the fact that the Austrians had intercepted part of Alexander's correspondence with Prince Adam Czartoryski, his chief confidant on Polish affairs, and were aware of the gist of his plans for Poland. Russian and Prussian appeals to German nationalism, on occasion calling for the overthrow of princes who supported Napoleon, infuriated the Austrians, partly for fear of chaos and partly because they alienated the Confederation of the Rhine monarchs whom Vienna was trying to woo. Baron vom Stein, Alexander's chief adviser on German affairs, was a particular Austrian bugbear.

From March 1813, however, Alexander increasingly bowed to Austrian wishes in this matter, stopping inflammatory proclamations by his generals and conceding to Austria the lead in all matters to do with Bavaria, Württemberg and southern Germany. Most importantly, the great majority of the Austrian political and military elite deeply resented the manner in which Napoleon had reduced Austria to the status of a second-rate power, annexing her territory and removing her influence from Germany and Italy. Given a good opportunity to reverse this process and restore a genuine European balance of power, most members of the Austrian elite would take it, by peaceful means if possible but running the risks inherent in war if necessary. The Austrian foreign minister, Count Clemens von Metternich, shared this mainstream viewpoint.[29]

In January 1813 Metternich's immediate priority was to free Austria from the French alliance and take up the role of neutral mediator without provoking Napoleon more than necessary in doing so. One aspect of this policy was to remove Schwarzenberg's corps from the *Grande Armée* and get it back safely over the Austrian border. Another was to work out peace terms on the basis of which Austria could mediate. Austria's goal was a European system in which Russia and France balanced each other, with Austria and Prussia restored to their previous strength and able to guarantee the independence of Germany. The Austrians also deeply wanted and needed a long and stable peace.[30]

To have any chance of success in its mediation, Metternich realized that Austria would need to rebuild its army so that it could threaten decisive intervention in the war. The problem here was that military expenditure had been cut savagely after the defeat of 1809 and the state bankruptcy of 1811. Many infantry battalions were mere skeletons; horses and equipment were in very short supply; most of the arms works had been closed. The finance ministry conducted a stubborn rearguard action on military expenditure in 1813, with money being disbursed very slowly even after budgets had been agreed. In addition, arms and uniforms workshops could not be re-created overnight and no sane manufacturer would give the Austrian government credit. Metternich also miscalculated how much time he had at his disposal. In early February he was convinced that Napoleon could not possibly have a large army in the field before the end of June. On 30 May he confessed his astonishment at 'the incredible speed with which Napoleon had re-created an army'. For all his great diplomatic skill, the speed and violence of Napoleonic warfare was alien to Metternich and could easily upset all his calculations. As with Prussia in 1805, Austria in 1813 dragged out negotiations with both warring camps before finally committing itself to the allies. Prussian policy had then been totally confounded by the disaster at Austerlitz. The same came near to happening to the Austrians in May 1813.[31]

Amidst all the tensions and uncertainties of Russo-Austrian relations in the spring and summer of 1813 it helped enormously that Nesselrode was in frequent and secret correspondence with Friedrich von Gentz, one of the leading intellectuals of the counter-revolution in Vienna and

Metternich's closest confidant. Gentz was exceptionally well informed about Metternich's own thinking and about the opinions and conflicts within Austrian ruling circles. Nesselrode had known Gentz for years and rightly trusted his deep commitment to the allied cause. Gentz could put in a good word for the allies in Metternich's ear. More importantly, he could explain to Nesselrode the severe constraints within which the foreign minister was operating, shackled as he was not just by the caution of Francis II and some of his advisers, but also by the deep and genuine difficulties facing Austrian rearmament.[32]

In comparison to the tortuous diplomacy conducted by Metternich in the first half of 1813, the movements of Schwarzenberg's observation corps are relatively easy to follow. In January 1813 Schwarzenberg's men stood directly in the path of a Russian advance through Warsaw and central Poland. As was the case with Yorck's corps at the other end of Napoleon's line, the 25,000 relatively fresh Austrian troops would have been a major obstacle to Kutuzov's overstretched army had it chosen to bar his way. But the Austrians had no interest in defending the Duchy of Warsaw and actually welcomed the Russian advance towards central Europe as a means of weakening and balancing Napoleon's power. They also had no wish to see their best troops sacrificed in battles with the Russian forces.

Ignoring French orders to cover Warsaw and retreat westwards, Schwarzenberg, on his government's instructions, concluded a secret agreement with the Russians to retreat south-westwards towards Cracow and Austrian Galicia. An elaborate charade was maintained with the Russians so that Vienna could claim that its troops' retreat had been necessitated by enemy outflanking movements. The only major force which now remained to cover central Poland was General Reynier's Saxon corps. This was overtaken and heavily defeated by Kutuzov's advance guard at Kalicz on 13 February 1813. The result of the Austrian retreat to the south-west was that by the end of February the whole of the Duchy of Warsaw had fallen into Russian hands with the exception of a handful of French fortresses and a small strip of land around Cracow.[33]

In the first week of March, with Berlin and all Prussia liberated, and with Miloradovich's and Wintzengerode's corps of Kutuzov's army positioned on the Polish border with Prussian Silesia, the first phase of the spring 1813 campaign was over. For the remainder of the month most of the Russian army was in quarters, resting after the winter campaign and attempting to feed itself and its horses, and to get its uniforms, muskets and equipment into some kind of order. Kutuzov issued detailed instructions to commanding officers about how to utilize this rest-period and they did their best to comply. While quartered near Kalicz, for example, the Lithuania (Litovsky) Guards Regiment trained every morning. All its muskets were repaired by skilled private craftsmen under the eagle eyes of the regiment's NCOs. Its battered wagons were also repaired. A fifteen-day supply of flour was baked into bread and biscuit against future emergencies. The regiment could not replenish its ammunition because the ammunition parks were still stuck along the army's line of communication, but each company built a Russian bath-house for itself. Material arrived for new uniforms and tailors' shops were immediately set up to turn this into uniforms.[34]

Although the Lithuania Guards Regiment enjoyed a rest in these weeks it received almost no reinforcements. This was true of almost all units in Kutuzov's and Wittgenstein's armies. The new reserve forces which had formed in Russia over the winter had been summoned to the front but they would not arrive until late May at the earliest. A handful of men dribbled back to the ranks from hospital or detached duties but they merely filled the gaps left by men falling out through sickness or dispatched from the regiments on essential tasks. At Kalicz, the Lithuania Guards had 38 officers and 810 men in the ranks but the Guards were usually far stronger than the bulk of the army. The Kexholm Regiment, for example, was down to just 408 men in mid-March.[35]

As was typical of Osten-Sacken's corps operating in south-west Poland, the Iaroslavl Regiment of Johann Lieven's 10th Infantry Division was much stronger than most of the units in Kutuzov's army. Even it, however, in mid-March had 5 officers and 170 men in hospital, and 14 officers and 129 men on detached duties. The latter included guarding the regimental baggage, helping the formation of reserves, escorting prisoners of war, collecting uniforms and equipment from the rear, and supervising the collection and dispatch of convalescents from hospitals. These detachments always required a disproportionate number of officers and were the inevitable consequence of a year's campaigning which had now resulted in lines of communication stretching back for hundreds of kilometres. But they meant that when the campaign's second phase began in April and the Russian forces advanced to meet Napoleon's main army they would do so in a thoroughly reduced, even in some cases skeletal, condition.[36]

While much of the Russian army was resting in March 1813 its light forces were gaining new laurels. Among their new exploits was a brilliant little victory near Lüneburg on 2 April where Chernyshev's and Dornberg's Russian 'flying columns' united to annihilate a French division under General Morand.

The most spectacular exploit of the light forces in March and April was, however, Tettenborn's seizure of Hamburg and Lübeck, amidst a popular insurrection against the French. In this region, whose prosperity depended on overseas trade, the Continental System and Napoleon's empire were deeply hated. The arrival of Tettenborn's cavalry and Cossacks was greeted with ecstasy by the population. Already on 31 January Tettenborn had written to Alexander to say that French rule was detested in north-west Germany and 'I am firmly convinced that we could quickly create a huge army there'. Now his predictions appeared to be coming true and his reports to Wittgenstein bubbled over with excitement and enthusiasm. On 21 March, for example, he reported that he expected to be able to form a large infantry force from local volunteers. Two days later he added that the formation of volunteer units was progressing 'with astonishing success'.[37]

In time unpleasant realities began to undermine the enthusiasm of this German patriot. The good burghers of Hamburg were not, as he had hoped, the German equivalents of the Spanish population of Saragossa, willing to see their houses destroyed over their heads and to fight in the ruins against French attempts to take their city. After initial enthusiasm, volunteering fell away sharply. Greatly outnumbered in Saxony by Napoleon, allied headquarters could spare no regular Russian or Prussian forces to support Tettenborn. The last hope of saving Hamburg from Marshal Davout's counter-offensive rested with Bernadotte's Swedish corps, whose first units began to disembark in Stralsund from 18 March. When Bernadotte refused to come to Hamburg's rescue, however, the city's cause was lost and Tettenborn evacuated his great prize on 30 May.

The circumstances in which Hamburg fell were the first act in the 'Black Legend' created by German nationalists against Bernadotte. Many further acts followed in 1813. It was whispered against him that he had no intention of fighting the French seriously since he wished to win their sympathy and replace Napoleon on France's throne. More realistically, Bernadotte was accused of caring nothing for the allied cause and of preserving his Swedish troops for the only war that mattered to him, which was the conquest of Norway from the Danes. The latter accusation had some force and Bernadotte, who infuriated both French and German nationalists, traditionally had a very bad press. But even one of his greatest critics, Sir Charles Stewart, who was the British envoy to Prussia, wrote in his memoirs that Bernadotte was correct not to commit Swedish forces to Hamburg.[38]

Bernadotte himself explained his actions to Alexander's envoys, generals Peter van Suchtelen and Charles-André Pozzo di Borgo. He stated that half of his troops and much of his baggage had not arrived due to contrary winds when the appeal from Hamburg came. His outnumbered men would have faced Davout to their front with hostile Danish forces in their rear. Acknowledging the seriousness of Hamburg's loss, Bernadotte argued that

despite all the misfortunes which this loss can bring, the defeat of the Swedish army would be a thousand times worse, and Hamburg would in that event be occupied for certain and the Danes would reunite with the French. Instead of this, I am concentrating my forces, I am organizing my troops and am receiving reinforcements from Sweden every day – and thereby I am making the French feel my presence and will stop them crossing the Elbe unless they do this in too great force.[39]

Though a big disappointment to German patriots, the Hamburg operation actually remained a great success from the point of view of allied headquarters. At the cost of a relative handful of Cossacks and cavalry, Napoleon's best marshal, Davout, and roughly 40,000 French troops were occupied in what was a strategic backwater at a time when their presence on the Saxon battlefields could have made a decisive difference. In addition, the chaos encouraged in north-western Germany by Tettenborn, Chernyshev and other 'partisan' leaders totally disrupted the horse-fairs which traditionally occurred in the region at this time. For the French this was a serious matter. The biggest headache faced by Napoleon as he strove to re-create the *Grande Armée* was the shortage of cavalry; 175,000 horses had been lost in Russia and this proved to be a more serious matter than the lost manpower. In 1813 'France was so poor in horses' (according to a nineteenth-century French expert) that even requisitioning private horses for the cavalry and other emergency measures 'could only provide 29,000 horses and even they were not in a state to enter military service immediately'. The Polish and north-east German studs were lost to Napoleon, and efforts to buy from the Austrians were rejected. The wrecking of the horse-fairs in north-western Germany was an additional blow, which further delayed the mounting and training of the French cavalry. Many thousands of French cavalrymen remained without horses in the spring 1813 campaign, and lack of cavalry very seriously undermined Napoleon's operations.[40]

Apart from the cavalry, however, Napoleon's efforts rapidly to rebuild his armies in the winter of 1812–13 were a triumphant success. The nature of this new *Grande Armée* is sometimes misunderstood. Contrary to legend, it was in reality by no means just a *mélange* of the 25,000 men who had crawled back across the Neman in December 1812 and a horde of 'Marie Louises', in other words young conscripts from the classes of 1813 and 1814. Even as early as January 1813 some fresh troops were available to reinforce Eugène's remnant of the old *Grande Armée*: above all, these were the 27,000 men of Grenier and Lagrange's divisions, which had never been committed to the Russian campaign. In addition, we have already encountered the French garrisons in Prussia which frightened Frederick William III in the winter of 1812–13.

Armies on campaign usually leave behind some sort of cadre in depots or along the lines of communication, from which their regiments can if necessary be reconstituted. For example, Napoleon's Guards in theory numbered 56,000 men on the eve of the 1812 campaign. The Guards units which entered Russia nominally comprised 38,000 men and had 27,000 actually present in the ranks when they crossed the Neman. The Young Guard regiments which invaded Russia were almost wiped out but two Young Guard battalions had remained in Paris in 1812, and two more in Germany. Around them and the four full Young Guard regiments in Spain a formidable new force could be created.[41]

Within France there were the reserve battalions of the regiments serving in Spain and in the farther-flung areas of the empire. In his study of the *Grande Armée* in 1813, Camille Rousset mentions them but gives no figure for the men they sent to it. The Prussian general staff history of the campaign reckons perhaps 10,000. French and Prussian sources also differ as to how many men were withdrawn from Spain. The smallest figure is 20,000 but all sources agree that the men from Spain were the elite of the troops deployed there. On top of this there were 12,000 good soldiers of the naval artillery stationed in France's ports and now incorporated into the new *Grande Armée*. Even the first wave of recruits, the 75,000 so-called cohorts, had already been under arms for nine months by the beginning of 1813. It was around this relatively large cadre that the true 'Marie Louises' were formed. These young men usually lacked neither courage nor loyalty: their great problem was endurance when faced by the gruelling demands of Napoleonic campaigning. Nevertheless, as it concentrated near the river Main Napoleon's new army was an impressive force. Initially, its more than 200,000 men faced barely 110,000 allied soldiers. If the Russians and Prussians had considerably more veterans, the French had Napoleon to even this balance.[42]

While Napoleon was mobilizing and concentrating his new armies Kutuzov was at headquarters in Kalicz, contemplating competing strategic options. Immediately after the signing of the Russo-Prussian alliance on 28 February Lieutenant-General Gerhard von Scharnhorst arrived at Russian headquarters in Kalicz to coordinate planning for the forthcoming campaign. There was no doubt, however, either that Russia was the senior partner in the alliance or that Kutuzov, field-marshal and commander-in-chief, would have the decisive say in strategy. Both at the time and subsequently Kutuzov was criticized from two diametrically opposed points of view.

One school of thought argued that the allied forces ought to have advanced decisively across Germany in March and early April 1813. Some of the Prussian generals and some later German historians took the lead here but Wittgenstein was also anxious to pursue Viceroy Eugène over the Elbe. Both those like Wittgenstein, who wished to attack Eugène at Magdeburg, and those who wanted to strike further south to disrupt Napoleon's planned offensive, believed this would allow the allies to mobilize powerful support from the German peoples and perhaps German princes. The opposite school of thought, almost exclusively Russian, sometimes blamed Kutuzov for having advanced so far from his base in Russia, and opposed any plan to cross the Elbe into the Saxon heartland until Russian reinforcements arrived.[43]

In an important letter written to his cousin, Admiral Login Golenishchev-Kutuzov, the commander-in-chief explained why the Russians had been forced to advance so deep into Germany.

Our movement away from our borders and so from our resources may seem ill-considered, particularly if you reckon the distance from the Neman to the Elbe and then the distance from the Elbe to the Rhine. Large enemy forces can reach us before we can be strengthened by reserves coming from Russia . . . But if you go into the circumstances of our activities in more detail, then you will see that we are operating beyond the Elbe only with light forces, of which (given the quality of our light forces) none will be lost. It was necessary to occupy Berlin and having taken Berlin how can you abandon Saxony, both because of its abundant resources and because it interdicts the enemy's communications with Poland. Mecklenburg and the Hanseatic towns add to our resources. I agree that our removal far from our borders also distances us from our reinforcements but if we had remained behind the Vistula then we would have had to wage a war like in 1807. There would have been no alliance with Prussia and all of Germany, including Austria, with its people and all its resources, would have served Napoleon.[44]

Kutuzov's response to those who urged a rapid advance across Germany is contained in the many letters he wrote to his subordinate generals, Winzengerode and Wittgenstein. The commander-in-chief admitted the advantages in occupying as much as possible of Germany in order to mobilize its resources, raise German morale and pre-empt Napoleon's plans. But the further the allies advanced the weaker their forces would become and the more vulnerable to a devastating counter-strike from the far larger army that Napoleon was building up in south-western Germany. Defeat would have more than merely military consequences: 'You must understand that any reverse will be a big blow to Russia's prestige in Germany.'[45]

Aleksandr Mikhailovsky-Danilevsky, who was serving at the time on Kutuzov's staff, recalled that there was constant tension between headquarters and Wittgenstein in March and April 1813, as Kutuzov tried to draw his subordinate's attention southwards to where Napoleon's main army was concentrating, and in particular to the line from Erfurt through Leipzig to Dresden along which the enemy was expected to advance. On the contrary, Wittgenstein was above all concerned to protect Berlin and the Prussian heartland which his corps had liberated and on whose borders it was mostly deployed in March 1813. Kutuzov and his chief of staff, Petr Volkonsky, were extremely concerned that unless Wittgenstein advanced to the south-west into Saxony there was every chance that Napoleon's advance would drive a wedge between him and the main allied forces and thereby enable the enemy to isolate and overwhelm first one allied army and then the other.[46]

In the circumstances Kutuzov and Volkonsky were basically correct. Given their acute shortage of troops, the allies had to concentrate their forces in the Dresden–Leipzig area in order to stop Napoleon driving eastwards along the Austrian border towards Poland. But the worries of Wittgenstein and his chief of staff d'Auvray about defending Berlin and Brandenburg were also legitimate and were shared by most senior Prussian commanders. If Napoleon reconquered these areas, Prussian mobilization of men and *matériel* would suffer a big setback. The basic problem of the allies in the spring of 1813 was that they needed to defend both the Prussian heartland around Berlin and southern Saxony. Unfortunately they lacked the resources to do this. The tension caused by conflicting strategic priorities and inadequate manpower to defend them continued throughout the spring campaign.

Clausewitz provides a realistic view on the allied situation which goes a long way towards justifying the strategy ultimately agreed by Kutuzov and Scharnhorst, and ratified by the Russian and Prussian monarchs. In his view Wittgenstein's wish to attack Eugène at Magdeburg made no sense: the viceroy would merely retreat if faced by superior numbers and would draw the allies away from the crucial Leipzig–Dresden operational line on which their links to Austria and to the Russian supplies and reinforcements in Poland depended. Mounting a pre-emptive strike into Thuringia, as some Prussian generals were urging, also made no sense. The advancing allied troops would face far superior numbers close to Napoleon's bases by April.

Unfortunately, however, the purely defensive strategy based on defence of the Elbe which some Russians advocated was also unlikely to work, given Napoleon's superiority in numbers and the fact that he held almost all the fortified crossing points over the river. By standing on the Elbe rather than further west, the allies would merely gift Napoleon extra time which they dearly needed to win over the Austrians and bring up Russian reinforcements. Though Clausewitz therefore approved of the allied strategy of advancing over the Elbe and seeking to delay Napoleon by offering battle near Leipzig, he was clear-eyed about the allied chances in this battle, given the French advantage in numbers. Surprise, added to the superiority of the allied veteran troops and of their cavalry, gave them some hope of victory but no more than that.[47]

On 16 March 1813 Blücher's Prussian corps crossed the Silesian border into Saxony. The next day Prussia declared war on France. Blücher was followed by the advance guard of Kutuzov's army, commanded by Winzengerode, who was subordinated to the Prussian general's command. Dresden, the Saxon capital, fell to Winzengerode on 27 March, after which the Russian and Prussian troops fanned out across Saxony towards Leipzig. Apart from the strategic reasons for occupying western Saxony, logistics also came into play. Silesia and the Lausitz (i.e. eastern Saxony) were largely manufacturing areas which depended even in normal circumstances on imported Polish grain. These provinces could sustain troops crossing them but the long-term deployment of the allied armies east of the Elbe was bound to be difficult and to impede efforts to mobilize resources in Silesia for the Prussian war effort.

The ever-aggressive Blücher dreamed of heading into Thuringia and Franconia to attack Napoleon's main army before it was ready. He knew that he could not do this on his own but his attempts to persuade Wittgenstein to join the offensive were unavailing. In fact even Blücher began to have his doubts about the wisdom of such a move. Like all the allied leaders, Blücher had his eyes on Austria, and in particular on Francis II. Like them too, memories of 1805 were burned into his consciousness: in that year probable Prussian intervention in the war had been wrecked by the premature allied attack at Austerlitz. He commented to Wittgenstein that everyone was warning him of the possible present-day parallels and that maybe on this occasion it was better to postpone the decision for as long as possible.[48]

Meanwhile Kutuzov and his army's main body remained in Kalicz, much to the Prussians' annoyance. The field-marshal saw no reason to disturb his men's rest. Having occupied Saxony he had no wish to advance further and his intelligence reports in March rightly concluded that Napoleon was not yet ready to attack him. On 2 April Frederick William arrived in Kalicz and inspected the Russian troops. The Guards, all in new uniforms, looked splendid but the king was dismayed by the small size of the Russian forces. The Prussians were beginning to realize how much the past year's campaigning had cost the Russians and how very great an effort Prussia would need to make for victory. Five days after the parade Alexander, Kutuzov and the Guards at last set off for Saxony.

En route, Captain Zhirkevich's battery of the Russian Guards artillery experienced another rather different inspection by Frederick William while passing through Liegnitz. The news that the king was in the city and wished to greet the Russian troops only reached Zhirkevich at very short notice. The Russian commander's preparations were then thrown into total confusion when the modest Frederick William suddenly emerged onto the insignificant steps of the first small house they passed on entering the city. A volley of commands more or less got the column into some variant of parade order in the narrow street but the excitement also stirred up the menagerie of ducks, geese and hens stacked on top of the gun caissons, who added their own cacophony to the military music. Behind the gun carriages and caissons followed a herd of sheep, calves and cows. They added to the confusion not just by their cries but also by attempting to array themselves into their own version of parade order too. Zhirkevich's embarrassment was increased by the fact that these animals had all been 'acquired' from the king's own province of Silesia, but Frederick William just smiled and told the Russian commander that it was good to see the troops looking so well and cheerful. The king could be morose, cold and ungracious but at heart he was a decent and well-meaning man. He also spoke and read Russian, albeit imperfectly, and he liked the Russians. It was lucky for Zhirkevich that his men's antics had been performed before Frederick William rather than Alexander or the Grand Duke Constantine. The latter would have taken a very dim view of the Guards' informality when on parade before an allied sovereign.[49]

For the Russian troops the march across Silesia and Saxony was something of a picnic. The weather was superb and, especially in Silesia, the Russian soldiers were greeted everywhere as allies and liberators. Though usually treated correctly by the Poles, the latter were seldom fully trusted by Russian officers. Much of Poland was poor at the best of times, and not improved by the passage of armies in 1812–13. By contrast, Silesia was rich and Saxony even richer. The Russian officers marvelled at the wealth, houses and lifestyles of Saxon peasant farmers. The blonde and buxom German young women were a joy to behold, though German 'vodka' seemed miserably thin and weak. Meanwhile, as they approached the Elbe, they could see on their left the romantic wooded slopes of the mountains dividing Saxony from Habsburg Bohemia.[50]

On 24 April Alexander and the Russian Guards entered Dresden, where they were to spend the Russian Easter. For the overwhelming majority of the Russian soldiers, both in Dresden and elsewhere in Saxony, the Easter services were a moving and uplifting experience. Serge Volkonsky, Prince Repnin-Volkonsky's brother and Petr Mikhailovich Volkonsky's brother-in-law, was an excellently educated, French-speaking officer of the Chevaliers Gardes. Nevertheless he recalls how the priests emerged from the church to greet the massed regiments with the Easter cry, 'Christ is risen', 'the prayer . . . dear to the heart of all Christians and for us Russians all the more strongly felt because our prayers are both religious and national. On account of both sentiments, for all the Russians present this was a moment of exaltation.' The time for prayers and picnics was drawing to a close, however. The same day that Alexander entered Dresden, Napoleon moved his headquarters forward from Mainz to Erfurt in preparation for his advance into Saxony.[51]

Meanwhile illness had forced Kutuzov to drop out en route to Dresden. The old field-marshal died in Bunzlau on 28 April. Kutuzov's death had no impact on allied strategy, which remained committed to stopping Napoleon's advance through Saxony. Alexander appointed Wittgenstein to be the new commander-in-chief. In many ways he was the most suitable candidate. No other general had won so many victories in 1812 and his reputation had been enhanced by the victorious campaign to liberate Prussia in 1813. Wittgenstein spoke German and French and could therefore communicate easily with Russia's allies. In addition, his concern for the defence of Berlin and the Prussian heartland endeared him to the Prussians and enabled him to empathize with their worries. One problem with Wittgenstein's appointment was that he was junior to Miloradovich, Tormasov and Barclay. The latter was still absent from the main army at the siege of Thorn but the other two full generals were deeply insulted. Tormasov departed for Russia and was no great loss. Miloradovich remained and was assuaged by daily messages of support and benevolence from Alexander.

None of this would have mattered too much had Wittgenstein chalked up a victory over Napoleon. Failure at the battle of Lutzen brought out the knives. Already prone to intervene in military operations, Alexander became even more inclined to do so as criticisms mounted of the new commander-in-chief. Unfortunately, these criticisms were often justified. Wittgenstein was out of his depth as commander-in-chief. Brave, bold, generous and even chivalrous, Wittgenstein was an inspirational corps commander but he could not master the much more complex requirements of army headquarters where authority could not always be exercised in face-to-face manner and painstaking administration and staff work were required to keep a large force operational. According to Mikhailovsky-Danilevsky, Wittgenstein's headquarters was chaotic, with little discipline or even elementary military security being exercised over the many hangers-on who came to infest it.[52]

In the last days of April, as Napoleon advanced from Erfurt towards Leipzig, the allies deployed just to the south of his line of march near the town of Lutzen. Either they must try to ambush Napoleon or they must retreat rapidly so that he could not reach Dresden before them and cut off their retreat over the Elbe. The choice was not difficult since to retreat without a battle when first encountering Napoleon would damage the troops' morale and the allies' prestige in Germany and Austria. A surprise attack which caught the enemy on the march might defeat him, or at the very least slow down his advance.

The allied plan was devised by Diebitsch. He aimed to catch part of the enemy army while it was strung out on the march and to destroy it before the rest of Napoleon's corps could come to its aid. The consensus is that the plan was good but its execution very flawed. This is not surprising. Wittgenstein brought with him his own staff. Almost all top positions at headquarters changed on the eve of the battle. To take but one example: Ermolov was replaced as chief of artillery by Prince Iashvili, who had previously headed the artillery of Wittgenstein's corps. Ermolov was already in some disfavour because of his failure to bring up the artillery parks with ammunition supplies at sufficient speed, but the sudden transfer of responsibility to Iashvili resulted in the new artillery chief not knowing the whereabouts even of all the ammunition that was to hand. Further confusion occurred because this was the first time that large Russian and Prussian forces had fought side-by-side.

Diebitsch's plan included columns moving at night to take up positions for attack by 6 a.m. on 2 May. Predictably, confusion occurred, columns bumped into each other and even the first allied line was not deployed until five hours later. Matters were not helped by the fact that the plans often arrived very late and were detailed but not always precise. To some extent the delay may even have worked in the allies' favour, however. During the five hours that elapsed, Napoleon and the bulk of his army was marching away from the battlefield and towards Leipzig, convinced that no battle would occur that day. In addition, had the battle of Lutzen commenced at dawn, Napoleon would have had a full summer's day to concentrate all his forces on the battlefield, with possibly dire results for the outnumbered allies.

The allies' initial target was Ney's isolated corps deployed near the villages of Grossgörschen and Starsiedel. It helped Wittgenstein that Ney had dispersed the five divisions of his corps and failed to take proper precautions. The initial attack by Blücher's Prussians took the enemy by surprise. The allied high command found itself equally surprised, however, by the fact that Marmont's corps was positioned in support of Ney and by the nature of the ground over which the battle was fought. This suggests that, despite their superiority in cavalry, allied reconnaissance was less than perfect. George Cathcart, the son of the British ambassador to Russia, was with Wittgenstein's headquarters. He commented that because of the undulating, cultivated terrain it was impossible to see from allied headquarters what lay beyond the first high ground where the enemy was positioned. The initial Prussian attack on Grossgörschen succeeded 'but Grossgörschen is only one of a cluster of nearly contiguous villages, interspersed with tanks, mill ponds, gardens etc., which furnished strong holding ground'. The villages on the battlefield were of 'stone houses with narrow, cobbled lanes and stone-walled gardens'.[53]

For the first time the allied troops encountered a fundamental difference between Saxon and Russian battlefields. On the latter, wooden villages offered no help to defenders. Solid Saxon stone walls and buildings were a very different matter and could sometimes be turned into small fortresses. Ney's troops were inexperienced but they were courageous and, in the nature of such soldiers, they drew strength from being able in part to fight behind fixed, stone defences. The Prussian infantry also showed extraordinary courage, urged on by officers desperate to wipe away the shame of Jena. The result was a ferocious battle that swung from side to side as villages were lost and then regained by fresh, well-ordered reserves whose swift counter-attacks caught the enemy before it had regained its breath and organized itself to defend its recent gains. The brunt of the fighting was borne by the Prussian infantry, with the Russians only entering the battle in their support well into the afternoon. From this moment Eugen of Württemberg's corps in particular was heavily engaged and suffered many casualties first in recapturing the villages and subsequently in holding off the growing threat to the allies' right flank.

The key to the battle was, however, that Ney's and Marmont's men were just able to hold the allied attacks long enough for first Napoleon himself and then other corps to arrive on the battlefield. It did not help the allied cause that faulty planning and reconnaissance meant that Miloradovich's corps remained inactive only a few kilometres from the battle. Even had Miloradovich's men been present, however, it would not have altered the outcome. Given the greatly superior French numbers of infantry and Napoleon's skill in using them, once the whole French army was concentrated on the battlefield victory was certain. By the late afternoon, with MacDonald threatening to turn the allies' right and Bertrand their left, Wittgenstein was being forced to commit his reserves at a time when Napoleon would soon have many fresh troops to hand.

Clausewitz argued that Lutzen was more a drawn battle than an allied defeat. At the end of the day the allies still stood on the battlefield and had inflicted more casualties than they had suffered. Their retreat was forced, not by defeat, but by the presence of overwhelming enemy numbers. According to Clausewitz, had they not fought at Lutzen this numerical inferiority would have forced the allies to retreat anyway without even slowing down the French advance to the degree achieved by the battle of Lutzen. There is something in this argument but also a touch of special pleading. It is true that Lutzen was not a serious defeat but it could well have become one with just two more hours of daylight.[54]

After the battle the allies made an orderly retreat across Saxony, recrossing the Elbe and reaching Bautzen in eastern Saxony on 12 May. For most of the way Miloradovich commanded the rearguard and did so with great skill. This allowed the rest of the army to move back in a calm and unhurried manner. At Bautzen the allies enjoyed almost a week's rest before Napoleon's troops fully caught up with them. The Russians by now had no equals in Europe when it came to rearguard actions and withdrawals. It would have taken far better cavalry than anything Napoleon possessed in 1813 to shake them. As a result of Lutzen, however, the King of Saxony, who had sat on the fence for two months, swung back into Napoleon's camp. The Saxon garrison of Torgau, the last fortified crossing of the Elbe not in French hands, was ordered to open its gates to Napoleon. Its commander, Lieutenant-General von Thielemann, delayed as long as possible and then fled with his chief of staff to the allied camp. Uncertainty as to whether Saxony would join the allies had constrained requisitioning in April. By the time King Frederick Augustus's position became clear it was too late for the retreating allies to milk the kingdom, whose rich resources were to sustain Napoleon's war effort for the next six months.[55]

The narrative of military operations in April and May 1813 at most tells only half of the story, however. Intensive diplomatic negotiations were going on simultaneously between the Austrians and the warring sides. This had a big impact on Russian strategy. In a letter to Bernadotte, Alexander claimed that all the battles which had occurred in Saxony in April and May had been fought in order to delay Napoleon and gain time for Austria to intervene, as it had promised repeatedly to do. At precisely the moment that Napoleon started his advance across Saxony the Austrians had launched their own diplomatic offensive. Having declared to both sides Austria's intention to mediate, Metternich sent Count Bubna to Napoleon and Count Philipp Stadion to allied head-quarters to discover the terms which the warring sides were willing to offer. Meanwhile Austria built up its army in Bohemia to add the threat of military intervention as an inducement to compromise.[56]

By this time Austria was tilting strongly towards the allies. Three months of negotiations with France and Russia had shown beyond doubt that Napoleon remained the enemy of the key Austrian objectives of regaining their lost territories and restoring some kind of balance of power in Europe. On these most fundamental issues the Russians and Prussians quite genuinely supported the Austrian position. If Vienna truly wanted to end France's dominion in Europe this could only be done in alliance with Petersburg and Berlin, and probably only by war. Just possibly the mere threat of Austrian intervention on the allies' side would induce Napoleon to make enough concessions to satisfy Vienna. Some Austrians hoped for this and the Russians and Prussians feared it. Around this key issue revolved the diplomatic negotiations between Austria, France and the allies in the late spring and summer of 1813.

On 29 April, three days before the battle of Lutzen, Metternich sent two important letters to Baron Lebzeltern, his representative at allied headquarters. The Austrian foreign minister noted continuing allied distrust of Vienna and set out to explain why the years of financial crisis since 1809 had so retarded military preparations. Metternich wrote that recent Austrian statements to Napoleon should leave him in no doubt about Vienna's position. When Stadion arrived at allied headquarters he would explain the peace terms Vienna was putting to Napoleon and leave the Russians and Prussians confident as to Austria's firm intention to act on them once its army was ready. In his first letter the Austrian foreign minister wrote that 'by the twenty-fourth of May we will have more than 60,000 men in the Bohemian border districts; in total we will have two field armies mobilized of between 125,000 and 130,000 men and a reserve of at least 50,000'. In his second letter, seeking to ease allied fears that their advance into Saxony was too risky, he added that

if Napoleon wins a battle it will be useless for most certainly the Austrian armies will not permit him to pursue his success: if he loses his fate is decided ... the emperor desires nevertheless that their Russian and Prussian majesties should have no doubt about the intervention of our Bohemian army which, I repeat, will stop any advance that the French armies might attempt against the allies in the case of victory; under no circumstances should this worry them.[57]

Stadion's instructions were issued on 7 May. They stated that even the minimal conditions which Austria would offer to Napoleon included the return of most Austrian and Prussian lost territories, the extinction of the Duchy of Warsaw and of all French territory in Germany east of the Rhine, and the abolition or at least modification of the Confederation of the Rhine. Austria bound itself to discover before the end of May whether Napoleon would accept these terms and listen to the voice of compromise. Metternich argued that the Austrian demands had deliberately been kept moderate because she sought a lasting European peace which could only be built on the consent of all the great powers. Stadion must reassure the allied monarchs that Austria's position would be changed neither by Napoleon's victories nor by his defeats on the battlefield. He must discover allied terms for peace but also create the basis for military cooperation in the event that Austrian armed mediation failed to sway Napoleon.[58]

Philipp Stadion reached allied headquarters at nine in the morning on 13 May, eleven days after the battle of Lutzen and one week before the battle of Bautzen. He met Nesselrode twice that day. In a report to

Alexander written on 13 May Nesselrode summarized the Austrian position as explained by Stadion. Vienna would insist on the restoration of the territories lost by it in 1805 and 1809. It would support whatever restoration of Prussian territory was stipulated in the Russo-Prussian treaty of alliance. It would demand the extinction of the Duchy of Warsaw, of all French territory east of the Rhine, and of the Confederation of the Rhine itself. If Napoleon did not accept these conditions by 1 June Austria would enter the war, regardless of what had happened on the battlefield between then and now. Stadion would agree with the allies the principles of a plan for joint military operations. Nesselrode commented correctly that 'without doubt the conditions set out will never be accepted by France'. He added that 'Count Stadion promises formally in the name of his court that no evasive or dilatory response by Napoleon will hold her back beyond the end of this period from executing the plan of operations which will have been agreed between her and the allied courts'.[59]

Nesselrode was a very calm and experienced diplomat. It is inconceivable that he misinterpreted Stadion, deliberately or otherwise, on so crucial a matter. Stadion himself was a former Austrian foreign minister. For all his hatred for Napoleon and the French Empire in Germany, he would never deliberately have misled the Russians. To do so would have been hugely risky both in military terms and in its impact on Austro-Russian relations. Perhaps Stadion allowed his enthusiasm too free a rein in interpreting his instructions, though it is impossible to know what was said between him and Metternich before his departure to allied headquarters. Whoever was to blame, however, there is no doubt that what Stadion told Nesselrode did not represent the true state of affairs in Vienna.

In the first place it was by no means certain that Francis II would take the uncompromising line suggested by Stadion in the event of Napoleon rejecting any of the Austrian minimal conditions, seeking delay, or winning victories over the allies on the battlefield. In addition, when Nesselrode three weeks later finally got to meet Field-Marshal Schwarzenberg and General Radetsky, the two key officers of the Army of Bohemia, they assured him that it had never been conceivable for the Austrian army to cross the Bohemian frontier before 20 June. Russian bafflement and suspicion was inevitable. Did Stadion speak for Metternich? What were the slippery foreign minister's true views and did he speak for Francis II? Did any Austrian statesman understand, let alone control, what the army was doing to prepare for war?[60]

Categorical Austrian assurances of support were a powerful additional reason for the allies to risk another battle against Napoleon by stopping their retreat at Bautzen. Nevertheless, though there were excellent reasons for trying to gain time and delay Napoleon, the decision was a very risky one. At the battle of Bautzen on 20–21 May the allies could muster only 96,000 men: Napoleon had double that number present by the end of the battle and his superiority was even greater as regards infantry, which would be the decisive arm on the battlefield. On the map the terrain at Bautzen seemed to favour a stout defence. When they arrived on the scene, as was their habit, the Russian troops immediately began to dig entrenchments and fortifications. Although individual strong points were formidable, however, the position was divided up into a number of sectors by streams and ravines. It would be very difficult to coordinate the defence or move reserves from one sector to another. Above all, the allied position was too extended for such a relatively small force. The Russians had four times fewer men per kilometre than had been the case at Borodino.

Count Langeron arrived at Bautzen with Barclay de Tolly's detachment just four days before the battle. After the fall of Thorn they had marched at speed to the rescue of the main army. At the battle of Bautzen Langeron's corps, under Barclay's overall command, stood on the far right flank of the allied line, against which Napoleon's decisive stroke – as it turned out – was to be directed, under the command of Marshal Ney. In his memoirs Langeron commented that the ground offered many advantages to its defenders but 25,000 men were needed to hold it; he had only 8,000. Eugen of Württemberg's corps was on the allied left flank. Like Langeron, he recognized that the decision to stand at Bautzen had been taken above all for political reasons. In his view, 'given how much we were outnumbered and given the very extended position we were holding we could not expect victory in the battle but just to inflict losses on the enemy and to conduct an orderly retreat protected by our numerous cavalry'.[61]

Fighting the leading general of the day at a two-to-one disadvantage, the danger was that they would be routed. Even another Friedland, let alone an Austerlitz, would probably have destroyed this allied coalition, as had happened to so many before it. A victory equal to Friedland was actually within Napoleon's grasp on 21 May and would probably have occurred but for the mistakes of Marshal Ney.

Napoleon's plan was simple and potentially devastating. On 20 May his limited attacks and feints would pin the allied main body along the whole defensive line which ran from the foothills of the Bohemian mountains on their left to the Kreckwitz heights on their right. These attacks would continue on 21 May. Given French numbers, it was easy to make these attacks very convincing and even to force the allies to commit part of their reserve to stop them. But the crucial stroke would be made on 21 May by Ney and Lauriston's corps on Barclay's position on the far right of the allied position near Gleina. In overwhelmingly superior numbers they would drive through Barclay and into the allied rear, cutting across the only roads which would allow the allies to make an orderly retreat eastwards to Reichenbach and Görlitz, and threatening to push the enemy in disorderly rout southwards over the Austrian frontier. This plan was fully viable and was indeed helped by Alexander's obsession that the main threat would come on his left, with Napoleon attempting to lever the allies away from the Bohemian frontier and thereby wreck the chances of coordinating operations with the Austrians. In contrast, Wittgenstein correctly understood that the main danger would come in the north. By now Alexander had lost confidence in Wittgenstein, however, and was almost acting himself as de facto commander-in-chief. Moreover, Wittgenstein did not help matters by telling the emperor that Barclay commanded 15,000 men whereas in reality he had barely half that many.[62]

On 20 May the battle went according to Napoleon's plan. Fierce fighting raged down the whole allied front as far north as the Kreckwitz heights and Alexander committed part of his reserves to drive back what he saw as the French threat on his left. Meanwhile Barclay's men were bothered by nothing more than a few skirmishers. On the next morning battle was renewed from the Bohemian foothills to Kreckwitz, but Ney and Lauriston also entered the fray.

The battle on the far right began at about nine in the morning. Barclay quickly realized that there was no hope of stopping the overwhelming numbers with which he was faced. All he could hope to do was fight a delaying action on the heights near Gleina and protect the key lines of retreat as long as possible. Langeron commented that in particular his 28th and 32nd Jaeger regiments showed both skill and heroism that morning, holding off the French until the last minute and allowing the Russian artillery to escape after inflicting heavy casualties. Barclay himself went forward among his jaegers, inspiring them by his quiet courage in extreme danger. For all the Russians' coolness and the temporary respite won by a counter-attack by Kleist's Prussians, the situation became increasingly desperate as Ney's pressure built up and part of Lauriston's corps threatened to envelop Barclay's right flank. When the village of Preititz finally fell to the French at three in the afternoon it would have been easy for Lauriston to move forward to cut the vital allied line of retreat down the road to Weissenburg.

Instead, providentially, Ney allowed himself to become over-excited by the ferocious struggle occurring to his right on the Kreckwitz heights, where Blücher was holding out against an attack by Soult, whose force included Bertrand's corps and Napoleon's Guards. Instead of pushing south-east towards the allied line of retreat, Ney not only directed his own corps south-westwards against Blücher but also ordered Lauriston to support him. Faced by these overwhelming numbers, old Blücher, still haranguing his men to fight like the Spartans at Thermopylae, was persuaded, very unwillingly and just in time, to retreat down the road which Barclay's men were still keeping open. The Russian Guards and heavy cavalry were ordered up to cover the retreat.

The allied right and centre moved down the road to Reichenbach and Weissenburg, the left down the parallel road through Loebau to Hochkirch. This retreat was essentially a flank march across the front of much more numerous enemy forces after two days of exhausting battle. Langeron comments that 'it was nevertheless achieved in the greatest order and without suffering the slightest loss, just like all the other retreats that this admirable Russian army made during the war, thanks to its perfect discipline, its obedience and to the innate courage of the Russian officers and soldiers'. No doubt Langeron was a biased witness but Baron von Odeleben, a Saxon officer on Napoleon's staff, watched the Russian rearguard on 21 May and recorded that 'the Russians retired in the greatest order' and 'made a retreat, which may be considered as a *chef d'œuvre* of tactics . . . although the lines of the allies had been, as it were, thrown on the centre, the French could not succeed, either in cutting off a part of their army, or capturing their artillery'.[63]

For Napoleon, the outcome of Bautzen was a great disappointment. Instead of a decisive victory he had merely pushed the allies back along their line of retreat after losing 25,000 men as against 10,850 Russian and Prussian casualties. His pursuit of the retreating allies brought him no more joy. The day after Bautzen, on 22 May, the French caught up with the Russian rearguard at Reichenbach. Its retreat was blocked by a traffic jam in the streets of the town but this did not fluster its commanders, Miloradovich and Eugen of Württemberg. Once again Odeleben was watching:

The dispositions made for the defence of the height in question confer the highest honour on the commander of the Russian rearguard. The road to Reichenbach, which comes out opposite the hill, turns where it leaves the town. The Russian general took advantage of the position until the last moment, and his troops did not withdraw until the French came up in such strong numbers that resistance became totally impossible. Directly after, he was seen defending another height between Reichenbach and Markersdorf, where he again arrested the march of the French.[64]

This was Eugen's 'retreat in echelon' in action and the snail-like progress it imposed on the French infuriated Napoleon and inspired him to such impatient rage that he took over the command of the advance guard himself. That evening the Russian rearguard took up yet another defensive position behind the village of Markersdorf. When Napoleon pressed on through the village the first shot of the Russian artillery mortally wounded his Marshal of the Court and closest friend, Géraud Duroc. Four days later at Hainau the Prussian cavalry ambushed and routed an incautious French advance guard under General Maison. As usual, these exploits of the allied rearguards bought their comrades the time to make an orderly retreat, but in the last ten days of the spring 1813 campaign they actually achieved much more than this. What Napoleon saw of the allies was a far superior enemy cavalry and imperturbable Russian rearguards like those whom he had pursued all the way to Moscow in the previous year without achieving anything. He would have been less than human had he not shuddered at renewing the same game with the very inferior cavalry he possessed in May 1813. What the allied rearguard hid totally from him were the deep dissensions and potential confusion affecting allied headquarters at this time.

The dissension above all stemmed from the fact that the allies were facing very difficult strategic dilemmas. If Austrian intervention was indeed imminent the priority should probably be to hug the Silesian border with Bohemia and prepare to link up with the invading Habsburg forces. If Austrian help was delayed or failed altogether, however, such a move could be fatal. The Prusso-Russian army could easily find itself outflanked from the east and trapped against a neutral border by Napoleon. At a minimum, attempting to remain near the Silesian–Bohemian border would make it difficult to feed the army for any length of time and would risk its communications back to Poland from where its supplies and reinforcements were coming.

This was anathema to Barclay de Tolly, who replaced Wittgenstein as commander-in-chief on 29 May. Months of campaigning, added to Wittgenstein's inept administration, had reduced the Russian army to a degree of confusion with corps, divisions and even regiments disordered and mutilated by detachments and special assignments. Wittgenstein did not even know where all his units were, let alone their numbers. By late May the men were also beginning to go hungry. Barclay's solution to these problems was to retreat across the Oder into Poland in order to reorganize his army. He promised that this reorganization would be completed within six weeks. By retreating to their own supply bases the Russians' problem of feeding the army and restoring its structure could quickly be solved. In addition, scores of thousands of reinforcements were now arriving in the theatre of operations. These included Fabian Osten-Sacken's formidable divisions, packed with more veterans than any other corps apart from the Guards; Dmitrii Neverovsky's excellent 27th division; Peter Pahlen's cavalry; and tens of thousands of reserves formed in Russia over the winter of 1812–13. Thousands of men were about to return from hospital and needed a breathing space to be fitted back into their regiments.

If Barclay's solution made good sense in narrowly Russian military terms, however, it was political dynamite. For the Prussians it would have meant abandoning Silesia and allowing Napoleon to detach a number of corps to reconquer Berlin and Brandenburg. It would probably also have doomed Austrian intervention, certainly in the short run and perhaps for ever. On 31 May, after the news of Bautzen had reached Vienna, the Hanoverian envoy wrote that

the fears of the emperor [i.e. Francis II] of a French invasion grow from day to day. Perhaps they are increased by anxiety lest the Russian emperor abandon the cause. People go as far as to fear that if the allies are pushed back to the Vistula, in a few months Bonaparte will be reinforced by the class of 1814 and will just leave an observation corps of 100,000 opposite the allies and will fall on Austria with the rest of his forces. To avoid this misfortune people are saying that Austria must move at top speed to get peace negotiations underway.

For all Metternich's fine words about Austrian policy not being affected by military events, Stadion was terrified by the impact on Austrian behaviour of the allied army retreating into Poland and he was entirely correct to be so.[65]

Initially Alexander deferred to the Prussians and to the need to hug the Bohemian border and keep in close touch with the Austrians. The army was ordered to swing south, off the line of retreat to Poland, and to take up position near Schweidnitz and the old fortified position at Bunzelwitz where Frederick II had defied the Austrians in the Seven Years War. On the Prussians' advice Alexander believed that, if necessary, the allies could fight Napoleon there on favourable ground. On arrival, however, it quickly became clear that the local authorities had done nothing to execute Frederick William's orders to rebuild the old defences and that the only favourable ground in the neighbourhood could not be held by a force of 100,000 men. The Silesian Landwehr, which was supposed to be present in force to reinforce the army, was nowhere to be found. In addition, difficulties in feeding the troops soon became acute.[66]

The basic reason for this was, as already noted, that Upper Silesia depended even in peacetime for food supplies from Poland and could not suddenly accommodate the entire allied army, concentrated as it had to be with the enemy in the offing. Although Kutuzov, back in April, had begged Stein to create food magazines in eastern Saxony nothing had been done: this was just one part of Stein's overall failure efficiently to mobilize Saxon resources while the allies occupied the kingdom. Barclay partly blamed Wittgenstein, pointedly noting in a letter to him that 'when first taking over the supreme command of the armies and looking into the question of victualling, it became clear to me that no preparatory measures had been taken to secure food. While the troops were in the Duchy of Warsaw and Saxony earlier they were fed exclusively by requisitioning in the area where they were deployed or through which they were marching, and the requisitioning lasted only so long as they were there. Almost no reserve supplies were created anywhere in the rear for the army.' Inevitably too, the intendant-general, Georg Kankrin, came in for criticism as the army began to go hungry. On 4 June he responded plaintively to Barclay by stating that the Prussians were providing almost nothing and on Prussian territory he could not requisition food or 'exert any authority and no one asked me about the possibility of feeding the troops when the route to Schweidnitz was chosen'.[67]

With the army going hungry, and the Austrian timetable for intervention visibly receding, a Russo-Prussian conference on 2 June backed a retreat towards the river Oder. Petr Volkonsky had already ordered the army's treasury to be escorted back to Kalicz and for preparations to be made to destroy the bridges over the Oder once the army had passed. Meanwhile the Prussian leaders were in uproar as their campaign to liberate their country reached its nadir.

General L'Estocq, the fierce military governor of Berlin, reported to Chancellor Hardenburg on 30 May that the French were heading for the Oder crossings 'in order to push on towards Poland and set off an insurrection there. The inconceivable level of tolerance shown in Warsaw has prepared the ground for this rather well.' The attempt to turn Silesia into a new Spain and launch a mass insurrection against the invading French had proved a damp squib. Had it mobilized against the French, l'Estoq believed that the Landsturm (i.e. the 'home guard') might have absorbed the efforts of thousands of enemy soldiers. In fact it had done nothing. He commented that 'the Silesian nobility want nothing to do with the Landsturm which easily explains why such miserable departures from duty and obedience happen', adding that the commander of the Landsturm 'must be charged as a traitor to the Fatherland and must immediately be shot'. Meanwhile at the conference of 2 June Blücher and Yorck argued that if the Russians retreated over the Oder the Prussian army must detach itself from them in order to defend what was left of Prussian territory.[68]

In this week of supreme crisis, as his whole strategy threatened to fall apart, Alexander showed outstanding leadership. Amidst Austrian prevarication, Prussian hysteria and the griping of his own generals he remained admirably calm, reasonable and optimistic about final victory. As in September 1812 his calm courage was partly sustained by faith in God's will and mercy. In late April he had taken a day out of the war to make an unannounced visit to the community of the Moravian brothers at Herrnhut, where he remained in deep conversation with the brothers for two hours and without an escort. His spirit had also been buoyed by the Easter services at Dresden, after which he wrote to Aleksandr Golitsyn that 'it would be hard for me to express to you the emotion which I felt in thinking over everything that has happened during the past year and where Divine Providence has led us'.[69]

Miraculously, Alexander's optimism was to be rewarded, as Napoleon bowed to Austrian pleas and agreed to an armistice which would last until 20 July and be accompanied by peace negotiations. Faced with this option, Napoleon's initial ploy had been to try to enter into negotiations directly with the Russians. Only when Alexander rejected this approach did Napoleon accept Austrian mediation and order his envoys to sign the armistice on 4 June. Subsequently he was to write that this was one of the worst decisions of his life.

The reasons Napoleon gave at the time for his decision were the need to get his cavalry in order and to take preparations against possible Austrian intervention. He might have added other good reasons too. His troops were exhausted, sick lists were mounting alarmingly and would undoubtedly rise further if he plunged forward into Poland. As his communications lengthened, so too would their vulnerability to allied raiding parties. In fact on the eve of the armistice a large force under Aleksandr Chernyshev and Mikhail Vorontsov was on the point of seizing Leipzig, far in Napoleon's rear, with its garrison and its vast stores. This was a reminder of the need to create fortified, secure bases for his future campaign. Nevertheless, good though all these reasons were, they did not outweigh the enormous advantages Napoleon would have gained by pressing on into Poland, dividing the Russians and Prussians, and terrifying the Austrians away from intervention. Napoleon's subsequent self-criticism was correct. In all probability had he continued the spring 1813 campaign for just a few more weeks he could have secured a very favourable peace.

Barclay could not believe his luck. He had asked for six weeks to restore his army and Napoleon had given it to him, without the need to risk a break with the Prussians or the Austrians, or indeed even to reorganize his corps in the midst of military operations. When Langeron heard the news of the armistice he 'went to Barclay's headquarters and he received me with a great burst of laughter: this explosion of happiness was by no means normal with Barclay. He was always cold, serious and severe in spirit and in his manner. The two of us laughed together at Napoleon's expense. Barclay, all the generals and our monarchs were drunk with joy and they were right to be so.'[70]

10

Rebuilding the Army

During the truce of summer 1813 the Russian army was transformed. By the time the autumn campaign began it was not just rested, well fed and reorganized but also much larger than had been the case in May. To understand how this happened requires us to retrace our steps a little and to look at events behind the front lines. In part this means understanding the complicated process of raising, training and equipping the hundreds of thousands of conscripts who reinforced the field armies in 1812–14. Just moving these forces from the Russian heartland to German battlefields was a challenge. In the autumn of 1812 the main training area of the reserve armies was in Nizhnii Novgorod province, some 1,840 kilometres even from Russia's frontier with the Duchy of Warsaw. The war ministry reckoned that it took fifteen weeks of marching to cover this distance.[1]

Once in Poland and Germany, Russian armies had to be fed and supplied while operating a huge distance from their home bases. One way of putting this in perspective is to remember that more than half a million Russian soldiers served outside the empire's borders in 1813–14, and this in a Europe where only two cities had populations of more than 500,000. It is equally useful to recall Russia's experience in the Seven Years War (1756–63), when Russian armies operated in the same German regions as in 1813. Their efforts were crucially undermined by the need to retreat eastwards hundreds of kilometres every autumn because they could not supply themselves on Prussian soil. For the Russians in 1813–14, to defeat Napoleon was only half the problem. Getting large armies to the battlefield in a state to fight him was as great a challenge and an achievement.[2]

In accordance with Barclay de Tolly's January 1812 law on the field armies, as Russian troops advanced westwards a network of military roads spread across eastern and central Europe. It began well within the Russian Empire and stretched all the way to the front lines. Down these roads travelled the great majority of the reinforcements, ammunition and other supplies which kept the Russian army strong and in the field. At regular intervals along these roads food depots and hospitals were set up, and town commandants appointed. These commandants had detachments of up to 100 Bashkir and Kalmyk cavalry at their disposal, who if properly supervised were formidable military police. The commandant's job was to make sure that roads and bridges were in good repair, and hospitals and depots properly supplied and administered. He registered the arrival and departure of all units on his stretch of road, reporting all movements to headquarters every ten days. The military roads made it much easier to ensure that troops en route to the front line were properly watched over, fed and cared for. The system was also a disincentive to desertion or marauding.[3]

The January 1812 (OS) army law also set out in some detail how Russian soldiers were to be supplied and fed when serving abroad. A sharp distinction was made between operating on the territory of allies, where all such matters were regulated by treaties between the states involved, and campaigning on enemy soil. The law made no allowance for neutrals: their territory should be treated in the same way as that of enemies. On hostile or neutral territory the army must supply itself from the land by requisition. Its day-to-day upkeep must not be the responsibility of the Russian treasury. Requisitioning should be carried out in orderly fashion, however, in order to preserve the troops' discipline and protect the local population and economy. Wherever possible this must be done through the local administration, overseen by officials of the army's intendancy. The intendant-general of the field army was ex officio to be the governor-general of all occupied territory and all officials were bound to obey his orders under threat of severe penalties for disobedience. Receipts were to be given for all food and materials requisitioned in order to prevent disorder and allow the local authorities to equalize burdens by repaying the holders of these receipts from their tax revenues.[4]

In the first half of 1813 Russian armies operated above all in Prussia and Poland. Well before the alliance with Frederick William was signed Alexander had agreed to pay for food requisitioned in Prussia. One-fifth of the value was to be paid immediately in Russian paper rubles, the rest subsequently in return for receipts. The instigator of this policy was Stein, who argued for it on political grounds and because it made no sense to ruin the population of a future ally, all of whose meagre resources would soon be needed for the war effort. This concession to the Prussians was never repeated when Russian troops were campaigning on Saxon and French territory.[5]

Immediately after the Russo-Prussian treaty of alliance was signed, the two governments came to an agreement on the upkeep of Russian forces operating on Prussian territory. Prussian commissars attached to Russian corps would requisition the necessary food in return for receipts. The commissars would then either arrange for food to be supplied from stores or for troops to be quartered on the population. The terms of repayment for the overall upkeep of the Russian forces on Prussian soil were generous. Food prices were calculated on a six-month average across the whole of Prussia, not at the hugely inflated rates of the districts in which masses of troops were actually operating. Three-eighths of the cost was to be covered by shipping grain from Russia to the Prussian ports, which the Russians were intending to do anyway for their own army. A further three-eighths would be in receipts, repayable after the end of the war. The final two-eighths was to be paid in paper rubles. Completely avoided was any requirement for the Russians to part with scarce silver and gold coin.[6]

The situation in the Duchy of Warsaw was very different, for this was conquered enemy territory. Polish food was to be crucial to the Russian war effort in 1813. Without it the Russian army could not have remained in the field in the summer and autumn of that year. The fact that all this requisitioned food was free was also vital for the Russian treasury. Though precision is impossible, the contribution of the Duchy of Warsaw to feeding and supplying both the Russian field armies and the Reserve Army, which was quartered on Polish territory from spring 1813, amounted to tens of millions of rubles.[7]

Russian policy in Poland was ambivalent, however. On the one hand, the Poles had to be milked if the Russian war effort was to be sustained. On the other hand, the emperor was anxious to win the loyalty of the Poles, whom he wished to make his future subjects. Kutuzov's proclamation setting up the Polish provisional government in March 1813 promised that 'all classes should feel His Imperial Majesty's care for them and through this, and also through the abolition of conscription, would experience how great was the difference between his fatherly administration and the former one, which had been forced to plunder in order to satisfy the insatiable thirst for conquest of masters who called themselves allies'. Promised full pay, full protection for persons and property, and strict punishment for any bad behaviour by the troops, the overwhelming majority of Polish officials in the Duchy of Warsaw stayed in their jobs. This was a great benefit to the Russians, who could not remotely have found the cadres to run Poland themselves. It did mean, however, that most officials in Poland would only requisition energetically for the Russians if their own lives and careers were clearly at stake.[8]

The new provisional government was headed by two Russians: its deputy head was Alexander's old friend, Nikolai Novosiltsev, a shrewd and tactful political operator whose appointment showed just how high a priority winning over the Poles was for the emperor. The head of the government, and simultaneously the governor-general of the Duchy, was the former intendant-general of Kutuzov's army, Vasili Lanskoy, who was himself now replaced by Georg Kankrin. Lanskoy's appointment underlined the even higher priority of using Poland to feed the Russian army, though most generals soon came to believe that he had 'gone native' and was serving Polish rather than Russian interests. For the Russians, however, the big problem was not in Warsaw but at provincial level. Despite what was said in the army law, it was impossible for the overstretched army's intendancy to spare officials to oversee the Polish provincial administration. Nor could the army spare front-line officers. Kutuzov had appealed to Alexander to send officials from the Russian interior instead and this is what was done. But the number and quality of these officials was well below what was needed.[9]

On the whole, from January until the middle of May 1813 the feeding of the troops went well and caused few clashes. This was especially true in Prussia and in Prussian settlements in the Duchy of Warsaw, where the population detested Napoleon and saw the Russian troops as liberators. Even in Polish areas matters usually went reasonably well, though Kutuzov's advance guard moving through the centre of the Duchy of Warsaw subsisted on biscuit for most of January and only received its wartime meat and vodka rations from the beginning of February. The Poles undoubtedly suffered but not as much as civilian populations in areas conquered by Napoleon or, in the Seven Years War, by Frederick the

Great. The Russians imposed neither conscription nor a war indemnity. Their leaders tried with some success to sustain discipline and protect the civilian population. For example, on 18 February 1813 Kankrin published instructions for the feeding of the Russian troops from Polish stores or by the households on which they were quartered. After spelling out the troops' proper rations, which for soldiers operating abroad included meat and spirits three times a week, he encouraged the local population to report any excessive demands or misbehaviour by the soldiers. Given the men's exhaustion and the way in which traditional distrust of Poles had been fed by the events of 1812, the regular troops appear to have behaved remarkably well. On 23 March, writing from Kalicz, Kutuzov told his wife that 'our soldiers' behaviour surprises everyone here and the morals shown by the troops even surprise me'.[10]

For six weeks from mid-May 1813, however, the army faced a crisis as regards food supply. Barclay explained the reasons for this crisis in a key memorandum for Alexander. He stated that the army's problems were the consequence of a year's campaigning back and forth across an enormous area in a manner which had no precedent in history. Disorder was inevitable. 'The army has drawn far ahead of the supplies prepared in Russia and has almost no food reserve left with its units.' According to the terms of the convention, the Prussian government was supposed to feed Russian troops when they were on Prussian soil. In Silesia, however, the Prussians did not have enough in their magazines to feed even their own troops in May 1813. A little could be done if one was prepared to purchase supplies with silver but the army's treasury was almost empty. It had received thus far in 1813 less than one-quarter of the money owed it by the ministry of finance. In the longer term, however, the answer to the army's needs was not the use of limited Russian funds to buy food but instead effective requisitioning in the Duchy of Warsaw. The key aims of Barclay's memorandum were to get Alexander to force the finance minister, Dmitrii Gurev, to release funds immediately and to make the governor-general of Warsaw, Vasili Lanskoy, carry out the army's plan for massive requisitioning in the Duchy. Barclay concluded by stating that unless Alexander did this, 'I cannot guarantee that we will not face catastrophic consequences which will have a fatal impact on our soldiers and on military operations'.[11]

In his report Barclay told Alexander that the only thing which had saved the soldiers from starvation in early June was the providential arrival of the mobile magazine of Chichagov's former Army of the Danube. The large store of biscuit it carried had tided the troops over for a number of weeks. Initially put together in Podolia and Volhynia in the summer of 1812, the 2,340 surviving carts of this magazine had struggled forward through snow and mud for 1,000 kilometres or more, despite the fact that heavily loaded peasant carts were supposed to be able to operate over distances of only 150 kilometres. Many of the carts had been hastily constructed of unseasoned wood. Most were of light construction and all were low slung with small wheels. In the autumn and spring mud it was almost impossible for horses to pull them. In comparison to Austrian carts, noted the magazine's commander subsequently, the Russian civilian ones in his magazine carried less goods, were more fragile, and required more horses.

Matters were not improved by the fact that initially many of these carts were drawn by oxen. Given their voracious appetites, it was impossible for a train pulled by oxen to move in winter. In January and February 1813 therefore the mobile magazine had come to a halt and its oxen had been turned into rations. Urged on by Kutuzov, the mobile magazine had got under way again once spring arrived, its oxen replaced by requisitioned horses, but its Heath Robinson appearance was accentuated by the fact that most of the horses were having to pull the carts with furnishings initially designed for oxen. Many of the drivers had never had to deal with horses before, had not been paid since departure, and were in some cases individuals whom their landlords were trying to get rid of. In the circumstances it was a miracle that the magazine turned up.[12]

The arrival of the mobile magazine bought enough time for the Prussians to get their system for supplying the Russians back in order. Once it became clear that the armistice would last for weeks, it was possible to disperse the army into quarters. The Russian cavalry commanders were always extremely concerned about their horses' proper feeding: now their regiments could be redeployed to areas well behind the front where oats were plentiful. Meanwhile the Prussian authorities had been helpful in organizing a deal between Kankrin and private Prussian contractors, who offered 55,000 daily rations of flour and bread partly on credit and partly for paper rubles. In a theatre of operations the first deficit item was always carts. The arrival in mid-July of 4,000 carts of the main army's mobile magazine was therefore a huge asset. Kankrin divided some of the mobile magazines' carts into echelons to bring up supplies from Poland by stages. Others were utilized to pick up food purchased from or provided by the Prussians, which had previously been impossible to transport.[13]

By the time the main army's magazine arrived, Alexander had already responded effectively to Barclay's appeal for money. He immediately commandeered for army headquarters almost 2.5 million paper rubles of ministry of finance funds held in Germany[14] and he ordered Gurev to remit the remainder immediately, commenting that he himself was a witness to the army's urgent needs. Faced with a direct imperial command, Gurev wrote to Barclay on 13 July that he had already sent him 4.8 million silver and 4 million paper rubles, and more was on the way.[15]

From the perspective of headquarters Gurev's delay in sending money already agreed in the military budget was indefensible. Inevitably, the finance minister saw things differently. Even before Napoleon's invasion, budget deficits could only be covered by the printing of paper money and fears of financial collapse were common. As a result of the war, expenditure shot up and revenues shrank. Nearly 25 per cent of anticipated revenue had failed to arrive in 1812. In the first quarter of 1813 things were worse: only 54 per cent of expected revenues had come in by late April. Gurev blamed 'the shock felt throughout the state in 1812, when on top of normal taxes, both traditional and newly established in that year, the population was burdened by the mobilization of the militia, by recruit levies, by military demands, duties and contributions: by a very conservative estimate all this amounted to over 200 million rubles'. Faced with a vast looming deficit all Gurev could do was to reduce expenditure wherever possible and fill the gap with additional printing of paper money. In April 1813 he predicted that if the war lasted throughout 1814 and its financing continued as at present then 'no means will remain to rescue us from the final destruction of our financial system'.[16]

Although Gurev feared hyper-inflation within Russia he tended to believe that the enormous amount of economic activity linked to repairing the damage caused by Napoleon's invasion would mop up much of the newly issued paper money. So too would growing Russian external trade now the Continental System was destroyed once and for all. The finance minister's true source of panic was the large amounts of Russian paper money which the Field Army was spending abroad. No foreigner would wish to hang on to this money, nor would private individuals use it in payment for goods and services provided by other Germans. Therefore the entire sum was likely to be remitted back to Russia for exchange, with dire consequences for the ruble's rate against foreign currencies.

Gurev warned that if the paper ruble's exchange rate collapsed, the Field Army's financing would become impossible. To avoid this he dragged his heels as regards remitting funds to army headquarters and got the committee of ministers to agree to a number of proposals, including paying officers and men abroad only half their pay with the remainder to be given them on return to Russia. Gurev's argument, partly true, was that officers and men serving abroad to a great extent lived off the land and did not need much cash. Nevertheless, had it been implemented, the impact of this policy on the morale of the troops can easily be imagined: the army was already very badly paid by European standards and was fighting an exhausting campaign on foreign territory in a cause many even of the officers did not understand.[17]

Faced with peremptory orders from the emperor, Gurev would have released funds for the army in all circumstances but he was also greatly encouraged in this direction by news of a large impending British subsidy, of which he had despaired. In 1812 Alexander had not requested a British subsidy. This was partly a question of pride. In addition, fighting on his own territory he could finance the war without great difficulty. Perhaps for this reason, it was actually many months after diplomatic relations with Britain were restored that Alexander got round to appointing an ambassador in London. Once Russian armies advanced across the empire's borders, however, the matter became urgent and the emperor nominated Christoph Lieven and sent him to London in January 1813 with a message for the British government: 'In the present circumstances every dispatch of troops abroad is becoming very expensive for me. It requires the emission of metallic currency which totally undermines our rate of exchange. This would have a serious effect on our finances which they could not ultimately sustain, since the state's revenues are bound to shrink considerably this year as a result of the complete devastation of some provinces.' Lieven was ordered both to ask for a subsidy and to present the British government with a scheme for 'Federal Paper Money'. This paper was to bear interest and to be redeemable immediately after the war. It was to be guaranteed by the

British, Russian and Prussian governments, and was to be used to pay for part of the Russian and Prussian war effort. The scheme had been devised in Petersburg with the help, among others, not just of Stein but of the British financier Sir Francis d'Ivernois.[18]

Given British resistance to subsidies in 1806–7, Alexander may have expected tough negotiations in London. In fact Lieven found that the British were willing to offer Russia £1.33 million in subsidy and that a further £3.3 million would accrue as their share of the Federal Paper scheme. In the context of overall British overseas payments and subsidies these sums were relatively modest. The war in the Peninsula had cost the British £11 million in 1811 and all subsidies represented less than 8 per cent of the cost of Britain's own armed forces. When calculated in paper rubles, however, £4.6 million was a mighty sum, which in principle should cover almost all Russian projected expenditure on the campaign in Germany for the remaining seven months of 1813. To be sure, the cash was slow to arrive, exchange and discounting costs took their toll, and some predictions on expenditure proved optimistic, but the British subsidy went some way towards calming Gurev's worries at least for a time.[19]

If Alexander's orders to Gurev were peremptory, his instructions to the governor-general of Warsaw, Vasili Lanskoy, were positively brutal. On 12 June Kankrin had set out the army's requirement from the Duchy for 3 million kilos of flour, 400,000 kilos of groats, 250,000 litres of vodka, 330,000 kilos of meat and 1,000 cattle on the hoof, and a huge amount of oats for the horses. Barclay wrote to Lanskoy the next day that 'all the supplies assigned from the provinces of the Duchy of Warsaw are to be levied immediately for it is these supplies alone which can guarantee the army's victualling . . . the slightest slowness or deficits can lead to the troops suffering from severe hunger and can wreck the army's condition and its ability to conduct military operations'. When Lanskoy pleaded the Duchy's poverty and the foodstuffs already requisitioned by the army, he received one of the fiercest letters written by the emperor during the whole course of 1812–14. Telling his governor-general that the fate of the army, the war and of Europe depended on this requisition, Alexander warned him that he would bear personal responsibility for any failure to levy the full amount and deliver it to the army on time and by requisitioned Polish civilian carts.[20]

After receiving this command from Alexander, Lanskoy of course caved in totally, telling local officials that 'no excuses of any sort will be accepted from anyone', but Barclay remained unconvinced that the Polish provincial administration would carry out the requisition promptly and strictly. He therefore sent two special commissars to watch over them, armed with all the powers provided for in the Field Army law when it came to dealing with obstruction by officials in conquered territory. He gave these commissars an open letter commanding all officials 'to execute the orders concerning the requisitioning and dispatch of supplies to the letter and without any deviation: any slowness, mistakes or, still worse, disobedience . . . will without fail result in a court martial under the army's regulations for field courts martial and on a charge of treason'. Meanwhile orders went out to the commanding officer in the Duchy, General Dokhturov, to use his troops to enforce the levy. The Ukrainian mounted militia, in some cases of little use against the French, were formidable when it came to requisitioning Polish peasants' carts to transport the supplies.[21]

Immediately after the armistice was signed Barclay got down to the business of reorganizing, re-equipping and training his troops. For this task he was the perfect leader. On 10 June he issued an order of the day to the soldiers and their commanding officers. He told the troops that they had not been defeated, and that they had lost not a gun nor an unwounded prisoner of war to the enemy. The armistice meant not peace but a chance to concentrate Russian and allied strength and make the preparations essential for a new and victorious campaign. Commanding officers were instructed that 'their duty during the armistice period will be to devote all their efforts to ensuring that weapons, equipment and suchlike are in proper order; to maintaining the soldiers' health; to preserving strict order and discipline; to training inexperienced soldiers in military skills; in a word to bringing each unit to a state of perfect readiness to achieve new victories'.[22]

During the two-month truce the measures taken earlier to re-uniform the troops bore fruit. On 16 July Kankrin reported that enough canvas for summer trousers and enough boots had now arrived for the entire army. In March Alexander had authorized the expenditure of 3.5 million rubles to pay for new coats and tunics for most units of the line. These were provided by private contractors in Königsberg and arrived during the armistice. Initially the cost was expected to be greater but Barclay de Tolly found and requisitioned a large store of excellent cloth in Posen in February initially earmarked for Napoleon's army. This met the needs not just of Barclay's own corps but also of the Guards. Still better, it was paid for by the Polish taxpayer.[23]

Meanwhile, immediately after the armistice was signed and as an urgent priority, Barclay ordered a check on all muskets to try to reduce the number of different weapons and calibres in battalions. Captain Radozhitsky was one of the artillery officers assigned to this job. He wrote in his memoirs that he checked 30,000 firearms in ten days and came to the conclusion that the main problem lay with men returning from hospital who were simply given the first gun available before being dispatched to their regiments. He also stated that many soldiers in the line infantry regiments had old and useless muskets, though in fact this was only true in some divisions. Thanks to the efforts of Radozhitsky and his comrades, muskets were swapped between battalions to ensure much greater uniformity and thereby make the supply of ammunition more efficient.[24]

None of these efforts by Barclay would have added up to much had he not got down immediately to sorting out the administrative confusion bequeathed, in part anyway, by Wittgenstein. It was after all hard to feed or re-equip men if headquarters did not know where units were or how many soldiers were actually in their ranks. Passing orders down the military hierarchy was impossible if divisions were apart from their correct corps, or regiments from their brigades and divisions. Another prerequisite for any kind of order in the army was reuniting detachments with their parent regiments and getting rid of temporary composite units. It was time too to reunite the shrunken reserve (i.e. second) battalions with the rest of their regiments. Immediately after the truce was agreed Barclay went to war on these issues. Within a week he had new tables issued listing the brigades, divisions and corps to which every regiment belonged and showing where all these units were to be deployed and quartered. He enjoyed about 95 per cent success in re-imposing a clear and logical structure on his army by the end of June. So long as 'partisan' units existed and combined a majority of Cossacks with detached squadrons of regular cavalry total success was impossible.[25]

There remained one vital task: to integrate into the Field Army the tens of thousands of reinforcements who arrived during the armistice. Some of these were men returning from hospital or from detachments. As veterans, they were particularly valuable. Most of the new arrivals, however, came from the 200,000-strong reserve units formed in Russia during the winter of 1812–13 from new conscripts. For each regiment on campaign, a reserve battalion of 1,000 men, divided into four companies, was created within Russia. When these new battalions were ready, Alexander's plan was that some of their companies would be dispatched to reinforce the armies in the field but a sufficient cadre would remain behind to train the next wave of recruits. These would bring the battalion back to full strength and allow, in time, yet more reinforcements to be sent to join the field armies. Similar arrangements were to be made for the artillery and cavalry. In the latter's case, for every regiment on campaign, two reserve squadrons, each of 201 men, would be formed within the empire.[26]

In all, more than 650,000 men were conscripted into the army in 1812–14. The great majority of these were netted in the three general call-ups between August 1812 and August 1813 (83rd, 84th, 85th recruit levies) which covered almost all the empire's provinces. In addition, however, a number of smaller call-ups targeted specific provinces. Since noble estates bore the burden of recruitment for the militia, these recruit levies above all targeted the 40 per cent of peasants who lived on state lands. The authorities realized that unless existing requirements were relaxed, they might not meet their quota of recruits. Therefore the age limit for new conscripts was raised to 40, the minimum height was reduced to just over one and a half metres, and men with minor physical defects were accepted. The huge demand for recruits meant that older and married men were conscripted in large numbers. Even if they survived the war, they faced decades of peacetime service. Tens of thousands of women would never see their husbands again but had no right to remarry, and many young families lost their main breadwinner.[27]

The 1810 regulations for state peasants required that recruitment records be kept which would guarantee both that obligations were fairly shared among households and that the burden of conscription fell on big families with many adult males rather than on small families which it would ruin.[28] In 1812 recruit boards were ordered by the war ministry to check these records and at least in Riazan province – for which the sources are exceptionally full – the records were actually submitted along with the conscripts to show that due process had been observed.[29]

Pamfil Nazarov was a state peasant conscripted into the army in September 1812. His memoirs are a unique insight into conscription as seen from below. Nowhere in the memoirs does Nazarov suggest that his recruitment was unjust. On the basis of his family's previous record of conscription and of the number of its adult males the Nazarov household was in line to provide a recruit. As was always the case, the peasant communal government targeted households, not individuals. It was up to the household itself to decide whom to send into the army. In this era most peasant households were extended families, including a number of married brothers and their children. It was notorious that the head of the household generally sent his nephews and even brothers into the army rather than his own sons. But in the Nazarov family it was clear that Pamfil was the only possible choice. Both his elder brothers were married: one had children, the other was weak. His younger brother was still under age.

Pamfil on the contrary was a strong, unmarried lad of 20. None of his family wanted to lose him: an atmosphere of misery reigned for days, with both Pamfil and his mother in particular sometimes overcome with tears. In September 1812 Napoleon was marching into the Russian heartland. Pamfil's own province, Tver, was threatened and Moscow fell in the midst of his induction into the army. Pamfil was untouched by any feeling of patriotism or awareness of the broader political context, however. Instead he was possessed by numb misery and fear at the prospect of being ripped out of his accustomed world of family and village, and thrust into the alien and brutal life of a soldier. Resigned fortitude, and in Pamfil's case prayer and obedience to God's will, were his only support, as was true of the overwhelming majority of peasant conscripts in these years.

Pamfil was accompanied by his brothers and grandfather to the recruit board in the town of Tver. The governor of Tver province presided ex officio over the board and himself inspected Pamfil briefly. The medical inspection was barely more thorough. Once Pamfil stated that he was in good health it amounted to no more than a check on his teeth and a brief glance at his body. There followed immediately the two great induction rituals of the Russian conscript: Pamfil's forehead was shaved and he took the military oath. Within a few days the recruits were sent to Petersburg: given the need for speed they travelled by cart. Once assigned to his regiment Pamfil Nazarov experienced some of the other typical aspects of the young conscript's rite of passage. The shock of being thrust so suddenly into an alien and harsh world made him very ill: during his two-week fever his money and clothes were stolen. A fist in the face from a junior NCO for whom Pamfil refused to do an illegal favour was also typical, as was a caning when he made a mess of his first shooting practice with powder and lead.

Nevertheless, not everything in Pamfil Nazarov's military life was pure suffering and shipwreck. The Grand Duke Constantine personally inspected the new recruits and assigned them to their regiments in Petersburg. At 1.6 metres Pamfil was too short for the Preobrazhenskys or Semenovskys, but Constantine assigned him to the light infantry of the Guards, meaning in this case the Finland Regiment. As a Guardsman Pamfil got better pay and a real uniform, rather than the shoddy recruit uniform which was the lot of most conscripts in 1812–13. Service in the Guards was no picnic: the Finland Guards suffered heavy casualties at both Borodino and Leipzig. Nevertheless the Guards regiments were in general held in reserve: service in them on campaign was not the weekly meat-grinder experienced by some regiments of the line infantry. Though wounded at Leipzig, Pamfil Nazarov was back in the ranks by the fall of Paris and he and his comrades took pride in their achievement. Unlike most men conscripted in 1812 he was to see his family again: as a reliable and exemplary Guardsman he was allowed three home leaves in the eleven years following the war. Even more unusually, Pamfil learned to read and write while serving in the Finland Regiment. When he retired after twenty-three years of service in the Guards he became a monk and was one of only two private soldiers in the Russian army of this era to write his memoirs.[30]

So long as recruits met the height and medical requirements, on private estates the government left it to the landowners to decide which of their serfs to send to the army. Richer peasants, and indeed most of their middling neighbours, preferred to put the burden of conscription on poorer villagers, who paid less of the village's collective tax burden. The landowner might share the view of the peasant commune that conscription should be used to rid the village of marginal or 'uneconomic' families. On the other hand, some aristocratic landowners did attempt to uphold fair conscription procedures and to protect vulnerable peasant families. Whether they succeeded depended greatly on their estates' managers because wealthy aristocrats owned many properties, and were themselves in any case most often to be found in Petersburg, Moscow or on service. Success might also depend on the nature of peasant society on a specific estate. Particularly in the more commercialized and less purely agricultural estates, it might be hard for a distant landowner to control the richer peasants.

The more than 70,000-hectare estate of Baki in Kostroma province was one of Charlotta Lieven's ten properties.[31] Hundreds of kilometres north of Moscow, Baki was no place for agriculture. The 4,000 or more peasants who lived on the estate were self-sufficient as regards food but the estate's wealth was derived from its enormous forests. The richer peasants were in reality merchants: they owned barges on which they shipped the produce of the forests down the Volga, sometimes all the way to Astrakhan on the shores of the Caspian Sea. One of Baki's wealthiest peasants, Vasili Voronin, owned many barges and employed scores of peasants. The clerk of the peasant communal administration, Petr Ponomarev, was his son-in-law. As the only truly literate peasant on the estate Ponomarev was a very powerful intermediary between the two worlds of the estate manager and the peasantry. In 1800–1813 Voronin used his power to ensure, for example, that conscription never touched his family, their clients, or men who worked for him. The estate steward, Ivan Oberuchev, accepted the Voronins' power. Maybe there was an element of corruption here. Maybe Oberuchev just wanted a quiet life. Perhaps he would have argued that he was defending his employers' interests by recognizing the realities of power on the estate.[32]

Charlotta Lieven's instructions had been that the entire peasant community in its assembly should determine which households were eligible for conscription and that these families should then draw lots to decide the order in which their members would be called up. She had also ordered that smaller households must be spared. In 1812–13 these principles were ignored. Many sole breadwinners were targeted for conscription, with tragic consequences for wives and children left behind, for a family without an adult male lost its right to land. In Staroust, one of the estate's many villages, six men were conscripted and two of them were the only adult males in the household. As bad was the case of the Feofanov brothers, of whom two out of three were conscripted in 1812. Meanwhile the Makarov family, the cocks of the village with seven eligible males, not merely provided no recruits in 1812–14 but had never done so for the fifty years that recruitment records had existed on the estate.[33]

In 1813 Charlotta Lieven dismissed the estate manager and replaced him by Ivan Kremenetsky, who had previously worked as Barclay de Tolly's private secretary in the war ministry. Kremenetsky's subsequent investigation revealed that fifty households on the estate had provided no recruits in the more than three decades for which records existed. Kostroma was part of the third militia district: unlike in the first two districts, only part of its militia was embodied. Subsequently the government required forty new army recruits from Baki in order to equalize the burden of conscription across the country on private and state peasants.

Charlotta von Lieven ordered that exemption certificates – each costing 2,000 rubles – should be bought in place of all forty recruits and that the households who had failed to provide recruits in the past should pay for them. Seventeen peasant households contributed 2,000 rubles each, which was roughly the annual salary of a Russian major-general. It says something about the confusing reality of Russian society at that time that seventeen illiterate peasants from the backwoods of Kostroma could pay such large sums without ruining themselves. Though in the short run a sort of justice had prevailed, in the longer term Kremenetsky's tactics united the richer peasants against him and made the estate unmanageable and bankrupt. There was probably a moral to be drawn from this story. The emperor could not govern early nineteenth-century Russia without the nobility's support. Probably Baki, a microcosm of the empire, could not be governed, or at least effectively exploited, without the cooperation of its wealthy peasants.[34]

The emperor and Arakcheev were acutely aware of the need to get reinforcements to the field armies urgently. Harassed by the war minister, who was himself under pressure from the emperor, the governor of Novgorod responded in early March 1813 that he was enforcing conscription with great strictness but that in his province some villages were well over 700 kilometres from the provincial capital and at this time of year the 'roads' were a sea of mud.[35] No excuses saved the governor of Tambov province, who was dismissed in December 1812 for slowness and incompetence in running the recruit levy.

The governors themselves put pressure on their subordinates, and above all on the internal security troops, to complete the recruit levies as quickly as possible. These troops were usually of poor quality and hugely overburdened. In provinces affected by Napoleon's invasion internal security was a major issue, with peasants sometimes threatening to 'mutiny' and marauders roaming the villages and forests. Many men were away escorting prisoners of war, while some of the best officers had been detached to serve in Lobanov-Rostovsky's regiments. On top of this the internal security forces were obliged to escort vastly increased numbers of recruits to their training areas, which were usually hundreds of kilometres from their native provinces. The Riga Internal Security Battalion arrived in the town of Wenden in the province of Livonia on 2 February 1813 to help with the new recruit levy. On arrival it comprised 25 officers and 585 men: by the time it departed it had detached so many parties on escort and other duties that it was down to 9 officers and 195 men. Its troops were so exhausted and frustrated by sweeps through the countryside to catch conscripts in hiding that they sometimes seized any man they found by the roadside to make up their quota of recruits.[36]

The bureaucracy and the noble marshals strained every muscle to implement conscription but coercive mass mobilization for war was in many respects the *raison d'être* of tsarist administration. The system was meeting the challenge for which it was designed. Finding enough officers for the expanded army was often more difficult, partly because the pool of loyal and educated candidates was not enormous but above all because potential officers could seldom be coerced into the army. In 1812–14 generals in the field complained more often about a shortage of officers than of soldiers.

In 1812–14 much the biggest source of new officers was noble NCOs, usually called sub-ensigns in infantry regiments and junkers in the cavalry.[37] They were the equivalent of the British navy's midshipmen, in other words officer cadets who were learning on the job before receiving commissions. The great majority of peacetime infantry and cavalry officers won their commissions this way. The Russian army therefore went to war in June 1812 with a large number of young cadets ready to fill posts caused by casualties or by the army's expansion. They were almost always the first choice when vacancies occurred. In the Guards Jaegers, for instance, thirty-one young men were commissioned as ensigns in 1812–14 and of these eighteen had served as noble NCOs in the regiment before the war. All but one of the eighteen were commissioned in 1812. Subsequently the regiment had to draw on other sources for its new officers. This was a pattern familiar across the army.[38]

The next largest group of new officers were NCOs who were not the sons of nobles or officers.[39] Most of these men were commissioned into the regiments in which they had served as NCOs in peacetime, though Guards NCOs often transferred to line regiments. The two key requirements for promotion were courage and leadership in action, and literacy. Some rankers had been commissioned in the eighteenth century and in the first decade of Alexander's reign but wartime needs hugely increased the number in 1812–14. The key moment came in early November 1812 when, faced with a dire shortage of officers, Alexander ordered his commanders 'to promote to officer rank in the infantry, cavalry and artillery as many junkers and non-commissioned officers as are available, regardless of whether they are nobles, so long as they merit this by their service, their behaviour, by their excellent qualities and by their courage'.[40]

Once the army had exhausted the supply of potential officers from within its regiments it was forced to look elsewhere. One key source was cadets from the so-called Noble Regiment, the cut-price and accelerated version of a cadet corps which had been the ministry of war's main new initiative in the pre-war years to find additional officers for an expanding army. In 1808–11 the 'Regiment' had commissioned 1,683 cadets into the army. In 1812 it graduated a further 1,139, though many of these young officers only reached their units in early 1813. With so many cadets graduating and many of the Noble Regiment's instructors drafted to lead reserve units in late 1812 there followed a lull, but a new inflow of young men into the 'Regiment' began in the winter of 1812–13 and many graduated in 1814. By then, however, former cadets were outnumbered by the many young civil servants who were transferring into the army, sometimes under pressure from their bosses. A few of these men had served in the army before entering the civil service, as had a larger number of the many militia officers who transferred into regular regiments in 1813–14.[41]

In the winter and early spring of 1812–13 the new reserve formations were concentrated and trained in four main centres. Petersburg and Iaroslavl in north-west Russia prepared reinforcements for the Guards, the Grenadiers and Wittgenstein's corps. The 77,000 infantry and 18,800 cavalry reinforcements for Kutuzov's main body were concentrated near Nizhnii Novgorod, 440 kilometres east of Moscow. Andreas Kleinmichel and Dmitrii Lobanov-Rostovsky had been responsible for forming the regiments created on Alexander's orders immediately after

Napoleon's invasion. Now the emperor appointed them to command the new reserve formations in Iaroslavl and Nizhniii Novgorod respectively. More than seven weeks after orders had gone out to Kleinmichel, Alexander instructed Lieutenant-General Peter von Essen to train 48,000 reinforcements for Chichagov's army. Essen's headquarters was the fortress town of Bobruisk in Belorussia, 150 kilometres south-east of Minsk. Essen was so short of officers to train and command his recruits that great delays occurred. In the end, his battalions arrived in the theatre of operations three months after the other reinforcements and only just in time for the battle of Leipzig. Had similar delays occurred to the rest of the reserves, the Russian army would have played a far smaller role in the autumn campaign and Napoleon might well have defeated the allies in August and September 1813.[42]

In the late autumn and winter of 1812 Dmitrii Lobanov-Rostovsky struggled to begin the formation of his battalions amidst the chaos which followed Moscow's surrender. Alexander and Kutuzov, hundreds of kilometres apart with Napoleon between them, were sending him contradictory orders. He had lost touch with many of the officers and even the generals who were supposed to be helping him train the new battalions. Equipment was also a big headache. The destruction of the commissariat stores in Moscow made it unthinkable to provide proper uniforms, wagons or the copper kettles which the men used for cooking, the latter a particular problem for inexperienced recruits unused to scrounging for themselves.[43]

By the winter of 1812 Russia was also running short of muskets. Production at Tula had been disrupted and it took time for imported British muskets to arrive and even they did not fully cover demand. Early in November Alexander ordered Lobanov-Rostovsky to supply only 776 muskets for each 1,000-strong reserve battalion he was forming. Given the high drop-out rate from sickness and exhaustion among the new recruits, the remaining 224 men were supposed to acquire muskets from comrades who were left behind in the long march to join the army in the field. Though perhaps realistic and necessary, this policy cannot have helped the new recruits' morale.[44]

Given the immense difficulties faced by Lobanov, it was inevitable that the war ministry would be heavily criticized for its slowness in feeding and equipping his troops. In the circumstances, however, Aleksei Gorchakov and his subordinates performed reasonably well in the winter of 1812–13: the ministry's senior commissariat and victualling officers both went to Nizhnii Novgorod in person to help Lobanov. Their job was made even more difficult when Lobanov's troops set off in December on the long march from Nizhnii to their new deployment area at Belitsa in Belorussia, well over 1,000 kilometres away. The move made obvious sense. With the theatre of operations moving to Germany the reserves needed to be concentrated in the western borderlands. Having struggled to get arms and equipment to Nizhnii, however, the war ministry now had to redirect them in the middle of winter and through a countryside turned upside down by war.[45]

Arranging the march of scores of thousands of inexperienced troops was also not easy. While drowning in the detailed preparations which needed his attention, Lobanov-Rostovsky suddenly received urgent orders to divert part of his forces to suppress a mutiny in the Penza militia, 'in the name of His Imperial Majesty the Sovereign', 'without the slightest loss of time' and with 'extreme severity'. The mutiny was suppressed without difficulty but the tone of Count Saltykov's instructions reflected the central government's acute fear that a horde of armed peasant and Cossack militiamen might unleash mayhem in a region where Pugachev had roamed forty years before.[46]

Lobanov-Rostovsky reported his arrival in Belitsa to Alexander on 1 February 1813. It was at this point that his worst troubles began. His troops' deployment area covered three provinces: northern Chernigov, southern Mogilev and south-eastern Minsk. In today's terms this means north-central Ukraine and south-eastern Belarus, the region of Chernobyl. This was a poor area in 1812, much poorer and less densely populated than central Great Russia. Suddenly establishing a city of 80,000 men in this region in the middle of winter was a great challenge. Immense efforts went into housing, feeding and training the troops and providing medical services.[47]

These arrangements were barely in place, however, when Lobanov received two new commands from Alexander on 1 March. These orders breathed the impatient ruthlessness which was the hallmark of Aleksei Arakcheev, the emperor's assistant on all matters concerning reserves and the mobilization of the rear. The first wave of reinforcements was to be dispatched to the Field Army immediately. Lobanov was to inspect all departing units personally to ensure they were fully equipped and victualled. He was then to remove himself and the remainder of his troops hundreds of kilometres north-westwards to Belostok, on the Russo-Polish frontier. The emperor had decided to create a united Reserve Army which would be deployed in the Belostok area and would be responsible for training and dispatching all future reinforcements to the armies in the field. Even initially this Reserve Army was to be over 200,000 strong. Lobanov was appointed its commander and ordered to submit plans for the new Reserve Army's deployment immediately.[48]

Lobanov was not exaggerating when he responded to Alexander on 1 March that he feared that his physical powers could not sustain such burdens. The following month must surely have been among the most stressful in his life. Within a week he had submitted to Alexander a plan for the organization and quartering of the new Reserve Army. Immediately on receiving Alexander's orders on 1 March to dispatch the reinforcements at once, Lobanov responded that 'Your Majesty may do with me what you want and I place my head on the block', but it was totally impossible to execute this command. He did, however, promise to do everything possible to speed the troops' departure and proved as good as his word. By the middle of March he had dispatched 37,484 reinforcements to the Field Army.[49]

It was not just Lobanov, however, who suffered because of the Field Army's urgent need for reinforcements. Of the 37,000 men, 2,350 had died by the time the reinforcements reached Warsaw and a further 9,593 were left behind along the way because of illness or exhaustion. Reinforcements sent from Petersburg and Iaroslavl suffered similar losses. Lobanov subsequently put down most of these casualties to exhaustion: many of these men – almost all of them new recruits – had marched 3,000 kilometres or more in the past few months, through snow and mud, and latterly across a ravaged war zone where typhus raged. In time, most of the 9,000 men left behind would recover and rejoin their battalions. Nevertheless the scale of the losses bears witness to the immense difficulties Russia faced in getting reinforcements to the theatre of operations in these critical months.[50]

For all the difficulties overcome by Lobanov and his colleagues, it was General Andrei Kologrivov, tasked with forming the bulk of the army's cavalry reserves, who faced the greatest challenge in 1812–13. He was to do an outstanding job. Training cavalrymen was much more compli-cated than turning recruits into effective infantry. Given good raw material and efficient training cadres, acceptable foot soldiers could be ready in three months. Cavalry would take at least three times as long. The cavalry recruit needed the same initial drill as an infantryman. The peasant recruit had to stand up straight, know his right from his left, and march in step. In short, he had to become a soldier. The cavalry recruit needed to master both cold steel weapons and firearms. Amidst the rush to train recruits in wartime, in the cuirassier and dragoon regiments the job of skirmishing might initially be left to veterans. But a light cavalryman who knew nothing about skirmishing, firearms and outpost duty was a danger to his comrades.[51]

The biggest challenge came when the peasant recruit first encountered his horse. Unlike Cossacks, who were bred in the saddle, few peasants rode horses, though it helped Kologrivov that the great majority of his first 20,000 recruits came from the southern provinces of Orel, Voronezh, Tambov and Kiev where horses and in some districts studs were numerous. The Russian light cavalry and dragoon horses drawn from steppe herds were feisty animals. The brief but ferocious breaking-in of these horses often left them hard to handle initially. The recruit's life was also not made easier by the need in wartime to accept more mares than would otherwise have been the case. This did not contribute to order in a cavalry squadron packed with stallions. Despite these problems the cavalry recruit had to master his horse quickly. He must learn to ride first on his own and then in formation, carrying out increasingly complicated manoeuvres at ever greater speed. Crucially, he must also learn to water, feed and care for his horse properly, otherwise a cavalry regiment would quickly disintegrate amidst the strains of a campaign.[52]

In 1813–14 the Russian cavalry got its horses from a number of sources. The Field Army requisitioned or even occasionally bought a few horses in the countries through which it marched: its finest coup was to grab part of the King of Saxony's stud. In the spring of 1813, however, Alexander ordered that no more cavalry horses were to be purchased abroad, since they were far cheaper in Russia. All cavalrymen in the Field Army whose horses were lost were to be sent back to Kologrivov to receive new mounts and help in the formation of reserve squadrons.[53]

A small number of the horses acquired in Russia came from the state's own studs, both in the winter of 1812–13 and subsequently. These were fine animals but most were reserved for the Guards cuirassiers and dragoons.[54] A far larger number of horses were bought by the regiments' remount officers, in other words by the normal peacetime process. On their own, however, the remount officers could never have satisfied the hugely increased wartime demand. In addition, the price of horses went through the roof.[55] In September 1812 Alexander sent the head of the internal security troops, Evgraf Komarovsky, to levy horses in lieu of recruits in the provinces of Volhynia and Podolia. He secured more than 10,000 cavalry horses – sufficient for fifty full-strength squadrons – from the two provinces. As a result the scheme was extended to the whole empire, with Komarovsky in charge. In time he sent General Kologrivov a further 37,810 horses. In addition, beginning in the winter of 1812–13, the governors bought 14,185 horses for Kologrivov's cavalry. These huge numbers illustrate Russia's wealth in horses, especially when one recalls that they do not include the great number of animals acquired for the army's artillery and baggage trains.[56]

In addition to acquiring new horses, the army made great efforts to preserve the ones it already had. In December 1812 Kutuzov ordered cavalry commanders to 'remove all ill, wounded or very thin horses from the cavalry and settle them in Chernigov province once communications with it reopen'.[57] This policy of resting and rehabilitating horses in depots established behind the lines was to continue until the army reached Paris in 1814. What percentage of horses was detached in this first wave is impossible to say but it was certainly considerable. The 2nd Cuirassier Division alone sent away 164 horses out of a total of well under 1,000 and there is no reason to think it was untypical.[58]

In the early summer of 1813 a young lancer officer, Lieutenant Durova, returned to duty after sick leave. Durova was a unique officer since she was female, serving for many years while preserving her secret. Like all convalescents returning to active military service from Russia, she was assigned to the Reserve Army, a policy which helped greatly to refill its ranks with veterans. She was sent to the cavalry depot, which had now moved forward to Slonim, charged along with three other officers 'with fattening up the exhausted, wounded, and emaciated horses of all the uhlan regiments'. She adds that 'to my part fell one hundred and fifty horses and forty uhlans to look after them', which is a reminder of how very labour-intensive was the care of cavalry horses. Every morning after breakfast,

I go to inspect my flock in their place in the stables. From their cheerful and brisk capers I see that my uhlans ... are not stealing and selling the oats, but giving them all to these fine and obedient beasts. I see their bodies, previously distorted by emaciation, taking on their old beauty and filling out; their coats are becoming smooth and glossy; their eyes glow, and their ears, which were all too ready to droop, now begin to flick rapidly and point forward.[59]

Together with horses, Kologrivov above all needed trained cadres. By the winter of 1812 the Field Army's cavalry regiments had a great many under-strength squadrons, usually with a disproportionate number of officers and NCOs. At Alexander's suggestion, in most cavalry regiments Kutuzov created three, two or if necessary even just one full-strength squadron for service in the field. The remaining cadre of officers, NCOs and veterans was sent to help Kologrivov form reserve cavalry. In the spring 1813 campaign the Smolensk Dragoon Regiment, for example, deployed two squadrons with the Field Army. These now comprised 13 officers and 332 other ranks. Meanwhile 18 officers and 89 other ranks were sent to Slonim to join Kologrivov.[60] The detailed report on the Reserve Army which Lobanov submitted at the end of the war, packed with statistics, shows that the Reserve Army's cavalry had contained many more veteran soldiers and a much greater proportion of officers and NCOs than was the case with the infantry. Given the realities of cavalry training and service this was essential.[61]

The generous provision of horses, officers and veteran troopers goes a long way to explaining why Kologrivov made such a success of forming the cavalry reserves but it is far from the whole story. According to his aide-de-camp, the poet Aleksandr Griboedov, Kologrivov organized not just horse hospitals, blacksmiths and other obvious adjuncts to a depot for cavalry but also picked recruits with key skills, trained others and created workshops to manufacture horse furnishings, saddles and uniforms, thereby not just saving the state a great deal of money but also freeing himself from overdependence on the war ministry's commissariat.[62]

Between March and September 1813 Kologrivov sent 106 squadrons to the Field Army. In November 1813 he sent another 63 and had almost as many more ready for dispatch. Dmitrii Lobanov-Rostovsky spent much of his time inspecting units of the Reserve Army before their departure to the Field Army. His comments about the cavalry were always complimentary in all respects. He was usually satisfied with his infantry and artillery reserves too but the artillery's horses were a frequent cause of complaint, as was the infantry's equipment. Though he thought most of his departing infantry well trained, there were exceptions. In December 1813, for instance, he commented that the reserves now departing to reinforce Wittgenstein's corps were too young and needed more time to prepare for combat.[63]

Perhaps the fairest judges were foreigners, however, not least because they were inclined to make informed comparisons. On 8 June 1813 Sir Robert Wilson watched as Alexander inspected the Guards and Grenadier reserves just arrived from Petersburg and Iaroslavl. Aware that they had spent the last three months on the march, he was astonished by their appearance:

These infantry . . . and their appointments appeared as if they had not moved further than from barracks to the parade during that time. The horses and men of the cavalry bore the same freshness of appearance. Men and beasts certainly in Russia afford the most surprising material for powder service. If English battalions had marched a tenth part of the way they would have been crippled for weeks and would scarcely have had a relic of their original equipments. Our horses would all have been foundered, and their backs too sore even for the carriage of the saddle.[64]

Colonel Rudolph von Friederich was the head of the historical section of the Prussian general staff. He had no doubt that the Russian reserves who arrived during the armistice were much superior to most of the Prussian and Austrian reinforcements who joined their field armies at that time. The Russian was 'an excellent soldier, of course without any intellect, but brave, obedient and undemanding. Their arms, clothing and equipment were very good and on the whole they were well trained.' Above all, these soldiers who had survived months of gruelling marches were extremely tough and resilient. As to the cavalry, they were 'in general excellently mounted, well-trained and impeccably uniformed and equipped'. Friederich's only criticism of the Russian reinforcements was that 'only the jaeger regiments had been taught to skirmish'.[65]

As regards training, it helped that the great majority of the reserves had arrived in the Field Army's encampments by the end of June. Most reserve units were broken up and distributed among the army's battalions and squadrons. The July weather was fine and the Field Army's regiments possessed the free time and the veterans to help complete the reserves' training, including intensive shooting practice. Friedrich von Schubert was the chief of staff of Baron Korff's cavalry in Langeron's army corps. In his memoirs he wrote that

the reserve squadrons, new recruits and remounts arrived in the regiments from Russia and the training and exercising of the men and the horses lasted from morning until night: it was a very hectic, brisk but cheerful business . . . the same happened in the infantry and artillery . . . Our efforts paid off because at the end of the armistice the Russian army was in better condition than at the beginning of the war: fully up to strength, well-equipped, healthy, full of courage and enthusiasm for battle, and with a mass of experienced and tested generals, officers and soldiers in numbers it had never previously possessed.[66]

The Russian reinforcements moving westwards in the spring and summer filled not just the Field Army but also the allied strategic reserve, in other words the so-called Army of Poland which Alexander ordered General Bennigsen to form in early June.[67] Bennigsen's four infantry divisions had been blockading the fortresses of Modlin and Zamosc in the spring. Some of their units had also been performing an internal security role in Poland. At one point their combined strength was less than 8,000 men. By the end of the armistice, however, just these four divisions were 27,000 strong. In September Bennigsen's army, which included Count Petr Tolstoy's militia corps, advanced through Silesia to join the Field Army.[68]

But Bennigsen's army could not just set off to Saxony, uncovering the French garrisons besieged in Modlin and Zamosc and leaving the Duchy of Warsaw denuded of troops. When the autumn campaign began, Napoleon was poised in Silesia, within jumping distance of the Polish border. Many Poles awaited his arrival with impatience. If he advanced through Silesia, his fortresses at Danzig, Modlin and Zamosc would become very important. When Alexander ordered Bennigsen forward, he therefore instructed Dmitrii Lobanov-Rostovsky's Reserve Army to move across the Duchy of Warsaw and take over his role of blockading Modlin and Zamosc, watching Warsaw and Lublin, and overawing the Polish population. At the same time Lobanov was to continue with his troops' training and to prepare to dispatch further reinforcements to the Field Army.[69]

In the last months of the war the Reserve Army played a crucial and successful role in Alexander's strategy. By deploying Lobanov's men across the Duchy of Warsaw the emperor had released Bennigsen's army to make what proved to be a major contribution to the autumn 1813 campaign. The Reserve Army's blockade of Modlin and Zamosc led to the fall of both these fortresses in the winter of 1813. Throughout this period the Reserve Army's reinforcements continued to flow to the Field Army in Germany and France. At the end of the war, strengthened by troops released by the fall of Danzig and by the first wave of recruits from the 85th recruit levy, the Reserve Army was at unprecedented strength, with more than 7,000 officers and 325,000 men on its rolls. As always, paper strengths did not accurately reflect the numbers actually present in the ranks. Moreover, many of the soldiers were not yet fully trained or armed, and almost one-quarter were sick. Nevertheless, had the struggle with Napoleon continued there would have been no doubt of Russia's ability to pull its weight on the battlefield. Also to the point, at a moment when other powers might contest Alexander's right to Poland, not merely did he have a formidable army in the field to deter them, he could also point to a fresh force of well over a quarter of a million men positioned in the region which he was claiming.[70]

11

Europe's Fate in the Balance

The armistice between Napoleon and the allies was agreed on 4 June. Initially it was set to continue until 20 July. Subsequently, at Austria's insistence, the allies very unwillingly agreed to extend it until 10 August. During the armistice a peace conference opened in Prague, with Austria mediating between the two sides. Before the conference convened Austria had secretly committed itself to joining the allied cause unless Napoleon agreed to the four minimal Austrian conditions for peace by 10 August. When he failed to do so Austria declared war and the autumn 1813 campaign began. Once this campaign started diplomacy largely took a back seat for three months. The Russians, Prussians and Austrians were agreed on the need to get Napoleon out of Germany and back across the Rhine, and were also agreed that this could only be achieved by military means. Had Napoleon won the initial battles it is possible that rifts would have reopened between the allies, and Austria would have resumed negotiations with Napoleon. In fact, however, diplomacy was mostly confined to consolidating the alliance between the four great powers fighting Napoleon and drawing the smaller German states to their side. Unlike in the spring of 1813 all the decisive moments in the autumn campaign occurred on the battlefield.

On the eve of the armistice Alexander sent Nesselrode to Vienna to clear up misunderstandings and urge the Austrians to take a firmer stand against Napoleon. On the way he met Francis II and Metternich; the latter had decided that at this moment of supreme crisis it was essential for himself and his sovereign to be closer to events. Face-to-face negotiations might well reduce distrust and misunderstanding between the allies and Austria. They would certainly avoid the delays created as messengers shuttled to and from Vienna. For the next ten weeks European top-level diplomacy was concentrated in the small area between

Napoleon's headquarters at Dresden, allied headquarters at Reich-enbach in south-western Silesia, the great north-eastern Bohemian chateaux of Gitschin and Ratiborsitz, where many private meetings between the allied leaders occurred, and the Bohemian capital, Prague, where the peace conference took place.

Nesselrode had a series of discussions with Metternich, Francis II and the Austrian military leaders, Schwarzenberg and Radetsky, between 3 and 7 June. Both generals were enthusiastic supporters of entry into the war, so their explanations of the problems facing the Habsburg army's preparations carried conviction. Nesselrode trusted and saw eye-to-eye with Metternich, whom he had known for many years, and he brought back to allied headquarters a memorandum setting out Austrian views on peace conditions. He emerged from his conversations with all the Austrian leaders convinced that Francis II was indeed the main obstacle to Austria joining the allies but that his opposition was by no means insurmountable. There was no chance, however, of moving the Austrian monarch towards war until Napoleon had been offered and rejected very moderate and minimal terms of peace.

These minimal terms boiled down to four points. The Duchy of Warsaw must be re-partitioned between the Russians, Austrians and Prussians: Prussia must get back Danzig, and Napoleon must evacuate all the fortresses on Prussian and Polish territory: Illyria must be returned to Austria: Hamburg and Lübeck must regain their independence immediately, and other French-occupied towns on the North Sea and Baltic coastlines in due course. On the eve of Nesselrode's return to allied headquarters at Reichenbach, Metternich wrote to the anxious Philipp Stadion that he had enjoyed many good conversations with the Russian diplomat and that both men understood and appreciated their two countries' interests and positions. 'Nesselrode is very well disposed to us and will depart very happy. I believe that I can fully promise you this. His mission has been of real benefit.'[1]

After Nesselrode's return to Reichenbach a series of meetings between the Russian and Prussian leaders discussed their response to Metternich's memorandum and the peace terms which would satisfy the allies. The basic point was that the Russians and Prussians were stuck. They badly needed Austrian assistance. As Nesselrode reminded Christoph Lieven, 'recent events have shown us just what resources Napoleon still possesses'. Only Austrian intervention could swing the balance in the allies' favour. Given 'the extreme distaste which the Emperor Francis shows for war', the allies had no option but to accept Metternich's strategy of presenting very moderate terms to Napoleon and comforting themselves with the thought that 'however inadequate they seem to us, it is very unlikely that the enemy will accept the Austrian conditions, given what we know of Napoleon's character'. But of course there was a risk that Napoleon would surprise the allies by accepting the Austrian terms. As Metternich subsequently wrote to Stadion, 'no one could be a reliable judge' of how Napoleon would react when he finally woke up to the imminent threat of Austrian intervention, 'given the peculiar character of the man on whom in the last resort peace depends'.[2]

The Russian problem was that Alexander and Nesselrode were convinced that the Austrian minimal terms were wholly inadequate to guarantee a lasting peace. The very high stakes involved concentrated Russian thinking. More minor issues went out of the window. Alexander and Nesselrode concerned themselves exclusively with achieving a stable peace which would guarantee Russian security. They focused almost entirely on the German question, which they saw as the key Russian interest. Since their thinking was displayed not just in communications to other powers but also in secret internal memorandums there is no reason to doubt the sincerity of their views.

Both Alexander and Nesselrode were convinced that if Napoleon continued to control most of Germany there could be no true European balance of power and no security for Prussia, Austria or Russia. They believed that if Austria only regained Illyria it would still be at Napoleon's mercy. At a minimum it needed to get back Tyrol, the fortress of Mantua and a strategically defensible frontier in northern Italy along the river Mincio. Understandably, however, the Russians left the Austrians to worry about their own salvation and concentrated on defending Prussian security. The four Austrian conditions would have left Napoleon as master of the Confederation of the Rhine, with his brother Jérôme still on the throne of the kingdom of Westphalia. He would also hold almost the whole length of the river Elbe, including all its key fortified crossings. In these circumstances 'any hope for the independence of any part of Germany would be lost for good. Prussia would constantly be exposed to attacks which could come at any moment and against which it could only offer a feeble defence, and the Emperor Napoleon could almost at will make himself master of the

Baltic coastline, so that any hope of the security of trade would be entirely illusory.'[3]

Nesselrode wrote to Metternich that, if peace was concluded on the basis of the four Austrian points, it would only be a truce, which would allow Napoleon sufficient time to restore his armies and then reimpose his unchallenged domination of Europe. The sine qua non for any true peace was that Prussia and Austria had to be strong enough to balance France. The stronger they were, the less likely Napoleon would be to challenge the peace settlement. Nesselrode emphasized the uniquely favourable present circumstances. For the first time since 1793 the armies of the three eastern monarchies were potentially united and concentrated for battle in the same theatre. They were superior in numbers, spirit and organization to Napoleon. 'It would be difficult, maybe even impossible, to re-create a similar conjunction of circumstances if the present ones did not lead to a result which, after so many efforts and sacrifices, did not erect powerful barriers against France.' If peace was made on the Austrian terms, history would repeat itself. After a short breathing space Napoleon would once again confront Austria and Prussia, who would be too weak and exhausted successfully to resist him. As in the past, the issue would be resolved before Russia's distant armies could come to her allies' aid.[4]

The Treaty of Reichenbach between Austria, Russia and Prussia signed on 27 June set out the four minimal Austrian conditions and guaranteed that Austria would enter the war unless Napoleon had accepted them by the expiry of the armistice on 20 July. The allies made it clear to Metternich, however, that although they would enter negotiations on this basis they would only sign a peace if it included other terms which would end Napoleon's domination of Germany and guarantee Prussian security. Relations between Austria and the allies reached their lowest ebb when Metternich returned from discussions with Napoleon in Dresden and imposed an extension of the armistice until 10 August. Some of the loudest denunciations of this extension came from Baron Stein. In his case the normal allied view that Austrian peace terms were inadequate was enhanced by fierce disagreement with Metternich about the war's ultimate goals. Stein wanted a reborn and more united German confederation with a constitution guaranteeing civil and political rights. He appealed to German nationalist feeling to achieve this. Since April 1813, however, Stein's influence with Alexander had been in decline as Germany failed to revolt against Napoleon and the allies' need for Austrian assistance became more pressing. Now he attempted to strike back, claiming that Metternich was pulling the wool over allied eyes and that with half a million Russians, Prussians and Swedes ready to take the field against 360,000 enemy troops Austrian help was probably unnecessary anyway. Previously he had supported Nesselrode because the latter shared Stein's view that Russia should commit herself wholeheartedly to the liberation of Germany from Napoleon. Now, however, he called Nesselrode Metternich's dupe, a well-meaning but empty weakling.[5]

In reality Nesselrode was right and Stein was wrong. The allies could not have driven Napoleon out of Germany without Austrian help. At the very moment when Stein was writing these denunciations Metternich was moving quietly to swing Austria towards the allied camp. With peace negotiations now in the offing, Metternich wrote to Francis II that it was essential that he and the emperor were in complete agreement as to future policy. The peace negotiations might have three outcomes. The two sides might agree terms, in which case Austria need only rejoice. Metternich did not need to spell out to Francis how unlikely this outcome was, since the Austrians were well aware how far apart the opposing sides were as regards acceptable peace terms. A second and somewhat likelier possibility was that Napoleon would accept the Austrian minimal terms and the allies would reject them. Metternich wrote that Austria could not determine in advance what to do in this event since to some extent it would depend on contexts and circumstances. Under no circumstances could it side with France, however, and the defeat or dissolution of the allied coalition would be a great threat to Austrian security. Armed neutrality might be a short-term option but it would be very difficult to sustain for any length of time and the only other alternative would be to join the allies.

Metternich's memorandum concentrated, however, on the third and likeliest possibility, which was that Napoleon would reject the Austrian terms. In that case Metternich's unequivocal advice was that Austria must declare war. He concluded his memorandum with a question: 'Can I count on Your Majesty's firmness in the event that Napoleon does not accept Austria's conditions for peace? Is Your Majesty resolutely determined in that case to entrust a just cause to the decision of arms – both those of Austria and of the whole of the rest of united Europe?'[6]

Francis responded that any decent man must desire stable and lasting peace and that this was all the more true for a sovereign like himself who bore responsibility for the well-being of 'his good subjects' and their 'beautiful lands'. No greed for territory or other advantages could justify war. But he trusted Metternich's judgement: 'To a great extent I have you to thank for the present excellent political situation of my monarchy.' Therefore he agreed with his foreign minister's conclusions. In the event that Napoleon accepted Austria's terms and the allies rejected them he would await Metternich's advice. If Napoleon rejected the Austrian terms then the monarchy would declare war on France.[7]

In the end therefore everything depended on Napoleon and he played into the allies' hands. The French representatives at the Prague peace conference arrived late and without powers to negotiate terms. Nothing could have done more to confirm Austrian suspicions that Napoleon was merely playing for time and had no interest in peace. Not until two days before the armistice was due to expire did Napoleon make a serious diplomatic move. On 8 August Caulaincourt, one of the two French delegates to the peace conference, visited Metternich's quarters to enquire what price Austria required to stay neutral or join the French camp. Not until the day after the armistice expired did the French provide Metternich with a response to the four minimal peace conditions set out by Austria. Napoleon agreed to abandon the Poles and hand over much of Illyria to Austria. He conceded nothing as regards the north German ports, rejected Prussian annexation of Danzig, and required compensation for the King of Saxony to make up for the fact that he had lost his position as Duke of Warsaw. These conditions would never have satisfied Metternich and by now it was in any case too late. Austria had closed the peace conference and now declared war on France.

Ever since August 1813 most historians, French ones included, have condemned Napoleon's ineptitude in failing to use diplomacy to divide the allies and keep Austria neutral. Even the inadequate concessions presented to Metternich on 11 August might have made an impact on Francis II if put forward as a first move at the beginning of the peace conference. There was room to exploit differences in Austrian and Russo-Prussian war aims, as regards both German and Polish territories. If the peace conference could be extended to include Britain, Napoleon's chances of sowing dissension must improve further. All the continental powers resented the fact that, while their territories had been occupied and ravaged, the United Kingdom had remained inviolate and become seemingly ever richer. They hoped to achieve territorial concessions by Napoleon in Europe in return for British willingness to hand back French colonies.

Nevertheless, even if Napoleon erred in not using diplomacy more skilfully to explore potential splits among his enemies, it is possible to understand his point of view in the summer of 1813. Refusal seriously to explore peace terms was much less obvious a blunder than his initial agreement to the armistice. The French monarch feared that once he began making concessions the allies would raise their demands. He was correct: the Russians and Prussians intended to do just this. The concessions he was being urged to make in north Germany might conceivably be acceptable in the context of a general peace which would include the return of French colonies, but Napoleon could hardly be expected to concede these territories in a continental peace and thereby find himself naked when he had to bargain later with the British.

A fundamental issue underlay all these peace negotiations. The allies, and indeed Austria, wanted to restore something approaching a balance of power in continental Europe. Napoleon was committed to French empire or at least hegemony. His defenders might plausibly assert that unless he preserved some version of French dominion on the continent he had lost his war with Britain and the vastly powerful maritime empire which it had created. Napoleon's basic problem was that although the continental powers resented the British version of empire, the French version was a much more direct threat to their interests. No amount of clever diplomacy could alter this. The only way in which Napoleon could get the continental powers to accept his empire was by re-creating their terror of French military power, which the disaster of 1812 had undermined. This was not an impossible task in August 1813. Napoleon had good reason to believe that he could defeat the Russians, Prussians and Austrians because the chances were very evenly matched. This adds to the drama of the autumn 1813 campaign.

In numerical terms Napoleon's forces were inferior to the allies but not greatly so. The Russian and Prussian official histories put allied numbers in Germany at the beginning of the autumn campaign at just over half a million. Napoleon himself reckoned in early August that he could put 400,000 men in the field, not counting Davout's corps at Hamburg, which was subsequently able to detach 28,000 men from garrison duties for an offensive against Berlin. On 6 August his chief of staff reported 418,000 men in the ranks. Exact numbers available for action on the battlefield are impossible to calculate for either side: roughly speaking, however, in the first two months of the campaign Napoleon could put rather more than four men in the field to every five allies. It was fortunate for the allies that 57,000 French troops were facing Wellington in the Pyrenees and another small corps under Marshal Suchet was still attempting to hold Catalonia.[8]

After two months the odds would shift somewhat towards the allies. The only reinforcements Napoleon could expect were Augereau's small corps which was forming in Bavaria. There were dangers in moving Augereau forward, since this made it easier for Bavaria to switch sides, which is what happened in October. To some extent the Russians faced a similar dilemma in the Duchy of Warsaw, where Bennigsen's Army of Poland was both a strategic reserve and an occupation force. In the Russian case, however, it was possible to move Lobanov-Rostovsky's Reserve Army into the Duchy to replace Bennigsen's 60,000 troops when they set off for Saxony. A steady flow of Austrian recruits also joined Schwarzenberg's army in September and October. In addition, once one began looking beyond the 1813 campaign it was clear that Austria and Russia had greater reserves of untapped manpower than Napoleon, especially if he was forced to rely just on France's own population. Napoleon's best chance of defeating the allies would therefore come in the first two months of the autumn campaign. This thought is unlikely to have worried the French emperor. After all, most of his great victories had been won in less time than this.

They had been won by better soldiers than he commanded in August 1813, however. Above all, Napoleon remained very inferior to the allies in cavalry. His mounted arm had improved considerably during the armistice, chiefly in terms of numbers. Some good cavalry regiments subsequently arrived from Spain. The Guards cavalry was mostly competent, as were the Polish and some of the German regiments. But the bulk of Napoleon's French cavalry was still well inferior to the Russian reserves formed by Kologrivov, not to speak of the veteran Russian cavalrymen. In addition, all sources agree that the cavalry was the best arm of the Austrian army. The situation as regards artillery was if anything the opposite. French equipment was much less cumbersome than Austrian guns and caissons. The Prussian artillery was so weak that the Russians had to second some of their own batteries to a number of Prussian divisions in order to give them sufficient firepower. The Prussian general staff history concluded that French artillery officers were usually more skilful than their allied counterparts. The main allied advantage as regards artillery was numerical. If they could concentrate their three field armies and Bennigsen's Army of Poland on a single battlefield, the weight of their firepower should be overwhelming.[9]

The majority of both the allied and the Napoleonic infantry were recruits, most of whom had never seen action before August 1813. The French conscripts were younger than their allied peers, but on the other hand many of them had experienced the spring campaign, which was true neither of the Austrians nor of the Prussian Landwehr. The Russian reserves were also going into action for the first time but at least in their case they had enjoyed plenty of time to train and were usually very tough and resilient. Above all, however, the Russian infantry contained more veterans than its French counterpart. This meant not just the men who had served throughout the 1812 and spring 1813 campaigns, but also many thousands of veterans who returned to their regiments during the armistice from hospitals and detached duties. Not surprisingly, the Guards contained exceptionally large number of veterans. The Guards regiments had not seen action in the spring 1813 campaign, and many of them had received drafts of veteran troops from regiments of the line. During the armistice, for example, from Osten-Sacken's Army Corps the Belostok Regiment provided 200 veterans for the Lithuania (Litovsky) Guards and the Iaroslavl Regiment lost 94 to the Izmailovskys.[10]

The choice of Sacken's corps to provide cadres for the Guards was not an accident because his regiments contained exceptional numbers of veterans. A closer look at his units gives a good sense of the Russian infantry's rather diverse make-up in the autumn campaign.

Sacken commanded two infantry divisions, Dmitrii Neverovsky's 27th and Johann von Lieven's 10th. We have already encountered Neverovsky's men in the 1812 campaign. His regiments were all newly created just before the war began and were made up mostly from soldiers in garrison regiments. In 1812 they had performed magnificently. When Alexander met Neverovsky for the first time in 1813 he told him: 'Your division fought gloriously and I will never forget its service or yours.' Glory came at a very high price. When the Odessa Regiment left Vilna in December 1812, for instance, it had only 4 officers, 11 NCOs and

119 men in its ranks, having suffered more than 1,500 casualties in the 1812 campaign. The 27th Division had been so shattered that it was left behind to recuperate in Lithuania in the spring of 1813, only rejoining the army during the armistice. Neverovsky scrounged new uniforms and equipment for his men while they were in the rear, but finding reinforcements proved much harder. The experience of the Odessa Regiment was typical of the whole division. The overwhelming majority of the regiment's sick and wounded were in hospitals in Russia and Belorussia. Those who recovered were sent to join Lobanov's Reserve Army. Ultimately the Odessa Regiment received its share of reserve companies from Lobanov, but on the eve of the autumn campaign it still contained only 21 officers, 31 NCOs and 544 men. Roughly half these last were new recruits.[11]

Lieven's 10th Division was very different. His regiments were drawn from Chichagov's Army of the Danube. All of them had campaigned in the Balkans before 1812. Some of them had remained in reserve, guarding fortresses and frontiers in 1812 and the first half of 1813. None had experienced anything like the appalling casualties suffered by the main army's regiments at Borodino, during the pursuit of Napoleon from Moscow to the Berezina, and at Lutzen and Bautzen. On 1 June 1813 the three infantry regiments of Lieven's division for which records remain (the Iaroslavl, Kursk and Belostok regiments) had 120 officers, 253 NCOs and 3,179 men present in their ranks. The overwhelming majority of these men were veterans, many of whom had fought in the wars of Paul and of Catherine II. In the whole course of 1812, for instance, the Belostok Regiment received only fifty new recruits. To be sure, both the Belostok and Iaroslavl regiments lost men to the Guards in the summer of 1813 but not enough seriously to damage their quality. Even in wartime the Guards seem to have picked men in part because of their appearance, though no doubt they avoided anyone with a bad record. Of the 94 men chosen by the Izmailovsky Guards from the Iaroslavl Regiment, for example, only 39 were from the elite grenadiers and sharpshooters.[12]

Above all, the Guards took none of Lieven's NCOs and it was around this body of veterans that formidable fighting regiments were built and preserved. In the Kursk Regiment the 23 sergeant-majors (*fel'dfebeli*) and quartermaster-sergeants (*kaptenarmusy*) in the ranks had served on average sixteen years in the army and almost thirteen in the regiment.

The twenty-five most senior sergeants (*unterofitsery*) had been in the regiment for an average of eighteen years. The Belostok Regiment had been created only in 1807 but all but one of its twelve sergeant-majors had been in its ranks since then. The regimental sergeant-major, Boris Vasilev, aged 33, was a soldier's son. He had joined the Kronstadt Garrison Regiment as a drummer aged only 13 and became a company sergeant-major ten years later. Along with many other men from the Kronstadt Regiment, Vasilev was transferred to the newly created Belostok Regiment in 1807. He won a Military Medal four years later at the siege of Rushchuk in the Balkans. Still quite youthful but already very experienced, he was a competent, literate manager in peacetime but also a soldier with a fine combat record: to the extent that one can judge from the bare facts of his official record, he epitomized everything a regimental commander could desire in his senior sergeant-major.

In addition to its veteran NCOs, the Belostok Regiment also had a surprisingly large number of officers of lower-class origin, most though by no means all of whom were soldiers' sons, and all of whom became officers well before the 1812 campaign began. These men too were hardened veterans. Lieutenant Nikolai Shevyrev, for example, had served fifteen years in a garrison regiment before becoming a sergeant-major, and had joined the Belostok Regiment as it was forming and just after he had been promoted to officer rank. Men such as Vasilev and Shevyrev were worthy opponents of the promoted rankers who packed the junior-officer and NCO ranks of Napoleon's army in 1812. By August 1813, however, there can have been very few French units in Germany able to match the veteran cadres of the Kursk and Belostok regiments.[13]

Though his army was inferior to the allies in both numbers and quality, in other respects Napoleon enjoyed key advantages. As he himself pointed out to Count Bubna, Metternich's envoy, interior lines combined with a clear chain of command and his own undisputed leadership were very valuable in themselves. When opposed to a coalition made up of equal great powers with diverse interests, and with armies deployed in a huge semicircle from Berlin in the north to Silesia in the east and Bohemia in the south, these advantages ought to be decisive. In his memoirs, Eugen of Württemberg wrote that in August 1813 he had been optimistic about allied victory but having discovered after the war how disunited and conflict-ridden the allied leadership had been he was now very surprised by ultimate allied success.[14]

The allied commander-in-chief was the Austrian field-marshal, Prince Karl von Schwarzenberg. Before 1813 Schwarzenberg had shown himself to be a skilful ambassador and a competent and courageous commander of a division. His record of commanding larger units had been less impressive. Nothing in his personality or career suggested that he was a match for Napoleon as the commander of a huge army. Schwarzenberg was a patient, tactful, kind and honourable man. He believed in the allied cause and served it unselfishly and to the best of his ability. A *grand seigneur*, he had the manners and the lack of personal ambition appropriate to his status. In the manner of an Eisenhower, he could absorb and defuse conflicts between the many ambitious and aggressive personalities over whom he exercised command. Of course, the aristocratic Schwarzenberg was fluent in French, the lingua franca of the allied high command. As commander-in-chief, however, he was hampered by his lack of confidence in his own military ability, his awe of Napoleon, and the immense difficulty of commanding a coalition army of equal great powers, two of whose sovereigns insisted on travelling with his headquarters and second-guessing his decisions. Though he often found Alexander very difficult to handle, Schwarzenberg on the whole liked him. He echoed the consensus that the Russian monarch was 'good but weak'. Frederick William III on the contrary was 'a coarse, churlish and insensitive person whom I dislike as much as I value the poor, valiant Prussians'.[15]

For all his inadequacies, Schwarzenberg was the best man available for the post of commander-in-chief. The supreme commander had to be an Austrian, not a Russian. This reflected allied dependence on Austria in August 1813 as well as the fact that the largest allied army was deployed on Austrian territory. Even if the Austrians had been willing – which was far from the case – Alexander himself would never have accepted the job. Had he wished to be the supreme military commander, the position was his for the asking after Kutuzov's death in April 1813. Some of his generals urged him to take personal command then but Alexander was far too lacking in confidence in his military abilities to agree. Instead he preferred to operate from behind the shoulder of the actual commander-in-chief, to the latter's acute discomfort.

The emperor treated Schwarzenberg with more respect than he had

Wittgenstein. At the beginning of the autumn campaign, for example, one even finds him telling Wittgenstein to obey Schwarzenberg's orders when they conflicted with Alexander's own commands. Quite soon, however, confidence in the supreme commander began to fade and old habits to some extent returned. Schwarzenberg quickly learned that the only way to guarantee that Russian commanders would actually execute his orders was to consult in advance the emperor's representative at allied headquarters, Karl von Toll, and on any major matters to get Alexander's own approval. Inevitably this delayed and blurred decision-making to a degree which could have proved fatal.[16]

Consulting Alexander and Frederick William entailed listening to the opinions of their military advisers. In Alexander's case this meant above all Barclay de Tolly, Diebitsch and Toll. Always inclined to trust foreign 'military professors', Alexander now found a partial substitute for Pfühl in Major-General Antoine de Jomini, one of the most respected military writers of the time, who had deserted from Napoleon's army during the armistice. Alexander put even more trust in Napoleon's old rival General Moreau, who had defeated the Austrians at Hohenlinden in 1800 and whom he had invited into his entourage from American exile. For Schwarzenberg and his Austrian staff officers it was bad enough having to listen to the allied monarchs and their Russian and Prussian generals. Having to defer to Moreau and Jomini was the final straw. The commander-in-chief wrote to his wife about the frustrations of being 'surrounded by weaklings, fops of every sort, creators of eccentric schemes, intriguers, idiots, chatterers and fault-finders'. Mikhailovsky-Danilevsky commented in his diary that allied decision-making was sometimes akin to the deliberations of a popular assembly, quite unlike the clear-cut system of command which had existed – in his rather idealized memory – at Kutuzov's headquarters in 1812.[17]

If Schwarzenberg's power over the main army – the so-called Army of Bohemia – was conditional, it was almost non-existent as regards the two other allied armies. The Army of the North was commanded by Bernadotte and was deployed around Berlin. As the de facto sovereign of a large, independent country Bernadotte had to be given command of one of the armies and would be very difficult for any commander-in-chief to control. In so far as anyone at the main army headquarters could influence Bernadotte's actions, it was Alexander to whom the Swedish crown prince to some extent deferred. In any case, the whole area between Schwarzenberg's and Bernadotte's armies was held by Napoleon, so messengers between the two headquarters generally made a huge detour to the east and took many days to shuttle back and forth. Even Schwarzenberg's attempts to control General Blücher, the commander of the Army of Silesia, bore little fruit. By delay and by appealing to Alexander and Frederick William the Prussian general successfully resisted all the commander-in-chief's many efforts to draw the Army of Silesia into Bohemia in order to cover the main army's right flank. At least in the Army of Bohemia Schwarzenberg could give direct orders to the 120,000 men who formed its Austrian contingent. In the Army of Silesia and the Army of the North, however, there were no Austrian troops.

In principle, allied movements were supposed to follow the plan agreed at Trachenberg between 10 and 12 July by the Russians, Prussians and Swedes. The plan stated grandly that 'all the allied armies are to act offensively: the enemy camp will be the point at which they will join'. If Napoleon advanced against any one of the allied armies, the other two were to attack his rear. Only the Army of Silesia was explicitly ordered to avoid battle with Napoleon, above all because in early July the allied planners believed that it would only be 50,000 strong. The chief architect of the Trachenberg plan was Toll: although still-neutral Austria could not participate in the Trachenberg war-planning conference, he had travelled to Austrian headquarters for lengthy discussions with Schwarzenberg and Radetsky, who agreed with the Trachenberg plan's principles. Austrian caution did subsequently modify the plan in one respect: all allied armies were now enjoined to avoid battle against Napoleon himself unless the other allied armies were able to join in.[18]

In many ways the Trachenberg plan made good sense. Napoleon was in Germany and the only way to remove him was by a coordinated offensive of all the allied armies. Avoiding a battle between any one allied army and Napoleon's main forces under his personal command was also sensible. Whether it was achievable was another matter. An army which invaded Saxony and then retreated in the face of Napoleon's counter-movements would be doing a great deal of exhausting marching. Avoiding battle with Napoleon on your tail was anyway easier said than done. The Russian army would probably have the skill in rearguard actions and the endurance to sustain this strategy. Whether the Austrian army or the Prussian Landwehr could do so was a moot point. In the absence of radio or telephones it was in any case impossible to coordinate the concentric movements of three armies in anything but the barest outlines. Some armies were bound to move more quickly than others. As the allies closed in, Napoleon's chances of using his central position to strike one and hold off the others for a few crucial days would improve. The personalities of the three allied commanders added to this likelihood. Blücher was bold, aggressive and much inclined to take risks. He had no fear of Napoleon. Schwarzenberg and Bernadotte were the exact opposite in all respects.

At the beginning of the campaign Alexander seems to have had high hopes that Bernadotte would mount a vigorous offensive. Perhaps he was seduced by his respect for foreign, and above all Napoleonic, generals. In a letter to Bernadotte of 21 August, for example, he held out the prospect that with Napoleon seemingly moving eastwards the Swedish crown prince could storm into his rear, taking Dresden and Leipzig, occupying the defiles into Bohemia, and even dispatching light forces westwards to encourage the confederation of the Rhine princes to abandon their alliance with Napoleon. In fact, however, there was nothing in Bernadotte's past to suggest that he might be willing or able to carry out such grandiose offensive operations. Over the years he had shown himself to be an excellent administrator and a skilful politician but nothing more than a competent, if cautious, general.[19]

Bernadotte was also operating under serious constraints, some of them political. The Swedish elites who had offered him their crown had done so in the expectation that this would improve relations with Napoleon and maybe help their planned revenge against Russia. Instead Bernadotte had led Sweden into alliance with Alexander, abandoning what seemed a golden opportunity to regain Finland in the process. To justify this policy, Bernadotte had to deliver on his promise to take Norway from the Danish king in compensation. In one sense this bound him to the allies, because Napoleon would never agree to robbing his Danish ally. Allied victory was a necessary but far from sufficient condition as regards grabbing Norway for Sweden, however. Apart from anything else, this was a minor issue for the allied great powers. They would be very slow to commit their own troops against Denmark. Bernadotte would also be well advised to have Norway firmly in his grasp before the horse-trading began at a post-war peace conference. All this helps to explain why the crown prince was so determined to keep his Swedish corps intact during the autumn campaign. There was also a simpler reason. Of all the allied troops the Swedes were probably the worst. If their infantry got into serious combat with the French there was every chance they would be badly mauled. The likely result would be that Bernadotte would return to Sweden with no Norway and half an army. In that case his chances of gaining the throne on the king's death would probably be slim.[20]

The Army of the North also faced a strategic dilemma. If Napoleon advanced against Blücher or Schwarzenberg at the beginning of the campaign both had room to retreat. Schwarzenberg, for example, could move back on to his supply bases, fortresses and good defensive positions in central and southern Bohemia. With the two other allied armies and a horde of light cavalry moving into his rear there were strict limits to how long Napoleon could pursue either Blücher or Schwarzenberg. Bernadotte's army on the other hand was deployed right in front of Berlin. He himself might wish to retreat towards his own Swedish bases on the Baltic coastline but if he abandoned Berlin without a struggle he would face revolt from his Prussian generals, whose troops constituted the biggest contingent in his army. Bernadotte knew this and therefore planned to beat off any French attack on Berlin. His nervousness was increased by his conviction that seizing the Prussian capital would be Napoleon's first priority. He was actually not far wrong: Napoleon was obsessed by Berlin and directed two offensives against it, led by marshals Oudinot and Ney, in the first month of the war. Had the initial battles with the armies of Bohemia and Silesia gone successfully, Napoleon's next move would have been to move northwards against Bernadotte with his Guards and the bulk of his other reserves.[21]

The armies of Silesia and Bohemia were in a safer position than Bernadotte so long as they stood on the defensive. If Napoleon was to be driven out of Germany they could not do this for long, however. Once they invaded Napoleon's base in central Saxony they also would be vulnerable. In Schwarzenberg's case his troops would have to cross the Erzgebirge, in other words the mountain range that ran along the whole length of the Saxon–Bohemian frontier. The only two decent roads from Bohemia across the Erzgebirge were the highways to Dresden and Leipzig. As they crossed the range these were 100 kilometres apart. If Schwarzenberg spread his advancing columns across both highways and the mountain paths between them, there was a chance that Napoleon would pounce on one of his flanks before the rest of the army could come to his aid. Rapid lateral movement across the steep valleys and along the winding mountain paths of the Erzgebirge was difficult even for messengers, let alone large bodies of troops. On the other hand, if Schwarzenberg tried to concentrate most of his army on just one highway, logistical problems would mount and his columns would move very slowly. That would increase the possibility of Napoleon pouncing on the leading divisions of the allied army while the rest of Schwarzenberg's army was crawling forward in a long crocodile across the mountains.[22]

If Blücher's army was to invade central Saxony it had to cross the Elbe. All the fortified crossings were in Napoleon's hands, which meant that only he could move his troops across the river rapidly and in full security. The only way for Blücher to cross was by building pontoon bridges. For this he depended on his Russian pontoon companies, who did an outstanding job in getting the Army of Silesia across first the Elbe and later the Rhine. Their bridges were distinctly ramshackle affairs. A senior Russian staff officer in Blücher's army recalled that 'these bridges, which only lay a couple of feet above the surface of the water, had to be crossed with great care. They moved up and down all the time, horses had to be led, and any damage to the tarpaulin of one of the barges could immediately sink it.' Once the army had crossed the river, either it dismantled the bridge and abandoned its communications or it had to construct field fortifications to protect the bridgeheads. The latter could never be as strong as permanent fortresses and therefore required much bigger garrisons. An army crossed such bridges much more slowly than over a permanent structure. It therefore had a higher chance of being caught by the enemy while moving across a river. The nightmare for any commander was to be forced to cross such a bridge in a hurry with Napoleon on his tail. True disaster loomed if the weather then turned against them, damaged the pontoons or made the bridge impossible to cross.[23]

Inevitably, to see things just from the allied perspective is to forget that Napoleon too faced serious problems. By standing on the defensive in Saxony with a large army he doomed his men, and above all his horses, to hunger. The marches and counter-marches imposed by the allied Trachenberg strategy exhausted Napoleon's young conscripts. The hostility of the local population and, above all, his great inferiority in light cavalry made it difficult to gather intelligence. His main base at

Dresden, on which his army's supply of food, ammunition and fodder greatly depended, was inadequately fortified and only one day's march from the Austrian border. Odeleben, still in Napoleon's headquarters, relates these and other problems and recalls that Napoleon's great aim and hope in the autumn campaign was to pounce on allied mistakes. This hope was realistic given the theatre of operations, the problems of coalition warfare, and the failings of the allied commanders.[24]

Telling the story of the first weeks of the autumn 1813 campaign in Germany is complicated by the fact that fighting occurred on three distinct fronts. The main army under Schwarzenberg in the south, Blücher's Army of Silesia in the east and Bernadotte's Army of the North in front of Berlin operated independently and it is necessary to follow each of their campaigns in turn for the sake of clarity. Only after the first half of the autumn campaign was concluded and the three allied armies advanced into Saxony towards Leipzig is it possible to tell the story of the campaign as a single integrated narrative.

Predictably, of the three allied army commanders it was Blücher who was off to the quickest start after the expiry of the armistice. In fact, thundering that 'it's time to finish with diplomatic buffoonery', he went into action even before hostilities were supposed to start.[25] Egged on by Barclay, he seized as an excuse minor French infractions of the armistice terms and invaded the neutral zone between the opposing armies in Silesia on 13 August. This move made sense. In a province exhausted by the presence of two big armies in June and July 1813 the neutral zone around Breslau stood out because its harvest had barely yet been tapped. This was a prize worth cornering for oneself and denying to the enemy.

More important, Blücher's move seized the initiative and forced Napoleon to respond to allied movements rather than himself dictating events. The advance of the Army of Silesia, for example, diverted Napoleon's attention from Barclay's columns of Russian and Prussian troops, which at this time were marching south-westwards to join Schwarzenberg's army in Bohemia. Had the French attacked these columns while they were strung out on the march the consequences could have been serious. In addition, by seizing the initiative Blücher caught the French forces opposite him by surprise and pushed them right back out of the neutral zone and all the way over the river Bober. Blücher advanced with

Sacken's Army Corps of 18,000 Russian troops on his right, Yorck's 38,000 Prussians in the centre and Langeron's 40,000 Russians on his left.

Count Alexandre de Langeron, the senior Russian officer in Blücher's army, was one of the many French émigrés in Russian service. His first experience of battle had been in the American War of Independence. He had joined the Russian army besieging the Ottoman fortress of Izmail in 1790, partly out of a sense of adventure but also, so it was whispered, to escape the consequences of a duel with a bishop. Langeron won the respect of the Russians by the courage and enterprise he showed during the siege and he remained in Russian service for the rest of his life. The first time Langeron saw Paris in many years was when his troops stormed the heights of Montmartre outside the city's gates in March 1814. He worked his way up the army's ranks, fighting mostly against the Turks but also at Austerlitz, where his less than brilliant performance excited Alexander's anger and almost cost him his career. Subsequently Langeron had regained favour through his performance against the Turks, but few people doubted that the count was a competent rather than a brilliant general.[26]

Langeron cut something of a strange figure in Blücher's Russo-Prussian army. He was very much the southern Frenchman, dark in complexion with black eyes and hair. He had the charm, the wit and the conversation of the Old Regime Parisian salons. He wrote tragedies and songs. Extremely absent-minded, he loved word-games, puzzles and charades. At times he would march up and down, his head down, his hands behind his back, lost in his thoughts and riddles. On the battlefield, however, he was calm and imposing and had a good eye for terrain. He had learned to speak a fluent and voluble Russian but in a weird accent that was often incomprehensible to his soldiers. Nevertheless he was well liked by the men and the admiration was mutual. One of his most endearing characteristics was his enormous admiration for the courage, decency and self-sacrifice of the ordinary Russian soldiers whom – as he always put it – he had the great honour to command. Perhaps there was in this a touch of the colonial officer, who far preferred the doughty native peasantry to the vulgar and pushy bourgeois back at home. But Langeron was also generous, even chivalrous, to his officers, quick to give praise to others and often critical about himself.

As the senior Russian officer in Blücher's army, however, Langeron had some responsibility for good relations between the Russian and Prussian troops and their commanders. This presented problems. Langeron spoke no German and Blücher had not a word of French or Russian. Communications went through Blücher's chief of staff, Gneisenau, in the French language. Like most Frenchmen of his day, Langeron thought Germans were rather a joke, once commenting that 'the heaviness, the stiff formality, the slow imagination of this nation and their uncouthness do not make them agreeable to other people'. Gneisenau hated the French even more than Langeron disliked the Germans. In addition, Blücher's chief of staff was something of a radical, who dreamed of arousing the German people to the same level of nationalist frenzy which had seized France in the Revolution. A Frenchman with similar inclinations he would have hated but understood; an émigré count fighting against his own nation was a different matter.[27]

The command structure of the Army of Silesia in fact had the potential for disaster. Sacken and Blücher could at least communicate in German. In time they came to admire each other's qualities. Their good relations were an unanticipated blessing, however, because Sacken was a sharp-tongued and short-tempered man with a poor reputation as a subordinate. Even so, in comparison with Yorck he was an angel. The Prussian corps commander thought Blücher was an idiot and the much younger Gneisenau a mere theoretician of war and a dangerous radical. The fact that he was subordinated to this pair was an obvious disgrace to merit and common sense. It was with these senior commanders that the Army of Silesia woke up on 21 August to the fact that it now faced Napoleon himself, his Guards and the core of his reserves, which had raced up to support the corps retreating before Blücher's forces.

Blücher reacted in accordance with the Trachenberg plan. His corps retreated and refused to become engaged in a major battle. As one might by now expect, the Russians did this with cool professionalism. On the right wing, outside Bunzlau, Sacken waited calmly for the five hours that it took the corps of Ney, Marmont and Sebastiani to deploy against him. Then he left it to the disciplined skill of Lieven's infantry and Ilarion Vasilchikov's horsemen to mount a rearguard action that frustrated the enemy commanders and kept the French at a respectful distance. In the Belostok Regiment alone ten soldiers won military medals for their calmness, courage and skill in the rearguard action at Bunzlau on 21 August. The infantry was helped enormously by the fact that Vasilchikov was one of the ablest light cavalry commanders in Europe and his regiments were far superior in every way to the horsemen of General Sebastiani's French Second Cavalry Corps, by whom they were opposed.[28]

On the other wing of Blücher's army Langeron's rearguard also performed well under heavy pressure. Its cavalry was ably commanded by General Georgii Emmanuel, the son of a Serbian colonist in southern Russia. The overall commander of the rearguard was Aleksandr Rudzevich, a Crimean Tatar who had been baptized into the Orthodox Church at the age of 12. In principle, Rudzevich, a trained staff officer, was Langeron's chief of staff. In fact, however, Langeron used his quartermaster-general, Colonel Paul Neidhardt, in this role and employed Rudzevich as his troubleshooter wherever the going was toughest. He wrote in his memoirs that Rudzevich, unique in his combination of staff training and long combat experience in the Caucasus, was much the ablest general in his Army Corps. For once, Blücher and Gneisenau agreed wholeheartedly with Langeron's opinion. Gneisenau wrote to the Prussian chancellor, Hardenberg, that on 21 August Rudzevich's rearguard risked being cut off by very superior enemy forces. Many generals would have lost their balance and judgement in so dangerous a position but Rudzevich had reacted with intelligence, calm and courage, pushing the French back and getting his men across the river Bober under their noses.[29]

How the Prussian troops, and above all the Landwehr, would cope with mounting a rearguard action against Napoleon was more uncertain. In fact the Prussians fought with courage and discipline in the four-day retreat back from the river Bober to behind the river Katzbach, where Blücher's advance had commenced only eight days before. The Army of Silesia's marches and counter-marches exhausted the troops, however, and in particular the Prussian militia. The 6th Silesian Landwehr Regiment, for example, was 2,000 strong when Blücher's advance began; eight days later it had melted down to just 700 men. Above all, this was due to the speed of the army's advance and subsequent retreat. In addition, it took time for Blücher's staff to get into their stride: the Army of Silesia had after all only come together on the very eve of the campaign. In the retreat from the Bober to the Katzbach columns sometimes crossed or got entangled in baggage trains. Night marches were a particular source of exhaustion to Yorck's corps.

Given the personalities involved, it was inevitable that tempers would explode. After a furious argument with Blücher, Yorck sent in his resignation to Frederick William III, noting that 'it may be that my limited abilities do not enable me to understand the brilliant conceptions by which General Blücher is guided'.[30]

Blücher's worst problems were with Langeron. Though personalities played a part, a more basic issue was their main cause. When the Trachenberg plan was originally devised, of the three allied groupings the only one explicitly urged to caution was the Army of Silesia. This was because at that time it seemed that this army would be only 50,000 strong. By the beginning of the campaign its numbers had actually doubled but Blücher's instructions from the monarchs still urged him to avoid major battles. Blücher promptly responded that, if these were his orders, then the allies needed to find an alternative commander more suited to caution. Barclay and Diebitsch replied, no doubt in the monarchs' name, that of course no one could stop the commander of 100,000 men from seizing whatever opportunities presented themselves. On this assurance Blücher accepted the command.[31]

Langeron was informed of Blücher's initial instructions but not of the manner in which they had been changed by Barclay and Diebitsch. It is possible that this was an oversight amidst the frantic last-minute preparations to move Barclay's force into Bohemia. It is also possible that it was a deliberate ploy by Alexander to use Langeron to check Blücher. There is no doubt that the emperor remained very nervous about where Blücher's aggressive nature would lead. After receiving the news of the Army of Silesia's initial advance to the Bober, for instance, he wrote to Blücher that 'your recent battles which have been so glorious must not lead you to involve yourself in a full-scale engagement'.[32]

Whether deliberate or accidental, the treatment of Langeron was deeply unfair to both him and Blücher. Langeron had some reason to believe that he was acting in accordance with Blücher's instructions and Alexander's own wishes. He also had excellent reason to fear that if Napoleon was allowed just a few more days to pursue Blücher, the latter would stand and fight, whatever the odds. The commander-in-chief might indeed have had no choice in the matter since there was a limit to how much more retreating the Landwehr regiments could take before they disintegrated. In fact Blücher himself wrote to Alexander that if need be he would stand and fight against Napoleon even if seriously outnumbered, providing he could find a strong defensive position where he could deploy his artillery to advantage. Inevitably, Blücher was furious about the many occasions during the first two weeks of the campaign when Langeron disobeyed his orders in the name of caution. By 25 August he and Gneisenau had lost all patience and were determined to get Alexander to remove the Russian general.[33]

Very fortunately for the Army of Silesia, the Trachenberg plan worked as intended. By 23 August it was clear to Napoleon that he could spare no more time chasing Blücher. Schwarzenberg's army was invading Saxony and threatening the key supply base of Dresden. Turning back to confront this danger with the Guards and the corps of Marmont and Victor, Napoleon left Marshal MacDonald to cope with Blücher. Under his command would be Sebastiani's Second Cavalry Corps and the Third, Fifth and Eleventh Infantry corps. Though Napoleon left Third Corps to MacDonald, he ordered its commander, Marshal Ney, to hand over command to General Souham and himself to take control of the army facing Bernadotte in front of Berlin.

Before departing for Dresden Napoleon ordered MacDonald to advance over the river Katzbach and drive Blücher back beyond Jauer. After this his job was to keep the enemy pinned down in eastern Silesia, far away from the crucial theatre of operations in Saxony west of the Elbe. MacDonald ordered his men to advance over the Katzbach on 26 August. Meanwhile Blücher was immediately aware of the departure of Napoleon and much of the enemy army. He therefore ordered the Army of Silesia to resume offensive operations, beginning with an advance over the Katzbach, also planned for 26 August. The scene was set for the crucial battle which took place on that day. Neither commander expected the other to advance. The resulting confusion when the two advancing armies bumped into each other was increased because heavy rain greatly reduced visibility.

MacDonald's army advanced on a wide front. Two of his divisions, under generals Ledru and Puthod, were deployed well to the south near Schönau and Hirschberg. Their job was to tackle the small Russian Eighth Corps commanded by Count Emmanuel de Saint-Priest, another royalist émigré and Petr Bagration's former chief of staff, and threaten Jauer from the south-west. This move would outflank Blücher's army and endanger its communications and its baggage, which was concentrated in and near Jauer. Meanwhile at the other end of MacDonald's line the Third Corps, deployed near Liegnitz, was ordered to cross the Katzbach at that city and then push down the road from Liegnitz to Jauer behind the allied right flank. The remainder of MacDonald's army, made up of his own Eleventh and Lauriston's Fifth Corps was to advance directly over the Katzbach towards Jauer. Having detached Ledru and Puthod, these two corps only amounted to four infantry divisions but they would be supported by Sebastiani's cavalry.

There were dangers in dispersing the French army so widely. Mac-Donald seems to have assumed that Blücher would be static or in retreat. This was a very dangerous assumption when facing so aggressive an enemy. A senior Russian staff officer subsequently wrote that failure to reconnoitre the allied position was the key to the French defeat at the Katzbach. For this not just MacDonald but also the atrocious weather and the poor quality of the French cavalry was to blame.[34]

The terrain over which MacDonald was advancing and on which the battle was fought added to the dangers of poor reconnaissance. Roughly speaking, before the battle the two armies were divided by the river Katzbach, which flows south-westwards from Liegnitz. The French were on the north bank and the allies on the south. MacDonald's troops crossed the river and the battle took place on the south bank between the Katzbach and Jauer. The battlefield was divided into two distinct halves by the river Wütender Neisse, which flows from Jauer and joins the Katzbach at something approaching a right angle.

The northern half of the battlefield – in other words the area north of the Wütender Neisse – was a flat and treeless plateau which falls steeply into the valleys of the Katzbach to the north-west and the Wütender Neisse to the south-west. The plateau is never more than 75 metres above the rivers but its steep and thickly forested slopes makes it impossible for anyone on the French side of the rivers to see what is happening there, even on a clear day. The roads across the Katzbach climbed on to the plateau through steep and narrow defiles, especially the one near Weinberg up which most of the French troops advanced. On a muddy or icy day this lane is troublesome even today in a car. Getting thousands of men, horses and guns up this lane in August 1813 amidst mud and driving rain was much worse. There was also a considerable danger of being surprised by what one might find on the plateau.

On 26 August 1813 the French encountered roughly 60 per cent of Blücher's army on the plateau, in other words the whole of Yorck's and

Sacken's army corps. Sacken was on the right, with his open flank anchored in the village of Eichholz, in which the 8th and 39th Jaegers of Johann von Lieven's division were deployed. Beyond Eichholz to the north were Major-General Kretov's Cossacks. To the left (i.e. south) of the village, Sacken deployed his infantry, with Neverovsky's 27th Division in the front line and the remainder of Lieven's 10th Division behind in reserve. Ilarion Vasilchikov's hussar and dragoon regiments were deployed behind and just to the right of Eichholz. Between Sacken's Army Corps and the Wütender Neisse stood Yorck's Prussians. Langeron's troops were deployed in the southern half of the battlefield, in other words south of the Wütender Neisse. The ground here is very different to the plateau north of the river. It is dominated by two ridges which run from the banks of the Wütender Neisse to the wooded hills which mark the south-western border of the battlefield. These ridges provided commanding views and artillery positions. In addition, the two villages of Hennersdorff and Hermannsdorf could be turned into strong-points for Langeron's infantry.

MacDonald's plans began going wrong from early on 26 August. As a result of misunderstood orders Third Corps had marched away from Liegnitz on the previous day. By the time they got back to the area General Souham decided that it was too late to execute MacDonald's order to cross the Katzbach at Liegnitz and march from there to Jauer. The main reason given by Third Corps for disobeying MacDonald's orders was that the crossings at Liegnitz were no longer usable because of the heavy rain. This sounds dubious, because Sacken's Russians crossed at Liegnitz on 28 August after two days of further continuous rain. Whatever the reason, on 26 August Souham decided to move his corps down the north bank of the Katzbach instead, thereby linking up with MacDonald's main body and supporting their attack across the river.[35]

In principle this concentration of the French army sounds sensible. In practice, however, the narrow roads on the north bank of the Katzbach could not sustain the movement of so many men. Between the villages of Kroitsch and Nieder Crayn a massive traffic jam developed. It included Sebastiani's cavalry, as well as artillery and baggage. Into this jam headed the four divisions of Third Corps. Only one of these divisions, General Brayer's 8th Division, succeeded in pushing its way through this traffic jam and moving onto the plateau across the bridge and up the defile at Weinberg. Even Brayer was forced to leave all his artillery behind. MacDonald ordered the other three divisions of Third Corps to backtrack and seek to cross the river further towards Liegnitz. Two of these divisions ultimately forded the Katzbach near the village of Schmogwitz but by the time they approached the plateau the battle was over. In the end the only French units to play a role in the fight on the plateau were Brayer's men, General Charpentier's 36th Division of MacDonald's corps and Sebastiani's cavalry. Since Brayer's artillery was stuck at Kroitsch on the wrong side of the Katzbach this force did not even have its full complement of guns. As the French were opposed by the entire army corps of both Yorck and Sacken, in other words 60 per cent of Blücher's army, it is not at all surprising that they lost this battle.

Having given his own orders to advance across the Katzbach, Blücher was surprised to be informed at about 11 a.m. on 26 August that the French were also advancing across the river against both Langeron and Yorck. Since the picture provided by the retreating Prussian outposts was very confused, Colonel Baron von Müffling, the quartermaster-general, rode forward on his own to spy out French numbers and where they were headed. Müffling recalled that 'I was mounted on a mouse-coloured horse, and had on a grey cloak, so that in the pouring rain I was not visible at 100 paces'. Müffling discovered French cavalry and artillery deploying on the plateau between Nieder Weinberg and Janowitz, with infantry moving up behind them in the valley near Nieder Weinberg. Informed of this situation, Blücher ordered Yorck to attack the French and Sacken to deploy artillery on the Taubenberg hill just south-west of Eichholz. The Russian artillery would distract French attention north-wards and away from Yorck's advance. They would also support the Prussian infantry as and when they made their attack. Meanwhile Sacken's infantry would hold their position at Eichholz and watch out for possible further French columns coming onto the plateau from their right, north of Janowitz.[36]

At best it would take Yorck's infantry an hour's marching to reach the French. Meanwhile, however, long before Blücher's orders arrived Sacken had posted Colonel Brahms's 13th Russian Heavy Battery on the Taubenberg and had begun to bombard the French. The Taubenberg 'hill' is actually a very slight elevation but it commands the entire plateau north-westwards to the Katzbach and south-westwards to the Wütender Neisse. Having inspected the position allocated to his Army Corps,

Sacken was far too good a general not to have spotted the Taubenberg's advantages and acted immediately on his own initiative. Soon Brahms was joined by other Russian and Prussian batteries.

Meanwhile Yorck and Müffling had got into an argument as to how the Prussian troops were to advance. Yorck wanted them deployed in line, whereas Müffling argued that there was insufficient room for this on the plateau and that the manoeuvre would in any case waste precious time. When Blücher supported Müffling, Yorck sulkily complied and sent two of his brigades forward in column. Inevitably time was lost, but by about 3 p.m. Yorck's men were in action against French infantry on the edge of the plateau near the defile which leads down into the river valley by Ober Weinberg. In the pouring rain few muskets would fire but after a brief hand-to-hand fight the outnumbered French infantry fled down the defile towards the river crossing. At this point some of Sebastiani's cavalry charged the Prussians in order to rescue their infantry and allow them to disengage and re-form. With their muskets useless in the rain Yorck's infantry were very vulnerable to cavalry, and Colonel Jurgas, commanding the Prussian reserve cavalry brigade, tried to come to their rescue. To Yorck's rage, however, the Prussian cavalry's attack was poorly coordinated and failed. According to Müffling, who was with Yorck all this time, there then followed a strange hiatus, lasting perhaps fifteen minutes, in which Yorck's infantry and some 4,000 French cavalry faced each other without either quite daring to attack. Then suddenly, to Müffling's great surprise, the French cavalry turned tail and fled down the defiles into the river valley.

The reason for their flight was that Sebastiani's men had been attacked by Vasilchikov's Russian cavalry. From where Sacken and Vasilchikov stood near Eichholz, the position taken up by Sebastiani and by Brayer's infantry seemed the answer to a cavalryman's prayer. The plateau was perfect ground for cavalry, with no ditches, walls, trees or other obstacles. Moreover, Sebastiani's left flank was hanging in the air, open to attack. It seems that the French cavalry commander was expecting that the missing three divisions of Souham's corps would soon be advancing through Janowitz to his support. Whatever the reason, to offer an open flank to a general of Vasilchikov's calibre was asking for trouble. Vasilchikov sent out scouts to ensure that the villages to the north of Sebastiani's line were not occupied by infantry and that his men would not be ambushed as they advanced. Having discovered that they were empty he advanced and attacked the French from three directions simultaneously.

The Alexandria and Mariupol Hussar regiments attacked the enemy front and were supported by a brigade of dragoons. Meanwhile the Akhtyrka and Belorussia Hussar regiments moved out behind the village of Klein Tinz and charged into Sebastiani's flank. Between Klein Tinz and Janowitz, Vasilchikov's Cossacks stormed into the rear of the French cavalry. The Count de Venançon, a Piedmontese émigré serving as Sacken's quartermaster-general, wrote to Petr Volkonsky that 'I am not exaggerating when I say that never was a manoeuvre executed with more precision and intelligence, and it was crowned with complete success because the entire enemy left flank was taken from the rear and overwhelmed'. Sebastiani's cavalry fled down the defiles to the Katzbach, carrying with them Brayer's infantry and abandoning all the guns that the French had succeeded in getting up to the plateau. According to French accounts, Brayer's infantry retreated in good order and even covered the flight of Sebastiani's cavalry. Disorder only set in when the infantrymen were forced to cross the Katzbach in the growing darkness, under enemy fire and amidst the chaos of roads blocked by carts, guns and cavalry.[37]

It was not until well after the rout of the rest of the French forces that two remaining divisions of Souham's corps began to approach the battlefield from the ford at Schmogwitz. According to Russian accounts, their advance was slow and hesitant. As the French moved southwards from the ford at Schmogwitz towards the village of Schweinitz, they encountered skirmishers sent forward from Neverovsky's 27th Division to slow them down. Skirmishing began at about seven in the evening. The bulk of Neverovsky's and Lieven's divisions then moved forward, supported by many batteries of allied artillery. Outnumbered, and informed of the disaster that had befallen the rest of the army, General Ricard ordered his men to retreat back over the ford at Schmogwitz. With this retreat ended the fighting on the northern half of the battlefield.[38]

Meanwhile a very different battle had been fought on the southern half of the battlefield, south of the Wütender Neisse. Langeron had detached Saint-Priest's Eighth Corps to guard the approach routes to Jauer from Hirschberg and in his absence the rival forces were roughly matched. Langeron had more and better cavalry but faced superior numbers of infantry in the three French divisions deployed against him. Given the terrain, he should nevertheless have been able to hold his ground against the attacks of MacDonald, who led the French forces in person, all other things being equal.

In fact, however, they were anything but equal since Langeron appears to have been staging a fighting retreat rather than a battle. Obsessed with the threat to his left and to Jauer, Langeron put most of his effort into securing his line of retreat. Fearful that Maison's division was seeking to push beyond his left, Langeron dispatched Kaptsevich's Tenth Corps back to Peterwitz to guard the line of retreat to Jauer. This left him with just two small corps, Olsufev's Ninth and Prince Shcherbatov's Sixth, and Rudzevich's detachment to hold off MacDonald. In his memoirs, however, Shcherbatov writes that his corps was held in reserve until late afternoon and played no part in the fighting until after 4 p.m. In addition, almost all Langeron's heavy batteries had been dispatched to the rear in order not to block any retreat down the narrow, muddy roads. Of course, when all these detachments were added together, they gave the French overwhelming superiority on the battlefield in terms of both numbers and firepower. By late afternoon they had pushed Langeron off the heights between Hennersdorf and Schlaupe which commanded the whole southern half of the battlefield. The Russian troops fought hard but had no chance of holding on against such superior numbers.[39]

At this point Müffling arrived from Blücher's headquarters, where the news that Langeron had been driven out of his strong position was greeted with scorn. In his memoirs Müffling recounts that he found Langeron on the hill behind Schlaupe, in company with Rudzevich, Olsufev and Shcherbatov. Müffling told them of the victory north of the Wütender Neisse, sang Sacken's praises and urged them to counter-attack and regain the Hennersdorf Heights immediately. The other Russian generals agreed with enthusiasm but Langeron responded: 'Colonel, are you certain that the commander-in-chief is not deploying my corps to cover his retreat?' Müffling added: 'This was the fixed and firmly rooted idea of Count Langeron, which had misled him into his false measures.' If Langeron had any doubts about the truth of Müffling's message, however, it was dispelled by the evidence of his own eyes. Captain Radozhitsky, whose battery was deployed on the hill, recalled that through the rain it was suddenly possible to see Prussian troops in full pursuit of fleeing French battalions on the other bank of the Wütender Neisse. He heard Langeron, standing not far away, exclaim, 'Good God, they are running.'[40]

All this was enough to persuade Langeron to order an immediate counter-attack to retake the Hennersdorf position. Rudzevich attacked on the left, Olsufev in the centre, and for the first time Shcherbatov's corps came into action on the right. The momentum and unexpectedness of the attack drove the French back off the heights with little serious fighting, according to Russian sources. Thus the Pskov Regiment, part of Shcherbatov's corps, had waited in reserve all day until ordered forward after 4 p.m. for the counter-attack. The regiment advanced at rapid pace in textbook fashion: it attacked in battalion columns with skirmishers out in front and artillery moving forward in the intervals between the columns. According to the regimental history, their skirmishers drove back the French light infantry screen and began to shoot down men in the ranks of the battalions behind. At this point, seeing the Russian columns advancing to storm their position, the French infantry decamped at speed. In good patriotic fashion, the regimental history forgets to mention that Shcherbatov's attack towards Schlaupe was much helped by Prussian troops fording the Wütender Neisse to take the French in the rear. But the official Russian history of the campaign does mention this and pays tribute to the courage of the Prussian troops.[41]

For the French, the battle of the Katzbach was a defeat but not a disaster. What turned defeat into catastrophe was the pursuit which followed the battle. This was by far the most successful pursuit of a defeated enemy in 1813. On 26 August Langeron had, to put things mildly, not distinguished himself. His misunderstanding of Blücher's intentions and disobedience of his orders could have had disastrous consequences. The heroes of the day were Yorck's infantry, Vasilchikov and his cavalry, and Fabian von der Osten-Sacken. During the pursuit, however, it was Langeron's corps which achieved much the most spectacular results. This did not come across in Blücher and Gneisenau's account of the battle. It would, of course, take time for Blücher to forget Langeron's insubordination. Moreover the Prussian leaders had good reason to try to build up the Landwehr's self-respect and morale by glowing accounts of its merits. In a secret report, the Prussian military government of Silesia had no need to go in for propaganda, however.

Rejoicing in the liberation of their province and the destruction of MacDonald's army, their account of the pursuit of the defeated enemy ascribed the catastrophe which had overtaken the French to Langeron alone.[42]

This was to go too far, because Yorck and Sacken did also contribute to the French debacle. On the evening of the battle Blücher ordered both men to cross the Katzbach immediately and hasten the enemy's flight. This was impossible. The allied troops were far too tired, the Katzbach was in full flood, and the night was pitch-black. The next day Yorck did just manage to get across the bridge and fords near Weinberg but immediately ran up against a well-organized French rearguard. There was nothing surprising in this, since three-quarters of Souham's corps had barely been in action the previous day.

Meanwhile Sacken's attempts to get across the fords between Schmog-witz and Liegnitz were thwarted by the flooded river banks and the depth and current of the Katzbach river, which the constant heavy rain had turned into a torrent. The Russians lost a day by having to march all the way to Liegnitz and cross the Katzbach there. All this meant that the French had time to mount a relatively orderly, albeit dangerously rapid, retreat. Many stragglers and baggage were lost but no large units were cut off or destroyed. Nevertheless casualties were high. On 29 August, with the retreat far from over, Third Corps's roll-call revealed that 930 men were dead, 2,722 wounded and 4,009 missing. On 3 September Sacken reported to Petr Volkonsky that his army corps had captured 2 generals, 63 officers, 4,916 men and 50 guns since 25 August. By then the French had retreated right back out of Silesia and over the border into Saxony.[43]

Langeron's men set off in pursuit of the French before dawn on 27 August. Their commander no doubt felt the need to redeem his poor performance on the previous day. Once again Rudzevich commanded the advance guard though he was now strengthened by regiments of Baron Korff's cavalry corps and by the whole of Lieutenant-General Petr Kaptsevich's Tenth Corps. Almost none of Korff's and Kaptsevich's men had fought on 26 August and they were therefore full of beans. By contrast the French troops were exhausted after two weeks of ceaseless marches, pouring rain, little food, and a day's battle in which initial victory had turned suddenly into defeat and an exhausting night-time retreat. The chief of staff of Korff's cavalry corps wrote in his memoirs that 'it is incredible to what extent a lost battle and a few days of very bad weather depressed the morale of the French troops'. This is harsh. Even Wellington's infantry might have gone to pieces if abandoned by their commissariat and cavalry, and forced to mount rearguard actions with muskets unusable because of the rain against a mass of well-disciplined enemy cavalry, supported by horse artillery and thousands of fresh infantry. But it is true that the exceptionally exhausting last few days played to the strengths of the tough Russian soldiers and to the weaknesses of Napoleon's young conscripts. It is also true that although French élan was unmatchable when things were going well, in times of adversity French troops very often lacked the disciplined calm and solidity of the Russian infantry.[44]

On 27 August, when the Russians caught up with the French rear-guards, many of the latter collapsed. Near Pilgramsdorf, the Kharkov and Kiev Dragoon regiments under General Emmanuel rode down part of the French rearguard and captured 1,200 men. Another rearguard under Colonel Morand was overtaken by the Tver Dragoon Regiment and the Seversk and Chernigov mounted jaegers, commanded by Ivan Panchulidzev, a veteran cavalry general of Georgian origin. Morand fought bravely but with their muskets unusable his infantry squares caved in to a simultaneous assault from three sides by the Russian cavalry. With the infantry rearguards collapsing and the French cavalry nowhere to be seen, the floodgates threatened to open. Cossacks swarmed around the retreating French. Langeron reported that 'the level of losses and the disorder in the enemy ranks reminded me of their disastrous flight from Moscow to the Vistula'.[45]

MacDonald and his corps commanders decided that it would be fatal to try to rally their men or oppose the Russians. Their only chance was to outrun them and subsequently find a safe spot to regroup and rebuild the men's shattered morale. This was probably realistic but it guaranteed that huge numbers of stragglers would desert or be scooped up by the Russian cavalry and Cossacks. It also meant abandoning the detached divisions of Ledru and Puthod to their fate. Ledru escaped but Puthod decided to try to link up with MacDonald's fleeing corps. Marching north-westwards from Hirschberg, Puthod was shadowed all the way by Major-General Iusefovich's cavalry. The Russians intercepted Puthod's report to MacDonald which outlined his plans and his line of march. On 29 August they encircled and trapped his division near Löwenberg with its back to the river Bober, which the heavy rain had made imposs-ible to ford. General Rudzevich waited to press his attack until Prince Shcherbatov's Sixth Corps had arrived. Against such overwhelming odds resistance was pointless, and Puthod surrendered with more than 4,000 men and 16 guns. His division had begun the autumn campaign just two weeks before with over 8,000 men in its ranks. Very few of them escaped to serve Napoleon again.[46]

Not until the first week in September did the allied pursuit come to a halt. By then MacDonald's army had been pushed right back into Saxony and had lost 35,000 men even according to French sources. The Army of Silesia had also lost heavily but very many of its missing men were exhausted Prussian militiamen who would in time return to the ranks. This was far less true of the French wounded and missing, who had been overrun by the allied advance. Napoleon could not afford such losses. Nor could he afford to have Blücher established within striking range of Dresden, the Elbe crossings and the other allied armies. The disaster which had befallen MacDonald's army made it very unlikely that the emperor would be able to execute his plan to take his Guards and reserves north to deal with Bernadotte.

Victory hugely raised the morale and confidence of Blücher's army and resolved many of the tensions which had existed among its commanders. Langeron's disobedience was forgiven. Blücher's report to Alexander on the battle of the Katzbach won for Sacken promotion to full general and the Order of St George, second class. The day after the battle Blücher told every Prussian within earshot that victory had been owed in great part to Sacken's handling of his cavalry and artillery. The next time Sacken rode past Yorck's corps he was greeted with volleys of cheers from the Prussian troops. All this was balm for the soul of a man who for many years had seen himself as the victim of injustice and bad luck. The battle of the Katzbach was the turning point in Sacken's fortunes. He would die many years after the war a prince, a field-marshal and one of the most respected figures in Russia.[47]

However great Blücher's victories were, in the end the fate of the cam-paign would rest above all on the performance of the main allied army, in other words Schwarzenberg's Army of Bohemia. It contained many more troops than the armies of Bernadotte and Blücher combined. Only the Army of Bohemia could hope to confront and defeat Napoleon himself. Moreover, only the Army of Bohemia contained a large contingent of Austrian troops. Potentially, Austria remained the weak link in the coalition. If the main army was destroyed or seriously weakened and Bohemia was invaded, then there was a real chance that Austria would renew negotiations with Napoleon or even drop out of the war.

In June and July Schwarzenberg and Radetsky had assumed that if the Austrians joined the war Napoleon would strike first against them into Bohemia. The allies tended to share this view and in any case were anxious to calm Austrian fears in any way possible. From an early stage in joint military consultations, therefore, it was planned to send Wittgenstein and 25,000 men into Bohemia to reinforce the Austrians. As unexpected numbers of reserves and men returning from hospital flowed into the allied regiments plans became more ambitious. When Count Latour, Schwarzenberg's representative, arrived at allied headquarters on 22 July to carry forward joint planning he was surprised to discover that the allies had hugely increased the size of the force they intended to send into Bohemia to assist the Austrians. In addition to the whole of Wittgenstein's Army Corps, they also earmarked Lieutenant-General von Kleist's Prussian Army Corps and the Grand Duke Constantine's Reserve Army Corps, which included the Russian and Prussian Guards, the Russian Grenadier Corps and the three Russian cuirassier divisions. In all, 115,000 Russians and Prussians would now march from Silesia into Bohemia the moment war was renewed.

The Austrians had slightly mixed feelings about this. On the one hand this huge reinforcement, which included the best troops in the allied armies, made a great contribution to the defence of Bohemia. On the other hand enormous last-minute efforts were required to feed all these men. Worst of all, there was no way that Frederick William, let alone Alexander, would resign all control over their elite regiments and what was now unequivocally both the main allied army and the core of the allied war effort. With the Russian and Prussian divisions came the two monarchs, as distinctly unwelcome guests in Schwarzenberg's headquarters.[48]

Under no circumstances was Schwarzenberg a commander who would seize the initative and impose his will on Napoleon. But in August 1813 his only initial option was to await the arrival of the Russo-Prussian reinforcements and take precautions against any attempt by Napoleon to attack them on the march or to invade Bohemia. Radetsky rather hoped that Napoleon would invade. The allies would then have the possibility of catching his troops as they sought to emerge from the narrow defiles of the Erzgebirge rather than the other way round. The Austrian quartermaster-general also had justified fears about how quickly and efficiently the commanders of the various allied columns would coordinate their operations if they were launched on an offensive through the mountains and into Saxony. Even leaving aside problems of terrain and inter-allied cooperation, the Austrian army itself had an over-centralized and unwieldy command structure. In 1809 the Austrians had adopted the French system of separate all-arms corps. The lesson they drew from the war was that their senior generals and staffs could not be relied on to make this system work. Uniquely among the four main armies in 1813, they had therefore in part reverted to a centralized army high command dealing directly with divisions and ad hoc column commanders. Radetsky had good reason to fear that this arrangement would prove defective.[49]

Had he understood the internal arrangements of the Russian forces his pessimism would have increased. The Russians had gone to war in 1812 with a lean and rational command structure of corps, divisions and brigades. By the autumn of 1813, however, there had been many promotions to the ranks of major- and lieutenant-general. There were now, for example, far more lieutenant-generals than there were corps, and Russian lieutenant-generals thought it beneath their status to command mere divisions. The result was the emergence of many corps which in reality were little bigger than the old divisions. These 'corps' were subordinated to the seven larger units into which the Field Army was divided in the autumn campaign. Though these seven units were also confusingly called corps, to avoid bewilderment I call them Army Corps. Two such Army Corps (Grand Duke Constantine and Wittgenstein) were in the Army of Bohemia; two were in the Army of Silesia (Langeron and Sacken); two were in the Army of Poland (Dokhturov and Petr Tolstoy); one was in the Army of the North (Winzengerode). To a great extent the creation of mini-corps was merely a cosmetic concession to generals' vanity, but it did make the Russian command structure top-heavy and it complicated relations with the Prussians. A Russian corps commanded by a lieutenant-general could contain no more men than a Prussian brigade, which on occasion could be commanded by a mere colonel. Since both Russian and Prussian officers were acutely conscious of seniority and status, 'misunderstandings' were inevitable.[50]

A further cause of inefficiency was the position of Mikhail Barclay de Tolly. Having performed excellently during the armistice as commander-in-chief, Barclay now found himself de facto relieved of the supreme command and subordinated to Schwarzenberg. Apparently it took Alexander some days to summon up the courage to tell Barclay about this. To maintain his pride – perhaps indeed to retain his services – Barclay kept his official position as commander-in-chief of the Russian forces. In principle Russian corps in the armies of Silesia and the North were in operational terms subordinated to Bernadotte and Blücher, but in matters of administration and personnel to Barclay. Given the wide dispersal of these forces this was an unworkable arrangement which caused frustration on all sides.

Barclay's power over the Russian and Prussian forces in the Army of Bohemia was more real without being more rational. It would have been more efficient had orders passed directly from Schwarzenberg to the Army Corps commanders (Constantine, Wittgenstein and Kleist), rather than being delayed and distorted by having to go through Barclay. Even Wittgenstein's position was problematic in the first half of the autumn campaign. In principle he commanded Eugen of Württemberg's Second Corps and the First Corps of Prince Andrei Gorchakov, the brother of the minister of war. In practice, however, Eugen's corps was detached from the main body in August 1813 and Wittgenstein only actually controlled Gorchakov's men. As a result, Wittgenstein too was more or less redundant on occasion: in August he and Gorchakov often merely frustrated each other by both trying to do the same job.[51]

By the time the leading allied generals met at the council of war in Melnik on 17 August, there was no sign of any French advance into Bohemia: almost all of them now believed that Napoleon would probably attack Bernadotte and seek to take Berlin. Radetsky and Diebitsch, the two ablest staff officers present, both shared this view. In this case it was impossible for the main army to stand still behind the mountains and leave Bernadotte to his fate. If Napoleon was heading northwards, the allies could safely cross the mountains on a broad front with their main line of advance aiming to move via Leipzig into the enemy's rear. The council therefore decided to invade Saxony the moment the Russian and Prussian reinforcements arrived. Wittgenstein would advance on the right up the Teplitz highway from Peterswalde via Pirna to Dresden.

In the centre, Kleist's Prussians would march from Brux through Saida to Freiberg. Behind them would come Constantine's reserves. Meanwhile the main Austrian body would advance along the highway that led from Kommotau via Marienberg to Chemnitz and ultimately to Leipzig. Smaller Austrian forces would use the roads on either side of the highway, with Klenau's column on the Austrian extreme left.

The allied columns crossed the border into Saxony early in the morning of Saturday, 22 August. Even before they did so, however, intelligence arriving at headquarters was increasingly suggesting that Napoleon had not headed northwards against Bernadotte after all but was on the contrary in eastern Saxony facing Blücher. If true, this suggested that an advance towards Leipzig was pointless and was heading into nothing. Meanwhile Napoleon might destroy Blücher. He might also either march westwards and overwhelm Wittgenstein or use his control over the Elbe crossing at Königstein to strike south-westwards into the allied rear in Bohemia. These worries were not imaginary. Once the allies were deep in the Erzgebirge it would take at least four days to concentrate the whole army on Wittgenstein's flank in the event that he was attacked by Napoleon. Though the allied commanders could not know this, Napoleon had in fact written to his commander in Dresden, Marshal Saint-Cyr, that he cared nothing if the allies marched into western Saxony or cut his communications with France. What concerned him was that they should not seize the Elbe crossings and above all the huge supply base which he had built up for the autumn campaign in Dresden. Moreover Napoleon was indeed contemplating the possibility of striking via Königstein into the allied rear.[52]

If allied arrangements had been sufficiently flexible they would have changed their plans before their advance began and shifted its weight eastwards towards Dresden. Last-minute changes to the movements of this vast army with its very cumbersome command structure were extremely difficult, however. Therefore, as Schwarzenberg informed his wife in the evening of 20 August, 'we want to cross the border on 22 August and then quickly swivel towards the Elbe'. This plan was no problem for the Russians since it did not change the planned line of march of Wittgenstein or the Grand Duke Constantine. Even Kleist's Prussians did not have too far to march to get to the new area of concentration in the area of Dippoldiswalde and Dresden. For the

EUROPE'S FATE IN THE BALANCE

Austrians, however, it was a completely different matter. They had the furthest to go and they would have to move across dreadful mountain paths which snaked up and down over the steep valleys of one stream after another. Already on 23 August General Wilson had encountered Klenau's Austrians 'drenched to the bones; most of them without shoes, many without greatcoats'. Wilson recorded that the morale of Klenau's men, very many of them fresh recruits, seemed good but it was debatable whether it would remain that way with the rain pelting down, stomachs already empty, the Austrian commissariat wagons trailing well in the rear, and the paths dissolving into mud. It took Klenau's men sixteen hours to cross the last 32 kilometres cross-country to the Freiberg area. To reach Dresden they still had the even worse path through the Tharandt forest to negotiate.[53]

The initial allied shift eastwards had far more to do with protecting Wittgenstein and Bohemia than with seizing the opportunity to capture Napoleon's base at Dresden. By 23 August, however, intelligence revealed that Napoleon was in fact in Silesia, even further away to the east than the allies had realized. On the evening of 23 August Schwarzenberg wrote to his wife that allied headquarters would be at Dippoldiswalde by the next day and that the army would attack Dresden on the afternoon of 25 August if sufficient forces could be concentrated there in time. He then went a long way towards guaranteeing that this would not be the case by giving most of the Austrian army a rest-day on 24 August.[54]

The thinking behind this move was that there was less urgency than previously feared because Wittgenstein and Bohemia were not in immediate danger. No doubt too the kindly commander-in-chief listened to the howls of his Austrian generals about the miserable condition of their men. Uncertain in his own mind whether it would be possible to take Dresden on 25 August, Schwarzenberg wavered between describing the planned attack as a *coup de main* or simply a reconnaissance in force. Had Schwarzenberg been Blücher, Dresden would have been attacked on 25 August, even if half the Austrian troops had dropped out from exhaustion along the line of march. From this moment on, the Austrians enjoyed the reputation of being the slowest marchers of all the allied armies. George Cathcart, a British officer and the son of the ambassador to Russia, wrote politely of the 'comparative tardiness of their movements'. Alexandre de Langeron put things more bluntly:

'The Austrians are always late and it is their incurable slowness which constantly leads to their defeat.'[55]

The Austrian official history claims that when the moment planned for the attack came in the afternoon of 25 August not only their own troops but also Kleist's Prussians had not yet arrived. The decision was taken to postpone the attack until the next day. But on 26 August fierce arguments raged among the allied leaders as to whether an assault on Dresden was practicable. Frederick William III was committed to an attack and so, less fervently, was Schwarzenberg if and when sufficient troops had arrived. Alexander was always dubious and by the afternoon of 26 August was opposed to the idea. He drew on the advice of both Moreau and Toll, who thought that any attack would fail.

So too even by 25 August did Dresden's commander, Saint-Cyr. At nine in the morning of 25 August he reported to Napoleon that allied columns were approaching the city and seemingly planned an assault: 'This attack seems to me a bit belated, given Your Majesty's approach.' He added that since Murat had already shown himself in the front lines and the campfires of Napoleon's corps must be visible to the allies they could not be under any illusion about the emperor's imminent arrival. Whether Dresden could have been stormed on 26 August is doubtful. The city's defences had been restored and improved by Napoleon during the armistice: as he himself had discovered in the previous year at Smolensk, even out-of-date walls and improvised fortifications could greatly slow down an attacking force. Moreover, by 26 August Napoleon's reinforcements were already flowing into the city.[56]

Given the speed with which his own troops moved, it is perhaps not surprising that Schwarzenberg was baffled by Napoleon's feat in marching his three corps the 120 kilometres from Löwenberg in Silesia to the Dresden area in just three days. Though this frustrated allied plans to take Dresden, to some extent it fulfilled the purpose of the Trachenberg plan. By advancing into Napoleon's rear and threatening his key base at Dresden the Army of Bohemia had stopped him from pursuing and overwhelming Blücher. In retrospect, too, the allies could be thankful that Napoleon had satisfied himself with marching to the rescue of Dresden rather than carrying out his initial and much more daring plan to destroy Schwarzenberg's army.

When first he heard, on 22 August, that the allied army was concentrating towards Dresden with the likely aim of attacking the city Napoleon began to plan a devastating counter-move. So long as Saint-Cyr could hold out for a few days, Napoleon intended to march with his Guards and the corps of Marmont, Victor and Vandamme across the Elbe at Königstein into the allied rear and either destroy the enemy army before it could concentrate against him or at the least devastate its rear bases. Had Napoleon carried out this plan it is very possible that he could have ended the campaign within a fortnight with a victory on the scale of Austerlitz or Jena. He would have been across the allied line of retreat and able to pin Schwarzenberg's army within the Erzgebirge. Moreover, the speed and daring of his move would have paralysed and totally disoriented the slow-moving and divided allied leadership. When he arrived at Stolpen on 25 August, however, Napoleon changed his mind because both his trusted aide-de-camp, General Gourgaud, and Marshal Murat reported from Dresden that the city could not hold out against the allies unless reinforced immediately by the emperor and the corps he had brought from Silesia. So Napoleon turned his men towards the Saxon capital and left the move across the Elbe at Königstein to General Vandamme alone.[57]

Even without Napoleon's projected master stroke, matters looked grim for the allies by 27 August. They had finally made their attempt to storm Dresden in the late afternoon of 26 August and it had failed. By then Saint-Cyr's garrison had been reinforced by Napoleon. The city's defences proved just as hard to crack as Alexander, Moreau and Toll had feared. The allied leaders nevertheless decided to try again the next day, on the grounds that on 26 August less than half their army had participated in the fight. This decision was not in accordance with the Trachenberg plan, as modified by Schwarzenberg and Radetsky. Much more important, it was foolish. With Napoleon's three corps from Silesia now inside Dresden there was no chance of storming the city. Unless they took Dresden, however, the allies could not remain in front of it for long, since they could not feed themselves off the land in the Erzgebirge and their supply trains were having a terrible time struggling forward down the mountain paths. Even more important, the position they had taken up outside the city made them very vulnerable to a counter-attack by Napoleon.

One key problem was that outside Dresden the allies were strung out along a line of almost 10 kilometres. Safe behind their fortifications, Napoleon's troops occupied a line half as long. The city's walls and fortifications allowed the defenders to hold off attacks made by superior allied numbers. Meanwhile Napoleon could concentrate troops to counter-attack and exploit the weaknesses of his over-extended enemy. On the far right Wittgenstein was trying to hold a weak position, 4 kilometres long, with only 15,000 men. His corps was also under fire from French batteries deployed on the other side of the Elbe. Under heavy pressure on 27 August his troops were pushed back towards the allied centre, losing their hold on the Teplitz highway which was their main chance of a safe retreat to Bohemia. When Barclay was ordered to counter-attack to regain the lost ground he refused, arguing that amidst the mud and the pelting rain he would never be able to get his artillery back onto its present high ground once he had sent it forward to support the counter-attack of his infantry. George Cathcart was present at allied headquarters that day. In his opinion Barclay's fears were fully justified. Even the Austrian official history, often critical of Barclay, states that on this occasion he probably acted wisely.[58]

At the time, however, there was too much confusion at allied head-quarters on the Racknitz Heights for anyone to take up the matter with Barclay. Cathcart recalled that shortly after two o'clock in the afternoon 'a cannon shot struck Moreau (who at the moment might have been half a horse's length in advance of the emperor) in the right leg, and going through his horse, shattered his left knee'. Moreau died a week later. Had the ball hit the emperor the consequences would have been dramatic. The Grand Duke Constantine could never have replaced his brother as the linchpin of the coalition. He totally lacked Alexander's charisma or his diplomatic skills, and shared neither his brother's commitment to defeating Napoleon nor his ability to generate loyalty among senior Russian generals, who in some cases had doubts about whether the war in Germany really served Russian interests. Given Constantine's extreme shifts of mood and his own frequent outbursts against continuing the war, Europe might have witnessed dramatic changes in Russian policy reminiscent of those in the time of his father and grandfather.[59]

Meanwhile disaster had befallen the allied left wing, all of whose troops were Austrian. One problem here was that the allied left was cut off from the rest of the army by the steep Plauen gully. It was impossible to reinforce troops beyond the gully from the allied centre in any emergency. General Mesko, who commanded the Austrian troops on the far left, was supposed to be supported by Klenau's 21,000 men but the latter were so delayed on the road through the Tharandt forest that they never reached the battlefield. To an extent Schwarzenberg was the victim of the fact that his army had grown to a size which was impossible to control with the technology available at the time. By the time news reached the commander-in-chief from the army's wings it was far too late to react.

Nevertheless Schwarzenberg managed a difficult problem incompetently. It made no sense to mass so much of the allied cavalry in the centre, where much of it was unusable, and to leave Mesko's infantry with so little protection. Moreover, for all the difficulties of getting down the road through the Tharandt forest, one suspects that a Blücher, with the smell of impending battle in his nose, would have done more to galvanize his subordinates into overcoming obstacles. He certainly would not have followed Schwarzenberg's example in initially allowing Klenau's men a rest-day on 26 August as they passed through the forest. The next day, with Klenau's troops still just emerging from the forest and hours from the battlefield, Mesko's detachment was destroyed. On 27 August the French took 15,000 Austrian prisoners. Not only were Mesko's unfortunate men set on by overwhelming numbers of French cavalry and infantry, their muskets were unusable in the rain. Even so, more of them would have escaped if they had had better leadership from their general and their staff officers.[60]

On the afternoon of 27 August, even before he heard of the disaster which had befallen Mesko, Schwarzenberg was determined to retreat back into Bohemia. The allied attacks on the right and in the centre had failed and it was clear that it would be impossible now to capture Dresden. In that case it was pointless to expose the troops to hunger, cold and sickness by remaining outside the city in bivouacs, while Napoleon's men were often quartered cosily inside Dresden. The weather was atrocious. Sir Robert Wilson noted in his diary: 'Heavy rain and fierce wind. The worst English December day was never more bleak or soaking.' In addition, however, alarming news was coming in that Vandamme had crossed the Elbe at Königstein and now posed a threat to the allied right flank and to Schwarzenberg's communications with Bohemia.[61]

When Wittgenstein had marched up the Teplitz highway to Dresden he had detached Eugen of Württemberg to watch the crossing at Königstein. Eugen was given most of his own Second Corps and Major-General Gothard von Helfreich's 14th Division from First Corps. In all, this added up to 13,000 men and 26 guns. Eugen had only four squadrons of regular cavalry and one small Cossack regiment, but his command included almost half of Wittgenstein's infantry. Nevertheless it was far too weak for the task Eugen now faced. Vandamme's force included not just his own First Corps of three strong divisions but also three big infantry brigades and a cavalry division drawn from other corps. At roughly six in the morning of 26 August Eugen's pickets informed him that the French were beginning to cross the Elbe at Königstein and that the prisoners they had taken stated that Vandamme had roughly 50,000 men in his command.

Eugen appealed urgently to Barclay and Wittgenstein for help but this would inevitably take time to arrive. For the moment the only reinforcement he received was the temporary loan of one cuirassier regiment from the Grand Duke Constantine, whose Army Corps was marching up the Teplitz highway on the morning of 26 August in order to join in the assault on Dresden. With the Empress's Own Cuirassier Regiment came the commander of its brigade, the 23-year-old Prince Leopold of Saxe-Coburg. One of Leopold's sisters had married Grand Duke Constantine, another was the wife of Duke Alexander of Württemberg, Eugen's uncle, who was currently commanding the Russian corps besieging Danzig. Like Eugen, Leopold had been made a Russian major-general while still a child. Though he had served in East Prussia in 1807, Leopold had subsequently retired from military service and only rejoined the army during the 1813 armistice. In the following weeks the young prince was to show that he was an able and courageous commander of cavalry and thereby to take his first small steps towards fame. Many years after the war he was to become famous throughout Europe as the first king of the Belgians and, incidentally, Queen Victoria's uncle.

On the morning of 26 August, faced with a very dangerous situation, Prince Eugen remained calm and showed excellent skill and judgement. Given Vandamme's overwhelming superiority in numbers, all Eugen could hope to do was to delay his advance and gain time for reinforcements to arrive. He decided that his only chance of doing this was to stop the French from deploying out of the woods surrounding Königstein for as long as possible. A number of factors worked to his advantage. Vandamme moved slowly and failed to get his artillery into action until the battle was well under way. The Russian artillery was thereby able to break up the initial French efforts to form up in attack columns in front of the woods. In addition, even when the French did force their way forward from the woods Eugen occupied a strong position, protected in front by a gully and anchored in the villages of Krietzschwitz and Struppen. The Russians fought with skill and courage, skirmishing effectively. They suffered more than 1,500 casualties and inflicted more. Every reserve had to be committed, including even Leopold's cuirassiers, despite the fact that this was very poor ground for heavy cavalry. Eugen just hung on but it was clear that he would have no chance of holding his position the next day against overwhelming numbers whose commanders could smother the Russians with artillery fire and turn their flanks.[62]

On the evening of 26 August, having delayed the French for a day, Eugen knew that he must retreat. The question was in which direction. He could not simultaneously cover the right flank of the allied army before Dresden and the allied line of retreat down the highway to Bohemia. To do the former required a retreat to the north, while protecting the route into Bohemia meant moving southwards down the Teplitz highway. With the battle at Dresden in full swing and the allies aiming to storm the city Eugen decided that the top priority was to stop Vandamme marching northwards to roll up their right flank. This was a fully reasonable choice at the time it was made and with the information available to Eugen, but when Schwarzenberg decided on a general retreat the next day it meant that Vandamme was in a position to block the movement of Eugen or any other allied forces down the Teplitz highway back to Bohemia.

Schwarzenberg's orders for the retreat to Bohemia went out at six in the evening of 27 August. They were drawn up by Radetsky and Toll. The army was to retreat in three groups. Roughly half the Austrian troops, including Klenau's detachment and the remnants of the left wing, were to march almost due west to Freiberg and from there to turn south-west and rejoin the Chemnitz highway at Marienberg. This would take them back to Commotau. The rest of the Austrian forces, including Colloredo's men, were to retreat to Dippoldiswalde. From there half would march via Frauenstein and the other half via Altenberg back to Dux in Bohemia. Meanwhile all the Russians and Prussians under Barclay and Kleist – in other words half the entire army – would retreat south-eastwards via Dohna on to the Teplitz highway before the defile at Berggieshubel. From there they would retreat down the highway to Teplitz via Peterswalde.[63]

These orders were 'modified' by some of the generals to whom they were sent. In part this was because they were unrealistic and had been overtaken by events. Of the three groups, the only one to march more or less according to plan was the central Austrian column, which set off quickly in the early evening of 27 August and got away, exhausted but unscathed, to Dippoldiswalde. On the allied left, however, it was impossible for Klenau's men to follow the planned retreat westwards via Freiberg since the Freiberg road was already occupied by Murat. The Austrian commanders also flatly refused to take the next parallel road to the south since this led through the Tharandt forest and had caused them dreadful difficulties in their advance to Dresden. They therefore struck out to the south-west via Pretschendorf. From there some of the Austrian troops marched to Dux while others rejoined the Chemnitz highway at Marienberg and there turned left to march back to Commotau. Though the initial stages of this retreat were exhausting, dangerous and chaotic, by the night of 28 August the Austrian troops were no longer in danger of being cut off. They had been helped greatly by Murat's rather lackadaisical pursuit. Most of Murat's cavalry in any case headed too far to the west and lost touch with the main Austrian body.

By far the most dangerous situation occurred on the allied right wing, where Barclay and Kleist decided to ignore the proposed march-route for the Russian and Prussian forces. As overall commander of the allied right wing Barclay took responsibility for this decision though he may well have acted in agreement with Toll.[64] Instead of moving south-eastwards onto the Teplitz highway the Russians and Prussians headed due south over the Erzgebirge. Barclay had good reasons for this deviation from Schwarzenberg's orders. Prince Eugen's reports showed that Vandamme and 50,000 men were in a position to block any march down the Teplitz highway into Bohemia. The highway passed through defiles which could be held by half that number of men against a multitude. Meanwhile there was every reason to believe that if Barclay and Kleist headed down the Teplitz highway they would be pursued by much of Napoleon's army. A great danger existed that Barclay and Kleist's men would be trapped on the Teplitz highway between Napoleon and Vandamme with no possible means of escape.

Barclay therefore preferred the risk of retreating across the Erzgebirge. The Russians marched down the road to Dippoldiswalde and Altenberg. The Prussians made their way down the 'Old Teplitz Road' which went from Maxen via Glashütte and Barenstein before descending into the Teplitz valley through the defile near Graupen. Both roads were unsuitable for tens of thousands of troops, not to mention their baggage and artillery. The Old Teplitz Road was the worse of the two, especially in its final stage as it descended into the valley. On the other hand, Kleist had half as many men as Barclay's Russians and at least he had the Old Teplitz Road more or less to himself. The Russians on the contrary were trying to force their way down the Dippoldiswalde–Altenberg road in the wake of a large column of retreating Austrians. Even worse, when the retreat began a good deal of the Austrian baggage had still been trying to force its way up the road towards Dresden. A huge traffic jam was inevitable, especially near Altenberg and Dippoldiswalde where a number of country lanes joined the main road.

Marshal Saint-Cyr described the Dippoldiswalde–Altenberg road as 'nothing other than one continual defile'. General Wilson wrote that the retreating Russian troops had to squeeze 'through the most difficult roads, through the most desperate country, through the most impracticable woods that Europe presents'. The road only became truly steep in its last section as it wound down into the Teplitz valley. At that point the horses drawing the guns and wagons had a terrible time braking and many lost their horseshoes. For most of the journey the road wound up and down the hills through which it passed from leaving Dippoldiswalde to beyond Altenberg. The worst problem was that the road was extremely narrow along its entire route. Only one gun, cart or artillery caisson could pass at a time. The embankments on either side of the road were anything from 4 to 6 metres high. The dense pine forests came right down to the embankments on either side of the road. Infantry who marched off the road to leave room for guns and wagons could only pass in single file along the tops of the embankments. Any cart which broke down, and many did on the flinty surface, had to be lifted off the road and over the embankment by hand.[65]

On 28 August the rain poured down incessantly on the Russian troops, all of whom were cold and hungry and some of whom had their boots sucked off in the mud. Among the latter was Private Pamfil Nazarov, on his first campaign and marching in the ranks of the Finland Guards.

His regiment had begun to retreat late in the evening of 27 August and had marched through the night. At eight the next morning they stopped to cook their porridge but before it was ready the French arrived and they were forced to decamp. At one point during the day the exhausted, barefoot Guardsmen emerged from the forests into an open field and passed by Alexander and Barclay. Pamfil recalls that, on seeing the sad state of his Guards, 'the emperor began to cry bitterly and, taking a white handkerchief out of his pocket, began to wipe his cheeks. Seeing this, I also began to cry.'[66]

Fortunately for the Russians their rearguards performed with their usual calm discipline in adversity. So too did the Prussian and Austrian troops detailed to perform this duty. The terrain on the whole favoured rearguards and impeded rapid pursuit by cavalry. Having performed brilliantly in marching from Silesia and defeating the allies, the French troops and their commanders had every right to be exhausted. Perhaps the most important point, however, was that Napoleon had taken his eye off the pursuit and retired to Dresden, where most of his attention was directed to the bad news coming not just from MacDonald in Silesia but also from Marshal Oudinot, whose advance on Berlin had been defeated at Gross Beeren. The emperor appears to have been unaware of his opportunity to destroy Schwarzenberg's army. Perhaps this stemmed partly from the fact that he did not know the terrain of the Erzgebirge well, and in particular had no knowledge of the defiles on the Austrian side of the border. In the absence of Napoleon much of the energy and coordination went out of the pursuit.

For the allies the biggest danger was not the forces pursuing them from Dresden but Vandamme's detachment. When the retreat began on 27 August not merely did Vandamme's force greatly outnumber Eugen's but he was also positioned to its south. He could have shouldered Eugen aside and marched unopposed down the highway past Peterswalde and into the Teplitz valley, reaching the defiles leading from the Erzgebirge well before most of the Russian and Prussian units could escape from the mountains. It did not require many troops to block the key defiles at Teplitz and Graupen towards which Barclay and Kleist were heading. Had this been combined by an energetic and coordinated pursuit by Napoleon then the allied army could have been cut off in the mountains and forced to surrender. In fact Napoleon settled for a lesser goal, ordering Vandamme merely to march into the Teplitz valley and seize the enormous amount of baggage and artillery which would not be able to escape. Once in the Teplitz valley Vandamme might have used his initiative, blocked the defiles and astonished Napoleon by the extent of the damage he inflicted on the allied armies. Even had he confined himself to obeying Napoleon's orders, the loss of their artillery and supply trains would have been a crippling blow to the allies. Rebuilding the Army of Bohemia in time to renew the campaign in the autumn of 1813 would have been very difficult. Dissension between the allies, already growing fast because of the defeat at Dresden, could easily have destroyed the coalition.[67]

Much therefore turned on the struggle between Vandamme and Prince Eugen on the Teplitz highway. On 26 and 27 August Eugen received two reinforcements, one welcome, the other quite the opposite. The welcome reinforcements were the 6,700 men of Major-General Baron Gregor von Rosen's 1st Guards Infantry Division. The Preobrazhensky, Semenovsky, Izmailovsky and Jaeger regiments of the Guards, which made up this division, were the finest infantry in the Russian army, so this addition to Eugen's force was much more valuable than mere numbers might suggest. They were accompanied by a small detachment of Guards marines, mostly used for building bridges, and by Aleksei Ermolov, now the commander of the Guards Corps.

The unwelcome reinforcement was General Count Aleksandr Ostermann-Tolstoy, who arrived from headquarters on 26 August with instructions to take over command of all the forces on the allied right near Königstein. There might perhaps be some excuse for appointing a senior general to fulfil this role. Eugen was only 25 and had never commanded an independent detachment. Ostermann-Tolstoy was the wrong man for the job, however. It seems that Alexander was simply trying to rid himself of a nuisance who was infesting his headquarters and constantly waylaying the emperor with pleas to be given something to do. When on 25 August Alexander told Ostermann to take overall command opposite Königstein he had no idea that this was soon to become a vital post. Nevertheless Alexander's assignment of Ostermann was yet another example of how sensitivity to the feelings of senior generals was allowed to undermine the army's structure of command.

Even at the best of times Ostermann lacked the temperament or the tactical skill to command an independent detachment. Unfortunately too, August 1813 was far from the best of times, for it was no secret that Ostermann-Tolstoy had returned from sick leave in spring 1813 in an extremely excitable and even unbalanced frame of mind. In the three days that followed his arrival at Eugen's headquarters he was to be an enormous nuisance. The immediate source of Ostermann's hysteria was his fear that Alexander's precious Guards might come to grief while under his command.[68]

What made this obsession particularly dangerous was the orders Ostermann received when the army began its retreat in the evening of 27 August. These orders allowed him to abandon the Teplitz highway and retreat over the Erzgebirge if he believed that attempting to march down the highway would be too dangerous. Inevitably the very nervous Ostermann did believe this and ordered the entire force to retreat off the highway and into the mountains. Had this order been carried out disaster must have followed. His men would have been added to the traffic jam on the Dippoldiswalde road. Vandamme would have been free to march unopposed into the Teplitz valley. What saved the allied cause was Eugen's flat refusal to obey Ostermann's orders. Eugen had a very clear understanding of the need to stop Vandamme from getting into the valley and blocking the allied army's escape routes from the Erzgebirge. He was backed by Ermolov, who had an excellent map of the area and had studied the local terrain and grasped its implications for military operations. The decisive voice was Eugen's, however. As a royal prince and the emperor's first cousin he was not easily overruled. When Eugen offered to take full responsibility for all the consequences, Ostermann caved in and plans were made to retreat down the Teplitz highway on 28 August.[69]

This was a difficult and dangerous undertaking. Fortunately for the allies, Vandamme had done nothing to block the road on 27 August. This enabled the Russians to get much of their baggage away safely back to Bohemia. Nevertheless, most of his force was positioned south of the allied position at Zehista. He could still occupy the highway ahead of them on 28 August. To reach semi-safety at Peterswalde, just over the Austrian border, the allies had to carry out an 18-kilometre flank march under the noses of an enemy who had double their numbers. The risk of being attacked while on the march was great. The highway itself was much better than the roads over the Erzgebirge but it was far from perfect. The allies would have to pull their guns and their ammunition carts up and down 15-degree gradients in the pouring rain and on a stony road covered in fallen pine-needles and leaves, which at times were as slippery as ice. The biggest danger of all would come at the narrow defiles near Giesshübel and Hennersdorf, which could be blocked by relatively small enemy forces, but the whole march would be full of peril.[70]

Eugen decided that the allies' best chance was for his Second Corps and Helfreich's division to make a diversionary attack towards Krieschwitz and the Kohlberg heights, in other words in the direction of Königstein. He hoped that this would draw Vandamme's attention and his reserves northwards and allow the Guards to retreat safely through the Giesshübel and Hennersdorf defiles. The Guards would leave rearguards at both these danger-spots to cover the retreat of Eugen's men and, if necessary, to extract them from the clutches of the pursuing French. The plan went better than anyone had a right to expect. Eugen himself led the attack on Krieschwitz, while Ermolov attacked the Kohlberg heights with a force that included some of Eugen's regiments of the line and the Guards Jaegers. The Russians attacked with great determination. The Kohlberg heights, for example, changed hands three times before finally being stormed by the Guards Jaegers. Helfreich's 14th Division first lost and then recaptured Cotta. The French threw in reserves in the north but they did nothing to reinforce the small detachments they had sent to ambush the Russians at the Giesshübel and Hennersdorf defiles. The Preobrazhenskys broke through without too much difficulty at Giesshübel and the Semenovskys drove Vandamme's men off the road at Hennersdorf.

Disengaging Second Corps and Helfreich's men from the battle in the north and getting them down the highway was bound to be very difficult, but in the main the Russians succeeded even here, though at quite heavy cost. The Estland Regiment, part of Helfreich's division, lost 6 officers and 260 men, in other words one-third of its entire strength, in the battles on the Kohlberg and at the Giesshübel defile. Helfreich got his men back through Giesshübel safely but it took a counter-attack led by Eugen himself to disentangle one of Prince Shakhovskoy's brigades from the pursuing French. Four of Eugen's infantry regiments, commanded by Major-General Pyshnitsky, had been heavily engaged at Krieschwitz at the northern end of Eugen's line and were in fact cut off on the highway but they succeeded in taking to a side lane, evaded the French, and rejoined Second Corps on the evening of 29 August, in time for the second day of the battle of Kulm.[71]

By the evening of 28 August the whole of Eugen and Ermolov's force, with the exception of Pyshnitsky's regiments, had reached Peterswalde. This was an enormous village strung out for 3 or more kilometres along the main road. Eugen's men held the village and formed the army's rearguard while the Guards marched back into the Teplitz valley and took up a holding position at Nollendorf, on which Eugen's men could retreat in safety the next day. This plan was almost wrecked early in the morning of 29 August. Orders from Ostermann-Tolstoy seem to have persuaded Prince Shakhovskoy's rearguard to hang on in front of Peterswalde much longer than Eugen intended. When they finally did begin to retreat through the village at dawn on 29 August they were caught by French units attacking not just along the highway but also infiltrating into Peterswalde down side lanes. Amidst the dense early morning mist a panic ensued in the village streets among some of Shakhovskoy's regiments. Fortunately, enough Russian infantrymen remained steady to put up a fight in Peterswalde and delay the French pursuit. When the numerous but disorganized French units did begin to advance out of Peterswalde towards the Teplitz valley they were charged by Eugen's cavalry, headed by Leopold of Saxe-Coburg's cuirassiers. This bought Eugen sufficient time to restore order, reorganize a rearguard, and set off on a steady retreat to Nollendorf and the cover provided by the Guards.[72]

At Nollendorf Eugen found not just two regiments of Guards but also four regiments of Shakhovskoy's division which had got out of Peterswalde by side roads and made their own way back to allied lines. In his memoirs Eugen wrote that the Guards Jaegers skirmished very skilfully and held up the French pursuit long enough for him to take up position, reorganize his corps and send the two Guards regiments and most of his own units back to Ermolov. Eugen then stood at Nollendorf for roughly ninety minutes with two of Shakhovskoy's regiments and the Tatar Lancers as a rearguard. He himself then retreated past the small town of Kulm which gave its name to the two-day battle that followed. By midday Eugen and his rearguard had reached Ermolov's position at the village of Priesten, 2 kilometres beyond Kulm. Here he found Ostermann-Tolstoy, Ermolov and the entire force deployed for a major battle against Vandamme.[73]

Ostermann-Tolstoy had not initially intended to make a stand. Late in the evening of 28 August he had written warning Francis II to leave Teplitz since the enemy was heading in that direction in very superior numbers and Ostermann was unable to stop him. The Austrian monarch decamped but before doing so he warned Frederick William, who had just arrived in the town, about Ostermann's message. The Prussian king immediately understood the potentially catastrophic consequences if Vandamme was allowed to take control of the crucial passes out of the Erzgebirge near Teplitz, towards which both his own forces and the Russians were heading. Even Alexander himself was at risk, since he was still stuck in the mountains somewhere on the road from Altenberg. The king immediately sent first his aide-de-camp, Colonel von Natzmer, and then his chief military adviser, General von dem Knesebeck, to warn Ostermann that he must block the French advance on Teplitz at all costs. With their own emperor's safety at stake, there could be no question of refusing Frederick William's plea to make a stand. Ostermann and Ermolov therefore chose the next possible defensive position at Priesten, roughly 7 kilometres from Teplitz. The Guards were already deploying in this position by eight o'clock. Roughly two hours later Frederick William arrived for a long discussion with Ostermann and Ermolov. By then the sun was out and the Russian troops were enjoying their first clear, warm day for a week.

The Russian position was anchored in three villages: Straden in the north, Priesten in the centre, and Karwitz in the south. Had these been Saxon villages, with their stone farmhouses and churches, their massive barns and their stout boundary walls, the three villages would have been of great assistance to their defenders. In Bohemia at that time, however, almost all buildings were of wood with thatch or shingle roofs. Far from offering shelter to defenders the buildings burned quickly and could easily become death traps. The Eggenmühle, a sawmill behind the Russian left, and a nearby chapel – the so-called Leather Chapel – were the only buildings of even marginal use to the defenders. Even the sawmill burned down in the course of the battle, however, killing the wounded who had taken shelter there.

As to the ground on which Ostermann had more or less been forced to fight, it too was not of great use. Its main advantage was that the Russian left flank was firmly anchored in the steep foothills of the Erzgebirge and could not easily be turned. On the Russian right, the meadow stretching southwards from Priesten to Karwitz was bordered to the east by a stream, which helped the Russian cavalry keep the French at bay. But all the serious fighting on 29 August was confined to the centre and north of the Russian line, which stretched from Priesten to Straden. This was open ground, dotted with bushes, shrubbery, and the ditches which were the normal boundary-markers between the villagers' small gardens. The Teplitz highway, which ran just south of Priesten, was slightly raised above the surrounding land and offered some cover from French artillery to the east for men in or just behind the village.[74]

On the far left of the allied line, Straden was held by the Guards Jaegers and the Murom Regiment. In the centre Priesten was occupied by the skirmishers of the Reval regiment and the 4th Jaegers, with the rest of both regiments just behind the village in support. Eugen expected these men to delay a French attack, not to defeat it. They were ordered to fall back to the right and left of the village. French infantry advancing out of Priesten would face the fire of two of Eugen's batteries deployed a few hundred metres behind the village. Just behind the batteries were Shakhovskoy's infantry. To his left were Helfreich's battalions. The former were low on ammunition, the latter had almost none left. To a great extent they would be forced to rely on their bayonets.

On Helfreich's left were the three Guards regiments, the Semenovskys and Izmailovskys in the first line, with the Preobrazhenskys behind and the two Guards artillery batteries deployed just in front of the columns of infantry. Initially the only cavalry on the Russian centre and left were the Guards Hussars, which Ermolov placed behind his infantry. When the battle began the Russians had only parts of four regular cavalry and one Cossack regiment to hold their right flank between Priesten and Karwitz, but this was not to matter since the French cavalry made little serious effort to challenge them and Vandamme concentrated all his infantry on Straden and Priesten with the aim of breaking through by the quickest route to Teplitz. Astride the highway were Lieutenant-Colonel Bistrom's twelve guns of the First Guards Horse Artillery Battery. When the battle began the Russians had roughly 14,700 men to hand.

Vandamme underestimated his enemy. He was an arrogant man and he was also in a hurry. The prospect of a marshal's baton had been dangled in front of him if his advance into Bohemia succeeded. On the previous evening he had reported to Marshal Berthier that 'the enemy has fought in vain against our brave troops: he has been defeated on all occasions and is in a state of complete rout'. The moment his advance guard, the brigade of Prince Reuss, was ready Vandamme ordered it to attack the Russian left at Straden. The Guards Jaegers and the Murom Regiment resisted stoutly and when the Semenovskys came up in support Reuss's men were forced to withdraw. The attack was swiftly renewed, however, when three regiments of Mouton-Duvernet's division arrived on the scene and advanced towards the space between Straden and Priesten. Helfreich's battalions moved up to meet them, supported by the Tobolsk and Chernigov regiments from Shakhovskoy's division. Still further pressure built up after two o'clock when four regiments of General Philippon's division arrived on the battlefield. One headed for Straden and the other three attacked Priesten.

Straden, by now in flames, was abandoned by the Russians, who fell back on the sawmill (Eggenmühle) and the 'Leather Chapel'. Around these two points a ferocious hand-to-hand battle developed. Ermolov sent in two battalions of the Preobrazhenskys to support the Semenovskys, who were fighting there alongside Helfreich's and Shakhovskoy's men. Meanwhile Philippon's regiments burst into Priesten but were met by murderous canister fire when they tried to break out of the village. When Philippon's men retreated Eugen brought forward two of his batteries to the left of Priesten and directed their fire into the flank and the rear of the French troops who were fighting near the chapel and the sawmill. This forced a further French assault on the village in order to silence the batteries.

Eugen's exhausted battalions were all now committed and he appealed to Ermolov to release the Izmailovsky Guards to drive the French back. Ermolov refused and a ferocious argument ensued. According to Eugen's aide-de-camp, Ermolov shouted, 'the Prince is a German and doesn't give a damn whether the Russian Guards survive or not: but my duty is to save at least something of his Guard for the emperor'. In this moment some of the underlying strains in the Russian high command came out, but Ermolov's refusal was by no means just xenophobic and irrational: the Izmailovskys comprised two of the only three battalions he still held in reserve. Eugen appealed to Ostermann-Tolstoy, however, and the Izmailovskys were released. The two battalions stormed forward and drove back the French but themselves suffered very heavy casualties.[75]

The Prussian general staff history cannot be suspected of bias since there were no Prussian troops present on 29 August. It comments that the fighting at Priesten was among the most ferocious in the entire Napoleonic wars. Sir Robert Wilson, present on the battlefield that day, wrote that 'the enemy could not gain an inch of ground . . . Never was an action more gloriously fought by the Russians – never was success more important.' Charles Stewart, also at the battle of Kulm, wrote subsequently of the 'reckless bravery' and 'dauntless conduct of His Imperial Majesty's Guards'. Shortly after the counter-attack of the Izmailovskys, Ostermann-Tolstoy was hit by a cannon ball which tore off part of his arm. Carried to the rear, he told the stretcher party, 'I am satisfied. This is the price I paid for the honour of commanding the Guards.'[76]

Not long after that the second brigade of Philippon's division arrived on the battlefield and a final attempt was made to storm Priesten. Both Philippon's brigades attacked the village in two big columns. The Russian batteries left of Priesten were forced to withdraw and the village was overrun. By now the Russians only had two companies of the Preobrazhenskys in reserve and matters looked desperate. The two companies counter-attacked and were joined by some of Shakhovskoy's battalions, though the latter were exhausted by days of continuous fighting and had almost no ammunition left. Salvation came, however, from the Guards cavalry. During the battle the Guards Dragoons and the Guards Lancers had arrived from the defile at Graupen and had been deployed behind the Guards infantry. At the moment of crisis Diebitsch also arrived from Barclay to announce that large numbers of fresh infantry would shortly reach the battlefield. After a brief discussion with Eugen he rode over to the Guards Dragoons and led them forward against the French infantry who were surging forward around Priesten.

Nikolai Kovalsky was a young officer of the Guards Dragoons in 1813. He recalls how the regiment was led down narrow and sometimes precipitous paths from the mountains into the Teplitz valley by staff officers and by two local shepherds who acted as guides. Apparently, when Diebitsch rode up to the Guards Dragoons and initially ordered them to charge no one moved because no one knew who he was. Only when he opened his coat and displayed his orders and medals did he get a response. First one dragoon, then more and finally the whole regiment moved forward. Ermolov tried to stop this disorderly attack which he had not authorized but it was too late. Kovalsky records that the French cavalry panicked and fled at their approach and the infantry did the same after just one volley. The weak French response undoubtedly owed much to the fact that while the Guards Dragoons were threatening their front the Guards Lancers were driving deep into their right flank and their rear. Almost certainly it was the Lancers who did the most serious fighting because while the Dragoons' losses were relatively modest, the Lancers lost one-third of their officers and men during the battle.[77]

Nevertheless the Guards cavalry's attack was a triumphant success. By their own estimate, French losses were very heavy and Philippon's attack was shattered. Sir Robert Wilson wrote that 'the lancers and dragoons of the guard charged through garden-ground and ravines upon the right column, which threw down its arms and fled with the most rapid haste, but many hundreds were killed and several hundred made prisoners. The other column retired with more order but not less speed.' Though on a smaller scale, the episode reminds one of the attack of the British heavy cavalry on d'Erlon's infantry in the first stage of the battle of Waterloo. On that occasion, too, French infantry advancing in column and convinced that victory was in their grasp were hit unexpectedly by a mass of enemy cavalry. The Russian cavalry were much more disciplined than their British equivalents, however. With Gobrecht's cavalry brigade deployed in the rear of the French columns they needed to be. The Russian counter-attack was not followed, in British style, by a mad pursuit into the arms of the enemy's reserves. The order of the day of the commanding general of the Guards cavalry praised not just the courage and timing of the attack but also the 'perfect obedience and attention to words of command and trumpet calls' shown by the troops, and the fact that they remained 'always ready to resume excellent formation to confront and defeat the enemy'.[78]

The rout of Philippon's division ended the day's fighting. For the Russians it had been a day of genuine glory. Roughly 14,700 Russian soldiers had kept some 30,000 French troops at bay. But glory had been very costly. No fewer than 6,000 Russians were dead or wounded. Until the very last stage of the battle all the fighting had been done by the infantry: of these 12,000 men, 5,200 were casualties, 2,800 of whom were Guardsmen and the rest from Eugen's regiments. Among the wounded was Aleksandr Chicherin. Fixing a handkerchief to the tip of his sword so that his men could see him, Chicherin was hit in the shoulder blade while trying to lead forward his platoon of the Semenovskys. The doctors were unable to remove the bullet and he died in agony some weeks later in the Russian military hospital in Prague. On his deathbed he persuaded a rich relative to give 500 rubles to help soldiers of his regiment who had been wounded during the battle at Kulm.[79]

That evening the allied leaders in Teplitz decided to counter-attack the next day in order to drive Vandamme further from the defiles out of the Erzgebirge before he was reinforced by Napoleon, as all the allied generals expected him to be. The mood in Teplitz was anything but triumphant. The Dresden campaign had been a disaster and had cost huge numbers of men, especially in the Austrian regiments. Now Alexander's Guards had also suffered terribly. During the battle for Dresden leadership and coordination in the allied high command had been woeful. Tensions were now running high between the Russians and Prussians on the one hand and the Austrians on the other. The Austrians were accused of having marched slowly, which was true, and fought badly, which was mostly unfair. But it was the case that the new recruits from Bohemia who filled up the ranks of Mesko and Klenau's regiments were poorly clothed and trained, and had not been ready for the rigours of the campaign. On the other hand Schwarzenberg approached Francis II requesting permission to resign, justifiably exhausted and indignant at frequent Russo-Prussian disobedience to his orders. Meanwhile large numbers of Russian and Prussian troops were still stuck in the Erzgebirge and needed to be extracted and given time to recover.

One of the largest of these contingents was Lieutenant-General von Kleist's Prussian Army Corps, which had retreated from Dresden mostly down the Old Teplitz Road through Glashütte and Fürstenwalde. Although Saint-Cyr was supposedly pursuing the Prussians, in fact he lost touch with them after they left Glashütte. Kleist's men began to arrive at Fürstenwalde by four o'clock in the afternoon of 29 August. Shortly before then Frederick William's aide-de-camp, Count von Schweinitz, arrived with orders from the king for Kleist to get through the defiles into the Teplitz valley and go to the aid of Ostermann-Tolstoy. As Kleist told Schweinitz, by now it was too late in the day to do this and in any case his exhausted troops had to rest before being called on for further efforts. Schweinitz informed Kleist that the defiles out of the Erzgebirge at Teplitz and Graupen were completely choked by Russian troops and baggage. This meant that it was impossible for Kleist to get into the Teplitz valley from Fürstenwalde by marching south or south-west.

That evening another envoy, Colonel von Schöler, arrived from the monarchs with orders for Kleist to march south-eastwards via Nollendorf into Vandamme's rear. In fact, however, by the time Schöler arrived Kleist had already reconnoitred the road to Nollendorf and had decided on this move for himself. A key figure in this decision was Kleist's chief of staff, Lieutenant-Colonel Karl von Grolmann, who had studied Frederick the Great's campaigns in the region and knew the terrain well. Kleist's decision was extremely courageous. By marching on to the Teplitz highway at Nollendorf he would be between Vandamme's corps and the reinforcements which Kleist, Vandamme himself and indeed almost every other general in the neighbourhood assumed Napoleon was sending down the highway to support the incursion into Bohemia. Kleist and Grolmann knew and weighed the risks and nevertheless committed themselves to marching via Nollendorf from first light. The allied victory at the battle of Kulm on 30 August owed much to luck and accident but, contrary to some accounts, there was nothing accidental about Kleist's appearance in Vandamme's rear.[80]

Colonel von Schöler got back to allied headquarters at 3 a.m. on 30 August, woke Diebitsch and informed him of Kleist's intentions. For the first time the headquarters staff began to see the possibility of a resounding victory over Vandamme. At first light Diebitsch and Toll set off to reconnoitre the battlefield and plan the allied attack. By the normal standards of the Russian high command – or perhaps of human nature – Toll and Diebitsch ought to have been enemies. They were the ablest Russian staff officers of their day. Until Kutuzov's death Toll had been the leading influence at headquarters as regards strategy and had won the confidence of Alexander. When Wittgenstein took over the command, Toll was pushed aside and Diebitsch became the key adviser on strategy to both the commander-in-chief and the emperor. He preserved this position under Barclay de Tolly. There was initially some tension between Toll and Diebitsch. Most men would have been very jealous of the latter's success, not least because Diebitsch was eight years younger than Toll. Both men, and especially Toll, were famous for passionate temperaments, great energy and very strong wills. This could easily have made matters worse between them. Very soon, however, mutual respect won out. To the great credit of both men, they understood each other's intelligence, resolution and absolute commitment to victory and to the army's well-being. By the time of the autumn campaign they had become firm allies and close friends, which they remained until Diebitsch's death in 1831.[81]

The two generals returned to Barclay's headquarters convinced that the Russians must pin down Vandamme's right and centre between Straden and Priesten, while Colloredo and Bianchi's Austrian divisions, supported by Russian cavalry, worked their way through and around the French left flank in the south. They had spotted the weakness of Vandamme's left, his vulnerability to an outflanking movement, and the fact that the Austrian approach could to a great extent be concealed behind the Strisowitz heights. If, as was now expected, Kleist struck into Vandamme's rear at the same time as the Austrians were turning his flank, the possibilities of a decisive victory were clear. Without Kleist the allies outnumbered Vandamme by perhaps five to four. If the Prussians joined the battle, however, then allied superiority would be massive. Barclay, who commanded the allied forces on the battlefield, accepted Diebitsch's and Toll's suggestions and the counter-attack was launched in the morning of 30 August.[82]

For once in August 1813, things went more or less as the allied commanders had planned. It was in fact Vandamme who restarted the battle at seven o'clock by again trying to batter his way through the Russians at Straden. Overnight the First Guards Division had withdrawn into reserve, to be replaced by the Second Guards and the First Grenadier divisions. Pyshnitsky's regiments, cut off on 28 August, had rejoined Eugen's corps. The Russians stopped Vandamme's attack without much trouble. Colloredo went into action at about 9.30. He quickly spotted the possibilities of outflanking the French troops facing him. Barclay agreed to Colloredo's proposal to shift to his right and Bianchi's division moved up to fill the gap. The threat from the south caught the French by surprise and they were unable to stop the Austrian infantry's advance, which kept threatening to outflank them on their left. Within an hour the Austrian infantry was over the Strisowitz heights and advancing deep into Vandamme's left flank towards Kulm and Auschine. The Austrians were well supported by Russian cavalry, which overran one big French battery and kept the French infantry in a constant state of alarm. Austrian and Russian artillery got up onto all the heights to the south of Vandamme's position and inflicted heavy casualties on the French infantry as they tried to make a stand in Kulm and Auschine.

At this point Kleist's corps of 25,000 infantry and 104 guns joined the fray. Amidst the confusion of battle it was initially unclear both to the French and to the allied commanders whether these new troops were the Prussians or Napoleon's reinforcements. Colloredo, for instance, stopped his advance until the situation was clarified. Once Kleist's artillery opened fire, however, all doubts disappeared. Vandamme's situation was now desperate but he responded calmly and courageously. He accepted the need to sacrifice his artillery and planned to stage a fighting withdrawal in the west against the Russians and in the south against the Austrians, while breaking through to the east against the Prussian forces on the Teplitz highway. His plan partly succeeded in that much of his cavalry did break through Kleist's corps and make its escape up the highway. This happened above all because most of Kleist's units were Landwehr battalions filled with exhausted militiamen, very many of whom were seeing action for the first time. Trained infantry would have deployed across the road and stopped the cavalry's advance but the Landwehr battalions panicked and scattered into the surrounding forest. Kleist's corps did, however, rally in time to block the French infantry which were trying to retreat in their cavalry's wake.

By two o'clock in the afternoon the battle was over. Vandamme himself was captured by the Cossacks and delivered to the allied monarchs. The Russian officer who rescued him from these Cossacks recalls that, in the mistaken belief that he was a general, Vandamme handed over his sword to him. The gesture was accompanied by a rather theatrical speech: 'I surrender to you my sword which has served me for many years to the glory of my country.' By the time the speech was made for the third time, when Vandamme and his sword were finally handed over to Alexander, it had lost some of its sprightliness. The monarchs treated him politely but the German civilian population was less generous, since he was notorious throughout Germany for his cruelty and extortion. Everywhere he showed himself he was greeted with jeers, insults and sometimes stones: shouts of 'tiger', 'crocodile' and 'poisonous snake' were interspersed with good wishes for his trip to Siberia. In fact when he got to Moscow Vandamme was well treated by the local nobility until an indignant Alexander reminded the city's governor-general that Vandamme's harsh and avaricious behaviour had made him detestable even to his own troops. The emperor directed that Vandamme be removed to Viatka. This was not quite Siberia but it was the nearest thing to it in European Russia.[83]

The allies also claimed 82 guns and more than 8,000 prisoners, including Vandamme's chief of staff. At least as many Frenchmen were killed and wounded, and this came on top of the heavy casualties of the previous days. Vandamme's First Corps essentially ceased to exist. Even so, in terms of sheer numbers the allies had lost more men in the Dresden campaign as a whole than Napoleon. Not only could they afford to do so, however, but their biggest losses – Mesko's raw recruits – could quickly be replaced because the Austrian mobilization of manpower was finally cranking into top gear. Nor in any case were numbers the key point. Victory at Kulm made a huge difference to allied morale and unity. The great tensions between the allies created by defeat at Dresden were very much reduced, not least because of the fact that Kulm was in the fullest sense an allied victory. If the Russians were the heroes on 29 August, Colloredo's Austrians and Kleist's Prussians had made the biggest contribution to victory on the following day.

An officer in Alexander's entourage recalled that as the emperor rode across the battlefield of Kulm after Vandamme's surrender 'joy shone on his face, for this was the first total defeat of the enemy in which he had participated personally'. All his life he had dreamed of military glory. Until now his dreams had been mocked. At Austerlitz his army had been routed and he himself humiliated. In 1812 his closest advisers had conspired to remove him from the army as a nuisance, and the emperor was far too intelligent and sensitive not to have seen through their arguments. All his enormous efforts thus far in 1813 had led to defeat at Lutzen, Bautzen and Dresden. Now at last there was a spectacular victory and one which was owed above all to his Guards, who were the apple of his eye.

With his cup already overflowing, just after Vandamme had been dispatched to Teplitz the emperor received news of Blücher's victory at the river Katzbach. Even his normally restrained entourage burst into resounding cheers. Riding back to Teplitz, Alexander overtook carts carrying the Russian wounded. 'The emperor rode up to them, thanked them, asked them how he could help them, and called them his comrades in arms.' To do him justice, if he had never quite shared his men's hunger or their bivouacs, he had frequently risked his life on the battlefield and he had carried mental burdens of which few of them could conceive. To his dying day Alexander talked frequently of the two days of battle near Kulm. In time he was to witness other victories and triumphs, 'but the battle of Kulm remained always his favourite memory'.[84]

Rewards poured down on the heads of generals and even soldiers, with the partial exception of the brave men of Eugen's and Helfreich's divisions, whose enormous services and sacrifices were cast into the shade by the attention given to the Guards. Barclay de Tolly was awarded the Grand Cross of St George, the soldier's ultimate accolade, granted to only thirteen military leaders in the whole history of the Russian Empire.[85] Barclay richly deserved this award for everything he had done for the army as both war minister and commander-in-chief. Never did he deserve it less than in August 1813, however, when his performance was often mediocre. In this respect Barclay was rather typical of the allied leadership during the Dresden campaign.

Undoubtedly the allies had been extremely lucky. There can have been few victories in history won by such a chaotic and inefficient command structure. Not merely could the campaign have ended in disaster, in all logic it ought to have done so once the retreat from Dresden began. The allies owed much to luck, though also to the courage and endurance of their troops, especially of the Russians on the first day of the battle of Kulm. Some of the allied generals had performed well. Kleist had shown real courage in advancing into Vandamme's rear. Ermolov displayed inspiring leadership on the first day at Kulm, and Colloredo did well on the second. Above all, Eugen of Württemberg stands out as the allied general who contributed most to making victory possible.

But Napoleon and his generals had also made a big contribution. In Vandamme's case this had less to do with his performance at Kulm than in the three days before the battle, when he had allowed the Russians to hold his far larger corps at bay and to sneak back to Bohemia under his nose. Saint-Cyr was also to blame for losing touch with Kleist's corps and thereby allowing it to intervene in the battle of Kulm. Above all, however, the disaster was Napoleon's fault. He had explicitly ordered Vandamme to advance into Bohemia and equally explicitly had ordered the Young Guard to remain on the Teplitz highway right back at Pirna. These two commands were the key reasons for Vandamme's destruction. More important than the loss of a single corps was the fact that in the three days after the battle of Dresden Napoleon had it within his power to destroy the main allied army and end the war. Not merely did he fail to grasp this opportunity but he made a big contribution to turning possible total victory into a very serious defeat.

As usual, Napoleon remained calm in the face of defeat. Kulm was not the only blow. At the same time news came in of MacDonald's rout at the river Katzbach on 26 August and of the defeat of Marshal Oudinot's advance on Berlin at Gross Beeren by Bernadotte's Army of the North on 23 August.

Bernadotte's army was made up of three 'national' contingents: Swedes, Russians and Prussians. Of these the Swedes were the smallest and the Prussians the largest. In the middle were Winzengerode's Russian Army Corps of 32,000 men and 120 guns. Histories of the Army of the North's 1813 campaign are always dominated by the Prussian perspective. Not only were the Prussians the largest contingent but it was also they who played much the biggest role in the two battles which defeated Napoleon's attempts to seize Berlin: at Gross Beeren on 23 August and at Dennewitz on 6 September. The commander of Winzengerode's infantry was Count Mikhail Vorontsov, an outstanding general who distinguished himself on many occasions in 1812–14. The only time in which he and his troops had no chance to show their quality was, however, during the autumn 1813 campaign. By contrast, the role of the Prussian forces in the battles to defend their capital understandably became part of Prusso-German mythology.

So too did the ferocious conflicts between Bernadotte and his Prussian subordinates. The senior Prussian officer in Bernadotte's army was Friedrich Wilhelm von Bülow.

Bülow was an easier subordinate to deal with than Yorck, but that was not saying much. He was a clever, honest and well-educated man and a very competent general: he was also blunt, outspoken, self-confident and possessed of a violent temper. Bülow had little time for Frenchmen and none at all for the voluble Gascon renegade who had somehow clambered next to the Swedish throne and who, in Bülow's view, seemed certain to sell out the Swedes, the allies and anyone else who got in the way of his ambition. It did not help relations that after the rout at Jena-Auerstadt in 1806 Bülow's detachment had in fact surrendered to Bernadotte's corps. According to one neutral historian, the Prussian general never forgot this humiliation.[86]

Bülow and Bernadotte had different views on how best to fight the war. Left to his own devices Bernadotte would have staged a fighting retreat towards his bases on the Baltic coast in the event of an advance by Napoleon, which he was convinced would soon materialize. He was cautious, nervous and very much in awe of Napoleon's genius. Bülow, far more confident and aggressive, was not just determined to defend Berlin but wanted to attack the French forces threatening the city and keep them as far from the capital as possible. As often happened in the allied armies in 1812–14 differences of opinion on strategy were quickly interpreted in political terms and seen as betrayal of the common cause. The events in Hamburg in the spring had confirmed Prussian suspicions that Bernadotte was not committed to the liberation of Germany and might even be constrained by his own dreams of replacing Napoleon on the throne of France. The commander-in-chief's caution in the autumn campaign was soon interpreted in this light.[87]

Some Russians shared this dim view of Bernadotte. On 3 September Alexander's representative at Blücher's headquarters wrote to Petr Volkonsky to protest at Bernadotte's inactivity. As always, such letters to Volkonsky were really for the attention of Alexander: Volkonsky was merely a filter. Baron Tuyll wrote that 'the crown prince of Sweden has not taken one step forward in nine days, that is to say since 23 August, though according to the overall plan of operations this was the moment to undertake a vigorous offensive'.[88]

The emperor's chief representative at Bernadotte's headquarters was Charles-André Pozzo di Borgo. Alexander's instructions to Pozzo were to make sure that Bernadotte used his army to serve the common cause and not purely Swedish interests, let alone any hopes Bernadotte might have about his future role in French politics. So long as the latter were simply Bernadotte's happy daydreams they could be indulged, as must also be Sweden's legitimate claim to Norway after the war. But Pozzo was warned to be very much on his guard against Bernadotte and to ally himself with Sir Charles Stewart, the British representative at the crown prince's headquarters. Alexander told Pozzo that in this instance Russian and British interests were identical: they were to ensure that Bernadotte used all the troops entrusted to him in the common cause and did not either paralyse them or misuse them for purely Swedish and secondary operations. Pozzo was the perfect man for this commission. By 1812 Alexander had gathered into his entourage a considerable gang of what one might describe as dyed-in-the-wool foreign anti-Bonapartists. The Baron vom Stein was the most famous of these men and Winzengerode was also a charter-member of the group. The anti-Bonapartist credentials of Pozzo di Borgo were soundest of all: of Corsican descent, he had been an enemy of Napoleon in French and Corsican politics since 1793. Pozzo was just the right bloodhound to set on that veteran of French revolutionary politics, the former republican, Jean-Baptiste Bernadotte. Not surprisingly, both Sir Charles Stewart and Baron vom Stein thought highly of Pozzo.[89]

The Russian troops in Bernadotte's army seem on the contrary to have liked the crown prince and the feeling was mutual. With fine tact Bernadotte was much inclined to tell the Prussians and Swedes that they should model themselves on their splendid Russian comrades-in-arms. His headquarters were always guarded by Russian troops, whom he treated indulgently, making sure they were well fed and got their vodka. He tried hard to ensure that all his soldiers were quartered whenever possible in houses, making them bivouac only when strictly necessary. The Russian soldiers appreciated his attentiveness and rather took to Bernadotte's Gascon flamboyance and eccentricity. Bernadotte was also polite and popular in the circle of his Russian senior officers. Vladimir Löwenstern wrote in his memoirs that Bernadotte conducted a model campaign in the autumn of 1813 despite the difficulties of his position in front of Berlin. As to Aleksandr Chernyshev, who commanded the Russian 'flying detachments', and Mikhail Vorontsov, they seem to have reserved their bile for Winzengerode, whom they correctly saw as a third-rate general, much inferior to themselves.[90]

Winzengerode himself reported to Alexander that Bernadotte's headquarters' staff were slow-moving. Like virtually all observers, he complained that the crown prince 'acts with great caution' after the battle of Gross Beeren and had failed to exploit the allied victory. On the whole, however, Winzengerode seems to have enjoyed good relations with Bernadotte. Like his commander-in-chief, Winzengerode was not at all anxious to advance boldly into Napoleon's lair. In addition, he had his own axe to grind as regards the Prussians, above all because of their failure to supply his troops adequately, as they were supposed to do according to the Russo-Prussian convention. Winzengerode's complaints on this score began in July and continued throughout the campaign. In one of his earliest letters, for example, he complained that not only his own corps but even Russian batteries lent to the Prussians to make up for their shortage of artillery were going unfed.[91]

Faced by Prussian failure to supply their troops adequately, the Russians resorted to their usual ploy of squeezing the Poles. In the first week of August Barclay de Tolly had ordered another large requisition in Poland, designed to tap the current harvest and above all to feed the Russian corps in the Army of Silesia. The levy included huge amounts of flour for the soldiers and oats for the Russian horses, and 295,000 litres of vodka. The Prussian government appealed to Barclay to use some of this food to lessen the burden on the Berlin region of feeding Winzengerode's troops and their horses. One week after Barclay issued his orders for the new requisition, part of the levy was diverted to Winzengerode. This included more than 500,000 kilograms of groats for the men's porridge, 87,000 litres of vodka and 524,000 kilograms of meat.[92]

Immediately the armistice had ended on 10 August Winzengerode ordered raiding and scouting parties to move out around the western flank of Oudinot's army and into its rear. Rumours that Napoleon himself was moving up towards Oudinot's headquarters even persuaded the Russian commander that he might seize the French emperor. Löwenstern was given a detachment of Cossacks and the task of bagging Napoleon. Moving southwards before swinging into Oudinot's rear, Löwenstern's Cossacks promptly pillaged a juicy manor house they encountered en route. Löwenstern records that he gave the men one hundred lashes each and degraded an NCO but he could not get most of the plunder back because his Cossacks were much too experienced in hiding it away. Löwenstern's scouts quickly discovered that Napoleon was far away in Silesia. Much closer was Oudinot's weakly guarded treasury, on which Löwenstern pounced with glee. The Russian colonel was something of a pirate by nature. In Petersburg before the war he won and more often lost vast sums at cards. During the war he combined great courage and boldness in action with the seduction of women all the way from Vilna to Paris. Even so, he was in his way a rather honourable pirate. Although he records that prisoners of war were a big nuisance for a raiding party, he always took them along with him and he despised Figner for murdering his French captives.

Oudinot's treasury contained the equivalent of 2.4 million paper rubles in coin. Löwenstern insists in his memoirs that by Russian military convention the treasure was his, since he had captured it sword in hand. Getting it home safely was quite a challenge. Judging by Löwenstern's memoirs, evading the French was less of a problem than beating off 'allies' anxious to share his spoils. The first threat was his own Cossacks. Russian military convention may (or may not) have made Löwenstern the rightful owner of his spoil but Cossack convention was more democratic. The Cossacks were the descendants of full-time plunderers who traditionally divided up their booty equally, with a special bonus for their commander. No one had quite got round to codifying how this tradition might be modified when in the service of the emperor. To avoid misunderstandings, Löwenstern gave each Cossack 100 silver francs and promised them the same again when they got the booty back to Berlin. His next success was to outwit and evade the neighbouring raiding party of Cossacks under Colonel Prendel, who felt an urgent need to help protect Löwenstern's loot from the awful possibility of recapture by the French.

Having got back to Berlin Löwenstern then faced the most dangerous enemy of all in the person of the city's fierce military governor, General L'Estocq. At a time when Prussia was desperate for cash, L'Estocq saw no reason to allow piracy to succeed untaxed and under his nose. There followed a strange hide-and-seek across Berlin as the governor tried to discover Löwenstern's carts and their contents. By the time he found them Löwenstern had his loot safely hidden. He then paid off a number of possible threats to his haul. In his memoirs he adds that old acquaintances popped up from all sides and 'it was a real joy to me to be useful to my friends'. Prince Serge Volkonsky, Winzengerode's duty general, was very much an old friend. He records that Löwenstern's haul of foreign coin was so enormous that it depressed the exchange rate of the Prussian taler in the entire Berlin region. Judging by Löwenstern's memoirs, business also increased dramatically among the best whorehouses and champagne-sellers in the Prussian capital.[93]

Meanwhile Napoleon was making the first of his two attempts to take Berlin, led in this case by Marshal Oudinot. Napoleon's obsession with capturing Berlin was fortunate for the allies. Had he simply masked Bernadotte's army he could have transferred substantial forces elsewhere. Bernadotte is most unlikely to have gone over to a bold offensive. He would instead have sat down to besiege Wittenberg, since he was determined to hold a fortified crossing over the Elbe before moving across the river and exposing himself to a sudden counter-thrust from his former boss. Not merely did Napoleon order first Oudinot and then Ney to march on Berlin but he also gave them too few soldiers of too low quality to perform their assigned task. He did this partly because he despised the Prussian infantry and discounted its potential on the battlefield.

Oudinot bungled his advance and was defeated at Gross Beeren on 23 August by Bülow's corps. On 27 August, the day the allied retreat from Dresden began, a strong division under General Girard, advancing from Wittenberg to support Oudinot, was annihilated at Hagelberg. The Russians were not involved at Gross Beeren, with the important exception of Russian batteries permanently attached to Bülow's corps to make up for the Prussians' own shortage of artillery. Winzengerode's corps stood at the right of the allied line covering Berlin, whereas Oudinot attempted to break through on the left. The battle was over before the Russians had time to intervene. The French commander advanced in such a manner that his columns were widely separated and unable to support each other. Therefore the two Prussian corps of Bülow and Tauenzien were more than adequate to defeat him without Russian help. At Hagelberg, however, Chernyshev threw the enemy into confusion by charging with his Cossacks unexpectedly into their rear in the middle of the battle and made a big contribution to their disintegration.[94]

The second French advance on Berlin was led by Marshal Ney. It was defeated at the battle of Dennewitz on 6 September. Once again the French advanced against the allied left, which was manned by Bülow and Tauenzien's Prussians. On this occasion, as at Gross Beeren, Winzengerode's corps was deployed on the allied right and only part of its cavalry and artillery participated in the battle. Even they became involved only in its final stages. No one could blame the Russians for this. Their deployment and movements were subject to Bernadotte's orders. But the crown prince's actions have ever since been subject to severe criticism, especially of course from historians of a Prusso-German nationalist persuasion. On the other hand, Bernadotte has also had numerous defenders, including probably the best historian of the campaign, the Prussian general staff colonel and military historian, Rudolph von Friederich.[95]

Bernadotte's enemies argue that he moved too slowly to the Prussians' aid, left the dirty work to them, and then took credit for himself, the

Swedes and the Russians. His supporters claim on the contrary that he had no alternative but to deploy on a broad front to cover the various possible lines of advance on Berlin, and that once he discovered that Ney was moving against Bülow he came to the Prussians' aid with all possible speed. They stress the big contribution made by the Russian cavalry and artillery in the final stage of the battle. They also argue that even if Bülow had been forced to fall back at that time, by then the exhausted enemy army would merely have advanced into the jaws of the Russians and Swedes.

No one denies that the Prussian troops fought with great courage for many hours. Bülow himself directed his men with skill, calm and good timing. The Landwehr regiments performed far better than the militia units in Kleist's corps at the battle of Kulm one week before. Also unarguable is the fact that if Prussian courage and grit to a great extent won the battle of Dennewitz, the French commanders did much to lose it. Though in principle the Prussians should have been heavily outnumbered, in practice Ney never succeeded in getting all three of his corps into action on the battlefield. The story was a rather familiar one. Ney was present on the northern half of the battlefield. He became wholly absorbed in the struggle going on around him and lost his sense of the overall situation, summoning the whole of Oudinot's corps to his own assistance and thereby exposing Reynier's Saxon corps on his southern wing to defeat. Oudinot, deeply insulted at being removed from overall command, was happy to contribute to his successor's defeat by dumb obedience to stupid orders. Bülow took advantage of Oudinot's march northwards to launch a counter-attack against Reynier's Saxons. Shortly afterwards the Russian cavalry and horse artillery drove into Reynier's open left flank, turning defeat into rout. Ivan Liprandi wrote that the concentrated fire they brought down on the wavering Saxons was the most professional performance by the Russian artillery which he witnessed in the course of the entire war.[96]

The historian of the St Petersburg Dragoon Regiment, one of the Russian cavalry units which struck the French left towards the end of the battle, wrote that the Russian cavalry played a decisive role in rescuing the exhausted Prussian infantry, scattering the French artillery, panicking the enemy infantry into flight, and then overrunning some of their rearguards. General Kamensky, who wrote this history, complained that foreigners never recognized the Russian contribution, though in fact his analysis of the battle is not too far removed from that of Rudolph von Friederich. Serge Volkonsky was as biased a nationalist as any Prussian historian of the battle of Dennewitz. He wrote (absurdly) in his memoirs that 'the whole honour' of the victory belonged 'to Bernadotte's dispositions and to the boldness of the Russian and Swedish artillery and the attack of the Russian cavalry'. In a much lower key, the dispute has something in common with subsequent arguments about the Prussian role at Waterloo, and was an almost inevitable aspect of coalition warfare. It has to be said, however, that the Prussian army did far more hard fighting at Waterloo than the Russians at Dennewitz, as in fact the Russian official history made clear. The one point on which all Prussian and Russian sources agreed was that Bernadotte failed to pursue Ney's fleeing army with sufficient determination, at a time when a full-blooded pursuit might well have destroyed it.[97]

Even without this, Ney's army had suffered badly. The Russians reckoned that he had lost up to 18,000 men, including more than 13,000 prisoners. Since the latter were mostly scooped up during the cavalry's pursuit of the fleeing French their number does say something about the Russian contribution to victory. Overall, in the first month of the war Napoleon had lost 100,000 men and more than 200 guns. The allies had lost barely 50 guns and not more than 85,000 soldiers. Reinforcements were flowing in to fill the allied ranks. By the time the advance on Leipzig began at the beginning of October Schwarzenberg had replaced all the Austrians lost at Dresden, and the new recruits were on the whole better trained than Mesko's men had been in August. Russian ranks were replenished by more arriving reserves and men returning from hospitals. Above all, they were augmented by the nearly 60,000 men of Bennigsen's Army of Poland. It is true that almost half of Bennigsen's infantry were Count Petr Tolstoy's militia, who were only really usable for sieges, but the rest of his infantry and all his cavalry and artillery were good troops.[98]

12

The Battle of Leipzig

The battle of Dennewitz ended the first phase of the autumn campaign. The rest of September was a hiatus. The second and decisive phase of the campaign began in early October, culminating in the battle of Leipzig. Napoleon would have liked to break the stalemate in September and impose his will on the enemy in his usual fashion. His strategic situation and, above all, his losses made this impossible, however. At the beginning of the autumn campaign Napoleon had hoped to deal the allies a knockout blow by leading his Guards and reserves northwards to strike against Berlin. Such a move was now unthinkable: the men could not be spared from the armies watching Blücher and Schwarzenberg. Napoleon restored MacDonald's army to some degree of order and attempted an advance on Blücher but the latter merely withdrew and dared Napoleon to pursue him across eastern Saxony and Silesia, thereby abandoning Dresden to Schwarzenberg.

In mid-September Napoleon moved southwards down the Teplitz highway and into the Erzgebirge, with the aim of defeating the main allied army. Pursuing Schwarzenberg's powerful army and trying to bring it to battle deep in Bohemia was unlikely to be successful, however. Schwarzenberg could find plenty of strong defensive positions. Meanwhile Napoleon's communications would be vulnerable to swarming allied cavalry and Blücher – even perhaps Bernadotte – would be at the gates of Dresden and devastating his base in Saxony. By now, unless he decided to abandon central Germany, Napoleon's only real option was to wait for the allies to invade Saxony and then try to exploit their mistakes.

The initiative lay in the hands of the allies. No invasion of Saxony was possible, however, unless the Army of Bohemia advanced back across the Erzgebirge. Schwarzenberg was not yet willing to try this again. In part he needed time to receive and train the Austrian troops who were to fill the gaps left by the battle of Dresden. During the chaotic retreat through the mountains in late August many carts and more supplies and ammunition had been lost. These too needed to be replaced before there could be any thought of a further offensive. Many horses had lost their shoes amidst the mud and stones of the mountain roads and, above all, during the steep descent into the Teplitz valley. In September 1813 horseshoes were in very short supply in Bohemia and had to be shipped in from elsewhere.

In general, supplying the allied armies in northern Bohemia was difficult and resulted in many disagreements between the Austrian, Russian and Prussian troops. The Austrians accused the Russians of marauding. The Russians replied that their troops were forced to hunt for food because the Austrians were failing to feed them, as they were obliged to do by the agreement between the two governments which covered the upkeep of the Russian troops while they were stationed on Austrian territory. Kankrin subsequently stated that there was in principle nothing wrong with the Austro-Russian agreement: the only, and far more costly, alternative would have been to use private contractors. But the Austrians had failed to implement the terms of the agreement efficiently. Ultimately, one partial solution to problems of supply was to move much of the cavalry towards central Bohemia where forage was abundant, until the allies were ready to resume the offensive.[1]

Strategic considerations also delayed allied operations. The near-disaster in late August had confirmed existing Austrians fears about the perils of advancing down the roads through the Erzgebirge. It had also provided ample justification for their concern that Napoleon would use their advance into the Erzgebirge to strike into their right and rear in Bohemia. Schwarzenberg would not move forward again into Saxony unless he was confident that he was well protected against any such threat. The problem was set out rather well in a memorandum by Jomini of 3 September. The main army needed to invade Saxony with at least 170,000 men, of whom 20,000 must be left to watch Dresden. It could not simultaneously detach sufficient troops to guard the line of the Elbe south of Dresden against the kind of strike contemplated by Napoleon and actually attempted by Vandamme in August. Jomini's solution was the one favoured by Schwarzenberg and agreed by the monarchs: Blücher's army must march into Bohemia to protect the right flank of the main army as it advanced across the Erzgebirge. Should no threat materialize from Napoleon, the Army of Silesia could then itself join the invasion of Saxony by marching up the Teplitz highway to Dresden and beyond.[2]

The victory of Dennewitz and the arrival of reinforcements for the Army of Bohemia changed some of Jomini's numbers without altering the basic strategic issue. Not at all surprisingly, Blücher was deeply unwilling to lose his independence and become a mere adjunct of Schwarzenberg's lumbering army. He wrote to Knesebeck as follows: for the 'sake of the common good, preserve me from a union with the main army; what can such a vast mass of men achieve in terrain of that sort?' Another letter from Blücher, drafted by Gneisenau and dated 11 September, went directly to Alexander and stressed the impact on Bernadotte if Blücher moved away from him and towards Bohemia: 'The battle of 6 September [i.e. Dennewitz] has certainly changed the military position within the theatre but the crown prince of Sweden would probably straight away and with good reason fall into inactivity if he noticed that the Army of Silesia was moving a long way away from him.'[3]

Caution was required when writing on such delicate themes. Along with the letter, Blücher also sent his excellent staff officer, Major Rühle von Lilienberg, to pass on his views orally to Alexander and Frederick William. Rühle stressed Blücher and Gneisenau's opinion that 'so long as the crown prince is deployed on his own in a separate theatre of war we can expect no activity from him because of his political position'. The combination of written and oral urgings convinced the monarchs and had a decisive influence on the future of the campaign. Blücher was allowed to remain independent and to plan his crossing of the Elbe and link-up with Bernadotte. Nesselrode wrote to Pozzo to keep the crown prince in line during the forthcoming military operation. Meanwhile Bennigsen's Army of Poland would be diverted from its march across Silesia and would instead be brought southwards to Bohemia to guard Schwarzenberg's right and rear.[4]

On 13 September Alexander wrote to Blücher to tell him that General von dem Knesebeck was coming to him with instructions which would give Blücher wide leeway to plan his forthcoming operations. On the same day he wrote to Bennigsen ordering him to march to Bohemia. The emperor simply told Bennigsen, 'I think that it would be difficult to turn him [Blücher] from the direction he has taken', and gave the commander of the Army of Poland the march-routes he was to follow into Bohemia. He stressed the urgency of the movement and that Bennigsen was to report daily. Bennigsen received Alexander's orders at Hainau on 17 September. He immediately stirred up his corps commanders, allowing Count Tolstoy's militia just one day's rest at Liegnitz and telling their general to leave behind any units incapable of combat in the field. It would take Bennigsen's men at least two weeks, however, to reach Bohemia along bad roads, in areas already eaten out by passing troops and in dreadful weather. Bennigsen subsequently reported daily to Alexander on all these problems but he did add that the Austrian commissariat on this occasion had done a good job in keeping his army fed.[5]

While Bennigsen's men were on the march most of the allied troops were resting. Military operations were largely confined to the light troops which by now were swarming in Napoleon's rear and doing great damage to his supplies. Both east and west of Leipzig, Russian, Prussian and Austrian light cavalry and Cossacks forced Napoleon to divert ever larger escorts to supply trains. Even this did not guarantee safety. On 11 September a supply convoy west of Leipzig with an escort of 4,000 infantry and 1,500 cavalry was overwhelmed by an allied force. Alexander ordered Blücher to release six Cossack regiments which he wanted to redeploy behind enemy lines in western Saxony. Through Petr Volkonsky he requested Platov to lead them, writing him a letter of an exquisite politeness, worthy of the days when the ataman of the Don Cossacks was truly an independent potentate. Platov took the job and justified Alexander's trust. Near Pennig on 28 September, together with other allied light cavalry units, he routed General Lefebvre-Desnouettes's 2nd Guards Cavalry Division, which Napoleon had sent back to the rear to deal with the allied partisans.[6]

Even more spectacular were the operations of the Army of the North's Russian light forces commanded by Aleksandr Chernyshev. Chernyshev writes that he prevailed on Bernadotte to allow him ten days in which he could operate behind enemy lines west of the Elbe according to his own plans and initiative. His force consisted of five Cossack regiments, six weak squadrons of regular cavalry and four guns. Crossing the Elbe on the night of 14 September, Chernyshev decided to head westwards for Kassel, the capital of Jérôme Bonaparte's tottering puppet kingdom of Westphalia. His journal states that in part he preferred this goal to Leipzig because the French forces were so numerous and so well organized around the latter. Chernyshev argued that a successful attack on Kassel could spark off revolt throughout the region.

He moved quickly and secretly, covering 85 kilometres in one day alone, and attacked Kassel early in the morning of 29 September. A combination of surprise, courage, bluff and French awareness of their deep unpopularity among the local population led to the flight of King Jérôme, the surrender of his capital, and the capture of extensive stores and a war chest of 79,000 talers. Chernyshev was no pirate: he distributed 15,000 of the talers to his men and sent the rest back to Winzengerode, before evacuating the city. His journal states that if he had found sufficient weapons in the city he would have armed civilian volunteers and tried to hold on to Kassel until relieved. His raid had been a spectacular affair and his boldness and leadership were once again in evidence. On the other hand, unlike on previous occasions when his raids sometimes had major strategic value, it is not obvious what the temporary capture of Kassel contributed to the allied cause in autumn 1813. What really counted in terms of undermining Napoleon's position in western Germany was the secret negotiations Metternich was conducting with the Confederation of the Rhine states, which were now on the verge of bringing Bavaria into the allied camp. Above all what mattered was the massive battle about to take place at Leipzig, which would decide the fate of Germany and perhaps Europe. Unlike Platov and the other partisan commanders in Saxony, Chernyshev did not weaken Napoleon's main army by diverting its troops or stopping its supplies. On this occasion he was the star of a brilliant but largely irrelevant sideshow.[7]

Meanwhile Bennigsen's army was heading towards Bohemia. In its ranks marched a young militia officer called Andrei Raevsky. As a militiaman, Raevsky's perspective was somewhat different to that of the regular officers. His memoirs celebrate the self-sacrifice of nobles who have volunteered to abandon home and family despite in many cases having earned a peaceful retirement after years of service to their country. Full of pride that the cream of the local community is offering itself up as a patriotic sacrifice, he says not one word about the peasant militiamen they commanded. In that respect there is a strong contrast between Raevsky's memoirs and the diary of Aleksandr Chicherin, with its sensitive and humane comments about the men in the ranks of the Semenovsky Guards.

In most ways, however, Raevsky's memoirs are typical of the writings of Russian officers who made the long march through Poland and Silesia into Bohemia. He contrasted Polish squalor and poverty with the wealth and tidiness of Silesia. When he got to Bohemia he noted that the locals were fellow Slavs and added how much less pleasant they were than the Germans of Silesia. Not only were they much poorer and less clean, they were also far meaner and less welcoming than the Germans as regards the arriving Russian army. Like many of his peers, Raevsky was uplifted by a sense of Russian power, prestige and generosity. He felt proud that Russians were not just defeating Napoleon but also liberating Europe from his yoke. His memoirs are also in part a romantic travelogue. At Leutmeritz, for instance, he recalls that the Russian militia came upon the wagon-train of the main army: 'a long row of carts, horses beyond number, everywhere the smoke of campfires with the Bashkir and Kalmyks who crowd around them reminding one of the wild nomadic tribes who roam on the steppes of the Urals and on the banks of the stormy [river] Enisei'.[8]

At Leutmeritz Bennigsen received Alexander's orders for the coming campaign. His chief task was to defend the main army's bases and communications in Bohemia. If Napoleon invaded the province then Bennigsen was to fall back on the strong defensive position behind the river Eger. If on the contrary the French moved against the main army then Bennigsen was to advance up the Teplitz highway into their rear. On 30 September General Dokhturov's men arrived in the Teplitz valley and began to occupy the former bivouacs of the Army of Bohemia. The Leipzig campaign was about to begin.[9]

Schwarzenberg's advance guard began to move northwards on 27 September. On this occasion the Army of Bohemia would be using just one of the two highways through the Erzgebirge, in other words the road from Kommotau through Chemnitz to Leipzig. Inevitably this slowed down its movements. Both Schwarzenberg and Barclay were acutely conscious of the army's vulnerability to a sudden attack by Napoleon as it emerged from the mountains. With so much of the light cavalry away in raiding parties around Leipzig, reconnaissance was a problem. Wittgenstein and Kleinau commanded the leading allied corps: the former had no Cossacks and the latter only 1,200 light cavalry.

Despite Barclay's worries about supplies, the area between Chemnitz and Altenburg had never been fought over and food and fodder turned out to be relatively abundant. Schwarzenberg advanced out of the Erzgebirge with 160,000 men. Facing him were only 40,000 men under Joachim Murat. But the allied movements were so slow and uncoordinated that Murat was easily able to delay them and even score a number of minor victories in skirmishes. The pressure on his force was so weak that Murat believed that he was facing only part of the Army of Bohemia, with Schwarzenberg and the main body probably still poised to move on Dresden. Murat's reports to this effect misled Napoleon but the key result of Schwarzenberg's caution was that Napoleon was free to turn on Blücher and Bernadotte with the great majority of his army.[10]

Blücher's army began its march northwards to link up with Bernadotte on 29 September. On 3 October his Russian pontoon companies got Blücher's Prussians across the Elbe at Wartenburg. Though outnumbered, the French forces at Wartenburg held very strong positions, which Yorck's infantry stormed with great courage. Meanwhile Bernadotte kept his promise to cross the Elbe to join the Army of Silesia: all three of his corps crossed the river on 4 October at Rosslau and Aken. Winzengerode had orders from Bernadotte to attack Ney's rear if the French advanced against Blücher. The Army of Silesia headed southeastwards towards Düben with Yorck in the lead, followed by Langeron, with Sacken's corps bringing up the rear. Having abandoned their bases east of the Elbe Langeron's men were already having to scrounge food from the local countryside and some of them were beginning to go hungry. Captain Radozhitsky complained that marching in the wake of the Prussians was always unpleasant because they stripped the country bare, treating the Saxon population much worse than the Russians' behaviour towards the Poles when marching through the Duchy of Warsaw earlier in the year.[11]

For their own safety and if the campaign was to succeed the armies of Silesia and of the North had to act in unison. In practice neither Bernadotte nor Blücher could give orders to the other army commander: they had to agree on strategy. Given Blücher's boldness and Bernadotte's caution this was bound to be difficult. Blücher's aim was to link up with Schwarzenberg near Leipzig, pulling Bernadotte along with him, and thereby uniting the three allied armies for a decisive battle against Napoleon. In principle Bernadotte did not object to this strategy. If

Napoleon advanced on Leipzig to do battle with Schwarzenberg then Bernadotte was fully willing to move forward into his rear, as the Trachenberg plan demanded. Quite reasonably, however, Bernadotte feared that if he and Blücher marched on Leipzig before the Army of Bohemia arrived in the neighbourhood they would expose themselves to being attacked by the whole of Napoleon's forces. At the very least they needed to be clear about Schwarzenberg's whereabouts and Napoleon's movements before undertaking so risky a move. In addition, Bernadotte believed that Napoleon might well rely on Schwarzenberg's slowness and himself march northwards to destroy the other two allied armies before the Army of Bohemia could intervene. In this prediction Bernadotte was entirely correct and his caution was fully justified.

When the Leipzig campaign began Napoleon was in Dresden. Initially he found it hard to get a grasp of the allied movements, partly because of his lack of good cavalry but also because he could not easily believe that Blücher would be bold enough to cross the Elbe with his entire army, advancing into Napoleon's lair and abandoning his bases and supplies in Silesia. The emperor only marched out of Dresden on 7 September, heading for Meissen and Wurzen, which he reached on the following day. This was the logical route either if he was going to move towards Leipzig against Schwarzenberg or if he wanted to strike northwards against Blücher. Only once he reached Wurzen would he have to show his hand by either continuing westwards to Leipzig or marching north-eastwards down the east bank of the river Mulde towards Düben.

Meanwhile, however, Napoleon had made what was probably his greatest mistake of the campaign. Initially he had ordered Saint-Cyr to abandon Dresden and join the main body with his corps. Saint-Cyr had already withdrawn his outposts in the Erzgebirge when the emperor changed his mind and told him to remain in Dresden to defend the city. By now Dresden's supplies had been eaten up and its usefulness as a base was almost gone. Since the city was not properly fortified it was also much less valuable than the other crossing-points over the Elbe at Torgau, Wittenberg and Magdeburg. In any case the allied invasion of western Saxony gave Napoleon his best and last chance to win the 1813 campaign and save his position in Germany. He needed to concentrate all his forces for the decisive battle. In the event Bennigsen was able to use Count Tolstoy's corps of militia, almost useless on a battlefield, to blockade Saint-Cyr in Dresden while taking the great majority of his regular troops to join the allied army in time for the battle of Leipzig. In November 1813 Saint-Cyr's hungry garrison of Dresden, totally isolated after Napoleon's defeat at Leipzig, was to surrender: 35,000 men who could well have turned the battle of Leipzig in Napoleon's favour went into captivity, having made almost no contribution to his cause in the crucial month of October.[12]

On 9 September Blücher and Langeron were at Düben, with Langeron's corps quartered in and around the village enjoying a rest. Early in the afternoon the alarm was sounded. Napoleon was moving on Düben from Wurzen in great strength, with his advance guard already dangerously close. In his memoirs Langeron wrote that he and Blücher could easily have been captured. Clearly his cavalry's reconnaissance had failed badly. Probably this owed something to the detachment of Cossack regiments from Blücher's army to join Platov's raiding parties near Leipzig. It was also true that the forests in the neighbourhood impeded intelligence-gathering. These were not good excuses for failure on this scale, however. Though both Langeron and Blücher had high respect for generals Rudzevich and Emmanuel, who generally commanded the Russian advance guard, their opinion of the most senior cavalry commanders in Langeron's army corps was low. Langeron wrote that 'during the entire campaign my cavalry was paralysed by the negligence, laziness and lack of resolution of its leaders', by which he meant above all the overall commander of the cavalry corps, Lieutenant-General Baron Korff, a man by now much addicted to campaigning in gentlemanly style and comfort.[13]

Thanks to the calm of General Kaptsevich and the skilful rearguard action mounted by his Tenth Corps, Langeron got all his troops safely out of Düben and retreated to the north-west, crossing the river Mulde at Jessnitz: but Napoleon's advance cut off Sacken's army corps from the rest of the Army of Silesia. In his subsequent report to Barclay de Tolly, Sacken recounted that his army corps had crossed the Elbe on 4 October. During the next few days his cavalry, including a Kalmyk regiment, had conducted a number of successful skirmishes with the French. Suddenly, on 9 November, 'the corps found itself in the most dangerous situation it encountered in the course of the whole of this war'. His advance guard under Major-General Lanskoy found its path blocked by enemy forces 'in great strength'. Meanwhile Major-General

Iuzefovich's rearguard was pressed hard by all Sebastiani's cavalry, 6,000 infantry and eighteen guns arriving from the direction of Torgau. French troops seemed to be on all sides.

Fortunately, Sacken was never one to panic and his cavalry commanders, headed by Ilarion Vasilchikov, were very competent. They held off the French long enough for Sacken to get his infantry on the march down country lanes, through the forests towards the north of the French forces in his path. Arriving at the village of Presl at midnight, after a ten-hour march, Sacken found part of his cavalry there and Sebastiani not far away. However, the French cavalry commander allowed himself to be hoodwinked by the fact that 'our baggage train was sent off towards Elster on the river Elbe: he assumed that our corps would march in the same direction'. In fact Sacken sent his troops in the opposite direction – in other words north-westwards in the wake of the rest of the army. Sebastiani ended by missing most of the baggage and all Sacken's troops. For Sacken, the next stretch of his march – 'where the main road heads from Düben to Wittenberg' – was the most dangerous moment. His men passed down this road during the night. 'We deployed our jaegers on both sides of this road, and we passed between them with the enemy's bivouacs in view but the foe did not notice our movement.'[14]

In his memoirs Langeron comments:

A less bold general than Sacken would have retired in haste via Smiedeberg to the bridgehead at Wartenburg but Sacken was absolutely determined not to be separated from us and he was an audacious general, very skilful at marches: he passed within a mile of Napoleon during the night, outflanked him, cut between his army and its advance guards, and rejoined us by forced marches via Raguhn, where he crossed the Mühlde. He was never brought to action and he didn't lose so much as one soldier of his baggage train. It is hard to find a bolder or better executed manoeuvre.[15]

Sacken's exploits averted immediate disaster but the situation was still dangerous. Blücher and Bernadotte had agreed that both the Army of the North and the Army of Silesia would march westwards and take up position on the other (i.e. western) side of the river Saale. United, and with the river between them and Napoleon, they could wait in security while they discovered Schwarzenberg's whereabouts and Napoleon's intentions. If, as Blücher predicted, the emperor headed towards Leipzig to fight the Army of Bohemia, then he and Bernadotte could march safely down the west bank of the Saale and attack Leipzig from the north. If, as Bernadotte feared, Napoleon tried to retreat across the Saale or towards Magdeburg and Marshal Davout, then the joint armies would be well placed to block him. They were also within easy reach of the Elbe crossings at Rosslau and Aken, should Napoleon attempt an attack on Berlin or on the Russo-Prussian army's communications.

By now, however, Blücher and all the Prussian generals were deeply distrustful of Bernadotte and more convinced than ever that he was a potential traitor to the allied cause. Believing that the crown prince had promised to build a pontoon bridge for Yorck's corps to cross the Saale at Wettin, when the Prussians got there on 11 October and found no bridge they interpreted this as an underhand trick to force them to retreat northwards along the Saale towards the Elbe crossings – in other words to defer to Bernadotte's priorities. Instead, Blücher marched southwards to the next crossing upriver at Halle. Very fortunately for the Prussian commander, Napoleon's cavalry reconnaissance was poor and his attention was fixed northwards towards the Elbe, in which direction he was convinced that Sacken and much of the rest of the allied army was retreating. Had he turned his gaze westwards towards the Saale, his chances of catching Yorck's isolated corps, pinning it against the river and destroying it would have been excellent.

By 12 October both the Army of Silesia and the Army of the North were deployed on the west bank of the Saale, with their commanders trying to make sense of confusing and contradictory information. Inevitably both Blücher and Bernadotte interpreted this evidence to fit their preconceived views. To an extent their confusion is unsurprising since at this very time Napoleon was sitting in Düben unable to make up his mind whether to concentrate at Leipzig against Schwarzenberg or to strike either west across the Saale or northwards towards the Elbe. In a way it was the allied supreme commander who made up Napoleon's mind for him. Had Schwarzenberg used his four-to-one advantage to push back Murat, the latter would have been forced to abandon Leipzig and fall back northwards on Napoleon. At that point the emperor's only realistic option would have been to follow Bernadotte's prediction and force his way over the Saale or move further north towards Magdeburg. Instead, Schwarzenberg's lack of speed or resolution persuaded Napoleon in the late afternoon of 12 October that his best chance would be to concentrate on Leipzig and smash the Army of Bohemia before

Blücher and Bernadotte could intervene. Before taking this decision, however, on 11 October Napoleon had sent two corps on a raid towards Dessau and Wittenberg on the Elbe.

In the atmosphere of heightened tension and uncertainty then prevailing, not only Bernadotte but also Lieutenant-General von Tauenzien, the Prussian commander north of the Elbe, interpreted this raid as proof that Napoleon was aiming to strike towards Berlin. Tauenzien's report to Bernadotte that Napoleon himself and four full corps were moving northwards to cross the Elbe increased the crown prince's determination to get back across the river himself in order to protect his communications and the Prussian capital. Fortunately for the allied cause, the approach of Napoleon's corps had persuaded the allied commanders at Aken and Rosslau to dismantle the pontoon bridges across which Bernadotte was hoping to march.

Bernadotte's army was therefore stuck south of the Elbe long enough for new information to arrive from Blücher which suggested strongly that Napoleon was headed for Leipzig. Under strong pressure not just from the Prussians but also from the Russian and British envoys (Pozzo di Borgo and Charles Stewart) at his headquarters, Bernadotte turned south again. Even now he did so in very hesitant fashion, heading not directly for Leipzig but rather towards Blücher's rear at Halle. Even this move came to a halt on 15 October as an increasingly confused Bernadotte overreacted to reports of French columns advancing from the east and deployed his columns against this new but imaginary threat. The net result of all this confusion was that the Army of the North was too far from Leipzig to participate in the battle's first day on 16 October.

The battlefield at Leipzig is best seen as three distinct sectors. In the north, where Blücher and Bernadotte's men were deployed, the river Parthe flowed from east to west between the allied and Napoleonic armies. Near its banks were the villages of Möckern, Eutritzsch and Schönefeld, all of which saw ferocious fighting. So too did the area around the Halle Gate just to the north of Leipzig, where the river Parthe flows into the river Pleisse. All these places have been absorbed into the expanding city of Leipzig in the last two hundred years and virtually nothing remains of the battlefield.

The same is true for slightly different reasons of the second sector, west of Leipzig. This area is dominated by the rivers Elster and Pleisse, which flow in parallel and close together before joining near Leipzig. In

1813 this whole area was a maze of waterways, large and small. Most of the land between the waterways was swampy, and this was particularly so in October, after weeks of rain. The few villages and very few roads in this area were almost islands amidst the swamps and waterways. Nowadays all this area has been tidied up, drained and embanked. Save to a very limited extent at Dölitz, it is impossible to get any sense from today's terrain of the enormous difficulties facing any general who tried to deploy large numbers of troops in this area in 1813.

The third sector, south and east of Leipzig, is very different. Until very recently it was also much better preserved.[16] On the crucial first day of the battle fighting in this sector was confined to the area south of Leipzig along the line which stretched from Markkleeberg on the river Pleisse to Liebertwollkwitz and beyond that to the village of Seifertshain. The key feature of this area is the ridge that runs all the way from the banks of the Pleisse to Liebertwollkwitz, a distance of roughly five and a half kilometres.

George Cathcart, present at the battle, writes that Liebertwollkwitz stood

on the top of a hill which formed a regular glacis to it. A ridge ran all the way from the shoulder of the eminence of Liebertwollkwitz to the river Pleisse, passing in rear of Wachau and commanding it. This position could not fail to present itself to the eye of an experienced officer as the only one which that uninteresting country afforded for the purpose of covering Leipzig towards the south.[17]

The ridge at Liebertwollkwitz gave Napoleon many advantages. It provided excellent views over most of the terrain to the south and east. It offered a perfect firing line for a massive concentration of artillery. Behind its slope troops could be brought up out of the enemy's sight. For an enemy seeking to attack the ridge, Cathcart's use of the word 'glacis' to describe the terrain was deadly accurate. In particular the slope from Gossa in the south up to the ridge between Liebertwollkwitz and Wachau is a bare and open killing ground with no cover whatsoever.

As one of the best historians of the battle notes, 'the terrain very much favoured Napoleon's objectives'. In the south he had a splendid defensive position, which also had good potential as a springboard for a counter-offensive which could burst unexpectedly from behind the ridge at Liebertwollkwitz and strike allied forces who were pinned down by massed artillery fire from the heights above them. The terrain west of the city, beyond the Pleisse, made any attack from that direction immensely difficult. A relatively small defending force could block the few narrow approaches to the city and keep vastly superior numbers of enemy troops at bay almost indefinitely. Moreover the whole area east of the Pleisse was dotted with villages, whose houses were usually sizeable, built of stone and surrounded by stout garden walls. As one approached the city, the denser and more stoutly built the houses became, with the old gates and walls of Leipzig and its suburbs still providing its defenders with welcome cover.

Against this, the disadvantage of Napoleon's position was that the area east of the Pleisse did allow a huge army to deploy fully. If the allies were given the opportunity to bring their whole superiority in numbers and firepower to bear, then the emperor would be hard pressed to keep them at bay. If forced to retreat, his entire army would need to retire through the narrow streets of Leipzig, across the city's only bridge over the river Elster, and down the long causeway through Lindenau which led westwards to safety, and ultimately to the Rhine. If the allies took Lindenau catastrophe threatened, but the village and its approaches were so easily defensible that only gross carelessness would allow this to happen. Even without this, however, getting a huge army, its wounded and its baggage away through Leipzig and Lindenau was bound to be tricky, especially after a lost battle.[18]

Prince Schwarzenberg's operational plan for the battle seemed guaranteed, however, to ensure that Napoleon need not worry about defeat. The commander-in-chief could not be blamed for the fact that neither Bernadotte nor Bennigsen would reach the battlefield on 16 October. Bernadotte's hesitations have already been explained and Bennigsen's Army of Poland was advancing from Dresden as quickly as possible. Schwarzenberg was to blame, however, for planning to deploy Blücher's troops and most of the Army of Bohemia west of Leipzig, where the terrain ensured that most of them would never get to grips with the enemy. The core of the Austrian army was supposed to advance over the Pleisse at Connewitz and Dölitz. Subsequently it would roll up the right flank of Napoleon's line east of the river and cut off its retreat to Leipzig. This made no sense. Getting across the Pleisse would at best be very costly and time-consuming. Even if ultimately sheer numbers prevailed and some Austrian units got across the river, they would be advancing very close to Napoleon's reserves and would have no chance of exploiting their initial success.

Truly bizarre, however, was Schwarzenberg's plan to deploy the Grand Duke Constantine's reserve corps, containing the Russian and Prussian Guards, on the west bank of the Elster to support the Austrian attack. On top of this he aimed to use both Blücher's army and General Gyulai's Austrian 'corps' to attack Lindenau, on terrain which made the deployment of tens of thousands of troops inconceivable. Had Schwarzenberg's initial plan been executed, 54,000 troops would have been funnelled into the attack on Connewitz, 75,000 would have tried to reach Lindenau, and a mere 72,000 would have been left to oppose the bulk of Napoleon's army east of the river.[19]

This plan was so obviously mistaken that all Alexander's senior advisers protested and the emperor himself was mobilized to take on Schwarzenberg. Alexander was usually very tactful with the commander-in-chief and Schwarzenberg was a model of polite deference towards the monarch. On this occasion, however, the Austrian defended his plan stubbornly and there was a row. The upshot was that Blücher's line of advance was directed back to the east bank of the Elster: he was to march on Leipzig down the main road from Halle. The Grand Duke Constantine's reserve corps was also brought back to the east bank, though the Guards were only moved to Rotha, right by a bridge over the Pleisse and still 10 kilometres behind the front-line Russian divisions. But no amount of argument could shift Schwarzenberg from his basic idea of using the Austrian army on the west bank of the Elster.[20]

On this matter the commander-in-chief deferred to his chief of staff, General von Langenau, a Saxon officer who had transferred into the Austrian service only in 1813. Austrian sources admit that too much credence was given to Langenau's superior knowledge of the local terrain as a native of the area. Rather lamely, they suggest that only the heavy recent rains had made the ground west of the Elster truly impassable. They also claim that French cavalry had stopped Schwarzenberg from conducting a thorough personal reconnaissance of the area. One recent author has even suggested that Langenau may have been a traitor to the allied cause, though there is no evidence for this. Perhaps the likeliest explanation is that Langenau was better at planning battles from maps than from any eye for actual terrain. On a map, his plan to thrust over the Elster into Napoleon's flank and rear had a certain plausibility. If successful it would give the chief glory for victory to the Austrian forces in general and Langenau in particular. Possibly one need look no further for explanations for the bizarre deployment of the allied forces at Leipzig.[21]

One reason why Schwarzenberg liked the plan was that he had never initially intended to bring on a great battle at Leipzig. His aim throughout the October campaign had been to block Napoleon's retreat to the west and force the emperor to attack the allied forces standing in his path. Though not totally implausible as a strategic concept, his efforts to translate this idea into tactical deployments around Leipzig were a disaster. There was in any case a very basic problem with the Austrian plan. Napoleon had not concentrated his forces in Leipzig in order to retreat westwards. He was intending to smash the Army of Bohemia and win the campaign.

Napoleon took it for granted that the bulk of the enemy army would be deployed in the only sensible place, in other words east of the rivers Elster and Pleisse. His plan was to turn the allies' right flank east of Liebertwollkwitz, smash through their centre and drive Schwarzenberg's army into the Pleisse. Even without Bernadotte and Bennigsen the allies had 205,000 troops available on 16 October against Napoleon's 190,000. But Schwarzenberg's plan, even after modifications to appease Alexander, meant that on the key southern front 138,000 French troops would face 100,000 allies, of which Constantine's 24,000 reserves could not arrive on the battlefield for a number of hours. Of course the allies would outnumber Napoleon in other sectors but the terrain would make it impossible to use this superiority. On the first day at Leipzig Schwarzenberg therefore gave Napoleon a completely unnecessary chance to snatch victory against the odds and against the previous flow of the autumn campaign.[22]

On 16 October Blücher's army advanced on Leipzig from the north. Langeron took the village of Euteritzsch and Yorck's corps finally stormed Möckern after a ferocious struggle which lasted until the evening. The main point, however, was that Blücher had succeeded in pinning down two large French corps in the north, including Marmont's men, on whom Napoleon was depending for his attack on Schwarzenberg. Blücher's achievement at Leipzig was similar to his impact on the battle of Waterloo. By arriving on the battlefield much earlier than Napoleon had predicted, he diverted a key part of the strategic reserve on which the emperor was counting to decide the battle on its main front.

West of Leipzig, the advance on Lindenau of Gyulai's Austrian troops forced Napoleon to send the whole of Bertrand's Fourth Corps across the rivers to secure the village, and with it his line of retreat to the west. Further south, all the Austrian attempts to cross the river Pleisse near Connewitz and Dölitz got nowhere, to Schwarzenberg's increasing frustration. By late morning he was prepared to give way to Alexander's pleas and agree that Langenau's plan had failed. He therefore ordered the Austrian reserves to cross the Pleisse to help beat off Napoleon's attack. By now the allied situation east of the Pleisse was increasingly dire. The key question was whether the Austrian reserves would arrive in time to shore up the allied line.

Eugen of Württemberg's Second Russian Corps was deployed near the centre of the allied line east of the Pleisse, in front of the village of Gossa. In his memoirs Eugen wrote that from Gossa on 15 October Napoleon could be seen on the heights near Wachau inspecting his troops and handing out medals. Eugen and his officers expected themselves to be attacked the next day but 'we could not understand why Schwarzenberg decided on a general attack for the 16th when on the following day we would have been strengthened by 130,000 men of the Army of the North, the Army of Poland, and Count Colloredo's corps'. It seems that the allied high command wished to pin down Napoleon and feared that he would otherwise attack Blücher and Bernadotte, and perhaps even slip away to the north.[23]

To avoid this, the allied forces east of the Pleisse were ordered to attack in four columns from early in the morning of 16 October. On the left Kleist's Prussian corps and Helfreich's 14th Russian division would advance on Markkleeberg. To Kleist's right Eugen's Second Corps would attack Wachau, supported by Klux's Prussian brigade. The third column was commanded by Lieutenant-General Prince Andrei Gorchakov. It comprised Gorchakov's First Corps and Pirch's Prussian brigade. Gorchakov would attack Liebertwollkwitz from the south-west while the fourth column, made up of General Klenau's Austrians, would advance on the village from the south-east.

The night of 15/16 October was cold and very windy. Trees were uprooted and roofs damaged. The next morning Klenau's troops arrived late for the assault. Gorchakov had to wait for them with his regiments already deployed for the attack and under artillery fire. Kleist and Eugen advanced on time, however, moving forward on this still stormy October morning before it was fully light. By 9.30 Kleist had taken Markkleeberg and Eugen had moved into Wachau. The initial French response was mild, partly because they had not expected the allies to attack. Things soon changed, however: French infantry counter-attacked at both Wachau and Markkleeberg, and ferocious artillery fire began to pour down from the massed batteries on the ridge onto the Russian and Prussian troops. The latter nevertheless pushed forward their attacks with great courage. The French artillery colonel, Jean-Nicolas Noel, who was stationed at Wachau, recalled that the Russians and Prussians 'attacked with a determination which I had never before seen in our adversaries'.[24]

Casualties mounted quickly on both sides but especially among Eugen's Russians on the bare slopes east of Wachau. Already by eleven o'clock most of Eugen's artillery had been knocked out. There was nowhere to find cover and the French cavalry deployed east of Wachau were an additional threat to any infantry who broke formation. Rudolph von Friederich, the Prussian general staff historian, comments that 'it took all the tenacity and contempt for death of the Russian soldiers and all the heroic courage of Duke Eugen to stand one's ground in such a position'. By the end of the day two-thirds of Eugen's men were casualties. All his regimental commanders were killed or wounded. Eugen wrote in his memoirs that his troops had been similarly smothered in artillery fire for a time at Borodino but on the first day at Leipzig their ordeal 'lasted for much longer'.[25]

The heroism of Eugen's infantry was all the more impressive because his regiments had suffered very heavy casualties at Kulm only a few weeks before. The Murom and Reval regiments, for example, lost many men first in 1812, and then at both Kulm and Leipzig as part of Prince Ivan Shakhovskoy's Third Infantry Division. Officers and NCOs had needed to be drafted into the regiments from other units after Kulm to fill the gaps left by its killed and wounded veterans. Nevertheless many regimental old-timers remained in the ranks during the battle of Leipzig, including most of the Reval Regiment's sergeant-majors. An unusual number of illiterate but veteran senior sergeants had in fact been promoted to sergeant-major in the Reval Regiment in 1813. They included sergeant-majors Aleksei Fedorov, Mikhail Lashbin and Mina Afanasev, who between them had seventy years' service in the regiment. Lashbin was a state peasant from Tobolsk in Siberia and Afanasev a serf from Smolensk, but Fedorov was actually a Chuvash, one of the small, pagan peoples of the Volga region, though his family had become Christians. All three men held military medals, as did seven of the ten sergeant-majors in all. No other regiment whose records I have seen could equal this.[26]

Among the officers of the Murom Regiment who fought at Leipzig were lieutenants Ilia Shatov and Ivan Dmitrev. Both men had entered the Murom Regiment as privates more than twenty years before, had risen to sergeant-major and had then been commissioned in 1812. Both had fought with the regiment in East Prussia in 1807 but Shatov had even served in its ranks in Switzerland in 1799. The senior officer of the Murom Regiment to survive the battle of Leipzig was Petr Kladishchev, from a run-of-the-mill noble family of Riazan province, who became a colonel aged only 29. Kladishchev had joined the Murom Regiment at the age of 16 and never left it. He was decorated for courage in East Prussia in 1807, as well as at Vitebsk in 1812 and Bautzen in 1813. He was one of many young officers whose record of courage and leadership brought rapid wartime promotion. These men were much less visible than spectacular cases such as generals Chernyshev and Diebitsch. Nevertheless they made a crucial contribution to the army's performance.[27]

All morning and through the early afternoon of 16 October Eugen's regiments held their ground and preserved the allied line under the French bombardment. The French artillery commanders themselves subsequently paid tribute to the steadfast courage of the Russian infantry, who closed their ranks and held their positions in the face of terrifying losses. By late morning the battle had become a race. If Napoleon could concentrate his forces and attack before the allied reserves arrived, Eugen and Kleist's thinning infantry battalions would not be able to stop him from breaking through the allied line and crushing the Army of Bohemia against the banks of the Pleisse.

Alexander, Barclay and Diebitsch were acutely aware of this danger. The moment he arrived on the battlefield and could see the two armies' deployment amidst the October gloom, Alexander sent orders for the Guards to advance at speed from Rötha. From the time they received their orders it would take them three hours to reach the battlefield.

Nikolai Raevsky's Grenadier Corps was closer but his two divisions on their own would never suffice to shore up the whole allied line. Meanwhile, even after they had been released by Schwarzenberg shortly before midday, the Austrian reserves had to march south down the west bank of the Pleisse to the fords near Crobern, get themselves across the swollen river, and then turn northwards to come to the aid of Kleist's corps at Markkleeberg. For the Austrian infantry, this was a four-hour march. It was very fortunate that Alexander's insistence on bringing his Guards over to the east bank of the Pleisse meant that at this moment of supreme crisis they would not be competing with the Austrians for river crossings.[28]

Also luckily for the allies, Napoleon took longer than he had anticipated to organize and launch his counter-attack. He was waiting for Marmont but the latter was forced to stop while on the march southwards and race back to block Blücher at Möckern. Above all, Napoleon would not move until Marshal MacDonald's whole corps had come up on his left and had advanced against the Austrians towards Seifertshain. Only when MacDonald's threat in the east had developed would the emperor throw in his main forces against Kleist and Eugen. It was almost midday before MacDonald was in position and ready to attack. Though he then drove back Klenau's Austrians all the way to Seifertshain, at this point Austrian resistance stiffened and MacDonald's attack stalled. The sudden arrival to his east of thousands of Cossacks commanded by Matvei Platov distracted MacDonald's attention and also contributed to slowing his advance. Platov drew off Sebastiani's cavalry corps which was operating on MacDonald's eastern flank and without Sebastiani MacDonald lacked the means to outflank Klenau or the numbers to smash through the Austrian position at Seifertshain.

By the early afternoon Napoleon's attention had shifted westwards, towards Kleist's and Eugen's shrinking battalions. Against them he launched his Guards, most of his cavalry, Drouot's artillery reserve, and all the remaining infantry at his disposal.

By 3 p.m. Kleist's brigades were fighting desperately to hold Markkleeberg and had been forced out of Auenhain, with French cavalry in pursuit. The 2nd Russian Grenadier Division came up behind Auenhain but could not stop the French advance. Fortunately for the allies, the six excellent regiments of Count Nostitz's cuirassier corps arrived in the nick of time, scattered the French cavalry and restored the situation.

Nostitz's regiments were the first of the Austrian reserves to arrive from the west bank of the Pleisse but they were followed by more cavalry and then by Bianchi and Weissenwolf's infantry divisions. Count Weissenwolf's Grenadier battalions were among the best infantry in the Austrian army. Once they were on the scene Napoleon's chance of breaking through Kleist's position had disappeared. On the contrary, by the time evening approached and the battle ceased Weissenwolf's Grenadiers had recaptured Auenhain and it was Napoleon who was having to commit even part of his Old Guard to stop the Austrians advancing from Markkleeberg.[29]

While Kleist's Prussians and Russians were fighting for their lives at Markkleeberg and Auenhain during the afternoon of 16 October an even fiercer battle was raging to their right around the village of Gossa. This was the centre of the allied line east of the river Pleisse and behind Gossa the allied monarchs and their staffs were positioned on a small hill. The infantry leading the French advance came from Lauriston's Fifth Corps and Marshal Oudinot's Young Guard. Down the hill in their support came much of the French artillery reserve, including all the Guards artillery, commanded by General Drouot, who had good claim to be the finest artillery commander in Europe.

This was classic Napoleonic tactics. Having attacked the enemy flanks, the emperor was now deploying massive mobile firepower to smash through its weakened centre. The only visible infantry in front of Gossa was Eugen's shredded battalions, whose ranks had become even thinner after the prince had been forced to redeploy one of his second-line brigades to the left to counter the growing threat from the direction of Auenhain. General Diebitsch's account of the battle speaks of 'a storm of concentrated artillery fire never previously encountered in war' now descending on Eugen's battalions. Spotting the weakness of the allied infantry Murat launched his cavalry to sweep through the allied centre and overrun the artillery defending the village of Gossa and the approaches to the hill from which the allied monarchs, now joined by Schwarzenberg, were directing the battle. Perhaps the most important and certainly the most famous episode in the first day at Leipzig was the result.[30]

Sorting out what happened in a cavalry attack is even more difficult than imposing some kind of order on battles in general. Amidst the excitement, the dust and the speed with which events unfold, participants are seldom reliable witnesses. Because Murat's cavalry attack on 16 October was in many ways the high point of the day, putting the allied sovereigns and the very centre of the allied position at risk, it also aroused a competition as to who was responsible for the repulse of Murat's horsemen. The best eyewitness account of the action in any language is provided by George Cathcart. He was a professional cavalry officer and, standing near the monarchs on the hill behind Gossa, he had an excellent view of events without himself being involved in the mêlée. Equally important, Cathcart was relatively neutral, since there were no British troops involved.

Cathcart recalled that some 5,000 French cavalry were involved in the attack. As they formed up for the assault on the shoulder of the ridge by Liebertwollkwitz they were visible from allied headquarters on the hill behind Gossa. Apart from Eugen's infantry, the only visible allied force in their path was the Russian Guards Dragoon and Guards Lancer regiments. To their great credit, most of Eugen's shrunken infantry battalions formed so-called 'masses' against the cavalry and, with the soldiers standing back to back, retreated in good order, his right wing falling back into the village of Gossa itself. The Russian Guards light cavalry was caught before it had deployed, possibly because its commander, General Shevich, was killed by a cannon ball just as the action was about to start. In any case, two regiments could never have held back the equivalent of an entire cavalry corps. The lancers were pushed aside to the south-west, the dragoons directly southwards. The French cavalry overran part of the allied artillery, advanced past Gossa and came within a very few hundred metres of the hill on which the allied monarchs were watching events.

At this point the horsemen were brought to a halt by what Cathcart describes as

a small brook or drain [which] ran from Gossa towards the Pleisse . . . Its banks happened to be swampy and could only be passed with difficulty, and by a leap across a wide drain, unless by causeways made in two or three places by the farmers, for agricultural purposes. This obstacle was only partial, and a few hundred yards to the right, nearer Gossa, it ceased to be an impediment . . . But the enemy . . . were unexpectedly checked by this unforeseen obstacle; their crowding and confusion increased; and at that moment the Russian regiment of hussars of the guard, which Wittgenstein had sent . . . appeared in their rear.

This caused a panic. The unwieldy mass became noisy, and attempted to retire; the Russian light cavalry instantly followed them. The Emperor Alexander, who stood on the hill above, seized the opportunity to send off his own escort of Cossacks of the guard, amounting to several squadrons, under Count Orlov Denisov, who passed the stream at a favourable spot near Gossa, and took the retiring mass in flank. This completed the panic, which then became a flight, and the fugitives did not draw their bridles till they had regained the protection of their infantry.[31]

Cathcart does not mention the intervention of two Prussian cavalry regiments to which most German-language sources assign a role in the defeat of the French attack. Though he praises the Russian Guards cavalry, the main point of his narrative is the incompetence with which the attack was mounted. The French cavalry seemed to advance closely bunched together in columns and 'certainly in one body only, that is, with no sort of second line or reserve'. Inadequate discipline and leadership allowed them to be thrown into confusion 'by an insignificant obstacle' and then to be 'seized by a panic' and 'fly before a force of light cavalry, which altogether could not have amounted to 2000 men'. The fact that most of the French horsemen were heavy cavalry made their defeat by Cossacks, lancers and hussars all the more remarkable. Above all, Cathcart put down the rout to 'want of a second line on which to rally, and from which to take a fresh departure – a precaution without which no cavalry attack ought ever to be made'.[32]

A true 'cavalry patriot', in one respect Cathcart is clearly a little biased in his account of what he calls 'this remarkable cavalry affair'. He forgets the contribution of the Russian artillery. As the French cavalry approached his hill, Alexander turned to the commander of his artillery, Major-General Ivan Sukhozanet, and said: 'Look: whichever side gets its forces here first will win. Is your reserve artillery far away?' Only 25, Sukhozanet was another good example of how promotion on merit during the wars of 1805–13 had brought a number of excellent young officers into key positions. The son of a Polish officer, and himself without wealth or connections, Sukhozanet had done well in 1806–7 and thereby secured the notice of his superiors and transfer to the Guards artillery. For his performance under Wittgenstein in 1812 and then at Bautzen in 1813, he had won the St George's Cross and two promotions. Wittgenstein's elevation to commander-in-chief benefited officers close to him. In Sukhozanet's case it resulted in appointment as deputy to Prince Iashvili, the army's new commander of artillery. When Iashvili fell ill during the autumn campaign, Sukhozanet replaced him and Leipzig gave him the opportunity to distinguish himself under the emperor's eyes.[33]

Sukhozanet took this opportunity and justified Alexander's trust. To the emperor's question about the whereabouts of the artillery reserve, he replied, 'It will be here within two minutes.' Sukhozanet was better than his word. Two horse artillery batteries arrived immediately: one directly supported the attack of the Cossack Life Guards towards the east of the brook behind Gossa: Sukhozanet reported that 'it took the enemy columns by surprise and, opening up a punishing fire, brought them to a halt'. Meanwhile the other battery moved forward west of the brook and took up a flank position, from which it struck the packed ranks of the French cavalry to great effect. But for Sukhozanet and the Russian artillery the big test was still to come. As the French cavalry flooded back towards Liebertwollkwitz, their infantry moved on Gossa, supported by Drouot's massed artillery. Unlike at Borodino, however, on this occasion the Russian reserve artillery was well managed. Sukhozanet brought forward 80 guns from the reserve and, adding them to the batteries already in place, formed a line of more than 100 guns behind Gossa. This massive concentration of firepower took on Drouot's batteries and finally forced the French artillery to retreat. General Miloradovich had been at Borodino but he subsequently recalled that the artillery battle near Gossa on 16 October was the loudest he had ever heard in his life.[34]

Meanwhile the terrain had played a trick in the Russians' favour. From where Napoleon stood on the heights west of Liebertwollkwitz it was impossible to see what was happening behind the hill on which the allied monarchs were standing. In fact, as the French infantry were approaching Gossa the Russian and Prussian Guards infantry were arriving behind the allied centre. Their commander, Aleksei Ermolov, had ridden out with his aide-de-camp, Matvei Muromtsev, to scout the ground around Gossa and was almost caught by the French cavalry's attack. Fortunately, the Russians' horses were speedier than those of the French cavalrymen who pursued them but it had been a close shave. Some time before, Muromtsev had lost a bet to Ermolov. His forfeit was that at any moment when Ermolov began to whistle the first bars of an aria, Muromtsev was obliged to burst into song and complete the piece. Having regained the Russian lines, Ermolov began to whistle and Muromtsev launched into Leporello's famous aria from *Don Giovanni*. He recalls that Ermolov, 'at this moment, having just saved himself from death or captivity . . . completely preserved his composure, but I remember very well that my response was not expressed with anything like the same calmness'.[35]

Ermolov was a charismatic and inspiring figure at all times. In action he was larger than life, and his battlefield exploits and quips went the rounds of the Russian army. So too, in a quite different sense, did the behaviour of Aleksei Arakcheev. As the Semenovskys drew up behind the hill on which Alexander stood, Arakcheev rode down to talk to an old acquaintance, Colonel Pavel Pushchin. At this moment French batteries began to range in on the Semenovskys and a shell burst only 50 metres from where Pushchin and Arakcheev were talking. The count was an administrator, not a battlefield commander; Pushchin commented that this was the closest Arakcheev had come to French artillery during the Napoleonic Wars. Thoroughly alarmed by the explosion and learning from Pushchin that it was a shell, Arakcheev's face 'changed colour, he turned his horse round and departed at the gallop from the place of danger'. Russian officers saw cowardice as the greatest of vices. Most Guards officers loathed Arakcheev anyway, but his lack of physical courage was the final and unforgivable blot on his reputation.[36]

The French infantry which attempted to storm Gossa included Maison's division of Lauriston's Fifth Corps. Both Russian sources and General Griois, who commanded some of Drouot's batteries just behind Gossa, say that Oudinot's two Young Guard divisions also took part in the battle in the village. The initial allied 'garrison' of Gossa was made up of some of Eugen's battalions and three battalions of Pirch's Prussian brigade: both had been hotly engaged for hours and were very under strength. The St Petersburg and Tauride Grenadier regiments joined the defence of the village, as did the Guards Jaegers. Attack and counter-attack followed each other in a struggle for Gossa, which lasted for three hours. According to the Russians, each time the French were driven out, a fresh wave of enemy infantry forced their way back into the village. In the end the issue was decided by the Russian 2nd Guards Infantry Division, who stormed into the village from the south-west in battalion columns without firing a shot. Fighting literally under the eyes of the emperor, the Guards displayed exceptional courage. More than half the officers of the Finland Guards Regiment were killed or wounded. The commander of the regiment, Major-General Maksim Kryzhanovsky, was wounded four times before he allowed himself to be carried off the battlefield.[37]

For once, however, it was not an officer but a private soldier who earned most fame in the battle for Gossa. Leontii Korennoi was a grenadier in the Third Battalion of the Finland Guards. Like most grenadiers of the Guards, he was tall and broad-shouldered. He was a veteran, who had been in the Finland Regiment since its formation, having previously served in the Kronstadt Garrison Regiment. A married man, he became known as 'uncle' in the Finland Guards. At Borodino he had won a military medal for his courage in the skirmishing line. Now he surpassed himself. Gossa was a village of stone houses, stout garden walls and many lanes. Amidst the ebb and flow of the action, the commander of the Third Battalion of the Finland Guards, Colonel Gervais, and some of his officers were cut off by a sudden French counter-attack. At first with a handful of comrades and then alone, Korennoi held off the French while the officers escaped over the walls back to the rest of the battalion.

To their great honour, the French not only took Korennoi prisoner but presented him to Napoleon himself, who praised his courage and ensured that he was well looked after. Since the French army was itself not short of heroes, Korennoi's exploit must indeed have been remarkable to win such treatment. He got back to his regiment by the end of the battle, where his comrades regarded him as a figure virtually risen from the dead. Korennoi's bust was to occupy pride of place in the barracks of the Finland Guards until 1917 and the song of the regiment ('We remember Uncle Korennoi') was composed in his honour.[38]

While Leontii Korennoi was winning fame, Pamfil Nazarov was fighting his first real battle with the Finland Guards. He recalls that the Grand Duke Constantine rode down the ranks of the regiment before they advanced against Gossa, telling the Guardsmen to load their muskets and ordering them to advance. Like many of his comrades, Pamfil was wounded in the attack before he even reached the village, in his case in the right leg above the knee. He remembers too that his overcoat was shredded by bullets. Pamfil collapsed and lost much blood. He recalls how hot his blood seemed to him. Somehow he dragged himself back the 2 kilometres to the medical point, collapsing once more on the way and constantly threatened by the cannon balls that continued to whistle by. When he got to the casualty point he found the regimental ammunition, flags, musicians and doctor. After being bandaged, he tottered to a fire by which to spend this cold and rainy night. A comrade from the regiment gave him two salted cucumbers, a big boon.

After much bleeding in the night, Pamfil re-bandaged himself and set off to the rear, carrying his haversack and using his musket as a crutch. His leg swelled up from days of walking and in the end he had to find a cart to get him to a hospital. Finally he got to a field hospital in Plauen on 28 October, where there were so many wounded that he had to be placed in a chapel. On the other hand there were also many German doctors and medical assistants present. It was now twelve days since Pamfil's wound had been bandaged and it was infected. There followed days of agony as bandages were changed and ointment was injected directly into the wound twice daily on lint attached to a huge needle. He did not get back to his regiment until the beginning of 1814.[39]

Nevertheless the sacrifices of Pamfil and his comrades did achieve their goal. Gossa was held and Napoleon's great counter-attack stopped. That evening the young officers of Ermolov's staff put on an impromptu performance of Racine's *Phèdre* in the ruins of Gossa. In tactical terms the first day of Leipzig was a draw. Apart from Blücher's capture of villages north of Leipzig, the two armies occupied almost the exact positions where they had started the day. In reality, however, a draw signified an allied victory. If Napoleon was to hold Germany, he had to defeat the allies decisively on the battle's first day. Otherwise, with more than 100,000 fresh troops close at hand, allied strength would become overwhelming. This should have been clear to Napoleon by nightfall on 16 October, though as always clarity is far easier in retrospect than on the evening of a battle. The wisest policy would have been to organize an immediate orderly retreat, getting his baggage away as quickly as possible and building additional crossings over the river Elster to avoid the very dangerous dependence on a single bridge. In fact it was not until the evening of 17 October that he made any arrangements for a retreat and even then nothing was done to ease the army's passage out of Leipzig and over the Elster. Instead he wasted time talking to the captured General Meerveldt, whom he then sent back to Francis II, seemingly in the naive hope that the allies might negotiate and allow him to escape.

Very little action occurred on Sunday, 17 October. Neither Bernadotte nor Bennigsen was yet on the battlefield and, since Napoleon showed no sign of departing, the allied monarchs were content to let their men rest and await the arrival of reinforcements. The only significant fighting to occur that day was a brilliant charge by Ilarion Vasilchikov's hussar division, which delighted Blücher, himself an old hussar, and resulted in the French not only losing many men and guns but also pulling right back in the north-west to the suburbs in front of the Halle Gate. From here any further retreat was unthinkable: if the Russians burst through the Halle Gate into Leipzig, the line of retreat of Napoleon himself and the entire army would be cut. Once he received news that the Army of Bohemia would not attack that day, however, Blücher was forced to postpone Sacken's attempt to break into Leipzig from the north until 18 October.[40]

The last two days of the battle of Leipzig – 18 and 19 October – were in one sense an anticlimax. There were no daring movements or examples of inspired military leadership. It was often the French, fighting with skill and courage in the many stout buildings in and near Leipzig, who had the better of encounters at least in the short run. When thousands of men are losing their lives it is wrong to talk of a battle being 'boring', but for the military scholar, when compared to an Austerlitz or Cannae, Leipzig was indeed a 'boring' battle. The key point, however, is that 'boring' battles were exactly what the allies needed to fight. Given their army's unmanageable size, its multi-national composition and its chaotic command structure, any attempt to do something clever or complicated was bound to end in disaster. What was required was to pin Napoleon down in a spot where his army could be subjected to the full weight of allied superiority in men and guns. This is what the allies achieved in the last two days of the battle of Leipzig. By the afternoon of 18 October they had concentrated all their troops and 1,360 guns on the battlefield.

The morning of 18 October dawned bright and sunny. That day the allies formed a huge semicircle enclosing Leipzig to the east, north and south. They attacked Napoleon all along this line. Probably the best-known events on 18 October are the defection of some Saxon regiments to the allies, but the desertion of a very few thousand men was actually of little significance in a battle fought by half a million soldiers. More important was the fact that Bernadotte's almost 60,000-strong Army of the North only arrived on the battlefield in mid-afternoon. This in turn forced Bennigsen to spread his army more thinly and reduced the possibility of his outflanking the village of Probstheida from the east and thereby forcing its abandonment. Probstheida was the key strong-point of Napoleon's position south of Leipzig and he hung on to it all day, thanks to the strength of its buildings and the heroism of its French defenders, to which allied accounts pay tribute. On the allied side it was the Prussians who bore the brunt of the costly attempts to take the village but even the remnants of Eugen's corps were made to join in, despite their terrible losses on the previous day. Meanwhile three regiments of the Russian 1st Guards Division and the whole of the Prussian Guard stood by idly less than a kilometre away, despite not having fired a shot on the battle's first day.

To an extent this was the monarchs once again protecting their Guards, but it was also simply the logic of Napoleonic-era warfare to try to preserve elite units as reserves until the moment of crisis came in a campaign or battle. Sacken had no Guards but in fact he conducted his attempts to storm through the Halle suburb in similar fashion. He committed Neverovsky's 27th Division and Lieven's two jaeger regiments but the three veteran infantry regiments of the 10th Division were held in reserve throughout the battle despite the tremendous casualties of the rest of Sacken's corps as they tried to fight their way through Leipzig's northern suburbs.

Even without the field fortifications constructed by the French, the suburbs around the Halle Gate were a formidable obstacle. Just in front of them flowed the river Pleisse, while the hamlet of Pfaffendorf with its stout buildings formed a strong advance point to blunt any attempt to break into the town. The approaches to the Halle Gate were narrow and the Russian infantry was vulnerable to flanking fire, not just from Pfaffendorf but also from the walls of the Rosenthal park to their west. The Austrian official history, by no means Russophile in sympathy, commented that 'the Russian soldiers performed with wonderful bravery and their officers too did everything possible'.[41]

Colonel Petr Rakhmanov, the brave and exceptionally intelligent former editor of *Voennyi zhurnal* and the commander of one of Neverovsky's brigades, was killed here, as was Colonel Huene, the 27th

Division's artillery commander. We last encountered Dmitrii Dushen-kevich as a 15-year-old ensign during his first battle, at Krasnyi in August 1812. By October 1813 he was an aide-de-camp to Dmitrii Neverovsky. He recalls that on 18 October Neverovsky was as usual in the thick of the action, with buildings burning all around, and attack and counter-attack rapidly following each other in ferocious house-to-house fighting. Neverovsky was encouraging Rakhmanov's troops as they attempted to storm their way towards the Halle Gate when he was hit in the left leg by a bullet. He was carried out of the battle by his Cossack escort and died a few days later. As part of the centenary celebrations in 1912, his body was taken back to Russia and reburied near the position defended by his division at Borodino.[42]

By the end of 18 October the Russians had suffered serious casualties but were little nearer the Halle Gate than they had been that morning. Nevertheless, contrary to some accounts, their sacrifice was by no means in vain. Dombrowski's Polish division were the initial defenders of the Halle suburb and, as often happened when Poles encountered Russians, the fighting was particularly bitter. But as Russian pressure mounted, more and more French reinforcements were committed to defend this vital area. These included Brayer's 8th Division, as well as twelve bat-talions and three batteries of the Young Guard. As Langeron noted, Sacken's attack diverted all these men from reinforcing the defenders of Schönefeld against his attempts to capture this crucial village.[43]

Schönefeld was the key to Napoleon's position in the north, just as Probstheida was in the south. It too was made up of mostly two-storey, solidly built stone houses and their gardens, with the whole village surrounded by a stout wall. To complicate the Russians' problem further, just to the village's south was a walled cemetery which gave excellent cover to defenders. It was also difficult to outflank Schönefeld from the north since the village lay very close to the marshy banks of the river Parthe. In addition, the attack on Schönefeld ran into the normal problems facing any army attempting to take these Saxon vil-lages. Given sufficient numbers and courage, the attacking infantry would break into the village, albeit at the cost of heavy casualties. But they would then be subject to counter-attacks by fresh enemy troops concentrated out of fire behind the village and supported by their massed artillery. Bringing forward the attackers' own guns through or around the village in sufficient numbers to match these enemy batteries was extremely difficult. Captain Radozhitsky attempted to do just this at Schönefeld and found his batteries smothered by overwhelming canister fire at short range. Langeron's first two major attacks took Schönefeld and then lost it again. Only after Bernadotte deployed all his artillery and pounded the village from the south did Schönefeld finally fall at 6 p.m. Even then Langeron's men had to hold it against fierce French counter-attacks which lasted into the night.[44]

The fall of Schönefeld posed the risk that the allies would advance into the rear of Napoleon's troops south of Leipzig and cut off their retreat. In fact, however, even by the morning of 18 October Napoleon had decided to abandon Leipzig. The only issue was whether he would get most of his army and its baggage away safe and sound. Already, early on 17 October, Bertrand's corps had been ordered down the highway beyond Lindenau in order to secure Weissenfels and Napoleon's retreat to the west. His corps was replaced at Lindenau by troops sent by Marshal Ney. The army's baggage train began to move back through Leipzig too. Drawing in his perimeter and using the stout Saxon buildings as strong-points, Napoleon stopped the allies from breaking into his rear or cutting off his retreat on 18 October.

The big test would come on 19 October, when his rearguards needed to hold the allies at bay for long enough for Napoleon to squeeze most of his soldiers, his guns and his still considerable baggage through the streets of Leipzig and over the bridge which was the only route to safety. Inevitably, many of Napoleon's batteries had to remain on the battlefield as long as possible to protect the rearguard from the allies' overwhelming superiority in artillery. Equally inevitably, this would greatly worsen the traffic jam in Leipzig on 19 October. Above all, Napoleon had needlessly worsened the situation by failing to build extra bridges to span the Elster. The Russian official history blamed Napoleon's failure on 'the usual disorder of French military administration of that time'.[45]

The allied columns began their advance on Leipzig at 7 a.m. on 19 October. Meanwhile Napoleon had entrusted the task of forming a rearguard to Poniatowski's Polish corps and to MacDonald's corps of French, Italian and German divisions. It is probably realistic to note that if Napoleon retreated behind the Rhine very many of these non-French troops would abandon his cause anyway. Nevertheless the rearguards fought effectively outside Leipzig's walls, using the many buildings and other obstacles to delay the allied advance. Even so, by eleven in the morning the allies were beginning to break through the four gates into the inner city. By midday, though the fight put up by the rearguards had enabled most of Napoleon's troops to escape over the Elster, many thousands of men and a vast amount of artillery were still trying to force their way through the streets of Leipzig. In these circumstances it is not surprising that a catastrophe occurred.

On the far right of the allied line north of Leipzig the Halle Gate into the city was finally stormed by the 39th Jaegers of Lieven's 10th Division. This was a formidable unit, formed out of the Briansk Infantry Regiment in 1810. Most of its officers and every single NCO had served their entire careers in the regiment. The 39th Jaegers had fought against the Ottomans in 1809–12 and then had performed well under Sacken in 1812 and the first half of 1813. Used to tackling strong Ottoman fortresses, the regiment had overwhelmed the defenders of the Polish fortress town of Czenstochowa in no time in March 1813 by their accurate marksmanship, winning ceremonial silver trumpets for themselves and promotion to lieutenant-general for Johann von Lieven. At Leipzig the regiment was commanded by Mikhail Akhlestyshev, an excellent officer who was badly wounded in the final assault on the Halle Gate.[46]

Meanwhile Alexandre de Langeron's infantry was moving up in Sacken's support. Two of his jaeger regiments – the 29th and 45th – advanced westwards through the Rosenthal garden and around the city's northern wall, getting across an undefended bridge over a small branch of the Elster and advancing into the city past the Jakob Hospital. Both the 29th and 45th Jaegers had fought in all the key actions of the recent war against the Ottomans, from the siege of Khotin in 1806 through the attempts to storm Brailov and Jurja, and concluding with Kutuzov's annihilation of the main Ottoman army in the winter of 1811–12. In 1812 and the spring of 1813 they had served in Sacken's corps, winning many plaudits but suffering nothing like the casualties of the regiments which had fought at Borodino or pursued Napoleon from Tarutino to Vilna. When they arrived at Leipzig both regiments were still packed with veterans who had years of experience of sharpshooting, street-fighting and raiding parties.[47]

The advance of the 29th and 45th Jaegers past Jakob Hospital brought them shortly after midday to within close range of the only bridge over the main branch of the Elster, across which Napoleon's army was retreating. Explosive charges had been laid under the bridge. Amidst the chaos of the retreat, the officer in charge had abandoned his post to get clarification as to when to detonate the charges, leaving a mere corporal in command in his absence. Coming under accurate musket fire from the 45th and 29th Jaegers and armed with instructions to destroy the bridge when the enemy approached, the corporal quite understandably detonated the charges. Not only Napoleon but also a number of other memoirists subsequently blamed the corporal for the loss of the thousands of men and hundreds of guns which the bridge's destruction stranded in Leipzig. Rather obviously, when the fate of a huge army is allowed to depend on a single bridge and a solitary corporal the responsibility lies further up the military hierarchy.[48]

The allies lost 52,000 men at the battle of Leipzig, of whom the largest share – 22,000 – were Russians. It says a great deal for the discipline of the allied armies that despite three days of fighting and this level of casualties there was very little looting or disorder when they stormed into Leipzig. French losses were certainly greater. Perhaps they were only 60,000, as French accounts claim: on the other hand, by the time the army reached Erfurt it had only 70,000 men under arms and 30,000 unarmed stragglers, so overall casualties during or immediately after the battle must have been closer to 100,000. Three hundred guns and 900 ammunition wagons were also left behind in Leipzig. The allied victory was therefore unequivocal and led to the loss to Napoleon of all Germany east of the Rhine.[49]

Given their superiority in numbers this was a battle that the allies ought to have won. That they came close to losing it on the first day was above all the fault of Schwarzenberg. The battle of Leipzig was Napoleon's last chance to hold Germany and he was right to seize the opportunity that Schwarzenberg's mistakes gave him on the battle's first day. His failure to win decisively on 16 October owed much more to the courage and tenacity of the allied troops than to any mistakes made by Napoleon. Once the chance of victory on the first day had gone, however, the odds were hopelessly against Napoleon and he delayed his retreat too long and failed properly to prepare for it.

Among the allied leaders, the chief hero was Blücher. Without him the three allied armies would never have converged on Leipzig at all. Admittedly, he had taken some great risks and luck had been on his side. Blücher too was responsible for diverting Marmont's corps from Napoleon's attack on the Army of Bohemia on 16 October and for finally dragging Bernadotte onto the battlefield two days later. Great credit does also go to Alexander, however. Only his intervention could have forced Schwarzenberg to change the initial allied deployment for the battle. Without his insistence, the Russian reserves would never have arrived in time behind Gossa on 16 October. His nagging contributed to Schwarzenberg's release of the Austrian reserves in time as well. It is fair to conclude that without Alexander the battle of Leipzig would probably have been lost. The emperor had finally made amends on the battlefield for the disaster at Austerlitz.

Napoleon's retreat from Leipzig bore some resemblance to his retreat from Moscow. The French army moved at great speed, at the price of many stragglers and much indiscipline. Russian Cossacks and light cavalry harried the retreating columns, picking up thousands of prisoners. Schwarzenberg pursued Napoleon no more quickly than Kutuzov had done. Even Blücher was left well behind by the French and then swung too far to the north because he misjudged their line of retreat. The role of Chichagov was played by the Bavarian-Austrian army under Marshal Wrede, which tried to cut across Napoleon's march at Haynau and was defeated. Since the Bavarians had just changed sides the French took particular pleasure in this victory over 'traitors'. As at the Berezina, Napoleon's army showed great courage and resilience with its back to the wall and its very survival in question. Nevertheless Napoleon could not afford the almost 15,000 additional casualties he sustained at Haynau. On 2 November he crossed the Rhine back into France.

No doubt the retreat from Leipzig lacked many of the horrors of the march from Moscow to the Russian border exactly one year before. There was little snow, fewer avenging peasants and no tales of cannibalism. There was, however, plenty of typhus: Napoleon got back to the Rhine with perhaps 85,000 men but thousands succumbed to the disease within days. Meanwhile the allied armies occupied Frankfurt, the old 'capital' of the Holy Roman Empire, and moved up to the Rhine. Germany east of the river was theirs. The foundations of the European balance of power had been restored. The objectives of the Russo-Prussian-Austrian alliance had therefore largely been achieved. The 1813 campaign was over.

13

The Invasion of France

In the 1814 campaign military operations were entangled with diplomacy and with French domestic politics. This was the inevitable result of allied success in 1813. The treaties of alliance signed at Teplitz in September 1813 had committed the Russians, Prussians and Austrians to pushing Napoleon back across the Rhine and restoring German independence. By November 1813 this goal was achieved. The allies now had to decide whether to stick to their previous limited war aims or to increase them. If they chose to do the latter, then they needed to agree on new goals. Whatever they decided, they required a French government which would negotiate a peace settlement and then stick to it. War-weariness might well persuade Frenchmen to welcome peace in the short run but after twenty-two years of war the allies longed for lasting peace, not just a temporary armistice. Designing a settlement which would guarantee European peace and stability, satisfy the allied powers' interests and also be acceptable to French society was bound to be hard.[1]

Should the allies offer France its so-called 'natural frontiers' – in other words the border marked out by the Rhine, the Alps and the Pyrenees and envisaged in the Teplitz treaties? Or should they seek to reduce France to its 'historic' borders, meaning the territory ruled by the French king in 1792? This was not the same question as whether the allies should negotiate with Napoleon or try to overthrow him, but the issues were linked. It was perhaps conceivable that Napoleon would tolerate a peace based on 'natural borders', but only a great optimist could believe that he would see a settlement linked to the old royal frontiers as anything other than a temporary truce. The allies knew, however, that it was neither in their power nor in their interests to impose a regime on the French. Their armies could not occupy France for ever. Sooner rather than later they needed a French regime with sufficient legitimacy to accept a peace settlement and survive in power, once initial war-weariness had faded in French society. There was plenty of room for honest disagreement among the allies about what kind of French regime would best fit this bill. The one obvious point, though, was that the more a regime was seen to be imposed by the allies, the harder its task would be to win acceptance among the French people.

These questions were complicated and without clear answers. Suspicion and arguments in the allied camp were made far worse, however, by clashes of interest over the final peace settlement for Europe as a whole. Directly or indirectly, Napoleon had ruled over most of Poland, Germany, Italy and the Low Countries. The fate of all of these territories now had to be decided, and this had enormous implications for the power, status and security of all the allied states. Above all there was Poland, or more specifically the Duchy of Warsaw. The whole Duchy was former Prussian or Austrian territory. Alexander wanted it for Russia. The balance of power in east-central Europe between the three major continental allies was widely seen as turning on this issue. Disagreements about how Poland should be partitioned had broken up the First Coalition against Revolutionary France. They were the likeliest source of disintegration for the present coalition too. Nor could the Polish issue be kept separate from the question of how to deal with Napoleon and France. Faced with Russo-Prussian solidarity, Austria looked to France as a possible ally. If too weakened or humiliated by the peace, the French could not fulfil this role. On the other hand, a France indebted to Vienna for a moderate peace settlement and ruled by Francis II's son-in-law, Napoleon, might be a useful check to Russian power.[2]

Though some tensions existed between all the allied powers, the most important conflict was between Austria and Russia. One key area of rivalry was the Balkans. In 1808–12 the Russians seemed on the verge of conquering all of present-day Romania and turning Serbia into their client state, thereby increasing their prestige and leverage throughout the Balkans. Only the threat of Napoleon's invasion had persuaded Petersburg to draw back, but no one in Vienna could be naive enough to believe that this was the end of the story. More broadly, the Austrians feared growing Russian power, of which 1812 had been a reminder. Her geographical near-invulnerability, the quality of her army and the scale of her resources all made Russia an empire to be feared.

Nevertheless, one must not exaggerate: in 1814 Austria was not yet greatly inferior to Russia in power. We are still far from the era of 1914, by which time Russia had been strengthened by huge population growth and the Austrian army weakened by the conflicts between the Habsburg Empire's many nationalities. Even on their own in 1814 the Austrians could hope to put up a stout defence against Russia. Allied to Prussia they had every chance of defeating it. In many ways the main problem for Metternich in 1814 was Russo-Prussian solidarity, which increased Russian confidence and gave Russia a secure gateway into central Europe. The Russo-Prussian alliance threatened to isolate Austria and cut across Metternich's desire for a Germanic bloc which would largely exclude French or Russian influence from central Europe. Within that bloc Austrian resources and Habsburg history would give Vienna a natural pre-eminence. Meanwhile Metternich envisaged that peace and equilibrium in Europe as a whole would be protected by a balance of power between France and Russia.[3]

Austrian perspectives had some support within the Prussian government. When the Treaty of Kalicz had been negotiated between Russia and Prussia in February 1813 there had been much tension over the fate of Prussia's former territories in the Duchy of Warsaw. The Prussian king's closest military adviser, Major-General Karl von dem Knesebeck, shared the Austrian high command's fears about attempting to march on Paris and unseat Napoleon.[4]

Against Knesebeck stood Blücher, Gneisenau and the Army of Silesia. Their views are sometimes belittled as stemming from nothing but desire for revenge and military glory. This is unfair. The Army of Silesia's quartermaster-general, Baron Müffling, was a cool-headed staff officer, personally much closer to Knesebeck than to Gneisenau or Blücher. But he shared their view that lasting peace required Napoleon's removal. He believed that if the emperor remained in power, after a short respite to rest and regroup his resources he was certain to try to overturn any peace settlement. All his veterans currently in allied captivity or in hospitals would stand ready to support him. Meanwhile, Müffling added, as Napoleon advanced over the Rhine, the Russian army would be 1,000 kilometres away and unable to come to Prussia's assistance.[5]

In the end, Prussian policy depended on Frederick William III. The king shared Müffling's views and was satisfied with the deal struck at

Kalicz. Once Frederick William had gone through the agony of making the great decision to back Russia in February 1813 he was temperamentally very disinclined to review it. In any case he trusted and admired Alexander. The king was also grateful for the fact that the tsar had refused to abandon Prussia at Tilsit and had rescued his kingdom from Napoleon in 1813. Very soon the Russo-Prussian alliance was to be drawn even closer by the marriage of the king's eldest daughter to Alexander's younger brother and eventual heir, the Grand Duke Nicholas.[6]

Amidst the rivalries of the continental allies, Britain stood somewhat apart. Her role in the alliance which liberated Germany in 1813 was mostly limited to subsidizing her allies' armies. By the winter of 1813–14, however, matters had changed. With Germany free and a final peace in the offing, Britain moved to the centre of the picture. The continental allies knew by bitter experience that if Britain and France remained at war they would end by being dragged in. Demobilizing their armies, restoring their finances and rebuilding international trade would be difficult. Britain therefore had to be brought into the peace settlement and her continental allies hoped that she would help to reconcile the French to peace by restoring many of the overseas colonies conquered between 1793 and 1814.

In 1813 Britain's diplomatic representatives at the three allied courts had not been impressive. Lord Cathcart and Sir Charles Stewart were generals, more anxious to join in the campaign than to conduct negotiations. Meanwhile Lord Aberdeen, the 28-year-old envoy to Austria, could not even speak decent French and inevitably was eaten by Metternich. One Austrian source commented that 'of the three only Aberdeen had any aptitude for diplomacy though he had no experience. The other two lacked either aptitude or experience.' The allies appealed to London to send a political heavyweight who could conduct peace negotiations. In response there arrived at allied headquarters in January 1814 Viscount Castlereagh, one of the ablest foreign secretaries Britain has ever possessed.[7]

The basic point, however, was that Britain was by some margin the most powerful of the four allies. After its defeat in the American War of Independence, the United Kingdom had faced the combined challenge of the French, Spanish and Dutch fleets. Now in 1814 these fleets had largely been destroyed and the Royal Navy dominated the seas. Behind it stood by far the strongest merchant marine and shipbuilding industry in the world. Beyond those stood Britain's immense financial and commercial resources. Scotland and Ireland, the historical back-doors into England, were now firmly under London's control. To these fundamental elements in British power were added Wellington and his soldiers, the best army and the best general fielded by Britain in the last two centuries. In 1814 the allied monarchs knew that Wellington's advance deep into southern France was keeping Marshal Soult and more than 40,000 troops tied down, far from the key theatre of operations in the north. Even more important, the logic of international relations in Europe worked in Britain's favour. The continental allies might often resent Britain's wealth and security, but their key interests were always more at risk from their land neighbours. They shared Britain's commitment to a balance of power on the continent for reasons of their own security. But a continental balance of power meant that British maritime and colonial dominance could not be seriously challenged.[8]

This reality was reflected in the peace negotiations. Britain insisted that 'maritime rights' – in other words the international laws of the sea – should not be subject to negotiation. It got its way. The Russians were unhappy about this. The consul-general in London wrote that right up to the end of the war the Royal Navy was still seizing Russian ships and cargoes. Sometimes these ships did have false papers but it was in any case very difficult to prove the opposite to suspicious British officers. The Russian embassy was never informed that ships had been seized and all subsequent procedures were secret and slow. Even if the British ultimately accepted that the Russian ships were on legitimate business, the long delays caused ruinous losses. No apologies or compensation were ever offered, nor were British officers ever punished for mistaken or malicious seizure of ships. But in 1814 the Russian government had higher priorities than maritime law and could not afford to offend London.[9]

The most important territorial gains of the United Kingdom in 1793–1814 – impossible without maritime supremacy – had been made from Indian princes and were therefore not part of the peace negotiations. Nor was the informal British commercial empire which was moving into the void left by the collapse of Spanish interests in South America. The colonies taken from France and her allies were subject to negotiation and London showed wisdom and moderation in returning, for example, the rich East Indies territories to the Dutch. But Britain retained Malta, the Cape and a number of islands in the Indian Ocean which strengthened her hold over the sea-lanes. Some of Britain's war aims in Europe had already been achieved by December 1813. Spain, for example, had been liberated. The one big remaining priority was to get the French out of Belgium and to ensure that the Belgian coast was in friendly hands. Without this, wrote Castlereagh, the Royal Navy would need to remain on a permanent wartime footing. But no European power save France was opposed to this British interest, and at the very moment when Castlereagh was making his statement the Dutch revolt against Napoleon was promising to solve the Belgian problem in a manner acceptable to London. In these circumstances Britain was able to hold the balance among the allies, helping to moderate their quarrels and tilting against any of them whose power or pretensions seemed to threaten British interests.[10]

In 1814 most of this 'tilting' occurred against Russia, partly just because it was the most powerful of the continental allies and partly because Alexander's aims and manner sometimes appeared unclear and even intimidating to British eyes. To an even greater extent than was true of Metternich, Alexander directed his country's foreign policy. Whereas Metternich ran Austrian policy because his sovereign and indeed the Austrian elite as a whole shared his outlook and trusted him to defend their interests, Alexander controlled Russian policy because he was sovereign and autocrat. Far from expressing a consensus view of the Russian ruling elite, on some key issues the emperor was very much in a minority.

For many of Alexander's advisers the key point was that an exhausted Russia was pouring out its wealth and soldiers on issues which appeared far removed from the empire's own core interests. Aleksandr Chernyshev was not just very loyal but also a consummate courtier. Even he wrote to the emperor in November 1813 that 'of all the coalition powers, Russia is the one which most needs a speedy peace. Deprived of trade for many years, it needs to restore order to its finances; . . . the richest Russian provinces have been devastated and require help urgently. Only the end of the war will heal these wounds.'[11]

Very few of Alexander's advisers would have disagreed. Admiral Shishkov had opposed crossing the Neman into Germany. The idea of crossing the Rhine into France reduced him to near hysteria. The minister of finance, Dmitrii Gurev, issued warnings that a further year of war threatened the state with bankruptcy. Kutuzov was dead and Rumiantsev marginalized, but Jomini took up their old call, reminding the emperor that a powerful France holding the Rhine frontier and the Belgian coast was essential to Russian interests since only this could check 'formidable British power'. Of Alexander's senior generals, the Russian commanders in the Army of Silesia took the same line as Blücher. As a royalist émigré, Alexandre de Langeron had personal reasons for wanting to drive Napoleon off his throne but Fabian von der Osten-Sacken horrified the assembled dignitaries of Nancy, all desperate to sit on the fence, by calling on them to join him in a toast of 'death and destruction to the tyrant who has so long been the scourge of the French nation and the plague of Europe'. On the other hand, in Alexander's own headquarters many of his closest advisers were much more cautious and inclined towards a compromise peace.[12]

Karl Nesselrode dismissed the worries of his father-in-law, the minister of finance, in terms of which the emperor would certainly have approved: 'The troops are fed and more or less clothed at the expense of the countries in which they are waging war. The conventions with Prussia and Austria are wholly to our advantage, the revenues of the Duchy of Warsaw accrue to us alone. So I don't understand why the war should be so terribly expensive.' On the other hand, Alexander's chief assistant for diplomatic affairs disagreed with the emperor on the two key issues which were of overriding importance not just for the monarch but also for Russia's relations with its allies. These were the fate of Poland and the question of whether to march on Paris and seek to overthrow Napoleon. Though he knew that his advice would be unwelcome, Nesselrode showed moral courage by continuing to defend what he considered to be the state's true interests.[13]

Nesselrode had submitted his key memorandum on Polish affairs to Alexander back in January 1813. In it he argued that appeasing the Poles by establishing an autonomous Polish kingdom would not add substantially to Russia's strength and would have fatal political consequences. It would both alienate Vienna and infuriate patriotic Russians, who believed that recent Polish behaviour towards Russia made them unworthy of any concessions. In the longer term, it would be immensely difficult for the autocratic tsar to function simultaneously as constitutional king of Poland. Since nothing would ever wean Polish elites from hopes of independence, the final result of incorporating the Duchy of Warsaw into the empire might be the loss of the Polish-dominated provinces which currently were part of the empire's western borderlands.[14]

Nesselrode's views had not changed by the winter of 1813. Meanwhile he was also submitting to Alexander unpalatable advice about negotiations with Napoleon. Nesselrode wrote that the allies had fulfilled their war aims. The possibility now existed of a peace which 'will enable Your Majesty to labour in security for the good of his subjects and to heal the deep wounds caused by the war, while establishing the western borders of his empire to his advantage and being able to exert on other governments a benevolent and equitable influence, rooted in the memory of the services which You have rendered to them'. In comparison to this certainty, 'it is impossible to calculate the chances offered by a prolonged war fought for unclear and excessive goals'.[15]

Nesselrode's views weakened Alexander's trust in him. Countess Nesselrode wrote to her husband that he was far too close to Metternich both personally and in his opinions for his own good. Nesselrode's own private letters reveal a barely suppressed frustration with the emperor. This frustration was shared by many key figures in the allied leadership in early 1814. To them Alexander appeared not just overbearing but also at times driven by purely personal and petty motives. In one of his first reports to the British prime minister from allied headquarters, Lord Castlereagh wrote that 'I think our greatest danger at present is from the *chevalresque* tone in which the Emperor Alexander is disposed to push the war. He has a *personal* feeling about Paris, distinct from all political or military combinations. He seems to seek for the occasion of entering with his magnificent guards the enemy's capital, probably to display, in his clemency and forbearance, a contrast' to the destruction of Moscow.[16]

Castlereagh's comment showed insight. In 1814 Alexander did sometimes allow himself to be swayed by personal and even petty considerations which had little to do with Russian interests. He saw his role of victor and peace-giver as a personal apotheosis. He also remembered that in 1812 he had stood alone against a seemingly invincible enemy whose huge army had included strong Austrian and Prussian contingents. In the following year he had risked much and shown great skill and patience in dragging first Prussia and then Austria into his victorious coalition. By February 1814 he felt that the reward for his efforts was an undeserved level of distrust and criticism from not just his allies but also many of his advisers. A combination of exaltation and bruised feelings is never easy to deal with. To complicate matters, Alexander's views on international relations were never rooted purely in realpolitik. His long-held idealism about international cooperation was now being influenced by his new-found Christian beliefs in ways which the down-to-earth pragmatists who ran the foreign policies of the other powers found disconcerting.[17]

The key point, however, is not just to understand Alexander's emotions but also to recognize that the core of his policy was usually rational and also in many instances more correct than his critics allowed. Reconciling Polish aspirations with Russian security was a hugely important matter for his empire. Alexander's attempt to do this was generous and imaginative. In the end it failed but so have all subsequent Russian efforts to square this circle. Moreover, though it caused uncertainty and suspicion, the emperor's determination not to reveal his cards and to postpone discussion of Polish affairs until after the end of the war was wise. Any attempt to do otherwise would surely have broken up the coalition.

Of course Alexander understood the argument of some of his advisers that French power was essential to keep British ambitions in check. To some extent this had been part of the rationale underlying Russian policy at Tilsit and in the following years. Rumiantsev had wished to use Napoleon against Britain just as Metternich hoped to use him to balance Russia. But the basic point was that France was too powerful and Napoleon far too ambitious for either the Austrians or Russians to use safely. Attempts to do so merely condemned Europe to more years of conflict and instability. Alexander's insight that Napoleon would never honour any settlement acceptable to the allies, and that lasting peace could only be made in Paris, was correct. More than any other individual, he was responsible for Napoleon's overthrow. If leadership of the coalition had rested with Metternich and Schwarzenberg, there is every likelihood that the 1814 campaign would have ended with Napoleon on his throne, the allies behind the Rhine, and Europe condemned to unending conflict and chaos. On the day that Paris finally capitulated, Castlereagh's half-brother, Sir Charles Stewart, wrote that 'it would be injustice' not to recognize Alexander's achievement as the man who had led the allies to victory and thereby 'richly deserved the appellation of the liberator of mankind'.[18]

In early November 1813, however, when the allies reached Frankfurt and encamped on the Rhine, Paris still seemed far away. In Frankfurt, the allied leaders agreed on a combined political and military strategy. They would offer Napoleon peace on very moderate terms. As even Metternich admitted to one of his Austrian subordinates, there was every probability that the emperor would reject these terms. But the offer of peace would clarify allied aims and allow them to expose Napoleon's intransigence to the French people. Throughout the 1814 campaign a key allied tactic was to stress that they were fighting Napoleon's insatiable ambitions, not France and her legitimate interests and pride. They were terrified that Napoleon might succeed in mobilizing 'the nation in arms' against their invasion of France, just as his republican predecessors had done in 1792–4. On the contrary, if they could split Napoleon from the French nation, this might either increase the pressure on him to make peace or encourage the emergence of an alternative French regime with which the allies could negotiate.[19]

The biggest source of allied leverage would be military. Having seen how Napoleon had used the winter of 1812–13 to recover from disaster in Russia and create a new army, the allies were determined not to give him a second such opportunity. They therefore committed themselves to a full-scale winter invasion of France. If any of the allied leaders had doubts about this commitment, they were quickly dispelled by news from Paris that on 15 November Napoleon had summoned a further 300,000 men to the colours, on top of the 280,000 conscripts whose recruitment had already been announced in the autumn of 1813. The allied response to this was a ringing manifesto aimed at the French people. It stated that

the French government has just ordered a new levy of 300,000 conscripts. The justifications set out in the new law are a provocation against the allied powers . . . The allied powers are not making war against France . . . but against the domination which the Emperor Napoleon has for too long exercised beyond the borders of his empire, to the misfortune of both Europe and France . . . The allied sovereigns desire that France should be strong, great and happy because a strong and great France is one of the fundamental bases of the whole order of the world (*édifice sociale*) . . . But the allied powers themselves want to live in freedom, happiness and tranquillity. They want a state of peace which through a wise re-distribution of power and a just equilibrium will preserve their peoples henceforth from the calamities beyond number which have weighed on Europe for twenty years.[20]

The allied peace terms were conveyed to Napoleon by the Count de Saint-Aignan, a French diplomat and Caulaincourt's brother-in-law, whom they had captured during the pursuit of the French army after the battle of Leipzig. On 29 October Metternich and Alexander had agreed these terms. Now on 10 November Saint-Aignan wrote them down in the presence of Metternich himself, Nesselrode and Lord Aberdeen. France was offered its 'natural frontiers', in other words the Rhine, the Alps and the Pyrenees. This would have preserved its hold on Antwerp and the Belgian coast, in other words precisely the territory which Britain was most intent on denying her. She must renounce all her sovereign rights beyond these borders, though explicitly not the influence exercised by any great power on weaker neighbours. Although Napoleon must cease to be King of Italy, the allied offer did not totally exclude the possibility that the current viceroy, Eugène de Beauharnais, might replace him. It also, even more amazingly, included the promise that Britain would make great sacrifices for the sake of peace, which implied the return of many French colonies, and recognized the principle of 'liberty of trade and navigation'. Though in itself vague, this suggested that the peace conference would discuss the whole issue of 'maritime rights', which was anathema to the British government.[21]

Even Metternich might have recoiled had Napoleon instantly agreed these terms, which put strong constraints on Austrian influence in Italy. Neither Russia nor Britain would actually have signed a peace treaty based on these conditions. Nevertheless, if Alexander had agreed to these terms being offered that was no doubt in part because, like Metternich, he expected that Napoleon would reject them. Ever since the summer of 1812 Alexander had believed deep in his heart that a stable peace could only be signed in Paris and, if possible, with a French ruler other than Napoleon. To put this forward as a war aim would have horrified his allies, however, and Alexander was very careful to keep his opinions to himself. Even in November 1813, to speak of marching on Paris and toppling Napoleon was premature and dangerous, and most of all when in earshot of Metternich. For Alexander, the key point was that military operations were to continue in full vigour. He had always believed that in the end it was the fortunes of war which both would and should determine the final peace settlement. As for Aberdeen, no doubt he feared to stand out alone against the allied consensus. He was also, however, a babe-in-arms when faced with diplomats of the power and subtlety of Metternich or Alexander.[22]

The allies in fact quickly began to water down their offer. The manifesto issued to the French people on 1 December promised not France's natural frontiers but 'an extent of territory greater than France had ever known under its kings, because a courageous nation is not demoted in status simply because it has suffered defeats in a stubborn and bloody war, in which it has fought with its customary boldness'. In part this shift reflected London's horror at what Aberdeen had agreed. In addition, however, Alexander's basic belief that military and political events on the ground would determine the peace terms was proving true.[23]

As the allied armies approached the Dutch border, revolt broke out in the Netherlands. Events followed a pattern very similar to the insurrection in Hamburg and northern Germany in the spring of 1813. Like the citizens of Hamburg, the Dutch had been ruined by Napoleon's economic policies and longed for liberation. The advance guard of Winzengerode's Army Corps under Alexander Benckendorff raced across the Netherlands to support the revolt and secure Amsterdam. His infantry – the 2nd Jaegers and the Tula Regiment – covered 60 kilometres in less than thirty-six hours. Benckendorff's detachment also included a regiment of Bashkirs, exotic and improbable liberators of bourgeois Holland. Benckendorff's tiny force of fewer than 2,000 men then led the defence of Breda against a French counter-offensive. The earliest French history of the campaign paid tribute to Alexander Benckendorff, saying that he showed courage and initiative even in attempting the defence, let alone in pulling it off.[24]

Unlike in the previous year at Hamburg, the allies now had large masses of regular troops with which to back up their Cossacks and sustain the revolt. Bülow's Prussian corps moved into the Netherlands and within weeks had cleared most of the Low Countries. Quite apart from its political impact, the conquest of the Low Countries had important military consequences for the invasion of France. It opened up a possible supply line through rich and untouched country to the coast which allied armies operating in the Paris region could use. It also convinced Napoleon that the allied offensive in the winter of 1813–14 would come in the Low Countries. As a result he moved the best of his meagre reserves northwards.[25]

Meanwhile the allied leaders were planning an invasion over the Rhine but well to the south. Blücher and Gneisenau argued for an immediate attack while Napoleon's army was still small and disorganized. Prussian historians subsequently supported this strategy. But the allied armies were also exhausted, hungry and diminished by the autumn campaign. They too needed time to rest and reorganize themselves, and to establish military roads, magazines and hospitals in their rear. During the seven weeks they rested on the Rhine, the allies in fact drew in more and better reinforcements than Napoleon. When they moved forward at the end of the year, eastern France fell to them easily and they still far outnumbered Napoleon's forces. If the campaign later became more difficult, that had little to do with numbers: it was due to poor leadership and to the way in which political considerations were allowed to sabotage military operations.[26]

On 9 November Barclay de Tolly submitted his report to the emperor on the state of the Russian army at the close of the autumn campaign. He reckoned that 'for all our great victories, the present campaign has cost us . . . half our army'. In some units a much higher proportion of men were no longer in the ranks. 'Count Wittgenstein's cavalry does not have even one-quarter of the strength with which it left Silesia' in late August. Of the five front-line Army Corps only two were still fully viable and 'look like regular soldiers'. These two were the Grand Duke Constantine's Guards and Grenadiers of the Reserve Army Corps and Winzengerode's Army Corps in the Army of the North, 'which have seen less combat and have suffered less than the others'. In many units of the other three Army Corps (Wittgenstein, Langeron and Sacken) 'total disorganization' threatened unless action was taken quickly. 'The soldiers are suffering from a great shortage of ammunition, and an even greater lack of boots, shirts and tunics.' In some regiments not more than one hundred men were still in the ranks. Casualties among officers in the autumn campaign had been high and 'the shortage of officers is the reason why even these small remnants cannot be restored to proper order'. Many other sources, including regimental accounts and Blücher's reports to Alexander, confirm the picture drawn by Barclay and stress the army's urgent need for a pause to fill up its ranks, rest its troops, and restock with ammunition, food and equipment.[27]

During the seven weeks that the Russian army remained on the Rhine the situation was transformed. Stragglers and men from hospital rejoined their regiments. Units detached in the rear during the autumn campaign were brought forward. Prince Aleksei Shcherbatov's corps, for example, arrived from Berlin to reinforce Sacken. Above all, however, a further wave of reinforcements arrived from Lobanov-Rostovsky's Reserve Army. As a result, as had happened during the summer truce in 1813, the Russian army entered the 1814 campaign refreshed and at full strength. During the seven weeks on the Rhine 25,000 reinforcements arrived for Langeron and Sacken, and 19,000 for Wittgenstein and the Grand Duke Constantine from Lobanov. In all, 63 reserve squadrons reinforced the army's regular cavalry regiments, in other words more than 12,000 men, and there were more on their way. Langeron and Sacken had arrived on the Rhine with fewer than 30,000 men. By the beginning of the 1814 campaign they had 60,000.[28]

The reinforcements were generally in good order and of high quality. As usual, the cavalry were best. General Nikolai Preradovich inspected the reserve squadron which arrived to reinforce the Chevaliers Gardes on 18 November and reported that 'I found it to be in perfect order: the men are well turned out and the horses in good form'. Peter Wittgenstein also reported that the reserve units reaching his Army Corps were in excellent condition. Completely unlike the situation with Lobanov's first wave of reinforcements in the spring of 1813, on this occasion the units arrived at full strength, having shed very few sick or stragglers. Of course, there was a big difference between marching through a German autumn and a Belorussian winter, but the contrast also reflected the fact that Kankrin's management of the military roads, hospitals and magazines in the army's rear was working well.[29]

In one sense the movement of reinforcements had been almost too successful. The reserve companies had marched with only three-quarters of the men supplied with muskets, as in the spring. Since very few men dropped out, some soldiers in Sacken's Army Corps actually only received their muskets when large supplies were captured from the French in early January 1814. Equipment was also a problem. Alexander became almost hysterical when his beloved Guardsmen turned up with jaeger regiments' cross-belts and pouches. Everyone denounced the wretched state of the recruits' uniforms, which by now were often in tatters. In 1814 many line regiments presented a strange appearance, in some cases being dressed in captured French clothing. Sometimes new uniforms had actually been ordered for them in Germany, Poland and Bohemia but the speed of the army's advance meant that these were trailing along well in the rear. The plan had been that the officers who had led Lobanov's units to the Field Army should return to Poland to continue the training of new recruits. In fact, however, the line units were now so short of officers that some of Lobanov's cadre had to stay behind on the Rhine and join the 1814 campaign.[30]

Meanwhile the Prussians and Austrians were also resting and reinforcing their troops. Almost as important, the allies were mobilizing the resources of conquered Germany to sustain their new campaign against Napoleon. Responsibility for this was given to the so-called Central Administration, headed by Baron vom Stein and established right back in March 1813 to run territories conquered by the allies. Stein initially saw the Central Administration as a means not just of mobilizing German resources for the allied cause but also of laying the foundations for a post-war united German polity, in which the sovereignty of the ruling princes would be circumscribed by federal institutions and by elected assemblies. This plan was unacceptable both to Metternich and to the monarchs of the former Confederation of the Rhine, who united to undermine it. Historians have concentrated on this battle over politics, in which Alexander made no attempt to challenge Metternich.

The price paid by the princes to preserve their sovereignty was generous support for the allied war effort. On this point Metternich was just as firm as Stein. In their treaties with the allies, the princes pledged themselves to provide as many troops of the line as they had to Napoleon and then an equal number of Landwehr. They also contributed one year's gross state revenue, though not of course all at once and in cash. In the end the Bavarian and Württemberg corps fought in Schwarzenberg's army and five other German corps were also created. Some of these corps took over the task of blockading French fortresses and guarding allied bases and lines of communication. This freed large numbers of front-line Russian and Prussian troops to march into the Paris region and join the fight against Napoleon in February and March 1814. Without these reinforcements, the allied campaign would almost certainly have failed.[31]

For many of the allied leaders and generals the idea of marching on Paris and overthrowing Napoleon seemed very risky. For many centuries France had been Europe's most powerful country. No foreign army had taken Paris since 1415. As Kutuzov recalled in November 1812, a century before at the end of the War of the Spanish Succession France had faced most of Europe, whose armies had been led by two of the greatest generals in history, Prince Eugène of Savoy and the Duke of Marlborough. After six years of lost battles total defeat loomed, yet still the country had summoned up the resources to defeat the invasion and hold Europe at bay. France had done the same in 1792–4, though the seemingly chaotic republican regime had confronted not just all Europe but also civil war. If the allied invasion ignited French nationalism and mass resistance, no armies would be large enough to hold down so big a country and population. In addition, France's eastern frontier was protected by line after line of rivers – not only the Rhine but the Moselle, the Meuse and the Marne – and the Vosges mountains. To these natural defences were added the densest and most expensive chain of fortresses anywhere in the world, designed to block, divert and harass any invader seeking to use the highroads which led from the eastern borders into the French heartland. On top of all of this, the allies were attempting to invade in winter.[32]

A winter campaign was vital if Napoleon's mobilization of men and resources was to be pre-empted. It ensured that the emperor would not yet have enough trained men both to garrison his fortresses and put a large army in the field. On the other hand it had serious implications as regards the allied army's supply, movements and impact on the civilian population. By far the bulkiest item in any army's supplies was forage for its horses. No army could carry more than a fraction of this forage in its wagons. In winter there would be no grass in the fields. Most forage would therefore have to be requisitioned from local stores. So would much of the soldiers' food. The bigger the baggage trains, the more ponderous would be the army's movements, especially in winter when many side roads would be impassable. Against Napoleon, lack of mobility could prove fatal.

Relying on local supplies would only work well, however, if the local authorities aided requisitioning and the population did not resist. So long as the allies were on the move, relatively dispersed, and seemed likely to win, local cooperation was likely. Once the armies needed to concentrate in order to fight, problems would multiply, especially if they remained static and if Napoleon appeared to gain the upper hand. Nothing was more likely to incite popular resistance and help Napoleon than a vast enemy army living off the land, especially as hunger spread amongst its ranks and discipline declined. At this point the allied leaders' appeals to their soldiers for good behaviour and Christian forbearance were likely to fall on deaf ears. A vicious circle of civilian resistance and military brutality could easily be the result, with ever larger detachments forced to travel ever further in pursuit of hidden supplies. Barclay de Tolly predicted many of these problems but they were in fact self-evident for any half-literate general.[33]

In order to minimize some of these problems and in particular to outflank the French belt of fortresses the allies decided that their main thrust should be through Switzerland. From there they would strike north-westwards to the plateau of Langres. Once established at Langres they would decide whether the time was ripe to advance on Paris. Alexander set out all the advantages of this plan in a letter to Bernadotte of 10 November. In this letter he claimed that he had proposed the plan to the Austrians and Prussians, and they had accepted his idea. Subsequently, however, the emperor changed his mind and argued that the allies should respect Swiss neutrality. It seems that he did so because he was appealed to by Jomini and by his former tutor, Cesare de la Harpe, both of whom were Swiss citizens. The Austrians seemed prepared to give way but then invaded Switzerland anyway, citing support for their action from Swiss military and political leaders. Alexander was furious at being hoodwinked and then became even more annoyed when the Austrians began to intervene in Swiss domestic politics on the conservative side. In fact, it was he who was mostly in the wrong. Since the Swiss government had allowed France to recruit and move troops on its territory its neutrality was a sham. Perhaps, as the best Prussian historian of the campaign argues, the allied plan was in any case flawed, but once it had been agreed the Austrians had every reason to oppose changing it. Above all, Swiss domestic matters were of no importance to Russia and the emperor was allowing purely personal considerations to interfere with strategy and damage allied unity.[34]

In the end not only the Austrians but also the Russian Guards crossed the Rhine at Basle and marched through part of Switzerland. Their passage of the great river was delayed until 1 January by the Russian calendar, so that it could fall on the anniversary of the day one year before when the Russian army had crossed the Neman and begun its campaign to liberate Europe. For some foreign observers this was yet another example of Alexander's interference in military operations for petty, personal reasons, though in fact the delay did no harm.

Others who watched the parade as the Russian Guards crossed the Rhine had more serious thoughts. Sir Charles Stewart wrote that

it is impossible by any description to give an exaggerated idea of the perfect state of these troops; their appearance and equipment were admirable, and when one considered what they had endured, and contemplated the Russians, some of whom had emerged from Tartary bordering the Chinese empire, traversed their own regions and marched, in a few short months, from Moscow across the Rhine, one was lost in wonder, and inspired with a political awe of that colossal power. The condition in which the Russian cavalry appeared, reflected the highest reputation on this branch of their service; and their artillery was admirable.

But Stewart combined admiration with alarm, in a statement which says much about the allied coalition. 'I could not help, on seeing these Russian guards on that day, recurring to serious impressions with regards to this overgrown empire ... the whole system of European politics ought, as its leading principle and feature, to maintain, as an axiom, the necessity of setting bounds to this formidable and encroaching power.'[35]

From Basle the allied army headed for Langres. Lord Burghersh, the British military representative at Schwarzenberg's headquarters, was not impressed by the field-marshal's leadership.

Nothing could more singularly mark the caution which was observed on the invasion of France, than the movements of the allied armies at this moment. The object of the allies was to establish themselves at Langres, a distance, by the direct road, of five days' march from Basle. At the end of December not a single French soldier could have opposed their advance in this direction; yet complicated marches, turning the flanks of positions, inch by inch overcoming of obstacles of rivers and chains of hills, all these scientific manoeuvres were resorted to; so that, instead of being in possession of the place on the 26th or 27th of December, it was not occupied till the 17th of January.[36]

Pavel Pushchin of the Semenovskys wrote in his diary during the march to Langres that the roads were awful, the weather atrocious and the local French population very poor. Since France had always been held up to them as the pinnacle of European civilization, many other Russian officers were also very surprised by the poverty they encountered. Their diaries and memoirs offer a strong contrast between French poverty and the prosperity they had so admired in Saxony and Silesia. Initially the French population appeared cowed and apathetic, showing no enthusiasm either to defend Napoleon or to support the Bourbons. Inevitably the huge invading army caused destruction and looting. An officer of the Guards Dragoons recalls that his men had an unerring instinct when it came to finding the hidden treasures of the chateau in which they were quartered. In the end the regiment's colonel succeeded in tracking down most of the loot and restoring it to its owners. Where the Guards cavalry led, Cossacks were hardly likely to be reticent and most of their officers had fewer scruples than a colonel of the Guards. Very soon after crossing into France Alexander was writing to Platov to complain that even some Cossack generals and colonels were plundering French homes and farms. For Alexander this was not just inherently shameful but also dangerous, since it risked provoking the people's war which the allies were desperate to avoid.[37]

While Schwarzenberg's large army was advancing almost unopposed to Langres, the much smaller Army of Silesia was embarking on a more dangerous march across the Middle Rhine and through the main belt of French fortresses and rivers. Alexander's instructions to Blücher of 26 December ordered him to cross the Rhine and advance to link up with the main army but left up to him his precise line of advance. The one point on which he insisted was that 'the key issue is to maintain the link between the two armies so that they are always in a position to unite for a battle'. Blücher was forced to leave almost all of Langeron's Army Corps to blockade the great fortress of Mainz and all of Yorck's Army Corps to watch the fortresses of Metz, Thionville and Luxemburg. Pressing forward just with Sacken's Army Corps and a small detachment led by Lieutenant-General Zakhar Olsufev, Blücher had barely 27,000 men under his command. The field-marshal was never averse to risk but his position was greatly helped by the fact that his Cossacks had captured key enemy dispatches and he was well informed about French numbers and deployment. With Napoleon in Paris mobilizing new troops and much of the Field Army's elite reserves deployed towards the Low Countries, Blücher knew that he was opposed by an exhausted and thinly spread enemy screen, whose total disposable numbers barely exceeded his own and whose forces were split up into detachments commanded by no fewer than three marshals. This emboldened him to push the French back over the Moselle, the Meuse and the Aisne before heading south-westwards to link up with Schwarzenberg.[38]

By the end of January 1814 the allies had conquered a huge swath of eastern France, thereby denying its manpower, taxes and food supplies to Napoleon. This was a big additional blow to Napoleon's war machine at a time when his attempts to mobilize French resources were already facing unprecedented difficulties and opposition. The formidable system of conscription, at its most effective in the period 1810–13, was at last beginning to run down in the face of Napoleon's insatiable demands. Most of the conscripts summoned to the depots in November 1813 did not turn up, and could not have been armed, equipped or officered even had they done so. Napoleon had not expected the allies to invade in winter and their offensive threw his plans to levy a new *Grande Armée* into disarray. In addition, Alexander rightly insisted that the large French forces besieged in Dresden, Danzig, Modlin and the other fortresses in central Europe must become prisoners of war when in due course each of these towns surrendered in the winter of 1813–14. He refused to ratify terms of surrender which would have allowed them to return to France, where some of them would undoubtedly have ended up training and forming a cadre for Napoleon's recruits. By the end of January 1814 Napoleon's position was looking increasingly desperate. Alexander's strategy of allowing military operations to determine the limits of the final peace settlement seemed on the point of achieving the result he desired – in other words Napoleon's defeat and overthrow.[39]

The first major battle on French soil occurred at the end of January. Napoleon had left Paris for his headquarters at Châlons on 25 January. From there he marched south-eastwards, hoping to catch and destroy Blücher's force before it could link up with Schwarzenberg. Fortunately for Blücher, the Russian cavalry captured a staff officer with Napoleon's plans. Also lucky was the fact that Peter Pahlen and part of the main army's cavalry was nearby. Pahlen delayed the advancing French and covered the march of Blücher's troops towards Brienne, where they arrived after midday on 29 January.

Late on that winter afternoon Napoleon's infantry attacked Brienne in three columns. Blücher's headquarters was in the chateau of Brienne, from which he had an excellent view of the advancing enemy. He immediately spotted that the French left-hand column was vulnerable to a cavalry attack and ordered Ilarion Vasilchikov to charge into the enemy flank and rear, which brought the French infantry to a halt. Later that evening, however, on the other allied flank, French infantry burst into Brienne in the darkness past Olsufev's small corps. Blücher and Sacken only just escaped capture and one of the latter's key staff officers was killed. Once the initial surprise had passed, the Russian troops rallied and Blücher retreated to link up with the main army on the heights of Trannes just a few kilometres south of Brienne. But Sacken was furious with Olsufev, whom he blamed for the whole episode.[40]

Napoleon followed Blücher and established his headquarters in the village of La Rothière, just north of the heights at Trannes. For two days the armies watched each other without moving. By midday on 1 February Napoleon believed that the allies were aiming to move around his western flank and ordered his reserves away from La Rothière to watch them. Soon afterwards, however, it became clear that Blücher was on the point of attacking the French line. Napoleon had fewer than 50,000 men to cover a front of 9.5 kilometres, which was too few. His right flank rested on the river Aube at the village of Dienville. The village of La Rothière was in the centre of his line, which stretched out to La Giberie on his left. Blücher commanded Sacken's and Olsufev's troops from the Army of Silesia, which stood in his centre opposite La Rothière. On their left were Gyulai's Austrian Army Corps, which he ordered to attack Dienville. On the right was the Württemberg Army Corps under their crown prince, whose task it was to assault La Giberie. On their own these troops barely outnumbered the French but the allies had more than double their number available within range of the battlefield.

Gyulai's attack on the strong French position at Dienville failed. The crown prince of Württemberg also had great difficulties deploying enough troops in the narrow defiles and swampy terrain around La Giberie to push back the French defenders. In the end he was rescued by Wrede's Bavarian corps which came up behind the enemy left flank and forced Marshal Marmont to retreat. Schwarzenberg had not ordered Wrede to join the battle but the Bavarian commander had marched to the sound of the guns on his own initiative.

By far the fiercest fighting occurred in and around La Rothière, however. Three-quarters of all allied casualties occurred here. Sacken's infantry assaulted La Rothière in two columns: Johann Lieven attacked from the front down the road and Aleksei Shcherbatov moved forward a few hundred metres to the east. This was the first time that the Army of Silesia had fought under Alexander's eye and Sacken was determined to impress. The Prussian official history writes that 'Lieven's column attacked the village with their bands playing and the soldiers singing'. With a snow storm blowing into their backs, the Russian infantry stormed into the village with their bayonets, without pausing to fire. Major-General Nikitin, the commander of Sacken's artillery, was unable to drag all of his guns forward to support the attack because of the heavy mud. So he left thirty-six guns behind and double-harnessed the rest. Between them Lieven and Shcherbatov cleared La Rothière after bitter fighting, only then to face a ferocious counter-attack in the early evening from Napoleon's Guards. In this fighting both Marshal Oudinot and Lieven were wounded. In the end, the issue was decided by the Russian reserves, in this case the 2nd Grenadier Division, which came up to support Sacken and drove the enemy out of La Rothière once and for all. The French lost 73 guns and 5,000 men, the allies barely fewer. But the main element in the allied victory was moral. In the first battle of the campaign, Napoleon had been defeated on French soil. His troops' morale slumped. In the following days many French soldiers deserted and set off for their homes.[41]

Sacken's report on the battle concluded with a courtier's flourish: 'On this memorable and triumphant day Napoleon ceased to be the enemy of mankind and Alexander can say, I will grant peace to the world.' Language like this was dangerously premature. Napoleon was not dead yet and the Army of Silesia was to be punished for its overconfidence in just a few days' time. For Sacken himself, however, the battle had been a triumph. For his victories in 1813 he had been promoted to full general and awarded a string of decorations. Now Alexander granted him the very coveted Order of St Andrew and made him a present of 50,000 rubles. Probably most important for Sacken, however, was the emperor's remark to him on the day after the battle: 'You have conquered not only your foreign but also your domestic enemies.' The old battle with Bennigsen dating back to 1807 which had embittered Sacken and threatened his career was now decided in his favour. His great enemy would end his life as a general and a count. Sacken would race past him, both a field-marshal and a prince.[42]

The day after the battle the allied leaders held a conference in the chateau of Brienne to decide future strategy. When the time to begin the meeting arrived, apparently Blücher was nowhere to be found and the various dignitaries scattered to track him down. It was Alexander who discovered him, deep in the wine cellars, plucking the best bottles from the racks. The conference decided that the main army and the Army of Silesia must split up, allegedly because it was impossible to feed them if they remained together. Schwarzenberg would advance on Paris from the south along the river Seine. Blücher would approach from the west along the Marne.[43]

In many ways this was to revert to the model of 1813 and to face the same dangers. Napoleon would be operating on interior lines between the two allied armies. By now he would be well attuned to Schwarzenberg's caution and slowness, and to Blücher's boldness and willingness to run risks. In the autumn of 1813 Napoleon had missed his chance to exploit this weakness. Now it had returned in even more clear-cut form. Unlike in the autumn, Napoleon would not have to exhaust himself by marching great distances to strike one or other allied army. Since all military operations were taking place in a small area, he could hope to defeat one enemy army and race back to face the other in a handful of days. Moving in his own country, he could mobilize local knowledge, transport and manpower to use side roads, tap food supplies and be forewarned about enemy actions. He also controlled most of the key river crossings. In addition, in February 1814 Blücher was even more inclined to take risks than before since he shared the widespread view that Napoleon's demise was imminent. By 7 February he and Alexander were discussing how to quarter the troops when they reached Paris.[44]

Meanwhile Schwarzenberg was even more cautious than in the previous year. The great numerical superiority of the allies seems to have merely increased his worries about the difficulties of commanding and feeding so vast an army. He was intensely concerned about the security of his long line of communications stretching back to Basle and across the Rhine. He exaggerated the size of Napoleon's army and, still more, of the force which Marshal Augereau was trying to form in Lyons, believing that Augereau might strike into the allied rear in Switzerland. In these circumstances Schwarzenberg was very opposed to any further move forwards. As he wrote to his wife on 26 January, 'any advance on Paris is in the highest degree contrary to military science'.[45]

To do the commander-in-chief justice he was not alone among the allied generals in this view. Knesebeck argued that it would be very difficult to feed the army in the region around Troyes through which they would have to approach Paris. The various allied corps could only move up and down the north–south highways leading to the capital since the side roads were almost impassable at this time of year. Lateral movements and mutual support among the allied corps would therefore be slow at best. Meanwhile Napoleon could feed himself from the fertile areas west of Paris and could use interior lines and better lateral roads which he controlled to concentrate and strike against the lumbering allied columns. If Napoleon's throne was threatened, no doubt he would fight to the death. What evidence was there that the French nation would desert him? Ultimately, to advance on Paris was to gamble on French politics. Might this not prove as deceptive as Napoleon's gamble in 1812 that occupying Moscow would lead to peace?[46]

Schwarzenberg's views and plans were strongly influenced by political considerations. In his view, the advance to Langres had been a means to exert additional leverage on Napoleon and force him to make peace on terms acceptable to the allies. Even now, after all these years, Schwarzenberg had not really grasped Napoleon's mentality or his way of war. Metternich's influence on the commander-in-chief was also very important. On a number of occasions in January 1814 he advised Schwarzenberg to delay operations and allow time for peace negotiations. By appointing Caulaincourt as minister of foreign affairs and seemingly accepting the allied peace terms conveyed by Saint-Aignan, Napoleon appeared to be open to compromise. With a peace congress finally about to commence at Châtillon on 3 February, Schwarzenberg, Metternich and Francis II were less inclined than ever to push forward in the days immediately following La Rothière or to let military operations determine policy and define the peace settlement. Because the commander-in-chief was an Austrian, Habsburg political perspectives could quietly derail allied military strategy.[47]

Meanwhile Alexander did his best to undermine Metternich's diplomatic strategy at Châtillon. When the congress began its deliberations on 5 February the Russian delegate, Count Razumovsky, announced that he had not yet received his instructions. Russian delaying tactics could not be hidden, however, unlike Metternich's advice to Schwarzenberg, and quickly annoyed their allies. By now the allies had toughened considerably the peace terms on offer. At Frankfurt they had proposed

France's natural frontiers. At Châtillon they offered the 'historic' frontiers of 1792. Metternich pinned Alexander down by presenting the allies with a memorandum which forced them to decide whether or not to make peace with Napoleon if he accepted these terms. It also required them to decide, if they rejected Napoleon, whether they should commit themselves to the Bourbons or decide on some way by which the French might choose an alternative ruler.[48]

Faced with these questions, Alexander found himself without support. He believed that if Napoleon accepted the allied terms, he would simply regard the peace as a temporary truce and would start a new war at the first suitable opportunity. His military genius and his aura added tens of thousands of invisible soldiers to any army he commanded. So long as he sat on France's throne, many of his former allies beyond France's borders would never believe that the peace settlement was permanent. Both the British and the Prussians wanted to sign a peace with Napoleon, however, so long as he accepted France's 1792 borders and immediately handed over a number of fortresses as a pledge of his commitment. None of the allies shared Alexander's view that their armies should first take Paris and then gauge French opinion on the nature of the regime with which to sign peace. To them this policy seemed too unreliable. The last thing the allies wanted was to incite popular revolt, or to find themselves involved in a French civil war. But if Napoleon did fall, then in the British, Austrian and Prussian view the only alternative was the return of the Bourbons, in the person of the family's legitimate head, Louis XVIII.[49]

Alexander was unenthusiastic about the restoration of the Bourbons. In part this simply reflected his low opinion of Louis XVIII, who had lived in exile in Russia for a number of years and had not impressed the emperor. Alexander was no legitimist. If anything, he had a touch of radical chic. His grandmother, Catherine II, had sought to impress Voltaire and Diderot. Alexander enjoyed winning the plaudits of Germaine de Staël, whose own preferred candidate to rule France was Marshal Bernadotte. Alexander himself briefly toyed with Bernadotte's candidacy. This infuriated his allies and even led to murmurings that the emperor was trying to put a Russian client on the French throne.[50]

In fact this was not the point and Alexander contemplated a number of possible candidates, of whom the crown prince of Sweden was but one. The basic issue was Alexander's belief that a society as sophisticated and modern as France could only be ruled by a regime which respected civil rights and allowed representative institutions. That regime must also accept part of the Revolution's legacy if it was to survive. The emperor doubted whether the restored Bourbons would do any of these things. As always with Alexander, he was most believable when telling people what they did not want to hear. Even as late as 17 March, he told a royalist emissary, the Baron de Vitrolles, that he had considered not just Bernadotte but also Eugène de Beauharnais and the Duke of Orléans as possible rulers who, unlike Louis XVIII, would not be prisoners of memories and supporters who demanded revenge for the past. The emperor staggered Vitrolles by saying that even a wisely ordered republic might suit France best.[51]

Above all, Alexander wanted a stable France which would live in peace with itself and with its neighbours. Better than anyone the emperor understood the enormous difficulties of bringing a Russian army across Europe and the unique circumstances which had made this possible. It might never be possible to repeat this effort. As he said to Lord Castlereagh amidst the arguments that raged among the allies in early February, it was precisely for this reason that Russia required a peace settlement which would endure, not a mere armistice. It was on these grounds that he opposed any peace with Napoleon. But it was the same anxiety which led him to look at alternatives to the Bourbons. In fact Alexander underestimated Louis XVIII and came in time to accept with good grace the Bourbons' restoration. But his fears were not groundless, as the overthrow of the incompetent Charles X subsequently showed.[52]

After fierce arguments with his allies in the second week of February 1814 Alexander was forced to give way, however. The fact that towards the end of this week news began to arrive of Blücher's defeat by Napoleon only confirmed the dangers of Russia's isolation. The emperor had to agree that if a restoration was to occur, then the only possible choice was the head of the royal house, Louis XVIII. More important from Alexander's perspective, he had to accept that the negotiations at Châtillon would continue and that the allies would ratify a peace with Napoleon if he accepted the 1792 frontiers and surrendered a number of fortresses. On the other hand, the allies did also agree that if Napoleon refused the allied conditions, then they would continue the war until victory was achieved over him. Frederick William III provided some balm to Alexander's injured feelings by refusing to join Metternich in threatening withdrawal from the war should the Russian monarch refuse to back down. The king insisted that so long as the Russians remained in the field, the royal army would fight alongside them.[53]

Meanwhile near disaster had befallen Blücher. After the conference in Brienne on 2 February he marched northwards with Sacken's and Olsufev's 18,000 Russians. Blücher aimed to unite with the 16,500 men of Yorck's Army Corps who were advancing just north of the river Marne towards Château Thierry and the nearly 15,000 Prussians and Russians under generals Kleist and Kaptsevich who were approaching Châlons from the east. A French corps under Marshal MacDonald was retreating in front of Yorck, and Blücher ordered Sacken to hurry forward to try to cut it off. Meanwhile he himself stopped with Olsufev's detachment at Vertus, waiting for Kleist and Kaptsevich to arrive. MacDonald in fact evaded Sacken's clutches but the attempt to catch him took Sacken's troops all the way to La Ferte-sous-Jouarre, well to the west of Château Thierry on the south bank of the Marne. Blücher's army was now dispersed over a distance of more than 70 kilometres, which made communications difficult and mutual support often impossible.

The details of the military operations which followed were complicated but the essence was simple. Napoleon thrust northwards through Sézanne into the middle of Blücher's army and defeated one isolated allied detachment after another. Since Blücher was the greatest Prussian hero of the Napoleonic Wars, some Prussian memoirists and historians had an understandable tendency to protect his reputation. They offered a number of partial excuses for his defeat. Correctly, they argued that if Schwarzenberg had pressed Napoleon's rear then the Army of Silesia would have been in no danger. Instead, not merely did the main army crawl forward, its commander-in-chief also withdrew Wittgenstein's Army Corps to the west, instead of leaving it as a link to Blücher. The field-marshal's defenders also argued that if Lieutenant-General Olsufev had destroyed the key bridge across the Petit Morin stream the moment danger threatened from the south, Napoleon could never have achieved his march into the middle of Blücher's army. Undoubtedly too, the allies had poor maps and incorrect information about local roads – as tended to be the case in fighting on foreign soil. Both Blücher and Sacken, for example, believed that the road along which Napoleon marched northwards from Sézanne was impassable for an army. Nevertheless the basic point remains that although in close proximity to the enemy, Blücher scattered his army to such an extent that it could not concentrate for battle and he could not exercise effective command. He made this mistake partly because he believed that Napoleon was on the verge of final defeat and Paris was his for the plucking.[54]

On 10 February Napoleon advanced from Sézanne and overwhelmed Olsufev's small corps at Champaubert. The emperor had just been reinforced by thousands of experienced cavalry arrived from Spain. Olsufev had a total of seventeen horsemen. A nimbler commander might have retreated in time to save his men but Olsufev was still smarting from Sacken's criticism for not having held his ground at Brienne two weeks before. Though his junior generals begged him to fall back on Blücher, Olsufev insisted on sticking to his orders to hold his position and seems to have believed that Blücher was himself advancing from the east into the enemy rear. Napoleon claimed to have taken 6,000 prisoners, which was a remarkable achievement since Olsufev's 'corps' numbered 3,690, of whom almost half escaped with their flags and many of their guns under cover of the winter night and the nearby forests. The key point, however, was that Napoleon and 30,000 men were now standing halfway between Sacken's 15,000 troops at La Ferte and Blücher's 14,000 near Vertus, directly on the road which connected the two wings of the Army of Silesia.[55]

The safest option would have been for Sacken to retreat north of the river Marne and join up with Yorck at Château Thierry. Yorck urged this on Sacken but to no effect. Sacken's orders from Blücher were to march back down the road which led eastwards through Champaubert to Étoges, where he was supposed to reunite with Olsufev and Blücher himself. These orders had been issued before Blücher had a clear understanding of Napoleon's movements and were now out of date but Sacken did not know this. He set out on the evening of 10 February. He knew that Yorck had been ordered by Blücher to cross the Marne and support him but did not know that the Prussian general had queried these orders and delayed his movement. When he received his orders Sacken had no way of knowing that Napoleon was astride the road down which he was expecting to march.

Late in the morning of 11 February Sacken bumped into the enemy advance guard just west of the village of Montmirail. Soon afterwards he learned from prisoners that Napoleon himself and his main army were present. With the battle in full flow, the Russian commander then received a message from Yorck to say that the road southwards from the Marne to Montmirail was so bad that only a minority of his infantry and none of his guns could advance to the Russians' rescue. Allied maps showed this to be a paved road whereas in reality it was a country track which the recent thaw had turned into deep mud.

Thanks to his infantry's discipline and steadiness Sacken succeeded in extricating his corps with most of its baggage and artillery and retreated during the evening and the night down the awful road which led north-wards to the river Marne at Château Thierry. Fires were lit every two hundred paces to guide the infantry along the way. In the drenching rain, with their muskets useless, the Russian infantry had both to march in compact masses to keep the enemy cavalry at bay and on occasion to break ranks in order to pull their artillery out of the mud. Though very outnumbered, Ilarion Vasilchikov and his splendid cavalry regiments greatly helped to protect the infantry and to drag away most of the guns. Napoleon pressed the retreating Russians hard and by the time they finally got across the Marne they had lost 5,000 men. Russian casualties would have been far higher had it not been for the courageous rearguard actions of Yorck's Prussian infantry. Sacken was a hardbitten old cam-paigner and 'politician'. The day after the battle, finally tracked down by his nervous and exhausted staff, who had lost him in the course of the retreat, he was as calm and self-assured as always. In the best traditions of coalition warfare, in his official report he blamed the defeat on the Prussians, and in particular on Yorck's failure to obey Blücher's orders and support him in good time.[56]

Having defeated Yorck and Sacken, Napoleon was preparing to march south to block Schwarzenberg when he learned to his astonishment on 13 February that Blücher was advancing down the road which led to Montmirail. Blücher had misinterpreted the retreat of the French forces watching the road and believed that Napoleon was already heading south against the main army. Instead, having reached Vauchamps by the morning of 14 February, Blücher found himself confronted by Napoleon himself and the bulk of his army, which greatly outnumbered the allied force. Like Sacken's troops three days before, Blücher's infantry was forced to retreat in square for many miles under heavy pressure. At least Sacken's foot soldiers had Vasilchikov's cavalry and Yorck's Prussians to help them. Blücher's 16,000 infantry on the contrary were retreating on their own, in broad daylight, through excellent cavalry country and with very few horsemen to help them. Unlike Sacken's veterans, most of the 6,000 Russians in Lieutenant-General Kaptsevich's corps were new recruits, in action for the first time. Their musketry was at times more enthusiastic than effective. One-third of the men became casualties but, as French observers recognized, it was a tribute to the great courage and discipline of the Russian and Prussian infantry that Blücher's whole detachment was not destroyed.[57]

In the course of five days' fighting Blücher's army had lost almost one-third of its men. Napoleon was ecstatic. Already on the evening of 11 February he was writing to his brother Joseph, 'this army of Silesia was the allies' best army', which was true enough. Much less truthfully, he added: 'The enemy army of Silesia no longer exists: I have totally routed it.' Even a week later, when there had been time to weigh the true results of the battle, he claimed in a letter to Eugène de Beauharnais to have taken more than 30,000 prisoners, which meant that 'I have destroyed the Army of Silesia'. The reality was very different. On 18 February, the day after Napoleon wrote this letter, 8,000 men of Langeron's Army Corps arrived to reinforce Blücher and there were many more Russian and Prussian units of the Army of Silesia, now relieved from blockading fortresses, on the march. Hundreds of prisoners of war were recaptured and many missing men returned to the ranks in the days immediately after the battle. Within a matter of days, Blücher's army was again as strong as it had been on 10 February.[58]

Ironically, in the end it was Napoleon himself who suffered most from his victories against Blücher. After the battle of La Rothière Napoleon very grudgingly granted Caulaincourt full powers to accept the allied peace conditions. On 5 February the foreign minister was told that 'His Majesty gives you carte blanche to bring the negotiations to a happy end, to save the capital and to avoid a battle on which the last hopes of the nation would rest'. Caulaincourt was bewildered by these instructions and asked for clarification, enquiring whether he was supposed to concede all the allied demands immediately or whether he still had some time for negotiation. Before there was time to reply, Napoleon had defeated Blücher and his tone had changed completely.[59]

On 17 February he revoked Caulaincourt's full powers and instructed him to accept nothing less than the so-called Frankfurt conditions, in other words France's natural frontiers. He justified his stance by saying that he had been prepared to accept the allied terms in order to avoid risking everything on a battle. Since he had faced that risk and taken more than 30,000 allied prisoners, the situation had changed entirely. He had smashed the Army of Silesia and now was marching to destroy Schwarzenberg's army before it could escape across the French border. Four days later he wrote an arrogant letter to Francis II, stating that he would never settle for anything less than France's natural frontiers. He added that even if the allies had succeeded in imposing the 1792 frontiers, such a humiliating peace could never have endured. To his brother Joseph he was even more explicit: 'If I had accepted the historical borders I would have taken up arms again two years later, and I would have said to the nation that this was not a peace that I had signed but a forced capitulation.' In fact the heady smell of victory made Napoleon now aspire to more even than France's natural frontiers. To Eugène de Beauharnais he wrote that France might now be able to hold on to Italy. Napoleon's words and actions in these days played directly into Alexander's hands and justified everything the Russian emperor had said to his allies. It is true that to some extent the French and Russian monarchs were pursuing the same strategy of allowing military operations to determine the peace settlement. But Alexander was more realistic about the true balance of military power and the likely outcome of the campaign. Above all, he had some sense of limits and compromise, and a far more sensitive grasp of the connections between diplomacy and war.[60]

None of this was yet clear to the allies in mid-February 1814, however, when their cause was at its lowest ebb. After defeating Blücher Napoleon raced south to deal with Schwarzenberg. This was the Napoleon of old whose speed and boldness stunned opponents, rather than the commander who in 1812–13 had been more inclined to rely on sheer numbers of men and weight of concentrated artillery firepower. Certainly he was far too speedy for Schwarzenberg. The main army had crawled forward along the river Seine, enjoying a number of rest-days en route to recover from its exertions. Even so, by 16 February Schwarzenberg's army was within three to four days of Paris. Each of his four front-line Army Corps (Bianchi's Austrians, the Württembergers, the Bavarians, Wittgenstein's Russians) had its own road. But the four columns were a good 50 kilometres apart and a combination of mud, the river Seine and the poor condition of the side roads made lateral communication very slow, as Knesebeck had predicted. Schwarzenberg believed that this was the only way his army could move or feed itself but it made the allies very vulnerable to a concentrated enemy attack. The Russian and Austrian reserves were still south of the Seine. To make things worse, Wittgenstein became so impatient with Schwarzenberg's slowness that he pushed forward alone and further isolated himself on the allied right flank. In particular, the 4,000 men of his advance guard, under Peter Pahlen, had been sent all the way forward to Mormant and were totally exposed, as Pahlen and Alexander himself warned.[61]

Before Wittgenstein could react, Napoleon pounced on the morning of 17 February. Pahlen was a fine rearguard commander but his 4,000 men stood no chance against overwhelming odds. His cavalry escaped but almost all his infantry were killed or taken prisoner. This included, for example, 338 men of the Estland Regiment, of which only 3 officers and 69 men remained in the ranks by the evening of 17 February. The regiment had fought with great courage under Wittgenstein in 1812 and then again at Kulm and Leipzig in 1813. To do him justice, Wittgenstein took full responsibility for the debacle and completely exonerated Pahlen, but the gentlemanly behaviour of its commanding general was not much consolation for the soldiers of the Estland Regiment, who had deserved a better fate. Napoleon's advance then bundled the whole allied army back across the Seine. Schwarzenberg's only thought was to retreat south-westwards to safety towards Troyes and Bar-sur-Aube. This he achieved, helped in part by the fact that a sudden shift in the weather froze the ground and allowed the retreating allied columns to move off the roads and across the country.[62]

Inevitably the military disasters of mid-February added to the existing tensions among the allies. Alexander and Frederick William blamed Schwarzenberg for not helping Blücher and believed – in part correctly – that he had advanced slowly for political reasons. Unpleasant rumours went round that the Austrians were deliberately preserving their own troops and 'bleeding' the Russians and Prussians so as to be in a stronger position when the war ended and a peace congress divided up the spoils among the allies. This was certainly unfair as regards Schwarzenberg, who was much too honourable a man to act in this way. Schwarzenberg's own interpretation of events was that Blücher and his associates had finally come by their just deserts for taking absurd risks and 'manoeuvring like pigs'. He wrote to Francis II on 20 February that the 6,000 men the main army had lost in the last few days were a relatively cheap proof that the advance had been a mistake from the start, as he had always predicted would be the case.[63]

Meanwhile grumbling grew in the ranks as regiments marched and counter-marched over an ever more exhausted terrain, knowing in their bones that their generals lacked confidence and were at war with each other. As always, retreat and growing hunger sapped morale and discipline. General Oertel, now the army's provost-general, was given orders to coordinate the efforts of all the commandants along the lines of communications to stamp out marauding. Trofim Evdokimov, a soldier of the Izmailovsky Guards, even tried to kill one of Alexander's own aides-de-camp when the latter intervened to stop him plundering.[64]

It was in the second week of February that problems in feeding the men and horses really began to hit hard. As Barclay wrote on 10 February, such problems were inevitable the moment the army began to halt its advance or to concentrate for battle: 'No country would long be able to sustain the enormous mass of the concentrated allied forces.' Units stole supplies designated for neighbours or allies. The Russians complained bitterly that the Austrian intendancy controlled the line of communications back through Switzerland and favoured their own supply columns. As always, the horses were the hardest problem and finding hay in the middle of winter a growing nightmare for the cavalry. Foraging expeditions travelled ever further for increasingly meagre rewards. The Courland Dragoons, for example, found that 'foraging expeditions required the sending out of virtually entire cavalry regiments and vast efforts only succeeded in collecting very insignificant quantities of food and forage'.[65]

If this was unpleasantly reminiscent of the French experience around Moscow in 1812, so too was the growing resistance of the French peasantry to allied requisitioning and plunder. Even by 29 January Kankrin was reporting that 'unless pressed very hard, the population provides nothing'. Subsequently, with Napoleon's fortunes improving, local French authorities often became more inclined to heed his orders to resist the allies. Peasants sometimes abandoned their ruined villages to take shelter in the forests and raid allied supplies moving down the roads. Sections of Kankrin's mobile magazine moving up from Switzerland were ambushed. Vladimir Löwenstern lost 80,000 rubles' worth of horses and other property when a French patrol sneaked out of the nearby artillery depot and ambushed a Russian supply train resting in the village of Mons-en-Laonnois, massacring its Cossack escort. General Winzengerode wished to burn the village down in reprisal but was dissuaded. But Barclay de Tolly ordered that the 'criminals' who had attacked Kankrin's supply columns 'must be punished as an example to terrify others', with public hangings and posters displayed throughout the neighbourhood to deter further attacks. Kankrin was an efficient, level-headed and by now very experienced head of the army's intendancy. If even he was saying by 4 March that problems of supply were worse than at any time since the war began in 1812, things were clearly very serious.[66]

14

The Fall of Napoleon

Within four weeks of taking the field Napoleon had thrown the allies into disarray and seemed to have stopped the invasion in its tracks. He had gone far towards restoring the reputation for invincibility and military genius which had been badly dented in 1812 and 1813. In fact, however, at the very moment that Kankrin was despairing the situation was turning in the allies' favour in all three crucial areas of the war, in other words supply, diplomacy and military operations.

As regards supply, one important factor was that most of Kankrin's mobile magazines commanded by majors Lisanevich and Kondratev struggled their way from the Rhineland through to the army, which they then kept supplied with biscuit for a month. Lisanevich and Kondratev were unsung heroes of the Russian war effort, whose achievement in getting so large a part of the mobile magazines – including the great majority of its original carts and horses – all the way from the Danube and Belorussia through Germany and Switzerland to central France was remarkable. En route they had defeated snowdrifts, floods, cattle plagues, ambushes and the never-ending breakdowns of their overloaded peasant carts. No doubt the biscuit they carried for the troops, much of it baked in the autumn of 1812 and then dried out after getting damp that winter, cannot have been very appetizing. But it was a great deal better than nothing and, as in 1813, the magazines' carts, which Kankrin used to shuttle food to and from depots along the lines of communication and to evacuate the wounded, were a godsend. Very importantly, he was also able to send Major Kondratev's whole mobile magazine to Joinville in Lorraine, through which he was opening up a completely new supply line for the Russian troops' exclusive use, thereby ending their dependence on the overloaded road back through Switzerland and on Austrian commissariat officials.[1]

Opening up this new supply line depended on the cooperation of David Alopaeus, the governor-general of occupied Lorraine. In January 1814 Baron Stein's Central Administration had been given responsibility for running conquered French territory. Austrian officials were to run the provinces between Schwarzenberg's army and the Rhine. The Prussians governed France's northern provinces, in other words the area adjacent to the Low Countries and the Lower Rhine. The central area, conquered by Blücher's army in January, was run by the Russians, whose governor-general, Alopaeus, was stationed in Nancy. Alopaeus was not initially very sympathetic to Kankrin's appeals, since he was already having to feed Blücher's army and was scared that if he imposed still more requisitioning peasant resistance might spread beyond control. Though Lorraine was richer than the provinces administered by the Austrians, it contained many French fortresses, which were very weakly blockaded, sometimes by forces smaller than their garrisons. Sorties to link up with local peasant bands were a constant threat. In addition, Alopaeus complained that the carts he needed to transport the supplies never returned from the army and that Russian commissariat officials were much less numerous and efficient than their Prussian counterparts.[2]

Kankrin must have gritted his teeth on reading this complaint, since his lines of supply ran all the way back to Russia and his shortage in particular of German- and French-speaking officials was inevitably chronic. As he reported to Barclay, he had been forced to strip even his own secretariat in order to find men to troubleshoot along the supply lines.[3] But he needed the help of Alopaeus far too much to afford resentment. As he wrote to Barclay, 'the new operational line for food supplies is a matter of crucial importance'. In fact relations quickly warmed, with the governor-general writing that, 'as you see, we don't lack goodwill, nor is there a total lack of the supplies which you need. But we do suffer from a severe lack of transport and of officials to oversee it.' In response, Kankrin sent every official he could scrape up, together with Kondratev's carts. Meanwhile the mobile magazine of the Army of Silesia also arrived providentially at Nancy, providing Alopaeus and Kankrin with an additional large reserve of carts. If this did not fully solve Kankrin's problems, it did end the immediate emergency and held out the prospect of putting the army's supply on a much more stable basis.[4]

Meanwhile, thanks to Napoleon, matters were looking much brighter for the allies on the diplomatic front too. His intransigence undermined Metternich's strategy and reminded the Austrians how dangerous it would be to rely on Napoleon and isolate themselves from their allies. As Metternich knew, even the British military representative at allied headquarters was becoming very impatient with Schwarzenberg's delaying tactics. Since Castlereagh's arrival at headquarters an informal political understanding had developed between him and Metternich. But both men realized that there were limits beyond which Britain could not go in its desire to accommodate Vienna. British public opinion would distrust any peace with Napoleon. So too would the government.[5]

While Castlereagh was negotiating at allied headquarters, the Russian ambassador in London, Christoph Lieven, was speaking to the prime minister, Lord Liverpool, and the Prince Regent. Both men opposed signing a peace with Napoleon. The Prince Regent's views precisely mirrored Alexander's, as Lieven reported:

It would be to betray the desires of Providence . . . not to establish on unshakeable foundations a peace which had already cost so much blood . . . never had the world seen so powerful means united to achieve this. But these means were unique and the moral and physical forces of the allies could never be re-constituted to this level at any future time. Now was the time to ensure the well-being of Europe for centuries – while any peace made with Napoleon, however advantageous its conditions, could never give the human race anything other than a shorter or longer truce. The history of his entire life provided one example after another of bad faith, atrocity and ambition; and the blood of all Europe would only have flowed for a very doubtful respite if peace depended on treaties signed with this everlasting source of disturbance.[6]

Castlereagh could sign a treaty with Napoleon so long as this secured Belgium and was accompanied by formidable barriers against renewed French aggression, and so long as there appeared to be no other force available in France with which to make peace. Under no circumstances, however, could he accept France's 'natural frontiers'. Even Austrian hints about such terms would drive Castlereagh into Alexander's arms. By the end of February, therefore, Metternich had every reason to seek a compromise. So too, however, did the Russian emperor. His political isolation from his allies in early February, coupled with Napoleon's military victories, showed the dangers of intransigence. As a result, on 1 March 1814 the four allied great powers signed the Treaty of

Chaumont, pledging themselves only to accept a peace based on France's historic borders, an independent and extended Netherlands, and a German confederation of sovereign states dominated by Austria and Prussia. At least as important, the treaty was also a military alliance between the four powers, designed to last for twenty years after the peace was signed and to uphold this peace by joint military action if France attempted to breach its terms. The Treaty of Chaumont could not determine whether the allies would make peace with Napoleon or some alternative French regime. All the allied leaders knew that to a great extent this would have to depend on the French themselves. Nevertheless the treaty was in both real and moral terms a big boost to allied unity.[7]

Ultimately, however, it was military operations that were most likely to determine Napoleon's fate. Only total defeat could persuade him to accept, even temporarily, the 1792 frontiers. Equally, the emperor's defeat was the likeliest catalyst for a revolt of the French elites against his rule. In the second half of February defeat once again seemed far away. Schwarzenberg's army was in full retreat. Initially the plan was to summon Blücher to march south to join with the main army and offer battle but by the time the Army of Silesia arrived in the vicinity on 21 February Schwarzenberg had changed his mind. The commander-in-chief insisted on detaching most of his Austrian troops southwards to block what he considered to be a growing threat to his communications from Marshal Augereau's army in Lyons. This gave him an excellent reason – his critics used the word 'excuse' – to continue his retreat southwards and avoid a battle. Blücher was outraged and Alexander seriously considered removing himself and the Russian corps from the main army and joining up with Blücher.

In the end a compromise was hammered out in a conference of the allied leaders at Bar-sur-Aube on 25 February. Schwarzenberg would continue his retreat as far as Langres if necessary, where he would be joined by the newly arriving Austrian reserves. If Napoleon was still pursuing him he would turn at Langres and fight a defensive battle. Meanwhile Blücher was to march northwards and, it was hoped, draw Napoleon off Schwarzenberg's back by threatening Paris. If, as was expected, Napoleon turned round and pursued Blücher, Schwarzenberg was to resume the offensive. Bülow and Winzengerode's Army Corps of Bernadotte's former Army of the North had in the meantime marched from the frontiers of Holland towards Paris and were now approaching

Soissons on the river Aisne. They would come under Blücher's command, as would the newly formed Saxon corps of the German federal forces, whose job it would be to hold the Low Countries. Even without the Saxons, Blücher's combined army would total over 100,000 men, which by now was considerably more than Napoleon's entire force. Alexander's instructions to the Prussian field-marshal reflected both his awareness that only Blücher had the confident aggression necessary for victory and his great fear that a repetition of Blücher's earlier carelessness might wreck the allied cause. They concluded with the words, 'as soon as you have coordinated the movements of your various corps we wish you to commence your offensive, which promises the happiest results so long as it is based on prudence'.[8]

Blücher set off northwards immediately. Unlike during his earlier offensive towards Paris, on this occasion the Russian cavalry was deployed to guard all the roads from the south. By 2 March it was clear from their reports that Napoleon was pursuing the Army of Silesia with a large force. The first objective of Blücher's manoeuvre had thus been achieved. The next task was to unite with Winzengerode and Bülow, who were currently surrounding Soissons, which was important because its bridge offered a secure passage over the river Aisne. Vladimir Löwenstern was sent into the town as an emissary by the allied commanders. He used all his gambler's tricks of bluff, aggression and charm to persuade the French commandant to surrender Soissons on 2 March.

Napoleon was furious, ordered the commandant to be shot, and claimed that if the city had not surrendered he would have pinned Blücher with his back to the Aisne and destroyed his army. Most Prussian historians angrily deny this and claim that the Army of Silesia could have crossed the Aisne elsewhere. On the other hand, some of General von Bülow's supporters were only too happy to argue that their hero had rescued Blücher from a tight spot. Inevitably they neglected to mention that the chief agent of this rescue was not a Prussian but Löwenstern. To an even greater extent than normal in 1813–14, the Russian role is neglected and what actually happened is obscured amidst a cacophony of French and German nationalism and machismo. Probably the Prussian historians are right and Blücher would have escaped Napoleon's clutches, but some at least of the allied force would have needed to cross the river over the Army of Silesia's Russian pontoon bridges, never an easy task with Napoleon in the offing and made no easier by the Aisne's flooding banks.[9]

The French army crossed the river Aisne at Berry-au-Bac to the east of Soissons on 5 March. Napoleon intended to advance on Laon; he was under the illusion that the allies were retreating and that all he would meet would be more or less determined rearguards. Blücher decided to pounce on the French as they advanced towards Corbeny and Laon. He deployed Winzengerode's 16,300 infantry under the command of Mikhail Vorontsov on a plateau just to the west of the Laon road near the village of Craonne. Correctly, he believed that the emperor could never push on to Laon with this force on his flank and would need to concentrate first on defeating Vorontsov. Fabian von der Osten-Sacken's Army Corps was deployed some kilometres behind Vorontsov on the plateau to support him in case of need. While Vorontsov's Russians were pinning down Napoleon and occupying his attention, Blücher intended to march 10,000 cavalry under Winzengerode and the whole of Lieutenant-General von Kleist's Prussian Army Corps around the French northern flank and into their rear. Meanwhile Bülow would shield Laon and Blücher's communications with the Low Countries, while part of Alexandre de Langeron's force would remain behind to hold Soissons.

There were problems with Blücher's plan. Langeron's and Bülow's men would take no part in the battle and were therefore to some extent wasted. The terrain over which Winzengerode and Kleist were supposed to make their flank march was not properly reconnoitred and turned out to be very difficult. Rocks, hills, streams and broken ground caused great delays even to the cavalry, let alone the guns. A better general than Winzengerode might well have overcome these difficulties but with him in command the whole flank movement crawled along and finally had to be abandoned.

As a result, in the battle of Craonne on 7 March Vorontsov fought alone for most of the day against an ever-increasing proportion of Napoleon's army. Fortunately his position was very strong. The height held by the Russians became famous in the First World War as the Chemin des Dames. It stretched about 17 kilometres from east to west and was narrow, in some cases being only a few hundred metres wide. The Russians could therefore hold their line in depth while the steep sides of the plateau made it very difficult for the French to outflank their position. Vorontsov deployed his artillery skilfully and he put the 14th Jaegers into the stout farm buildings at Heurtebise in front of his main line in order to blunt and delay the French attack. This was a crack regiment, with its ranks full of elite sharpshooters from the former combined grenadier battalions of Winzengerode's Army Corps, which had been disbanded just before the campaign began. For once it was the Russians who enjoyed the advantage of fighting from behind stout walls and the 14th Jaegers put up a formidable performance on 7 March.[10]

The battle began shortly after ten o'clock in the morning of 7 March when Marshal Ney's corps, 14,000 strong, advanced against the left of the Russian line. Ney attacked prematurely before other infantry divisions were on hand to support his advance. His young conscripts fought with great courage but they were advancing over difficult ground in the face of many well-sited Russian batteries. Not surprisingly, their repeated attacks failed. When General Boyer's excellent division of units withdrawn from Spain arrived on the scene Napoleon threw it into the fray immediately. It fought its way past the farm of Heurtebise and up onto the plateau, allowing four French batteries to climb the slopes and deploy in its support. Vorontsov, however, launched a counter-attack which threw both Boyer and Ney back off the plateau. Not until the early afternoon, when Charpentier's infantry and a number of cavalry brigades joined the attack, was the Russian position in serious danger.

At this point orders came from Blücher for Vorontsov to retire and for the whole army to retreat northwards and concentrate at Laon. The orders were sensible. Once the flank attack had come to nothing it made no sense to expose Vorontsov and Sacken to a battle against the whole French army. Inevitably this was not how matters seemed to Vorontsov in the midst of the fray. His men had fought with great courage to pin down Napoleon. Now their sacrifice appeared to be in vain. A warrior's pride made it very difficult for him to retreat from a battle in which thus far victory had been on his side. In any case, at least in the short run it was easier to hold one's ground than to retreat in orderly fashion in the face of a numerically superior enemy who would be emboldened by the sight of his enemy withdrawing.

Only after repeated orders from Sacken did Vorontsov begin his withdrawal. He remained calm throughout, as did his men, and the French cavalry had no success in their efforts to break into the Russian infantry squares or capture their guns. At the narrow defile near the village of Cerny, Vorontsov halted his retreat to give time for Ilarion Vasilchikov's cavalry to arrive. When Sacken received Blücher's orders to retreat he had got his infantry away immediately but he sent Vasilchikov forward to cover Vorontsov's regiments as they made their way across the more open plateau west of Cerny. Together Vasilchikov and Vorontsov kept the pursuing French at a respectful distance, particularly after they had combined to ambush one enemy detachment which pursued them too incautiously. Towards the western end of the plateau it once again narrowed and the French were forced to bunch together in close columns to continue their advance. At these points the very competent commander of Sacken's artillery, Major-General Aleksei Nikitin, had deployed a number of batteries and their concentrated fire stopped the pursuit and inflicted heavy casualties, before the Russian guns slipped away unscathed under the protection of Vasilchikov's cavalry.[11]

Since Britain had no troops in the allied army, Lord Burghersh – its military representative at headquarters – was a relatively impartial observer. He called the Russian performance at Craonne 'the best fought action during the campaign'. Vorontsov, Vasilchikov and their troops had certainly shown great skill, discipline and courage. The performance of Vorontsov's infantry was particularly striking because few of his regiments had seen serious combat since the spring of 1813 and for many of his men this was their first experience of battle. The French subsequently claimed victory because Blücher's plan had failed and because they held the battlefield at the end of the day. In this narrow sense they were indeed victorious, just as they had been 'victorious' in these terms in every Russian rearguard action during their advance to Moscow in 1812. But the Russians left behind no guns and very few prisoners. Clausewitz sums up the battle of Craonne by saying that 'the Russians defended themselves at Craonne so successfully that the main goal, to reach Laon undisturbed, was achieved . . . this was accomplished by exceptionally brave soldiers, a very self-possessed commander and an excellent position'.[12]

The Russians lost 5,000 men. The earliest full French account puts their own casualties at 8,000 and since they were very disinclined indeed to overstate their losses this figure may be accurate. Subsequently, however, French historians chipped away at the numbers and Henri Houssaye wrote that 'the Russians lost 5,000, the French 5,400'. A contemporary French expert tweaked the figures still further, claiming that the allies lost 5,500 men and Napoleon only 5,000. Presumably this was in order to stake an additional claim to victory. In the same spirit 29,000 Frenchmen are said to have faced 50,000 allies, which may be true if one counts every soldier within a day's march of the battle but completely distorts what actually happened on the battlefield on 7 March. In reality all of this juggling of statistics is irrelevant, though it does help to illustrate the historian's difficulties in getting at the truth. Even if in fact the Russians and the French had lost the same number of men at Craonne, the basic point was that Napoleon could no longer afford this kind of attrition.[13]

Napoleon followed up Blücher to Laon and on 9 March attacked the Russo-Prussian forces there. Once again he believed that he was likely to face only a rearguard and drastically underestimated the size of the allied army. In fact Blücher had concentrated all his corps near Laon, almost 100,000 men, and outnumbered the French by more than two to one. In addition, Napoleon's army was divided in two, with the emperor advancing up the road from Soissons and Marmont up the road from Rheims. Communication between the two wings was very difficult because of the Russian light cavalry and the swampy terrain. Not at all surprisingly, Napoleon's attack on 9 March failed. After darkness set in that evening the Prussians themselves surprised and routed Marmont in one of the most successful night attacks of the war. Napoleon's army was now at the allies' mercy. He was saved by Blücher's breakdown, which paralysed the Army of Silesia. The immense strains of the previous two months had ruined the health of the 72-year-old field-marshal. After Prussia's defeat in 1806–7 Blücher had suffered a breakdown, a side effect of which was alarming hallucinations about giving birth to an elephant. Now staff officers who came to him for orders found him in another world and unable to respond to their enquiries. Any light on his eyes caused him great suffering.[14]

The next few days revealed the fragility of the coalition armies' command structure and just how much the Army of Silesia had depended on Blücher's drive, courage and charisma. In principle the army's senior full general was Alexandre de Langeron but there was no chance of Yorck or Bülow obeying him. Langeron himself dreaded the idea of having to take over command and argued that Gneisenau should do so, as Blücher's chief of staff and the man best informed of the commander-in-chief's intentions. Neither Yorck nor Bülow much respected Gneisenau, however, and in addition he was junior to both of them. Yorck chose this moment to act the prima donna and resign his command, only returning to duty after Blücher scrawled an appeal to him which was supported by the pleas of Prince William of Prussia, one of Yorck's brigade commanders and the king's brother. Deprived of Blücher's strength and inspiration, Gneisenau lost confidence and courage. He fell prey to one of his congenital failings, the belief that Prussia was being betrayed by her allies. The result was that for more than a week after the battle of Laon the Army of Silesia spread out in search of food but played no useful role in the war.[15]

The inactivity of the Army of Silesia allowed Napoleon to escape, rest and then pounce on the 12,000-strong detachment led by Emmanuel de Saint-Priest, Bagration's chief of staff back in 1812, which had taken Rheims on 12 March. Although Napoleon had suffered at least 6,000 casualties at Laon, reinforcements arrived from Paris, bringing his army back up to 40,000 men. This was more than sufficient to defeat Saint-Priest, particularly since Napoleon caught the allies by surprise. To some extent this was Saint-Priest's fault for not taking proper precautions but it was hard to predict that Blücher's army would stand still, lose all track of Napoleon and fail to provide any warning as to his movements. Part of Saint-Priest's force was made up of Prussian Landwehr, who had dispersed in search of food and put up little resistance when the French attacked on 13 March. Saint-Priest's Russian regiments from his own Eighth Corps were made of sterner stuff, however, and put up a stiff fight, despite the fact that their general himself was severely wounded and out of action from the beginning of the battle.

The core of Russian resistance was the Riazan Regiment, an old unit with a fine fighting record, founded by Peter the Great in 1703. In the current war the regiment had fought at Borodino, Bautzen and Leipzig, where 35 per cent of its officers were killed or wounded and thirty-two of its men won military medals. General Saint-Priest himself was popular with his troops, of whom he took good care, for instance using a captured French treasury to buy new clothes for his soldiers in the winter of 1813–14. He had a particularly strong relationship with the Riazan Regiment, which he called 'the Guards of the Eighth Corps'. The regiment's inspiring commander was Colonel Ivan Skobelev, the son of a state peasant, who had served twelve years in the ranks before receiving his commission. Amidst the chaos on 13 March the Riazan Regiment's third battalion built a breastwork in front of the main gate of Rheims and beat off French efforts to break into the city. Meanwhile, initially 2 kilometres outside the city's walls, the regiment's first battalion formed a square against the French cavalry and fought their way back to where their comrades of the third battalion were holding out, carrying the wounded Saint-Priest in their midst. The two battalions of the Riazan Regiment then formed the core of the Russian rearguard, commanded by Skobelev, which held up the French for long enough for most of the Eighth Corps to escape from Rheims and rally beyond the city. The Riazan Regiment itself was cut off but escaped through the city's back streets with the help of a local royalist guide.[16]

After defeating Saint-Priest, Napoleon gave his troops two days' rest at Rheims before heading south to tackle Schwarzenberg. Meanwhile the first three weeks of March had been a time of great tension at allied headquarters, above all for Alexander. The emperor was not without military talent but he was nervous and lacked confidence. His correspondence in March 1814 reveals great fears that history was about to repeat itself. Once again Schwarzenberg was advancing with infuriating caution and slowness at a time when Blücher's army was running considerable risks. The emperor was constantly attempting to prod Schwarzenberg forward while enquiring anxiously about the safety of Blücher and Saint-Priest, and bemoaning the fact that news from them was so infrequent. On 12 March there were angry scenes at headquarters when Alexander interrogated Metternich about the existence of secret Austrian orders to Schwarzenberg constraining the main army's movements. Meanwhile Frederick William III shouted out that the Austrians were betraying the allied cause and exposing the Prussian and Russian soldiers of Blücher's army to destruction. Inevitably, when news arrived of Saint-Priest's defeat this did nothing to calm Alexander's fears. Remembering events in February, he was terrified that, once again, Wittgenstein's Army Corps and Pahlen's advance guard were isolated and vulnerable to a sudden attack. Langeron recalls that Napoleon's speed and audacity in February had thrown the allied commanders off balance: 'We believed that we could see him everywhere.' Of no one was this more true than Alexander.[17]

Nevertheless, Alexander was correct to believe that Napoleon's strategy would now be to strike into the main army's right flank and rear in the hope of isolating and destroying one of its Army Corps. In fact by now if Napoleon was to attack the main army this was his only option. He had been forced to leave marshals Marmont and Mortier with 20,000 men to watch Blücher's 100,000. Marshal MacDonald was guarding the southern approaches to Paris with 30,000 men against Schwarzenberg's 122,000. This left Napoleon with barely 20,000 men when he marched southwards from Rheims on 17 March in the hope of surprising Schwarzenberg. He could expect to be joined by a few thousand reinforcements from Paris while on the march but even if he then united with MacDonald the allied main army would still outnumber him by more than two to one. On 21 March, when the emperor found himself confronted by the whole of Schwarzenberg's army at Arcis-sur-Aube, he knew that his offensive had failed and that he had no option but to retreat.

It was at this point that the allied decision to invade France in winter and pre-empt Napoleon's efforts to raise a new army truly justified itself. The emperor had no reserves left in his depots and two months of ceaseless marches and battles had shattered his army. After retreating from Arcis Napoleon really had only two options left. He could retreat on his capital and concentrate every soldier and National Guard he could scrape together for the defence of Paris. His presence would overawe any opposition forces in the capital. Entrenched in the hills, gardens and buildings surrounding Paris even 90,000 men under Napoleon's personal command would be a formidable nut for the allies to crack.[18]

The other option – the one adopted by Napoleon on 22 March – was to strike against the allies' communications to the Rhine. During the campaign Schwarzenberg had shown himself to be in general very cautious and in particular extremely nervous about any threats to his rear. It was therefore reasonable for Napoleon to believe that, if he himself attacked Schwarzenberg's communications with his main army, the allied commander-in-chief would retreat from the Paris region and try to protect his bases and supply lines. Nothing in the way Schwarzenberg had previously fought the campaign suggested that he would take the risk of turning his back on Napoleon and marching on Paris. If, however, the allies did do this then Napoleon needed to be able to sacrifice his capital, as Alexander had sacrificed Moscow. One of his greatest weaknesses in 1814 was that he felt he could not do this, for political reasons. Events were to prove him correct. French armies had occupied Moscow, Vienna and Berlin without any serious domestic opposition emerging against the Romanov, Habsburg or Hohenzollern monarchs. Within one week of the allies' arrival in Paris not just Napoleon but also his dynasty had been swept away. Napoleon's belief that his own throne was more fragile than those of the legitimate monarchs who opposed him was justified. On the other hand, in 1813–14 he had done much to persuade French elites that he was fighting more for his own glory than for French interests.[19]

On 22 March Schwarzenberg and Alexander did not know in which direction Napoleon was heading. Petr Volkonsky wrote to Gneisenau on 22 March that Napoleon had masked his movements by leaving large cavalry screens behind him. The allies intended to follow hot on his heels. If the enemy attacked the Army of Silesia then on this occasion the main army would be right on his tail and would strike his rear. If he took any other direction, the two armies would unite and then advance against him and seek battle. That very evening Blücher discovered exactly where the enemy was heading because his Cossacks had captured a French courier with a letter from Napoleon to Marie-Louise saying that he was intending to attack the allies' communications and thereby draw them well away from Paris.[20]

A copy of the letter was immediately sent to the main army head-quarters where its implications were discussed in a council of war held in Pougy on the afternoon of 23 March. Of Alexander's closest Russian military advisers only Petr Volkonsky was in Pougy at the time, and he never spoke up publicly in such meetings. The most basic point, however, was that by the time the allied armies could be turned round Napoleon would have two days' start on them. Nothing could now stop him from getting into the allied rear. Any attempt to race back to protect allied bases would put tremendous strains on army morale and discipline, not least because the troops would be marching into areas already ravaged by war, where they would find it very difficult to feed themselves. For the moment therefore the allied leaders stuck to their existing plan to link up with Blücher and then advance to meet the enemy and give battle. Meanwhile urgent orders went out to town commandants and commanders of troops in the rear to get as many supplies, transport columns and reinforcements as possible under protection or away from the main roads. The ever-nervous provost-general, Oertel, had pre-viously been chided for over-reacting to imagined threats to the Russian lines of communication. Now urgent orders went out to him from

Barclay to take emergency measures to preserve Russian bases, supplies and treasuries. Oertel did well on this occasion and reported his arrangements to Barclay, a fellow Balt, in Latvian, a language which the commander-in-chief understood. If the orders were intercepted, it would be a very unusual Frenchman who could decipher them.[21]

On the evening of 23 March Schwarzenberg, Alexander, Frederick William and their staffs set off from Pougy to Sompuis where they arrived early in the morning of the next day. On the way they were given more enemy dispatches captured by the Russian cavalry. These told of the low morale of Napoleon's troops and their generals, and also revealed that Paris's depots and arsenals were empty. Most important was a letter to Napoleon from his police chief Savary, who wrote that he could not answer for the capital's loyalty if the allied armies approached. That same night news arrived from the south that Bordeaux had gone over to the Bourbons and that the city had been occupied by Wellington. Nevertheless when Schwarzenberg and Frederick William left Sompuis on the morning of 24 March the allied plan was still to unite their two armies and then go in search of Napoleon.

Not long afterwards, at approximately ten o'clock, Alexander summoned Barclay, Diebitsch and Toll, showed them the intercepted letters and the troops' current positions on the map, and asked for their advice about the best course of action. He put two options to them: either the allies could pursue Napoleon or they could march on Paris. It may be that Alexander had already talked to Volkonsky, who had spoken up in private for moving on Paris. Barclay on the contrary was a cautious and not very imaginative strategist: he argued for continuing with the current policy of combining with Blücher and then going in search of Napoleon. Diebitsch did not disagree openly with his superior but argued that they should also send a strong corps to take Paris at the same time. Toll was always a less 'political' and tactful person than Diebitsch. Disagreeing with a boss was second nature to him. He argued that a single detached corps could never take Paris. Instead both armies should head for the capital, sending off a flying column mostly made up of cavalry to shadow Napoleon and report his movements.[22]

The emperor was probably expecting and hoping for Toll's view, which he adopted instantly. Alexander sent an aide-de-camp to find Schwarzenberg and Frederick William, and ask them to wait for him. He caught up with them on a little hill near the village of Plancy and in the fine early spring weather Toll spread his map on the ground and an impromptu outdoor conference took place. The Prussian king immediately agreed to Alexander's proposal and Schwarzenberg too took little persuading, despite the objections of some of his staff. The idea of turning one's back on Napoleon and marching on the French capital was not a total surprise to Schwarzenberg. It had been in the air for some time and his ablest staff officer, Lieutenant-General Radetsky, had apparently argued for it privately on the previous day. It is nevertheless striking that the previously very cautious commander-in-chief agreed to so daring a move without much delay or opposition. There is no certain evidence as to why he did so but one can make a plausible and informed guess.[23]

Though a march on Paris was bold, the alternatives were also risky. Only ten days before, Schwarzenberg had been bemoaning the difficulties of squeezing food out of 'impoverished Champagne, which has been supporting us for three months'. Moving the combined allied armies through this region in pursuit of Napoleon would be very difficult. Actually a threat to Paris was probably the likeliest way to draw Napoleon away from the allied rear. The area around Paris was rich and untouched by war. Once they arrived there the allies would have far less trouble feeding themselves than if they pursued Napoleon or remained static. The main army currently held more than enough food in its carts to keep it going until it reached this area. On 25 March one Russian corps reported that it had eight days of supplies still in its regimental carts. Four days later Kankrin told Barclay that the 200 carts of Lisanevich's mobile magazine currently with the army still carried four days' biscuit rations. As Kankrin and Francis II both noted, with the main army heading north there was also now a good chance of opening up a new line of supply through the wealthy and largely untouched Low Countries.[24]

Barclay de Tolly was not inclined to easy compliments, but he wrote to Kankrin at this time saying that 'I have complete confidence in your zeal and your sensible arrangements for the good of the service'. The praise was merited because the allied intendancy responded well to the challenge of simultaneously protecting its rear bases and feeding its own advancing army. But if the army's supply officers made an advance possible, political and military reasons made it seem desirable in Schwarzenberg's eyes. With the congress of Châtillon closed and negotiations with Napoleon suspended, it was clear that military victories were the only way to secure peace. Taking Paris was the best means either to force Napoleon to accept allied peace terms or to encourage French elites to get rid of him. The recent fireworks at headquarters must have made Schwarzenberg realize that Russian, Prussian and even British patience with his cautious strategy was wearing very thin. Even some of his senior Austrian officers were complaining about the inglorious role played by their army thus far in the campaign. Probably all these thoughts were in the commander-in-chief's mind when he ordered his army to march on Paris. In addition, it is a happy commander who starts an operation knowing the position, weakness and worries of his enemies.[25]

Ferdinand Winzengerode was ordered off in pursuit of Napoleon with 8,000 cavalry. He was told to try to hoodwink the emperor into believing that the whole allied army was pursuing him and to keep allied head-quarters well informed as to enemy movements. Meanwhile the two allied armies began their march towards Paris early in the morning of 25 March. The bulk of the main army marched down the road which led from Vitry through Fère-Champenoise to Sézanne, with the cavalry of Peter Pahlen and Prince Adam of Württemberg as its advance guard. A few kilometres to the south Barclay and the army's reserve units marched in parallel along side roads and across country. To the north of the main army, Langeron's and Sacken's troops advanced down the road from Châlons to Bergères. Ahead of them rode the cavalry divisions of Baron Korff and Ilarion Vasilchikov. The scent of victory had led to the semi-recovery of Blücher. He travelled with his troops in a carriage, visible to all, wearing a lady's green silk hat with a very broad brim to shade his eyes. The weather had turned fine and the allied troops at last felt that they were moving forward under confident and united leadership. Morale soared.

Shortly after eight in the morning of 25 March Pahlen and Prince Adam bumped into Marshal Marmont's corps drawn up across the road to Fère-Champenoise, near the village of Soudé Sainte-Croix. Nearby was Marshal Mortier's corps. Together the two marshals commanded 12,300 infantry, 4,350 cavalry and 68 guns. Even counting Cossacks, this well outnumbered the 5,700 horsemen and 36 guns of Pahlen and Prince Adam, but the French marshals could see large enemy forces in the distance and began to retreat. Even after the arrival of 2,500 Austrian cuirassiers the French infantry squares were still safe enough, though their cavalry was driven off and two light infantry regiments were cut off in Soudé Sainte-Croix and forced to surrender.

Things began to look ominous only around two in the afternoon, when the Russian heavy cavalry arrived on the scene. The Chevaliers Gardes and Horse Guards had not seen serious action since Borodino and their commanding general, Nikolai Preradovich, begged Barclay to allow the 1st Cuirassier Division to take part in the battle. Their appearance more or less coincided with the onset of a violent rain and hailstorm, which blew directly in the faces of the French infantry as they were trying to pass through the deep gully near Conantray. With their muskets useless and under accurate fire from the Guards horse artillery two French squares collapsed and were ridden down by the Russian cuirassiers and the Württemberg cavalry. Panic ensued among much of the rest of the French infantry, many of whom took to their heels. In the end Marmont and Mortier escaped but they lost one-third of their men and most of their guns to an enemy which they always outnumbered and which did not include any infantry.[26]

Part of the reason they escaped at all was that towards five in the afternoon heavy gunfire was heard in the rear of the allied cavalry. For a time there was uncertainty on all sides as to which troops were in sight and what the gunfire meant. In fact this was two small French divisions, mostly of National Guardsmen, escorting a vast artillery and supply train, and pursued by Korff's and Vasilchikov's cavalry from the Army of Silesia. The French column, commanded by generals Pacthod and Amey, was roughly 5,000 strong. It initially encountered Korff's cavalry at about eleven in the morning on the road from Châlons. Baron Korff had begun the 1812 campaign on the heavy side. By 1814 he was very large and becoming rather lazy. Disliking bivouacs, he had retired on the previous night to the nearby chateau of Sillery, accompanied by his subordinate generals. Meanwhile his Cossacks had uncovered a store of 60,000 bottles of wine into which all of Korff's cavalry dived with joy. Not surprisingly, they got off to a rather slow start the next morning.[27]

By midday, however, the French were in full retreat down the road from Châlons to Bergères which passes near Fère-Champenoise. By now they were surrounded not only by Korff's men but also by the much more formidable Ilarion Vasilchikov. In all, the Russians had 4,000 cavalry and three batteries of horse artillery. The French generals abandoned their baggage train in mid-afternoon but even this did not save them. Already having exhausted themselves and suffered heavy casualties against Korff and Vasilchikov, their position became hopeless when their retreat took them straight into the arms of the main army's cavalry and horse artillery at Fère-Champenoise. In the end the entire column was killed or taken prisoner.

The battle of Fère-Champenoise is often described as a tale of French heroism. At one level this is entirely just. Pacthod and Amey's National Guardsmen showed a courage, discipline and endurance of which veterans would have been proud. Not all of Marmont and Mortier's regiments did as well, however. Moreover, the achievement of the allied cavalry was also remarkable. Sixteen thousand horsemen, of whom three-quarters were Russian, had defeated 23,000 French troops, most of them infantry, killing or capturing half of them and taking almost all their guns. The battle of Fère-Champenoise is well compared to Dmitry Neverovsky's desperate fight against Marshal Murat at Krasnyi in August 1812, though the numerical odds against Neverovsky were much greater. Like the French at Fère-Champenoise, a large proportion of Neverovsky's men had been new recruits who showed great courage and discipline during their first battle. The Russian generals succeeded at Fère-Champenoise where Murat failed at Krasnyi partly because, unlike him, they got their horse artillery to the battlefield. They also coordinated their attacks and adapted their tactics to the terrain much more skilfully.[28]

With Marmont and Mortier in flight, the road to Paris was open. The only real chance of defending the capital was if Napoleon and his army could return in time. Even if the emperor arrived on his own he was likely to galvanize and coordinate the defence, and overawe potential traitors in the city. Not until 27 March, however, was Napoleon aware of the fact that he had been tricked and that the enemy armies were advancing on Paris. By now the allies had three days' march on him. After consulting with Caulaincourt, Bassano and his marshals he decided that he must abandon his assault on the allied rear and race back to save his capital, but it was too late. By the time he approached the city in the late evening of 30 March the battle of Paris had been lost and his capital was on the point of surrender. Worse still, Napoleon's enemies in Paris were stirring. On the emperor's orders his wife, son and government left Paris on the eve of the battle so as not to be captured. With all the key figures in the Bonapartist regime gone and the allies on the point of occupying Paris, the moment had arrived for Napoleon's opponents to seize the initiative. Along with all other top officials, Talleyrand had been ordered to leave Paris but he contrived to evade these orders without seeming openly to flout Napoleon's authority.[29]

On the other side of the lines, now only a few kilometres away, was Karl Nesselrode, to whom Talleyrand had slipped so much secret advice and information in the years before 1812. When Napoleon launched his assault on allied communications on 22 March, almost all the allied diplomats had been cut off from headquarters and had scuttled southwards to safety, to the undisguised glee of many of the generals, who were glad to be rid of them. The one exception was Nesselrode, who had got away just in time from Chaumont to find his way back to Alexander's side. On 28 March, the very day that it was decided that Napoleon's empress, son and government should leave the capital, Nesselrode wrote to his wife from a village near Paris that he was enjoying 'an exquisite capon', which Marshal Ney's wife had sent to her husband from Paris along with some bottles of liqueur. The Cossacks had intercepted the present and tactfully donated it to their emperor's table. With Francis II, Metternich, Castlereagh and Hardenberg all absent, there was never any doubt that Alexander would speak for the allies should their armies reach Paris. To have Nesselrode by his side was an additional advantage, however, especially when it came to negotiating with Talleyrand. As victory loomed and Alexander's hopes were realized, the tension that had existed between the two men disappeared.[30]

The Russian army approached Paris through a rich countryside amidst fine spring weather and with the smell of victory in the air. Vladimir Löwenstern ate peacock for the first time to celebrate. Peter Pahlen contemplated all the beautiful young ladies he would meet in the French capital. Ivan Radozhitsky recalled his men telling each other that when they got to Paris the emperor would give them each a ruble, a pound of meat and a tumbler of vodka. As his battery marched down the highway the cry rang out, 'stand to the right, stand to the left', as happened when a general or the emperor himself was passing through a marching column. Down the middle of the highway charged Vaska, a goat which the soldiers had adopted as a mascot, to hoots of 'make way, make way, Vaska is off to Paris'.[31]

In the early evening of 29 March, the emperor's staff, including

Aleksandr Mikhailovsky-Danilevsky, ascended a slight rise towards the village of Clichy. Many years later he recalled that

the sun had just set, and a cool breeze refreshed the air after the heat of the day; there was not a cloud in the sky. All at once, on the right hand, we got a momentary glimpse of Montmartre, and the tall spires of the capital. 'Paris! Paris!' was the general cry. We pointed out and strained our eyes to grasp the huge but indistinct mass rising above the horizon. Forgotten in a moment were the fatigues of the campaign, wounds, fallen friends and brothers: overwhelmed with joy, we stood on the hill from which Paris was barely visible in the distance. Since that day, more than twenty years have passed . . . but the remembrance of that memorable scene is still so vivid, that it comes over us with all the freshness of a recent event, making the heart swell with that triumphant exaltation which then filled every breast.[32]

In the longest campaign in European history, in less than two years the Russian army had marched from Vilna to Moscow and then all the way back across Europe to Paris. With the enemy capital in sight at last, speed was now essential. Paris must be taken before Napoleon arrived to galvanize and reinforce its defence. The Bavarians and Sacken's Army Corps had been left at Meaux to guard the allied rear in case Napoleon attempted to march on Paris by the most direct route. But that night orders went out to all other corps for a full-scale assault on Paris on the very next day, 30 March. On the allied right, the Army of Silesia was to attack the capital from the north, heading for Montmartre and La Chapelle. On the left the Württemberg corps was to advance from the east along the north bank of the Seine, past the chateau of Vincennes. General Gyulai's Austrians would support the Württembergers. Peter Wittgenstein had returned to Russia, handing over command of his Army Corps to Nikolai Raevsky. He would lead the attack in the centre towards Romainville and Pantin. In all, the attacking force added up to 100,000 men. Behind Raevsky, to be used if necessary, stood the Grand Duke Constantine's Reserve Army Corps, made up of the Guards and Grenadiers.[33]

The position held by the French was very strong. The heights of Montmartre to the north and of Romainville in the centre were major obstacles for an attacking army, around which the capital's defence could be anchored. As one would expect on the outskirts of one of Europe's greatest cities, the whole area was also a maze of stone buildings and walls. Napoleon, however, had done nothing to strengthen the city's natural defences. Moreover, there were only 38,000 men to hold a long defence line, and of these many thousands were National Guardsmen with minimal training and unreliable muskets. Under the overall authority of Napoleon's brother Joseph, Marshal Mortier was responsible for defending the northern sector against the Army of Silesia and Marshal Marmont the eastern sector against the allied main army. All three men knew that unless the defenders were willing to fight in the streets of Paris and bury themselves under the city's rubble, their chances of success were slight. If the whole allied assault force had attacked simultaneously early in the morning of 30 March, the city would probably have fallen by lunchtime.

In fact, allied plans went awry. It was clear even on the evening of 30 March that the Württembergers and Austrians were still so far in the rear that they could not launch their attack until early the following afternoon. Meanwhile the aide-de-camp carrying Schwarzenberg's orders to Blücher got lost in the dark, which meant that most of the Army of Silesia would only be ready to attack at eleven o'clock, six hours later than planned. As a result, the initial allied assault was only made by the 16,000 men of Raevsky's Army Corps in the allied centre. Fortunately for the Russians they found the key village of Romainville undefended and were able to seize it before Marmont had time to send troops to occupy it. They also took the village of Pantin early in the morning. But it was all they could do to hold these strongholds against French counter-attacks in the morning of 30 March.

All attempts to break forward out of the villages came to nothing. The Prussian Guards infantry, not in action since the spring of 1813, stormed forward out of Pantin with great courage but was stopped in its tracks with heavy casualties. Amidst the buildings, walls and gardens all formation was lost and the battle dissolved into confused skirmishing and fire-fights. Barclay de Tolly moved up the two Russian Grenadier divisions in Raevsky's support and came up to the front line himself to coordinate operations. Very sensibly, he got most of the regiments back into battalion columns ready for a new push, but ordered Raevsky not to mount a major new attack until the Württembergers were in position on his left and the Army of Silesia was absorbing Mortier's full attention on his right.[34]

Shortly before three o'clock in the afternoon all the allied corps were in line and ready to attack. The Crown Prince of Württemberg pushed forward past the chateau of Vincennes against slight opposition, threatening to unhinge the whole French right flank by the Seine. The advance of Yorck's Army Corps from the north into their rear forced the French troops fighting near the village of Pantin to retreat. In the centre Raevsky's men and the Grenadier divisions attacked in overwhelming force and took all the key French positions within ninety minutes. Russian artillery batteries were brought forward and now ringed Paris to the east from close range. On the far right of the allied line, Langeron's Army Corps stormed up the heights of Montmartre. In fact by the time the Russians took these heights Marshal Marmont was already seeking to capitulate, though there was no way that either the Russians or the French at Montmartre could yet know this.

The allies had suffered 8,000 casualties, three-quarters of them Russian, but Paris was theirs. A great wave of rejoicing went through the Russian ranks. The Guards began polishing their equipment and getting out their best uniforms in preparation for the greatest parade of their lives down the streets of Paris. On the heights of Montmartre the infantry bands blasted out regimental marches. The officer whom Langeron sent into Paris to arrange a truce with the nearest French troops came back hours later and in a state of bliss, having drunk too many toasts to victory. His commanding general forgave him. Langeron's regiments from the former Army of the Danube had marched a long way and fought many battles for this moment.[35]

The really difficult battle was just about to begin, however, and it would be political rather than military. Unless their generals blundered on a grand scale, sheer weight of numbers and the superior quality of their troops were likely to bring the allies victory and the capitulation of Paris on 30 March. The French capital was of political rather than military importance, however. Much would depend on whether the allies could turn the fall of Paris to their political advantage. Of course, the allied leaders in general and Alexander in particular were acutely aware of this. Schwarzenberg issued a proclamation stressing that the allies fought Napoleon, not France, and sought peace and prosperity for all. As his army approached Paris, Alexander issued orders to his generals and pleas to his allies to preserve the strictest discipline and treat the civilian population well, stressing the great importance of cultivating French opinion. The man whom Alexander sent into Paris to arrange the capitulation was Colonel Mikhail Orlov, the same young intelligence officer who had accompanied Aleksandr Balashev to Napoleon's headquarters in Vilna in June 1812. Orlov's first words to Marshal Marmont were, 'His Majesty desires to preserve Paris for France and for the sake of the whole world.' Allied troops were to be quartered in Parisian barracks, not in private homes, and the National Guard was to be retained to preserve calm and normality on the streets. For the next few days Alexander was a perfect embodiment of charm, tact and flattery as regards the Parisians. This was a role at which he excelled.[36]

On the next day, Sunday, 31 March 1814, the allied armies entered Paris. The sun shone and Paris revelled in a crisp spring morning. Alexander emerged from his headquarters at eight o'clock, wearing the undress general's uniform of the Chevaliers Gardes. Mounting his grey 'Mars', a gift from Caulaincourt when the latter was ambassador in Petersburg, he rode off with his suite to join Frederick William and Schwarzenberg. Greeted by salutes and thunderous cheers from their troops, the allied leaders rode through Montmartre and into the centre of the city. Their escort was provided by the Cossack Life Guard in their scarlet tunics and dark-blue baggy trousers, the same troops who had guarded Alexander throughout the campaigns of the last two years. On the Champs-Elysées the monarchs and Schwarzenberg stopped and reviewed their regiments as they marched past. The parade included the Prussian Guards, a division of Austrian Grenadiers and even a regiment of Guards from Baden. By universal consent, however, the Russian Guards were the finest-looking troops in Europe and it was they who stole the show.[37]

Both for the Guards and, above all, for Alexander this was a supreme moment of pride and personal fulfilment, but it did also have a political aspect. For the Parisian crowds, to see thousand upon thousand of these superb troops in their splendid uniforms marching in perfect formation as if in peacetime was a reminder of allied power and the hollowness of Napoleon's claims that the invaders were on the edge of exhaustion. But if the allies handed out a political lesson they also received one. Thus far the allied monarchs had encountered few signs of popular enthusiasm for the Bourbons in the areas they had conquered. It was far from predictable that things would be different in Paris where so many beneficiaries of the Revolution and Napoleon lived. In fact, however, especially as they entered central Paris the monarchs were greeted by huge crowds shouting support for the allied cause and the monarchy, and bearing the white cockade and the white flag of the Bourbons. Two days later Alexander was to admit to a royalist politician that public support for a restoration was 'much greater than I could have imagined'. After the parade the monarchs and Schwarzenberg rode to Talleyrand's mansion on the nearby rue Saint-Florentin, where Alexander was to stay for his crucial first few days in Paris. On watch around the Hôtel de Talleyrand that night were the men of the First (Emperor's Own) Company of the First Battalion of the Preobrazhenskys. This was the battalion that had mounted guard at Tilsit seven years before.[38]

While the troops were entering Paris that morning, Nesselrode was already on his way to the rue Saint-Florentin. On the previous day, while waiting in Marmont's mansion to agree the terms of the city's capitulation, Mikhail Orlov had been approached by Talleyrand with the request 'to convey the deepest respects of the Prince of Benevento [i.e. Talleyrand] to His Majesty the Emperor of Russia'. Orlov was a clever and well-informed intelligence officer and had no doubt as to Talleyrand's meaning. 'Prince – I replied softly – you may be sure that I will bring this open offer to His Majesty's notice.' The young officer recalled that 'a slight, barely noticeable smile passed quickly across the prince's face'. Now on 31 March Nesselrode was coming to enlist Talleyrand's help in toppling Napoleon and replacing him with a stable regime both legitimate in French eyes and willing to endorse the peace settlement. As Alexander made clear to the French leaders he met that evening, these were his only priorities. Though he outlined to them a number of possible scenarios as regards France's future government, he stressed that it was for the French themselves to choose between them.[39]

For the emperor, Talleyrand was the perfect ally, and not merely because of his political skills and his connections. Like Alexander, he was no great partisan of the Bourbons. Even on 30 March he was by no means committed to a restoration. He was determined that if the monarchy was to return, it should be constrained by a constitution and should accept much of what had changed in France since 1789. In his heart he would probably have preferred a regency for Napoleon's infant son, with himself as the power behind the throne. Alexander was no different. With Napoleon alive, free and still full of ambition, however, such a regency had obvious dangers. In the conference between the allied leaders and French politicians which took place in Talleyrand's salon during the night of 31 March the key moment arrived when it came to drafting the allies' proclamation to the French people. No one doubted that they would rule out negotiating with Napoleon. When it came to the clause also excluding negotiations with members of the Bonaparte family, Alexander 'cast a glance towards Prince Schwarzenberg who agreed with a nod of his head, as did the King of Prussia'. Even after this Alexander's mind was not entirely made up. As late as 5 April Caulaincourt believed that Alexander was still open to the idea of a regency and Talleyrand and his associates deeply feared this. By then, however, it would have been very difficult for Alexander to reverse course and abandon those Frenchmen who had committed themselves to the restoration under his protection and encouragement.[40]

Following the scenario which Alexander had outlined back in February, the allied declaration called upon the Senate to meet, to elect a provisional government and to draw up a new constitution. Under Talleyrand's direction, a rump of the Senate agreed to this on 1 April, electing Talleyrand and his four associates as ministers. The next day the Senate deposed Napoleon and the Bonaparte family and released all French soldiers from their oath of allegiance. With Paris clearly heading towards the restoration of the monarchy the biggest issue now was the position of the army. If Napoleon's army at Fontainebleau continued to support him there was a strong chance that the allies would find themselves in the middle of a French civil war. Not merely did they dread the time and costs involved: it was also self-evident that this would hugely damage the legitimacy of any regime they supported in France. Quite apart from his doubts about the Bourbons, this factor also had to influence Alexander's thoughts about the continuing possibility of a regency for Napoleon's infant son. Only the defection of Marshal Marmont's corps on 5 April from Napoleon's army ended Alexander's doubts and made the restoration of the monarchy certain.[41]

For the first crucial days in Paris Alexander led and spoke for the coalition. During his time in Paris he made some mistakes. Though his effort to press the cause of moderation and the senatorial constitution on Louis XVIII was understandable, it was actually unnecessary and contributed to initially poor relations between Russia and the restored French monarchy. A more serious blunder was to allow Napoleon the sovereignty of Elba, which caused allied and Russian fears at the time, later justified. Undoubtedly this was in part the product of Alexander's desire to be, and to be seen to be, generous to a defeated foe. It was not easy in the circumstances of the time to find any safe solution to the problem posed by Napoleon, however, as Castlereagh recognized in a letter to the British secretary for war which is not included in his collected correspondence. Castlereagh wrote that the French Provisional Government had supported Alexander's offer because they were scared of civil war and desperate to get the emperor away from his army at Fontainebleau. Elba had its dangers but there were no obvious better alternatives. Although Castlereagh did not mention this, any constraint on Napoleon's freedom was impossible because it was ruled out by the agreement with Marmont when he brought his corps over to the allies. The British foreign secretary did, however, write that Elba was a better alternative than Napoleon's apparent desire to live in England, which the British Government certainly would not welcome.[42]

On the whole, however, Alexander's performance in Paris was a great success. He had charmed the French, kept in line with his allies, and established a regime in Paris which had the best chance of retaining legitimacy while accepting a lasting peace. Alexander had been much criticized for arguing that once the allies reached Paris they would be able to find and encourage French opponents to Napoleon, but events had proved him right. If he retained doubts about the Bourbons, these were shared by many Frenchmen and by Alexander's allies. As Schwarzenberg wrote to his wife at the time, the removal of Napoleon was a boon to mankind but he had little faith in the restored monarchy. For him as for Alexander, and in a manner very familiar in politics, the Bourbons were simply the least bad alternative at the allies' disposal. With the monarchy restored and peace with France signed, Alexander left Paris on 3 June 1814.[43]

While Alexander had been busy negotiating, his army had been experiencing life in and around the French capital. Vladimir Löwenstern set himself up with an expensive Parisian mistress and a fine carriage, paid for partly by 10,000 rubles won at cards. The Guards officers received a special allowance to enable them to enjoy and grace Paris. Humble officers of the line were not so lucky. Aleksandr Zaitsev, an innocent young ensign of the Kexholm Regiment, was quickly separated from his meagre earnings when he dared to visit the gambling dens and the young ladies of the Palais Royal. As to the soldiers, only the Guards were quartered in Paris and they were subjected to strict discipline and constant parades. The news that they were going home was greeted with joy. First to depart were the irregular cavalry – Cossacks, Bashkirs and Kalmyks: they were not the best peacetime ambassadors for a Russia anxious to conciliate the French civilian population and to be seen as a pillar of European order and civilization. Soon afterwards the regiments of the line began the long march home, many of them enjoying feasts in the Prussian towns through which they passed, as a mark of gratitude from Frederick William III. As always, the Guards were different, most of them being carried home to Petersburg by the Russian fleet which had spent the last eighteen months based in British ports.[44]

15

Conclusion

Not much more than a year after the Russian army left France they were back again, as a result of the 'Hundred Days', in other words Napoleon's escape from Elba and attempt to overthrow the 1814 settlement. On the eve of Waterloo a Russian army of 150,000 men had just reached the Rhine and Karl von Toll had just arrived in Belgium to coordinate operations with Wellington and Blücher. Part of what had been won in 1814 had needed to be reconquered in 1815 at the cost of many lives, though in this case not Russian ones.

Although this might seem to make the 1814 campaign pointless, in fact this is untrue. If the allies had signed a compromise peace with Napoleon in March 1814 he would have been in a much stronger position to challenge the peace settlement than was actually the case in 1815 after his escape from Elba. He would have had longer to plan his revenge and would have been able to pick his moment. His position within France would also have been stronger. By 1815 the restored monarchy had many supporters and even Napoleon's chief bulwark, the army, was riven with tensions between those who had compromised with the Bourbons and the hard core of Bonapartist loyalists.

Above all, the international situation would have been more favourable. In the end in 1814 the allies could unite with relative happiness around the restoration of the monarchy. A compromise peace with Napoleon would have been much less acceptable, above all for Alexander. Attempting subsequently to achieve agreement among the allies on a European settlement would have been all the harder. Even without this, the Congress of Vienna looked at one point as if it was going to result in a renewed European war. With Napoleon poised in Paris to exploit allied dissensions and his former allies awaiting his resurgence the dangers of further wars would have been great. In fact by the time

Napoleon re-established himself in Paris in 1815 the allies had achieved agreement on the peace settlement and were united in their determination not to let him unravel it. That made his defeat nearly certain. In June 1815 Napoleon had to risk everything by trying to destroy Wellington's and Blücher's armies before the main allied armies could intervene. He knew that even if he succeeded in doing this, he still faced probable defeat at the hands of the massive Russian, Austrian and Prussian forces already approaching France's borders.

The Hundred Days made little difference to the terms of the peace settlement. France more or less retained its 1792 borders. Russia got most but not all of the Duchy of Warsaw. Prussia was compensated with part of Saxony and was given Westphalia and the Rhineland in order to secure their defence against French revanchism. The very loose German Confederation which was created under Austrian and Prussian leadership far from satisfied the hopes of German nationalists or liberals, though these were much fewer on the ground than subsequent nationalist historians claimed. This was even more true in Italy, which after 1815 was made up of a number of illiberal states under a rather benevolent Habsburg hegemony.

For the Russians, the key elements in the settlement were Poland and Germany. As regards the former, many of Nesselrode's dire predictions proved correct. Alexander did consider seriously the idea of a federalized Russia with representative institutions, into which the constitutional Polish kingdom might fit more easily than into the present autocratic empire. Understandably, however, given Russian realities at the time, he retreated from this idea. Soon enough the contradictions between the monarch's role as autocratic tsar and constitutional king of Poland became glaring. The 1830 Polish rebellion ended the experiment of constitutional rule in Poland. Meanwhile the revolt of Russian officers in the so-called Decembrist movement of 1825 owed much to injured Russian national pride at the Poles being given freedoms denied to the Russian elites. In the century which followed 1815 the Poles contributed much to the Russian Empire's economy. In political terms, however, both the Polish and Jewish populations of the former Duchy of Warsaw caused the Russian government many problems. Nor was it even clear that the annexation of the Duchy had strengthened Russia's strategic position. On the contrary, by 1900 it could be seen as a potential trap for the Russian army. By then the German settlement of 1815 also looked a mistake from the perspective of Russian interests. A France bordering on the Rhine would have eased many Russian concerns about the challenge of Germany's growing power.

Of course, it is unfair to judge the efforts of statesmen using retrospective knowledge. Some of the difficulties caused by annexing the Duchy of Warsaw could have been – and indeed were – anticipated. But from the Russian perspective there were actually no easy answers to the Polish problem, to an even greater extent than was true of the British in Ireland. Nor could anyone predict that the weak Prussia of 1814 would be transformed by the Industrial Revolution and German unification into a menace to itself and Europe. Nevertheless a knowledge of subsequent European history does give emphasis to the question of whether the enormous sacrifices of the Russian people in 1812–14 had been worthwhile.

This is not just a matter of how much the Russian population suffered during the war. As is always true, victory legitimized and consolidated the existing regime, which in Russia was rooted in autocracy and serfdom. The sense that Russia was victorious and secure removed an incentive for radical domestic reform. The conservative regime of Nicholas I, who ruled from 1825 until 1855, was partly rooted in an assumption of Russian power and security. This assumption was only undermined by defeat in the Crimean War of 1854–6, which unleashed a swath of modernizing reforms under Nicholas's son, the Emperor Alexander II. In 1815, however, Russia did not have the means – which meant above all the educated cadres – to carry out radical reforms of the type undertaken two generations later. It is naive to believe that defeat by Napoleon would have unleashed a programme of successful liberalization in Russia. Even less well founded is the belief that Nicholas's conservatism was the basic cause of Russia's growing backwardness in 1815–60 vis-à-vis north-western Europe. The Industrial Revolution had dynamics well beyond the control of the Russian government of that era. It required levels of education and population density which Russia lacked, and the bringing together of coal and iron deposits, which in Russia's case was only possible with the introduction of the railway.

In any case, the question whether the sacrifices made in 1812–14 were worthwhile implies that the Russians had a choice. Then as always, ordinary Russians of course had little choice. The whole logic of the political system was designed to deny this. In 1807–14, however, the Russian government in reality also had few options. By the second half of 1810 the brilliantly run Russian intelligence operations in Paris gave Alexander every reason to expect attack. The very extensive military intelligence provided in 1811 confirmed this. No doubt if Alexander had caved in to all Napoleon's demands war might have been avoided for a time. By 1810, however, it was clear that the price of adhering to Napoleon's Continental System would be the undermining of the financial base of Russia's position as a great power. Russia's growing weakness would make it easy for Napoleon to restore a greater Poland, which was within both his power and his interests. Returning part of its Adriatic coastline to Austria could easily reconcile the Habsburgs to this new European order. Compensating the King of Saxony by destroying Prussia would have satisfied two French interests simultaneously. If full-scale French empire in Europe was impossible, French hegemony was not – at least for a time. No Russian government would have allowed this to happen without fighting. In the barely credible event that a Russian monarch had tried to do this, he would have been overthrown. Perhaps subsequent European history would have been happier had French hegemony lasted. But no one can expect Alexander's government to have foreseen or accepted this.

As some of Alexander's advisers had predicted, one result of Napoleon's destruction was a great increase in British power. For a century after Waterloo Britain enjoyed global pre-eminence at a historically small price in blood and treasure. Russian pride and interests sometimes suffered from this, most obviously in the Crimean War. In the long run, too, British power meant the global hegemony of liberal-democratic principles fatal to any version of Russian empire. But this is to look way into the future: in 1815 Wellington and Castlereagh disliked democracy at least as much as Alexander I did. Under no circumstances could Russian policy in the Napoleonic era have stopped Britain's Industrial Revolution, or its effects on British power. Moreover, in the century after 1815 Russia grew greatly in wealth and population, benefiting hugely from integration into the global capitalist economy whose main bulwark was Britain. In the nineteenth as in the twentieth century Russia had much less to fear from Britain than from land-powers intent on dominating the European continent.

There is no great puzzle as to why Russia fought Napoleon. How it fought him and why it won are much bigger and more interesting questions. To answer these questions requires one to demolish well-established myths. It is not surprising that these myths dominate Western thinking about Russia's role in Napoleon's defeat. No Western scholar or soldier has ever studied these years from a Russian perspective on the basis of the Russian evidence. Interpreting any country's war effort through the eyes of its enemies and coalition partners is bound to be problematic, still more so in an era when European nationalism was just beginning its march.

Much more interesting and difficult is the task of challenging Russian national myths. Naturally, by no means are all these myths untrue. The Russian army and people showed great heroism and suffered hugely in 1812. The truly bizarre and unique element in Russian mythology about the defeat of Napoleon is, however, that it radically underestimates the Russian achievement. The most basic reason for this is that the Russia which defeated Napoleon was an aristocratic, dynastic and multi-ethnic empire. Mining the events of the Napoleonic era just for Russian ethno-national myths and doing so in naive fashion inevitably leaves out much about the war effort.

At one level it is absurd to call Leo Tolstoy the main villain in this misunderstanding. A novelist is not a historian. Tolstoy writes about individuals' mentalities, values and experiences during and before 1812. But *War and Peace* has had more influence on popular perceptions of Napoleon's defeat by Russia than all the history books ever written. By denying any rational direction of events in 1812 by human actors and implying that military professionalism was a German disease Tolstoy feeds rather easily into Western interpretations of 1812 which blame the snow or chance for French defeat. By ending his novel in Vilna in December 1812 he also contributes greatly to the fact that both Russians and foreigners largely forget the huge Russian achievement in 1813–14 even in getting their army across Europe to Paris, let alone defeating Napoleon en route. One problem with this is that marginalizing or misunderstanding as crucial an actor as Russia results in serious errors in interpreting why and how Napoleon's empire fell. But it is also the case that to understand what happened in 1812 it is crucial to realize that Alexander and Barclay de Tolly always planned for a long war, which they expected to begin with a campaign on Russian soil that would exhaust Napoleon but that would end in a Russian advance into

Europe and the mobilization of a new coalition of anti-Napoleonic forces.

One key reason why Russia defeated Napoleon was that its leaders out-thought him. In 1812 Napoleon failed to understand Russian society and politics, or to exploit Russia's internal weaknesses. In the end he ruined his cause by delaying in Moscow in the naive hope that salvation would come from Alexander, the Russian elites or even a Cossack revolt. By contrast, Alexander well understood the strengths and weaknesses of his enemy and used this insight to full effect. Before the invasion he realized exactly what kind of war Napoleon wanted and needed. The Russians planned and executed the opposite kind of war – a drawn-out defensive campaign and a 'people's war' which would play to their strengths and Napoleon's weaknesses. In the first year of the war Russian strategy succeeded beyond their expectations. Napoleon's entire army was virtually destroyed. This owed much to luck and to Napoleon's mistakes. Events certainly did not precisely follow Alexander's plans. Had they done so, Napoleon would have been stopped and worn down on the river Dvina. But in war events very seldom do go precisely according to plan, particularly in a defensive campaign which necessarily surrenders the initiative to the enemy. Nevertheless the basic Russian concept of 'deep retreat' was sound and worked. It would not have done so without luck and enemy mistakes, but the resolution and moral courage of Mikhail Barclay de Tolly was also crucial, as above all were the fortitude, discipline and skill of the Russian rearguards and their commanders.

It should be no surprise to anyone that the Russian army fought with more skill in 1813–14 than in 1812. Even more than in most activities there is a vast difference between training for war and its reality. Experience is a crucial teacher. Whether one looks at low-level tactics – such as the use of jaegers – or at the competence of staffs, there is no doubt that the army of March 1814 was much more formidable than had been the case two years before. In comparison to the disaster of 1806–7 when Bennigsen's army starved in East Prussia, the performance of Georg Kankrin in feeding and supplying the Russian troops as they crossed almost the whole of Europe was also outstanding. No one who has read accounts of how the army fought at Kulm, Leipzig or Craonne – to take but three examples – could subscribe to old myths about how the soldiers lacked the patriotic motivation they had felt in 1812. This is not to deny that officers and men may have fought with special desperation at Borodino after weeks of retreat and in the Russian heartland. As in most armies, however, the key to performance on the battlefield was usually loyalty to comrades and to one's unit. In the Russian case this included messmates in the artel but also the regiment, which for so many of these soldiers was their lifetime home.

The Russian regiment was very much part of an Old Regime rather than a modern, national army. This merely underlines the fact that it was the European Old Regime which defeated Napoleon. It had absorbed some aspects of modernity such as the Prussian Landwehr and it had allied itself to British economic power, which was much more truly modern than was Napoleon's absolutist empire. Nevertheless the main cause of Napoleon's defeat was that the three great dynasties fought side by side for the first time since 1792 and that the Russian army was on the scene from the start, rather than having to pick up the pieces after Napoleon had defeated the Austrians or Prussians. It did help enormously that Napoleon's army had been destroyed in 1812 and that he fought in 1813 with younger and less skilled troops. But during the spring 1813 campaign the Russian army too was still hugely weakened by its efforts in the previous year and the Prussian army was mostly raw and struggling to train, arm and equip itself. The same was true of both the Prussians and the Austrians at the start of the autumn 1813 campaign. In fact, right down to the battle of Leipzig, the 1813 campaign was a very close-run business and could easily have gone in Napoleon's favour. This contributes to the story's drama.

Of course it is not surprising that Russians find it easier to identify with the battle of Borodino, fought under Kutuzov outside Moscow, than with the battle of Leipzig, fought in Germany under Barclay de Tolly and Schwarzenberg in defence of a concept of Russian security rooted in the European balance of power. As with the British and 1940, standing alone, united and undaunted is the finest of all wartime memories. But even from the narrowest and most selfish conception of Russian or British interests 1940 and 1812 were not enough. To remove the enemy threat meant taking the war beyond the country's borders, and it required allies. In 1941 Hitler and Tojo kindly provided the British with these allies. In 1813 Alexander had to take the great risk of invading central Europe with his exhausted and weakened army to mobilize his potential allies, at times almost needing to grab them by the scruff of the neck in order to get them to serve their own and Europe's interests. The courage, skill and intelligence he showed in first creating the allied coalition and then leading it to Paris was remarkable.

Alexander acted in this way first and foremost because of a correct view that this is what the interests of Russia – empire, state and people – demanded. This is not to deny that Nikolai Rumiantsev was also partly correct in seeing growing British economic hegemony across the globe as the most important underlying reality of the age. This certainly helps one to put the Napoleonic Wars into global perspective and to understand their logic. But for Russia in 1812–13 the overriding priority had to be the ending of Napoleonic control of Germany. So long as Napoleon held Germany he would be much more powerful than Alexander. The financial costs of sustaining Russian security against the threat he represented would soon become intolerable. Vital Russian security and economic interests could therefore not be protected. In the winter of 1813–14, with Germany liberated, the arguments for and against invading France and seeking to topple Napoleon were more evenly balanced. Perhaps Alexander believed that by so doing it would be easier to satisfy his ambitions in Poland, but the Russian documents show clearly that this was not his main motivation. On the contrary, the emperor believed that so long as Napoleon ruled neither the German settlement nor European peace would be secure.

The basic point was that Alexander was convinced that Russian and European security depended on each other. That is still true today. But perhaps there is some inspiration to be drawn from a story in which the Russian army advancing across Europe in 1813–14 was in most places seen as an army of liberation, whose victories meant escape from Napoleon's exactions, an end to an era of constant war, and the restoration of European trade and prosperity.

Appendix 1
The Russian Army in June 1812

First Western Army: General M. B. Barclay de Tolly
Chief of Staff: Lieutenant-General N. I. Lavrov
Quartermaster-General: Major-General S. A. Mukhin
Duty General: Colonel P. A. Kikin
Chief of Artillery: Major-General Count A. I. Kutaisov
Chief Engineer: Lieutenant-General Kh. I. Trusson

First Infantry Corps: Lieutenant-General Count P. Kh. von Wittgenstein
5th Infantry Division: Major-General G. M. Berg
  1st Brigade: Major-General K. F. Kazachkovsky
  Sevsk Infantry Regiment; Kaluga Infantry Regiment
  2nd Brigade: Major-General Prince A. B. Sibirsky
  Perm Infantry Regiment; Mogilev Infantry Regiment
  3rd Brigade: Colonel G. N. Frolov
  23rd and 24th Jaeger regiments
  5th Field Artillery Brigade: Lieutenant-Colonel Muruzi
  5th Heavy and 9th and 10th Light batteries
  Reserve: 2 Combined Grenadier battalions
14th Infantry Division: Major-General I. T. Sazonov
  1st Brigade: Colonel D. V. Lialin
  Tenge Infantry Regiment; Navagin Infantry Regiment
  2nd Brigade: Major-General G. von Helfreich
  Estland Infantry Regiment; Tula Infantry Regiment
  3rd Brigade: Colonel S. V. Denisev
  25th and 26th Jaeger regiments
  14th Field Artillery Brigade: Colonel E. E. Staden
  14th Heavy and 26th and 27th Light batteries
  Reserve: 2 Combined Grenadier battalions
Cavalry: 3rd Brigade of 1st Cavalry Division: Major-General M. D. Balk
  Riga Dragoon Regiment; Iamburg Dragoon Regiment
  5th Brigade of 1st Cavalry Division: vacant
  Grodno Hussar Regiment; 3 Don Cossack regiments
1st Reserve Artillery Brigade: Major-General Prince L. M. Iashvili
  27th and 28th heavy batteries; 1st and 3rd Horse Artillery batteries; 1st and 2nd Pontoon
    companies.

Second Infantry Corps: Lieutenant-General K. F. Baggohufvudt
4th Infantry Division: Major-General Prince Eugen of Württemberg
  1st Brigade: Colonel D. I. Pyshnitsky
  Kremenchug Infantry Regiment; Minsk Infantry Regiment

2nd Brigade: Major-General I. P. Rossi
Tobolsk Infantry Regiment; Volhynia Infantry Regiment
3rd Brigade: Colonel E. M. Pilar von Pilchau
4th and 34th Jaeger regiments
4th Field Artillery Brigade: Colonel A. I. Voeikov
4th Heavy and 7th and 8th Light batteries
17th Infantry Division: Lieutenant-General Z. D. Olsufev
1st Brigade: Major-General I. S. Alekseev
Riazan Infantry Regiment; Beloozero Infantry Regiment
2nd Brigade: Major-General P. A. Tuchkov
Willmanstrand Infantry Regiment; Brest Infantry Regiment
3rd Brigade: Colonel Ia. A. Potemkin
30th and 48th Jaeger regiments
17th Field Artillery Brigade: Colonel I. I. Dieterichs
17th Heavy and 32nd and 33rd Light batteries
Cavalry: from 8th Brigade of 2nd Cavalry Division
Elizavetgrad Hussar Regiment; 6 guns of 4th Horse Artillery Battery

Third Infantry Corps: Lieutenant-General N. A. Tuchkov
1st Grenadier Division: Major-General Count P. A. Stroganov
1st Brigade: Colonel P. F. Zheltukhin
Life Grenadier Regiment; Count Arakcheev Grenadier Regiment
2nd Brigade: Major-General A. I. Tsvilenev
Pavlovsky Grenadier Regiment; Ekaterinoslav Grenadier Regiment
3rd Brigade: Major-General B. B. Fock
St Petersburg Grenadier Regiment; Tauride Grenadier Regiment
1st Field Artillery Brigade: Colonel V. A. Glukhov
1st Heavy and 1st and 2nd Light batteries
Reserve: 2 Combined Grenadiers battalions
3rd Infantry Division: Lieutenant-General P. P. Konovnitsyn
1st Brigade: Major-General A. A. Tuchkov
Reval Infantry Regiment; Murom Infantry Regiment
2nd Brigade: Lieutenant-Colonel I. M. Ushakov
Kopore Infantry Regiment; Chernigov Infantry Regiment
3rd Brigade: Major-General Prince I. L. Shakhovskoy
20th and 21st Jaeger regiments
3rd Field Artillery Brigade: Lieutenant-Colonel F. E. Tornov
3rd Heavy and 5th and 6th Light batteries
Cavalry: from 2nd Brigade of the Guards Cavalry Division
Cossack Life Guard Regiment; 1st Teptiarsky Cossack Regiment; 2nd Horse Artillery Battery

Fourth Infantry Corps: Lieutenant-General Count P. A. Shuvalov
11th Infantry Division: Major-General N. N. Bakhmetev
1st Brigade: Major-General P. N. Choglokov
Kexholm Infantry Regiment; Pernau Infantry Regiment
2nd Brigade: Major-General P. A. Filisov
Polotsk Infantry Regiment; Elets Infantry Regiment
3rd Brigade: Colonel A. I. Bistrom
1st and 33rd Jaeger regiments
11th Field Artillery Brigade: Lieutenant-Colonel A. Kotliarev
2nd Heavy and 3rd and 4th Light batteries
23rd Infantry Division: Major-General A. N. Bakhmetev
1st Brigade: Major-General N. M. Okulov

Rylsk Infantry Regiment; Ekaterinburg Infantry Regiment
  2nd Brigade: Major-General F. P. Aleksopol
  Selenginsk Infantry Regiment; 18th Jaeger Regiment
  2nd Combined Grenadier Brigade: Colonel A. I. Efimovich
  5 Combined Grenadier battalions
  23rd Field Artillery Brigade: Lieutenant-Colonel L. L. Gulevich
  23rd Heavy and 43rd and 44th Light batteries
Cavalry: from 8th Brigade of 2nd Cavalry Division
  Izium Hussar Regiment and 6 guns of 4th Horse Artillery Battery

Fifth Reserve Corps: Grand Duke Constantine
Guards Infantry Division: Major-General A. P. Ermolov
  1st Brigade: Major-General Baron G. V. von Rosen
  Preobrazhensky Guards Regiment; Semenovsky Guards Regiment
  2nd Brigade: Colonel M. E. Khrapovitsky
  Izmailovsky Guards Regiment; Lithuania (Litovsky) Guards Regiment
  3rd Brigade: Colonel K. I. Bistrom
  Finland Guards Regiment; Guards Jaeger Regiment; Guards Marines Battalion
  Guards Artillery Brigade: Colonel A. Kh. Euler
  1st and 2nd Guards Heavy batteries, 1st and 2nd Guards Light batteries, Marine Guards
    artillery detachment
  1st Combined Grenadier Brigade: Colonel Prince G. M. Cantacuzene
  4 Combined Grenadier battalions
1st Cuirassier Division: Major-General N. I. Preradovich
  Guards Cuirassiers Brigade: Major-General I. E. Shevich
  Chevaliers Gardes Regiment; Horse Guards Regiment
  1st Cuirassier Brigade: Major-General N. M. Borozdin
  His Majesty's Life Cuirassier Regiment; Her Majesty's Life Cuirassier Regiment; Astra-
    khan Cuirassier Regiment
  1st and 2nd Guards Horse Artillery batteries: Colonel P. A. Kozen

Sixth Infantry Corps: General D. S. Dokhturov
7th Infantry Division: Lieutenant-General P. M. Kaptsevich
  1st Brigade: Colonel D. P. Liapunov
  Pskov Infantry Regiment; Moscow Infantry Regiment
  2nd Brigade: Colonel A. I. Aigustov
  Libau Infantry Regiment; Sofia Infantry Regiment
  3rd Brigade: Major-General A. I. Balla
  11th and 36th Jaeger regiments
  7th Field Artillery Brigade: Lieutenant-Colonel D. F. Devel
  7th Heavy and 12th and 13th Light batteries
24th Infantry Division: Major-General P. G. Likhachev
  1st Brigade: Major-General I. D. Tsybulsky
  Ufa Infantry Regiment; Shirvan Infantry Regiment
  2nd Brigade: Colonel P. V. Denisev
  Butyrki Infantry Regiment; Tomsk Infantry Regiment
  3rd Brigade: Colonel N. V. Vuich
  19th and 40th Jaeger regiments
  24th Field Artillery Brigade: Lieutenant-Colonel I. G. Efremov
  24th Heavy and 45th and 46th Light batteries
Cavalry: from 11th Brigade of 3rd Cavalry Division
  Sumi Hussar Regiment; 7th Horse Artillery Battery

First Cavalry Corps: Lieutenant-General F. P. Uvarov
    1st Brigade of Guards Cavalry Division: Major-General A. S. Chalikov
    Guards Dragoon Regiment; Guards Lancer Regiment
    2nd Brigade of Guards Cavalry Division: absent
    Guards Hussar Regiment
    4th Brigade of 1st Cavalry Division: Major-General I. I. Charnysh
    Kazan Dragoon Regiment; Nezhin Dragoon Regiment
    5th Horse Artillery Battery

Second Cavalry Corps: Major-General Baron F. K. von Korff
    6th Brigade of 2nd Cavalry Division: Colonel N. V. Davydov
    Pskov Dragoon Regiment; Moscow Dragoon Regiment
    7th Brigade of 2nd Cavalry Division: Major-General S. D. Panchulidzev
    Kargopol Dragoon Regiment; Ingermanland Dragoon Regiment
    5th Brigade of 1st Cavalry Division: absent
    Polish Lancer Regiment; 6th Horse Artillery Battery

Third Cavalry Corps: Major-General Count Peter von der Pahlen
    9th Brigade of 3rd Cavalry Division: Major-General S. V. Diatkov
    Courland Dragoon Regiment; Orenburg Dragoon Regiment
    10th Brigade of 3rd Cavalry Division: Major-General A. A. Skalon
    Siberia Dragoon Regiment; Irkutsk Dragoon Regiment
    11th Brigade of 3rd Cavalry Division: absent
    Mariupol Hussar Regiment

Cossack Flying Corps: General M. I. Platov
    Don Cossack Ataman Regiment; 7 other Don Cossack regiments
    1st and 2nd Bug Cossack regiments; 1st Bashkir Regiment
    Simferopol and Perekop Tatar Horse regiments
    Stavropol Kalmyk Regiment
    2nd Don Cossack Artillery Brigade

Army reserve:
    29th and 30th Heavy batteries
    5 pioneer companies; 2 pontoon companies; 4 mobile veterans companies; 6 mobile
    artillery parks

Second Western Army: General Prince P. I. Bagration
Chief of Staff: Major-General Count E. de Saint-Priest
Quartermaster-General: Major-General M. S. Vistitsky
Duty General: Colonel S. N. Marin
Chief of Artillery: Major-General Baron K. F. von Löwenstern
Chief Engineer: Major-General E. F. Forster

Seventh Infantry Corps: Lieutenant-General N. N. Raevsky
26th Infantry Division: Major-General I. F. Paskevich
    1st Brigade: Colonel A. I. Liphardt
    Ladoga Infantry Regiment; Poltava Infantry Regiment
    2nd Brigade: Colonel N. F. Ladyzhensky
    Nizhnii Novgorod Infantry Regiment; Orel Infantry Regiment
    3rd Brigade: Colonel F. G. Gogel
    5th and 42nd Jaeger regiments
    26th Field Artillery Brigade: Lieutenant-Colonel G. M. Schulmann
    26th Heavy and 47th and 48th Light batteries

12th Infantry Division: Major-General P. M. Koliubakin
 1st Brigade: Colonel M. N. Ryleev
 Smolensk Infantry Regiment; Narva Infantry Regiment
 2nd Brigade: Colonel K. K. Panzerbiter
 Aleksopol Infantry Regiment; Novoingermanland Infantry Regiment
 3rd Brigade: Major-General I. I. Palitsyn
 6th and 41st Jaeger regiments
 12th Field Artillery Brigade: Lieutenant-Colonel Ia. I. Sablin
 12th Heavy and 22nd and 23rd Light batteries
Cavalry: from 14th Brigade of 4th Cavalry Division
 Akhtyrka Hussar Regiment; 8th Horse Artillery Battery

Eighth Infantry Corps: Lieutenant-General M. M. Borozdin
2nd Grenadier Division: Major-General Prince Karl of Mecklenburg-Schwerin
 1st Brigade: Colonel I. Ia. Shatilov
 Kiev Grenadier Regiment; Moscow Grenadier Regiment
 2nd Brigade: Colonel I. F. von Buxhoeweden
 Astrakhan Grenadier Regiment; Fanagoria Grenadier Regiment
 3rd Brigade: Colonel V. A. Hesse
 Siberia Grenadier Regiment; Little Russia Grenadier Regiment
 2nd Field Artillery Brigade: Colonel A. A. Boguslavsky
 11th Heavy and 20th and 21st Light batteries
2nd Combined Grenadier Division: Major-General Count M. S. Vorontsov
 1st Brigade: 4 Combined Grenadier battalions
 2nd Brigade: 6 Combined Grenadier battalions
 3rd Reserve Artillery Brigade: absent
 31st and 32nd Heavy batteries
2nd Cuirassier Division: Major-General O. F. von Knorring
 2nd Cuirassier Brigade: Major-General N. V. Kretov
 Ekaterinoslav Cuirassier Regiment; Military Order Cuirassier Regiment
 3rd Cuirassier Brigade: Major-General I. M. Duka
 Glukhov Cuirassier Regiment; Little Russia Cuirassier Regiment; Novgorod Cuirassier
  Regiment

Fourth Cavalry Corps: Major-General Count K. K. von Sievers
 12th Brigade of 4th Cavalry Division: Major-General I. D. Panchulidzev
 Kharkov Dragoon Regiment; Chernigov Dragoon Regiment:
 13th Brigade of 4th Cavalry Division: Colonel E. A. Emmanuel
 Kiev Dragoon Regiment; New Russia Dragoon Regiment
 From 14th Brigade of 4th Cavalry Division
 Lithuania Lancer Regiment; 10th Horse Artillery Battery

Cossack Detachment: Major-General N. V. Ilovaisky
 8 Don Cossack regiments; 3rd Bug Cossack Regiment
 1st Don Horse Artillery Battery

Army reserve:
  2 pioneer and 1 mining company; 1 pontoon company; 3 mobile veterans companies;
  6 mobile artillery parks

En route to Second Army:
27th Infantry Division: Major-General D. P. Neverovsky
 1st Brigade: Colonel M. F. Stavitsky
 Odessa Infantry Regiment; Ternopol Infantry Regiment

2nd Brigade: Colonel A. Ia. Kniazhnin
Vilna Infantry Regiment; Simbirsk Infantry Regiment
3rd Brigade: Colonel A. V. Voeikov
49th and 50th Jaeger regiments
27th Field Artillery Brigade: Colonel Arapetov
49th Heavy and 53rd and 54th Light batteries
2 Combined Grenadier battalions

Third Reserve Army: General A. P. Tormasov
Chief of Staff: Major-General I. N. Inzov
Quartermaster-General: Colonel R. E. Rennie
Duty General: Colonel K. F. Oldekop
Chief of Artillery: Major-General I. Kh. von Sievers

Corps of General S. M. Kamensky
18th Infantry Division: Major-General Prince A. G. Shcherbatov
  1st Brigade: Major-General P. E. Bernados
  Vladimir Infantry Regiment; Tambov Infantry Regiment
  2nd Brigade: Major-General Prince N. N. Khovansky
  Kostroma Infantry Regiment; Dnieper Infantry Regiment
  3rd Brigade: Major-General V. D. Meshcherinov
  28th and 32nd Jaeger regiments
  18th Field Artillery Brigade: Lieutenant-Colonel Pashchenko
  18th Heavy and 34th and 35th Light batteries
  Combined Grenadier Brigade: Lieutenant-Colonel Timashev
  6 Combined Grenadier battalions
Cavalry: from 14th Brigade of 8th Cavalry Division
  Pavlograd Hussar Regiment; 11th Horse Artillery Battery

Corps of Lieutenant-General E. I. Markov
15th Infantry Division: Major-General F. V. Nazimov
  1st Brigade: Major-General F. F. Padeisky
  Kozlov Infantry Regiment; Kolyvan Infantry Regiment
  2nd Brigade: Lieutenant-Colonel F. I. Ushakov
  Kurin Infantry Regiment; Vitebsk Infantry Regiment
  3rd Brigade: Major-General Prince V. V. Viazemsky
  13th and 14th Jaeger regiments
  15th Field Artillery Brigade: Lieutenant-Colonel A. D. Zasiadko
  15th Heavy and 28th and 29th Light batteries
9th Infantry Division: Major-General E. E. Udom
  1st Brigade: Colonel A. M. Seliverstov
  Nasheburg Infantry Regiment; Iakutsk Infantry Regiment
  2nd Brigade: Colonel A. A. Reichel
  Apsheron Infantry Regiment; Riazhsk Infantry Regiment
  3rd Brigade: Colonel I. D. Ivanov
  10th and 38th Jaeger regiments
  9th Field Artillery Brigade: Colonel Liapunov
  9th Heavy and 16th and 17th Light batteries
Cavalry: from 17th Brigade of 5th Cavalry Division
  Aleksandria Hussar Regiment; 12th Horse Artillery Battery

Corps of Lieutenant-General Baron F. von der Osten-Sacken
  18 reserve (i.e. second) battalions and 16 reserve squadrons of cavalry
  Lubny Hussar Regiment

4th Reserve Artillery Brigade; 33rd Heavy and 13th Horse Artillery batteries
Cavalry Corps of Major-General Count C. de Lambert
5th Cavalry Division: Major-General Count C. de Lambert
  15th Brigade: Major-General A. N. Berdiaev
  Starodub Dragoon Regiment; Tver Dragoon Regiment
  16th Brigade: Major-General I. A. Khrushchev
  Zhitomir Dragoon Regiment; Arzamas Dragoon Regiment
  17th Brigade; Tatar Lancer Regiment
8th Cavalry Division: Major-General E. I. Chaplitz
  24th Brigade: Major-General P. K. Musin-Pushkin
  Vladimir Dragoon Regiment; Taganrog Dragoon Regiment
  26th Brigade; Serpukhov Dragoon Regiment
  4th Reserve Artillery Brigade; 34th Heavy Battery and 4th Pontoon Company
Cossack detachment:
  5 Don Cossack regiments; 2 Kalmyk regiments; 2 Tatar regiments; 1 Bashkir regiment

Army of the Danube: Admiral P. V. Chichagov
Chief of Staff: Lieutenant-General I. V. Sabaneev
Quartermaster-General: Major-General B. M. Berg
Duty General: Major-General A. E. Ansio
Chief of Artillery: Major-General V. D. Rezvoi

Corps of General Count A. de Langeron
22nd Infantry Division: Major-General S. A. Tuchkov
  1st Brigade: Major-General M. A. Shkapsky
  Viatka Infantry Regiment; Staroskol Infantry Regiment
  2nd Brigade: absent
  Vyborg Infantry Regiment
  3rd Brigade: Colonel I. N. Durnovo
  29th and 45th Jaeger regiments
  22nd Field Artillery Brigade: Colonel Kolotinsky
  22nd Heavy and 41st and 42nd Light batteries
Cavalry: 16th Brigade of 6th Cavalry Division: Major-General Count I. V. von Manteuffel
  St Petersburg Dragoon Regiment; Livonia Dragoon Regiment
  2 Don Cossack and 1 Ural Cossack regiments; 14th Horse Artillery Battery

Corps of Lieutenant-General P. K. von Essen
8th Infantry Division: Lieutenant-General P. K. von Essen
  1st Brigade: Colonel V. N. Shenshin
  Archangel Infantry Regiment; Ukraine Infantry Regiment
  2nd Brigade: Major-General G. G. Engelhardt
  Schlüsselberg Infantry Regiment; Staroingermanland Infantry Regiment
  3rd Brigade: 37th Jaeger Regiment
  8th Field Artillery Brigade: Colonel Bastian
  8th Heavy and 14th and 15th Light batteries
Cavalry: from 19th Brigade of 6th Cavalry Division: Seversk Dragoon Regiment
  From 21st Brigade of 7th Cavalry Division: Smolensk Dragoon Regiment
  1 Don and 1 Ural Cossack regiment
  15th Horse Artillery Battery; 1 pontoon company

Corps of Lieutenant-General A. L. Voinov
10th Infantry Division: Major-General Count J. A. von Lieven
  1st Brigade: Colonel A. P. Zass
  Belostok Infantry Regiment; Crimea Infantry Regiment

2nd Brigade: Kursk Infantry Regiment
3rd Brigade: Colonel I. P. Belokopytov
8th and 39th Jaeger regiments
10th Field Artillery Brigade: Lieutenant-Colonel Verbovsky
10th Heavy and 18th and 19th Light batteries
Cavalry: from 19th Brigade of 6th Cavalry Division: Kinburn Dragoon Regiment
From 20th Brigade of 6th Cavalry Division: Belorussia Hussar Regiment
1 Don Cossack and 2 Ural Cossack regiments
7th Reserve Artillery Brigade; 38th Heavy and 50th Light batteries

Corps of Lieutenant-General A. P. Zass
16th Infantry Division: Major-General M. L. Bulatov
1st Brigade: Okhotsk Infantry Regiment
2nd Brigade: Major-General T. I. Zbievsky
Kamchatka Infantry Regiment; Mingrelia Infantry Regiment
16th Field Artillery Brigade: Colonel Pohl
16th Heavy and 31st Light batteries
Cavalry: 7th Cavalry Division: Lieutenant-General A. P. Zass
21st Brigade: Pereiaslavl Dragoon Regiment
22nd Brigade: Major-General Count Paul von der Pahlen
Dorpat Dragoon Regiment; Tiraspol Dragoon Regiment
23rd Brigade: Chuguev Lancer Regiment; 2 Don Cossack regiments
7th Reserve Artillery Brigade: 39th Heavy and 50th Light batteries
Army reserve: Lieutenant-General I. V. Sabaneev
Olonets Infantry Regiment; Iaroslavl Infantry Regiment; 7th Jaeger Regiment; Olviopol
Hussar Regiment; 1 Don Cossack regiment
16th Horse Artillery Battery; 1 miner and 2 pioneer companies

Detachment in Serbia: Major-General N. I. Lüders
16th Infantry Division: Major-General N. I. Lüders
1st Brigade: Neishlot Infantry Regiment
3rd Brigade: Major-General S. Ia. Repninsky
27th and 43rd Jaeger regiments
30th Light Battery of 16th Field Artillery Brigade
Cavalry: from 20th Brigade of 6th Cavalry Division
Volhynia Lancer Regiment; 2 Don Cossack regiments
18th Horse Artillery Battery

Riga Corps: Lieutenant-General I. N. von Essen
24 reserve (i.e. second) battalions; 18 recruit depot (i.e. fourth) battalions
1 company pioneers and 1 company miners

Finland Corps: Lieutenant-General F. F. von Steinhel
6th Infantry Division: Major-General V. S. Rakhmanov
1st Brigade: Major-General E. S. Gorbuntsov
Briansk Infantry Regiment; Nizov Infantry Regiment
3rd Brigade: Colonel M. L. Treskin
Azov Infantry Regiment; 3rd Jaeger Regiment
6th Field Artillery Brigade: Lieutenant-Colonel Schulmann
6th Heavy and 11th Light batteries
21st Infantry Division: Major-General N. I. Demidov
1st Brigade: Colonel A. T. Maslov
Petrovsk Infantry Regiment; Podolia Infantry Regiment
2nd Brigade: Colonel Baron F. F. von Rosen

Neva Infantry Regiment; Lithuania Infantry Regiment
3rd Brigade: Colonel F. E. Knipper
2nd and 44th Jaeger regiments
21st Field Artillery Brigade: Colonel Hüne
21st Heavy and 40th Light batteries
25th Infantry Division: Major-General P. Ia. Bashutsky
1st Brigade: Colonel A. E. Peucher
1st Marine Regiment; 2nd Marine Regiment
2nd Brigade: Colonel M. F. Naumov
3rd Marine Regiment; Voronezh Infantry Regiment
3rd Brigade: Colonel A. I. Wedermeier
31st and 47th Jaeger regiments
25th Field Artillery Brigade: Colonel Argun
Cavalry: 27th Cavalry Brigade: Major-General I. I. Alekseev
Finland Dragoon Regiment; Mitau Dragoon Regiment; 3 Don Cossack regiments

First Reserve Corps: Lieutenant-General Baron E. I. Müller-Zakomelsky
27 reserve (i.e. second) battalions and 33 reserve cavalry squadrons

Second Reserve Corps: Lieutenant-General F. F. Oertel
18 reserve (i.e. second) battalions and 6 reserve squadrons; 3 Don Cossack regiments

Bobruisk Detachment: Major-General G. A. Ignatev
12 reserve (i.e. second) battalions; 1 pioneer and 2 miner companies

Smolensk Reserve Corps: Major-General Baron F. F. von Winzengerode
27 recruit depot (i.e. fourth) battalions; 12 recruit depot squadrons
2nd Reserve Artillery Brigade: Colonel Matsylev
46th and 51st Heavy, 59th, 60th, 61st and 62nd Light and 20th and 24th Horse Artillery batteries

Kaluga Reserve Corps: General M. A. Miloradovich
42 recruit depot (i.e. fourth) battalions; 18 recruit depot squadrons

Appendix 2
Russian Army Corps at the beginning of the autumn 1813 campaign*

Army of Bohemia

Army Corps of General Count Peter von Wittgenstein: 43 battalions, 19 squadrons, 4 Cossack regiments, 92 guns: total strength = 31,913 men

First Infantry Corps: Lieutenant-General Prince Andrei I. Gorchakov
5th Infantry Division: Major-General V. P. Mezentsev
  Brigade: Perm Infantry Regiment; Mogilev Infantry Regiment
  Brigade: Kaluga Infantry Regiment; Sevsk Infantry Regiment; Grand Duchess Catherine's Battalion
  Brigade: 23rd and 24th Jaeger regiments
14th Infantry Division: Major-General Gothard von Helfreich
  Brigade: Tenge Infantry Regiment; Estland Infantry Regiment
  Brigade: 25th and 26th Jaeger regiments
  3rd Heavy and 6th and 7th Light Artillery batteries

Second Infantry Corps: Lieutenant-General Prince Eugen of Württemberg
3rd Infantry Division: Major-General Prince I. L. Shakhovskoy
  Brigade: Murom Infantry Regiment; Reval Infantry Regiment
  Brigade: Chernigov Infantry Regiment; Selenginsk Infantry Regiment
  Brigade: 20th and 21st Jaeger regiments
4th Infantry Division: Major-General D. I. Pyshnitsky
  Brigade: Tobolsk Infantry Regiment; Volhynia Infantry Regiment
  Brigade: Kremenchug Infantry Regiment; Minsk Infantry Regiment
  Brigade: 4th and 34th Jaeger regiments
  5th Heavy and 13th and 27th Light batteries
1st Hussar Division: Lieutenant-General Count Peter von der Pahlen
  Grodno, Sumi, Olviopol and Lubny Hussar regiments
  4 Don Cossack regiments
  6th and 12th Horse Artillery batteries

Reserve Army Corps of the Grand Duke Constantine: 47 battalions, 87 squadrons, 3 Cossack regiments and 182 guns = 43,498 men

Fifth (Guards) Infantry Corps: Lieutenant-General A. P. Ermolov
1st Guards Division: Major-General Baron Gregor von Rosen

* This does not include the Reserve Army, Duke Alexander of Württemberg's Army Corps besieging Danzig, or other detachments blockading enemy fortresses.

Brigade: Preobrazhensky Guards Regiment; Semenovsky Guards Regiment
Brigade: Izmailovsky Guards Regiment; Guards Jaeger Regiment; Marine Guards
  Battalion
2nd Guards Division: Major-General I. F. Udom
Brigade: Lithuania (Litovsky) Guards Regiment; Life Grenadier Guards Regiment
Brigade: Pavlovsky Guards Regiment; Finland Guards Regiment
2nd Guards Heavy and 1st and 2nd Guards Light batteries

Third (Grenadier) Corps: Lieutenant-General N. N. Raevsky
1st Grenadier Division: Major-General P. N. Choglokov
Brigade: Count Arakcheev Grenadier Regiment; Ekaterinoslav Grenadier Regiment
Brigade: Tauride Grenadier Regiment; St Petersburg Grenadier Regiment
Brigade: Kexholm Grenadier Regiment; Pernau Grenadier Regiment
2nd Grenadier Division: Lieutenant-General Prince Karl of Mecklenburg-Schwerin
Brigade: Kiev Grenadier Regiment; Moscow Grenadier Regiment
Brigade: Astrakhan Grenadier Regiment; Fanagoria Grenadier Regiment
Brigade: Siberia Grenadier Regiment; Little Russia Grenadier Regiment
33rd Heavy and 14th Light batteries
Reserve Cavalry: Lieutenant-General Prince D. V. Golitsyn
1st Cuirassier Division: Major-General N. I. Preradovich
Brigade: Chevaliers Gardes; Horse Guards
Brigade: His Majesty's Life Cuirassiers; Her Majesty's Life Cuirassiers
1st and 2nd Guards Horse Artillery batteries: Colonel Kozen
2nd Cuirassier Division: Major-General N. V. Kretov
Brigade: Ekaterinoslav Cuirassier Regiment; Pskov Cuirassier Regiment
Brigade: Glukhov Cuirassier Regiment; Astrakhan Cuirassier Regiment
3rd Cuirassier Division: Major-General I. M. Duka
Brigade: Military Order Cuirassier Regiment; Starodub Cuirassier Regiment
Brigade: Little Russia Cuirassier Regiment; Novgorod Cuirassier Regiment
Guards Light Cavalry Division: Major-General I. G. Shevich
Brigade: Guards Dragoon Regiment; Guards Lancer Regiment
Brigade: Guards Hussar Regiment; Cossack Guards Regiment
Lancer Division: Major-General Baron E. I. Müller-Zakomelsky
Chuguev Lancer Regiment; Serpukhov Lancer Regiment; 2nd Tatar Lancer Regiment
Ataman Cossack Regiment and 2 other Don Cossack regiments
1st Don Cossack Horse Artillery Battery
Reserve artillery:
1st Guards Heavy Battery; 1st, 14th, 29th, 30th Heavy batteries
Marine Guards artillery detachment: 1st, 3rd, 10th, 23rd Horse Artillery batteries

Army of Silesia

Army Corps of Lieutenant-General Baron Fabian von der Osten-Sacken: 24 battalions,
  30 squadrons, 12 irregular cavalry regiments, 60 guns = 17,689 men
10th Infantry Division: Lieutenant-General Count Johann von Lieven
Brigade: Iaroslavl Infantry Regiment
Brigade: Crimea Infantry Regiment; Belostok Infantry Regiment
Brigade: 8th and 39th Jaeger regiments
16th Infantry Division: Major-General S. Ia. Repninsky
Brigade: Okhotsk Infantry Regiment; Kamchatka Infantry Regiment
27th Infantry Division: Lieutenant-General D. P. Neverovsky
Brigade: Vilna Infantry Regiment; Simbirsk Infantry Regiment
Brigade: Ternopol Infantry Regiment; Odessa Infantry Regiment
Brigade: 49th and 50th Jaeger regiments

Cavalry: Lieutenant-General I. V. Vasilchikov
  Brigade from 3rd Dragoon Division
  Smolensk Dragoon Regiment; Courland Dragoon Regiment
2nd Hussar Division: Major-General S. N. Lanskoy
  Brigade: Belorussia Hussar Regiment; Akhtyrka Hussar Regiment
  Brigade: Aleksandria Hussar Regiment; Mariupol Hussar Regiment
  8 Don Cossack regiments; 1 Kalmyk and 1 Bashkir regiment; 2 other Cossack regiments
Artillery: Major-General A. P. Nikitin
  10th and 13th Heavy, 24th and 35th Light, and 18th Horse Artillery batteries
  1 company of pioneers

Army Corps of General Count A. de Langeron: 53 battalions, 37 squadrons, 176 guns =
  43,531 men

Sixth Infantry Corps: Lieutenant-General Prince A. G. Shcherbatov
7th Infantry Division: Major-General F. I. Talyzin
  Brigade: Pskov Infantry Regiment; Moscow Infantry Regiment
  Brigade: Libau Infantry Regiment; Sofia Infantry Regiment
  Brigade: 11th and 36th Jaeger regiments
18th Infantry Division: Major-General P. E. Benardos
  Brigade: Vladimir Infantry Regiment; Tambov Infantry Regiment
  Brigade: Dnieper Infantry Regiment; Kostroma Infantry Regiment
  Brigade: 28th and 32nd Jaeger regiments

Eighth Infantry Corps: Lieutenant-General Count E. de Saint-Priest
11th Infantry Division: Major-General Prince I. S. Gurelov
  Brigade: Ekaterinburg Infantry Regiment; Rylsk Infantry Regiment
  Brigade: Elets Infantry Regiment; Polotsk Infantry Regiment
  Brigade: 1st and 33rd Jaeger regiments
17th Infantry Division: Major-General Georg Pilar von Pilchau
  Brigade: Riazan Infantry Regiment; Beloozero Infantry Regiment
  Brigade: Wilmanstrand Infantry Regiment; Brest Infantry Regiment
  Brigade: 30th and 48th Jaeger regiments

Ninth Infantry Corps: Lieutenant-General Z. D. Olsufev
9th Infantry Division: Major-General E. E. Udom
  Brigade: Nasheburg Infantry Regiment; Apsheron Infantry Regiment
  Brigade: Riazhsk Infantry Regiment; Iakutsk Infantry Regiment
  Brigade: 10th and 38th Jaeger regiments
Detachment of General A. Ia. Rudzevich: 15th and 13th Infantry divisions:
  Brigade (15th Division): Vitebsk Infantry Regiment; Kozlov Infantry Regiment
  Brigade (15th Division): Kuriia Infantry Regiment; Kolyvan Infantry Regiment
  Brigade (13th Division): 12th and 22nd Jaeger regiments

Tenth Infantry Corps: Lieutenant-General P. M. Kaptsevich
8th Infantry Division: Major-General Prince A. P. Urusov
  Brigade: Archangel Infantry Regiment; Schlüsselberg Infantry Regiment
  Brigade: Staroingermanland Infantry Regiment
  Brigade: 7th and 37th Jaeger regiments
22nd Infantry Division: Major-General P. P. Turchaninov
  Brigade: Viatka Infantry Regiment; Staroskol Infantry Regiment; Olonets Infantry Regiment
  Brigade: 29th and 45th Jaeger regiments

Cavalry Corps: Lieutenant-General Baron Friedrich von Korff
3rd Dragoon Division: Major-General A. N. Berdiaev
  Tver Dragoon Regiment; Kinburn Dragoon Regiment
1st Dragoon Division: Major-General N. M. Borozdin
  Moscow, Kargopol, Mitau, New Russia Dragoon regiments
4th Dragoon Division: Major-General G. A. Emmanuel
  Kharkov Dragoon Regiment: Kiev Dragoon Regiment
1st Mounted Jaeger Division: Major-General S. D. Panchulidzev
  Chernigov, Arzamas and Seversk Mounted Jaeger regiments
2nd Mounted Jaeger Division: Major-General Count Paul von der Pahlen
  Livonia and Dorpat Mounted Jaeger regiments
Irregular cavalry
  5 Don Cossack, 3 Ukrainian Cossack and 1 Kalmyk regiment

Artillery of Langeron's Army Corps:
  2nd, 15th, 18th, 32nd, 34th and 39th Heavy batteries; 3rd, 19th, 28th, 29th, 32nd, 33rd
  and 34th Light batteries; 8th Horse Artillery Battery and 2nd Don Cossack Horse
  Artillery Battery; 3 pioneer and 3 pontoon companies

Army of the North:

Army Corps of Lieutenant-General Baron F. von Winzengerode: 29 battalions, 48 squadrons,
  20 irregular cavalry regiments, 96 guns = 29, 639 men

Detachment of Lieutenant-General Count M. S. Vorontsov
21st Infantry Division: Major-General V. D. Laptev
  Brigade: Petrovsk, Podolia and Lithuania Infantry regiments
  Brigade: Neva Infantry Regiment: 44th Jaeger Regiment
  31st Heavy and 42nd Light Artillery batteries
24th Infantry Division: Major-General N. V. Vuich
  Brigade: Shirvan and Ufa Infantry regiments
  Brigade: Butyrki and Tomsk Infantry regiments
  Brigade: 19th and 40th Jaeger regiments
  46th Light Artillery Battery
Cavalry: Major-General Count Gothard von Manteuffel
  St Petersburg Dragoon Regiment; Elizavetgrad Hussar Regiment; Iakhontov Volunteer
  Cavalry Regiment
  5 Don Cossack, 1 Bug and 1 Ural Cossack regiment

Detachment of Major-General Harpe
  Navagin, Tula, Sevsk infantry regiments
  2nd, 13th, 14th Jaeger regiments
  3 Combined Grenadier battalions

Cavalry detachment of Major-General Count Joseph O'Rourke
  Nezhin Mounted Jaeger, Pavlograd Hussar, Polish Lancer and Volhynia Lancer
  regiments
  6 Don Cossack, 1 Siberian Cossack and 1 Bashkir regiment

Cavalry detachment of Major-General A. I. Chernyshev
  Finland Dragoon Regiment; Riga Dragoon Regiment; Izium Hussar Regiment
  5 Don Cossack regiments; 4 guns of 8th Horse Artillery Battery

Army Corps artillery
  31st Heavy, 42nd and 46th Light Artillery batteries; 8 guns of 8th Horse Artillery Battery

Army of Poland:

Commander: General Levin von Bennigsen: 43 battalions of army and 27 battalions of
  militia infantry: 40 squadrons of army regular cavalry, 10 regiments of irregular cavalry,
  7 squadrons of militia cavalry: 198 guns = 59,033 men

Advance Guard: Lieutenant-General E. I. Markov
16th Infantry Division: Major-General M. L. Bulatov
  Neishlot Infantry Regiment; 27th and 43rd Jaeger regiments
13th Infantry Division: 2nd Brigade: Major General Ivanov
  Saratov Infantry Regiment: Penza Infantry Regiment
Cavalry: Major-General S. V. Diatkov and Major-General N. V. Dekhterev
  Orenburg and Vladimir Lancer regiments; 1st Combined Hussar Regiment; 1st Combined
    Lancer Regiment
  4 Don Cossack regiments, 1 Ural Cossack regiment, 4 Bashkir regiments
  1 regiment Siberian Cossack militia and 1 regiment Penza militia cavalry
Artillery: 16th Heavy, 56th Light and 30th and 10th Horse Artillery batteries

Right Flank Army Corps: General D. S. Dokhturov
12th Infantry Division: Major-General Prince N. N. Khovansky
  Brigade: Smolensk Infantry Regiment; Narva Infantry Regiment
  Brigade: Aleksopol Infantry Regiment; Novoingermanland Infantry Regiment
  Brigade: 6th and 41st Jaeger regiments
26th Infantry Division: Major-General I. F. Paskevich
  Brigade: Ladoga Infantry Regiment; Poltava Infantry Regiment
  Brigade: Nizhnii Novgorod Infantry Regiment; Orel Infantry Regiment
  Brigade: 5th and 42nd Jaeger regiments
13th Infantry Division: Brigade of Major-General Axel Lindfors
  Velikie Luki Infantry Regiment: Galits Infantry Regiment
Cavalry detachment: Lieutenant-General E. I. Chaplitz
  Combined Dragoon Regiment: 1st and 2nd Combined Mounted Jaeger regiments; 2nd
    Combined Lancer Regiment; Taganrog, Siberia and Zhitomir Lancer regiments
Artillery: 26th and 45th Heavy, 1st and 47th Light, 2nd Horse Artillery batteries
  1 company miners
Army Corps reserve artillery: 22nd Heavy, 18th, 48th, 53rd Light, and 9th Horse Artillery
  batteries

Left Flank Army Corps: Lieutenant-General Count P. A. Tolstoy

Militia Corps of Major-General N. S. Muromtsev
  4 regiments of Nizhnii Novgorod militia infantry; 1 regiment of Nizhnii Novgorod and
    1 regiment of Kostroma militia cavalry; 1 Ural Cossack regiment
  52nd Heavy and 22nd Horse Artillery batteries

Militia Corps of Major-General Titov
  3 regiments of Penza militia infantry; 1 regiment of Riazan militia infantry and 1 regiment
    of Riazan militia jaegers; 1 regiment of Riazan militia cavalry; 2 squadrons of Kazan
    militia cavalry
  64th Light Artillery Battery

Notes

Abbreviations

AGM	*Arkhiv grafov Mordvinovykh*
BL	British Library
Correspondance de l'Empereur Alexandre	*Correspondance de l'Empereur Alexandre Ier avec sa sœur la Grande Duchesse Cathérine 1805–1818*, ed. Grand Duke Nicholas, SPB, 1910
Entsiklopediia	V. Bezotosnyi *et al.* (eds.), *Otechestvennaia voina 1812 goda: Entsiklopediia*, Moscow, 2004
Eugen, *Memoiren*	*Memoiren des Herzogs Eugen von Württemberg*, 3 vols., Frankfurt an der Oder, 1862
IV	*Istoricheskii vestnik*
Kutuzov	L. G. Beskrovnyi (ed.), *M. I. Kutuzov: Sbornik dokumentov*, Moscow, 1954, vols. 4i, 4ii, 5
MVUA	*Materialy voenno-uchenago arkhiva (1812, 1813)*
PSZ	*Polnoe Sobranie Zakonov Rossiiskoi Imperii*
RA	*Russkii arkhiv*
RD	*Relations diplomatiques*
RGVIA	Rossiiskii gosudarstvennyi voenno-istoricheskii arkhiv
RS	*Russkaia Starina*
SIM	*Sbornik istoricheskikh materialov izvlechennykh iz arkhiva S.E.I.V. kantseliarii*
SIRIO	*Sbornik imperatorskago russkago istoricheskago obshchestva*
SPB	St Petersburg
SVM	Stoletie voennago ministerstva
TGIM	Trudy gosudarstvennogo istoricheskogo muzeia
VIS	*Voenno-istoricheskii sbornik*
VPR	*Vneshniaia politika Rossii*
VS	*Voennyi sbornik*

Chapter 1: Introduction

1 Much of this introduction is drawn from my article, 'Russia and the Defeat of Napoleon', *Kritika*, 7/2, 2006, pp. 283–308. That article includes comprehensive footnotes, and interested readers should consult it as regards references to most of the secondary literature. This introductory chapter also skims across many topics covered in more detail later in the book, at which point I will make the necessary citations to literature in the notes.

2 For the key works in English on and around this subject, see Additional Reading.

3 The one exception is Christopher Duffy: see his *Austerlitz*, London, 1999, and *Borodino*

and the War of 1812, London, 1999: both of these are reprints by Cassell of books published some years previously. Both books are brief and were written when Russian archives were shut to foreigners. Duffy's main works on Russia cover an earlier period.

4 Of course by this I mean the primary sources: there is much splendid French secondary literature on the Napoleonic era. See my article in *Kritika*, n. 14.

5 *Memoiren des Herzogs Eugen von Württemberg*, 3 vols., Frankfurt an der Oder, 1862.

6 For example, the memoirs of Friedrich von Schubert, the chief of staff of Baron Korff's cavalry corps: *Unter dem Doppeladler*, Stuttgart, 1962.

7 Carl von Clausewitz, *The Campaign of 1812 in Russia*, London, 1992.

8 Clausewitz's judgements on the later stages of the campaign are more mellow: conceivably it helped that by then he was serving under Peter Wittgenstein, at whose headquarters all the key officers were German.

9 The first three volumes of Rudolph von Friederich (*Die Befreiungskriege 1813–1815*) cover the spring and autumn campaigns of 1813 and the campaign of 1814: *Der Frühjahrsfeldzug 1813*, Berlin, 1911; *Der Herbstfeldzug 1813*, Berlin, 1912; *Der Feldzug 1814*, Berlin, 1913.

10 See the five volumes of *Geschichte der Kämpfe Österreichs: Kriege unter der Regierung des Kaisers Franz. Befreiungskrieg 1813 und 1814*, Vienna, 1913.

11 This is most true as regards Henry Kissinger, *A World Restored*, London, 1957.

12 See e.g. Anthony D. Smith, 'War and Ethnicity: The Role of Warfare in the Formation, Self-Images, and Cohesion of Ethnic Communities', *Ethnic and Racial Studies*, 4/4, 1981, pp. 375–97.

13 Above all thanks to Peter Hofschroer's two volumes: *1815: The Waterloo Campaign*, London, 1998 and 1999.

14 The tart comment by F. Zatler in 1860 that logistics is the big weakness of military history still largely remains true: *Zapiski o prodovol'stvii voisk v voennoe vremia*, SPB, 1860, p. 95. The best published source on Russian logistics in 1812–14 remains the report submitted to Alexander I by Georg Kankrin and Mikhail Barclay de Tolly: *Upravlenie General-Intendanta Kankrina: General'nyi sokrashchennyi otchet po armiiam ... za pokhody protiv Frantsuzov, 1812, 1813 i 1814 godov*, Warsaw, 1815. There is a useful candidate's dissertation by Serge Gavrilov, *Organizatsiia i snabzheniia russkoi armii nakanune i v khode otechestvennoi voiny 1812 g. i zagranichnykh pokhodov 1813–1815 gg.: Istoricheskie aspekty*, SPB, 2003. On Napoleonic logistics, see Martin van Creveld, *Supplying War: Logistics from Wallenstein to Patton*, Cambridge, 1977, ch. 2.

15 There is an interesting recent work on the horse in war by Louis DiMarco, *War Horse: A History of the Military Horse and Rider*, Yardley, 2008.

16 On Wellington and the history of Waterloo, see Malcolm Balen, *A Model Victory: Waterloo and the Battle for History*, London, 1999, and Peter Hofschroer, *Wellington's Smallest Victory: The Duke, the Model-Maker and the Secret of Waterloo*, London, 2004. Buturlin's work was originally published in French in 1824: *Histoire militaire de la campagne de Russie en 1812*. Mikhailovsky-Danilevsky's first published campaign history was on the 1814 campaign: *Opisanie pokhoda vo Frantsii v 1814 godu*, 2 vols., SPB, 1836. His history of 1812 was published in Petersburg in 1839 in four volumes: *Opisanie otechestvennoi voiny 1812 goda*. The next year his two-volume history of the 1813 campaign was published: *Opisanie voiny 1813 g.*

17 On Russian historiography of the Napoleonic Wars, see I. A. Shtein, *Voina 1812 goda v otechestvennoi istoriografii*, Moscow, 2002, and the article by V. P. Totfalushin in *Entsiklopediia*, pp. 309–13.

18 B. F. Frolov, '*Da byli liudi v nashe vremia': Otechestvennaia voina 1812 goda i zagranichnye pokhody russkoi armii*, Moscow, 2005.

19 See the discussion and bibliography in D. Lieven, *Empire: The Russian Empire and its Rivals*, London, 2001.

20 There are some parallels in Chinese and Turkish historiography concerning the Manchu and Ottoman empires.

21 Anyone touching this theme owes much to John Keegan, *The Face of Battle*, London, 1978, pp. 117–206. There were great similarities and relatively few differences between the values of the British officers he discusses and their Russian counterparts.

22 Pamfil Nazarov and Ivan Men'shii.

23 J. P. Riley, *Napoleon and the World War of 1813*, London, 2000, is an interesting and original study of world war in 1813 by a senior British officer. It is true that the Anglo-American war of 1812–14 was directly linked to the Napoleonic Wars though not part of them: see Jon Latimer, *1812: War with America*, Cambridge, Mass., 2007.

Chapter 2: Russia as a Great Power

1 See the chapters by Paul Bushkovitch and Hugh Ragsdale in D. Lieven (ed.), *The Cambridge History of Russia*, Cambridge, 2006, vol. 2, pp. 489–529, for surveys of Russian foreign policy in the eighteenth century.

2 On Catherine and her reign, the bible is Isabel de Madariaga, *Russia in the Age of Catherine the Great*, London, 1981. On the 'Greek project', see Simon Sebag Montefiore's splendid *Prince of Princes: The Life of Potemkin*, London, 2000, pp. 219–21, 241–3.

3 The fullest recent survey of eighteenth-century Ottoman developments is Suraiya Faroqhi (ed.), *Turkey*, vol. 3: *The Later Ottoman Empire 1603–1839*, Cambridge, 2003. On the Ottoman army, see Virginia Aksan, *Ottoman Wars 1700–1870: An Empire Besieged*, Harlow, 2007. I attempted Russo-Ottoman comparisons in D. Lieven, *Empire: The Russian Empire and its Rivals*, London, 2001, ch. 4, pp. 128 ff.

4 There is a vast literature on the European Old Regime. For the long view of state formation in Europe, see Charles Tilly, *Coercion, Capital and European States: A.D. 990–1992*, Oxford, 1990. Equally thought-provoking are Perry Anderson, *Lineages of the Absolutist State*, London, 1974, and Brian Downing, *The Military Revolution and Political Change*, Princeton, 1992.

5 The best recent survey of the Russian peasantry is by David Moon, *The Russian Peasantry, 1600–1930*, London, 1999. On comparative European landholding by elites, see D. Lieven, *Aristocracy in Europe 1815–1914*, Basingstoke, 1992, chs. 1 and 2, pp. 1–73.

6 The exact figure is 7.3 per cent, and is derived from the nearly 500 generals included in *Entsiklopediia*. On education and Enlightenment in the Baltic provinces, see G. von Pistohlkors, *Deutsche Geschichte in Osten Europas: Baltische Länder*, Berlin, 1994, pp. 266–94.

7 The best source is the official history of Russian military engineering: I. G. Fabritsius, *Glavnoe inzhenernoe upravlenie*, SVM, 7, SPB, 1902. On doctors see: A. A. Baranov, 'Meditsinskoe obespechenie armii v 1812 godu', in *Epokha 1812 goda: Issledovaniia, istochniki, istoriografiia*, TGIM, vol. 1, Moscow, 2002, pp. 105–24.

8 D. G. Tselerungo, *Ofitsery russkoi armii, uchastniki Borodinskogo srazheniia*, Moscow, 2002, p. 81. The best source on the origins of the general staff is N. Glinoetskii, 'Russkii general'nyi shtab v tsarstvovanie Imperatora Aleksandra I', *VS*, 17/10, 1874, pp. 187–250. See also: P. A. Geisman, *Vozniknovenie i razvitie v Rossii general'nago shtaba*, SVM, 4/1/2/1, especially pp. 169 ff: 'Svita Ego Imperatorskago Velichestva po kvartirmeisterskoi chasti'.

9 This is to borrow the term used by John Brewer in the context of eighteenth-century Britain.

10 The Russian statistics are inexact because the government only counted the number of subjects who owed compulsory military service. This did not include women, nobles, priests, merchants or all non-Russian minorities. For the basic statistics on European populations, see R. Bonney (ed.), *Economic Systems and Finance*, Oxford, 1995, pp. 315–19 and 360–76. For a more detailed breakdown of the European population in 1812, see the statistics compiled by Major Josef Paldus which are contained in the appendix to *Geschichte der Kämpfe Österreichs: Kriege unter der Regierung des Kaisers Franz. Befreiungskrieg 1813 und 1814*, vol. 1: O. Criste, *Österreichs Beitritt zur Koalition*,

Vienna, 1913. All these statistics have to be watched carefully. For example Paldus's figure for the Russian population is much too low, though it may well be that he is using estimates for ethnic Russians rather than for all subjects of the emperor. Bonney cites P. G. M. Dickson for the Habsburg figure (*Finance and Government under Maria Theresa 1740–1780*, 2 vols., Oxford, 1987, vol. 1, p. 36), but Dickson does not include the population of the Habsburg Netherlands or Italy.

11 On Russian pay and rations, see F. P. Shelekhov, *Glavnoe intendantskoe upravlenie: istoricheskii ocherk*, SVM, 5, SPB, 1903, pp. 87, 92. On Wellington's troops, see Matthew Morgan, *Wellington's Victories*, London, 2004, pp. 33, 74.

12 E. K. Wirtschafter, *From Serf to Russian Soldier*, Princeton, 1990, ch. 4, pp. 74–95.

13 On Russian conscription, see Janet Hartley, *Russia, 1762–1825: Military Power*, London, 2008, ch. 2, pp. 25–47. On French conscription, see Isser Woloch, *The New Regime: Transformations of the French Civil Order, 1789–1820s*, London, 1994, ch. 13, pp. 380–426, and David Hopkin, *Soldier and Peasant in French Popular Culture*, Woodbridge, 2003, pp. 125–214. On the nation in arms, see MacGregor Knox, 'Mass Politics and Nationalism as Military Revolution: The French Revolution and After', in MacGregor Knox and Williamson Murray (eds.), *The Dynamics of Military Revolution. 1300–2050*, Cambridge, 2001, ch. 4, pp. 57–73.

14 'Zapiski I. V. Lopukhina', *RA*, 3, 1914, pp. 318–56, at p. 345. On the militia and the debate that surrounded its mobilization, see V. V. Shchepetil'nikov, *Komplektovanie voisk v tsarstvovanie imperatora Aleksandra I*, SVM, 4/1/1/2, SPB, 1904, pp. 18–40, 69–72.

15 I. Merder, *Istoricheskii ocherk russkogo konevodstva i konnozavodstva*, SPB, 1868: the quote is on pp. 84–5. V. V. Ermolov and M. M. Ryndin, *Upravlenie general-inspektora kavalerii o remontirovanii kavalerii. Istoricheskii ocherk*, SVM, 3/3.1, SPB, 1906. This is a key work.

16 Marquess of Londonderry, *Narrative of the War in Germany and France in 1813 and 1814*, London, 1830, p. 31. Sir Robert Wilson, *Campaigns in Poland. 1806 and 1807*, London, 1810, p. 14.

17 Apart from Merder, see Shelekhov, *Glavnoe intendantskoe upravlenie*, for the purchase and upkeep of horses: e.g. purchase prices are on p. 104. A useful modern history of the Russian cavalry is A. Begunova, *Sabli ostry, koni bystry*, Moscow, 1992. On the incident with the Austrians, see T. von Bernhardi, *Denkwürdigkeiten aus dem Leben des kaiserlichen russischen Generals der Infanterie Carl Friedrich Grafen von Toll*, 5 vols., Leipzig, 1858, vol. 4, book 7, pp. 183–4.

18 There are two extremely useful unpublished Russian candidates' dissertations (i.e. roughly equivalent to a contemporary British Ph.D.) on the military economy: S. V. Gavrilov, *Organizatsiia i snabzheniia russkoi armii nakanune i v khode otechestvennoi voiny 1812g i zagranichnykh pokhodov 1813–1815gg: Istoricheskie aspekty*, candidate's dissertation, SPB, 2003, and V. N. Speranskii, *Voenno-ekonomicheskaia podgotovka Rossii k bor'be s Napoleonom v 1812–1814 godakh*, Gorky, 1967. The basic statistics on raw materials are in Gavrilov, pp. 39–42. Speransky is a mine of useful information: his only weakness appears to be that he neglects the crucial production of field artillery at the Petersburg arsenal. See the following note for references to this production. Viktor Bezotosnyi kindly confirmed that the arsenal did indeed produce most Russian field artillery.

19 For the basic statistics, see L. Beskrovnyi, *The Russian Army and Fleet in the Nineteenth Century*, Gulf Breeze, 1996, pp. 196–7. Speranskii, *Voenno-ekonomicheskaia*, pp. 38–58, on production at the Petrozavodsk and other works. On the artillery's equipment, guns and tactics in 1812–14, see A. and Iu. Zhmodikov, *Tactics of the Russian Army*, 2 vols., West Chester, Ohio, 2003, vol. 2, chs. 10–15. See also: Anthony and Paul Dawson and Stephen Summerfield, *Napoleonic Artillery*, Marlborough, 2007, pp. 48–55.

20 On the three arms works, the best introduction are the articles in *Entsiklopediia*, pp. 296, 654 and 724–5.

21 Speranskii, *Voenno-ekonomicheskaia*, ch. 2, especially pp. 82 ff., 362 ff. Much the most

detailed primary source on the Tula works is an exceptionally interesting article by
P. P. Svinin, 'Tul'skii oruzheinyi zavod', *Syn Otechestva*, 19, 1816, pp. 243 ff. Though
naively Soviet-era in many of its judgements, V. N. Ashurkov, *Izbrannoe: Istoriia
Tul'skogo kraia*, Tula, 2003, contains interesting details.

22 On the French tests, see K. Alder, *Engineering the Revolution: Arms and Enlightenment
in France, 1763–1815*, Princeton, 1997, p. 339. On English criticism, see Philip Haythornthwaite, *Weapons and Equipment of the Napoleonic Wars*, London, 1996, p. 22. Speranskii, *Voenno-ekonomicheskaia*, pp. 458–9, on the sources of the muskets distributed to
the army in 1812–13.

23 Even Wellington's men did not usually expect to beat off attacks by musketry alone.
Volleys were followed up by rapid counter-attacks with the bayonet.

24 Two recent surveys of Russian finance and taxation are: Peter Waldron, 'State Finances',
in Lieven (ed.), *Cambridge History of Russia*, vol. 2, pp. 468–88, and Richard Hellie,
'Russia', in R. Bonney (ed.), *The Rise of the Fiscal State in Europe c. 1215–1815*, Oxford,
1999, pp. 481–506.

25 All these statistics should be viewed with a certain scepticism. The Russian ones are
specially to be distrusted because of uncertainties as to whether sums are being cited in
silver or paper rubles. Most of the statistics are drawn from Bonney, *Economic Systems*,
pp. 360–76. The French figure is from Michel Bruguière, 'Finances publiques', in J. Tulard
(ed.), *Dictionnaire Napoléon*, Paris, 1987, pp. 733–5. The British figure is from J. M.
Sherwig, *Guineas and Gunpowder: British Foreign Aid in the Wars with France 1793–
1815*, Cambridge, Mass., 1969, p. 96.

26 W. M. Pintner, *Russian Economic Policy under Nicholas I*, Ithaca, NY, 1967, ch. 5.
There is a useful table on p. 186 which shows the volume of paper money issued annually
and its value vis-à-vis the silver currency. A well-informed source stated that the peasants'
obligation to feed the soldiers for very inadequate compensation from the state was a
well-established custom: L. Klugin, 'Russkaia soldatskaia artel', RS, 20, 1861, pp. 90,
96–7.

27 Most of the subsequent discussion is gleaned from basic texts, with the addition of some
of my own ideas: see in particular Paul W. Schroeder, *The Transformation of European
Politics 1763–1848*, Oxford, 1994; H. M. Scott, *The Emergence of the Eastern Powers,
1756–1775*, Cambridge, 2001; H. M. Scott, *The Birth of a Great Power System 1740–
1815*, Harlow, 2006; A. N. Sakharov *et al.* (eds.), *Istoriia vneshnei politiki Rossii: Pervaia
polovina XIX veka*, Moscow, 1995.

28 Isabel de Madariaga, *Britain, Russia and the Armed Neutrality of 1780*, London, 1962.
There is a good description of the realities behind these disputes over maritime rights in ch.
1 of Ole Feldbaek, *The Battle of Copenhagen 1801*, Barnsley, 2002. Pitt's miscalculation is
analysed by Jeremy Black, 'Naval Power, Strategy and Foreign Policy, 1775–1791', in
Michael Duffy (ed.), *Parameters of British Naval Power 1650–1850*, Exeter, 1998,
pp. 93–120.

29 Apart from the general diplomatic histories, see in particular H. Heppner, 'Der Öster-
reichisch-Russische Gegensatz in Sudosteuropa im Zeitalter Napoleons', in A. Drabek
et al. (eds.), *Russland und Österreich zur Zeit der Napoleonischen Kriege*, Vienna, 1989,
pp. 85 ff.

30 Elise Wirtschafter, 'The Groups Between: *raznochintsy*, Intelligentsia, Professionals', in
Lieven, *Cambridge History of Russia*, vol. 2, pp. 245–63, is a good introduction to the
evolution of the Russian middle classes. On state and society in the Napoleonic era,
Nicholas Riasanovsky, *A Parting of Ways: Government and the Educated Public in Russia
1801–1855*, Oxford, 1976, remains valuable.

31 Jerzy Lukowski, *The Partitions of Poland*, Harlow, 1999, is a reliable introduction to
this issue.

32 J. Hartley, *Alexander I*, London, 1994, pp. 58–72. A. A. Orlov, *Soiuz Peterburga i
Londona*, Moscow, 2005, ch. 1, pp. 7 ff.

33 The key text for this is Alexander's instructions for his envoy to the British government,

Nikolai Novosil'tsev: *VPR*, 1st series, 2, pp. 138–46 and 151–3, 11/23 Sept. 1804. See also Patricia Grimsted, *The Foreign Ministers of Alexander I*, Berkeley, 1969, pp. 32–65.

34 On the 1805 campaign, see above all two recent works: R. Goetz, *1805 Austerlitz: Napoleon and the Destruction of the Third Coalition*, London, 2005; Frederick W. Kagan, *Napoleon and Europe 1801–1805: The End of the Old Order*, Cambridge, Mass., 2006.

35 For an interesting defence of Prussian policy, see Brendan Simms, *The Impact of Napoleon: Prussian High Politics, Foreign Policy and the Crisis of the Executive 1797–1806*, Cambridge, 1997. Russia's foreign minister in 1806, Prince Adam Czartowski, was very unsympathetic to the Prussian dilemma. See W. H. Zawadski, *A Man of Honour: Adam Czartoryski as a Statesman of Russia and Poland 1795–1831*, Oxford, 1993, pp. 61–136.

36 The best source on this is Shelekhov, *Glavnoe intendantskoe upravlenie*, chs. VI–XIV; F. Zatler, *Zapiski o prodovol'stvii voisk v voennoe vremia*, SPB, 1860, is also an excellent source and provides statistics on relative population densities on pp. 23 and 78–9: even in 1860, after decades of rapid population growth, densities in Belorussia and Lithuania were one-quarter of what one found in Silesia, Saxony, Bohemia or north-eastern France. Gavrilov, *Organizatsiia*, p. 59. On salaries, see *PSZ*, 30, 23542, 17 March 1809 (OS), pp. 885–6. In 1809 the salaries of all junior officers had to be raised 33 per cent to offset the depreciation of the paper ruble.

37 There is a good, detailed article on this in Drabek *et al.* (eds.), *Russland und Österreich* by Rainer Egger: 'Die Operationen der Russischen Armee in Mahren und Österreich ob und unter der Enns im Jahre 1805', pp. 55–70.

38 See above all E. Weber, *Peasants into Frenchmen*, Stanford, Calif., 1976, especially ch. 6, pp. 67 ff.

39 This statistic is based on a survey I carried out of 1,500 NCOs whose details are recorded in the personnel records (*formuliarnye spiski*) in RGVIA, Fond 489. I included all NCOs whose records were legible and who were not the sons of soldiers and clergy, from the following regimental lists: Preobrazhensky Guards (Ed. Khr. 1); Little Russia Grenadiers (Ed. Khr. 1190); Kherson Grenadiers (Ed. Khr. 1263); Murom (Ed. Khr. 517), Chernigov (Ed. Khr. 1039), Reval (Ed. Khr. 754), Kursk (Ed. Khr. 425) infantry regiments; the 39th (Ed. Khr. 1802) and 45th (Ed. Khr. 1855) Jaegers; His Majesty's Life Cuirassiers (Ed. Khr. 2114) and the Mitau (Ed. Khr. 2446), Borisogleb (Ed. Khr. 2337), Narva (Ed. Khr. 2457), Iamburg (Ed. Khr. 2631) and Pskov (Ed. Khr. 212) dragoons; the 2nd (Ed. Khr. 3798), 5th (Ed. Khr. 3809) and 10th (Ed. Khr. 3842) artillery brigades.

40 There is much information on this in A. N. Andronikov and V. P. Fedorov, *Prokhozhdenie sluzhby*, SVM, 4/1/3, SPB, 1909, pp. 1–59, and Shchepetil'nikov, *Komplektovanie*, pp. 41–55.

41 On the artel, see the comments of William Fuller in *Strategy and Power in Russia, 1600–1914*, New York, 1992, pp. 172–3; also L. Klugin, 'Russkaia soldatskaia artel'', pp. 79–130; Andronikov and Fedorov, *Prokhozhdenie sluzhby*, pp. 112–14. On the formation of new regiments, see A. A. Kersnovskii, *Istoriia russkoi armii*, 4 vols., Moscow, 1992, vol. 1, p. 206.

42 Eugen, *Memoiren*, vol. 2, p. 49; S. F. Glinka, *Pis'ma russkogo ofitsera*, Moscow, 1987, p. 347.

43 In 1806, for example, a circular from Alexander's Personal Military Chancellery stressed that 'the transfer of officers from one regiment to another is wholly contrary to the emperor's wishes': Andronikov and Fedorov, *Prokhozhdenie sluzhby*, p. 112. In 1812 Baron Cyprian von Kreutz became chief of the Siberian Lancer Regiment. Next year his two young brothers-in-law transferred into the regiment. Within thirty months one of them had been promoted twice and the other three times: RGVIA, Fond 489, Opis 1, Ed. Khr. 2670, fos. 34–45: 'Spisok o sluzhbe i dostoinstv Sibirskago ulanskago polka generaliteta' and 'Spisok o sluzhbe i dostoinstv Sibirskago ulanskago polka rotmistrov i shtab-rotmistrov'. See the personnel records e.g. of the Preobrazhensky Guards (Ed. Khr. 1), the Little Russia and Kherson Grenadiers (Ed. Khr. 1190 and 1263), the Kursk

and Briansk (39th Jaegers) regiments (Ed. Khr. 425 and 1802) and the Pskov Dragoons (Ed. Khr. 212).

44 On Karneev, see RGVIA, Fond 489, Ed. Khr. 1, fo. 506: 'Formuliarnyi spisok leib gvardii Preobrazhenskago polka, generalam, shtab i ober ofitseram i drugim chinam', dated 1 Jan. 1808 (OS). On the Briansk, Narva and Grenadier regiments, see the sections on NCOs in their personnel records listed in n. 39 above. On soldiers' sons and NCOs, see *Komplektovanie, SVM*, pp. 173–208. On Russian NCOs, see D. G. Tselerungo, 'Boevoi opyt unter-ofitserov russkoi armii – uchastnikov Borodinskago srazheniia', in *Otechestvennaia voina 1812 goda: Istochniki, pamiatniki, problemy. Materialy XII vserossisskoi nauchnoi konferentsii. Borodino, 6–8 sentiabria 2004 g.*, Moscow, 2005, pp. 21–6.

45 Much the best evaluation of the Russian army's performance in 1805–7 is in vol. 1 of Zhmodikov, *Tactics*.

46 Eugen, *Memoiren*, vol. 1, p. 136.

47 This information comes from the biographical sketch which introduced Osten-Sacken's own diaries when these were published by *Russkii arkhiv* in 1900: *RA*, 1, 1900, pp. 6–25.

48 'Iz zapisok fel'dmarshala Sakena', *RA*, 1, 1900, pp. 161–80. Langeron's memoirs are a useful source on this dispute, since he had a healthy respect for both Bennigsen and Sacken. Langeron's letter to Bennigsen, dated 10 Dec. 1816, is in vol. 1, pp. xxvii–xxix, of *Mémoires du Général Bennigsen*, 3 vols., Paris, n.d. The comments in his own memoirs are in *Mémoires de Langeron, Général d'Infanterie dans l'Armée Russe: Campagnes de 1812, 1813, 1814*, Paris, 1902, pp. 15–18.

49 The best source on the views of both Alexander and his advisers is the many letters of Prince Aleksandr Kurakin to the Dowager Empress Marie, in *RA*, 1, 1868. See also A. Gielgud (ed.), *Memoirs of Prince Adam Czartoryski*, 2 vols., London, 1888, vol. 2, pp. 174–83. V. Sirotkin, *Napoleon i Aleksandr I*, Moscow, 2003, is a good introduction to opinion within the Russian ruling elite on foreign policy.

50 S. Tatishcheff, *Alexandre I et Napoléon*, Paris, 1894, Alexander to Lobanov, 4/16 June 1807, p. 121.

51 D. N. Shilov, *Gosudarstvennye deiateli Rossiiskoi imperii*, SPB, 2001, pp. 377–9. Grand Duke Nikolai Mikhailovich, *Russkie portrety*, SPB, n.d., vol. 4, part 1, no. 62.

52 On Aleksandr Kurakin's career, see S. N. Shipov and Iu. A. Kuz'min, *Chleny gosudarstvennogo soveta Rossiiskoi imperii*, SPB, 2007, pp. 412–16. Lobanov's reports on the initial negotiations are in *RS*, 98, 1899, pp. 594–5, Lobanov to Alexander, 7/19 June 1807. See also *RA*, 1, 1868, Kurakin to Empress Marie, 10/22 June 1807, pp. 183–7.

53 It seems that in his initial drafts Tolstoy depicted the Kuragins in more sympathetic terms: K. B. Feuer, *Tolstoy and the Genesis of War and Peace*, Ithaca, NY, 1976, p. 71. On the ancestry of Lobanov and Kurakin, see N. Ikonnikov, *La Noblesse de Russie*, 2nd edn., vols. A1–Z2, Paris, 1958–66: vols. H1, pp. 211–16 and I1, pp. 426–31.

54 On Constantine, see E. Karnovich, *Tsesarevich Konstantin Pavlovich*, SPB, 1899. On Paul, see R. McGrew, *Paul I of Russia*, Oxford, 1992, and H. Ragsdale (ed.), *Paul I: A Reassessment of his Life and Reign*, Pittsburgh, 1979.

55 V. I. Genishta and A. T. Borisovich, *Istoriia 30-go dragunskago Ingermanlandskago polka 1704–1904*, SPB, 1904, pp. 119–21, describes Lieven's role in preparing the army for the 1805 campaign.

56 Lieven's personnel record is in RGVIA, Fond 489, Opis 1, Delo 7062, fo. 356: as was true of many officers, he omitted to mention his parents' property. See his self-appraisal in a letter to his fiancée, Dorothea, who was the god-daughter of the Empress Marie: J. Charmley, *The Princess and the Politicians*, London, 2005, p. 7.

57 S. W. Jackman (ed.), *Romanov Relations*, London, 1969, Grand Duchess Anna to Grand Duke Constantine, 2 April 1828, p. 149.

58 See e.g. Tatishcheff, *Alexandre*, pp. 140, 183, and A. Vandal, *Napoléon et Alexandre Premier*, 3 vols., Paris, 1891, vol. 1, pp. 61–7. The instructions are in *VPR*, 1st series, 3, note 414, pp. 754–60.

59 Alexander did relinquish the Ionian Islands and Cattaro, which Russia could in any case never defend once at war with the Ottomans and Britain. It received the more useful Belostok district in return.

60 The treaties of peace and alliance are in *VPR*, 1st series, vol. 3, nos. 257 and 258, pp. 631 ff.

61 These comments on Alexander's preferences and perceptions are drawn from the instructions he gave to Kurakin and Lobanov: *VPR*, 1st series, vol. 3, note 414, pp. 754-60.

62 For a list of regimental artisans, see I. Ul'ianov, *Reguliarnaia pekhota 1801-1855*, vol. 2, Moscow, 1996, p. 212. On the Church in the army, see L. V. Mel'nikova, *Armiia i pravoslavnaia tserkov' Rossiiskoi imperii v epokhu Napoleonovskikh voin*, Moscow, 2007, pp. 45-56, 116-37.

63 The key work on officers' profiles is Tselerungo, *Ofitsery russkoi armii*.

64 The information on the Preobrazhenskys comes from: RGVIA, Fond 489, Opis 1, Ed. Khr. 1, fos. 455-560: 'Formuliarnyi spisok leib gvardii Preobrazhenskago polka, generalam, shtab i ober ofitseram i drugim chinam', dated 1 Jan. 1808. Only occasionally in the personnel records of line regiments can one spot that officers have neglected to mention serf-owning: see for one example the three Dolzhikov brothers in the Narva Dragoons who had family serfs as orderlies: RGVIA, Fond 489, Opis 1, Ed. Khr. 2457, 'Spisok o sluzhbe . . . Narvskago dragunskago polka', fos. 95 ff. for the list of batmen and lines 6 ff. and 27 ff. for the personnel records of the brothers. It is much easier to spot omissions among the prominent officers of the Preobrazhensky officers, let alone in the generals' personnel records in Fond 489, Opis 1, Delo 7602.

65 The quote is from *Zapiski Sergeia Grigorovicha Volkonskago (dekabrista)*, SPB, 1902, p. 70. See e.g. L. G. Beskrovnyi (ed.), *Dnevnik Aleksandra Chicherina, 1812-1813*, Moscow, 1966, for excellent insights into the cultured young Guards officers' mentality. Two such strikes were in the Semenovskys on the eve of 1812 and in the Guards artillery in January 1814: P. Pototskii, *Istoriia gvardeiskoi artillerii*, SPB, 1896, pp. 285-6; *Dnevnik Pavla Pushchina*, Leningrad, 1987, pp. 49-50.

66 On Lazarev, see http:www.svoboda.org/programs. For examples of ex-rankers being censured for poor behaviour after the war, see e.g. the cases of lieutenants Beliankin and Kirsanov of the 45th Jaegers (RGVIA, Fond 489, Opis 1, Delo 1855, fos. 19-20) or of three officers of the Iamburg Lancers (Lt. Krestovskii, *Istoriia 14-go Ulanskago Iamburgskago E.I.V. velikoi kniagini Marii Aleksandrovny polka*, SPB, 1873, appendices). Of course, many ex-rankers flourished.

67 'Imperator Aleksandr I: Ego kharakteristika po sochineniiu N. K. Shil'dera', *RS*, 99/3, 1899, pp. 98-114, at p. 99.

68 The catalogue of the excellent recent exhibition at the Hermitage on Alexander contains articles with many insights into his personality: *Aleksandr I: 'Sfinks ne razgadannyi do groba'*, SPB, 2005.

69 Quoted in N. Shil'der, *Imperator Aleksandr pervyi: Ego zhizn' i tsarstvovanie*, 4 vols., SPB, 1897, vol. 3, a letter to Alexander from Professor Parrot, p. 489.

70 D. V. Solov'eva (ed.), *Graf Zhozef de Mestr: Peterburgskie pis'ma*, SPB, 1995, no. 72, de Maistre to de Rossi, 20 Jan./1 Feb. 1808, p. 99.

71 There is a dearth of work on provincial society and administration under Alexander. The reign of Catherine II and the period from the 1861 Emancipation to 1917 are much better covered. For a good overview of local administration, see Janet Hartley, 'Provincial and Local Government', in Lieven (ed.), *Cambridge History of Russia*, vol. 2, pp. 446-67.

72 The book which best expresses Alexander's dilemmas is S. V. Mironenko, *Samoderzhavie i reformy: Politicheskaia bor'ba v Rossii v nachale XIX v.*, Moscow, 1989.

73 Metternich to Hardenberg, 5 Oct. 1812, in W. Oncken, *Österreich und Preussen in Befreiungskriege*, Berlin, 1878, vol. 1, no. 3, pp. 378-80.

74 *RD*, 5, no. 520, Caulaincourt to Champagny, 19 Sept. 1810, pp. 138-40.

Chapter 3: The Russo-French Alliance

1 N. F. Dubrovin, 'Russkaia zhizn' v nachale XIX v.', *RS*, 29/96, 1898, pp. 481–516.

2 *RD*, 4, no. 334, Caulaincourt to Champagny, 3 Oct. 1809, pp. 110–16.

3 e.g. *RD*, 1, no. 52, Caulaincourt to Champagny, 25 Feb. 1808, pp. 161–74; 2, no. 165, Caulaincourt to Napoleon, 8 Sept. 1808, pp. 344–6; 3, no. 187, Caulaincourt to Champagny, 15 Jan. 1809, pp. 27–32.

4 *Zapiski Sergeia Grigorovicha Volkonskago (dekabrista)*, SPB, 1902, pp. 60–62.

5 A. Vandal, *Napoléon et Alexandre Premier*, 3 vols., Paris, 1891, vol. 1, pp. 196–7. *SIRIO*, 89, 1893, no. 15, Tolstoy to Rumiantsev, 26 Oct./7 Nov. 1807, pp. 183–5; no. 86, Tolstoy to Alexander, Dec. 1807, pp. 312–13; no. 111, Tolstoy to Rumiantsev, 25 April/7 May 1808, pp. 519–27.

6 *Correspondance de l'Empereur Alexandre*, no. 12, Catherine to Alexander, 25 June 1807, pp. 18–19. On the French émigrés in Russia, see André Ratchinski, *Napoléon et Alexandre Ier*, Paris, 2002.

7 *VPR*, 4, no. 219, Stroganov to Alexander, 1/13 Feb. 1809, pp. 490–91.

8 On Mordvinov, see e.g. *AGM*, 4, pp. xliv–xlv: see in particular his memorandum on the Continental System dated 25 Sept. 1811 (OS), pp. 479–86. For Gurev's statement, see C. F. Adams (ed.), *John Quincy Adams in Russia*, New York, 1970, p. 277. Since official policy on the surface remained committed to the French alliance until the moment Napoleon crossed the border, diplomats usually camouflaged this view. The main but by no means only exception was Petr Tolstoy, who was already arguing for rapprochement with Britain as early as the summer of 1808. See e.g. *SIRIO*, 89, 1893, no. 111, Tolstoy to Rumiantsev, 25 April/7 May 1808, pp. 519–27; no. 176, Tolstoy to Rumiantsev, 26 July/7 Aug. 1808, pp. 631–5. But see also e.g. *VPR*, 4, no. 101, Alopaeus to Rumiantsev, 18/30 April 1808, pp. 233–5, for just one of many examples of other Russian diplomats expressing very 'Tolstoyan' views.

9 *Mémoires du Général Bennigsen*, 3 vols., Paris, n.d., vol. 1, 4th letter, pp. 33–52; vol. 3, annex 53, pp. 377–95.

10 The main English-language source on Speransky remains Marc Raeff's classic *Mikhail Speransky: Statesman of Imperial Russia*, The Hague, 1969, but at the very least the anglophone reader should also turn to John Gooding, 'The Liberalism of Michael Speransky', *Slavonic and East European Review*, 64/3, 1986, pp. 401–24.

11 For de Maistre's views, see D. V. Solov'eva (ed.), *Graf Zhozef de Mestr: Peterburgskie pis'ma*, SPB, 1995, no. 72, de Maistre to de Rossi, 20 Jan./1 Feb. 1808, pp. 98–101. For Caulaincourt, see *RD*, 1, no. 18, Caulaincourt to Napoleon, 13 Jan. 1808, pp. 48–51. Count A. de Nesselrode (ed.), *Lettres et papiers du Chancelier Comte de Nesselrode 1760–1850*, Paris, n.d., vol. 3, Nesselrode to Speransky, 2/14 April 1810, pp. 251–2. See also Joanna Woods, *The Commissioner's Daughter: The Story of Elizabeth Proby and Admiral Chichagov*, Witney, 2000.

12 *RA*, 2, 1876, Prozorovsky to Golitsyn, 23 July/4 Aug. 1807, pp. 157–9. On the British angle, see Brendan Simms, *Three Victories and a Defeat: The Rise and Fall of the First British Empire, 1714–1783*, London, 2007.

13 On Ireland, see S. J. Connolly, *Religion, Law and Power: The Making of Protestant Ireland 1660–1760*, Oxford, 1992, pp. 249–50.

14 On the global context, see Christopher Bayly, *The Birth of the Modern World 1780–1914*, Oxford, 2004, part 1, chs. 1–3, pp. 27–120; John Darwin, *After Tamerlane: The Global History of Empire*, London, 2007, ch. 4, 'The Eurasian Revolution', pp. 158–217.

15 *RD*, 5, no. 563, Caulaincourt to Champagny, 14 Dec. 1810, pp. 235–43.

16 Adams, *Adams*, p. 209.

17 Ibid., pp. 87, 432.

18 The debate on the origins of the Industrial Revolution seldom bothers even to mention Russia as a potential candidate. Apart from the reasons set out in the text, it is generally assumed that industrial take-off required a densely concentrated population. See e.g. the

interesting discussion in Kenneth Pomeranz, *The Great Divergence: China, Europe and the Making of the Modern World Economy*, Princeton, 2000.

19 *RD*, 4, no. 334, Caulaincourt to Champagny, 3 Oct. 1809, pp. 110-16; no. 423, 11 March 1810, pp. 325-8.

20 P. Bailleu (ed.), *Briefwechsel König Friedrich Wilhelm III's und der Königin Luise mit Kaiser Alexander I*, Leipzig, 1900, no. 157, Alexander to Friedrich Wilhelm, 2 Nov. 1807, pp. 167-8. *VPR*, 4, no. 146, Kurakin to Rumiantsev, 16/28 Aug. 1808, pp. 320-21, is merely one of many Russian appreciations on the damage done to any hopes of peace by Napoleon's debacle in Spain. Another is no. 198, Rumiantsev to Alexander, 16/28 Dec. 1808, p. 441.

21 N. Shil'der: 'Nakanune Erfurtskago svidaniia 1808 goda', *RS*, 98/2, 1899, pp. 3-24, Marie to Alexander, 25 Aug. 1808 (OS), pp. 4-17. The Erfurt convention is in *VPR*, 4, no. 161, pp. 359-61.

22 *RS*, 98/2, 1899, Alexander to Marie, n.d. but certainly late Aug. 1808, pp. 17-24.

23 *Correspondance de l'Empereur Alexandre*, no. 19, Alexander to Catherine, 26 Sept. 1808, p. 20.

24 This paragraph is based on reading all the Russian diplomatic correspondence in these six months and it is impossible to cite all the relevant dispatches. The key ones are: *VPR*, 4, no. 131, Kurakin to Alexander, 2/14 July 1808, pp. 291-8; no. 143, Alexander to Kurakin, 14/26 Aug. 1808, pp. 316-17; no. 144, Rumiantsev to Kurakin, 14/26 Aug. 1808, pp. 317-19; no. 150, Alexander to Kurakin, 27 Aug./8 Sept. 1808, pp. 331-2; no. 174, Rumiantsev to Alexander, 26 Oct./7 Nov. 1808, pp. 387-9; no. 186, Anstedt to Saltykov, 22 Nov./4 Dec. 1808, pp. 410-12; no. 217, Rumiantsev to Alexander, 30 Jan./11 Feb. 1809, pp. 485-7; no. 220, Alexander to Rumiantsev, 2/14 Feb. 1809; no. 224, Alexander to Rumiantsev, 10/22 Feb. 1809, pp. 502-4; no. 246, Rumiantsev to Anstedt, 11/23 March 1809, pp. 543-5.

25 *SIRIO*, 89, 1893, no. 94, Rumiantsev to Tolstoy, March 1808, pp. 496-7; no. 112, Tolstoy to Rumiantsev, 26 April/8 May 1808, pp. 525-7.

26 *Correspondance de l'Empereur Alexandre*, Marie to Catherine, 23 Dec. 1809 (OS), pp. 251-7; Catherine to Marie, 26 Dec. 1809 (OS), pp. 259-60.

27 On the non-ratification of the convention, see *RD*, 4, no. 410, Caulaincourt to Champagny, 26 Feb. 1810, pp. 296-9; Barclay de Tolly's memorandum is reproduced in *MVUA 1812*, 1/2, pp. 1-6.

28 *VPR*, 4, no. 221, Rumiantsev to Kurakin, 2/14 Feb. 1809, pp. 496-7.

29 The statistics are drawn from A. A. Podmazo, 'Kontinental'naia blokada kak ekonomicheskaia prichina voiny 1812 g.', *Epokha 1812 goda: Issledovania, istochniki, istoriografiia*, 137, TGIM, Moscow, 2003, vol. 2, pp. 248-66, and M. F. Zlotnikov, *Kontinental'naia blokada i Rossiia*, Moscow, 1966, ch. IX, pp. 335 ff. For Caulaincourt's comment, see *RD*, 2, no. 179, Caulaincourt to Napoleon, 9 Dec. 1808, pp. 387-8.

30 Adams, *Adams*, pp. 236-8, 364; J. Hanoteau (ed.), *Mémoires du Général de Caulaincourt, Duc de Vicenze*, 3 vols., Paris, 1933, vol. 1, pp. 282-3. *AGM*, vol. 4, no. 1050, 25 Sept. 1811, pp. 479-86 for Nikolai Mordvinov's memorandum on the Continental System.

31 *SIRIO*, 121, 1906, Chernyshev to Barclay de Tolly, 31 Dec. 1811/12 Jan. 1812, pp. 196-202. V. M Bezotosnyi, *Razvedka i plany storon v 1812 godu*, Moscow, 2005, pp. 51-5.

32 The quote is from a letter to Rumiantsev from Chernyshev dated 6/18 June 1810: *SIRIO*, 121, 1906, no. 7, pp. 55-8.

33 Nesselrode (ed.), *Nesselrode*, vol. 3, 5/17 July 1811, pp. 375-9.

34 The memorandum is reprinted in N. K. Shil'der, *Imperator Aleksandr pervyi: Ego zhizn' i tsarstvovanie*, 4 vols., SPB, 1897, vol. 3, pp. 471-83, but note the comment in *VPR*, 5, note 246, pp 692-3, which corrects Shil'der's error as to when this report reached Alexander.

35 All this is drawn from Chernyshev's reports to Alexander, Barclay de Tolly and Rumiantsev published in *SIRIO*, 121, 1906, parts 2 and 4, pp. 32-108 and 114-204. The quote

is from report no. 6, to Barclay, dated Nov. 1811, pp. 178–87. Chernyshev's one error was a moment of carelessness on departure in 1812 which allowed his agent in the War Ministry to be caught. Vandal, *Napoléon et Alexandre*, vol. 3, pp. 306–18, 377, 393, discusses Chernyshev's activities. Some details differ: for example, he writes that the War Ministry's 'book' was produced every fortnight. More importantly, he underestimates the scale and impact of Chernyshev's role, let alone the importance of his and Nesselrode's information combined.

36 Bailleu (ed.), *Briefwechsel*, no. 192, Frederick William to Alexander, 19/31 Oct. 1809, pp. 204–5. Nesselrode (ed.), *Nesselrode*, vol. 3, Nesselrode to Speransky, 6/18 Aug. 1811, pp. 382–5. The most detailed description of Chernyshev's activities is ch. 2 of General A. Mikhailovskii-Danilevskii, *Zhizneopisanie kniazia Aleksandra Ivanovicha Chernysheva ot 1801 do 1815 goda*, reprinted in *Rossiiskii arkhiv*, 7, Moscow, 1996, pp. 13–40.

37 *SIRIO*, 121, 1906, no. 12, Chernyshev to Barclay, received 3 March 1812, pp. 204–10.

38 *VPR*, 6, Barclay de Tolly to Alexander, 22 Jan./3 Feb. 1812, pp. 267–9.

39 By far the best source in English on these men and issues is Alexander Martin, *Romantics, Reformers, Reactionaries: Russian Conservative Thought and Politics in the Reign of Alexander I*, De Kalb, Ill., 1997. There are also useful biographical details about Rostopchin in A. Kondratenko, *Zhizn' Rostopchina*, Orel, 2002.

40 All this discussion is drawn from Richard Pipes's excellent translation and analysis of Karamzin's work: see R. Pipes, *Karamzin's Memoir on Ancient and Modern Russia: A Translation and Analysis*, Ann Arbor, 2005; the quote is from p. 146.

41 Ibid., pp. 147–67.

42 *VPR*, 6, no. 137, Rumiantsev to Stackelberg, 28 March/9 April 1812, pp. 341–3; no. 158, Stackelberg to Rumiantsev, 29 April/11 May 1812, pp. 393–4.

43 Bailleu (ed.), *Briefwechsel*, no. 196, Frederick William to Alexander, 30 April/12 May 1812, pp. 214–18.

44 W. H. Zawadski, *A Man of Honour: Adam Czartoryski as a Statesman of Russia and Poland 1795–1831*, Oxford, 1993, pp. 188–205. See *VPR*, 6, p. 693, n. 98 for a detailed demolition of Vandal's statement that Russia was planning a pre-emptive strike in 1811.

45 W. Oncken, *Österreich und Preussen in Befreiungskriege*, 2 vols., Berlin, 1878, vol. 2, appendices, no. 30, Saint-Julien to Metternich, 13 Aug. 1811, pp. 611–14.

46 Bailleu (ed.), *Briefwechsel*, no. 198, Alexander to Frederick William, 14 May 1811, pp. 219–22; no. 208, Frederick William to Alexander, 19/31 March 1812, pp. 238–9.

47 I. G. Fabritsius, *Glavnoe inzhenernoe upravlenie*, SVM, 7, SPB, 1902, pp. 733–58. There is a new and interesting book on Ottoman warfare by Virginia Aksan: *Ottoman Wars 1700–1870: An Empire Besieged*, London, 2007. If it has a weakness it is that it says too little about actual battle and tactics.

48 *SIRIO*, 121, 1906, no. 13, Chernyshev to Rumiantsev, 13/25 July 1810, and no. 15, 5/17 Sept. 1810, pp. 75–80 and 88–95. For his account of his mission to Sweden, see *SIRIO*, 121, pp. 22–48.

49 The quote is from a letter from Bernadotte to Count Löwenhielm, the special Swedish emissary to Alexander, dated 7/19 March 1812 and published in *La Suède et la Russie: Documents et matériaux 1809–1818*, Uppsala, 1985, pp. 96–8. The text of the Russo-Swedish treaty of alliance is no. 66, pp. 105–11.

50 The phrase 'blundered towards empire' was suggested by Owen Connelly to describe Napoleon's campaigns: *Blundering to Glory: Napoleon's Military Campaigns*, Wilmington, Del., 1987.

51 The literature on Napoleon's empire is so immense that any attempt at a bibliography is impossible here. The best up-to-date general history in my opinion is Thierry Lentz, *Nouvelle histoire du Premier Empire*, 3 vols., Paris, 2004–7. In English, the best recent works include P. Dwyer (ed.), *Napoleon and Europe*, Harlow, 2001; M. Broers, *Europe under Napoleon*, London, 1996; S. Wolff, *Napoleon's Integration of Europe*, London, 1991.

52 See above all Christopher Bayly, *Indian Society and the Making of the British Empire*,

Cambridge, 1988, ch. 3, and the chapters by Michael Duffy, Patrick O'Brien and Rajat Kanta Ray in P. J. Marshall (ed.), *The Oxford History of the British Empire: The Eighteenth Century*, Oxford, 1998.

53 Rajat Kanta Ray, 'Indian Society and the Establishment of British Supremacy, 1765–1818', in Marshall (ed.), *British Empire*, pp. 509–29, at p. 525. On changing European views on overseas empire, see especially Jennifer Pitts, *A Turn to Empire: The Rise of Imperial Liberalism in Britain and France*, Princeton, 2005. On French (and other) views of eastern Europe, see Larry Wolff, *Inventing Eastern Europe: The Map of Civilization on the Mind of the Enlightenment*, Stanford, Calif., 1994.

54 This is to risk embroiling myself in a vast literature on the origins of nations: see e.g. A. D. Smith, *The Ethnic Origins of Nations*, London, 1986. The Napoleonic era provides fine opportunities to test national identities' strength and constituent elements, not just in Europe but in comparative terms across the globe: R. G. S. Cooper, *The Anglo-Maratha Campaign and the Contest for India*, Cambridge, 2003, illustrates the internal weaknesses of a polity which was Britain's toughest enemy in India. Compare this with e.g. M. Rowe (ed.), *Collaboration and Resistance in Napoleonic Europe*, Basingstoke, 2003.

55 The perfect model of an imperial conqueror is the Chinese Emperor Ch'in Shih-Huang, whom Sam Finer calls the ruler who left the biggest and most lasting mark on government. Measured against him, Napoleon's ambitions and impact appear puny: S. Finer, *The History of Government*, 3 vols., Oxford, 1997, vol. 1, pp. 472–3. For a fuller study of the First Emperor, see D. Bodde, 'The State and Empire of Ch'in', in D. Twitchett and M. Loewe (eds.), *The Cambridge History of China*, vol. 1: *The Ch'in and Han Empires 221 BC–AD 220*, Cambridge, 1986, ch. 1. Michael Doyle, *Empires*, Ithaca, NY, 1986, is perceptive as regards institutionalization.

56 On this and many other points discussed in this section, see the excellent Lentz, *Nouvelle histoire*, vol. 3: *La France et l'Europe de Napoléon 1804–1814*, Paris, 2007. As will be evident from the above, I agree with Professor Lentz on the question of ideology: see pp. 671–5 of his book.

57 *VPR*, 5, no. 142, Memorandum of F. P. Pahlen, not later than 14/26 Nov. 1809, pp. 294–5.

58 On Napoleon's 'Indian projects' and Russian fears that they would be forced to serve them, see V. Bezotosnyi, 'Indiiskie proekty Napoleona i Rossiia v 1812 g.', in *Epokha 1812 goda: Issledovaniia, istochniki, istoriografiia*, 161, TGIM, Moscow, 2006, vol. 5, pp. 7–22.

Chapter 4: Preparing for War

1 D. V. Solov'eva (ed.), *Graf Zhozef de Mestr: Peterburgskie pis'ma*, SPB, 1995, no. 72, 20 Jan./1 Feb. 1808, pp. 98–9.

2 On Arakcheev, see E. Davydova, E. Liatina and A. Peskov (eds.), *Rossiia v memuarakh: Arakcheev. Svidetel'stva sovremennikov*, Moscow, 2000, a very useful collection of contemporary recollections of Arakcheev. See also ch. 1 by K. M. Iachmenikov, 'Aleksei Andreevich Arakcheev', pp. 17–62, in *Russkie konservatory*, Moscow, 1997.

3 Solov'eva, *de Mestr*, no. 72, 20 Jan./1 Feb. 1808, p. 99.

4 Above all these were better canister ammunition and better sights.

5 P. Pototskii, *Istoriia gvardeiskoi artillerii*, SPB, 1896, chs. VI and VIII, pp. 99–153, is the best source on Arakcheev's role. There is a useful chapter also in V. N. Stroev, *Stoletie sobstvennoi Ego Imperatorskago Velichestva kantseliarii*, SPB, 1912, pp. 98–129. As regards memoirs, see above all 'Zapiski A. A. Eilera', *RA*, 11, 1880, pp. 333–99, at pp. 342–3, 348–50. F. Lange (ed.), *Neithardt von Gneisenau: Schriften von und über Gneisenau*, Berlin, 1954: 'Denkschrift Gneisenaus an Kaiser Alexander I', pp. 119–34, at p. 133.

6 See e.g. laws and decrees published in these years: *PSZ*, 30, 22756, 17 Jan. 1808, p. 27 (all reports to Alexander to go via Arakcheev); 22777, 25 Jan. 1808, pp. 42–3 (accounting);

22809, 5 Feb. 1808, p. 58 (no private letters); 23052, 2 June 1808, p. 284 (accurate service records); 23205, 5 Aug. 1808, pp. 486–508 (rules for the acceptance of cloth supplied).

7 *PSZ*, 30, 23923, 21 Oct. 1809, pp. 1223–7, on cloth supplies; *MVUA 1812*, 1/2, no. 8, Arakcheev to Barclay, 26 Jan. 1810, pp. 21–3. The regimental histories are the best source for Arakcheev's instructions on shooting practice and the upkeep of weapons: see e.g. V. V. Rantsov, *Istoriia 96-go pekhotnago Omskago polka*, SPB, 1902, pp. 114–17.

8 *MVUA 1812*, 1, no. 116, Barclay to Commissary-General, 4 June 1810, p. 53; *RD*, 4, no. 332, Caulaincourt to Champagny, 2 Oct. 1809, pp. 106–8.

9 On recruit uniforms, see e.g. *PSZ*, 30, 20036, 23 May 1808, pp. 272–4. On initial emergency measures regarding cloth supplies, 23121, 26 June 1808, pp. 357–68. S. V. Gavrilov, *Organizatsiia i snabzheniia russkoi armii nakanune i v khode otechestvennoi voiny 1812 g. i zagranichnykh pokhodov 1813–1815 gg.: Istoricheskie aspekty*, candidate's dissertation, SPB, 2003, pp. 117–20, 124.

10 The same was true in France: see K. Alder, *Engineering the Revolution: Arms and Enlightenment in France, 1763–1815*, Princeton, 1997, p. 466 for all the references to the failed effort to introduce interchangeable parts.

11 See above all the excellent chapter on small arms production in V. N. Speranskii, *Voenno-ekonomicheskaia podgotovka Rossii k bor'be s Napoleonom v 1812–1814 godakh*, Gorky, 1967, pp. 82–135. On the new musket and its calibre, *PSZ*, 30, 23580, 13 April 1809, pp. 908–11. On lead, 22827, 16 Feb. 1808, pp. 71–7, and also *MVUA 1812*, 4, no. 11, Kremer to Barclay de Tolly, 25 July 1811, pp. 82–5; no. 12, Barclay to Gurev, draft, pp. 85–6. P. Haythornthwaite, *Weapons and Equipment of the Napoleonic Wars*, London, 1996, p. 21.

12 *PSZ*, 30, 23297, 10 Oct. 1808, pp. 603–38.

13 'Dvenadtsatyi god: Pis'ma N. M. Longinova k grafu S. R. Vorontsovu', *RA*, 4, 1912, pp. 381–547, 13 Oct. 1812, pp. 534–5. I. P. Liprandi, *Materialy dlia otechestvennoi voiny 1812 goda: Sobranie statei*, SPB, 1867, ch. 10, pp. 199–211.

14 Much the best source on Barclay's background, values and early life is Michael and Diana Josselson, *The Commander: A Life of Barclay de Tolly*, Oxford, 1980.

15 See e.g. the comments of Eugen of Württemberg: Eugen, *Memoiren*, vol. 1, pp. 274–7.

16 Josselson, *Commander*, pp. 81–2. V. P. Totfalushin, *M. V. Barklai de Tolli v otechestvennoi voine 1812 goda*, Saratov, 1991, ch. 1.

17 The law is in *PSZ*, 31, no. 24975, 27 Jan. 1812 (OS), pp. 43–164. Gavrilov, *Organizatsiia*, pp. 61 ff. discusses it in detail.

18 The amendment is *PSZ*, 31, no. 25035, 13 March 1812 (OS), pp. 228–9. On the law, see P. A. Geisman, *Svita Ego Imperatorskago Velichestva po kvartirmeisterskoi chasti v tsarstvovanie Imperatora Aleksandra I*, SVM, 4/2/1, SPB, 1902, pp. 284 ff.

19 The law on forming the 13 new regiments is *PSZ*, 30, no. 24505, Jan. 1811, pp. 537–43; the law on internal security is vol. 30, no. 24704, pp. 783–802. On the new regiments' quality, see e.g. F. G. Popov, *Istoriia 48-go pekhotnago Odesskago polka*, 2 vols., Moscow, 1911, vol. 1, pp. 7–52; S. A. Gulevich, *Istoriia 8-go pekhotnago Estliandskago polka*, SPB, 1911, pp. 117–21.

20 A collection of documents on the internal security troops was published in Moscow in 2002: *Vnutrenniaia i konvoinaia strazha Rossii: Dokumenty i materialy*. For English-language readers John LeDonne provides a short guide in *Absolutism and Ruling Class*, Oxford, 1991, pp. 132–9. P. E. Shchegoleva (ed.), *Zapiski grafa E. F. Komarovskgogo*, SPB, 1914, pp. 183–7, is very revealing about the formation of the internal security troops and Alexander's attitude towards them. For Alexander's views on Balashev, see 'Zapiski Iakova Ivanovicha de Sanglena: 1776–1831 gg.', *RS*, 37, 1883, pp. 1–46, at pp. 20–25.

21 See in particular Lobanov's letter to Alexander of 8 May 1814 (OS): RGVIA, Fond 125, Opis 1/188a, Delo 153, fo. 65. It is only fair to add that Lobanov wrote that some of these officers were excellent.

22 In this period all regiments had so-called chiefs. They might be anything from colonels to senior generals. They bore responsibility for their regiment's training, finances and

administration. If they had no other job, then chiefs would actually command the regiment. In all circumstances they exercised a strong influence on their subordinate officers' behaviour.

23 Colonel Markov, *Istoriia leib-gvardii kirasirskago Eia Velichestva polka*, SPB, 1884, pp. 199–201; E. K. Wirtschafter, *From Serf to Russian Soldier*, Princeton, 1990, pp. 97–8.

24 M. A. Rossiiskii, *Ocherk istorii 3-go pekhotnago Narvskago general-fel'dmarshala kniazia Mikhaila Golitsyna polka*, Moscow, 1904, pp. 291–302.

25 P. Voronov and V. Butovskii, *Istoriia leib-gvardii Pavlovskago polka 1790–1890*, SPB, 1890, pp. 46–73; Popov, *Istoriia 48go*, vol. 1, pp. 26–8. For another example of how poor leadership contributed to desertion in individual squadrons, see Lt. Krestovskii, *Istoriia 14-go Ulanskago Iamburgskago E.I.V. velikoi kniagini Marii Aleksandrovny polka*, SPB, 1873, pp. 327–33.

26 The latest British work on Wellington's 95th Regiment makes these points convincingly: see Mark Urban, *Rifles*, London, 2003.

27 Hon. George Cathcart, *Commentaries on the War in Russia and Germany in 1812 and 1813*, London, 1850, p. 7.

28 On the regulations for training jaegers and recruits, see A. I. Gippius, *Obrazovanie (Obuchenie) voisk*, SVM, 4/1, book 2, SPB, 1903, pp. 76–7, 81–2. On the history of the jaegers, see e.g. Rantsov, *Istoriia 96-go*, pp. 1–36. The three-volume history of the Russian infantry by I. Ulianov, *Reguliarnaia pekhota 1801–1855*, Moscow, 1995–8, is a very useful summary of regulations, uniforms, weaponry and tactics: fortunately, it includes the jaegers. Lange, *Gneisenau*, pp. 130–31.

29 The two light infantry regiments of the Guard have excellent histories which tell one a great deal about jaegers in this era: *Istoriia leib-gvardii egerskago polka za sto let 1796–1896*, SPB, 1896, and S. Gulevich, *Istoriia leib gvardii Finliandskago polka 1806–1906*, SPB, 1906.

30 *Mémoires de Langeron, Général d'Infanterie dans l'Armée Russe: Campagnes de 1812, 1813, 1814*, Paris, 1902, pp. 74–5. On the 2nd Jaegers, see Rantsov, *Istoriia 96-go*, pp. 81–3. On the 10th Jaegers, see N. Nevezhin, *112-i pekhotnyi Ural'skii polk: Istoriia polka 1797–1897*, Vilna, 1899, pp. 35–8.

31 Digby Smith, *Napoleon against Russia: A Concise History of 1812*, Barnsley, 2004, p. 92. M. I. Bogdanovich, *Istoriia otechestvennoi voiny 1812 goda*, 3 vols., SPB, 1859–60, vol. 2, p. 456.

32 I read all the issues of *Voennyi zhurnal* for 1810–12. It is impossible to cite them all.

33 The two key works on the origins of the general staff are Geisman, *Svita*, SVM, and N. Glinoetskii, 'Russkii general'nyi shtab v tsarstvovanie Imperatora Aleksandra I', *VS*, 17/10, Oct. 1874, pp. 187–250 and 17/11, Nov. 1874, pp. 5–43.

34 Volkonsky's former subordinate, Mikhailovsky-Danilevsky, damns him with faint praise: A. I. Mikhailovskii-Danilevskii, *Memuary 1814–1815*, SPB, 2001, pp. 156–7.

35 Glinoetskii, 'Russkii general'nyi shtab', *VS*, 17/11, Nov. 1874, p. 11.

36 RGVIA, Fond 489, Opis 1, Ed. Khr. 1, fos. 215 ff.

37 All these statistics are drawn from S. V. Shvedov, 'Komplektovanie, chislennost' i poteri russkoi armii v 1812 godu', in *K 175-letiiu Otechestvennoi voiny 1812 g.*, Moscow, 1987, pp. 120–39. The older statistics provided in Geisman, *Vozniknovenie*, SVM, p. 298, are higher. As Adam Czartoryski commented, 'I have so often seen in Russia 100,000 men on paper represented only by 65,000 effectives': A. Gielgud (ed.), *Memoirs of Prince Adam Czartoryski*, 2 vols., London, 1888, vol. 2, p. 221.

38 The basic rules on the structure and wartime deployment of regiments are in *PSZ*, 31, nos. 24400 and 24526, pp. 420–24 and 553–8.

39 The likeliest reason for this was that the Guards veterans companies, the marine regiments and the many other military units and institutions in Petersburg provided a more than sufficient rear cadre so there was no need to leave the second battalions behind.

40 For Alexander's view, see *SIM*, 1, no. 56, Alexander to Essen, 3 Aug. 1812 (OS), pp. 46–7. When he arrived in Riga, General von Steinhel supported Essen's view: 'The

troops here are reserve battalions, weak in numbers and inferior in combat-readiness to front-line units': *SIM*, 13, no. 3, Steinhel to Arakcheev, 7 Sept. 1812 (OS), pp. 205–7.

41 For picking one's way through the complicated changes in policy and nomenclature as regards recruit depots and reserve formations, the outstanding *Entsiklopediia* on 1812 is immensely useful.

42 The key document on the distribution of the fourth battalions is a memorandum attached to a letter of Alexander to Wittgenstein dated 3 Aug. 1812 (OS): *SIM*, 1, no. 58, pp. 47–9.

43 On the Noble Regiment, see M. Gol'mdorf, *Materialy dlia istorii byvshego Dvorianskago polka*, SPB, 1882: the statistics are from p. 137. On attracting officers, see also A. N. Andronikov and V. P. Fedorov, *Prokhozhdenie sluzhby*, SVM, 4/1/3, SPB, 1903, pp. 2–9, 100–182.

44 N. Shil'der, *Imperator Aleksandr pervyi: Ego zhizn' i tsarstvovanie*, 4 vols., SPB, 1897, vol.3, pp. 98–102. This will be covered in more detail in Ch. 7. The instructions to Lobanov to form twelve new regiments on the basis of voluntary contributions were enclosed in a letter from Barclay of 10 May 1812 (OS): RGVIA, Fond 125, Opis 1/188a, Delo 15, fos. 2–10. Estimates of costs are contained in a letter from the governor of Voronezh to Balashev on 24 June 1812 (OS): RGVIA, Fond 125, Opis 1/188a, Delo 16, fos. 92–3.

45 *MVUA 1812*, 1/2, no. 1, pp. 1–6.

46 For Wolzogen's view, see his memorandum of 13 Oct. 1811 (OS) in *MVUA 1812*, 5, no. 139, Wolzogen to Barclay, pp. 273–9. For the minister's own view that an offensive strategy was the better option, see e.g. a memorandum by him of Jan. 1811: *MVUA 1812*, 7, no. 16 (additional), pp. 187–9.

47 *MVUA 1812*, 2, no. 56, Plan of Military Operations, Feb. 1811, pp. 83–93.

48 Alexander of Württemberg's useful memorandum is in *MVUA 1812*, 10, no. 143, pp. 253–75; for Bagration, see e.g. *MVUA 1812*, 12, no. 103, Bagration to Barclay, 12 June 1812 (OS), pp. 107–9; for Volkonsky, *MVUA 1812*, 11, no. 260, 29 April 1812 (OS), pp. 324–33.

49 There are very many documents on the difficulties of feeding the troops but see e.g. a report from Barclay to Alexander of 4 April 1812 (OS) in which he states that food and particularly fodder is a great problem, the roads are impassable, he cannot requisition since a state of war has not yet been proclaimed but has no money to buy food, and is keeping sickness rates down so long as the units are well dispersed; *MVUA 1812*, 11, no. 41, 4 April 1812 (OS), pp. 54–5.

50 Again, there are very many memorandums on this theme in *MVUA* but the best summary of the problem is in I. G. Fabritsius, *Glavnoe inzhenernoe upravlenie*, SVM, 7, SPB, 1902.

51 For Wolzogen's views, see his memorandum above (n. 6). Bogdanovich, *Istoriia ... 1812 goda*, vol. 1, pp. 407–11, describes the terrain well. Oppermann's report to Barclay is dated 10 Aug 1811 (OS): *MVUA 1812*, 4, no. 56, pp. 207–9.

52 The two key works on the Pfühl plan in particular and Russian planning in general are V. M. Bezotosnyi, *Razvedka i plany storon v 1812 godu*, Moscow, 2005, pp. 85–108, and V. V. Pugachev, 'K voprosu o pervonachal'nom plane voiny 1812 goda', in *K stopiati-desiatiletiiu otechestvennoi voiny*, Moscow, 1962, pp. 31–46. I owe a great deal to both works.

53 'Analiticheskii proekt voennykh deistvii v 1812 P. A. Chuikevicha', in *Rossiiskii arkhiv*, 7, 1996, pp. 41–57.

54 Josselson, *Commander*, pp. 41–2; *Correspondance de l'Empereur Alexandre*, no. 73, Alexander to Catherine, 18 Sept. 1812 (OS), pp. 86–93; Comte de Rochechouart, *Souvenirs de la Révolution, l'Empire et la Restauration*, Paris, 1889, pp. 167–8. Rostopchin's letter is quoted in A. G. Tartakovskii, *Nerazgadannyi Barklai*, Moscow, 1996, p. 73.

55 F. von Schubert, *Unter dem Doppeladler*, Stuttgart, 1962, pp. 212–13: 'Russia would have been irretrievably lost'. *Metternich: The Autobiography 1773–1815*, London, 2004,

p. 153. *MVUA 1812*, 7, *prilozheniia*, no. 21, 'Plan voennykh deistvii', Johann Barclay de Tolly, 1811, pp. 217–42, at p. 218.

56 It is impossible to cite all this correspondence: see e.g. a typical letter from Lieutenant-General Baggohufvudt to Barclay, dated 9 Feb. 1812 (OS): *MVUA 1812*, 9, no. 50, p. 128.

57 Most of these retreats are too famous to require references, but see C. Esdaile, *The Peninsular War*, London, 2002, p. 412, for the impact on British discipline of the retreat from Burgos ('many units went to pieces'). The quote comes from Gordon Corrigan, *Wellington: A Military Life*, London, 2001, p. 227. For Bagration, see his letter to Alexander of 6 June 1812 (OS): *MVUA 1812*, 13, no. 57, pp. 48–50.

58 See e.g. the comments by the historian of the Iamburg Lancer Regiment: Lieutenant Krestovskii, *Istoriia . . . Iamburgskago . . . polka*, pp. 102–3. The English-speaking reader will get some sense of Suvorov's 'doctrine' from P. Longworth, *The Art of Victory*, London, 1965. Christopher Duffy, *Russia's Military Way to the West*, London, 1981, is a very good introduction to the eighteenth-century Russian army's history, including the evolution of its 'doctrine'.

59 *MVUA 1812*, 1/2, no. 60, Diebitsch to Barclay, 9 May 1810 (OS), pp. 87–91; the anonymous report is not dated but clearly originates from the winter of 1811–12: see *MVUA 1812*, 7, no. 13, pp. 175–83.

60 C. F. Adams (ed.), *John Quincy Adams in Russia*, New York, 1970, p. 426. Longinov's letter to S. R. Vorontsov is dated 28 July 1812 (OS): *RA*, 4, 1912, pp. 481–547, at p. 490.

61 *MVUA 1812*, 16, no. 2, Alexander to Barclay, 7 April 1812 (OS), pp. 180–81, on the significance of the alliance and the impossibility now of a pre-emptive strike; 13, no. 190, Arenschildt to Münster, 22 May (3 June) 1812, pp. 189–94.

62 *MVUA 1812*, 12, no. 260, Memorandum by Volkonsky, 29 April 1812 (OS), pp. 324–33.

63 *MVUA 1812*, 13, no. 65, Barclay to Bagration, 6 June 1812 (OS), p. 56.

64 *MVUA 1812*, 13, no. 94, pp. 96–7, and no. 103, pp. 107–9: Bagration to Barclay.

65 *MVUA 1812*, 13, no. 57, Bagration to Alexander, 6 June 1812 (OS), pp. 48–50.

Chapter 5: The Retreat

1 Statistics from S. V. Shvedov, 'Komplektovanie, chislennost' i poteri russkoi armii v 1812 godu', in *K 175-letiiu Otechestvennoi voiny 1812 g.*, Moscow, 1987, p. 125.

2 See Appendix 1. The table is drawn from *MVUA 1812*, 17, pp. 51–4.

3 See e.g. Paulucci's letter to Alexander of 14 July 1812 (OS) in *MVUA 1812*, 14, no. 130, pp. 128–9.

4 For biographical information on Toll, see D. N. Shilov, *Gosudarstvennye deiateli Rossiiskoi imperii*, SPB, 2001, pp. 671–4. The comments are drawn from N. Murav'ev, 'Zapiski Nikolaia Nikolaevicha Muraveva', *RA*, 3, 1885, pp. 5–84, at p. 81.

5 P. Grabbe, *Iz pamiatnykh zapisok: Otechestvennaia voina*, Moscow, 1873, pp. 17–19, 60, 74–7.

6 Murav'ev, 'Zapiski', p. 53. P. Pototskii, *Istoriia gvardeiskoi artillerii*, SPB, 1896, pp. 155–6.

7 Ludwig von Wolzogen, *Mémoires d'un Général d'Infanterie au service de la Prusse et de la Russie (1792–1836)*, Paris, 2002, pp. 106, 115. V. von Löwenstern, *Mémoires du Général-Major Russe Baron de Löwenstern*, 2 vols., Paris, 1903, vol. 1, pp. 217, 247–8.

8 *SIM*, 5, nos. 1 and 2, Ermolov to Alexander, 1 and 10 Aug. 1812, pp. 411–17. V. Kharkevich (ed.), *1812 god v dnevnikakh, zapiskakh i vospominaniiakh sovremennikov*, 4 vols., Vilna, 1900–1907, vol. 1, p. 183 ('Iz zapisok Vistitskago').

9 S. N. Golubeva (ed.), *General Bagration: Sbornik dokumentov i materialov*, Moscow, 1945, no. 102, Ermolov to Bagration, 30 June 1812 (12 July NS), pp. 189–90. There is a vast literature on the Decembrists, much of which discusses Ermolov: see e.g. M. A. Davydov, *Oppozitsiia ego velichestva*, Moscow, 1994. For Alexander's comment:

'Zapiski Iakova Ivanovicha de Sanglena: 1776-1831 gg.', *RS*, 37, 1883, pp. 1-46, 539-56, at p. 551.

10 See, above all, R. I. Sementkovskii, *E. F. Kankrin: Ego zhizn' i gosudarstvennaia deiatel'nost'*, SPB, 1893.

11 *Correspondance de l'Empereur Alexandre*, no. 73, Alexander to Catherine, 18 Sept. 1812 (OS), pp. 86-93. For Alexander's key statement on the need to beware public opinion, see *VS*, 47/1, 1904, no. 19, Alexander to Barclay, 24 November 1812 (OS), pp. 231-3.

12 On Wittgenstein, see *MVUA 1812*, 13, no. 173, Barclay to Alexander, 18 June 1812 (OS), pp. 183-4; Baggohufvudt's letter is quoted in I. I. Shelengovskii, *Istoriia 69-go Riazanskago polka*, 3 vols., Lublin, 1911, vol. 2, p. 143.

13 *Mémoires du Général Bennigsen*, 3 vols., Paris, n.d., vol. 3, p. 77; see *Mémoires de Langeron, Général d'Infanterie dans l'Armée Russe: Campagnes de 1812, 1813, 1814*, Paris, 1902, e.g. p. 35, for the view that Bennigsen was Russia's best tactician.

14 On Barclay's frustrating efforts to create a mobile magazine, see e.g. V. P. Totfalushin, *M. V. Barklai de Tolli v otechestvennoi voine 1812 goda*, Saratov, 1991, pp. 29-31.

15 See Pushchin's diary: V. G. Bortnevskii (ed.), *Dnevnik Pavla Pushchina: 1812-1814*, Leningrad, 1987, pp. 46-7. Aleksei Nikitin, for instance, notes that most of the Polish Lancer Regiment deserted at Vitebsk: 'Vospominaniia Nikitina', in Kharkevich (ed.), *1812 god*, vol. 2, pp. 140-41. This may be an exaggeration.

16 M. M. Petrov, 'Rasskazy sluzhivshego v 1-m egerskom polku polkovnika Mikhaila Petrova o voennoi sluzhbe i zhizni svoei', in *1812 god: Vospominaniia voinov russkoi armii*, Moscow, 1991, pp. 112-355, at pp. 176-7.

17 N. E. Mitarevskii, *Rasskazy ob otechestvennoi voine 1812 goda*, Moscow, 1878, pp. 13-23. The story about the priests comes from the reminiscences of Ivan Liprandi, the quartermaster general of Sixth Corps: Kharkevich, *1812 god*, vol. 2, p. 5: 'Zamechaniia I. P. Liprandi'.

18 *MVUA 1812*, 13, no. 203, Uvarov to Alexander, 19 June 1812 (OS), pp. 206-7.

19 Armand de Caulaincourt, *At Napoleon's Side in Russia*, New York, 2003, p. 43. V. M. Bezotosnyi, *Razvedka i plany storon v 1812 godu*, Moscow, 2005, pp. 58-9, 100-101.

20 *Correspondance de Napoléon Ier*, 32 vols., Paris, 1858-70, vol. 24, no. 18925, Napoleon to Clarke, 8 July 1812, pp. 33-4.

21 On Orlov's mission, see e.g. the diary of Nikolai Durnovo for 21 and 22 June 1812 (OS), in A. G. Tartakovskii (ed.), *Voennye dnevniki*, Moscow, 1990, pp. 79-80.

22 Grabbe, *Iz pamiatnikh*, pp. 22-35.

23 *MVUA 1812*, 13, no. 296, Barclay to Alexander, 25 June 1812 (OS), pp. 302-3 and no. 323, 27 June 1812 (OS), pp. 331-3.

24 On the engineers, see I. G. Fabritsius, *Glavnoe inzhenernoe upravlenie*, SVM, 7, SPB, 1902, pp. 392-5.

25 See the discussion in Bezotosnyi, *Razvedka*, pp. 112-13, where it is argued that the so-called Pfühl plan was a cunning ploy on Alexander's part to avoid responsibility for a policy of strategic withdrawal which he considered necessary but did not want to acknowledge.

26 Löwenstern, *Mémoires*, vol. 1, p. 208. *MVUA 1812*, 17, Alexander to Bagration, 5 July 1812 (OS), pp. 275-6. Shishkov reproduces the letter to Alexander in his memoirs and discusses the conversations between the three men: N. Kiselev and I. Iu. Samarin (eds.), *Zapiski, mneniia i perepiska Admirala A. S. Shishkova*, 2 vols., Berlin, 1870, vol. 1, pp. 141-8.

27 For Bagration's 'system', see e.g. his order of the day to his troops of 7 July 1812 and his earlier letter to Arakcheev: *General Bagration*, nos. 95, pp. 179-80, and 103, which is simply dated June 1812 and is on pp. 190-91. For his proposed diversion, see *MVUA 1812*, 13, no. 120, Bagration to Alexander, 26 June 1812, pp. 131-3.

28 I. Radozhitskii, *Pokhodnyia zapiski artillerista s 1812 po 1816 god*, 3 vols., Moscow, 1835, vol. 1, p. 67.

29 See e.g. Löwenstern, *Mémoires*, vol. 1, p. 209. In defence of Ostermann-Tolstoy, see I. I. Lazhechnikov, 'Neskol'ko zametok i vospominanii po povodu stat'i "Materialy dlia biografii A. P. Ermolova" ', *Russkii vestnik*, 31/6, 1864, pp. 783–819. On Ostermann-Tolstoy's appearance, see Serge Glinka, *Pis'ma russkogo ofitsera*, Moscow, 1987, p. 316.

30 On the Ingermanland Dragoons, see V. I. Genishta and A. T. Borisovich, *Istoriia 3-go dragunskago Ingermanlandskago polka 1704–1904*, SPB, 1904, pp. 172–5, and *prilozhenie 7*. One cannot be absolutely sure that all five promoted NCOs were not nobles but they were certainly not *junkers*, in other words officer cadets. See G. P. Meshetich, 'Istoricheskie zapiski voiny rossiian s frantsuzami i dvadtsat'iu plemenami 1812, 1813, 1814 i 1815 godov', in *Vospominaniia voinov russkoi armii: Iz Sobraniia otdela pis'mennykh istochnikov gosudarstvennogo istoricheskogo muzeia*, Moscow, 1991, pp. 39–102, at pp. 42–3.

31 Radozhitskii, *Pokhodnyia zapiski*, pp. 32–3.

32 Here as elsewhere in this chapter my narrative owes much to M. Bogdanovich, *Istoriia otechestvennoi voiny 1812 goda*, 3 vols., SPB, 1859–60, supported in all moments of uncertainty by *Entsiklopediia*. On the decision to retreat from Vitebsk, see e.g. Barclay's explanation to Alexander of 22 July 1812 (OS), *MVUA 1812*, 14, no. 196, pp. 195–6.

33 See e.g. Barclay's letter to Alexander of 15 July 1812 (OS) in *MVUA 1812*, 14, no. 136, pp. 136–7. On Peter Pahlen, see M. Bogdanovich, 'Graf Petr Petrovich fon der Palen i ego vremia', *VS*, 7/8, 1864, pp. 410–25. General Gourgaud as usual defends Napoleon from these attacks but does so partly by blurring the timing of the Russian decision to retreat: Général Gourgaud, *Napoléon et la Grande Armée en Russie ou Examen critique de l'ouvrage de M. le Comte de Ségur*, Paris, 1826, pp. 132–6.

34 Duc de Fezensac, *Souvenirs militaires*, Paris, 1863, pp. 221–2; Philippe de Ségur, *History of the Expedition to Russia, 1812*, 2 vols., Stroud, 2005, vol. 1, p. 145.

35 'Zapiski Paskevicha', in Kharkevich (ed.), *1812 god*, vol. 1, pp. 82–119, at p. 96. 'Zhurnal uchastnika voiny 1812 goda', *VIS*, 1/3, 1913, pp. 155–72, at pp. 152–3.

36 *SIM*, 5, no. 1, 1 August 1812 (OS), Ermolov to Alexander, pp. 411–14.

37 *MVUA 1812*, 14, no. 257, Alexander to Barclay, 28 July 1812 (OS), pp. 263–4. N. Dubrovin (ed.), *Otechestvennaia voina v pis'makh sovremennikov*, Moscow, 2006, no. 60, Alexander to Barclay, 30 July 1812 (OS), pp. 68–9.

38 *MVUA 1812*, 16, no. 59, Barclay to Alexander, 9 Aug. 1812 (OS), pp. 47–8.

39 *MVUA 1812*, 16, no. 92, Barclay to Alexander, 16 Aug. 1812 (OS), pp. 76–7; 17, Barclay to Chichagov, 31 July 1812 (OS), pp. 167–8; Barclay to Kutuzov, 17 Aug. 1812 (OS), pp. 186–7.

40 Löwenstern, *Mémoires*, vol. 1, p. 220. Bogdanovich, *Istoriia . . . 1812 goda*, vol. 1, pp. 234–5.

41 *MVUA 1812*, 14, no. 277, Bagration to Barclay, 30 July 1812 (OS), pp. 280–81.

42 Golubeva (ed.), *General Bagration*, no. 129, Bagration to Arakcheev, 29 July 1812 (OS), p. 226.

43 e.g. Popov, *Istoriia 48-go pekhotnago Odesskago polka*, 2 vols., Moscow, 1911, vol. 1, pp. 7–26. D. V. Dushenkovich, 'Iz moikh vospominanii ot 1812 goda do 1815 goda', in *1812 god v vospominaniiakh sovremennikov*, Moscow, 1995, pp. 103–35.

44 Baron Fain, *Manuscrit de Mil Huit Cent Douze*, Paris, 1827, p. 359.

45 Dushenkovich, 'Iz moikh vospominanii', in *1812 god v vospominaniiakh*, p. 111.

46 'Zapiski Paskevicha', in Kharkevich (ed.), *1812 god*, vol. 1, pp. 99–103.

47 There is a good discussion of these issues in A. G. Tartakovskii, *Nerazgadannyi Barklai*, Moscow, 1996, pp. 103–8.

48 'Zamechaniia I. P. Liprandi na "Opisanie Otechestvennoi voiny 1812 goda" Mikhailovskago-Danilevskago', in Kharkevich (ed.), *1812 god*, vol. 2, pp. 1–35, at pp. 15–16. Dushenkovich, 'Iz moikh vospominanii', p. 111.

49 P. A. Geisman, *Svita Ego Imperatorskogo Velichestva po kvartirmeisterskoi chasti v tsarstvovanie Imperatora Aleksandra I*, SVM, 4/2/1, SPB, 1902, pp. 313–14. The best source on overburdening is the memoirs of Nikolai Muravev: 'Zapiski'.

50 Much the best sources on this action are Bogdanovich, *Istoriia ... 1812*, vol. 1, pp. 285–9, and Eugen, *Memoiren*, vol. 2, book 2, pp. 18–41.

51 F. von Schubert, *Unter dem Doppeladler*, Stuttgart, 1962, p. 97.

52 Kharkevich (ed.), *1812 god*, vol. 1, p. 13 ('Zapiski Shcherbinina') and pp. 219–24 ('Iz vospominanii grafa Orlova-Denisova'). *SIM*, 5, no. 2, Ermolov to Alexander, 10 Aug. 1812 (OS), pp. 414–17.

53 T. Lentz, *Nouvelle histoire du Premier Empire*, 3 vols., Paris, 2004–7, vol. 2, p. 324.

54 Schubert, *Doppeladler*, pp. 203–4.

Chapter 6: Borodino and the Fall of Moscow

1 The best source on Riga's defences is I. G. Fabritsius, *Glavnoe inzhenernoe upravlenie*, SVM, 7, SPB, 1902, pp. 355–9. As always, M. I. Bogdanovich, *Istoriia otechestvennoi voiny 1812 goda*, 3 vols., SPB, 1859–60 (here vol. 1, pp. 340–43) and the many relevant entries in *Entsiklopediia*, are also invaluable. See *VS*, 53/11, 1910, pp. 30–38 for the memoirs of General Emme, the commandant of the Riga fortress: these are interesting but perhaps a little unfair to General Essen.

2 I derive all troop strengths for 1812 from the relevant entries in *Entsiklopediia*, unless otherwise stated. For Wittgenstein's instructions, see *MVUA 1812*, 17, Barclay to Wittgenstein, 4 July 1812 (OS), pp. 134–5.

3 Bogdanovich, *Istoriia ... 1812*, vol. 1, pp. 351–2, makes the point about experience in the Finnish war but see too e.g. two regimental histories: Captain Geniev, *Istoriia Pskovskago pekhotnago general-fel'dmarshala kniazia Kutuzova-Smolenskago polka: 1730–1831*, Moscow, 1883, pp. 178–82; S. A. Gulevich, *Istoriia 8-go pekhotnago Estliandskago polka*, SPB, 1911, pp. 128–41. On morale in Wittgenstein's corps and the impact of victory, see V. Kharkevich (ed.), *1812 god v dnevnikakh, zapiskakh i vospominaniiakh sovremennikov*, 4 vols., Vilna, 1900–1907, 'Zapiski A. I. Antonovskago', vol. 3, pp. 72–3.

4 See e.g. comments by Mikhailovsky-Danilevsky, in A. G. Tartakovskii (ed.), *Voennye dnevniki*, Moscow, 1990, pp. 333, 345.

5 On d'Auvray, see e.g. F. von Schubert, *Unter dem Doppeladler*, Stuttgart, 1962, p. 58; on Sukhozhanet, see e.g., N. M. Zatvornitskii, *Pamiat' o chlenakh voennago soveta*, SVM, 3/4, SPB, 1906, pp. 141 ff.

6 On Diebitsch, see e.g. the comments of Aleksandr Chicherin: L. G. Beskrovnyi (ed.), *Dnevnik Aleksandra Chicherina, 1812–1813*, Moscow, 1966, p. 135. *Dnevnik Pavla Pushchina*, SPB, 1896, p. 111.

7 *Correspondance de Napoléon Ier*, 32 vols., Paris, 1858–70, vol. 24, no. 19100, Napoleon to Berthier, 19 Aug. 1812, pp. 158–9.

8 Marshal Gouvion Saint-Cyr, *Mémoires pour servir à l'histoire militaire sous le Directoire, le Consulat et l'Empire*, Paris, 1831, vol. 3, pp. 79–81; *MVUA 1812*, 17, Wittgenstein to Alexander, 6 Aug. 1812 (OS), pp. 284–5.

9 Gulevich, *Istoriia ... Estliandskago polka*, pp. 137–41.

10 Saint-Cyr, *Mémoires*, vol. 3, p. 87.

11 *MVUA 1812*, 17, no. 32, p. 295: Wittgenstein to Alexander: the letter is dated 25 Aug. (OS) but it seems clear that these reports to the emperor are dated by when Alexander received them rather than when they were written. The sum of 14 million comes from Bogdanovich, *Istoriia ... 1812 goda*, vol. 2, p. 72. The figure for the 1811 budget comes from F. P. Shelekhov, *Glavnoe intendantskoe upravlenie*, SVM, 5/1, SPB, 1903, p. 373. The slight vagueness as regards the number of provinces is caused by complications in defining the word province in the Russia of 1812. Some border districts and Asiatic regions were not called provinces.

12 See e.g. the comments of Major-General Prince Vasili Viazemsky, who commanded a brigade in Tormasov's army: Tartakovskii (ed.), *Voennye dnevniki*, pp. 199–215.

13 Langeron calls this army 'one of the best in Europe'. As deputy commander of this force his view is biased but it was to be proved by the Army of the Danube's performance.

Mémoires de Langeron, Général d'Infanterie dans l'Armée Russe: Campagnes de 1812, 1813, 1814, Paris, 1902, p. 7.

14 *VPR*, 6, no. 164, Russo-Turkish peace treaty, pp. 406–17.

15 The two key letters from Alexander to Chichagov were written on 6 and 22 July (OS): *VIS*, 2/3, 1912, pp. 201–6.

16 *MVUA 1812*, 16, Alexander to Barclay, 7 April 1812 (OS), pp. 181–2.

17 The instructions are *VPR*, 6, no. 145, 21 April 1812, pp. 363–5.

18 *VPR*, 6, no. 197, Rumiantsev to Alexander, 5/17 July 1812, pp. 486–90.

19 *MVUA 1812*, 13, no. 321, Tuyll to Barclay, 26 June/8 July 1812, pp. 329–30. *VIS*, 2/3, 1912, Alexander to Chichagov, 13 June 1812 (OS), pp. 196–8. On Austrian promises, see in particular Francis II's conversation with Stackelberg: *VPR*, 6, no. 158, Stackelberg to Rumiantsev, 29 April/11 May 1812, pp. 393–6.

20 For march-routes and times, see *MVUA 1812*, vol. 17, pp. 197–8.

21 V. von Löwenstern, *Mémoires du Général-Major Russe Baron de Löwenstern*, 2 vols., Paris, 1903, vol. 1, p. 250. *VS*, 47/1, 1904, no. 19, Alexander to Barclay, 24 Nov. 1812 (OS), pp. 231–6.

22 S. Panchulidzev, *Istoriia kavalergardov*, SPB, 1903, vol. 3, p. 180.

23 N. M. Konshin, 'Zapiski o 1812 gode', *IV*, 8, 1884, pp. 263–86, at pp. 281–2. A. M. Valkovich and A. P. Kapitonov (eds.), *Borodino: Dokumental'naia khronika*, Moscow, 2004, no. 27, Kutuzov to Alexander, 19 Aug. 1812 (OS), pp. 24–5. *Kutuzov*, vol. 4i, Moscow, 1954, no. 125, Kutuzov to E. I. Kutuzova, 19 August 1812 (OS), p. 108.

24 Langeron, *Mémoires*, p. 28. Many wounded were actually abandoned at Mozhaisk but this was exceptional.

25 Carl von Clausewitz, *The Campaign of 1812 in Russia*, London, 1992, pp. 175–6.

26 Antoine de Jomini, *The Art of War*, London, 1992, pp. 64–5, 230, 233–8.

27 Eugen, *Memoiren*, vol. 2, pp. 70–72.

28 F. Glinka, *Pis'ma russkogo ofitsera*, Moscow, 1987, p. 293.

29 See the comments by Konovnitsyn and General Kreutz (who commanded some of the rearguard's cavalry) in Kharkevich (ed.), *1812 god*, vol. 2, pp. 70–72, 124–5; also Mikhailovsky-Danilevsky's reminiscences about Konovnitsyn in Tartakovskii (ed.), *Voennye dnevniki*, pp. 313–16. Bogdanovich, *Istoriia . . . 1812*, vol. 2, pp. 129–36.

30 Ivan Radozhitskii, *Pokhodnyia zapiski artillerista s 1812 po 1816 god*, 3 vols., Moscow, 1835, vol. 1, pp. 131–2.

31 For the record of this committee, see *Kutuzov*, vol. 4i, no. 82, pp. 71–3. For the issues behind the choice, see A. G. Tartakovskii, *Nerazgadannyi Barklai*, Moscow, 1996, pp. 130–37. A. A. Podmazo, 'K voprosu o edinom glavnokomanduiushchem v 1812 godu', in *Otechestvennaia voina 1812 goda: Istochniki, pamiatniki, problemy. Materialy X vserossiiskoi nauchnoi konferentsii. Borodino, 3–5 sentiabria 2001 g.*, Moscow, 2002, pp. 140–46.

32 *Dnevnik Pavla Pushchina*, 19 Aug. 1812 (OS), p. 59. *Correspondance de l'Empereur Alexandre*, nos. 70 and 73, Alexander to Catherine, 8 Aug. and 18 Sept. (OS), pp. 81–2, 86–93.

33 The literature on Kutuzov is immense. Probably the best summary is by N. A. Troitskii, *Fel'dmarshal Kutuzov: Mify i fakty*, Moscow, 2002.

34 On relations among the leading generals, see above all V. Bezotosnyi, 'Bor'ba general'skikh gruppirovok', in *Epokha 1812 goda: issledovaniia, istochniki, istoriografiia*, TGIM, Moscow, 2002, vol. 1, but also Lidiia Ivchenko, *Borodino: Legenda i deistvitel'nost'*, Moscow, 2002, pp. 6–18.

35 In addition to the sources listed in the previous note, see *Mémoires du Général Bennigsen*, 3 vols., Paris, n.d., vol. 3, pp. 77–84. On one dispute, concerning the design of the Raevsky Battery, see I. P. Liprandi, *Materialy dlia otechestvennoi voiny 1812 goda: Sobranie statei*, SPB, 1867, 176–8.

36 Clausewitz, *Campaign*, p. 148.

37 The secondary literature on Borodino is vast: English-language readers should start with A. Mikaberidze, *The Battle of Borodino*, Barnsley, 2007, which provides a clear and fair

interpretation, above all from the Russian perspective. Duffy, *Borodino*, remains a good, brief introduction. As almost always, the place to start in the case of Russian-language work is the entry in *Entsiklopediia* (in this case 'Borodinskoe srazhenie', pp. 80–92), which gives a good summary of the best contemporary Russian interpretation of the battle. The Russian literature on military operations in 1812 is immense, detailed and often very good. An example of this is the three long articles which A. A. Smirnov devotes to the battle at Shevardino on 5 September: these cover tsarist, Soviet and post-Soviet historiography respectively. See *Epokha 1812 goda: Issledovaniia, istochniki, istoriografiia*, TGIM, Moscow, vol. 3, 2004, pp. 320–51; vol. 4, 2005, pp. 239–71; vol. 5, 2006, pp. 353–68: 'Chto zhe takoi Shevardinskii redut?'

38 There is a good description of this deployment and its implications in the memoirs of a young staff officer in Fifth Corps, Nikolai Muravev: see 'Zapiski Nikolaia Nikolaevicha Murav'eva', *RA*, 3, 1885, pp. 225–62, at p. 250. For a discussion of casualties caused by artillery fire, see: A. A. Smirnov, 'Somnitel'nye vystrely', in *Problemy izucheniia istorii otechestvennoi voiny 1812 goda*, Saratov, 2002, pp. 150–4.

39 Mark Adkin, *The Waterloo Companion*, London, 2001, pp. 120–21, 284–301.

40 The distances are from *Entsiklopediia*, pp. 80–83. Barclay's report to Kutuzov is in Valkovich and Kapitonov (eds.), *Borodino: Dokumental'naia khronika*, no. 331, 26 Sept. 1812 (OS), pp. 249–51. In his excellent book *Tactics and the Experience of Battle in the Age of Napoleon*, London, 1998, Rory Muir states on p. 15 that the Russians had 36,000 men per mile in comparison to 24,000 in Wellington's army. These calculations are always difficult to make but I suspect that if one looked at where the Russian army actually fought rather than where it was initially deployed the figure would be even higher.

41 For example, Barclay through Löwenstern urged the commander of the Guards cavalry to try to keep his men, the army's ultimate elite reserve, under cover. General Shevich responded that there was no cover to be found. Löwenstern, *Mémoires*, vol. 1, p. 264. Grabbe, for example, writes that Ermolov told him to order the troops covering the Raevsky Redoubt to lie down in order to reduce the impact of artillery fire but that they refused to do so: P. Grabbe, *Iz pamiatnykh zapisok: Otechestvennaia voina*, Moscow, 1873, p. 77.

42 The best description from the Russian viewpoint is the official history of the Russian corps of military engineers in this period: Fabritsius, *Glavnoe inzhenernoe upravlenie*, pp. 760–65, covers Borodino but needs to be read in the context of other sections on sieges in 1812 and on the structure and tasks of the corps of military engineers at that time. Bogdanovich has a sensible description of the fortifications, which he describes as 'very weak' in *Istoriia ... 1812*, vol. 2, pp. 142–3. Inevitably the English-language secondary literature usually just repeats established myths of French origin. Thus the recently published *Fighting Techniques of the Napoleonic Age*, London, 2008 (edited by Robert Bruce *et al.*), writes of 'the daunting defences of the ... massive Russian redoubt': p. 113.

43 Bogdanov's memoirs are reproduced in *Borodino v vospominaniiakh sovremennikov*, SPB, 2001, pp. 169–71.

44 Fabritsius, *Glavnoe inzhenernoe upravlenie*, pp. 762–4. Clausewitz, *Campaign*, p. 151.

45 Liprandi, *Materialy*, pp. 177–80.

46 Mikaberidze, *Borodino*, pp. 75–6, handles these issues well. Even young (and at this point retired) Lieutenant Glinka records seeing from Borodino bell-tower how Napoleon's troops massed on the left towards the evening of 6 September and recalls 'the general opinion' of Russian officers he met that day that Napoleon would attack the Russian left: *Pis'ma*, pp. 18, 299.

47 Löwenstern, *Mémoires*, vol. 1, pp. 261–2.

48 Mikaberidze, *Borodino*, pp. 49–53, discusses numbers and provides a table showing the many differing estimates by historians and contemporaries.

49 On Miloradovich's reinforcements, see his report to Alexander of 18 Aug. 1812 (OS), in Valkovich and Kapitonov (eds.), *Borodino: Dokumental'naia khronika*, pp. 21–2.

50 Philippe de Ségur, *History of the Expedition to Russia, 1812*, 2 vols., Stroud, 2005, vol. 1, p. 255.

51 *Correspondance de Napoléon Ier*, vol. 24, no. 19182, p. 207.

52 Ségur, *History*, vol. 1, pp. 251–2. On this occasion General Gourgaud, *Napoléon et la Grande Armée en Russie ou Examen critique de l'ouvrage de M. le Comte de Ségur*, Paris, 1826, pp. 213–15, is wholly correct in his defence of Napoleon's decision.

53 The official report of the regiment's commander, Karl Bistrom, rather confuses the reader by its details, as does the regiment's official history: Valkovich and Kapitonov (eds.), *Borodino: Dokumental'naia khronika*, no. 293, Bistrom to Lavrov, 31 Aug. 1812 (OS), pp. 168–70; *Istoriia leib-gvardii egerskago polka za sto let 1796–1896*, SPB, 1896, pp. 84–6. On Barclay, see Grabbe, *Iz pamiatnykh*, p. 74. For rumours, see e.g. Tartakovskii (ed.), *Voennye dnevniki*, p. 107, diary of Ivan Durnovo.

54 Complete casualty figures for other ranks are provided in the *prilozhenie* (appendix) 4 of Valkovich and Kapitonov (eds.), *Borodino: Dokumental'naia khronika*, pp. 332–54. On the French artillery, see A. P. Larionov, 'Izpol'zovanie artillerii v Borodinskom srazhenii', in *K stopiatidesiatiletiiu otechestvennoi voiny*, Moscow, 1962, pp. 116–31 at p. 127.

55 Jomini, *Art of War*, pp. 202–3.

56 T. von Bernhardi, *Denkwürdigkeiten aus dem Leben des kaiserlichen russischen Generals der Infanterie Carl Friedrich Grafen von Toll*, 5 vols., Leipzig, 1858, vol. 4, p. 74.

57 I. Ul'ianov, *1812: Russkaia pekhota v boiu*, Moscow, 2008, pp. 164–5.

58 On Kutaisov, see A. A. Smirnov, *General Aleksandr Kutaisov*, Moscow, 2002.

59 Thanks to their translator and editor, Alexander Mikaberidze, Ermolov's memoirs are now available in English: *The Czar's General*, Welwyn Garden City, 2007. His account of this episode is on pp. 159–61. Löwenstern's account is in *Mémoires*, vol. 1, pp. 257–9.

60 On the deployment of artillery at Borodino, see Larionov, 'Izpol'zovanie', *passim*. P. Pototskii, *Istoriia gvardeiskoi artillerii*, SPB, 1896, pp. 181–2, explains these failings by Kutaisov's death. For Liprandi's views, see Kharkevich (ed.), *1812 god*, vol. 2, 'Zamechaniia I. P. Liprandi', pp. 28–9.

61 For Paskevich's account, see I. F. Paskevich, 'Pokhodnyia zapiski', in *1812 god v vospominaniiakh sovremennikov*, Moscow, 1995, pp. 72–105, at pp. 102–3.

62 Pototskii, *Istoriia*, p. 178, for Norov's comment. Kharkevich (ed.), *1812 god*, vol. 2, pp. 176–84, for the excellent memoirs of Lieutenant-Colonel Vasilii Timofeev of the Izmailovskys. For the Finland Regiment, see S. Gulevich, *Istoriia leib gvardii Finliandskago polka 1806–1906*, SPB, 1906, pp. 204–20. For the Lithuania Regiment, see N. S. Pestreikov, *Istoriia leib-gvardii Moskovskago polka*, SPB, 1903, vol. 1, pp. 59–83.

63 Eugen, *Memoiren*, vol. 2, pp. 110–11; Bogdanovich, *Istoriia ... 1812 goda*, vol. 2, pp. 219, 226.

64 Together the Preobrazhenskys and Semenovskys lost fewer than 300 men on 7 Sept.: Valkovich and Kapitonov (eds.), *Borodino: Dokumental'naia khronika*, p. 342.

65 D. Chandler, *The Campaigns of Napoleon*, London, 1993, p. 807, writes that Napoleon's decision was probably correct.

66 The most recent analysis of the second attack on the redoubt is by V. N. Zentsov, 'Borodinskoe srazhenie: Padenie "bol'shogo reduta"', in *Borodinskoe pole: Istoriia, kul'tura, ekologiia*, Moscow, 2000, pp. 31–55.

67 'Zhurnal uchastnika voiny 1812 goda', *VIS*, 3/2, 1913, pp. 163–4.

68 Radozhitskii, *Pokhodnyia zapiski*, vol. 1, p. 168.

69 Valkovich and Kapitonov (eds.), *Borodino: Dokumental'naia khronika*, pp. 332–5. Mikaberidze, *Borodino*, p. 209.

70 V. M. Bezotosnyi, *Donskoi generalitet i ataman Platov v 1812 godu*, Moscow, 1999, pp. 33–4, 62–4, 75–83. The memoirs of Fedor Akinfov, Miloradovich's aide-de-camp, are very useful for this period: 'Iz vospominanii Akinfova', in Kharkevich (ed.), *1812 god*, vol. 2, pp. 205–12.

71 Countess Edling's memoirs in A. Libermann (ed.), *Derzhavnyi sfinks*, Moscow, 1999,

p. 177, for Kutuzov's words to Alexander. *Kutuzov*, vol. 4i, no. 105, Kutuzov to Rostopchin, 17 August 1812 (OS), pp. 90–91.

72 As usual, the best summary account of the council of war is in *Entsiklopediia*, pp. 666–7. Mikaberidze's translation of Ermolov's memoirs gives a strong sense of the game played between him and Kutuzov over responsibility for Moscow's abandonment: *The Czar's General*, pp. 168–72. Bennigsen's letter to Alexander of 19 Jan. 1813 (OS) in *VS*, 1, 1903, pp. 235–8, puts his side of the argument.

73 S. I. Maevskii, 'Moi vek ili istoriia generala Maevskago, 1779–1848', *RS*, 8, 1873, pp. 135–67, at p. 143.

74 'Iz vospominanii Akinfova', in Kharkevich (ed.), *1812 god*, vol. 1, pp. 205–12. Maevskii, 'Moi vek', pp. 143–4.

75 The most up-to-date surveys are, as usual, in *Entsiklopediia*: see especially the pieces on Moscow (pp. 476–9) and the fire (pp. 482–4). For the figure on private property destroyed, see Bogdanovich, *Istoriia . . . 1812 goda*, vol. 3, p. 28. For the evacuation of the wounded, see Mikhailovskii-Danilevskii, *Memuary 1814–1815*, SPB, 2001, p. 189, for a subsequent conversation with Wylie. Also S. Gavrilov, *Organizatsiia i snabzheniia russkoi armii nakanune i v khode otechestvennoi voiny 1812 g. i zagranichnykh pokhodov 1813–1815 gg.: Istoricheskie aspekty*, SPB, 2003, pp. 143–4.

76 On the barges, see the records of the post-war inquiry in *Kutuzov*, vol. 4ii, *prilozhenie* no. 20, pp. 717–18.

77 As always, A. I. Popov, *Velikaia armiia v Rossii: Pogonia za mirazhom*, Samara, 2002, pp. 178 ff., has an excellent discussion of these issues.

78 V. N. Speranskii, *Voenno-ekonomicheskaia podgotovka Rossii k bor'be s Napoleonom v 1812–1814 godakh*, candidate's dissertation, Gorky, 1967, pp. 386–8. *Kutuzov*, vol. 4i, no. 294, Kutuzov to Voronov, 7 Sept. 1812 (OS), p. 250.

Chapter 7: The Home Front in 1812

1 P. A. Chuikevich, 'Analiticheskii proekt voennykh deistvii v 1812. P. A. Chuikevicha', *Rossiiskii Arkhiv*, 7, 1996, p. 46. S. N. Golubeva (ed.), *General Bagration: Sbornik dokumentov i materialov*, Moscow, 1945, no. 57, 'Plan kampanii 1812 goda, predstavlennyi P. I. Bagrationom Aleksandru I', pp. 130–38. Janet Hartley provides a very useful survey of Russian society's resistance to Napoleon in 'Russia and Napoleon: State, Society and the Nation', in M. Rowe (ed.), *Collaboration and Resistance in Napoleonic Europe*, Basingstoke, 2003, pp. 186–202.

2 N. Shil'der, *Imperator Aleksandr Pervyi: Ego zhizn' i tsarstvovanie*, 4 vols., SPB, 1897, vol. 3, pp. 100–103.

3 *MVUA 1812*, 17, Barclay to Asch, 21 July 1812 (OS), pp. 157–8.

4 L. G. Beskrovnyi (ed.), *Narodnoe opolchenie v otechestvennoi voine 1812 goda: Sbornik dokumentov*, Moscow, 1962, no. 2, 6 July 1812 (OS), pp. 14–15.

5 The statistics come from Beskrovnyi (ed.), *Narodnoe opolchenie*, no. 205, pp. 218–19: these are the final reports of Lieutenant-General Tyrtov, the commander of the Tver militia. C. F. Adams (ed.), *John Quincy Adams in Russia*, New York, 1970, p. 452.

6 The outstanding work on Russian popular (and other) resistance to Napoleon is A. I. Popov, *Velikaia armiia v Rossii: Pogonia za mirazhom*, Samara, 2002. Popov also contributed many excellent articles, on 'People's War', peasant disturbances, partisans and adjacent topics, to *Entsiklopediia*. There are parallels here with Spain, where Charles Esdaile shows that many of the guerrillas were regular cavalrymen. The Russian case was much more clear-cut, however, as one would expect. Unlike in Spain, the Russian state had not collapsed. See Charles Esdaile, *Fighting Napoleon: Guerrillas, Bandits and Adventurers in Spain 1808–14*, London, 2004.

7 Beskrovnyi, *Narodnoe opolchenie*, no. 140, Kutuzov to Alexander, 23 Oct. 1812 (OS), pp. 155–6; see e.g. no. 89, pp. 113–17, and no. 121, p. 142, for descriptions of individual actions.

8 Popov, *Velikaia armiia*, pp. 185–229. A. G. Tartakovskii (ed.), *Voennye dnevniki*, Moscow, 1990, diary of Prince D. M. Volkonsky, p. 146. For an older but still useful view of peasant disturbances, see V. I. Semevskii, 'Volneniia krest'ian v 1812 gi. sviazannyia s otechestvennoi voinoi', in A. K. Dzhivelegov, S. P. Melgunov and P. I. Pichet (eds.), *Otechestvennaia voina i russkoe obshchestvo*, 7 vols., Moscow, 1911, vol. 5, pp. 74–113.

9 See the many interesting documents in RGVIA, Fond 1, Opis 1ii, Delo 2584: 'O vozmushcheniiakh krest'ian i ob usilenii sredstv k poimke beglykh rekrut, dezertirov i kazakov': fos. 41–2: d'Auvray to Gorchakov, 1 Nov. 1812 (OS), describes the rout of the dragoons, and fo. 35: Wittgenstein to Gorchakov, 6 Nov. 1812 (OS), explains why military operations have to come first.

10 *SIM*, 2, no. 312, Alexander to Gorchakov, 9 Nov. 1812 (OS), pp. 171–2.

11 There is an immense literature on Moscow in 1812 with many interesting materials contained, for example, in the multi-volume series compiled by P. I. Shchukin: *Bumagi otnosiashchiiasia do otechestvennoi voiny 1812 goda*, Moscow, 1897–1908. N. Dubrovin (ed.), *Otechestvennaia voina v pis'makh sovremennikov*, Moscow, 2006, contains a number of Rostopchin's letters to Balashev: see in particular nos. 55 and 62, 23 July and 30 July 1812 (OS), pp. 60–63, 70–71. English-speaking readers need to look no further than an excellent article by Alexander Martin, 'The Response of the Population of Moscow to the Napoleonic Occupation of 1812', in Eric Lohr and Marshall Poe (eds.), *The Military and Society in Russia, 1450–1917*, Leiden, 2002, pp. 469–89.

12 Dubrovin, *Otechestvennaia voina*, no. 47, 15 July 1812 (OS), pp. 54–6. Shil'der, *Imperator Aleksandr*, vol. 3, p. 90. L. V. Mel'nikova, *Armiia i pravoslavnaia tserkov' Rossiiskoi imperii v epokhu Napoleonovskikh voin*, Moscow, 2007, pp. 57–90, 100–115.

13 *PSZ*, 22, 16187, 21 April 1785 (OS), p. 348.

14 Compare for example the language of Alexander's decree to Governor Suponev of Vladimir with Suponev's own subsequent reference to the emperor's 'commands': RGVIA, Fond 125, Opis 1, Delo 16, fos. 21, 23–8: Suponev to Lobanov-Rostovsky, 11 June 1812 (OS), and Alexander to Suponev, 13 May 1812 (OS). As regards service in the militia and its evasion, see e.g. N. F. Khovanskii, *Uchastie Saratovskoi gubernii v otechestvennoi voine 1812 g.*, Saratov, 1912, pp. 41–64; I. I. Prokhodtsev, *Riazanskaia guberniia v 1812 godu*, Riazan, 1913, pp. 277–528.

15 See the memoirs of Countess Edling, reprinted in A. Libermann (ed.), *Derzhavnyi sfinks*, Moscow, 1999: 'Grafinia Roksandra Skarlatovna Edling: Zapiski', pp. 157–236, at pp. 174–5. On sabotaging the estate tax, see e.g. Prokhodtsev, *Riazanskaia*, pp. 8–21.

16 'V. V. Viazemskii: Zhurnal 1812 g.', in *Russkie dnevniki: 1812 god*, Moscow, 1990, pp. 185–225, at p. 211.

17 Khovanskii, *Uchastie*, pp. 31–3.

18 *Upravlenie General-Intendanta Kankrina: General'nyi sokrashchennyi otchet po armiiam . . . za pokhody protiv Frantsuzov, 1812, 1813 i 1814 godov*, Warsaw, 1815, pp. 11, 44. L. G. Beskrovnyi, *Otechestvennaia voina 1812 goda*, Moscow, 1962, pp. 245–7. S. Gavrilov, *Organizatsiia i snabzheniia russkoi armii nakanune i v khode otechestvennoi voiny 1812 g. i zagranichnykh pokhodov 1813–1815 gg.: Istoricheskie aspekty*, SPB, 2003, p. 121.

19 V. V. Tivanov, *Finansy russkoi armii*, Moscow, 1993, p. 79.

20 *PSZ*, 32, nos. 24975 and 25035, 27 Jan. and 13 March 1812 (OS), pp. 43–164 and 228–9. *Upravlenie General-Intendanta*, p. 134. *Kutuzov*, vol. 4i, no. 387, Kutuzov to Kaverin, 13 Sept. 1812 (OS), p. 305: the same letter went to the governors of Riazan, Orel, Tver and Tula.

21 The estimate is by Tivanov, *Finansy*, p. 66, but is based on the discussion in M. I. Bogdanovich, *Istoriia otechestvennoi voiny 1812 goda*, 3 vols., SPB, 1859–60, vol. 2, pp. 31–90.

22 The key documents for Kleinmichel's operation are in *SIM*, 1, no. 3, Alexander to Gorchakov, 27 June 1812 (OS), pp. 5–11; no. 9, Alexander to Kleinmichel, 27 June 1812 (OS), pp. 14–15; no. 21, Alexander to Kleinmichel, 6 July 1812 (OS), pp. 23–4. There is

a fine new book on the Russian marines which includes extensive coverage of the Napoleonic era: A. Kibovskii and O. Leonov, *300 let Rossiiskoi morskoi pekhoty*, Moscow, 2007.

23 RGVIA, Fond 125, Opis 1/188a, Delo 16, e.g. fos. 18–19, Suponev to Lobanov, 6 June 1812 (OS); fo. 21, Suponev to Lobanov, 11 June 1812 (OS); fos. 23–8, copies of Alexander's orders to Suponev, dated 13 May 1812 (OS). See Prokhodtsev, *Riazanskaia*, p. 168, for a list of these provinces.

24 RGVIA, Fond 125, Opis 1/188a, Delo 16, fos. 2–3, Pasynkov to Lobanov, 18 June 1812 (OS); fos. 90–91, Shter to Lobanov, 6 July 1812 (OS).

25 RGVIA, Fond 125, Opis 188a, Delo 16, fos. 6–7, Pasynkov to Lobanov, 23 July 1812 (OS); fos. 100–101, Shter to Lobanov, 18 July 1812 (OS).

26 RGVIA, Fond 125, Opis 1/188a, Delo 16, fos. 6–7, Pasynkov to Lobanov, 23 July 1812 (OS); fos. 284–5, Prince Grigorii Golitsyn to Lobanov, 9 July 1812 (OS). *RA*, 6, 1866, pp. 922–7: 'Avtobiograficheskie zametki Grafa Arakcheeva'.

27 Prokhodtsev, *Riazanskaia*, pp. 174–82, 210–22; *Entsiklopediia*, p. 297.

28 RGVIA, Fond 125, Opis 1/188a, Delo 16, fos. 92–3, Shter to Balashev, 24 June 1812 (OS); Delo 19, fos. 77–81, Urusov to Lobanov, 23 July 1812 (OS). Prokhodtsev, *Riazanskaia*, p. 188.

29 RGVIA, Fond 125, Opis 1/188a, Delo 16, fos. 29 and 32, Dolgorukov to Lobanov, 6 Aug. and 3 Sept. 1812 (OS).

30 RGVIA, Fond 125, Opis 1/188a, Delo 19, fos. 2–4, Gorchakov to Lobanov, 20 Aug. 1812 (OS); fos. 134–40, 'Spisok o vsekh shtab i ober ofitserakh postupivshikh na sluzhbu'.

31 *Kutuzov*, vol 4ii, Kutuzov to Alexander, 9 October 1812 (OS), pp. 62–3. Prokhodtsev, *Riazanskaia*, pp. 224–7. RGVIA, Fond 125, Opis 1/188a, Delo 16, fos. 100–101, Shter to Lobanov, 18 July 1812 (OS).

32 Beskrovnyi, *Narodnoe opolchenie*, no. 3, 18 July 1812 (OS), pp. 15–16, is the text of this manifesto.

33 The statistic comes from an article by V. I. Babkin, the leading Soviet-era expert on the militia: 'Organizatsiia i voennye deistviia narodnogo opolcheniia v otechestvennoi voine 1812 goda', in *K stopiatidesiatiletiiu otechestvennoi voiny*, Moscow, 1962, pp. 134–62, at p. 145.

34 Beskrovnyi, *Narodnoe opolchenie*, no. 117, pp. 137–9: regulations of the Kaluga militia committee, 25 July 1812 (OS).

35 Prokhodtsev, *Riazanskaia*, p. 228. A few of these men did receive new uniforms produced abroad: see Ch. 10. The minister added that even in wartime not all wool could be assigned for uniforms.

36 Beskrovnyi, *Narodnoe opolchenie*, no. 354, Tolstoy to Alexander, 28 Sept. 1812 (OS), p. 368.

37 Bogdanovich, *Istoriia . . . 1812 goda*, vol. 2, p. 56.

38 Apart from Babkin and Bezotosnyi, the fullest source on the militia is the many volumes compiled by V. R. Apukhtin for the centenary of 1812: see e.g. *Narodnaia voennaia sila: Dvorianskiia opolcheniia v otechestvennoi voine*, Moscow, 1912. Apukhtin is as determined to sing the nobles' glory as Babkin is to downplay their contribution. Prokhodtsev, *Riazanskaia*, pp. 229–621, is an immensely informative study of the Riazan militia.

39 Speranskii, *Voenno-ekonomicheskaia podgotovka*, pp. 381, 392, 407–23. *Kutuzov*, vol. 4i, no. 18: memorandum by Müller-Zakomel'sky, 10 July 1812 (OS), p. 20.

40 *SIM*, 1, no. 81, Alexander to Kutuzov, 24 Aug. 1812 (OS), pp. 64–5.

41 A. I. Ulianov, 'Tarutinskii lager: "neudobnye" fakty', in *Ot Tarutino do Maloiaroslavtsa: K 190-letiiu Maloiaroslavetskogo srazheniia*, Kaluga, 2002, pp. 23–36.

42 Radozhitskii, *Pokhodnyia zapiski*, vol. 1, p. 172. Viazemskii, 'Zhurnal', p. 215. *Correspondance de l'Empereur Alexandre*, nos. 33 and 37, Catherine to Alexander, 6 Sept. and 23 Sept. 1812 (OS), pp. 107–8, 119–22.

43 Meshetich, 'Istoricheskie zapiski', p. 50. L. G. Beskrovnyi (ed.), *Dnevnik Aleksandra Chicherina, 1812–1813*, Moscow, 1966, pp. 14–16.

44 On Tishchenko, see *MVUA 1812*, 19, pp. 335–6. *Istoriia leib-gvardii egerskago polka za sto let 1796–1896*, SPB, 1896, p. 88. V. Kharkevich (ed.), *1812 god v dnevnikakh, zapiskakh i vospominaniiakh sovremennikov*, 4 vols., Vilna, 1900–1907, vol. 2, p. 200: 'Opisanie srazhenii'.

45 *Dnevnik Chicherina*, pp. 18–19, 28. *Dnevnik Pavla Pushchina*, Leningrad, 1987, pp. 61–2.

46 'Edling', pp. 172–3, makes this point about mutual distrust.

47 E. F. Komarovskii, *Zapiski grafa E. F. Komarovskago*, SPB, 1914, p. 195. Shil'der, *Imperator Aleksandr*, vol. 3, pp. 88–90.

48 Shil'der, *Imperator Aleksandr*, pp. 90–92. 'Edling', pp. 174–5.

49 Sir Robert Wilson, *The French Invasion of Russia*, Bridgnorth, 1996, pp. 115–16.

50 Ibid., pp. 116–17.

51 Ibid.

52 'Edling', pp. 178–9.

53 *Correspondance de l'Empereur Alexandre*, nos. 33, 38, 39, Catherine to Alexander, 6, 23 and 28 Sept., 1812 (OS), pp. 83–4, 93–6 and 98–9; nos. 73 and 74, Alexander to Catherine, 18 and 24 Sept. 1812 (OS), pp. 86–93, 96–8.

54 Elizabeth to the Margravine of Baden, 7 and 9 Sept. 1812, in Grand Duke Nikolai Mikhailovich, *L'Impératrice Élisabeth, épouse d'Alexandre Ier*, 4 vols., SPB, 1908–9, vol. 2ii, pp. 443–5.

55 Quoted in F. Ley, *Alexandre Ier et sa Sainte-Alliance (1811–1825)*, Paris, 1975, pp. 49–55; 'Edling', pp. 176–9.

56 See Michaud's account of the conversation in Shil'der, *Imperator Aleksandr*, vol. 3, *prilozheniia*, document VII, pp. 509–10.

Chapter 8: The Advance from Moscow

1 *Kutuzov*, vol. 4i, no. 187, Kutuzov to Alexander, 27 Aug. 1812 (OS), pp. 154–5; no. 241, Alexander to Kutuzov, 31 Aug. 1812 (OS), pp. 194–5.

2 The plans were set out in Alexander's letter of 31 Aug. (OS) and also in the draft instructions to Chichagov, Tormasov, Wittgenstein and Steinhel which Chernyshev brought with him to Kutuzov's headquarters. For the latter see *prilozheniia* 6, 7, 8 and 9 in *Kutuzov*, vol. 4i, pp. 463–70.

3 *Kutuzov*, vol. 4i, no. 322, Chernyshev to Alexander, 10 Sept. 1812 (OS), pp. 265–8.

4 Chernyshev's own account of these actions is in RGVIA, Fond 846, Opis 16, Delo 3386, fos. 2ii–3ii: 'Zhurnal voennykh deistvii General Adiutanta Chernysheva'. *MVUA 1812*, 20, no. 1, Wittgenstein to Alexander, 6 Nov. 1812 (OS), p. 4.

5 Eugen, *Memoiren*, vol. 2, pp. 169, 173. A. Brett-James (ed.), *General Wilson's Journal 1812–1814*, London, 1964, p. 75.

6 A good translation of Davydov's memoirs was recently published in English: *In the Service of the Tsar against Napoleon: The Memoirs of Denis Davydov*, trans Prince G. Trubetskoy, London, 2006.

7 T. J. Binyon, *Pushkin: A Biography*, London, 2002, p. 130.

8 I. Radozhitskii, *Pokhodnyia zapiski artillerista s 1812 po 1816 god*, 3 vols., Moscow, 1835, vol. 1, pp. 205–6. On Figner, see an anonymous article entitled 'Uverennost' v zvezde svoego schastiia', *Rodina*, 8, 2002, pp. 47–50.

9 *MVUA 1812*, 18, no. 124, Davydov to Konovnitsyn, 21 Sept. 1812 (OS), p. 101.

10 P. Grabbe, *Iz pamiatnykh zapisok: Otechestvennaia voina*, Moscow, 1873, pp. 97–8; V. von Löwenstern, *Mémoires du Général-Major Russe Baron de Löwenstern*, 2 vols., Paris, 1903, vol. 1, p. 296.

11 S. G. Volkonskii, *Zapiski Sergeia Grigorovicha Volkonskogo (dekabrista)*, SPB, 1902, pp. 170–71, 189–94; Löwenstern, *Mémoires*, vol. 2, pp. 7, 182. *Kutuzov*, vol. 4ii, no. 163, Kutuzov to Alexander, 20 Oct. 1812 (OS), p. 175. For Arakcheev's efforts to reduce his own contributions, see his angry correspondence with Governor Sumarokov of

Novgorod in the summer and autumn of 1812 and his appeals for help to Balashev: P. I. Shchukin (ed.), *Bumagi otnosiashchiiasia do otechestvennoi voiny 1812 goda*, vol. 4, Moscow, 1899, pp. 118–27.

12 See, above all, G. Bibikov, 'Aleksandr Khristoforovich Benkendorf (1781–1844): Istoricheskii ocherk', *Vestnik MGU*, 1, 2007, pp. 36–60. Also an informative letter from Johann to Christoph Lieven, dated 5 Jan. 1811 (OS): BL Add. Mss 47410, p. 56.

13 *Zapiski Benkendorfa, 1812 god: Otechestvennaia voina. 1813 god. Osvobozhdenie Niderlandov*, Moscow, 2001, pp. 70–71.

14 All these statistics are drawn from *Kutuzov*, vol. 4i, no. 439, Kutuzov to Alexander, 22 Sept. 1812 (OS), pp. 353–61, and *prilozheniia*.

15 For example, on 22 September Kutuzov's order of the day warned that remounts would soon be arriving from many sources and told his regiments to prepare to collect them. One such source was Tula province, whose governor had been told by Kutuzov to purchase 500 horses and send 2,000 militia horses to the army's regular cavalry: *Kutuzov*, vol. 4i, nos. 287, 296, 320, pp. 246–7, 251, 264: the first two documents are letters of 6 and 7 Sept. (OS) to Governor Bogdanov, the third is an order of the day of 10 September.

16 Babkin, 'Organizatsiia', p 145. L. G. Beskrovnyi (ed.), *Narodnoe opolchenie v otechestvennoi voine 1812 goda: Sbornik dokumentov*, Moscow, 1962, nos. 452, 453, pp. 473–7. The first document is a report of 23 July (OS) from the Don region to Platov on the universal mobilization. The second is Platov's October report to Alexander I on the results of the mobilization. See also V. M. Bezotosnyi, *Donskoi generalitet i ataman Platov v 1812 godu*, Moscow, 1899, pp. 92–6.

17 Viscount de Puybusque, *Lettres sur la Guerre de Russie en 1812*, Paris, 1816, pp. 142–4.

18 For Kutuzov's comment, see A. I. Mikhailovskii-Danilevskii, *Opisanie otechestvennoi voiny v 1812 godu*, repr. Moscow, 2008, p. 384. *Kutuzov*, vol. 4i, no. 531, Alexander to Kutuzov, 2 Oct. 1812 (OS), pp. 431–2.

19 A. P. Ermolov, *The Czar's General*, ed. and trans. A. Mikaberidze, Welwyn Garden City, 2007, pp. 178–80, covers Tarutino and Ermolov's views on the command structure in the English translation of his memoirs. Prince Aleksandr Golitsyn, Kutuzov's aide-de-camp, describes his rage in *VS*, 53/12, 1910, pp. 21–35, at p. 29: 'Zapiska o voine 1812 goda A. B. Golitsyna'.

20 Barclay's letter to Alexander of 24 Sept. 1812 (OS) on this score is in *MVUA 1812*, 18, no. 148, pp. 118–22.

21 N. A. Troitskii, *Fel'dmarshal Kutuzov: Mify i fakty*, Moscow, 2002, quotes Raevsky on pp. 232–3.

22 By far the fullest recent account of the battle is by V. A. Bessonov, 'Tarutinskoe srazhenie', in *Epokha 1812 goda: Issledovaniia, istochniki, istoriografiia*, TGIM, Moscow, 2006, vol. 5, pp. 101–53.

23 Eugen, *Memoiren*, vol. 2, pp. 175–82, gives a graphic but fair account.

24 Bennigsen's view is best put in a letter to his wife of 10 Oct. 1812 (OS): no. 177, pp. 223–5 in N. Dubrovin (ed.), *Otechestvennaia voina v pis'makh sovremennikov*, Moscow, 2006. The casualty figures are from Bessonov, 'Tarutinskoe', pp. 142–3, though A. I. Ulianov cites higher ones in *Entsiklopediia*, p. 694. Kutuzov's report to Alexander on Tarutino is in *Kutuzov*, vol. 4ii, no. 16, Kutuzov to Alexander, 7 Oct. 1812 (OS), pp. 16–19.

25 P. de Ségur, *History of the Expedition to Russia, 1812*, 2 vols., Stroud, 2005, vol. 2, pp. 75–8, recalls some of Napoleon's thinking on the various possibilities. Napoleon himself spelled them out in a number of letters and memorandums written in Moscow in October 1812: see *Correspondance de Napoléon Ier*, 32 vols., Paris, 1858–70, vol. 24, especially no. 19237, notes, undated, pp. 235–8, but also his letters to Berthier of 5 and 6 Oct. and to Maret of 16 Oct.: nos. 19250, 19258, 19275, pp. 246–7, 252–4, 265–6.

26 Ségur, *History*, vol. 2, pp. 82–3; A. de Caulaincourt, *At Napoleon's Side in Russia*, New York, 2003, pp. 136–8; Duc de Fezensac, *Souvenirs militaires*, Paris, 1863, p. 258. Brett-James, *Wilson's Journal*, p. 80. On the astonishing level of plundering in the Italian

campaign, see Martin Boycott-Brown, *The Road to Rivoli*, London, 2001, pp. 287-8, 306, 335-6.

27 The key report from Dokhturov to Kutuzov, written at 9.30 p.m. on 22 October, is in *Kutuzov*, vol. 4ii, no. 59, pp. 75-6.

28 The best account of the battle is by A. Vasil'ev, *Srazhenie pri Maloiaroslavtse 12/24 oktiabria 1812 goda*, Maloiaroslavets, 2002; see p. 27 for the information on the 6th Jaegers. The entries on the battle and the monastery in *Entsiklopediia*, on pp. 437-9 and 472, are very useful too.

29 Kutuzov's account is in his report to Alexander of 16 Oct. 1812 (OS), which enclosed his army's journal of military operations: *Kutuzov*, vol. 4ii, no. 119, pp. 128-34.

30 Sir Robert Wilson, *The French Invasion of Russia*, Bridgnorth, 1996, p. 234.

31 His comment about England is cited by Troitskii, *Fel'dmarshal Kutuzov*, p. 278.

32 Many of Wilson's letters both to the emperor and to his compatriots are published in Dubrovin (ed.), *Otechestvennaia voina*. They were drawn from police files. Bennigsen's letter of 8 October (OS) asking Alexander to return to headquarters is published in *MVUA 1812*, 19, pp. 344-5.

33 N. Shil'der, *Imperator Aleksandr pervyi: Ego zhizn' i tsarstvovanie*, 4 vols., SPB, 1897, vol. 3, p. 124.

34 See e.g. Alexander's comments to Wilson in Vilna in December 1812 or the Grand Duchess Catherine's annoyance about Kutuzov's huge popularity and how unworthy of it he was: *Wilson's Journal*, p. 95. *Correspondance de l'Empereur Alexandre*, no. 46, Catherine to Alexander, 25 Nov. 1812 (OS), pp. 108-9.

35 *Kutuzov*, vol 4ii, no. 192, pp. 195-201, journal of military operations. *MVUA 1812*, 19, e.g. Ermolov to Kutuzov, 18 Oct. 1812 (OS), p. 73; Platov to Kutuzov, 20 Oct. 1812 (OS), p. 78.

36 P. B. Austen, *1812: Napoleon's Invasion of Russia*, London, 2000, p. 47.

37 F. Glinka, *Pis'ma russkogo ofitsera*, Moscow, 1987, p. 371.

38 S. V. Gavrilov, *Organizatsiia i snabzheniia russkoi armii nakanune i v khode otechestvennoi voiny 1812 g. i zagranichnykh pokhodov 1813-1815 gg.: Istoricheskie aspekty*, candidate's dissertation, SPB, 2003, p. 109, for the statistics quoted here.

39 *Kutuzov*, vol 4i, no. 536 and annex, Kutuzov to Lanskoy, 3 Oct. 1812 (OS), pp. 439-40. See also Gavrilov, *Organizatsiia*, pp. 158-9.

40 RGVIA, Fond 103, Opis 210/4, Sv. 1, Delo 1: fos. 1-2, Kutuzov's circular to twelve governors of 15 Sept. 1812 (OS); fos. 28-9, Lanskoy's report to Kutuzov of 9 Oct. (OS).

41 RGVIA, Fond 103, Opis 210/4, Sv. 1, Delo 1: fos. 38-9: Major-General Potulov to Bennigsen, 11 Oct. 1812 (OS); NB the letter was received on 16 Oct.; fos. 77-8, Lanskoy to Kutuzov, 11 Nov. (OS); fo. 97, Santi to Kutuzov, November but no day given; fos. 113-14, Lanskoy to Kutuzov, 11 Dec. (OS); fos. 126-7, Lanskoy to Kutuzov, 15 Dec. (OS); fos. 137-8, Lanskoy to Kutuzov, 23 Jan. 1813 (OS). On winter clothing, see e.g. *Kutuzov*, vol. 4i, no. 387, Kutuzov to Kaverin, 13 Sept. 1812 (OS), p. 305.

42 See e.g. Kutuzov's letters to Nikolai Bogdanov, the governor of Tula, of 19 and 24 Oct. (OS): *Kutuzov*, vol. 4ii, nos. 159 and 196, pp. 169-70 and 205-6.

43 *Kutuzov*, vol. 4ii, no. 195, pp. 203-4, 24 Oct. 1812 (OS): an Order of the Day. Mikhailovskii-Danilevskii, *Opisanie 1812*, p. 457, writes that 74 million rubles' worth of property was destroyed in Smolensk province in 1812. Gavrilov, *Organizatsiia*, p. 159.

44 Eugen, *Memoiren*, vol. 2, pp. 204-7. *Entsiklopediia*, p. 170, states that the Russians lost 1,800 men, the enemy 7,000. Radozhitskii, *Pokhodnyia zapiski*, vol. 1, pp. 250-51.

45 *Kutuzov*, vol. 4ii, *prilozhenie* 21, p. 719, has a table showing the temperature month-by-month in 1812 in various places with statistics indicating how much this diverged from the norm. Anyone using this table must remember that the months are according to the Russian calendar. R. M. Zotov, *Sochineniia*, Moscow, n.d., p. 611, on how winter came suddenly in 1812. It would be tedious to list all the Russian sources which criticize French excuses about the weather, but see e.g. V. Kharkevich (ed.), *1812 god v dnevnikakh, zapiskakh i vospominaniiakh sovremennikov*, 4 vols., Vilna, 1900-1907, vol. 1,

pp. 80–81, for General Kreutz's comments. Baron Fain, *Manuscrit de Mil Huit Cent Douze*, Paris, 1827, pp. 151–2.

46 Radozhitskii, *Pokhodnyia zapiski*, vol. 1, pp. 256–67.

47 Puybusque, *Lettres*, pp. 105–15: 7, 10, 12 Nov. 1812. Fezensac, *Souvenirs*, p. 276.

48 T. von Bernhardi, *Denkwürdigkeiten aus dem Leben des kaiserlichen russischen Generals der Infanterie Carl Friedrich Grafen von Toll*, 5 vols., Leipzig, 1858, vol. 4, p. 307.

49 Eugen, *Memoiren*, vol. 2, pp. 241–50. Löwenstern, *Mémoires*, vol. 1, p. 348.

50 Both M. I. Bogdanovich, *Istoriia otechestvennoi voiny 1812 goda*, 3 vols., SPB, 1859–60, vol. 3, pp. 101–46, and *Entsiklopediia*, pp. 379–80, give accurate and fair accounts. Eugen, *Memoiren*, vol. 2, pp. 268–70 explains Ney's escape from the Russian perspective.

51 *Dnevnik Pavla Pushchina*, Leningrad, 1987, pp. 71–2.

52 Eugen, *Memoiren*, vol. 2, p. 275.

53 Gavrilov, *Organizatsiia*, pp. 154–71. *Upravlenie General-Intendanta Kankrina: Generalnyi sokrashchennyi otchet po armiiam ... za pokhody Frantsuzov, 1812, 1813, 1814 godov*, Warsaw, 1815, p. 79. On the troops' exhausting marches down snow-bound side roads, see *Zapiski o pokhodakh 1812 i 1813 godov ot Tarutinskago srazheniia do Kul'mskago boia*, SPB, 1834, part 1, p. 40. The book is anonymous because its author, V. S. Norov, had been imprisoned after the Decembrist rising of 1825 and wrote it in custody.

54 There are interesting sidelights on this from Kutuzov's discussions with the captured Puybusque: *Lettres*, especially as recorded in his letters of 11 and 18 Dec. 1812 (OS), pp. 141 ff. Note too Kutuzov's earlier comments to Wilson and Bennigsen discussed in this chapter and his later conversations with Alexander and Shishkov which I will discuss in Ch. 9.

55 The letter is in a footnote on p. 282 of *Kutuzov*, vol. 4ii, no. 295.

56 Kutuzov's two letters to Chichagov are in *Kutuzov*, vol. 4ii, no. 295, 3 Nov. 1812 (OS), pp. 282–3, and no. 363, 10 Nov. 1812 (OS), pp. 344–5. His letter to Wittgenstein of 8–9 November is in the same volume, no. 349, pp. 334–5. His comment to Ermolov is cited by V. S. Norov who was an aide-de-camp and an officer of the Guards Jaegers, one of the Guards regiments entrusted to Ermolov. See Norov's *Zapiski*, p. 75. Ermolov quotes the first but not the second sentence in his memoirs and he was best placed to know exactly what Kutuzov said. Norov may have been embellishing his tale. But the words he ascribes to Kutuzov do sum up an attitude which comes across in many accounts, including Ermolov's: see A. P. Ermolov, *Zapiski A. P. Ermolova 1798–1826*, Moscow, 1991, pp. 243–6.

57 Carl von Clausewitz, *The Campaign of 1812 in Russia*, London, 1992, pp. 213–14.

58 The basic narrative here comes from Bogdanovich, *Istoriia ... 1812*, vol. 2, ch. XXXI, pp. 442 ff. and vol. 3, ch. XL, pp. 205 ff. See RGVIA, Fond 846, Opis 16, Delo 3419: 'Iskhodiashchii zhurnal Generala Sakena', fos. 4i–ii, Sacken to Kutuzov, 21 Feb. 1813 for his complaint that he and his men had sacrificed themselves for the common good without hope of personal recognition.

59 Bogdanovich, *Istoriia ... 1812*, vol. 3, pp. 206–35. A. G. Tartakovskii (ed.), *Voennye dnevniki*, Moscow, 1990, pp. 211–25, covers the advance to the Berezina.

60 Bogdanovich, *Istoriia ... 1812*, vol. 3, p. 236.

61 See Oertel's letter to Chichagov of 3 Nov. 1812 (OS): *MVUA 1812*, 21, pp. 115–17; Chichagov to Alexander, 17 Nov. 1812 (OS): *SIRIO*, 6, 1871, pp. 56–8.

62 *MVUA 1812*, 19, Wittgenstein to Alexander, 19 Oct. 1812 (OS), p. 265.

63 Marshal Gouvion Saint-Cyr, *Mémoires pour servir à l'histoire militaire sous le Directoire, le Consulat et l'Empire*, Paris, 1831, vol. 3, pp. 201–3.

64 Bogdanovich, *Istoriia ... 1812*, vol. 3, pp. 198–204. *MVUA 1812*, 19, Wittgenstein to Alexander, 26 Oct. 1812 (OS), p. 268; Wittgenstein to Alexander, 31 Oct. 1812 (OS), pp. 270–72. Gavrilov, *Organizatsiia*, p. 163. See e.g. Alexander's letter to Kutuzov of 30 Oct. 1812 (OS) in *SIM*, 2, no. 270, pp. 140–41, and Kutuzov's letter to Wittgenstein of 3 Nov. (OS) on the same danger in *Kutuzov*, vol. 4ii, no. 293, pp. 280–81.

65 V. Kriuchkov, *95-i pekhotnyi Krasnoiarskii polk: 1797–1897*, SPB, 1897, p. 172. Gavrilov, *Organizatsiia*, p. 161, on requisitioning in Mogilev province.

66 Ermolov, *Zapiski*, pp. 244–8.

67 P. Pototskii, *Istoriia gvardeiskoi artillerii*, SPB, 1896, pp. 207–10. (Norov), *Zapiski*, pp. 76–7; *Istoriia leib-gvardii egerskago polka za sto let 1796–1896*, SPB, 1896, pp. 88–94.

68 S. Gulevich, *Istoriia leib gvardii Finliandskago polka 1806–1906*, SPB, 1906, pp. 256–61. (Norov), *Zapiski*, pp. 76–7.

69 Chichagov's letters to Alexander constitute his first defence of his actions: see *SIRIO*, 6, 1871, pp. 51–67: 17 and 18 Nov. 1812 (OS). In the memoir material, perhaps the best defence comes in an article by General Ivan Arnoldi: 'Berezinskaia pereprava', *VS*, 53/9, 1910, pp. 8–20. The main recent defence is by I. N. Vasilev, *Neskol'ko gromkikh udarov po khvostu tigra*, Moscow, 2001.

70 *Kutuzov*, vol. 4ii, no. 363, Kutuzov to Chichagov, 10 Nov. 1812 (OS), pp. 344–5. Clausewitz, *Campaign*, p. 210.

71 Ermolov, *Zapiski*, p. 251.

72 Bogdanovich, *Istoriia . . . 1812*, vol. 3, pp. 255–61. Mikhailovskii-Danilevskii, *Opisanie 1812*, p. 519.

73 Arnol'di, 'Berezinskaia pereprava', pp. 11–12.

74 The best Russian descriptions are Bogdanovich, *Istoriia . . . 1812*, vol. 3, pp. 263–76, and Vasil'ev, *Neskol'ko gromkikh udarov*, pp. 190–200, 248–68.

75 Bogdanovich, *Istoriia . . . 1812*, vol. 3, pp. 270–72, 277–84, 297. Vasil'ev, *Neskol'ko gromkikh udarov*, pp. 235–48, 268–85. Clausewitz, *Campaign*, pp. 204–8.

76 Ermolov, *Zapiski*, pp. 254–5.

77 Both Bogdanovich, *Istoriia . . . 1812*, vol. 3, p. 288, and Bernhardi, *Denkwürdigkeiten*, vol. 4, p. 319, make this point.

78 *Kutuzov*, vol. 4ii, no. 563, Kutuzov to Alexander, 19 Dec. 1812, pp. 551–4. N. Murav'ev, 'Zapiski Murav'eva', *RA*, 3, 1885, pp. 389–90. The numbers do not include Osten-Sacken's corps.

79 I. I. Shelengovskii, *Istoriia 69-go Riazanskago polka*, 3 vols., Lublin, 1911, vol. 2, p. 192. *Upravlenie General-Intendanta*, pp. 108–16.

80 *Upravlenie General-Intendanta*, pp. 114–16.

81 *Kutuzov*, vol. 4ii, no. 516, Kutuzov to Alexander, 1 Dec. 1812 (OS), pp. 494–5.

Chapter 9: 1813: The Spring Campaign

1 C. F. Adams (ed.), *John Quincy Adams in Russia*, New York, 1970, pp. 458–9. *VPR*, 7, no. 120, Rumiantsev to Alexander, 27 June/9 July 1813, pp. 293–4; no. 158, Rumiantsev to Alexander, 18/30 Sept. 1813, pp. 386–9.

2 Countess Choiseul-Gouffier, *Historical Memoirs of the Emperor Alexander I and the Court of Russia*, London, 1904, p. 148.

3 S. I. Maevskii, 'Moi vek ili istoriia generala Maevskago', *RS*, 8, 1873, p. 253.

4 'Grafinia Roksandra Skarlatovna Edling: Zapiski', in A. Libermann (ed.), *Derzhavnyi sfinks*, Moscow, 1999, p. 181.

5 See e.g. the comments by Sir Charles Stewart, later Marquess of Londonderry, in his *Narrative of the War in Germany and France in 1813 and 1814*, London, 1830, pp. 33, 242–3.

6 On seduction, see e.g. V. von Löwenstern, *Mémoires du Général-Major Russe Baron de Löwenstern*, 2 vols., Paris, 1903, and Boris Uxkull, *Arms and the Woman: The Intimate Journal of an Amorous Baltic Nobleman in the Napoleonic Wars*, London, 1966. The Guards officers' memoirs bear out David Bell's point about the links between sex and war in aristocratic military culture: D. A. Bell, *The First Total War*, London, 2007, pp. 23–4.

7 For Shishkov's conversation with Kutuzov, see N. Kiselev and Iu. Samarin (eds.), *Zapiski, mneniia i perepiska Admirala A. S. Shishkova*, 2 vols., Berlin, 1870, vol. 1, pp. 167–9.

For Toll's memorandum, see T. von Bernhardi, *Denkwürdigkeiten aus dem Leben des kaiserlichen russischen Generals der Infanterie Carl Friedrich Grafen von Toll*, 5 vols., Leipzig, 1858, vol. 3, book 5, pp. 469–70.

8 *VPR*, 7, no. 12, Nesselrode to Alexander I, early Feb. 1813, pp. 33–4.

9 L. G. Beskrovnyi (ed.), *Pokhod russkoi armii protiv Napoleona v 1813 g. i osvobozhdenie Germanii: Sbornik dokumentov*, Moscow, 1964: no. 24, Chernyshev to Kutuzov, 1/13 Jan. 1813, p. 23.

10 'Perepiska markviza Paulushi s imperatorom Aleksandrom, prusskim generalom Iorka i drugimi litsami', in K. Voenskii (ed.), *Akty, dokumenty i materialy dlia istorii 1812 goda*, 2 vols., SPB, 1910–11, vol. 2, pp. 330–443.

11 See F. Martens (ed.), *Sobranie traktatov i konventsii, zakliuchennykh Rossiei s inostran-nymi derzhavami*, vol. 7: *Traktaty s Germaniei 1811–1824*, SPB, 1885, no. 254, pp. 40–62.

12 See F. Reboul, *Campagne de 1813: Les préliminaires*, 2 vols., Paris, 1910, vol. 1, pp. 194–6, on Yorck's numbers.

13 See Paulucci's letter to Alexander I of 27 Dec. 1812 (OS), in Voenskii, *Akty*, vol. 2, pp. 400–402, and Wittgenstein's angry letter to Chichagov about Paulucci's idiotic behaviour: *MVUA* 1813, vol. 2, no. 24, Wittgenstein to Chichagov, 4 Jan. 1813 (OS).

14 Beskrovnyi (ed.), *Pokhod*, no. 16, pp. 14–15.

15 Ibid., no. 7, 6/18 Dec. 1812, pp. 6–8, and no. 53, 25 Jan./6 Feb. 1813, for two important memorandums by Stein to Kutuzov about feeding the Russian troops and utilizing the Prussian administration.

16 There are any number of documents to this effect, but see e.g. Wittgenstein's report to Kutuzov of 31 Dec. 1812/12 Jan. 1813 (Beskrovnyi (ed.), *Pokhod*, no. 21, pp. 19–20) in which he states that the troops' behaviour in Königsberg had been exemplary and the local population had greeted them as liberators and was providing food through local Prussian officials in the manner prescribed by Kutuzov's orders.

17 E. Botzenhart (ed.), *Freiherr vom Stein: Briefwechsel, Denkschriften und Aufzeich-nungen*, 8 vols., Berlin, 1957–70, vol. 4, Stein to Alexander I, 27 Feb./11 March 1813, pp. 234–6.

18 The discussion of Frederick William's attitudes and policies in the following paragraphs owes much to T. Stamm-Kuhlmann, *König in Preussens grosser Zeit*, Berlin, 1992, pp. 365 ff.

19 W. Oncken, *Österreich und Preussen in Befreiungskriege*, 2 vols, Berlin, 1878: the discussion of the Knesebeck mission is in vol. 1, pp. 137–56, with the Knesebeck quotation on p. 166.

20 Beskrovnyi (ed.), *Pokhod*, no. 33, 10/22 Jan. 1813, Chernyshev to Kutuzov, pp. 31–3.

21 Ibid., no. 48, 22 Jan./3 Feb. 1813, Chernyshev to Kutuzov, pp. 43–4.

22 On the battle on the Warthe, see Chernyshev's journal: RGVIA, Fond 846, Opis 16, Delo 3386, fos. 6ii–7i, and his report to Wittgenstein of 31 Jan./11 Feb. 1813 in RGVIA, Fond 846, Opis 16, Delo 3905, fo. 2ii; on Benckendorff, see Beskrovnyi (ed.), *Pokhod*, no. 80, 15/27 Feb. 1813, Wittgenstein to Kutuzov, pp. 80–81.

23 See e.g. Reboul, *Campagne de 1813*, vol. 2, ch. 5, and Gouvion Saint-Cyr, *Mémoires pour servir à l'histoire militaire sous le Directoire, le Consulat et l'Empire*, vol. 4, Paris, 1831, ch. 1.

24 RGVIA, Fond 846, Opis 16, Delo 3386, fo. 8.

25 See e.g. reports by Benckendorff to Repnin of 22 Feb. (10 Feb. OS) and of Chernyshev to Wittgenstein on the previous day: RGVIA, Fond 846, Opis 16, Delo 3905, fo. 8ii; Beskrovnyi (ed.), *Pokhod*, no. 86, 20 Feb./4 March 1813, Wittgenstein to Kutuzov, p. 89.

26 RGVIA, Fond 846, Opis 16, Delo 3416, fos. 1–2.

27 A. G. Tartakovskii (ed.), *Voennye dnevniki*, Moscow, 1990: A. I. Mikhailovskii-Danilevskii, pp. 319–20.

28 On the treaty, see Martens, *Sobranie traktatov*, vol. 7, pp. 62–82. For Stein's views on Poland, see Botzenhart, *Stein*, vol. 4, Stein to Münster, 7/19 Nov. 1812, pp. 160–62.

29 Oncken, *Österreich*, vol. 1, pp. 359–60; vol. 2, p. 287. *VPR*, no. 50, Nesselrode to Stackelberg, 17/29 March 1813, pp. 118–22. Beskrovnyi (ed.), *Pokhod*, no. 131, Kutuzov to Winzengerode, 24 March/5 April 1813, p. 132.

30 The fullest source on Austrian policy remains Oncken's two volumes, *Österreich und Preussen*. Apart from general works on the diplomacy of the period already cited, see E. K. Kraehe, *Metternich's German Policy*, vol. 1: *The Contest with Napoleon 1799–1814*, Princeton, 1963, and the essays in A. Drabek *et al.* (eds.), *Russland und Österreich zur Zeit der Napoleonischen Kriege*, Vienna, 1989.

31 Oncken, *Österreich*, vol. 1, p. 423: no. 19, Instructions for Lebzeltern, 8 Feb. 1813; vol. 2, pp. 323–4, conversation with Count Hardenberg, 30 May 1813. On military preparations, see the first two volumes of *Geschichte der Kämpfe Österreichs: Kriege unter der Regierung des Kaisers Franz, Befreiungskrieg 1813 und 1814*, vol. 1: O. Criste, *Österreichs Beitritt zur Koalition*, Vienna, 1913; vol. 2: W. Wlaschutz, *Österreichs entscheidendes Machtaufgebot*, Vienna, 1913.

32 Count A. de Nesselrode (ed.), *Lettres et papiers du Chancelier Comte de Nesselrode 1760–1850*, Paris, n.d., vol. 5, e.g. Gentz to Nesselrode, 16 Jan. 1813, pp. 12–21; 28 Jan. 1813, pp. 27–31; 10 March 1813, pp. 35–44; 12 March 1813, pp. 44–7; 17 March 1813, pp. 48–51; 18 March 1813, pp. 51–5; Nesselrode to Gentz, 14/26 March 1813, pp. 58–60; Gentz to Nesselrode, 11 April 1813, pp. 64–70; 16 April 1813, pp. 70–78; 2 May 1813, pp. 83–90; 16 May 1813, pp. 96–101; 13 June 1813, pp. 104–7; 23 July 1813, pp. 122–4. On Gentz's position in Vienna, see Helmut Rumpler, *Österreichische Geschichte 1804–1914*, Vienna, 1997, pp. 78–80.

33 Most of the later negotiations were conducted by Fabian von der Osten-Sacken and most of the relevant documents are in his journal of outgoing correspondence: RGVIA, Fond 846, Opis 16, Delo 3403. The Austrians passed on considerable information about Polish movements. The text of the original armistice is in Martens, *Sobranie traktatov*, vol. 3, no. 67, pp. 70–91. Subsequent agreements are in *VPR*, 7, p. 118, and no. 74, pp. 184–5.

34 *Kutuzov*, vol. 5, no. 320, Order of the Day, 16 Feb. 1813 (OS), pp. 282–4. N. S. Pestreikov, *Istoriia, leib-gvardii Moskovskago polka*, SPB, 1903, vol. 1, pp. 115–19.

35 Pestreikov, *Istoriia*, vol. 1, p. 115; on the Kexholm Regiment, see B. Adamovich, *Sbornik voenno-istoricheskikh materialov leib-gvardii Keksgol'mskago imperatora Avstriiskago polka*, vol. 3, SPB, 1910, p. 300.

36 On the Iaroslavl Regiment, see RGVIA, Fond 489, Opis 1, Delo 1098, fos. 46–71.

37 Beskrovnyi (ed.), *Pokhod*, no. 59, Tettenborn to Alexander, 31 Jan. 1813, pp. 54–6. For his reports to Wittgenstein, see RGVIA, Fond 846, Opis 16, Delo 3905: the two reports cited are Tettenborn to Wittgenstein, 9 March 1813 (OS) (fos. 22ii–23i) and 11 March 1813 (OS) (fos. 24ii–25i).

38 Londonderry, *Narrative*, p. 63.

39 J. von Pflugk-Harttung, *Das Befreiungsjahr 1813: Aus dem Geheimen Staatsarchivs*, Berlin, 1913, no. 136, conversation of Bernadotte with Pozzo and Suchtelen, June 1813, pp. 175–7.

40 R. von Friederich, *Die Befreiungskriege 1813–1815*, vol. 1: *Der Frühjahrsfeldzug 1813*, Berlin, 1911, pp. 196–7; C. Rousset, *La Grande Armée de 1813*, Paris, 1871, pp. 96–7; A. Vallon, *Cours d'hippologie*, 2 vols., Paris, 1863, vol. 2, p. 473. I am grateful to Professor Thierry Lentz for bringing Vallon's work to my attention.

41 A. Uffindell, *Napoleon's Immortals*, Stroud, 2007, pp. 76, 88–90.

42 The two key sources here are Rousset, *Grande Armée*, chs. I–XII; Friederich, *Frühjahrsfeldzug*, pp. 162–80. Friederich states that Napoleon withdrew about 40,000 veterans from Spain: Scott Bowden writes that 'the Army of Spain immediately provided 20,000 proven veterans for Napoleon's new *Grande Armée*', so the difference between the figures may be a question of the precise period involved. S. Bowden, *Napoleon's Grande Armée of 1813*, Chicago, 1990, p. 29.

43 *Mémoires de Langeron, Général d'Infanterie dans l'Armée Russe: Campagnes de 1812, 1813, 1814*, Paris, 1902, p. 190.

44 Beskrovnyi (ed.), *Pokhod*, no. 141, Kutuzov to Golenishchev-Kutuzov, 28 March/9 April 1813, p. 142.

45 Ibid., no. 131, Kutuzov to Winzengerode, 24 March/5 April 1813, p. 132.

46 Tartakovskii, *Voennye dnevniki*, p. 329: this is an extract from Mikhailovsky-Danilevsky's diary for 1813. Beskrovnyi (ed.), *Pokhod*, no. 105, Kutuzov to Wittgenstein, 8/20 March 1813, pp. 107–8; no. 123, Kutuzov to Wittgenstein, 17/29 March 1813, pp. 125–6; no. 94, Wittgenstein to Kutuzov, 26 Feb./10 March 1813, pp. 95–6; no. 150, Volkonsky to d'Auvray, 8/20 April 1813, pp. 151–2.

47 K. von Clausewitz, *Der Feldzug in Russland und die Befreiungskriege von 1813–15*, Berlin, 1906, pp. 196–202.

48 Pflugk-Harttung, *Befreiungsjahr*, no. 82, Blücher to Wittgenstein, *c.* 20 April 1813, pp. 106–7: no. 45, Scharnhorst to Volkonsky, 22 March 1813, pp. 62–5.

49 P. Pototskii, *Istoriia gvardeiskoi artillerii*, SPB, 1896, pp. 220–21.

50 I. Radozhitskii, *Pokhodnyia zapiski artillerista s 1812 po 1816 god*, 3 vols., Moscow, 1835, vol. 2, pp. 22–5.

51 S. G. Volkonskii, *Zapiski Sergeia Grigorovicha Volkonskogo (dekabrista)*, SPB, 1902, p. 232: there are many similar comments, e.g. by young staff officers, as a group the best educated men in the army.

52 Tartakovskii, *Voennye dnevniki*, pp. 333, 345.

53 Hon. George Cathcart, *Commentaries on the War in Russia and Germany in 1812 and 1813*, London, 1850, pp. 122–30. J. P. Riley, *Napoleon and the World War of 1813*, London, 2000, pp. 79–89 (the description of the villages is on p. 80).

54 Clausewitz, *Feldzug*, p. 209.

55 On this, see Botzenhart, *Stein*, vol. 4, memorandums and correspondence with Scharnhorst, Hardenberg and Nesselrode in April 1813, pp. 274–6, 289–90, 293–4, 299–300, 304–6.

56 *VPR*, no. 102, Alexander to Bernadotte, 26 May/7 June 1813, pp. 238–42; Oncken, *Österreich*, vol. 2, no. 46, Stadion to Metternich, 3 June 1813, pp. 660–63.

57 Oncken, *Österreich*, vol. 2, nos. 33 and 34, Metternich to Lebzeltern, 29 April 1813, pp. 630–34.

58 Ibid., vol. 2, no. 38, Instructions for Stadion, 7 May 1813, pp. 640–44.

59 *VPR*, no. 80, Nesselrode to Alexander, 1/13 May 1813, pp. 196–7.

60 *VPR*, no. 101, Nesselrode to Alexander, 24 May/5 June 1813, pp. 236–7.

61 Langeron, *Mémoires*, pp. 169–78. Eugen, *Memoiren*, vol. 3, p. 39.

62 In addition to the basic texts already cited (Bogdanovich, Friederich, Chandler, Riley and Hofschroer), Baron Müffling's memoirs are a vital source on this, but his figure of 5,000 for Barclay's corps should be discounted since Langeron, who commanded this unit, states that 8,000 men were present that day: Baron Karl von Müffling, *The Memoirs of Baron von Müffling: A Prussian Officer in the Napoleonic Wars*, London, 1997, pp. 36–8.

63 Langeron, *Mémoires*, p. 189. Baron von Odeleben, *A Circumstantial Narrative of the Campaign in Saxony in the Year 1813*, 2 vols., London, 1820, vol. 1, p. 95.

64 Odeleben, *Narrative*, vol. 1, p. 103.

65 Oncken, *Österreich*, vol. 2, pp. 323–4, and no. 46, Stadion to Metternich, 3 June 1813, pp. 660–63.

66 For Alexander's view on Schweidnitz, see RGVIA, Fond 846, Opis 16, Delo 3905, fo. 51ii, Volkonsky to Wittgenstein, 11 May 1813 (OS); Müffling, *Memoirs*, pp. 44–9.

67 RGVIA, Fond 103, Opis 4/210, Sv. 17, Delo 34, fo. 18, Kankrin to Barclay de Tolly, 23 May 1813; RGVIA, Fond 103, Opis 4/210, Sv. 17, fos. 158–9, Barclay to Wittgenstein, 26 June 1813. Botzenhart, *Stein*, vol. 4, Kutuzov to Stein, 6/18 April 1813, p. 287.

68 RGVIA, Fond 846, Opis 16, Delo 3905, fo. 55ii, Volkonsky to d'Auvray, 19 May 1813 (OS); Pflugk-Harttung, *Befreiungsjahr*, no. 135, L'Estocq to Hardenburg, 30 May 1813, pp. 171–5; M. I. Bogdanovich, *Istoriia voiny 1813 g. za nezavisimost' Germanii*, 2 vols., SPB, 1863, vol. 1, pp. 299–301.

69 F. Ley, *Alexandre Ier et sa Sainte-Alliance (1811–1825)*, Paris, 1975, pp. 63–5. On Alexander's behaviour, see e.g. Oncken, *Österreich*, vol. 2, p. 330.

70 Langeron, *Mémoires*, p. 199.

Chapter 10: Rebuilding the Army

1 RGVIA, Fond 1, Opis 1/2, Delo 2888, fos. 11–13.

2 John Keep, 'The Russian Army in the Seven Years' War', in E. Lohr and M. Poe (eds.), *The Military and Society in Russia, 1450–1917*, Leiden, 2002, pp. 197–221. For an overall view of logistics in the Seven Years War campaigns, see F. Szabo, *The Seven Years War in Europe 1756–1763*, Harlow, 2008.

3 *MVUA 1813*, 1, pp. 119–20. The army law of January set out the basic arrangements for military roads: see *PSZ*, 32, no. 24975, 27 Jan. 1812 (OS), pp. 116–18. *Kutuzov*, vol. 5, no. 461, Order of the Day, 15 March 1812 (OS), pp. 416–17.

4 *PSZ*, 32, no. 24975, 27 Jan. 1812 (OS), part 3, pp. 107–58.

5 *Kutuzov*, vol. 5, no. 255, Kutuzov to Stein, 31 Jan. 1813 (OS), pp. 214–15; L. G. Beskrovnyi (ed.), *Pokhod russkoi armii protiv Napoleona v 1813 g. i osvobozhdenie Germanii: Sbornik dokumentov*, Moscow, 1964, no. 7, Stein memorandum to Alexander, 6/18 Dec. 1812, pp. 6–8, and no. 53, Stein to Kutuzov, 25 Jan./6 Feb. 1813, pp. 47–8.

6 F. Martens (ed.), *Sobranie traktatov i konventsii, zakliuchennykh Rossiei s inostrannymi derzhavami*, vol. 7: *Traktaty s Germaniei 1811–1824*, SPB, 1885, no. 258, pp. 88–96. See also p. 123 of *Upravlenie General-Intendanta Kankrina: General'nyi sokrashchennyi otchet po armiiam . . . za pokhody protiv Frantsuzov, 1812, 1813 i 1814 godov*, Warsaw, 1815.

7 In late 1813, for example, the Russian war ministry calculated that in the previous four months it had spent 3.9 million rubles feeding units of the Reserve Army deployed within the empire, and only 1.1 million on the much more numerous forces stationed in the Duchy. Even this 1.1 million was only due to Alexander's order that the Reserve Army's meat and spirits rations should be paid for by the Russian treasury, and no longer by the Poles: ministry of war memorandum for Prince Aleksei Gorchakov, 30 Dec. 1813 (OS), RGVIA, Fond 846, Opis 16, Delo 3441, fos. 100–101.

8 *Kutuzov*, vol. 5, no. 370, Law on the Provisional Government of the Duchy of Warsaw, 1/13 March 1813, pp. 329–35; quotation on p. 332.

9 *Kutuzov*, vol. 5, no. 34, Kutuzov's proclamation to the Polish population, 27 Dec. 1812 (OS), p. 29, and no. 326, Kutuzov to Alexander, 18 Feb. 1813 (OS), p. 291. *MVUA 1813*, vol. 2, no. 96, Vorontsov to Chichagov, 1 Feb. 1813 (OS), p. 70.

10 For Kankrin's instructions, see RGVIA, Fond 474, Opis 1, Ed. Khr. 1204, fos. 4i–ii. *Kutuzov*, vol. 5, no. 442, Kutuzov to his wife, 11 March 1813 (OS), p. 400. Adamovich, *Sbornik*, III, pp. 302–5, has interesting statistics on victualling the Kexholm Regiment in the advance guard in January–April. On Frederick's treatment of Saxony, see Szabo, *Seven Years War*, pp. 119–20.

11 RGVIA, Fond 103, Opis 208a, Sv. 28, Delo 31, fos. 161–7, Barclay to Alexander, 18 June 1813 (OS). There is another copy of this letter in Opis 4/210, Sv. 17, Delo 34, fos. 100–106.

12 There are two key reports on Chichagov's mobile magazine: see RGVIA, Fond 103, Opis 4/210, Sv. 18, Delo 76, fos. 20–25: report of Lisanevich to Kankrin, 5 Dec. 1813 (OS); RGVIA, Fond 103, Opis 4/210, Sv. 17, Delo 34, fos. 184–7: report by Major Alekseev to Kankrin, 25 June 1813 (OS). See also *Kutuzov*, vol. 5, Kutuzov to Chichagov, 31 Jan. 1813 (OS), pp. 212–13.

13 On the deal with Adelsohn and co., see RGVIA, Fond 103, Opis 4/210, Sv. 17, Delo 34, fos. 240–41, 317–18. The first document is a report by a senior Prussian court official, Count de Bethusy, dated 25 July. The second is a report submitted by Adelsohn himself on 8 November. On the main army's magazine, see in particular the reports by Kankrin to Barclay of 6, 10 and 16 July 1813 (OS): RGVIA, Fond 103, Opis 4/210, Sv. 17, Delo

34, fos. 207–8, 226, 251–3. On peasant carts' operational limits, see Keep, 'Russian Army', p. 215.

14 This was mostly money in the so-called exchange offices set up to remit back to Russia paper rubles which foreigners had received and which they wished to exchange for their own currencies.

15 Alexander's orders to Gurev are in *SIM*, 3, no. 136, Alexander to Gurev, 14 June 1813 (OS), pp. 100–101. Two of Gurev's letters to Barclay, dated 28 June and 1 July (OS), are of interest: see RGVIA, Fond 103, Opis 208a, Sv. 28, Delo 31, fos. 125 and 219.

16 *SIM*, 1, section B, 'Sekretnyia ofitsial'nyiia svedeniia o polozhenii nashikh finansov v 1813g i ob izyskanii sredstv k prodolzheniiu voennykh deistvii v chuzhikh kraiakh': no. 1, memorandum by Gurev of 24 April 1813 (OS), pp. 47–50 and 54.

17 Ibid., pp. 55–63.

18 *VPR*, 7, nos. 13 and 14, Alexander to Lieven, 20 Jan./1 Feb. 1813, pp. 36–9.

19 *VPR*, 7, no. 55, Lieven to Alexander, 25 March/6 April 1813, pp. 132–7; no. 84, Gurev to Nesselrode, 5/17 May 1813, pp. 203–6. E. Botzenhart (ed.), *Freiherr vom Stein: Briefwechsel, Denkschriften und Aufzeichnungen*, 8 vols., Berlin, 1957–70, Stein to Kochubei, 31 May 1813, pp. 350–51. The biggest remaining problem was the exchange costs of British treasury bills on the continent.

20 Kankrin's list is in RGVIA, Fond 103, Opis 4/210, Sv. 17, Delo 34, fos. 64–5: Kankrin to Barclay, 30 May 1813 (OS); Barclay's letter to Lanskoy, dated 31 May (OS) is on fo. 66 of the same Delo. Alexander's orders to Lanskoy are in *SIM*, 3, no. 140, 14 June 1813, pp. 102–3.

21 RGVIA, Fond 103, Opis 4/210, Sv. 17, Delo 34: Lanskoy to Barclay, 22 June 1813 (OS), fos. 167–8; Open orders to Major Vinokurov, 18 June 1813 (OS), fo. 135; Vinokurov to Barclay, 23 Aug. 1813 (OS), fos. 311–12; Lieutenant-Colonel Lekarsky to Barclay, 27 July 1813 (OS), fos. 313–14).

22 Beskrovnyi (ed.), *Pokhod*, no. 184, Order of the Day, 29 May/10 June 1813, pp. 195–6.

23 *Kutuzov*, vol. 5, no. 300, Kutuzov to Barclay, 9 Feb. 1813 (OS), pp. 259–60; no. 258, Kutuzov to the commandant of Königsberg (Major-General Count Sievers), 2 Feb. 1813 (OS), pp. 216–18; no. 441, Kutuzov to Alexander, 11 March 1813 (OS), pp. 398–9.

24 RGVIA, Fond 103, Opis 3/209b, Sv.10, Delo 117, fo. 6: report by Kankrin on boots and trousers. Radozhitsky, *Pokhodnyia*, vol. 2, pp. 156–9. RGVIA, Fond 103, Opis 209b, Sv. 11, Delo 2, fos. 104–10: report by Major-General Prince Gurialov to d'Auvray, 13 July 1813 (OS) on muskets.

25 *MVUA 1813*, 1, pp. 97–132.

26 *Kutuzov*, vol. 4ii, pp. 575–7. Alexander set out his plan to Kutuzov in a letter dated 29 November 1812 (OS): *SIM*, 2, no. 367, pp. 211–13.

27 V. V. Shchepetil'nikov, *Komplektovanie voisk v tsarstvovanie imperatora Aleksandra I*, SVM, 4/1/1/2, SPB, 1904, pp. 55–62. The average age of conscripts into the Moscow Dragoons in 1813 was 28 – four years above the peacetime average. See RGVIA, Fond 489, Opis 1, Ed. Khr. 2442, fos. 94–119: note that, although the document states that the men joined in 1812, in fact very many did so in 1813. Forty per cent of conscripts into the Kherson Grenadier Regiment in late 1812 and 1813 were married: see RGVIA, Fond 489, Opis 1, Ed. Khr. 1263. The folio numbers are indecipherable but the list of new recruits comes after the *formuliarnyi spisok* of NCOs on fos. 43 ff.

28 V. A. Aleksandrov, *Sel'skaia obshchina v Rossii (XVII-nachalo XIX v.)*, Moscow, 1976, pp. 244–5.

29 I. I. Prokhodtsov, *Riazanskaia guberniia v 1812 godu*, Riazan, 1913, p. 119. RGVIA, Fond 1, Opis 1/2, Delo 2636, fo. 11, for the ministry's circular urging recruit boards to check the records submitted by the state peasant administration.

30 V. Lestvitsyn (ed.), 'Zapiski soldata Pamfila Nazarova', *RS*, 9/8, 1878, pp. 529–43.

31 These records are held in the British Library as Additional Manuscript 47427 of the Lieven papers.

32 On the estate, see Edgar Melton, 'Household Economies and Communal Conflicts on a Russian Serf Estate, 1800-1817', *Journal of Social History*, 26/3, 1993, pp. 559-86.

33 On Staroust, see BL Add. MSS. 47424, fos. 47-53. Melton, 'Household Economies', p. 569, for the Leontev case, in which the estate management's efforts to allow the wife of a conscripted man to be the breadwinner and keep his land were rejected by the commune. All other individual cases are drawn by me from Add. MSS. 47427.

34 Charlotta's instructions for the 'wealth tax' are in BL Add. MSS. 47427: they and the lists providing sums to be raised from each household are contained in fos. 122-41. See also Melton, 'Household Economies', p. 569.

35 RGVIA, Fond 1, Opis 1/2, Delo 2636, fo. 53.

36 S. E. Charnetskii, *Istoriia 179-go pekhotnago Ust-Dvinskago polka: 1711-1811-1911*, SPB, 1911, p. 26.

37 I used above all the service records (*formuliarnye spiski*) in RGVIA. The regiments covered were: the Kherson (Ed. Khr. 1263) and Little Russia (Ed. Khr. 1190) Grenadiers; the Murom (Ed. Khr. 517), Kursk (Ed. Khr. 425), Chernigov (Ed. Khr. 1039), Reval (Ed. Khr. 754), Selenginsk (Ed. Khr. 831) and Belostok (Ed. Khr. 105) infantry regiments; the 29th (Ed. Khr. 1794), 39th (Ed. Khr. 1802) and 45th (Ed. Khr. 1855) Jaegers; His Majesty's Life Cuirassier Regiment (Ed. Khr. 2114), the Iamburg (Ed. Khr. 2631), Siberia (Ed. Khr. 2670), Moscow (Ed. Khr. 2442), Borisogleb (Ed. Khr. 2337) and Pskov (Ed. Khr. 212) Dragoon regiments and the Volhynia Lancers (Ed. Khr. 2648). In addition, the appendices of three regimental histories have lists of officers giving dates when they were commissioned. These are the Guards Jaegers (*Istoriia leib-gvardii egerskago polka za sto let 1796-1896*, SPB, 1896, *prilozheniia*, pp. 56 ff.); the Guards Lancers (P. Bobrovskii, *Istoriia leib-gvardii ulanskago E.I.V. gosudarnyi Imperatritsy Aleksandry Fedorovny polka*, SPB, 1903, *prilozheniia*, pp. 140 ff.); Her Majesty's Life Cuirassier Regiment (Colonel Markov, *Istoriia leib-gvardii kirasirskago Eia Velichestva polka*, SPB, 1884, *prilozheniia*, pp. 73 ff.). In all there were 341 new officers, of whom 43 per cent were former sub-ensigns or junkers. This does not comprise all the newly commissioned officers in these regiments, since some of the service records are from January or July 1813. That also biases the results towards men who had served as noble NCOs.

38 *Istoriia leib-gvardii egerskago polka*, *prilozheniia*, pp. 56 ff., is a mine of information.

39 Of the new officers surveyed, 20 per cent were formerly non-noble NCOs. In fact a handful of these men were nobles but had not yet reached even the rank of sub-ensign or junker. But this was far fewer than the twelve non-noble NCOs commissioned into other regiments, so the statistic of one in five holds good. In reality Russian society was more blurred than the sharp legal distinctions between estates admitted. A halfway house was the many petty Polish noble NCOs from lancer regiments who received commissions in the Russian lancer units which in 1813 were created out of some dragoon regiments.

40 *SIM*, 2, no. 249, Alexander to Wittgenstein, 26 Oct. 1812 (OS), pp. 119-21.

41 In my survey, 8.5 per cent of the officers came from the Noble Regiment and 7 per cent were former civil servants but the bias towards the first half of the war undoubtedly underestimates their importance. Another source of officers was the military orphanages, where the sons of dead officers were educated. On the Noble Regiment, see M. Gol'mdorf, *Materialy dlia istorii byvshego Dvorianskago polka*, SPB, 1882; the statistics are from p. 137. Alexander wrote on 18 December 1812 (OS) to Count Saltykov that there were superfluous civil officials and what the state needed at present were officers. Men unwilling to transfer to the army should therefore be dismissed: *SIM*, 2, no. 417, pp. 253-4. On 29 December 1812 he ordered that the Noble Regiment be 'restarted', which reflects the reality that it had more or less come to a halt amidst the emergency of 1812: *SIM*, 2, no. 412, Alexander to Viazmitinov, 17 Dec. 1812 (OS), p. 250.

42 *Mémoires du Général Bennigsen*, 3 vols., Paris, n.d., vol. 3, pp. 278-9 (letter to Alexander I of 24 June (OS)). RGVIA, Fond 125, Opis 188a, Delo 70: Essen's report on his troops' condition upon departure from their training camps is on fo. 4 and the list of men dispatched on fo. 5.

43 *SIM*, 11, no. 13, Lobanov-Rostovsky to Alexander I, 16 Nov. 1812 (OS), pp. 109–11.

44 *Kutuzov*, vol. 4ii, pp. 578–80. This was in a report by the inspector-general of artillery, Müller-Zakomelsky, dated 3 Jan. 1813 (OS). *SIM*, 11, no. 12, 14 Nov. 1812 (OS), is Lobanov's acknowledgement to Alexander that he had received this order. V. N. Speranskii, *Voenno-ekonomicheskaia podgotovka Rossii k bor'be s Napoleonom v 1812–1814 godakh*, candidate's dissertation, Gorky, 1967, pp. 385–454 is excellent on small-arms production in 1812–14.

45 RGVIA, Fond 125, Opis 188a, Delo 163, fos. 31–2: Gorchakov to Lobanov-Rostovsky, 31 March 1813 (OS).

46 *SIM*, 11, Saltykov to Lobanov-Rostovsky, 19 Dec. 1812 (OS), p. 199.

47 The two key sources on the Reserve Army in this period are Lobanov-Rostovsky's reports to Alexander I for 7 Jan.–6 Aug. 1813 (RGVIA, Fond 125, Opis 188a, Delo 47) and the journal of outgoing correspondence of Lobanov's headquarters for 1 Jan.–1 April 1813 (RGVIA, Fond 125, Opis 188a, Delo 42).

48 Alexander's orders are in *SIM*, 3, no. 52, Alexander to Lobanov-Rostovsky, 5 Feb. 1813 (OS), pp. 39–42. Lobanov's initial response to the movement orders is in RGVIA, Fond 125, Opis 188a, Delo 147, fos. 17–18: letter dated 15 Feb. 1813 (OS).

49 RGVIA, Fond 846, Opis 16, Delo 3441, fos. 31–2: Lobanov to Alexander, 17 Feb. 1813 (OS).

50 For Lobanov's report, see RGVIA, Fond 125, Opis 188a, Delo 47, fos. 26–9. For Neverovsky's report to the emperor, see RGVIA, Fond 125, Opis 188a, Delo 39, fos. 28–9. The statistics come from the same Delo and are on fos. 31–2. Lobanov's letters to Alexander I of 9 May (fos. 62–4) and 18 July (fos. 104–5) 1813 (OS) (in RGVIA, Fond 125, Opis 188a, Delo 47) state that of 9,000 sick left behind in Belitsa 7,000 had already rejoined their units and more were expected to do so. The reserve companies of the Guards Jaeger Regiment, for example, left Petersburg with 704 men and arrived in Silesia with 481; see *Istoriia leib-gvardii egerskago polka*, p. 113.

51 Even the Chevaliers Gardes at Kulm put out skirmishers: see S. Panchulidzev, *Istoriia kavalergardov*, SPB, 1903, vol. 3, p. 314.

52 The best shorthand guide to the Russian cavalry of this era (including useful illustrations of horse furnishings, how to hold the reins and use a sword, and how to deploy to skirmish and charge, etc.) is Alla Begunova, *Sabli ostry, koni bystry*, Moscow, 1992.

53 See e.g. Arakcheev's letter to Kutuzov of 31 March 1813 (OS) and Alexander's letter to the Grand Duke Constantine of the same date: RGVIA, Fond 103, Opis 4/20, Sv. 3, Delo 22, fos. 42 and 43.

54 Kologrivov received 269 fine horses from the state studs in December 1812, for example: all were for the Guards and he gave only one even to the Guards Lancers: *MVUA 1812*, 20, Kologrivov to Gorchakov, 12 Dec. 1812 (OS), p. 153.

55 V. V. Ermolov and M. M. Ryndin, *Upravlenie general-inspektora kavalerii o remontirovanii kavalerii*, SVM, 13, SPB, 1906, pp. 126–7.

56 RGVIA, Fond 846, Opis 16, Delo 3442, is devoted to this mission. See also Komarovsky's memoirs: *Zapiski Grafa E. F. Komarovskago*, SPB, 1914, pp. 200 ff. Ermolov and Ryndin, *Upravlenie*, SVM, 13, pp. 134–6.

57 *Kutuzov*, vol. 4ii, no. 513, memorandum, pp. 488–90: no date but probably late November.

58 A. Grigorovich, *Istoriia 13-go dragunskago voennago ordena general-fel'dmarshala Grafa Minikha polka*, 2 vols., SPB, 1907 and 1912, vol. 2, pp. 32–3. Even in late October (OS) the five cuirassier regiments of this division had barely 1,000 other ranks present.

59 N. Durova, *The Cavalry Maiden: Journals of a Female Russian Officer in the Napoleonic Wars*, ed. and trans. Mary Fleming Zirin, Bloomington, Ill., 1989, p. 168.

60 V. Godunov, *Istoriia 3-go ulanskago Smolenskago Imperatora Aleksandra III-go polka 1708–1908*, Libava, 1908, pp. 133–4. At Slonim they were joined by the 8 officers and 155 veterans of the former reserve squadron, the 7th, which had been deployed in the rear at Olviopol in 1812.

61 The report is entitled 'Otnoshenie Generala ot Infanterii kniaz'ia Lobanova-Rostovskago s otchetami o raspredelenii v rezervy voinov i loshadei'. Together with a covering letter from Lobanov to Gorchakov dated 14 April 1815 (OS), it is to be found in RGVIA, Fond 1, Opis 1/2, Delo 3230. The Reserve Army's cavalry corps had dispatched 543 officers and 21,699 other ranks to the Field Army. Since the formation of the Reserve Army 1,749 officers, 33,423 veteran other ranks and 38,620 recruits had served in its cavalry corps. The Reserve Army's infantry corps had dispatched 635 officers and 61,843 other ranks to the Field Army; 3,662 officers, 116,904 veterans and 174,148 recruits had served in the infantry corps during the existence of the Reserve Army. It is important to remember that these statistics do not include the 'first wave' of reinforcements dispatched by Kologrivov and Lobanov in the spring of 1813 before the Reserve Army was created.

62 A. S. Griboedov, *Sochineniia*, Moscow, 1953: 'O kavaleriiskikh rezervakh', pp. 363–7.

63 For the statistics, see Ermolov and Ryndin, *Upravlenie*, p. 136. For Lobanov's comments on cavalry training, see e.g. his report to Alexander of 4 Feb. 1814 (OS) in RGVIA, Fond 125, Opis 188a, Delo 153, fo. 21. RGVIA, Fond 125, Opis 188a, Delo 47, no. 135: Lobanov to Alexander, 29 Nov. 1813 (OS), on Wittgenstein's men.

64 A. Brett-James (ed.), *General Wilson's Journal, 1812–1814*, London, 1964, p. 147.

65 Rudolph von Friederich, *Die Befreiungskriege 1813–1815*, vol 2: *Der Herbstfeldzug 1813*, Berlin, 1912, pp. 18–26.

66 Friedrich von Schubert, *Unter dem Doppeladler*, Stuttgart, 1962, p. 311.

67 *SIM*, 3, no. 131, Alexander to Bennigsen, 25 May (OS) 1813, pp. 96–8.

68 *MVUA 1813*, 1, Barclay to Bennigsen, 14 June 1813 (OS), p. 123. On troop strengths, see M. I. Bogdanovich, *Istoriia voiny 1813 g. za nezavisimost' Germanii*, 2 vols., SPB, 1863, vol. 1, pp. 722–7. Essen's battalions, intended for Sacken and Langeron's regiments, were attached to regiments in Bennigsen's army rather than merged into them, in order to preserve their own regimental identity: see e.g. Lieutenant Lakhtionov, *Istoriia 147-go Samarskago polka 1798–1898*, SPB, 1898, pp. 66–7.

69 *SIM*, 3, no. 150, Alexander to Bennigsen, 10 July 1813 (OS), pp. 107–9. Lobanov passed on these instructions in an order of the day dated 16 July 1813 (OS): RGVIA, Fond 125, Opis 188a, Delo 149, fo. 35.

70 The statistics are from Lobanov's final report and accounting for the Reserve Army, with a covering note from him to Gorchakov dated 14 April 1815. The figure of 325,000 includes 45,783 supernumerary other ranks, in other words men not yet formally assigned to units. As always, theoretical numbers will have been considerably larger than the number of men actually present in the ranks. See RGVIA, Fond 1, Opis 1/2, Delo 3230 *passim*. On sickness, see RGVIA, Fond 125, Opis 188a, Delo 144, fo. 12, Essen to Lobanov, 8 May 1814 (OS).

Chapter 11: Europe's Fate in the Balance

1 *VPR*, no. 101, Nesselrode to Alexander, 24 May/5 June 1813, pp. 236–7. W. Oncken, *Österreich und Preussen in Befreiungskriege*, vol. 2, Berlin, 1878, Metternich to Stadion, 6 June 1813, pp. 663–4; 8 June 1813, pp. 664–5.

2 *VPR*, no. 104, Nesselrode to Lieven, 2/14 June, pp. 246–9; Oncken, *Österreich*, vol. 2, Metternich to Stadion, 30 July 1813, pp. 680–81.

3 *VPR*, no. 118, Alexander's instructions to Anstedt, 26 June/8 July 1813, pp. 283–92 (quotation from p. 286).

4 *VPR*, no. 107, Nesselrode to Metternich, 7/19 June 1813, pp. 257–8.

5 E. Botzenhart (ed.), *Freiherr vom Stein: Briefwechsel, Denkschriften und Aufzeichnungen*, 8 vols., Berlin, 1957–70, vol. 4, Stein to Gneisenau, 11 July 1813; to Münster, 17 July 1813; to Alexander, 18 July 1813, pp. 372–81.

6 Oncken, *Österreich*, vol. 2, pp. 402–5.

7 Ibid., pp. 405–8.

8 R. von Friederich, *Die Befreiungskriege 1813–1815*, vol. 2: *Der Herbstfeldzug 1813*,

Berlin, 1912, pp. 26, 31; M. I. Bogdanovich, *Istoriia voiny 1813 g. za nezavisimost' Germanii*, 2 vols., SPB, 1863, vol. 1, p. 448. The figure given by C. Rousset (*La Grande Armée de 1813*, Paris, 1871, p. 180) is 425,000 soldiers ready for battle, of whom 365,000 were in the ranks of Oudinot, Ney and Napoleon's three armies. In August 1813 Davout in Hamburg and Girard in Magdeburg were able to contribute 40,000 men to the advance on Berlin.

9 Friederich, *Herbstfeldzug*, pp. 33, 348.

10 N. S. Pestreikov, *Istoriia leib gvardii Moskovskago polka*, SPB, 1903, vol. 1, pp. 129-30. RGVIA, Fond 489, Opis 1, Delo 1098, fo. 220, on the men detached from the Iaroslavl Regiment.

11 F. G. Popov, *Istoriia 48-go pekhotnago Odesskago polka*, 2 vols., Moscow, 1911, vol. 1, pp. 119-27.

12 RGVIA, Fond 489, Opis 1, Delo 1098, fos. 177-94 and 271-391 (Iaroslavl Regiment); Delo 105, fos. 194i-195ii (Belostok Regiment); Delo 106, fos. 111-13 (Kursk Regiment).

13 All this information comes from the two regiments' service records in RGVIA, Fond 489, Opis 1, Dela 105 and 106. In the Belostok Regiment, 10 of the 29 sub-lieutenants, lieutenants and staff captains were of lower-class origin. None of the more senior officers and none of the ensigns was.

14 Oncken, *Österreich*, vol. 2, Bubna to Metternich, 9 Aug. 1813, pp. 684-6. Eugen, *Memoiren*, vol. 3, pp. 64-8.

15 Karl Fürst Schwarzenberg, *Feldmarschall Fürst Schwarzenberg: Der Sieger von Leipzig*, Vienna, 1964, p. 233.

16 RGVIA, Fond 846, Opis 16, Delo 3399, Volkonsky to Wittgenstein, 9/21 Aug. 1813, fo. 11.

17 A. G. Tartakovskii (ed.), *Voennye dnevniki*, Moscow, 1990, p. 355; Schwarzenberg, *Schwarzenberg*, p. 233.

18 L. G. Beskrovnyi (ed.), *Pokhod russkoi armii protiv Napoleona v 1813 g. i osvobozhdenie Germanii: Sbornik dokumentov*, Moscow, 1964, Trachenberg Conference, 28–30 June/10–12 July 1813, p. 462; *Geschichte der Kämpfe Österreichs: Kriege unter der Regierung des Kaisers Franz, Befreiungskrieg 1813 und 1814*, vol. 3: E. Glaise von Horstenau, *Feldzug von Dresden*, Vienna, 1913, pp. 3–6.

19 RGVIA, Fond 846, Opis 16, Delo 3399, Alexander to Bernadotte, 9/21 Aug. 1813, fos. 2–3.

20 On the Swedish army, see Marquess of Londonderry, *Narrative of the War in Germany and France in 1813 and 1814*, London, 1830, pp. 72–4. On Bernadotte, the latest book is C. Bazin, *Bernadotte*, Paris, 2000.

21 The best appreciation of Bernadotte's position is in the Prussian general staff's history: Friederich, *Herbstfeldzug*, pp. 146–8. See also M. Leggiere, *Napoleon and Berlin*, Stroud, 2002, for a fine account of operations in the northern theatre and the mobilization of Prussian resources.

22 The best angle on this is the two volumes of the Austrian staff history, which discuss the planning and execution of Schwarzenberg's initial advance to Dresden in August and subsequent move on Leipzig. See Horstenau, *Dresden*, pp. 63–106; *Geschichte der Kämpfe Österreichs: Befreiungskrieg 1813 und 1814*, vol. 5: Max von Hoen, *Feldzug von Leipzig*, Vienna, 1913, especially pp. 127–34.

23 F. von Schubert, *Unter dem Doppeladler*, Stuttgart, 1962, pp. 336–7.

24 Baron von Odeleben, *A Circumstantial Narrative of the Campaign in Saxony in the Year 1813*, 2 vols., London, 1820, vol. 1, p. 140.

25 The quotation is from Bogdanovich, *Istoriia . . . 1813*, vol. 2, p. 22.

26 On the French emigration in Russia in general, see A. Ratchinski, *Napoléon et Alexandre Ier*, Paris, 2002; on Langeron and Richelieu, see L. de Crousaz-Cretet, *Le Duc de Richelieu en Russie et en France*, Paris, 1897, especially pp. 18–20. Langeron's personality and career are summarized by Emmanuel de Waresquiel in J. Tulard (ed.), *Dictionnaire Napoléon*, Paris, 1999 edn., 2 vols., vol. 2, pp. 144–6.

27 On Langeron, see especially Schubert, *Doppeladler*, pp. 163–7. For the quotation, see Langeron, *Mémoires de Langeron, Général d'Infanterie dans l'Armée Russe: Campagnes de 1812, 1813, 1814*, Paris, 1902, p. 205.

28 On the action at Bunzlau, see in particular E. Nikolaev, *Istoriia 50 pekhotnago Belostokskago, Ego Vysochestva Gertsoga Saksen-Al'tenburgskago polka*, SPB, 1907, pp. 71–3. Friederich, *Herbstfeldzug*, p. 122, notes the poor quality of Sebastiani's regiments.

29 Langeron, *Mémoires*, p. 220; J. von Pflugk-Harttung, *Das Befreiungsjahr 1813: Aus dem Geheimen Staatsarchivs*, Berlin, 1913, no. 196, Gneisenau to Hardenberg, 25 Aug. 1813, pp. 276–8.

30 Yorck's letter is quoted by Bogdanovich, *Istoriia . . . 1813*, vol. 2, p. 42. Bennigsen also complained about Blücher's strategy: see his letter to Alexander of 14/26 Aug., written from Kalicz: RGVIA, Fond 846, Opis 16, Delo 3385, fos. 191–2.

31 Marshal Gouvion Saint-Cyr, *Mémoires pour servir à l'histoire militaire sous le Directoire, le Consulat et l'Empire*, Paris, 1831, vol 4, no. 8, Protocole de la conférence de Trachenberg: no. 9, Instructions pour S. Ex. M. de Blücher, pp. 347–53.

32 Alexander's letter to Blücher is in RGVIA, Fond 846, Opis 16, Delo 3399, fos. 7ii–8i.

33 Blücher's letter to Alexander, undated but received on 27 Aug., is in RGVIA, Fond 846, Opis 16, Delo 3911, fos. 215i–ii.

34 RGVIA, Fond 846, Opis 16, Delo 3911, fo. 247ii: Venançon to Volkonsky, 16/28 Aug. 1813, on MacDonald's failure to reconnoitre the allied position.

35 The best source on the movements of Third Corps is the journal compiled by Captain Koch: *Journal des opérations du IIIe Corps en 1813*, Paris, 1999. The description of the corps's role at the Katzbach is on pp. 54–60.

36 Müffling's description of the battle comes in two sections of his memoirs, which were written and published years apart because some of his comments would have caused offence if published earlier: see Baron Karl von Müffling, *The Memoirs of Baron von Müffling: A Prussian Officer in the Napoleonic Wars*, London, 1997, pp. 58–75 and 317–24. The quotation is on p. 60.

37 RGVIA, Fond 846, Opis 16, Delo 3911, fos. 246ii–247i: Venançon to Volkonsky, 16/28 Aug. 1813. Venançon's long report is much the best account of the battle from the perspective of Osten-Sacken's corps. Koch gives the best French eyewitness account and Müffling is the best Prussian source. Bogdanovich provides an excellent detailed account too, which Friederich confirms.

38 Apart from the general works and Koch, the history of the Odessa Regiment, which was part of Neverovsky's 27th Division, is useful on this little-remarked last episode in the battle: Popov, *Istoriia 48-go*, pp. 139–41.

39 Prince A. G. Shcherbatov, *Moi vospominaniia*, SPB, 2006, p. 87.

40 Müffling, *Memoirs*, pp. 67–8. I. Radozhitskii, *Pokhodnyia zapiski artillerista s 1812 po 1816 god*, 3 vols., Moscow, 1835, vol. 2, p. 202.

41 Captain Geniev, *Istoriia Pskovskago pekhotnago general-fel'dmarshala kniazia Kutuzova-Smolenskago polka: 1700–1831*, Moscow, 1883, pp. 216–17; Bogdanovich, *Istoriia . . . 1813*, vol. 2, p. 65.

42 Pflugk-Harttung, *Befreiungsjahr*, no. 219: Silesian military government to the military governor of Berlin, 28 Aug. 1813, pp. 283–4.

43 Koch, *Journal*, p. 64; RGVIA, Fond 846, Opis 16, Delo 3403, fos. 24i–25i: Sacken to Volkonsky, 3 Sept. 1813.

44 Schubert, *Doppeladler*, p. 321.

45 Beskrovnyi (ed.), *Pokhod*, no. 216, Journal of Military Operations, 23 Aug./4 Sept. 1813, pp. 245–7. Apart from Bogdanovich, there is a good account of the pursuit in Prince N. B. Golitsyn, *Zhizneopisanie generala ot kavalerii Emmanuelia*, Moscow, 1844, pp. 97–104.

46 The statistics are drawn from George Nafziger, *Napoleon at Dresden*, Chicago, 1994, pp. 77, 301.

47 Bogdanovich, *Istoriia . . . 1813*, vol. 2, p. 78.

48 Horstenau, *Dresden*, pp. 1–11.

49 The key sources on Austrian organization and preparations are the first three volumes of *Befreiungskrieg 1813 und 1814* authored by O. Criste (*Österreichs Beitritt zur Koalition*, Vienna, 1913), Wlaschutz (*Österreichs entscheidendes Machtaufgebot*, Vienna, 1913) and Glaise von Horstenau. See e.g. Horstenau's comment in *Dresden*, p. 78. See also, however, a very interesting conversation with Radetsky recorded in Wilson's diary: A. Brett-James (ed.), *General Wilson's Journal 1812–1814*, London, 1964, 20 Aug. 1813, p. 63.

50 See e.g. an indignant protest from Vorontsov to Barclay on hearing that he was being subordinated to Bülow, who had become a lieutenant-general one month after Vorontsov himself. Barclay accepted the protest and subordinated him to Winzengerode. RGVIA, Fond 103, Opis 4/210, Sv. 53, Delo 18, fos. 15–16: Vorontsov to Barclay, 9 July 1813 (OS).

51 See e.g. Barclay's letter to Sacken of 10 Sept. 1813 (OS), one of many such examples: *MVUA 1813*, 1, p. 202; Eugen, *Memoiren*, vol. 3, pp. 145–6.

52 Saint-Cyr, *Mémoires*, vol. 4, no. 15, Napoleon to Saint-Cyr, 17 Aug. 1813, pp. 365–8.

53 Horstenau, *Dresden*, pp. 78–117. Brett-James, *Wilson's Journal*, p. 165.

54 Horstenau, *Dresden*, pp. 103, 106–7, 123–4.

55 Hon. George Cathcart, *Commentaries on the War in Russia and Germany in 1812 and 1813*, London, 1850, p. 29. Langeron, *Mémoires*, p. 256.

56 Horstenau, *Dresden*, p. 159; Friederich, *Herbstfeldzug*, p. 69; Bogdanovich, *Istoriia . . . 1813*, vol. 2, p. 127. Saint-Cyr, *Mémoires*, vol. 4, no. 26, Saint-Cyr to Napoleon, 25 Aug. 1813, pp. 383–4.

57 A quick guide to Napoleon's initial plan is conveyed in a letter to the Duc de Bassano of 24 August: Saint-Cyr, *Mémoires*, vol. 4, no. 21, 24 Aug. 1813, pp. 377–8.

58 Cathcart, *Commentaries*, pp. 231–2. Horstenau, *Dresden*, p. 270.

59 Cathcart, *Commentaries*, p. 228. On Constantine's views, see e.g. *RA*, 1, 1882, pp. 142–54.

60 These points are all made by Horstenau, *Dresden*, pp. 257–68, 277–86: since he was the official Austrian historian of the campaign he had no reason to exaggerate the failings of Austrian leadership, so one can assume that his judgements are fair. See also Friederich, *Herbstfeldzug*, pp. 76–8.

61 Brett-James, *Wilson's Journal*, 30 August 1813, p. 169.

62 All the general histories of the campaign go into detail about the crucial events of 26–30 August on the allied right. Apart from Friederich and Bogdanovich, there is a full description in *Geschichte der Kämpfe Österreichs: Befreiungskrieg 1813 und 1814*, vol. 4: Maximilian Ehnl, *Schlacht bei Kulm*, Vienna, 1913. Apart from Eugen's own memoirs, it is also important to read the memoirs of his chief of staff, General von Helldorff: *Zur Geschichte der Schlacht bei Kulm*, Berlin, 1856. All subsequent histories draw heavily on the three volumes written between 1844 and 1852 by Colonel Aster of the Saxon army about the autumn 1813 campaign. Nevertheless one must go back to Aster himself because his works contain significant details omitted from the later histories: on the events on the right wing, see H. Aster, *Die Kriegsereignisse zwischen Peterswalde, Pirna, Königstein und Priesten im August 1813 und die Schlacht bei Kulm*, Dresden, 1845. For obvious reasons it is far harder to find detailed French coverage of these events: Rousset, *Grande Armée*, for example, says little on the debacle though he does cite important correspondence of Vandamme. Saint-Cyr also publishes useful documents but like all the other French participants is anxious to exonerate himself from blame. Fezensac puts most of the blame on Vandamme though he is also critical of Saint-Cyr and Napoleon. His is the best-informed account from the French side: *Souvenirs militaires*, Paris, 1863, pp. 403–29.

63 The clearest and most detailed description of the intended march-routes is in Horstenau, *Dresden*, pp. 293–6.

64 There is a useful discussion of this decision in T. von Bernhardi, *Denkwürdigkeiten aus dem Leben des kaiserlichen russischen Generals der Infanterie Carl Friedrich Grafen von Toll*, 5 vols., Leipzig, 1858, vol. 3, book 6, pp. 175–83.

65 Saint-Cyr, *Mémoires*, vol. 4, no. 30, Saint-Cyr to Berthier, 29 Aug. 1813, pp. 386–7; Brett-James, *Wilson's Journal*, 30 Aug. 1813, p. 172; the best description of the road is in P. Pototskii, *Istoriia gvardeiskoi artillerii*, SPB, 1896, pp. 261–3.

66 P. Nazarov, 'Zapiski soldata Pamfila Nazarova', *RS*, 9/8, 1878, p. 535.

67 The key order to Vandamme, issued at 4 p.m. on 28 August by Berthier in Napoleon's name, is reprinted as no. 5, p. 204, in the appendices of Ehnl, *Kulm*.

68 The memoirs of Eugen and of Colonel von Helldorff who served on his staff might be seen as biased against Ostermann-Tolstoy, though Aleksei Ermolov also remarked that at the battle of Kulm Ostermann-Tolstoy was more trouble than the French. Helldorff writes that the whole army knew that Ostermann-Tolstoy had mental problems in 1813 after returning from sick leave: Helldorff, *Kulm*, p. 17. Many other memoirs confirm that Ostermann-Tolstoy was in no fit state to command troops in August 1813. In his defence, see I. I. Lazhechnikov, 'Neskol'ko zametok i vospominanii po povodu stat'i "materialy dlia biografii A. P. Ermolova" ', *Russkii vestnik*, 31/6, 1864, pp. 783–819.

69 Eugen, *Memoiren*, vol. 3, pp. 131–3; L. von Wolzogen, *Mémoires d'un Général d'Infanterie au service de la Prusse et de la Russie (1792–1836)*, Paris, 2002, p. 169; Pototskii, *Istoriia*, p. 250. Helldorff says that Ermolov initially supported Ostermann but then backed down for fear of annoying Eugen and therefore bringing Alexander's wrath down on his own head: *Kulm*, pp. 29–30.

70 The best description of the highway and the terrain is in *Istoriia leib-gvardii egerskago polka za sto let 1796–1896*, SPB, 1896, pp. 125–30.

71 Apart, as always, from Bogdanovich, some of the regimental histories offer excellent descriptions of the events of 28 August. The history of the Guards Jaegers, cited in the previous note, is probably the best, but see also e.g. S. A. Gulevich, *Istoriia 8-go pekhotnago Estliandskago polka*, SPB, 1911, pp. 178–81.

72 Helldorff's description of these events, of which he was an eyewitness, is on pp. 35–8 of *Kulm*.

73 Eugen, *Memoiren*, vol. 3, p. 149.

74 All the general histories describe the terrain well, but Bogdanovich, Friederich and Ehnl presumably take it for granted that a reader will know that Bohemian villages were built of wood and say nothing about buildings. It is because he provides small but crucial details of this sort that Aster is so important: on houses, for example, see Aster: *Kriegsereignisse . . . Kulm*, pp. 14–15.

75 Helldorff, *Kulm*, p. 45.

76 Friederich, *Herbstfeldzug*, p. 88; Brett-James, *Wilson's Journal*, p. 173; Londonderrry, *Narrative*, p. 124. *Istoriia leib-gvardii egerskago polka*, p. 135.

77 For Kovalsky's account, see 'Iz zapisok pokoinago general-maiora N. P. Koval'skago', *Russkii vestnik*, 91/1, 1871, pp. 78–117, especially p. 102; 'Zapiski N. N. Murav'eva-Karskago', *RA*, 24/1, 1886, pp. 5–55, especially pp. 22–6; P. Bobrovskii, *Istoriia leib-gvardii ulanskago E.I.V. gosudarynyi Imperatritsy Aleksandry Fedorovny polka*, SPB, 1903, p. 231.

78 On French losses, see Muravev's conversation with Vandamme's chief of staff: 'Zapiski', p. 25; Brett-James, *Wilson's Journal*, p. 173; Bobrovskii, *Istoriia leib-gvardii ulanskago . . . polka*, p. 230.

79 L. G. Beskrovnyi (ed.), *Dnevnik Aleksandra Chicherina, 1812–1813*, Moscow, 1966, pp. 252 ff.; 'Zapiski N. N. Murav'eva', 24/1, 1885, p. 26.

80 This point is well documented by Friederich, *Herbstfeldzug*, pp. 90–92, and Ehnl, *Kulm*, pp. 112–18, so there is no reason why the fable still exists.

81 Bernhardi, *Denkwürdigkeiten*, p. 454.

82 Ehnl, *Kulm*, p. 132, writes that 41,000 allied infantry and 10,000 cavalry faced 39,000 French infantry and 3,000 cavalry. Given Vandamme's casualties on 28 and 29 August, the figure for his infantry seems too high.

83 P. A. Kolzakov, 'Vziatie v plen marshala Vandama 1813 g.', *RS*, 1, 1870, pp. 137–44.

Bogdanovich, *Istoriia . . . 1813*, vol. 2, p. 704; *SIM*, no. 254, Alexander to Rostopchin, 22 Dec. 1813, p. 164.

84 Tartakovskii, *Voennye dnevniki*: Mikhailovsky-Danilevsky's journal for 1813, p. 360.

85 This does not count members of the Romanov family or foreigners.

86 Hoen, *Feldzug von Leipzig*, p. 274: neutral in the sense that Hoen was an Austrian.

87 Friederich, *Herbstfeldzug*, pp. 144–8; Leggiere, *Napoleon and Berlin*, ch. 7 and especially pp. 137–41.

88 RGVIA, Fond 846, Opis 16, Delo 3911, fos. 213–4, Thuyl to Volkonsky, 21 Aug./ 2 Sept. 1813.

89 *VPR*, no. 141, Alexander's instructions to Pozzo, 31 July/10 Aug. 1813, p. 345; Botzenhart, *Stein*, vol. 4, Stein to Munster, 7 and 10 Aug. 1813, pp. 390–92; Londonderry, *Narrative*, p. 179.

90 V. von Löwenstern, *Mémoires du Général-Major Russe Baron de Löwenstern*, 2 vols., Paris, 1903, vol. 2, pp. 136–7, 184–5; S. G. Volkonskii, *Zapiski Sergeia Grigorovicha Volkonskago (dekabrista)*, SPB, 1902, pp. 264–5, 306–7.

91 RGVIA, Fond 846, Opis 16, Delo 3911, Winzengerode to Alexander, 7/19 Aug. 1813, fos. 148–9; 22 Aug./3 Sept. 1813, fos. 289–91; RGVIA, Fond 103, Opis 4/210, Sv. 53, Delo 18, fo. 7: Kankrin to Lotthum, 1/19 July 1813.

92 RGVIA, Fond 103, Opis 4/120, Sv. 18, Delo 57, fos. 5–6: Barclay to Lanskoy, 28 July 1813 (OS); Sv. 53, Delo 18, fo. 25, Barclay to Kankrin, 8 Aug. 1813 (OS).

93 Löwenstern, *Mémoires*, vol. 2, pp. 100, 146–78; Volkonskii, *Zapiski*, pp. 258–9; V. M. Bezotosnyi, *Donskoi generalitet i ataman Platov v 1812 godu*, Moscow, 1899, pp. 109–18.

94 Friederich, *Herbstfeldzug*, pp. 139–73, provides an excellent analysis and description.

95 A recent full account in English of both the battle and some of the disputes that surrounded it is in Leggiere, *Napoleon and Berlin*, ch. 11. Leggiere is more hostile to Bernadotte than is Friederich, *Herbstfeldzug*, pp. 177–91.

96 V. Kharkevich (ed.), *1812 god v dnevnikakh, zapiskakh i vospominaniiakh sovremennikov*, 4 vols., Vilna, 1900–1907, vol. 2, p. 28.

97 Major-General E. S. Kamenskii, *Istoriia 2-go dragunskago S-Peterburgskago generalafel'dmarshala kniazia Menshikova polka 1707–1898*, Moscow, 1900, pp. 225–37. Volkonskii, *Zapiski*, p. 266.

98 Bogdanovich, *Istoriia . . . 1813*, vol. 2, pp. 275, 281.

Chapter 12: The Battle of Leipzig

1 The treaty is in F. Martens (ed.), *Sobranie traktatov i konventsii, zakliuchennykh Rossiei s inostrannymi derzhavami*, vol. 3: *Traktaty s Avsrtieiu*, SPB, 1876, no. 71, pp. 126–38. Kankrin's comments are in *Upravlenie General-Intendanta Kankrina: General'nyi sokrashchennyi otchet po armiiam . . . za pokhody protiv Frantsuzov, 1812, 1813 i 1814 godov*, Warsaw, 1815, pp. 72–6.

2 L. G. Beskrovnyi (ed.), *Pokhod russkoi armii protiv Napoleona v 1813 g. i osvobozhdenie Germanii: Sbornik dokumentov*, Moscow, 1964, no. 214, Jomini to Alexander, 21 Aug./ 2 Sept. 1813, pp. 241–2.

3 The letter to Knesebeck is quoted by Rudolph von Friederich, *Die Befreiungskriege 1813–1815*, vol. 2: *Der Herbstfeldzug 1813*, Berlin, 1912, pp. 214–15; the letter to Alexander is printed in Beskrovnyi (ed.), *Pokhod*, no. 232, Blücher to Alexander, 30 Aug./11 Sept. 1813, pp. 268–9.

4 Rühle's words are quoted by Friederich in *Herbstfeldzug*, p. 215: *VPR*, no. 162, Nesselrode to Pozzo, 21 Sept./3 Oct. 1813, pp. 393–4.

5 RGVIA, Fond 846, Opis 16, Delo 3399, nos. 50 and 51, Volkonsky to Blücher, Volkonsky to Bennigsen, 1/13 Sept. 1813, fos. 21ii–22ii; Delo 3416, 'Zhurnal voennykh deistvii Pol'skoi armii', fos. 12i–14i.

6 M. I. Bogdanovich, *Istoriia voiny 1813 g. za nezavisimost' Germanii*, 2 vols., SPB, 1863, vol. 2, pp. 336–41; RGVIA, Fond 846, Opis 16, Delo 3399, Volkonsky to Platov, 4 Sept. 1813 (OS), fos. 24ii–25i.

7 Chernyshev's journal covers the raid in fos. 26–31 of RGVIA, Fond 846, Opis 16, Delo 3386. Bogdanovich, *Istoriia . . . 1813*, vol. 2, pp. 342–55, provides a narrative, though my conclusions are very different from his.

8 A. Raevskii, *Vospominaniia o pokhodakh 1813 i 1814 godov*, Moscow, 1822, pp. 1–77.

9 RGVIA, Fond 846, Opis 16, Delo 3416, fos. 16i–17ii.

10 The best and most detailed narrative is in *Geschichte der Kämpfe Österreichs: Kriege unter der Regierung des Kaisers Franz. Befreiungskrieg 1813 und 1814*, vol. 5: M. von Hoen, *Feldzug von Leipzig*, Vienna, 1913; on Schwarzenberg's fears see RGVIA, Fond 846, Opis 16, Delo 3399, Volkonsky to Oppermann, no. 97, 24 Sept. 1813 (OS), fos. 38i–39i; on victualling, see A. A. Eiler, 'Zapiski A. A. Eilera', *RS*, 1/11, 1880, p. 367 and *Pokhod*, no. 254, Barclay to Wittgenstein, 20 Sept./2 Oct. 1813, pp. 296–7.

11 RGVIA, Fond 846, Opis 16, Delo 3385, Bernadotte to Winzengerode, 2 Oct. 1813, fo. 57i; I. Radozhitskii, *Pokhodnyia zapiski artillerista s 1812 po 1816 god*, 3 vols., Moscow, 1835, vol. 2, p. 246.

12 It is true that some of the 35,000 were sick, but the basic point remains valid: on Bennigsen's deployment of troops at Dresden, see *Feldzug der kaiserlichen Russischen Armee von Polen in den Jahren 1813 und 1814*, Hamburg, 1843, pp. 33–6.

13 *Mémoires de Langeron, Général d'Infanterie dans l'Armée Russe: Campagnes de 1812, 1813, 1814*, Paris, 1902, pp. 222, 298.

14 RGVIA, Fond 846, Opis 16, Delo 3403, fos. 27i–28ii, Sacken to Barclay, 1 Oct. 1813 (OS).

15 Langeron, *Mémoires*, pp. 299–300.

16 I visited the battlefield on two occasions, before major construction began on the motorway which will provide a bypass for Leipzig and in the process ruin much of the southern battlefield.

17 Hon. George Cathcart, *Commentaries on the War in Russia and Germany in 1812 and 1813*, London, 1850, p. 298.

18 Friederich, *Herbstfeldzug*, p. 294.

19 Ibid., p. 295.

20 Bogdanovich cites Alexander's words: *Istoriia . . . 1813*, vol. 2, p. 439.

21 Hoen, *Feldzug von Leipzig*, pp. 402–10. The possibility of treason is raised by Digby Smith (*1813 – Leipzig, Napoleon and the Battle of the Nations*, London, 2001, p. 69) but no evidence is provided. My own explanation is partly drawn from Ludwig von Wolzogen, *Mémoires d'un Général d'Infanterie au service de la Prusse et de la Russie (1792–1836)*, Paris, 2002, pp. 179–82.

22 The statistics come from Friederich, *Herbstfeldzug*, pp. 296–300.

23 Eugen, *Memoiren*, vol. 3, p. 230.

24 J.-N. Noel, *With Napoleon's Guns*, London, 2005, pp. 180–81.

25 Friederich, *Herbstfeldzug*, p. 232; *Mémoires du Général Griois*, Paris, n.d., p. 202; Eugen, *Memoiren*, vol. 3, p. 232. Smith, *Leipzig*, p. 86, argues that Eugen should have moved his corps out of the line of fire or at least ordered them to lie down. But the prince could not just decamp and leave a hole in the allied line. Moreover, Russian troops (or Prussian and Austrian ones) were not trained to lie down in sight of enemy guns. Even Wellington's infantry might have hesitated to do so on an open glacis with a mass of enemy cavalry nearby.

26 RGVIA, Fond 489, Opis 1, Delo 754, fos. 38 ff.

27 All this information comes from the personnel records (*posluzhnye spiski*) of the Murom Regiment in RGVIA, Fond 489, Opis 1, Ed. Khr. 517: each rank has its separate *posluzhnoi spisok*, beginning on fo. 2.

28 See for instance a report from Diebitsch to Barclay timed at 8 a.m. on 16 October in which the former urges that the Guards be moved forward immediately: unless this was

done 'the distance to Rotha is so great that they will never arrive in time': Beskrovnyi (ed.), *Pokhod*, no. 283, Diebitsch to Barclay, 4/16 Oct. 1813, p. 329.

29 As one might expect, the Austrian official history gives most attention to this part of the battle but its account is largely confirmed by Bogdanovich: the Austrians and Russians were not very fond of each other even in 1813 and had become a good deal less so by the time they got round to writing their official histories of the campaign. On the whole, a good rule of thumb is to believe the Russian history when it praises the Austrians, and vice versa. If in doubt, Friederich is often a remarkably fair and neutral arbiter. Hoen, *Feldzug von Leipzig*, pp. 471–82; Bogdanovich, *Istoriia ... 1813*, vol. 2, pp. 461–4; Friederich, *Herbstfeldzug*, pp. 308–12.

30 Beskrovnyi (ed.), *Pokhod*, no. 300, Diebitsch's account of the battle of Leipzig, 1813, pp. 360–81, at pp. 363–5.

31 Cathcart, *Commentaries*, pp. 306–7.

32 Ibid., pp. 307–8.

33 Ibid., p. 308; P. Pototskii, *Istoriia gvardeiskoi artillerii*, SPB, 1896, pp. 271–2; A. Mikaberidze, *The Russian Officer Corps in the Revolutionary and Napoleonic Wars, 1795–1815*, Staplehurst, 2005, p. 382.

34 Bogdanovich, *Istoriia ... 1813*, p. 460; Pototskii, *Istoriia gvardeiskoi artillerii*, pp. 270–73. Beskrovnyi (ed.), *Pokhod*, no. 299, Sukhozhanet to Iashvili, 29 Dec. 1813/ 10 Jan. 1814, pp. 358–60; no. 300, Diebitsch's account of Leipzig, 1813, pp. 365–7.

35 'Vospominaniia Matveia Matveevicha Muromtseva', *RA*, 27/3, 1890, pp. 366–94, at p. 378.

36 *Dnevnik Pavla Pushchina*, Leningrad, 1987, p. 128.

37 S. Gulevich, *Istoriia leib gvardii Finliandskago polka 1806–1906*, SPB, 1896, pp. 303–13; *Istoriia leib-gvardii egerskago polka za sto let 1796–1896*, SPB, 1906, pp. 144–50; Griois, *Mémoires*, pp. 202–3.

38 Gulevich, *Istoriia leib gvardii Finliandskago polka*, pp. 312–15.

39 'Zapiski soldata Pamfila Nazarova', *RS*, 9/8, 1878, pp. 536–7.

40 There is a good description of Vasilchikov's attack in Smith, *Leipzig*, pp. 166–8.

41 Hoen, *Feldzug von Leipzig*, pp. 619–27.

42 D. V. Dushenkovich, 'Iz moikh vospominanii ot 1812 goda', in *1812 god v vospominani-iakh sovremennikov*, Moscow, 1995, pp. 124–6.

43 Langeron, *Mémoires*, p. 330.

44 Ibid., pp. 326–34; Radozhitskii, *Pokhodnyia zapiski*, vol. 2, pp. 269–74.

45 Bogdanovich, *Istoriia ... 1813*, vol. 2, pp. 550–51.

46 On the 39th Jaegers, see RGVIA, Fond 489, Opis 1, Ed. Khr. 1802, *passim*, but also Sacken's reports after the fall of Czenstochowa (RGVIA, Fond 846, Opis 16, Delo 3403, fos. 8ii–9i: Sacken to Kutuzov, 25 March 1813 (OS)) and the battle of Leipzig; Beskrovnyi (ed.), *Pokhod*, no. 293, pp. 349–51: Sacken to Barclay, 18/30 Oct. 1813.

47 See RGVIA, Fond 489, Opis 1, Delo 1855, fos. 2 ff., for the 45th Jaegers ('Spisok ... 45go Egerskago polka' dated 1 July 1813) and Delo 1794, fos. 2 ff., for the 29th Jaegers ('29-go egerskago polka ... o sluzhbe ikh i po prochim', dated 1 Jan. 1814). Beskrovnyi (ed.), *Pokhod*, no. 300, Diebitsch's account, pp. 379–82; Langeron, *Mémoires*, p. 343.

48 Smith, *Leipzig*, p. 272, on attempts to shift responsibility.

49 On allied losses, see e.g. Smith, *Leipzig*, p. 298; on French statistics, see J. Tulard (ed.), *Dictionnaire Napoléon*, Paris, 1987, p. 354; on lost guns, see Hoen, *Feldzug von Leipzig*, pp. 652–4.

Chapter 13: The Invasion of France

1 F. Martens (ed.), *Sobranie traktatov i konventsii, zakliuchennykh Rossiei s inostrannymi derzhavami*, vol. 3: *Traktaty s Avstrieiu*, SPB, 1876, no. 70, pp. 111–26, and vol. 7: *Traktaty s Germeniei 1811–1824*, SPB, 1885, no. 259, pp. 96–112, for Russia's treaties with Austria and Prussia. The Austro-Prussian treaty was identical.

2 See e.g. a letter from Count Münster, the Hanoverian statesman, to the Prince Regent (the future George IV of Britain) about the arguments over military and diplomatic policy towards France in January: 'The main factor in all these disagreements is that Russia has not stated how far it wishes to extend its borders in Poland.' A. Fournier, *Der Congress von Chatillon: Die Politik im Kriege von 1814*, Vienna, 1900, sect. IV, no. 1, Münster to Prince Regent, 30 January 1814, pp. 295–6.

3 There is a large literature even in English about Metternich and his policies. The two great pillars of this literature are Paul W. Schroeder, *The Transformation of European Politics 1763–1848*, Oxford, 1994, and Henry Kissinger, *A World Restored*, London, 1957. Schroeder's book in particular is a splendid piece of scholarship. Alan Sked punctures some of the more elevated interpretations of Metternich's 'system' in *Metternich and Austria*, London, 2008. As regards this book's focus, in other words Metternich's role in Napoleon's overthrow, I have some sympathy with his scepticism.

4 On Knesebeck's views, see R. von Friederich, *Die Befreiungskriege 1813–1815*, vol. 3: *Der Feldzug 1814*, Berlin, 1913, pp. 81–2.

5 Baron Karl von Müffling, *The Memoirs of Baron von Müffling: A Prussian Officer in the Napoleonic Wars*, London, 1967, pp. 92–3, 100–101, 418–19.

6 On Frederick William, see Chapter 9, n. 18.

7 Fournier, *Congress*, p. 10. Paul Schroeder tries to defend Aberdeen, not altogether convincingly, in 'An Unnatural "Natural Alliance": Castlereagh, Metternich, and Aberdeen in 1813', *International History Review*, 10/4, Nov. 1988, pp. 522–40. VPR, 7, no. 191, Alexander's instructions to Lieven and Pozzo di Borgo, 6 Dec. 1813, pp. 492–500.

8 N. A. M. Rodger, *The Command of the Ocean*, London, 2004, pp. 572–3, sets out the elements of British power.

9 VPR, 7, no. 249, Dubachevsky to Rumiantsev, 2 April 1814, pp. 230–37.

10 Castlereagh's statement is in a key letter to Aberdeen on British war aims, dated 13 November 1813. See Marquess of Londonderry (ed.), *Correspondence, Despatches, and Other Papers of Viscount Castlereagh*, 12 vols., vol. 9, London, 1853, pp. 73–6.

11 VPR, 7, no. 180, n.d. but not later than 20 Nov. 1813: Chernyshev to Alexander, pp. 447–51.

12 VPR, 7, no. 171, Gurev to Nesselrode, 3 Nov. 1813, pp. 429–31; N. Kiselev and I. Iu. Samarin (eds.), *Zapiski, mneniia i perepiska Admirala A. S. Shishkova*, 2 vols., Berlin, 1870; A. de Jomini, *Précis politique et militaire des campagnes de 1812 à 1814*, 2 vols. in 1, Geneva, 1975, vol. 2, pp. 231–2; Fournier, *Congress*, annex VI, Hardenberg's diary, 27 Feb. 1814, p. 364.

13 VPR, 7, no. 197, Nesselrode to Gurev, 19 Dec. 1813, pp. 512–14. Count A. de Nesselrode (ed.), *Lettres et papiers du Chancelier Comte de Nesselrode 1760–1850*, Paris, n.d., vol. 6, pp. 152–3: Nesselrode to his wife, 16 Jan. 1814.

14 SIRIO, 31, 1881, pp. 301–3: 'Memoire présenté par le comte de Nesselrode sur les affaires de Pologne'.

15 VPR, 7, no. 207, Nesselrode to Alexander, 9 Jan. 1814, pp. 539–41.

16 *Nesselrode*, vol. 6, pp. 161–3, Nesselrode to his wife, 28 Feb. 1814; Countess Nesselrode to her husband, 9 April 1814, pp. 188–90. *Castlereagh*, vol. 9, Castlereagh to Lord Liverpool, 30 Jan. 1814, pp. 212–14.

17 See Baron Hardenberg's comments in his diary entry for 27 Feb.: Fournier, *Congress*, p. 364.

18 *Castlereagh*, vol. 9, Stewart to Castlereagh, 30 March 1814, pp. 412–13.

19 Fournier, *Congress*, Metternich to Hudelist, 9 Nov. 1813, p. 242.

20 The manifesto is reproduced in Baron Fain, *Manuscrit de Mil Huit Cent Quatorze*, Paris, 1825: no. 5, pp. 60–61.

21 Fournier, *Congress*, p. 8, mentions the agreement between Alexander and Metternich in Meiningen. Fain, *Manuscrit de Mil Huit Cent Quatorze*, nos. 1 and 2, pp. 49–56, gives Saint-Aignan's report to Napoleon and his memorandum stating the allied terms.

22 On Alexander's innermost thoughts, see 'Grafinia Roksandra Skarlatovna Edling:

Zapiski', in A. Libermann (ed.), *Derzhavnyi sfinks*, Moscow, 1999, p. 181; *SIRIO*, 31, 1881: 'Considérations générales sur la politique du Cabinet de Russie à la fin de la Campagne de 1813', pp. 343–5. For Castlereagh's very measured subsequent 'advice' to Aberdeen, see *Castlereagh*, vol. 9, Castlereagh to Aberdeen, 30 Nov. 1813, pp. 73–6.

23 Fain, *Manuscrit de Mil Huit Cent Quatorze*, no. 5, pp. 60–61.

24 Benckendorff's own account is in *Zapiski Benkendorfa, 1812 god: Otechestvennaia voina. 1813 god. Osvobozhdenie Niderlandov*, Moscow, 2001, pp. 205–38. On the jaegers, see V. V. Rantsov, *Istoriia 96-go pekhotnago Omskago polka*, SPB, 1902, pp. 187–90. The French comment is by Captain Koch in *Mémoires pour servir à l'histoire de la campagne de 1814*, 3 vols., Paris, 1819, vol. 1, p. 69.

25 The fullest recent study of events in the Netherlands is M. V. Leggiere, *The Fall of Napoleon: The Allied Invasion of France 1813–1814*, Cambridge, 2008, pp. 100–104, 145–87. For the background to the revolt, see Simon Schama, *Patriots and Liberators*, London, 2005.

26 See e.g. Friederich, *Feldzug*, pp. 6–10.

27 *VPR*, 7, no. 172, Barclay to Alexander, 9 Nov. 1813, pp. 431–3. For Blücher, see e.g. his report to Alexander of 23 Nov.: RGVIA, Fond 846, Opis 16, Delo 3915, fos. 121–2. The historian of the Riazan Regiment wrote that 'the storming of Schönefeld had weakened the regiment and the march to the Rhine almost destroyed it': I. I. Shelengovskii, *Istoriia 69-go Riazanskago polka*, 3 vols., Lublin, 1911, vol. 2, p. 246.

28 For most of these statistics, see M. I. Bogdanovich, *Istoriia voiny 1814 goda vo Frantsii*, 2 vols., SPB, 1865, vol. 1, pp. 35–40, 48–9. He states that 45 squadrons had arrived by 27 December from Lobanov but 18 more were on the way, and in fact still more arrived subsequently. See e.g. Lobanov's report to Alexander of 15 Nov. 1813 (OS) in RGVIA, Fond 125, Opis 1, Delo 148, fos. 44–7.

29 S. Panchulidzev, *Istoriia kavalergardov*, SPB, 1903, vol. 3, p. 433. Barclay reported to Alexander that of the 6,250 men on the rolls of the reserve units reaching Wittgenstein, only 48 had been left behind in hospital en route: *MVUA 1813*, 1, Barclay to Alexander, 22 Dec. 1813 (OS), p. 276.

30 *MVUA 1813*, 1, Barclay to Alexander, 30 Nov., 1 and 22 Dec. 1813 (OS), pp. 258–60, 276; Barclay to Army Corps GOCs, 21 Dec. 1813 (OS), p. 275. Bogdanovich, *Istoriia...1814*, vol. 1, p. 80. *SIM*, 4, no. 3, Alexander to Lobanov, 3 Jan. 1814 (OS), p. 3. On the general appearance of the line army in the 1814 campaign, see Il'ia Ul'ianov, 'I eti nas pobedili', *Rodina*, 8, 2002, pp. 74–8; Oleg Sheremet'ev, 'Katat' shineli, gospoda', *Rodina*, 6, 2006, pp. 53–9.

31 Bogdanovich's and Friederich's histories of the 1814 campaign say something about this, but the key text is by Peter Graf von Kielmansegg, *Stein und die Zentralverwaltung 1813/14*, Stuttgart, 1964.

32 For Kutuzov's comments, see Count de Puybusque, *Lettres sur la Guerre de Russie en 1812*, Paris, 1816, pp. 153 ff., 18 Dec. 1812. For the fortresses, see a recent work by Paddy Griffith, *The Vauban Fortifications of France*, Oxford, 2006.

33 See e.g. Barclay's report to Alexander of 9 Nov. 1813 (*VPR*, 7, no. 172, pp. 431–3), but also his letter to Kankrin of 29 Jan. 1814 (OS), in RGVIA, Fond 103, Opis 4/210, Sv. 18, Delo 17, fo. 128.

34 For the Austrian view on this, see Karl Fürst Schwarzenberg, *Feldmarschall Fürst Schwarzenberg: Der Sieger von Leipzig*, Vienna, 1964, pp. 268–71. Jomini's line is inevitably different: see Jomini, *Précis*, vol. 2, pp. 224–5, 228–31. Friederich, *Feldzug*, pp. 9–15, gives a balanced account but argues that going through Switzerland was probably unnecessary. Alexander's letter to Bernadotte is in *VPR*, 7, no. 174, pp. 434–6. His indignant letter to Schwarzenberg of 5 Jan. 1814 is in RGVIA, Fond 846, Opis 16, Delo 3399, fo. 108.

35 Marquess of Londonderry, *Narrative of the War in Germany and France in 1813 and 1814*, London, 1830, pp. 254–5. Perhaps Stewart's feelings at the time were not as clear-cut as this last sentence, written in 1830, implies.

36 Lord Burghersh, *The Operations of the Allied Armies in 1813 and 1814*, London, 1822, pp. 72–3.

37 *Dnevnik Pavla Pushchina*, Leningrad, 1987, pp. 142–3. I. Radozhitskii, *Pokhodnyia zapiski artillerista s 1812 po 1816 god*, 3 vols., Moscow, 1835, vol. 3, pp. 36–9. 'Iz zapisok pokoinago general-maiora N. P. Koval'skago', *Russkii vestnik*, 91/1, 1871, pp. 106–7. RGVIA, Fond 846, Opis 16, Delo 3399, fos. 120i–ii, Alexander to Platov, 24 Jan. 1814 (OS).

38 RGVIA, Fond 846, Opis 16, Delo 3399, fos. 99ii–100i, Alexander to Blücher, 14 Dec. 1813 (OS). For reasons of space this is an abbreviated account: for a fuller one, see Leggiere, *Fall of Napoleon*, chs. 10–16, and Friederich, *Feldzug*, pp. 60–72.

39 These points are covered by Leggiere, *Fall of Napoleon*, and Friederich, *Feldzug*, but on the running down of conscription see Isser Woloch, *The New Regime: Transformations of the French Civil Order, 1789–1820s*, London, 1994, ch. 13, pp. 380–426.

40 For accounts of the battle, see Friederich, *Feldzug*, pp. 89–95; Bogdanovich, *Istoriia . . . 1814*, vol. 1, pp. 108–13; James Lawford, *Napoleon: The Last Campaigns. 1813–15*, London, 1976, pp. 68–101. Sacken's own rather laconic report on the battle is in RGVIA, Fond 846, Opis 16, Delo 3403, fos. 34ii–35ii, Sacken to Barclay, 17 Jan. 1814 (OS).

41 Quotation from Friederich, *Feldzug*, p. 103. See Sacken's letter to Barclay de Tolly of 27 Jan. 1814 (OS), in RGVIA, Fond 846, Opis 16, Delo 3403, fo. 37i.

42 RGVIA, Fond 846, Opis 16, Delo 3403, fos. 36i–ii, Sacken to Barclay, 21 Jan. 1814 (OS). Bogdanovich, *Istoriia . . . 1814*, vol. 1, p. 128.

43 F. von Schubert, *Unter dem Doppeladler*, Stuttgart, 1962, p. 343, on Blücher and the wine cellar.

44 See Alexander's letter to Blücher of 26 Jan. 1814 (OS) in RGVIA, Fond 846, Opis 16, Delo 3399, fos. 121ii–122i.

45 Schwarzenberg, *Schwarzenberg*, pp. 276–300.

46 Friederich, *Feldzug*, pp. 81–2. Burghersh, *Operations*, pp. 91–103, 250–52.

47 Fournier, *Congress*, pp. 42–4, 58–63; see above all Francis II's reply (p. 277) to Schwarzenberg's letter of 8 Feb. (pp. 272–3). Schwarzenberg was clearly asking for instructions to stand still and these the emperor supplied. Schwarzenberg, *Schwarzenberg*, pp. 276–9, 293–9.

48 Fournier, *Congress*, pp. 105–14. The text of Metternich's memorandum is in *SIRIO*, 31, 1881, pp. 349–55.

49 Alexander's response to Metternich's questions is in *SIRIO*, 31, 1881, pp. 355–60. A summary of the British, Austrian and Prussian views is in Fournier, *Congress*, pp. 285–9.

50 For Madame de Staël's view on Alexander, see her *Ten Years' Exile*, Fontwell, 1968, pp. 377–82. On Alexander's view of Louis, see Philip Mansel, *Louis XVIII*, London, 2005, p. 164. On Bernadotte's candidacy, see F. D. Scott, 'Bernadotte and the Throne of France 1814', *Journal of Modern History*, 5, 1933, pp. 465–78. There is nothing in the Russian military or diplomatic correspondence of 1814 which suggests more than a passing interest in Bernadotte's candidature. In 1813 Alexander had written that Bernadotte's private hopes for the French crown could be indulged so long as they did not impede his contribution to the allied cause. In 1814 the emperor may even have encouraged Bernadotte's hopes as a way of luring him back from his campaign against Denmark.

51 Baron de Vitrolles, *Mémoires et relations politiques*, 3 vols., Paris, 1884, vol. 1, pp. 115–20.

52 For the conversation with Castlereagh, see T. von Bernhardi, *Denkwürdigkeiten aus dem Leben des kaiserlichen russischen Generals der Infanterie Carl Friedrich Grafen von Toll*, 5 vols., Leipzig, 1858, vol. 4ii, p. 58.

53 Fournier, *Congress*, pp. 105–37; Friederich, *Feldzug*, pp. 156–64.

54 See e.g. Karl von Clausewitz, *Der Feldzug von 1812 in Russland, der Feldzug von 1813 bis zum Waffenstillstand und der Feldzug von 1814 in Frankreich*, Berlin, 1862, pp. 361–71. Müffling, *Memoirs*, pp. 115–45. Friederich, *Feldzug*, pp. 117–47, is as always admirably fair and balanced.

55 Major-General Kornilov was the senior officer of Olsufev's corps who escaped: his report

on the battle is in M. Galkin, *Boevaia sluzhba 27-go pekhotnago Vitebskago polka 1703–1903*, Moscow, 1908, pp. 223–4. On Olsufev's losses, see: Napoleon to Joseph, 10 Feb. 1814, in A. du Casse (ed.), *Mémoires et correspondance politique et militaire du Roi Joseph*, Paris, 1854, p. 85.

56 The basic narrative is from Friederich, *Feldzug*, pp. 129–34, and Bogdanovich, *Istoriia . . . 1814*, vol. 1, pp. 186–96. Sacken's official report to Barclay, dated 3 Feb. 1814 (OS), is in RGVIA, Fond 846, Opis 16, Ed. Khr. 3403, fos. 37ii–39i. The description of Sacken the day after the battle is from Bernhardi, *Denkwürdigkeiten*, vol. 4i, p. 393. There is a good description of the retreat in the history of the Pskov Infantry Regiment: Captain Geniev, *Istoriia Pskovskago pekhotnago general-fel'dmarshala kniazia Kutuzova-Smolenskago polka: 1700–1831*, Moscow, 1883, pp. 233–6.

57 Koch, *Mémoires*, vol. 1, pp. 267–8. There is a good description of this retreat in Müffling, *Memoirs*, pp. 128–36.

58 Bogdanovich, *Istoriia . . . 1814*, vol. 1, pp. 206–8. Du Casse, *Mémoires . . . du Roi Joseph*, Napoleon to Joseph, 11 Feb. 1814, pp. 88 ff. *Correspondance de Napoléon Ier*, 32 vols., Paris, 1858–70, vol. 27, Paris, 1869, no. 21295, Napoleon to Eugéne, 18 Feb. 1814, pp. 192–3.

59 Fain, *Manuscrit de Mil Huit Cent Quatorze*, nos. 12 and 13, Bassano to Caulaincourt, 5 Feb. and Caulaincourt to Bassano, 6 Feb. 1814, pp. 253–7.

60 Ibid., no. 26, Napoleon to Caulaincourt, 17 Feb. 1814, pp. 284–5. *Correspondance de Napoléon*, vol. 27, no. 21344, Napoleon to Francis II, 21 Feb. 1814, pp. 224–7; no. 21295, Napoleon to Eugène, 18 Feb. 1814, pp. 192–3. Du Casse, *Mémoires . . . du Roi Joseph*, Napoleon to Joseph, 18 Feb. 1814, pp. 133 ff.

61 For Alexander's warning to Wittgenstein, see RGVIA, Fond 846, Opis 16, Delo 3399, fo. 125ii, Alexander to Wittgenstein, 4 February 1814 (OS). On Pahlen and Wittgenstein, see M. Bogdanovich, 'Graf Petr Petrovich fon der Pahlen i ego vremiia', *VS*, 7/8, 1864, pp. 411–26, at pp. 418–19.

62 For Wittgenstein, see the previous note. On the Estland Regiment, see S. A. Gulevich, *Istoriia 8go pekhotnago Estliandskago polka*, SPB, 1911, p. 208.

63 Schwarzenberg, *Schwarzenberg*, pp. 281–8, for his comments about Blücher. Fournier, *Congress*, no. 14, pp. 277–8, for his letter to Francis II of 20 Feb. and no. 13, p. 277, for Francis's instructions to remain south of the Seine until it was clear whether or not the peace negotiations would succeed. Count Münster's letter to the Prince Regent of 23 Feb. describes allied suspicions of Austrian 'bleeding' tactics: Fournier, *Congress*, no. 9, p. 302.

64 On frustration in the ranks, see Sabaneev's letter to P. M. Volkonsky of 20 Feb. (OS): RGVIA, Fond 846, Opis 16, Delo 4166, fo. 65i, and on orders to Oertel and the Evdokimov case his letters of 28 Jan. (OS) to Major-General Oldekop (fo. 40i) and to the Grand Duke Constantine of 24 Jan. (fo. 42i).

65 The voluminous correspondence above all between Barclay and Kankrin in RGVIA, Fond 103, Opis 4/210, Sv. 18, Delo 17, gives a detailed sense of the army's efforts to feed itself and the problems they encountered: see in particular fos. 128i–ii, Barclay to Kankrin, 29 Jan. 1814 (OS); fos. 153i–ii, Barclay to Kankrin, 9 Feb. 1814 (OS); fos. 160i–ii, Kankrin to Barclay, 14 Feb. 1814 (OS). M. Dandevil', *Stoletie 5-go dragunskago Kurliandskago Imperatora Aleksandra III-go polka*, SPB, 1903, p. 105.

66 RGVIA, Fond 103, Opis 4/120, Sv. 18, Delo 17, fos. 109–10, Kankrin to Barclay, 17 Jan. 1814 (OS); fos. 172–5, Kankrin to Barclay, 20 Feb. 1814 (OS); fo. 218, Barclay to Oertel, 7 March 1814 (OS). V. von Löwenstern, *Mémoires du Général-Major Russe Baron de Löwenstern*, 2 vols., Paris, 1903, vol. 2, pp. 315–20.

Chapter 14: The Fall of Napoleon

1 RGVIA, Fond 103, Opis 4/120, Sv. 18, Delo 17, fos. 68–70, Kankrin to Barclay (enclosing Lisanevich's own report: fos. 70–71), 14 Jan. 1814 (OS); fos. 73–5, Barclay to Kankrin, 15 Jan. 1814 (OS) (on how the mobile magazine should be used); fo. 127, Kankrin to

Barclay, 27 Jan. 1814 (OS) (on the magazines' survival almost intact); fo. 160, Kankrin to Barclay, 15 Feb. 1814 (OS) (on how the mobile magazines had already supplied biscuit rations for one month); fo. 204, Kankrin to Barclay, 27 Feb. 1814 (OS) (on the dispatch of Kondratev's magazine to Joinville).

2 RGVIA, Fond 103, Opis 4/210, Sv. 18, Delo 17, fos. 50–52: Stein's letter to Barclay explaining the arrangements to administer occupied territory and defining the districts, dated 25 Jan. (NS) 1814. For Alopaeus's initial responses see: fos. 188–9, Kankrin to Barclay, 22 Feb. 1814 (OS), and fos. 201–3, Alopaeus to Barclay, 23 Feb. 1814 (OS). See also Peter Graf von Kielmansegg, *Stein und die Zentralverwaltung 1813/14*, Stuttgart, 1964, part 4, pp. 98 ff.

3 RGVIA, Fond 103, Opis 4/210, Sv. 12, Delo 126, fos. 52–3, Kankrin to Barclay, 22 Jan. 1814 (OS).

4 RGVIA, Fond 103, Opis 4/210, Sv. 18, Delo 17, fo. 204, Kankrin to Barclay, 27 Feb. 1814 (OS); fos. 205–7, Alopaeus to Kankrin, 25 Feb. (OS).

5 A. Fournier, *Der Congress von Chatillon: Die Politik im Kriege von 1814*, Vienna, 1900, no. 27, Metternich to Stadion, 9 March 1814, pp. 334–5. Lord Burghersh, *The Operations of the Allied Armies in 1813 and 1814*, London, 1822, pp. 177–85, for a retrospective, 'sanitized' view.

6 Dispatch from Lieven to Nesselrode, 26 Jan. 1814, enclosed in a letter from Castlereagh to Liverpool, 18 Feb. 1814: Marquess of Londonderry (ed.), *Correspondence, Despatches, and Other Papers of Viscount Castlereagh*, 12 vols., vol. 9, London, 1853, pp. 266–73.

7 F. Martens (ed.), *Sobranie traktatov i konventsii, zakliuchennykh Rossiei s inostrannymi derzhavami*, vol. 3: *Traktaty s Avstrieiu*, SPB, 1876, no. 73, pp. 148–65.

8 RGVIA, Fond 846, Opis 16, Delo 3399, fos. 131ii–132i. *SIRIO*, 31, 1881, pp. 364–5, has the protocol of the meeting of 25 February. M. Bogdanovich, *Istoriia voiny 1814 goda vo Frantsii*, 2 vols., SPB, 1865, vol. 1, pp. 268–70.

9 K. von Clausewitz, *Der Feldzug von 1812 in Russland, der Feldzug von 1813 bis zum Waffenstillstand und der Feldzug von 1814 in Frankreich*, Berlin, 1862, pp. 375–7; Baron Karl von Müffling, *The Memoirs of Baron von Müffling: A Prussian Officer in the Napoleonic Wars*, ed. P. Hofschroer, London, 1997, pp. 146–71; V. von Löwenstern, *Mémoires du Général-Major Russe Baron de Löwenstern*, 2 vols., Paris, 1903, vol. 2, pp. 325–34. *Correspondance de Napoléon Ier*, 32 vols., Paris, 1858–70, vol. 27, no. 21439, Napoleon to Joseph, 5 March 1814, pp. 288–9. Henri Houssaye, *Napoleon and the Campaign of 1814: France*, Uckfield, 2004, pp. 116–41, tends to be an uncritical apologist for the Bonapartist line. Bogdanovich, *Istoriia . . . 1814*, vol. 1, pp. 299–307.

10 For the basic narrative from rival sides, see Bogdanovich, *Istoriia . . . 1814*, vol. 1, pp. 309–29; Houssaye, *Napoleon*, pp. 142–59. R. von Friederich, *Die Befreiungskriege 1813–1815*, vol. 3: *Der Feldzug 1814*, Berlin, 1913, pp. 214–22, is semi-neutral and accurate. On Heurtebise, and the battle of the Russian jaegers, see S. I. Maevskii, 'Moi vek, ili istoriia generala Maevskogo, 1779–1848', *RS*, 8, 1873, pp. 268–73. He commanded the 13th Jaeger Regiment during the battle.

11 Apart from the works cited in the previous note, see specifically on the Russian retreat, Ivan Ortenberg, 'Voennyia vospominaniia starykh vremen', *Biblioteka dlia chteniia*, 24/6, 1857, pp. 18–33, at pp. 18–19.

12 Burghersh, *Operations*, p. 196. Clausewitz, *Feldzug*, 1862, p. 379.

13 Bogdanovich, *Istoriia . . . 1814*, vol. 1, pp. 324–5; Captain Koch, *Mémoires pour servir à l'histoire de la campagne de 1814*, 3 vols., Paris, 1819, vol. 1, pp. 399–400. Houssaye, *Napoleon*, p. 157. Alain Pigeard, *Dictionnaire de la Grande Armée*, Paris, 2002, pp. 648–9. Friederich, *Feldzug*, writes that 15,000 Russians actually fought 21,000 French soldiers on the battlefield of Craonne.

14 There is a good description of meeting Blücher at this time in F. von Schubert, *Unter dem Doppeladler*, Stuttgart, 1962, pp. 345–6.

15 Friederich, *Feldzug*, pp. 243–8; Müffling, *Memoirs*, pp. 167–76.

16 I. I. Shelengovskii, *Istoriia 69-go Riazanskago polka*, 3 vols., Lublin, 1911, vol. 2,

pp. 251–75. Skobelev was actually an *odnodvorets*, in other words the descendant of free peasant colonists who had manned the southern frontier regions of Muscovy in the fifteenth and sixteenth centuries. By Alexander's reign the burdens and constraints on *odnodvortsy* were roughly the same as those of the state peasantry.

17 Alexander's correspondence in RGVIA, Fond 846, Opis 16, Delo 3399, contains a mass of letters expressing these worries: see e.g. fos. 147ii and 151i for letters of 28 Feb. (OS) to Schwarzenberg urging him to press forward more quickly, and of 5 March (OS) to Nikolai Raevsky, who had replaced Wittgenstein, warning him not to become isolated and to expect an attack by Napoleon at any moment. For the scenes at GHQ, see Karl Fürst Schwarzenberg, *Feldmarschall Fürst Schwarzenberg: Der Sieger von Leipzig*, Vienna, 1964, pp. 306–8, 483–4. *Mémoires de Langeron, Général d'Infanterie dans l'Armée Russe: Campagnes de 1812, 1813, 1814*, Paris, 1902, p. 423.

18 Langeron, *Mémoires*, pp. 434–7, has a good discussion of these two options.

19 T. von Bernhardi, *Denkwürdigkeiten aus dem Leben des kaiserlichen russischen Generals der Infanterie Carl Friedrich Grafen von Toll*, 5 vols., Leipzig, 1858, vol. 4ii, pp. 292–4, cites Napoleon's own subsequent conversations on this point.

20 RGVIA, Fond 846, Opis 16, Delo 3399, fo. 154ii, Volkonsky to Gneisenau, 10 March 1814 (OS). The basic narrative of events is the same in Friederich, *Feldzug*, and in Bogdanovich, *Istoriia . . . 1814*.

21 Friederich, *Feldzug*, pp. 281–2. On previous criticism of Oertel, see RGVIA, Fond 103, Opis 4/120, Sv. 12, Delo 126, fo. 71: Barclay to Oertel, 16 Feb. 1814 (OS). A. Mikhailovskii-Danilevskii, *Opisanie pokhoda vo Frantsii v 1814 godu*, SPB, repr. 1841, pp. 284–5.

22 The only witness of this discussion to leave a detailed account is Toll: see Bernhardi, *Denkwürdigkeiten*, vol. 4ii, pp. 310–14. Bernhardi is right to dismiss Austrian claims to authorship of the plan, for which there is no evidence and which make a nonsense of Schwarzenberg's actions. One cannot rule out Volkonsky's role so easily, however. According to Mikhailovsky-Danilevsky, Alexander himself told him of Volkonsky's advice. If Mikhailovsky had merely recorded Volkonsky's role in his published history one could easily dismiss it as one of his many efforts to please still-living grandees of Nicholas's reign by praising their role in the war. But he says the same in a manuscript not intended for publication in which in general he is critical of his former boss: Mikhailovskii-Danilevskii, *Memuary 1814–1815*, SPB, 2001, pp. 33–5. See also, however, Diebitsch's brief account in a letter to Jomini of 9 May 1817, published in Langeron, *Mémoires*, pp. 491–3.

23 Schwarzenberg, *Schwarzenberg*, p. 323.

24 Ibid., pp. 308–9. RGVIA, Fond 103, Opis 4/210, Sv. 18, Delo 17, fos. 227–8, 235, 238–9, Kankrin to Barclay: 12, 13, 17 March 1814 (OS).

25 An interesting letter of 17 March from Count Latour to Radetsky states that the Austrian army had lost prestige because it was generally blamed for twice doing nothing and leaving the Army of Silesia to its fate: Fournier, *Congress*, no. 17, pp. 281–2. For Barclay's compliment to Kankrin, see his letter of 10 March 1814 (OS), in RGVIA, Fond 103, Opis 210/4, Sv. 17, Delo 17.

26 For the Russian angle, see the excellent and detailed account by Bogdanovich, *Istoriia . . . 1814*, vol. 1, pp. 456 ff. For the French view – on this occasion not too dissimilar – see Houssaye, *Napoleon*, pp. 296–311. Friederich, *Feldzug*, pp. 287–90, is fair and intelligent as always. There is a recent account in English by Digby Smith, *Charge: Great Cavalry Charges of the Napoleonic Wars*, London, 2003, pp. 207 ff., but as with most of the English-language literature on 1813–14 it very much underestimates the Russian impact, in this respect following its German-language sources. This chapter, for example, gives the impression that Württemberg's cavalry played the leading role at Fère-Champenoise, which is far from true.

27 Langeron, *Mémoires*, pp. 446–8.

28 See n. 26 above for the main sources. See Ch. 5, pp. 162–4, for the battle of Krasnyi. Mikhailovsky-Danilevsky was present at Fère-Champenoise and gives a good description

of the final stages of the battle: *Opisanie 1814*, pp. 294–313. P. Pototskii, *Istoriia gvardeis-koi artillerii*, SPB, 1896, pp. 300–310, has interesting details on the role of the Guards horse artillery.

29 For an excellent and succinct interpretation of Talleyrand's views and role in 1814, see Philip Dwyer, *Talleyrand*, Harlow, 2002, pp. 124–40. For Napoleon's movements and the Council of Regency, Houssaye, *Napoleon*, pp. 317–70.

30 Count A. de Nesselrode (ed.), *Lettres et papiers du Chancelier Comte du Nesselrode 1760–1850*, Paris, n.d., vol. 5, pp. 183–4, 28 March 1814.

31 Löwenstern, *Mémoires*, vol. 2, p. 376. I. Burskii, *Istoriia 8-go gusarskago Lubenskago polka*, Odessa, 1913, pp. 115–17. I. Radozhitskii, *Pokhodnyia zapiski artillerista s 1812 po 1816 god*, 3 vols., Moscow, 1835, vol. 3, pp. 109–10.

32 Mikhailovskii-Danilevskii, *Opisanie 1814*, p. 327.

33 There is a detailed narrative of the battle in Bogdanovich, *Istoriia ... 1814*, vol. 1, pp. 506–60, and Friederich, *Feldzug*, pp. 301–10.

34 Bogdanovich, *Istoriia ... 1814*, vol. 1, pp. 534–7. Eugen, *Memoiren*, vol. 3, pp. 278–90.

35 Langeron, *Mémoires*, pp. 465–73.

36 See e.g. his orders to Langeron: RGVIA, Fond 846, Opis 16, Delo 3399, fo. 160ii, 16 March 1814 (OS), and his plea to Wrede, in Mikhailovskii-Danilevskii, *Opisanie 1814*, p. 324. M. F. Orlov, 'Kapitulatsiia Parizha 1814 g.', *VS*, 37/6, 1864, pp. 287–309.

37 See e.g. Castlereagh's comment to the Prince Regent that the Russian Guards were 'the most splendid that can be imagined': *Castlereagh*, vol. 9, 30 Jan. 1814, pp. 210–12.

38 Burghersh, *Operations*, pp. 250–52. Baron de Vitrolles, *Mémoires et relations politiques*, 3 vols., Paris, 1884, vol. 1, p. 316.

39 Orlov, 'Kapitulatsiia', p. 300. Vitrolles, *Mémoires*, vol. 1, pp. 311–12.

40 On Talleyrand see n. 29 above. J. Hanoteau (ed.), *Mémoires du Général de Caulaincourt, Duc de Vicenze*, 3 vols., Paris, 1933, vol. 3, pp. 207–30. Houssaye, *Napoleon*, pp. 470–99. For Talleyrand's own account of these days, see *Mémoires du Prince de Talleyrand*, Paris, 1891, pp. 156–67.

41 All the key documents of these days are reproduced between pp. 403 and 416 of *SIRIO*, 31, 1881: these include the various allied declarations, senatorial resolutions, Marmont's statements and a short commentary by Nesselrode.

42 For Alexander's letter to Louis XVIII of 17 April, see *SIRIO*, 31, 1881, pp. 411–12. *Castlereagh*, vol. 9, pp. 450–51, reproduces Charles Stewart's letter to Bathurst of 7 April denouncing the offer of Elba but there is no mention of his brother's letter to Bathurst of 13 April: this is published as no. 4, pp. 420–3, in Baron Fain, *Manuscrit de Mil Huit Cent Quatorze*, Paris, 1825. Since there is nothing that is implausible in the content of the letter and no reason to think that Fain invented it, the likeliest interpretation is that it was not included in the collection by Lord Londonderry because he did not think it reflected well on his brother. He does include many other letters to Bathurst. In Castlereagh's defence, he was seeking to sustain a fait accompli created by others.

43 Schwarzenberg, *Schwarzenberg*, p. 337.

44 Löwenstern, *Mémoires*, vol. 2, pp. 342, 419–23. A. Zaitsev, *Vospominaniia o pokho-dakh 1812 goda*, Moscow, 1853, pp. 29–34. P. Nazarov, 'Zapiski soldata Pamfila Naza-rova', *RS*, 9/8, 1878, pp. 539–40. RGVIA, Fond 846, Opis 16, Delo 3399, fo. 172ii, Volkonsky to Barclay, 2 April 1814 (OS), on the immediate departure of the irregular cavalry. Radozhitskii, *Pokhodnyia zapiski*, vol. 3, pp. 236–7, on the tremendous reception given to the returning Russian troops in Silesia, thanks partly to the king, who had given 3 million talers for parties and meals in their honour. *Dnevnik Pavla Pushchina*, Leningrad, 1987, pp. 166–73, on the Guards' journey home.

Bibliography

For abbreviations, see list on p. 543.

Archives

1. Rossiiskii gosudarstvennyi voenno-istoricheskii arkhiv:
Fond 1: Chancellery of the War Ministry
Fond 46: A. S. Kologrivov
Fond 103: M. B. Barclay de Tolly
Fond 125: D. I. Lobanov-Rostovsky/Reserve Army
Fond 140: M. G. Titov
Fond 474: Otechestvennaia voina 1812g + kampaniia 1813 i 1814 gg. (campaigns of 1812–14)
Fond 489: Formuliarnye spiski (personnel records)
Fond 846: Military Scientific Archive (voenno-uchenyi)
Fond 9194: L. L. Bennigsen/Army of Poland

2. British Library
Lieven papers: Additional Manuscripts 47410, 47424, 47427

Published Documents

Akty, dokumenty i materialy dlia istorii 1812 goda, ed. K. Voenskii, 2 vols., SPB, 1910–11.
'Aperçu des transactions politiques du Cabinet de Russie', *Sbornik imperatorskago russkago istoricheskago obshchestva*, 31, 1881.
Arkhiv grafov Mordvinovykh, ed. V. A. Bilbasov, SPB, 1902, vol. 4.
Das Befreiungsjahr 1813: Aus den Geheimen Staatsarchivs, ed. J. von Pflugk-Harttung, Berlin, 1913.
Borodino: Dokumental'naia khronika, ed. A. M. Val'kovich and A. P. Kapitonov, Moscow, 2004.
Briefwechsel König Friedrich Wilhelm III's und der Königin Luise mit Kaiser Alexander I, ed: P. Bailleu, Leipzig, 1900.
'Bumagi A. I. Chernysheva za tsarstvovanie Imperatora Aleksandra Igo', *Sbornik imperatorskago russkago istoricheskago obshchestva*, 121, 1906.
Bumagi otnosiashchiasia do otechestvennoi voiny 1812 goda, ed. P. I. Shchukin, 10 vols., Moscow, 1897–1908.
Chuikevich, P. A., 'Analiticheskii proekt voennykh deistvii v 1812 P. A. Chuikevicha', *Rossiiskii Arkhiv*, 7, 1996.
Correspondance de l'Empereur Alexandre Ier avec sa sœur la Grande Duchesse Cathérine 1805–1818, ed. Grand Duke Nicolas, SPB, 1910.

Correspondance de Napoleon Ier, 32 vols., Paris, 1858–70.

Correspondence, Despatches and Other Papers of Viscount Castlereagh, ed. Marquess of Londonderry, vol. 9, London, 1853.

Fel'dmarshal Kutuzov: Dokumenty, dnevniki, vospominaniia, ed. Iu. N. Gulaev and V. T. Soglaev, 2 vols., Moscow, 1995.

Freiherr vom Stein: Briefwechsel, Denkschriften und Aufzeichnungen, 8 vols., ed. E. Botzenhart, Berlin, 1957–71.

General Bagration: Sbornik dokumentov i materialov, ed. S. N. Golubeva, Moscow, 1945.

L'Imperatrice Elisabeth, épouse d' Alexandre Ier, ed. Grand Duke Nicolas, 4 vols., SPB, 1908–9.

'Iz zapisok fel'dmarshala Sakena', *RA*, 22, 1900.

Karamzin's Memoir on Ancient and Modern Russia, ed. and trans. R. Pipes, Ann Arbor, 2005.

Materialy voenno-uchenogo arkhiva: Otechestvennaia voina 1812 goda, vols. 1–21, SPB, 1900–1914.

Materialy voenno-uchenogo arkhiva: Voina 1813 goda, vols. 1–2, SPB, 1915–16.

M. I. Kutuzov: Sbornik dokumentov, ed. L. G. Beskrovnyi, vols. 4i, 4ii, 5, Moscow, 1954–6.

'Nakanune Erfurtskago svidaniia 1808 goda', *RS*, 98, 1899.

Narodnoe opolchenie v otechestvennoi voine 1812 goda, ed. L. G. Beskrovnyi, Moscow, 1962.

Neithardt von Gneisenau: Schriften von und über Gneisenau, ed. F. Lange, Berlin, 1954.

Nesselrode, Count A de (ed.), *Lettres et papiers du Chancelier Comte de Nesselrode 1760–1850*, vols. 3, 4, 5, Paris, n.d.

Otechestvennaia voina v pis'makh sovremennikov, ed. N. Dubrovin, Moscow, 2006.

Pis'ma glavneishikh deiatelei v tsarstvovanie Imperatora Aleksandra I, ed. N. Dubrovin, Moscow, 2006.

Pokhod russkoi armii protiv Napoleona v 1813 g i osvobozhdenie Germanii: Sbornik dokumentov, ed. L. G. Beskrovnyi, Moscow, 1964.

Pol'noe Sobranie zakonov Rossiiskoi Imperii, 1807–14, vols. 30, 31, 32.

'Posol'stvo Grafa P. A. Tolstago v Parizhe v 1807 i 1808 gg.', *Sbornik imperatorskago russkago istoricheskago obshchestva*, 89, 1893.

Les Relations diplomatiques de la Russie et la France 1808–12, ed. Grand Duke Nicolas, 6 vols., SPB, 1905–6.

Sbornik istoricheskikh materialov izvlechennykh iz arkhiva Sobstvennoi Ego Imperatorskago velichestva kantseliarii, ed. N. Dubrovin, vols. 1–15, SPB, 1876–1915.

Shishkov, A. S., *Zapiski, mneniia i perepiska A. S. Shishkova*, ed. N. Kiselev and I. Iu. Samarin, 2 vols., Berlin, 1870.

Sobranie traktatov i konventsii zakliuchennykh Rossiei s inostrannymi derzhavami, SPB, 1876 and 1885, editor: F. F. Martens, vols. III and VII

La Suède et la Russie: Documents et materiaux 1809–1818, Uppsala, 1985.

Upravlenie General-Intendanta Kankrina: General'nyi sokrashchennyi otchet po armiiam (krome Pol'skoi i Rezervnoi) za pokhody protiv Frantsuzov, 1812, 1813, i 1814 godov, Warsaw, 1815.

Vneshnaia politika Rossii XIX i nachala XX veka: Dokumenty Rossiiskogo Ministerstva Inostrannykh Del, 1st series, ed. A. L. Narochnitskii, vols. 4, 5, 6, 7, Moscow, 1962–70.

Voennyi zhurnal, SPB, 1808–11.

'1807 god: Pis'ma s dorogi ot kniazia A. B. Kurakina k gosudaryne-imperatritse Marii Feodorovne', *RA*, 1, 1868.

Memoirs, Diaries, Private Letters

Arnol'di, I., 'Berezinskaia pereprava', *VS*, 53/9, 1910.

Benckendorff, Count A., *Zapiski Benkendorfa*, Moscow, 2001.

Bennigsen, L. L., *Mémoires du Général Bennigsen*, 3 vols., Paris, n.d.

Bernhardi, T. von, *Denkwürdigkeiten aus dem Leben des kaiserlichen russischen Generals der Infanterie Carl Friedrich Grafen von Toll*, 5 vols., Leipzig, 1858.

Beskrovnyi, L. G. (ed.), *Dnevnik Aleksandra Chicherina, 1812–1813*, Moscow, 1966.

Borodino v vospominaniiakh sovremennikov, SPB, 2001.

Bortnevskii, V. G. (ed.), *Dnevnik Pavla Pushchina*, Leningrad, 1987.

Choisseul-Gouffier, Countess, *Historical Memoirs of the Emperor Alexander I and the Court of Russia*, London, 1904.

Dushenkovich, S. V. 'Iz moikh vospominanii ot 1812 goda', in *1812 god v vospominaniiakh sovremennikov*, Moscow, 1995.

Edling, Countess R., 'Grafinia Roksandra Skarlatovna Edling: Zapiski', in A. Libermann (ed.), *Derzhavnyi sfinks*, Moscow, 1999.

Eiler, A. A. 'Zapiski A. A. Eilera', *RS*, 1/11, 1880.

Ermolov, A. P., *Zapiski A. P. Ermolova 1798–1826*, Moscow, 1991.

Fezensac, Duc de, *Souvenirs militaires*, Paris, 1863.

Gielgud, A. (ed.), *The Memoirs of Prince Adam Czartoryski*, 2 vols., London, 1888.

Glinka, S. F. *Pis'ma russkogo ofitsera*, Moscow, 1987.

Golitsyn, Prince A., 'Zapiska o voine 1812 goda A. B. Golitsyna', *VS*, 53, 1910.

Grabbe, P., *Iz pamiatnykh zapisok: Otechestvennaia voina*, Moscow, 1873.

Griboedov, A. S. *Sochineniia*, Moscow, 1953.

Griois, C.-P.-L., *Mémoires du Général Griois*, Paris, n.d.

Hanoteau, J. (ed.) *Mémoires du Général de Caulaincourt, Duc de Vicenze*, 3 vols., Paris, 1933.

Kharkevich, V. (ed.), *1812 god v dnevnikakh, zapiskakh, i vospominaniiakh sovremennikov*, 4 vols., Vilna, 1900–1907.

Komarovskii, E. F., *Zapiski grafa E. F. Komarovskogo*, SPB, 1914.

Konshin, N. M., 'Zapiski o 1812 gode', *IV*, 4, 1884.

Langeron, A de, *Mémoires de Langeron, Général d'Infanterie dans l'Armée Russe: Campagnes de 1812, 1813, 1814*, Paris, 1902.

Lazhechnikov, I. I., 'Neskol'ko zametok i vospominanii po povodu stat'i "materialy dlia biografii A. P. Ermolova" ', *Russkii vestnik*, 31/6, 1864.

Lestvitsyn, V. (ed.), 'Zapiska soldata Pamfila Nazarova', *RS*, 9/8, 1878.

Longinov, N. M., 'Dvenadtsatyi god: Pis'ma N. M. Longinova k grafu S. R. Vorontsovu', *RA*, 4, 1912.

Löwenstern, V. von, *Mémoires du Général-Major Russe Baron de Löwenstern*, 2 vols., Paris, 1903.

Maevskii, S. I., 'Moi vek ili istoriia generala Maevskago', *RS*, 8, 1873.

Mitarevskii, N. E., *Raskazy ob otechestvennoi voine 1812 goda*, Moscow, 1878.

Murav'ev, N., 'Zapiski Nikolaia Nikolaevich Muraveva', *RA*, 22, 23, 24, 25, 26, 28, 1885–91.

Muromtsev, M. M. 'Vospominaniia Matveia Matveevicha Muromtseva', *RA*, 27/3, 1890.

Norov, A. S., *Voina i mir 1805–1812 s istoricheskoi tochki zreniia*, SPB, 1868.

Norov, V. S., *Zapiski o pokhodakh 1812 i 1813 godakh ot Tarutinskago srazheniia do Kul'mskago boia*, SPB, 1834.

Orlov, M. F., 'Kapitulatsiia Parizha 1814 g.', *VS*, 37/6, 1864.

Ortenberg, I., 'Voennyia vospominaniia starykh vremen', *Biblioteka dlia chteniia*, 24/6, 1857.

Radozhitskii, I., *Pokhodnyia zapiski artillerista s 1812 po 1816 god*, 3 vols., Moscow, 1835.

Raevskii, A., *Vospominaniia o pokhodakh 1813 i 1814 godov*, Moscow, 1822.

Rochechouart, Comte de, *Souvenirs de la Révolution, l'Empire at la Restauration*, Paris, 1889.

Saint-Cyr, Gouvion, *Mémoires pour servir à l'histoire militaire sous le Directoire, le Consulat et l'Empire*, vols. 3, 4, Paris, 1831.

Schubert, F. von, *Unter dem Doppeladler*, Stuttgart, 1962.

Shcherbatov, Prince A. G., *Moi vospominaniia*, SPB, 2006.

Simanskii, L., 'Zhurnal uchastnika voiny 1812 goda', *Voenno-istoricheskii sbornik*, 3, 1913.

Solov'eva, D. V. (ed.), *Graf Zhozef de Mestr: Peterburgskie pis'ma*, SPB, 1995.

Tartakovskii, A. G. (ed.), *Voennye dnevniki*, Moscow, 1990.

Vitrolles, Baron de, *Mémoires et relations politiques*, 3 vols., Paris, 1884.

Volkonskii, S. G., *Zapiski Sergeia Grigorovicha Volkonskogo (dekabrista)*, SPB, 1902.

Vospominaniia voinov russkoi armii: Iz sobraniia otdela pis'mennykh istochnikov gosudarstvennogo istoricheskogo muzeia, Moscow, 1991.

Wolzogen, L von, *Mémoires d'un Général d'Infanterie au service de la Prusse et de la Russie (1792–1836)*, Paris, 2002.

Württemberg, Duke Eugen von, *Memoiren des Herzogs Eugen von Württemberg*, 3 vols., Frankfurt an der Oder, 1862.

Zaitsev, A., *Vospominaniia o Pokhodakh 1812 goda*, Moscow, 1853.

Key Secondary Literature

Adamovich, B., *Sbornik voenno-istoricheskikh materialov leib-gvardii Keksgol'mskago imperatora Avstriiskago polka*, SPB, 1910.

Aksan, V., *Ottoman Wars 1700–1870: An Empire Besieged*, Harlow, 2007.

Alder, K., *Engineering the Revolution: Arms and Enlightenment in France, 1763–1815*, Princeton, 1997.

Aleksandrov, V. A., *Sel'skaia obshchina v Rossii (XVII-nachalo XIX v.)*, Moscow, 1976.

Anderson, P., *Lineages of the Absolutist State*, London, 1974.

Babkin, V. I., 'Organizatsiia i voennye deistviia narodnogo opolcheniia v otechestvennoi voine 1812 goda', in *K stopiatidesiatiletiiu otechestvennoi voiny*, Moscow, 1962.

Bayly, C., *The Birth of the Modern World 1780–1914*, Oxford, 2004.

Bell, D. A., *The First Total War*, London, 2007.

Beskrovnyi, L. *The Russian Army and Fleet in the Nineteenth Century*, Gulf Breeze, 1996.

Bezotosnyi, V. M., 'Bor'ba general'skikh gruppirovok', in *Epokha 1812 goda: Issledovaniia, istochniki, istoriografiia*, TGIM, Moscow, 2002, vol. 1.

——, *Donskoi generalitet i ataman Platov v 1812 godu*, Moscow, 1999.

——, *Razvedka i plany storon v 1812 godu*, Moscow, 2005.

Bezotosnyi, V. P. et al (eds.), *Otechestvennaia voina 1812 goda: Entsiklopediia*, Moscow, 2004.

Bobrovskii, P., *Istoriia leib-gvardii ulanskago E.I.V. gosudarnyi Imperatritsy Aleksandry Fedorovny polka*, SPB, 1903.

Bogdanovich, M. I., *Istoriia otechestvennoi voiny 1812 goda*, 3 vols., SPB, 1859–60.

——, *Istoriia voiny 1813 g. za nezavisimost' Germanii*, 2 vols., SPB, 1863.

——, *Istoriia voiny 1814 goda vo Frantsii*, 2 vols., SPB, 1865.

Bonney, R. (ed.), *Economic Systems and Finance*, Oxford, 1995.

Bowden, S., *Napoleon's Grande Armée of 1813*, Chicago, 1990.

Burskii, I., *Istoriia 8go gusarskago Lubenskago polka*, Odessa, 1913.

Charnetskii, S. E., *Istoriia 179-go pekhotnago Ust-Dvinskago polka: 1711–1811–1911*, SPB, 1911.

Clausewitz, K. von, *Der Feldzug in Russland und die Befreiungskriege von 1813–15*, Berlin, 1906.

Creveld, M. van, *Supplying War: Logistics from Wallerstein to Patton*, Cambridge, 1977.

Dandevil', M. *Stoletie 5-go dragunskago Kurliandskago Imperatora Aleksandra III-go polka*, SPB, 1903.

Darwin, J., *After Tamerlane: The Global History of Empire*, London, 2007.

Dawson, P., and Summerfield, S., *Napoleonic Artillery*, Marlborough, 2007.

DiMarco, L., *War Horse: A History of the Military Horse and Rider*, Yardley, 2008.

Downing, B., *The Military Revolution and Political Change*, Princeton, 1992.

Drabek, A. *et al.*(eds.), *Russland und Österreich zur Zeit der Napoleonischen Kriege,* Vienna, 1989.

Dubrovin, N. F., *Russkaia zhizn' v nachale XIX veka*, SPB, 2007.

Dzhivelegov, A. K., Melgunov, S. P., and Pichet, P. I. (eds.), *Otechestvennaia voina i russkoe obshchestvo*, 7 vols., Moscow, 1911.

Esdaile, C., *Fighting Napoleon: Guerrillas, Bandits and Adventurers in Spain 1808-14*, London, 2004.

Fain, Baron, *Manuscrit de Mil Huit Cent Douze*, Paris, 1827.

——, *Manuscrit de Mil Huit Cent Quatorze*, Paris, 1825.

Feuer, K. B., *Tolstoy and the Genesis of War and Peace*, Ithaca, NY, 1976.

Fournier, A., *Der Congress von Chatillon: Die Politik im Kriege von 1814*, Vienna, 1900.

Friederich, R. von, *Die Befreiungskriege 1813-1815*, vol. 1: *Der Fruhjahrsfeldzug 1813*, Berlin, 1911; vol. 2: *Der Herbstfeldzug 1813*, Berlin, 1912; vol. 3: *Der Feldzug 1814*, Berlin, 1913.

Gavrilov, S. V., *Organizatsiia i snabzhenie russkoi armii nakanune i v khode otechestvennoi voiny 1812 g. i zagranichnykh pokhodov 1813-1815 gg: Istoricheskie aspekty*, candidate's dissertation, SPB, 2003.

Geniev, Captain, *Istoriia Pskovskago pekhotnago general-fel'dmarshala kniazia Kutuzova-Smolenskago polka*, Moscow, 1883.

Genishta, V. I., and Borisovich, A. T., *Istoriia 30-go dragunskago Ingermanlandskago polka 1704-1904*, SPB, 1904.

Geschichte der Kämpfe Österreichs: Kriege unter der Regierung des Kaisers Franz. Befreiungskrieg 1813 und 1814, 5 vols.:

    vol. 1: Criste, O., *Österreichs Beitritt zur Koalition*, Vienna, 1913.

    vol. 2: Wlaschutz, W., *Österreichs entscheidendes Machtaufgebot*, Vienna, 1913.

    vol. 3: Horstenau, E. Glaise von, *Feldzug von Dresden*, Vienna, 1913.

    vol. 4: Ehnl, M., *Schlacht bei Kulm*, Vienna, 1913.

    vol. 5: Hoen, Max von, *Feldzug von Leipzig*, Vienna, 1913.

Glinoetskii, N., 'Russkii general'nyi shtab v tsarstvovanie Imperatora Aleksandra I', *V S*, 17/10, 17/11, 1874.

Godunov, V., *Istoriia 3-go ulanskago Smolenskago Imperatora Aleksandra III-go polka*, Libava, 1908.

Gol'mdorf, M., *Materialy dlia istorii byvshego Dvorianskogo polka*, SPB, 1882.

Gooding, J., 'The Liberalism of Michael Speransky', *Slavonic and East European Review*, 64/3, 1986.

Gourgaud, General, *Napoléon et la Grande Armée en Russie ou Examen critique de L'ouvrage de M. le Comte de Ségur*, Paris, 1826.

Grigorovich, A., *Istoriia 13-go dragunskago voennago ordena general-fel'dmarshala Grafa Minikha polka*, 2 vols., SPB, 1907 and 1912.

Gulevich, S., *Istoriia 8-go pekhotnago Estliandskago polka*, SPB, 1911.

Haythornthwaite, P., *Weapons and Equipment of the Napoleonic Wars*, London, 1996.

Houssaye, H., *Napoleon and the Campaign of 1814: France*, Uckfield, 2004.

Istoriia leib-gvardii egerskago polka za sto let 1796-1896, SPB, 1896.

Ivchenko, L., *Borodino: Legenda i deistvitel'nost'*, Moscow, 2002.

Kamenskii, E., *Istoriia 2-go dragunskago S-Peterburgskago generala-fel'dmarshala kniazia Menshikova polka 1707-1898*, Moscow, 1900.

Karnovich, E., *Tsesarevich Konstantin Pavlovich*, SPB, 1899.

Keegan, J., *The Face of Battle*, London, 1978.

Keep, J., 'The Russian Army in the Seven Years' War', in E. Lohr and M. Poe (eds.), *The Military and Society in Russia, 1450-1917*, Leiden, 2002.

Khovanskii, N. F., *Uchastie Saratovskoi gubernii v otechestvennoi voine 1812 g.*, Saratov, 1912.

Kielmansegg, P. Graf von, *Stein und die Zentralverwaltung 1813/14*, Stuttgart, 1964.

Kissinger, H., *A World Restored*, London, 1957.

Klugin, L., 'Russkaia sol'datskaia artel' ', *RS*, 20, 1861.

Lieven, D., *Empire: The Russian Empire and its Rivals*, London, 2001.

Longworth, P., *The Art of Victory*, London, 1965.

McGrew, R., *Paul I of Russia*, Oxford, 1992.

Madariaga, I. de, *Britain, Russia and the Armed Neutrality of 1780*, London, 1962.

Markov, Colonel, *Istoriia leib-gvardii kirasirskago Eia Velichestva polka*, SPB, 1884.

Marshall, P. J. (ed.), *The Oxford History of the British Empire: The Eighteenth Century*, Oxford, 1998.

Martin, A., 'The Response of the Population of Moscow to the Napoleonic Occupation of 1812', in E. Lohr and M. Poe, (eds.), *The Military and Society in Russia, 1450–1917*, Leiden, 2002.

Mel'nikova, L. V., *Armiia i pravoslavnaia tserkov' Rossiiskoi imperii v epokhu Napoleonov-skikh voin*, Moscow, 2007.

Melton, E., 'Household Economies and Communal Conflicts on a Russian Serf Estate, 1800–1817', *Journal of Social History*, 26/3, 1993.

Mikhailovskii-Danilevskii, A. I., *Opisanie otechestvennoi voiny 1812 g.*, 4 vols., SPB, 1839.

——, *Opisanie pokhoda vo Frantsii v 1814 godu*, 2 vols., SPB, 1836. repr. in one vol., 1841.

——, *Opisanie voiny 1813 g.*, 2 vols., SPB, 1840.

Mironenko, S. V., *Samoderzhavie i reformy: Politicheskaia bor'ba v Rossii v nachale XIX v.*, Moscow, 1989.

Muir, R., *Tactics and the Experience of Battle in the Age of Napoleon*, London, 1998.

Nikolaev, E., *Istoriia 50 pekhotnago Belostokskago Ego Vysochestva gertsoga Saksen-Al'tenburgskago polka*, SPB, 1907.

Oncken, W., *Österreich und Preussen in Befreiungskriege*, 2 vols., Berlin, 1878.

Orlov, A. A., *Soiuz Peterburga i Londona*, SPB, 2005.

Panchulidzev, S., *Istoriia kavalergardov*, SPB, 1903, vol. 3.

Pestreikov, N., *Istoriia leib-gvardii Moskovskago polka*, SPB, 1903, vol. 1.

Pitts, J., *A Turn to Empire: The Rise of Imperial Liberalism in Britain and France*, Princeton, 2005.

Podmazo, A. A., 'Kontinental'naia blokada kak ekonomicheskaia prichina voiny 1812 g', in *Epokha 1812 goda: Issledovaniia, istochniki, istoriografiia*, TGIM, 137, Moscow, 2003, vol. 2.

Pomeranz, K., *The Great Divergence: China, Europe and the Making of of the Modern World Economy*, Princeton, 2000.

Popov, A. I., *Velikaia armiia v Rossii: Pogon'ia za mirazhom*, Samara, 2002.

Popov, F. G., *Istoriia 48-go pekhotnago Odesskago polka*, 2 vols., Moscow, 1911.

Pototskii, P., *Istoriia gvardeiskoi artillerii*, SPB, 1896.

Prokhodtsev, I. I., *Riazanskaia guberniia v 1812 godu*, Riazan, 1913.

Pugachev, V. V., 'K voprosu o pervonachal'nom plane voiny 1812 goda', in *K stopiatidesiati-letiiu otechestevennoi voiny*, Moscow, 1962.

Rantsov, V., *Istoriia 96-go pekhotnago Omskago polka*, SPB, 1902.

Ratchinski, A., *Napoléon et Alexandre Ier*, Paris, 2002.

Reboul, F., *Campagne de 1813: Les préliminaires*, 2 vols., Paris, 1910.

Rodger, N. A. M., *The Command of the Ocean*, London, 2004.

Rousset, C., *La Grande Armée de 1813*, Paris, 1871.

Rowe, M. (ed.), *Collaboration and Resistance in Napoleonic Europe*, Basingstoke, 2003.

Schwarzenberg, K. Fürst von, *Feldmarschall Fürst Schwarzenberg: Der Sieger von Leipzig*, Vienna, 1964.

Scott, H. M., *The Birth of a Great Power System 1740–1815*, Harlow, 2008.

——, *The Emergence of the Eastern Powers 1756–1775*, Cambridge, 2001.

Shelengovskii, I., *Istoriia 69-go Riazanskago polka*, 3 vols., Lublin, 1911, vol. 2.

Sherwig, J. M., *Guineas and Gunpowder: British Foreign Aid in the Wars with France 1793–1815*, Cambridge, Mass, 1969.

Shil'der, N., *Imperator Aleksandr pervyi: Ego zhizn' i tsarstvovanie*, 4 vols., SPB, 1897.

Shtein, I. A., *Voina 1812 goda v otechestvennoi istoriografii*, Moscow, 2002.

Shvedov, S. V., 'Komplektovanie, chislennost' i poteri russkoi armii v 1812 godu', in *K 175-letiiu Otechestvennoi voiny 1812 g.*, Moscow, 1987.

Simms, B., *The Impact of Napoleon: Prussian High Politics, Foreign Policy and the Crisis of the Executive 1797–1806*, Cambridge, 1997.

——, *Three Victories and a Defeat: The Rise and Fall of the First British Empire, 1714–1783*, London, 2007.

Sked, A., *Metternich and Austria*, London, 2008.

Smirnov, A. A., 'Chto zhe takoi Shevardinskii redut?', in *Epokha 1812 goda: Issledovaniia, istochniki, istoriografiia*, TGIM, 3, Moscow, 2004, pp. 320–51; vol. 4, 2005, pp. 239–71; vol. 5, 2006, pp 353–68.

——, *General Aleksandr Kutaisov*, Moscow, 2002.

Smith, A. D., 'War and Ethnicity: The Role of Warfare in the Formation, Self-Images and Cohesion of Ethnic Communities', *Ethnic and Racial Studies*, 44, 1981.

Speranskii, V. N., *Voenno-ekonomicheskaia podgotovka Rossii k bor'be s Napoleonom v 1812–1914 godakh*, candidate's dissertation, Gorky, 1967.

Stamm-Kuhlmann, T., *König in Preussens grosser Zeit*, Berlin, 1992.

Stoletie voennago ministerstva (SVM): 13 vols., SPB, 1902–10:

vol. 2, books 1 and 2: Kvadri, V. V., *Imperatorskaia glavnaia kvartira.*

vol. 4, part 1, book 1, section 2: Shchepetil'nikov, V. V., *Glavnyi shtab: Komplektovanie voisk v tsarstvovanie Imp. Aleksandra I.*

vol. 5, part 1, book 2, section 1: Geisman, P. A., *Glavnyi shtab: Vozkniknovenie i razvitie v Rossii general'nogo shtaba.*

vol. 4, part 1, book 2, section 3: Gippius, A. I., *Obrazovanie (obuchenie) voisk.*

vol. 5: Shelekhov, V. V., *Glavnoe intendantskoe upravlenie.*

vol. 7: Fabritsius, I. G., *Glavnoe inzhenernoe upravlenie.*

vol. 13, book 3: Ermolov V. V., and Ryndin, M. M., *Upravlenie General-inspektora kavalerii: O remontirovanii kavalerii.*

Stroev, V. N., *Stoletie sobstevennoi Ego Imperatorskago Velichestva kantseliarii*, SPB, 1912.

Svinin, P. P., 'Tul'skii oruzheinyi zavod', *Syn Otechestva*, 19, 1816.

Tartakovskii, A. G., *1812 god i russkaia memuaristika*, Moscow, 1980.

——, *Nerazgadannyi Barklai*, Moscow, 1996.

Tatishcheff, S., *Alexandre Ier et Napoléon*, Paris, 1894.

Tilly, C., *Coercion, Capital and European States: A.D. 990–1992*, Oxford, 1990.

Tivanov, V. V., *Finansy russkoi armii*, Moscow, 1993.

Totfalushin, V. P., *M. V. Barklai de Tolli v otechestvennoi voine 1812 goda*, Saratov, 1991.

Troitskii, N. A., *Fel'dmarshal Kutuzov: Mify i fakty*, Moscow, 2002.

——, *1812 velikii god Rossii*, Moscow, 2007.

Trudy Gosudarstvennogo Istoricheskogo Muzeia (TGIM), *Epokha 1812 goda: Issledovaniia, istochniki, istoriografiia*, vols. 1–7, Moscow, 2002–7.

Tselerungo, D. G., *Ofitsery russkoi armii, uchastniki Borodinskogo srazheniia*, Moscow, 2002.

Tulard, J. (ed.) *Dictionnaire Napoléon*, Paris, 1987; repr. in 2 vols., Paris, 1999.

Uffindell, A., *Napoleon's Immortals*, Stroud, 2007.

Ulianov, I., *Reguliarnaia pekhota 1801–1855*, 3 vols., Moscow, 1995–8.

Vandal, A., *Napoléon et Alexandre Premier*, 3 vols., Paris, 1891.

Vasilev, A., *Srazhenie pri Maloiaroslavtse 12/24 oktiabria 1812 goda*, Maloiaroslavets, 2002.

Wolff, L., *Inventing Eastern Europe: The Map of Civilization in the Mind of the Enlightenment*, Stanford, Calif., 1994.

Woloch, I., *The New Regime: Transformations of the French Civil Order, 1789–1820s*, London, 1994.

Zatler, F., *Zapiski o prodovol'stvii voisk v voennoe vremia*, SPB, 1860.

Zawadski, W. H., *A Man of Honour: Adam Czartoryski as a Statesman of Russia and Poland 1795–1831*, Oxford, 1993.

Zlotnikov, M. F., *Kontinental'naia blokada i Rossiia*, Moscow, 1966.

Additional Reading in English

As noted in the Introduction, the literature on Russia's war effort is sparse and often unreliable, mostly being derived from French and German sources. An exception is Alexander Mikaberidze, *The Battle of Borodino*, Barnsley, 2007. The same author has compiled a useful work on the Russian officer corps in the period: *The Russian Officer Corps in the Revolutionary and Napoleonic Wars, 1795–1815*, Staplehurst, 2005. Also valuable is Alexander and Iurii Zhmodikov, *Tactics of the Russian Army in the Napoleonic Wars*, 2 vols., West Chester, 2003, but this is a very limited edition and hard to get hold of. Christopher Duffy has made a great contribution to English-language readers' understanding of the Russian army but his main work covers the period before the Napoleonic wars: *Russia's Military Way to the West*, London, 1981, and *Eagles over the Alps: Suvorov in Italy and Switzerland 1799*, Chicago, 1999. He has also written two short books on the battles of Austerlitz and Borodino: *Austerlitz* and *Borodino and the War of 1812*, both reprinted in new editions by Cassell in London in 1999.

A number of Western scholars have written often excellent books in English which provide a background to the empire's war with Napoleon. See in particular William Fuller's splendid *Strategy and Power in Russia, 1600–1914*, New York, 1992, and Patricia Grimsted, *The Foreign Ministers of Alexander I*, Berkeley, 1969; Janet Hartley, *Alexander I*, London, 1994, and *Russia, 1762–1825: Military Power, the State and the People*, London, 2008; John Keep, *Soldiers of the Tsar, 1462–1874*, Oxford, 1985; John Le Donne, *The Grand Strategy of the Russian Empire, 1650–1831*, Oxford, 2004; Alexander Martin, *Romantics, Reformers, Reactionaries: Russian Conservative Thought and Politics in the Reign of Alexander I*, De Kalb, Ill., 1997; Alan Palmer, *Alexander I: Tsar of War and Peace*, London, 1974; Richard Pipes, *Karamzin's Memoir on Ancient and Modern Russia: A Translation and Analysis*, Ann Arbor, 2005; Nicholas Riasanovsky, *A Parting of Ways: Government and the Educated Public in Russia 1801–1855*, Oxford, 1976; David Saunders, *Russia in the Age of Reaction and Reform 1801–1881*, London, 1992; Elise Kimerling Wirtschafter, *From Serf to Russian Soldier*, Princeton, 1990.

Readers seeking background information on Russian government, society and culture might consult volume 2 of *The Cambridge History of Russia*, Cambridge, 2006, which I edited, and which contains many excellent contributions by experts in the field of Russian imperial history. Both in this volume and in the books listed in the previous paragraph can be found bibliographies that will lead the interested reader to the rather few academic articles in English on the era of Alexander I and relevant to the wars with Napoleon.

A number of memoirs originally written by Russians who participated in the wars have been translated into English: Nadezhda Durova, *The Cavalry Maiden: Journals of a Female Russian Officer in the Napoleonic Wars*, ed. and trans. Mary Fleming Zirin, Bloomington, Ill., 1989; Denis Davydov, *In the Service of the Tsar against Napoleon: The Memoirs of Denis Davydov*, ed. and trans. Gregory Troubetzkoy, London, 2006; Aleksei Ermolov, *The Czar's General: The Memoirs of a Russian General in the Napoleonic Wars*, ed. and trans.

Alexander Mikaberidze, London, 2006; Boris Uxkull, *Arms and the Woman*, trans. Joel Carmichael, London, 1966.

Some memoirs and commentaries by non-Russian participants in the wars are also available in English and are valuable for their insights into the Russian war effort. These include: C. F. Adams (ed.), *John Quincy Adams in Russia*, New York, 1970; A. Brett-James (ed.), *General Wilson's Journal 1812–1814*, London, 1964; Lord Burghersh, *The Operations of the Allied Armies in 1813 and 1814*, London, 1822; the Hon. George Cathcart, *Commentaries on the War in Russia and Germany in 1812 and 1813*, London, 1850; A de Caulaincourt, *At Napoleon's Side in Russia*, New York, 2003; Carl von Clausewitz, *The Campaign of 1812 in Russia*, London, 1992; the Marquess of Londonderry, *Narrative of the War in Germany and France in 1813 and 1814*, London, 1830; Baron Karl von Müffling, *The Memoirs of Baron von Müffling: A Prussian Officer in the Napoleonic Wars*, ed. Peter Hofschroer, London, 1997; Baron von Odeleben, *A Circumstantial Narrative of the Campaign in Saxony in the Year 1813*, 2 vols., London, 1820; Count P. de Ségur, *History of the Expedition to Russia, 1812*, 2 vols., Stroud, 2005.

English-language secondary literature on the Napoleonic wars as a whole is vast. As regards military operations the bible is David Chandler, *The Campaigns of Napoleon*, London, 1993, and, as regards diplomacy, Paul W. Schroeder, *The Transformation of European Politics, 1763–1848*, Oxford, 1994. Charles Esdaile, *Napoleon's Wars: An International History 1803–15*, London, 2007, is a good recent book on European international relations in this era. On the 1812 campaign an excellent recent work is Adam Zamoyski, *1812: Napoleon's Fatal March on Moscow*, London, 2004. Paul Austen's *1812: Napoleon's Invasion of Russia*, London, 2000 is based on French and allied memoirs and is extremely readable and moving. The 1813 campaign is less well covered in English, perhaps in part because German nationalism – the year's traditional theme – has not evoked much enthusiasm in anglophone circles since 1914. Jonathan Riley, *Napoleon and the World War of 1813: Lessons in Coalition Warfighting*, London, 2000, is thought-provoking. M. Leggiere, *Napoleon and Berlin*, Stroud, 2002; the three volumes by George Nafziger on 1813 (*Napoleon at Lutzen and Bautzen*; *Napoleon at Dresden*; *Napoleon at Leipzig*, Chicago, 1992, 1994, 1996); and Digby Smith, *1813 – Leipzig. Napoleon and the Battle of the Nations*, London, 2001, are also useful. As regards the 1814 campaign, the place to start for the English-speaking reader is James Lawford, *Napoleon: The Last Campaigns. 1813–15*, London, 1976, not least because of its excellent maps. Much the fullest account is M. V. Leggiere, *The Fall of Napoleon: The Allied Invasion of France 1813–1814*, whose first volume was published in Cambridge in 2008.

Index